Anne Boleyn

The Big Questions

Margaret Bolton

Ariana Press

*The principal office of history I take to be this:
to prevent virtuous actions from being forgotten,
and that evil words and deeds should fear
an infamous reputation with posterity*

Tacitus

*My business is to teach my aspirations
to conform themselves to fact,
not to try and make facts harmonise with my aspirations.*

Aldous Huxley

Copyright © 2025 Margaret Bolton

Published by Ariana Press, Kent, England: 2025

ISBN: 978-0952647416

DA 333.B6   942.65

All rights reserved. Neither this book nor any portion thereof may be reproduced or transmitted by any means – electronic, mechanical, photocopying, scanning, recording – or used in any manner whatsoever without the express written permission of the publisher except for the use of brief quotations in a book review or scholarly journal.

Margaret Bolton hereby asserts her moral right under Section 77 of the Copyright, Designs & Patents Act 1988 to be identified as the author of this work.

Contents

Introduction	1
How did Katherine of Aragon become Queen of England	5
What are the principal sources for the life of Anne Boleyn?	17
When was Anne Boleyn born?	52
Was Henry married when he met Anne?	74
Was Anne the cause of the breakdown of Henry's 'marriage' to Katherine?	136
Why did it take so long for Henry and Anne to marry?	182
When did Henry and Anne marry?	513
What was Anne's life like as queen?	522
Was Anne a Protestant?	539
Why did Anne fall?	557
Was Anne's conviction fair?	592
Why was Anne's marriage annulled?	604
Conclusion	612

Appendices

1. The bull and the brief	614
2. The love letters	617
3. Henry and Anne's wedding service	622
4. Anne's coronation	630
5. Anne's properties	637
6. Key relationships	643
7. Anne's judges	659
8. The cardinals involved	663
Index	678

In memory of
Ronald Quick
1923-2024
who always
encouraged me
and of my teachers
who gave me
a love for the subject

Introduction

Not another book on Anne Boleyn! Surely we all know about her romance with Percy, Henry's demand for a divorce from poor Katherine because of his lust for Anne, his many affairs (including her sister) which culminated in him having her framed and executed just so he could marry Jane Seymour? Well yes, we have been told all these things in many books, articles, and dramas, but the repetition does not make them true. Indeed, stories have a habit of growing in the retelling until the facts become lost all together.

This volume does not seek to be a conventional biography of Anne Boleyn. There is no attempt to discover what she was doing or wearing every day. Instead, it considers her life through a series of questions from "When was she born?" to "Why did she fall?" Some of the answers are relatively straightforward but others, such as "Why did it take so long for Henry and Anne to marry?" require considerably more detail. Too many studies focus on Anne's relationship with Henry from an almost exclusively English point of view but it needs to be seen in the wider European context. Anne and Henry did not live in isolation from the rest of the world and their options were limited due to wars, changing alliances and the machinations of Katherine's supporters. This volume aims to correct that bias and to show that the French, in particular, had a huge impact on the way events unfolded.

Just as Henry and Anne were impacted by what happened in their own day, so they were affected by things which had happened in the past. The story does not begin in 1527 when the annulment crisis began but in 1502 with the death of Prince Arthur, Henry's older brother and Katherine's husband. What prompted anyone at the time to imagine that Henry could marry his widow? Writers today generally assume that this was a perfectly normal event and that the application for permission from the pope was routine but it was not. No such permission had ever been granted in the entire history of the church and dispensations for such a case had been specifically prohibited by the Fourth Lateran Council. Much more attention needs to be given to the circumstances behind the grant and whether the precious dispensation was worth the paper it was written on. This matters because anyone who refers to Katherine as Henry's wife or to him seeking a divorce is expressing their conviction that Julius was legitimately elected pope and entitled to give such permission and their belief that judgments from Rome are of greater value than decisions of the English Parliament and the Archbishop of Canterbury, that canon law is superior to civil and common law and popes are superior to General Councils. This book will argue strongly against any such assumptions. A detailed analysis of Henry's theological position is provided which demonstrates not only the strength of his case but draws attention to his revolutionary use of Hebrew material.

The third goal of this work is to provide a convenient reference source for information which is not always easily available. To this end, a month by month account of events with commentary is provided for the crucial period from the start of the annulment crisis to the time when Anne became queen. This unusual approach enables readers to go on the journey with Henry and Anne and aims to ensure a fuller picture is given. As a famous novelist once commented, it is "surprisingly easy to prove anything one may desire by a process either of conscious or of unwitting selection."[1] Amongst the appendices, the texts of the dispensation and the infamous brief are compared. Anne's wedding and coronation services have been recreated and there is consideration of her property portfolio. Relationships between key characters in the story are provided in multiple simplified charts rather than complex trees to make it easier to see how people were connected. There is also a look at the political affiliations of cardinals, Henry's love letters and the reliability of various sources for the period.

Anne Boleyn continues to fascinate. Her story seems to have it all: royalty, romance, a sudden rise to power and an equally sudden fall leading to a gruesome death, arguably engineered by her husband. The interpretation varies according to whether the writer sees her as a strong, independent and ambitious woman or as a marriage-breaking temptress or an innocent victim of manipulative men. Often such viewpoints are based on the author's own views and upbringing, whether they are products of strict Victorian morality or of the post-Pill era where a woman's sexual activity and refusal to obey men are taken for granted. Some comments herein will be criticised for being judgmental but we cannot learn from the past unless we understand right and wrong. Objectivity toward evil is the first step toward its toleration and growth.

There is no doubt that the interest in Anne will continue and that portrayals of her will vary in line with changing fashions, but this should not prevent historians from seeking the actual truth based on an analysis of the evidence and an understanding of the culture of the period. This book is the result of my own attempt to do just that, through a process of rigorous academic study, leavened with a little humour.

---

1 Anthony Berkeley, *The Poisoned Chocolates Case* (1929), chapter 17.

Note on Conventions

The year is defined as beginning on 1st January rather than 25th March as it did in Tudor times.

Efforts to relate Tudor monetary values to their equivalent today are fraught with difficulty but here the presumption is that one pound in the period principally covered by this book (1525-1536) equates to seven thousand pounds today. This is based on the average labour value as given on eh.net which basically compares a labourer's wage in 1530 with the equivalent today. At the time, an unskilled man might earn 3d a day or between £3 and £4 a year while today, a full time worker on National Minimum Wage would get around £20,000. For further details on why this measure is used in preference to one based on the RPI, see Roderick Floud, 'Putting a Price on the Past', *History Today*, March 2019 vol. 69 issue 3 pp.40-45. It has been deemed necessary to use a figure because it helps put claims made by contemporaries into perspective. For example, the value of Henry's alleged bribes to supporters is shown to be a pittance compared to those paid by Katherine's supporters while the oft repeated stories relating to Thomas Boleyn's poverty are proved to be at best exaggerations or, more frankly, blatant lies.

The following abbreviations are used:

LP	Letters and Papers of Henry VIII
CSPS	Calendar of State Papers: Spain
CSPV	Calendar of State Papers: Venice
CSPM	Calendar of State Papers: Milan

All of these are freely available on british-history.ac.uk. Unless otherwise stated the reference is to the document number and not the page. e.g. LP 4.3205 is volume four of the Letters and Papers series, document 3205. Other abbreviations used are:

SP	State Papers of King Henry the Eighth (published by HMRC between 1831 to 1849)
PP	Account of the Privy Purse expenses of Henry VIII (ed. Nicolas 1827)

Modern spelling and punctuation has been used for all quotations.

To avoid confusion regarding people who change title or job during the period covered by this book, the same name is used throughout. For example, Anne's father is always called Thomas Boleyn rather than Rochford, Wiltshire or Lord Privy Seal. References to the pope all relate to the bishop of Rome although other people bore that title in Henry's day as they do today, such as the head of the Coptic Orthodox church.

Due to space restrictions no bibliography is included but all sources are referenced in full the first time they appear in each chapter.

How did Katherine of Aragon become Queen of England?

The life of Anne Boleyn is tied up with the life of Katherine of Aragon because at the time she met him, Henry was considered to be a married man and years were spent trying to rectify this situation. Any study of the quest made by Henry for an annulment of his "marriage" to Katherine of Aragon must begin over a quarter of a century before with a look at how they came to be united in the first place. Questions regarding what happened between 1501 and 1509 would play a key role in the annulment proceedings so it is vital to look at documents from that period and not simply rely on the recollections of people almost thirty years later which might or might not be accurate.

Henry VII, father of Henry VIII, came to the throne after winning the Battle of Bosworth and defeating Richard III who was widely believed at the time to have murdered the Princes in the Tower, an act felt by contemporaries to be so heinous that it relieved them of any debt of loyalty to him. The battle and Henry's subsequent marriage to the daughter of Edward IV, ended the Wars of the Roses but the years of bloodshed had impoverished the country and Henry faced various pretenders to his throne in the early years, most sponsored by foreign rulers keen to use their puppets as a means of taking control of England. After more than a decade, Henry had established himself and he sought a prestigious bride for his eldest son, Arthur, Prince of Wales. His choice fell on Katherine of Aragon.[1] Spain was wealthy and therefore potentially able to help support England should war break out with France. Spain also offered trading opportunities which it was hoped would benefit the English economy. It should be remembered that this was before Spain became associated with the dreaded Inquisition, and some fifty years before the burning of Protestant martyrs on pyres across England and the despatch of the Armada intent on invading the country. Spain, in 1501, was regarded as a friendly country and most people welcomed the idea of the heir to the throne marrying a Spanish princess who would eventually becoming their queen.

Katherine arrived in England on 2nd October 1501. She was two months shy of her sixteenth birthday and the groom was just over a month past his fifteenth birthday. They were therefore closely matched in age as well as in education. On 14th November 1501, Arthur and Katherine were married at St Paul's. On the morning after, Arthur was reported to have come out of the bedroom asking for a drink saying that he had spent a thirsty night deep in Spain.[2] Today, this statement is generally taken as a bit of youthful boasting or

---

1 She should properly be called Katherine of Castile but convention called her of Aragon and that practice is followed here.
2 LP 4.5574 deposition 3 from Sir Anthony Willoughby dated 28th June 1529. The same was reported in deposition 13.

even disregarded by authors whose support for Katherine means they are inclined to view any statement opposing her case as a lie dreamt up by a Machiavellian Henry VIII. However, whilst such a statement would seem in very bad taste to us, it was usual at the time. In some other European countries it was traditional to display the blood stained bedclothes next morning to show that consummation had taken place and that the bride had been a virgin. Where this did not happen, it was expected that the man would make the confirmation himself – the assumption being that a lady would find alluding to the process indelicate. In 1514 when King Louis XII of France married Henry VIII's sister Mary, he emerged from the bridal chamber to tell his courtiers that he had managed to mount her three times and he was looking forward to doing so again shortly.[3] During the annulment proceedings for Henry's "marriage" to Katherine, Arthur's words would be oft repeated as valid testimony of what happened with Henry making the point in the *Glasse of Truthe* that Arthur's claim was spoken at the time – in contrast to Katherine's almost thirty years later when her lawyers were advising her that arguing the union was not consummated was key to her remaining Queen.[4] Moreover, it is almost certain that Henry VII asked his son, Arthur, about what had happened the next day. A service of thanksgiving was scheduled for the successful completion of the marriage two days after the wedding and Henry would have wanted to know that they could do this in good faith. The King also approved the official record of the wedding which was published very soon after in which it was confirmed that the couple had "concluded and consummate the effect and complement of matrimony."[5]

As soon as the wedding celebrations were over, Katherine and Arthur departed toward their new home of Ludlow Castle. The Spanish ambassador had advised Henry VII that Katherine would be upset if forced to stay behind in London and abstain from sex if her husband went alone.[6] The journey to Ludlow would have taken several days and been an arduous journey, particularly in winter, but Arthur had a job to do and it was necessary that he go. On 20th December, both Arthur and Katherine were reported as being very well.[7] Sadly, three months later, Arthur died on April 2nd 1502. His death came as a tremendous shock to his parents indicating that he had not been regarded as sickly before he left.[8] Indeed, none of the ambassadorial reports or accounts of

---

3 CSPV 2.508; Erin Sadlack *The French Queen's Letters* (New York, 2011) p.70
4 Nicholas Pocock (ed.), *Records of the Reformation* (Oxford, 1870) vol. 2. p.416. The *Glasse of Truthe* (1532) is reproduced in this volume pp.385-421.
5 G. Kipling (ed.), *The receyt of the Ladie Kateryne* (EETS, 1990) p.47.
6 CSPS Supplement.1. There had been some discussion about Katherine staying behind with the Queen but she chose to go with her new husband following a discussion with him.
7 CSPS 1.314. The report was written by the Spanish ambassador.
8 Thomas Hearne (ed.) *John Leland's Collectanea* vol. 5 (London 1774) pp.373-4. It was later revealed by Maurice St John who was first cousin to Prince Arthur as well as his attendant in Ludlow, that the prince had sickened at Shrovetide which that

the wedding suggest that Arthur was anything but an ordinary healthy fifteen year old at the time. Katherine was also ill when he died which suggests that both had contracted a contagious disease such as the sweat.

Arthur's death made ten year old Prince Henry heir to the throne although he was not recognised as this for almost three months as people waited to see if Katherine was pregnant.[9] This is significant in light of later arguments about whether the marriage to Arthur had been consummated: if it had not been, Henry would have become heir immediately.

For Katherine's parents, Ferdinand and Isabella, Arthur's death created a problem. They had hoped that an alliance with England would give them support in their European wars and this was now in jeopardy. The marriage agreement had required them to pay Henry VII one hundred thousand crowns when the couple married with the same amount again before the end of the first year.[10] Understandably, they were reluctant to pay out the money due when there was no longer any chance of their daughter becoming queen and they went so far as to claim that because God had dissolved the marriage by death, they were no longer obliged to pay and should get their money back.[11] Thus, the very day that they learned of Arthur's death – 10th May 1502 – they proposed a solution: Katherine should marry Arthur's younger brother. Alternatively, they wanted their money and daughter back plus all the income to which she was entitled as the dowager Princess of Wales.[12] One can imagine Henry VII's reaction to this last. The fact that his son had died was unfortunate but long life was not something which could be guaranteed in a treaty. The contract required them to pay the outstanding sums before Katherine was entitled to her dower income. Her parents' refusal to do this left Katherine in severe financial straits, a situation which was to last for some years.

The idea of marrying Katherine to Prince Henry was not straightforward. Prince Henry was still only ten years old so below the age to enter into a marriage, let alone consummate one. Was Katherine to stay in England and wait for him to grow up? Most writers today refer to the need for a dispensation from the pope as if it was some routine event like applying for a parking permit. It was nothing of the sort. The Bible stated clearly that God had forbidden men from marrying their brother's wives and in the almost one

---

    year would have meant about February 20th.
9 Henry was first referenced as Prince of Wales in a grant of 22nd June 1502, *Calendar of Patent Rolls* 1494-1509 p.258
10 A crown was valued at 4s 2d so the total value of 200,000 crowns was £13,541 13s 4d which today would be worth around one hundred million pounds. The first 100,000 was paid at Richmond on 28th November 1501, CSPS 1.310
11 CSPS 1.317. The argument about returning the money went on for months. Ferdinand and Isabella claimed it was a Habsburg custom but no clause to this effect had ever been put in the original marriage treaty and the English advised that it was not in line with English law.
12 CSPS 1.317, 318. It was two days later before they thought to send their sympathy to Henry VII on the loss of his son.

thousand and five hundred years which had elapsed since the death of Jesus, nobody had ever been granted permission to do such a thing, not from Rome nor in the Orthodox churches. What Ferdinand and Isabella proposed was manifestly illegal. As this fact is so routinely ignored it is worth stressing.

> NOBODY HAD EVER BEEN GRANTED A DISPENSATION TO MARRY THEIR BROTHER'S WIFE BEFORE.

In 1392, the pope had refused an application from Bernard VII of Foix to marry his brother's widow on grounds he did not have authority to overturn God's law.[13] The Fourth Lateran Council of 1215 had agreed that the limits of consanguinity and affinity up to four degrees – and Henry's link to Katherine was first degree – must be "strictly observed" and "we wish the prohibition to be perpetual, notwithstanding earlier decrees on this subject issued either by others or by us. If any persons dare to marry contrary to this prohibition, they shall not be protected by length of years."[14]

Ferdinand and Isabella were confident, however, that Alexander VI (the notorious Borgia) would grant their request, even though most of the world would have thought the idea of a man marrying his sister-in-law to be as ridiculous as a man marrying his horse. After all, Alexander had in 1496 permitted Ferdinand's sister to marry her husband's half nephew and in 1500 allowed Manuel of Portugal to marry two of their daughters in succession, Isabella and Maria, both of which unions were forbidden by canon law.[15] Moreover, Ferdinand knew that the pope was desperate for Spanish support to get the French out of Naples, something which would not happen if the dispensation was refused.

Not everybody was convinced that Henry could or should marry Katherine. William Warham and Henry VII's mother both opposed the idea.[16] Warham had been involved in the negotiations for Katherine's match to Arthur and was Master of the Rolls and Keeper of the Great Seal as well as Bishop of London and a doctor of canon law. The king's mother, Margaret Beaufort, was

---

13 Bernard accepted the decision and married another woman in 1393.
14 Decrees 50 and 51
15 Lev 18:14 forbids marrying an uncle's wife: it does not mention half-uncles. The situation with regard sisters was mentioned in Lev 18:18 but the Hebrew is unclear whether this is an injunction against polygamy or siblings of the first wife though it does state that the regulation only applies during the lifetime of the first wife. In 1446, pope Eugenius IV had refused to permit the Dauphin to marry a sister of his late wife Margaret. See John Turrecremata, *Commentaria super Decreto Gratiani*, pars ii. c. 35, qu. 2. (Venice 1578)
16 Garrett Mattingly, *Catherine of Aragon* (1942) p.91; LP 4.5774. By the time the dispensation was granted, Warham was Lord Chancellor and Archbishop of Canterbury. The sickness of Henry Dean, his predecessor as Archbishop of Canterbury, had led to Warham taking on a number of his responsibilities before this date.

probably upset because one of her senior staff, who had gone on to serve Arthur as Vice-Chamberlain of his household, had reported at the time Arthur died, that Katherine's demands for frequent intercourse had left the prince too exhausted to recover from his sickness.[17] She therefore had no doubt that the union had been consummated and feared for the physical life of her only remaining grandson.

Henry VII, however, agreed to enter into negotiations for such a union and on 23rd June 1503 an agreement was made. This stated that the money paid for the marriage with Arthur was accepted as the first payment toward the union with Prince Henry and that final payment would only be made upon consummation.[18] It also declared that both families would petition the pope for a dispensation explaining:

> The papal dispensation is required, because the said Princess Katharine had on a former occasion contracted a marriage with the late Prince Arthur, brother of the present Prince of Wales, whereby she became related to Henry, Prince of Wales, in the first degree of affinity, and because her marriage with Prince Arthur was solemnised according to the rites of the Catholic Church, and afterwards consummated.[19]

Over twenty years later, Katherine was to deny that the marriage had been consummated but the question had been raised at the time. Warham, deputed by the King to negotiate the new treaty, was required to proffer legal advice and this would have meant ascertaining if a dispensation was needed for the impediment of affinity (consummated) or public honesty (non-consummated). The Spanish ambassador had checked with Katherine's confessor just after Arthur died, and Father Alessandro said that it had been consummated and suggested that Katherine might be pregnant which turned out not to be the case.[20] Katherine's parents advised they had not had confirmation so the said confessor wrote to Queen Isabella telling her this, a letter which mysteriously disappeared from the Spanish archives later on.[21] Katherine's duenna then wrote to the Queen disputing this statement and as late as April 1503, Isabella claimed to believe this.[22] Nonetheless, both Ferdinand and Isabella happily signed the treaty confirming that the match with Arthur was consummated on

---

17 LP 7.128. Philips died in 1506.
18 Added at Spanish insistence, CSPS 1.327.
19 CSPS 1.364. In the treaty with Spain of June 1503, it is stated that Katherine's union with Arthur "contractum, celebratum & consummatum fuerat" i.e. had been contracted, solemnised and consummated, Thomas Rymer, *Foedera* vol 13 (1727) p.78. The marriage treaty was negotiated by Warham and Foxe, both of whom were called in 1527 to testify to events of this period.
20 Garrett Mattingly, *Catherine of Aragon* (1942) p.49.
21 Patrick Williams, *Katherine of Aragon* (Stroud, 2013) p.128; CSPS 1.325.

24th and 30th September respectively.[23] Why would they do this if it was not true? Certainly, Spain was keen for an agreement with England because they wanted Henry's assistance in their war with France but the likelihood is that they had checked with Katherine herself.[24] There is no trace in the archives of any letters from her to her parents from the time of her arrival in England to this point but it does seem inconceivable that none was written which makes the absence suspicious. Neither Henry not Ferdinand were prone to spend money unnecessarily and they would have known that obtaining a dispensation following a consummated first marriage would be considerably more difficult and hence much more expensive than if it had not.

A couple of days after the treaty was agreed, Prince Henry and Katherine were formally betrothed. Unlike a modern engagement, this was a legally binding contract with both parties saying in response to the question "wilt thou take this man/woman to be thy lawful wedded husband/wife" "I will." Henry was three days short of his twelfth birthday. The decision to go ahead with a betrothal before any decision had been given from Rome was highly presumptuous given there was no precedent for such a marriage in Christian history.

Shortly after this, and notwithstanding the agreement, Katherine's father wrote to his ambassador at Rome, the man tasked with persuading the pope to grant the dispensation, saying that her marriage to Arthur had actually not been consummated and he had only accepted the clause to please the English.[25] Many writers have taken this letter at face value but it was written because a number of people around the pope had evidently said that no dispensation could be granted if she was not a virgin.[26] Ferdinand was a wily political strategist not an affable old duffer keen to humour some English monarch. He wanted the match to go ahead but wanted to protect himself if it did not. A virgin daughter would have been more marriageable elsewhere.

During the course of the attempt to obtain a dispensation, Alexander VI and then Pius III died and were replaced by Julius II who was elected on 1st November 1503. His first response, according to Cardinal Hadrian was to query

---

22 CSPS 1.327 dated 12th July where the Queen refers to Elvira's letter and CSPS 1.360 dated 11th April 1503. David Starkey, *Six Wives* (2004) p.83 notes the vested interest which Elvira had in making such a claim.
23 CSPS 1. 375, 378
24 CSPS 1.327, 344, 372.
25 He claimed he had generously agreed to say it had because "the right of succession depends on the undoubted legitimacy of the marriage," a comment which reveals the extent of doubt there was about the possibility of such a union ever being considered valid. CSPS 1.370 dated 10th August 1503.
26 Both Herbert and Henry VIII suggested that Katherine denied consummation in order to facilitate the grant of the dispensation. Lord Edward Herbert, *The Life and Reign of Henry VIII* (1672) p.8. Pocock, *Records*, vol.2 p.415. Some canon lawyers argued that an unconsummated marriage was not a full marriage so less of a problem.

whether as pope he would have authority to issue such a document.[27] However, a couple of weeks later on 4th February 1504, the same cardinal was to write again to Henry VII to tell him that Julius, following an approach by the representatives of Ferdinand and Isabella, had submitted consideration of the matter to the cardinals of Naples and Portugal but he warned there could be a delay as one of the French cardinals had objected to it.[28] He does not say why Cardinal George d'Amboise of Rouen opposed the dispensation. It could have been on religious grounds but it was more likely to have been political. France had no wish to see England and Spain united and Queen Isabella suspected the French wanted the young Prince Henry to marry instead one of their own princesses.[29] This protest was reported to the papal nuncio in Spain in March 1504.[30] Henry should have been encouraged by the choice of the two cardinals who had been deputed to advise the pope: Jorge da Costa of Portugal was ninety-seven and had been involved in the grant to Manuel I in 1500 while Oliviero Carafa of Naples, aged seventy-three, was a lifelong supporter of Aragon. Neither man was therefore independent. Indeed, Naples was held by Spain at the time of the discussion.[31]

Five months later on 6th July 1504, pope Julius II wrote to say that he would grant the dispensation for the marriage to take place saying that the delay was to allow time for the obstacles to be considered fully and commenting that the rumours that he planned to refuse it were unfounded.[32]

In August, as part of a bundle of documents sent from Spain, a papal brief of dispensation was received in England. The Spanish ambassador confirmed that Henry VII had given it directly to him without keeping a copy or showing it to his councillors, and the ambassador immediately showed it to Katherine.[33] This confirmed that her marriage to Arthur had been consummated. Significantly in light of later events, Katherine raised no objections.

On the basis of this, Henry and Katherine were married in the autumn of 1504. The event was so private that no record survives of the date or witnesses. Henry was thirteen so under age, Katherine eighteen. It may be presumed this was a spousals ceremony where the couple took vows using the present rather

27 Pocock, *Records* vol .1 p.2
28 James Gairdner (ed.) *Letters and Papers Illustrative of the reigns of Richard III and Henry VII* vol 2 (1863) document XXII p115
29 CSPS 1.327 dated 12th July 1502
30 LP 4. Appx.267. Ghinucci found the letter in the papal archives and sent it to Henry VIII who noted it supported his case.
31 It was Aragonese until the French took it in 1501 but reverted to Spain after the battle of Gangliano in December 1503.
32 Pocock, *Records* vol. 1 pp.5-6; CSPS 1.396
33 CSPS 1.398. This was the infamous "Spanish brief" which created so much fuss in 1528 and 1529, the document which Katherine denied having seen and claimed was incorrect because it stated that her union with Arthur had been consummated. It was sent from Rome to Spain because Katherine's mother, Queen Isabella, was ill, Gairdner, *Letters and Papers Illustrative*, vol.1 p.243

than future tense and it may have been before a lawyer in an ordinary room rather than in church.[34]

What had led to this decision by Julius II? Scenario A has the pope and his advisors spending hours in prayerful contemplation of the Bible before receiving a call from God to go boldly where no pope had ever gone before and issue a dispensation. Scenario B has Ferdinand and Isabella, worried that the pope's anxiety over his debts will prevent him finding time to attend to their request, offering him 80,000 ducats to ease his mind. What is certain and supported by documentary evidence, is that Katherine's parents arranged with the pope's banker to write off all his debts[35] and that the pope suddenly announced that he did have the necessary power and would issue the infamous dispensation. Whether there was a causal link between the payment and the pope's decision or it was coincidental that the debts were paid just as the pope had his Damascus moment is perhaps a matter of faith. In years to come, Katherine's supporters would claim the former while everyone else was more cynical and thought the latter. The money paid out was equivalent to £18,000 at the time or around £125 million today – a sure sign of the desperation felt by Katherine's parents and that their request for a dispensation was far from routine. To get a dispensation for their daughter Maria they had only needed to give Alexander VI a wealthy Archbishopric for his great-nephew.[36]

On 8th November, Henry VII, concerned that the actual bull of dispensation had not been received, complained to the pope and he asked that it be given to his ambassador there.[37] Dispensations were ordinarily issued as formal bulls not mere letters or briefs.

Whilst this missive was still en route to Rome, Ferdinand wrote to Henry VII saying that he was sending a copy of the dispensation to his new ambassador De Puebla.[38] Presumably this did not arrive for on 22nd February 1505, the pope wrote to Henry VII admitting that he still had the original. Confirming this was a bull sealed with lead, he said that a copy had been sent to Spain first because Isabella was dying and wanted to be assured of it. Had this not been the case, Henry's bull would have been sent at the same time. He was, however, now arranging for a suitable carrier to bring it to England.[39] On 17th

---

34 The officiant may have been a priest because many were canon lawyers but there was no need for this. Spousals were used when there was some reason why the full solemnisation could not go ahead in church but the families wanted to confirm the contract. The most common reason was that one or both of the parties was under age but they were also used when one of the parties was absent and being represented by a proxy.
35 LP 7.86. Pocock, *Records* vol, 2 p.513. The original document was removed from the archives after Henry's death. Suspicion must fall upon Queen Mary for this.
36 Patrick Williams, *Katherine*, p.99
37 CSPS 1.414
38 CSPS 1.407 dated 24th November 1504. Ferdinand does not specify if he has a brief or bull.
39 James Gairdner (ed.) *Letters and Papers Illustrative of the reigns of Richard III and Henry VII* vol.1 (1861) Document LXVII p.242. Pocock, *Records*. Vol. 1 pp.7-8.

March, the Bishop of Worcester, referring to the pope's recent letter, wrote to Henry VII and said that he had been deputed to bring it. He added that the fact that the dispensation had been sent to Spain first had been supposed to be a secret.[40] Presumably this bull arrived safely as there is no further correspondence about the matter. It would appear that the English filed the document away without reading it carefully, an omission which was to prove costly years later when the validity of the document came to be questioned.

Henry and Katherine should have repeated their vows when he came of age because vows taken by a minor were not binding unless the said minor confirmed them upon reaching maturity[41] but on the day before his fourteenth birthday in 1505, Henry made a formal protest at Richmond before Bishop Richard Foxe of Winchester renouncing the match saying that it had been arranged when he was a minor and he did not consent to it.[42] This rejection was encouraged by Archbishop Warham who continued to believe that marriage to a brother's wife was against divine law and would be displeasing to God.[43] It may be presumed that Henry's father was content with the action and approved it.

Around the same time, Henry wrote to the pope expressing his concern about his wife's behaviour. Katherine, he said, wanted to live the life of a nun and he was concerned that not only was she refusing to give up her frequent fasting when he told her to do so – as his wife, she had promised obedience – but he was worried that she was damaging her health and so risking the likelihood of them having healthy children when they did come together. Since Henry's original letter has not survived, it is impossible to know if this was sent just before or after his protestation although the likelihood is that it was before. The pope replied on 20th October 1505 advising Henry that he must exercise his authority and absolutely forbid Katherine from behaving in this manner and saying that Katherine must not disregard his commands.[44] In light of what was to follow over twenty years later, the letter is particularly interesting and demonstrates an early example of disobedience and disrespect on Katherine's part. Whether her behaviour contributed to her dire obstetric history is uncertain.

On 5th October 1507, De Puebla wrote to Ferdinand to say that King Louis XII of France had told the English ambassador that he wished Prince Henry to marry the sister of the Duc d'Angoulême and he added that Katherine

---

Isabella died on 26th November 1504.
40 CSPS 1.426
41 The same procedure had taken place with Arthur.
42 Gilbert Burnet, *The History of the Reformation* vol 4 (Pocock edition, Oxford 1865) pp.17-18
43 Henry Ansgar Kelly, *The Matrimonial Trials of Henry VIII* (1976) p.126. Warham said the protest should be made the day after rather than the day before Henry's fourteenth birthday as protests made before coming of age were invalid. The information was revealed in a deposition made by Bishop Foxe in 1527 and Warham did not dispute this.
44 Stephan Ehses, *Romische Dokumente* (Paderborn, 1893) pp.xliii-xliv

was upset because she had heard – he did not say who told her – that her marriage to Henry was "not yet rendered indissoluble."[45]   Meanwhile in June 1508, it was reported that Prince Henry would marry Eleanor, daughter of the late Archduke Philip, a man who had made a favourable impact on Henry when they met in 1506. [46] Nine months later, on 6th March 1509, ambassadors arrived from the King of the Romans to arrange a match between Prince Henry and the daughter of Albert of Bavaria.[47] How serious these negotiations were it is hard to say but Ferdinand had still not paid the money due as per the marriage treaty so it would not be too surprising if Henry VII was considering his options. In July 1508, he told the new Spanish representative Fuensalida that he considered his son free to marry where he chose.[48] It is possible that Henry was only pretending interest in other brides in order to encourage Ferdinand to pay up, but he may have felt that he could do better for his son since Katherine was not an heiress. In December 1507, he signed an agreement for his daughter Mary to marry Charles, the future Emperor which was clearly a very prestigious match and the couple were espoused a year later.[49] If Henry's match with Katherine was confirmed when he came of age, this would make a double link between the Tudors and the Habsburgs. Alternatively, a match with another country could broaden England's diplomatic ties and potentially add territory and wealth to the crown.

The situation changed suddenly on 21st April 1509 when Henry VII died and his son became Henry VIII at the age of seventeen. Until that time, Fuensalida had been pessimistic about Katherine's prospects. In September 1508 he had told Ferdinand that he suspected that should he pay the money due for Katherine's second marriage, Henry VII would poison her and keep the cash – a bizarre theory which Ferdinand treated with the contempt it deserved. Prompted by fears of losing the prized English match, Ferdinand finally sent the money to Fuensalida who promptly sent it back overseas saying that Henry VII was meeting with the French and discussing a league against Ferdinand and

---

45   CSPS 1.552 dated 5th October 1507. Marguerite d'Angoulême was the same age as Henry and would become a reformer and exert an influence on Anne Boleyn. Her brother Francis went on to reign as Francis I after the death of Louis XII. Ferdinand wrote to Katherine three months later to reassure her that he considered her marriage to Henry totally valid, indissoluble and secure. CSPS 1.575
46   Gairdner, *Letters and Papers Illustrative* vol. 1 Document LXV p.346. For the story of Henry being rather dazzled by Philip see David Starkey, *Henry: Virtuous Prince* (2008) pp. 215-219. Philip's wife was Katherine of Aragon's elder sister. Eleanor would later marry Francis I of France.
47   CSPS Supplement no 4
48   Duke of Alba (ed.), *Correspondencia de Gutierre Gomez de Fuensalida* (Madrid 1907) pp.460-1.
49   The original treaty is in Rymer, *Foedera*, vol.13 pp 236-239. An English summary is at CSPS 1.558. Confirmation of the marriage is at CSPS 1.602. This point is worth remembering given in later years, Katherine was to claim that she had to marry Henry as this was the only way to prevent war and maintain links between the countries. Mary's remained espoused to Charles until 1514.

had warships ready in the Thames. Just six days after the death of Henry VII, Fuensalida wrote that he had been told by two members of the royal council that Henry VII had told his son on his deathbed that he could marry whom he liked and one of the said councillors said that the new king was worried about the prohibition in the Bible on marrying a brother's wife.[50] This is important as it shows Henry's scruple pre-dated his romance with Anne Boleyn by almost twenty years and that it existed before he lost any of his children.

Fuensalida was astonished therefore to be summoned by the royal council on May 5th and be told that Henry VIII wished the marriage to go ahead as planned as part of an alliance between England, Spain and the Holy Roman Empire which would have as its objective the bridling of French ambitions. Katherine, who as recently as 9th March, had expressed her desire to enter a convent, wrote to her father to tell him the good news on the 6th May.[51]

On 11th May, Ferdinand, who had clearly not received this news but only heard of the death of Henry VII, wrote to Fuensalida to tell him that whereas he had refused the late king's requirements, he was willing to grant any made by the new king in order to expedite the match. In particular he must insist on it being consummated without delay and tell Henry that his previous vows could not be dissolved and that it would be a sin if he tried. In respect of Henry's scruples about the marriage being forbidden by God, he should reassure him that the pope had said it was fine. If that did not exert enough pressure on the young monarch, he was to remind him that the treaties signed by Ferdinand and Henry VII were legally binding on their successors so he had no choice. [52]

Henry exchanged marriage vows with Katherine on 11th June watched by Lord Shrewsbury and William Thomas. Thomas, his groom and friend, had also attended Katherine and Arthur and been with them in Ludlow.[53] The minister asked:

> Most illustrious Prince, is it your will to fulfil the treaty of marriage concluded by your father, the late King of England, and the parents of the Princess of Wales, the King and Queen of Spain; and, as the pope has dispensed

---

50   Mattingly, *Catherine*, pp.85, 91, 93. Fuensalida's letter of 26th April can be found on pp.515-517 of his correspondence. Henry VIII wrote to Eleanor's aunt on 27th June that he had married Katherine because it was his father's dying wish but it is probable that this was a diplomatic white lie to avoid hurting Eleanor's feelings or provoking war – LP 1.84
51   CSPS Supplement 3
52   CSPS 2.8. Letters took around eleven days to get from London to Spain.
53   Starkey, *Henry: Virtuous Prince* p.281. Thomas was the person mentioned on Henry's prayer roll which is kept by the National Archives and would testify to the number of times he escorted Arthur to Katherine's bed at the legatine court of 1529. He was one of the first people to receive grants in Henry's reign – LP 1.54. 18 and 19.

> with this marriage, to take the Princess who is here present for your lawful wife?
>
> The King answered: I will.
>
> Most illustrious Princess, is it your will to fulfil the treaty of marriage concluded by your parents the King and Queen of Spain, and the late King of England, and, as the pope has dispensed with this marriage, to take the King who is here present for your lawful husband?
>
> The Princess answered: I will.

Despite Ferdinand's instructions, Katherine refused to allow Fuensalida to attend.[54] On this occasion, the service was a full solemnisation before a priest and with a nuptial mass. The union was not just a legal contract but sacramental. During the service, the authorising bull of dispensation would have been read which referred to her union with Arthur having been "perhaps" consummated and Katherine made no comment.

Why did Henry do it? For years he had lived a very protected existence due to the unsurprising concern which his father had for the life of his sole son and heir.[55] Suddenly, he was free of parental constraint and he had a fortune to spend and crowds of adoring people wherever he turned. He could have commenced negotiations for an overseas princess but that would have taken months and he might not like what he got. His later experience of marrying Anne of Cleves without meeting her was to show the dangers of this approach. Katherine was on his doorstep. He knew her and liked her and, best of all to a seventeen year old red blooded male in search of a sex life, she was instantly available. He had been brought up to believe that bishops knew best and he accepted their advice that the pope's dispensation made it all right. In later years as a mature man, he would come to realise that he had been seriously ill advised.

On 16th June 1509, Ferdinand finally paid his contractual debt and eight days later, on 24th June, Henry and Katherine were crowned.[56] A new chapter in English history had begun.

---

54 CSPS 2.15 dated 18th May 1509.

55 Fuensalida on 9th May 1508 said that nobody was allowed to speak with Prince Henry but this may not have been entirely true but rather a case of Henry VII seeking to keep the Spanish ambassador away from his son. *Correspondencia* p.449. Fuensalida was forced to report that he had so upset the King that Henry VII refused to speak to him. CSPS Supplement no 4 dated 20th March 1509

56 CSPS 2.18

What are the principal sources for the life of Anne Boleyn?

There is an old police maxim, "Accept nothing, Believe nobody, Check everything" and this is advice applicable to the historian as much as the detective. The fact that a source is contemporary or close to it does not make it reliable. Consider today the vast number of books and websites purporting to tell the truth about the relationships of Charles and Diana, William and Harry, Andrew and Sarah. Virtually none of the authors have ever met any of the individuals about whom they write, let alone have they lived with them, grown up with them or been present at private conversations between them. Even when they have some link, such as once being a member of staff, their contact has been limited to one area of life so they have not seen the wider picture. The sixteenth century may not have had tabloid journalists and bloggers but it had royal watchers, people who lived on gossip. Chapuys is often quoted but his information mostly came from spies and what the government chose to tell him: he was not a councillor or man on the inside and he never spoke to Anne Boleyn. Cavendish, also often cited, was the Tudor equivalent of the twentieth century Paul Burrell. Not only did authors make mistakes but they usually had their own agendas. Before employing them as sources, it is necessary to consider why they were writing and whether they were in a position to know what they were talking about or if they were simply guessing or reporting rumours. The main sources which affect a study of Anne are shown below together with a note of which aspects of her life are to be found in them. Those familiar with Anne's life will recognise the stories referenced but they will be discussed later in the text.

Cavendish

George Cavendish, *Life of Wolsey, Metrical Visions* (both c.1556)

Author

George Cavendish, (bc.1500) was one of Cardinal Wolsey's staff and served him from around 1522 through to his death in 1530.[1] Thereafter, Cavendish retired to the country.

---

1 He says he witnessed the arrival of Wolsey's cardinal's hat from Rome in November 1515 but gives no indication that he was working for him at this time. The hat was taken in a spectacular procession which Cavendish says had the grandeur of a coronation George Cavendish, *The Life of Cardinal Wolsey* (ed. Samuel Singer, 1827) vol. 1 p.92

Reason for writing

He said he wrote "that all estates might see what it is to trust to fortune's mutability"[2] but also to defend his master's image against the "sundry surmises and imagined tales made about his proceedings and doings which I myself have perfectly known to be untrue."[3]

Viewpoint regarding Anne

Hostile. In *Metrical Lives,* he compares Anne with Athaliah who was a queen of Judah in the mid ninth-century BC. The Bible describes how she seized the throne and the rightful heir had to be hidden to escape her killing fury. After six years of wickedness which included murdering the godly and encouraging evil, she was herself publicly executed on the king's orders – 2 Kings 11:1-16; 2 Chronicles 22:2-3. Cavendish clearly was hinting that Anne had threatened Mary's life and suggesting she was responsible for the death of men like More and Fisher whom he saw as true men of God. In his *Life of Wolsey*, he describes her execution as one of the "wonderful works of God against such persons as forget God." [4]

Principal stories:
- Anne's engagement to Henry Percy
- Anne's vow of revenge on Cardinal Wolsey for breaking up this betrothal
- Henry's love for Anne from 1522 onwards
- the Bishop of Bayonne provoking the annulment
- Anne arranging a picnic to prevent Henry having further meetings with Wolsey at Grafton
- Katherine's performance in the court at Bridewell
- Anne being a factional leader
- the university opinions being sought and received before the legatine court was requested
- Henry not telling Wolsey that he wanted an annulment until after the Sack of Rome
- Anne being known as "the night crow"

Reliability

Cavendish was one of Wolsey's Gentlemen Ushers. He was part of a team of twelve whose role was to meet and greet guests of the Cardinal and to take them to him. If they were staying, he would be involved in ensuring they had suitable accommodation and in liaising with the kitchen staff for their refreshment. As an usher, Cavendish also took messages for Wolsey. He describes the role of the ushers as "daily waiters", not because they waited on

---

2   Vol. 2 p.6
3   Vol. 1 p.65
4   Ibid. p.130

tables but because they awaited instructions.[5] It must be assumed that the ushers worked in rotation to ensure Wolsey had service at all times of day.[6] When Wolsey went to France in 1527, Cavendish went ahead with letters and to check the arrangements. When Wolsey travelled in England, Cavendish was involved in finding him places to stay. When a high-ranking French delegation came to Hampton Court, Cavendish was one of three men responsible for ensuring the guest rooms had silk hangings on the beds. Cavendish would have worn a sumptuous uniform or livery to show he was one of Wolsey's staff and he would have accompanied Wolsey to certain major events where Wolsey wanted to enter with his retinue to show his importance. However, Cavendish was not a confidant of Wolsey. He would have seen Wolsey signing documents but not have been in any position to see the actual documents themselves or to read them. At banquets, he would have sat with other ushers in the corner and not at the table with the King and other ministers of state. He would not have attended meetings hence the dialogue and speeches he uses in his *Life* are speculative and Cavendish admits this by often adding the words "in effect". This is entirely in line with practices of the period. Reginald Pole commented of his own work: "I do claim truth for my account even though perhaps in the manner and arrangement I have adopted I cannot maintain that I have reproduced the actual words used for I was not present. But this much I can claim that there is nothing of any importance recorded in the speech I have written which I have not been given to understand either from his own account or those who shared his policy."[7]

By contrast, *Metrical Visions* is a fantasy in which Cavendish envisages a host of dead people coming to him as he sits under a tree and all confessing their faults, admitting that he was always right and they were utterly wrong.

Cavendish wrote his *Life* in the mid 1550s, some twenty to thirty years after the events he describes. Whether it was poor memory or indicative of his position in the household, there are a number of errors in his book. Boleyn enthusiasts only tend to read the sections in which he mentions Anne but Cavendish also gives a long account of relations with France and the war of the 1520s which is far from accurate. He routinely gets names wrong, such as describing Campeggio as Bishop of Bath and saying Henry appointed him thus when he visited England in 1518: in fact, Campeggio was appointed Bishop of Salisbury in 1524 when he was in Italy. Cavendish names Bridget's father as Richard Wiltshire when he was John. Cavendish claims that Cromwell defeated a Parliamentary bill against Wolsey which led to a charge of Praemunire being levelled instead: in fact, the Praemunire charge was made three months before Wolsey's case was mentioned in Parliament and there was no debate. One of the most famous incidents in his book is when Katherine throws herself on her

---

5 Ibid p.99
6 A further two ushers were employed in his private chamber.
7 Quoted in Arthur Ogle, *The Tragedy of the Lollards Tower* (1949) p.206, Thucydides in his *History of the Peloponnesian War* 1.22.1 similarly says he has given characters the words which were demanded by the occasion *in his opinion*.

knees before Henry at the legatine court and swears she was a virgin when she came to him. This appears in Shakespeare's play and in every novel and film made about the period. It is a moment of high drama, but curiously does not appear in any other account of the trial, including official reports or Campeggio's correspondence. This suggests it was something which Cavendish either dreamt up to add colour to his narrative or put in by genuine mistake based on statements Katherine made on other occasions.

His chronology is erratic to say the least. In 1527, he has Anne plotting to send Wolsey to France to get him out of the way so she can whisper evil lies about him to Henry. According to Cavendish, Wolsey goes whereupon the French assume he is there to arrange a match for Henry and Princess Renée and another for Henry's daughter with the Duke of Orléans. These scandalous suggestions are ignored by Wolsey who negotiates a great peace which he comes back and tells Henry about at Allington. Two weeks later there is a big celebration in London and only after that, does Henry suggest he wants to annul his union with Katherine, something which shocks the Cardinal. He arranges a meeting of bishops who advise on a European wide appeal to the universities. Having read their reports, Cavendish says Wolsey wrote to the pope urging the establishment of a legatine court involving himself and Campeggio.

Every single element of this scenario is wrong. Wolsey went to France having already negotiated a treaty of perpetual peace with France and Mary's marriage to Orléans which had been publicly celebrated. He went at the invitation of Francis I, not as a result of some plot of Anne Boleyn. Wolsey returned from France to see Henry at Richmond not Allington. The annulment process had begun some five months earlier and Wolsey had already held a hearing into the matter and told Francis about it. The universities were not asked to give their verdicts until 1530 – after the legatine court had been held and Wolsey's fall – with most not providing their views until after his death.

Frankly, the work seems to illustrate the comment that memory "usually chronicles the things that have never happened, and couldn't possibly have happened."[8] Cavendish did, however, see Anne Boleyn up close and regularly because she was a regular visitor to Wolsey's home. Whether he ever had cause to speak to her cannot be known. If he did, it was most likely only to answer a question like, "Where is the Cardinal at present?"

Clifford

Henry Clifford, *The Life of Jane Dormer, Duchess of Feria* (1643)

Author

Clifford was born in the 1570s and employed by Jane Dormer for at least eight years, probably longer. Jane joined the service of "Bloody" Queen

---

8 Cecily in Act 2 of Oscar Wilde's *The Importance of Being Earnest*

Mary around 1553. She was born in 1535 just a year before Anne's death and Clifford almost forty years after, so neither knew her.[9]

Reason for Writing

After Jane's death in 1613, her family commissioned Clifford to write her biography and gave him access to her papers.

Viewpoint regarding Anne

Hostile. Jane's great uncle, Sebastian Nudigate, had been executed by Henry for opposing the break with Rome and Clifford was himself a loyal Roman Catholic. Clifford's writing style is clever and sneaky. For example, he reports that an attempt was made to poison Bishop Fisher in the same paragraph as an account of Anne Boleyn loving to dance. He does not say she was responsible but the two topics clearly should be separate and his decision to unite them is designed to give the impression that she was. In a similar manner, he reports the rumour that Katherine of Aragon was poisoned and follows this with the words "the Lady Anne hated her extremely."

Principal Stories
- Anne mistaking Mary's curtsey at Mass as a sign of respect and Mary's rude response
- Anne losing her child after seeing Jane Seymour sitting on Henry's knee
- Mark Smeaton being the father of Elizabeth I
- Wolsey being the instigator of Katherine's troubles and telling the Emperor that Henry intended to marry Marguerite d'Alençon
- Anne's mother being a whore
- Anne being twenty-eight when she died
- Anne's father being one of those who pronounced her guilt and dying of grief "shortly after"
- Katherine claiming she was being punished for her parents' sin in demanding the death of the innocent son of the Duke of Clarence

Reliability

The way that the book is written makes it impossible to know what information Clifford got from Jane and what from other sources, and this makes the reliability hard to assess. The incident in the chapel probably came from Queen Mary herself because so few would have heard the exchange, but it could have been recalled by another lady-in-waiting who was in attendance on the day. The story of Anne losing the baby after seeing Jane Seymour on Henry's knee is taken from Sander as is the description of Bishop John Fisher as "the light not only of the kingdom of England but of the entire Christian

---

9   On p.59 of the 1887 edition of the memoir, it says that Jane died aged 67 but on p. xvii it quotes a letter dated 22nd March 1606 which says that she had celebrated her seventy-first birthday on January 6th.

world."[10] Anne's age is a hotly debated issue amongst historians. Clifford gives the same age as Camden but his references to Camden's book in his text, show he had read it. If Jane had been told the same age by Queen Mary, someone who would undoubtedly have known exactly how old Anne was, it would be strong corroborative evidence for 1506/7 but as there is no way of knowing whether Clifford took the age from Camden or from Jane, the information must be treated with caution. With regard Anne's father dying of grief "shortly after" Anne, she died in May 1536 and he in March 1539.

De Carles

Lancelot de Carles, *The Trial and Death of Queen Anne Boleyn* (1536)[11]

Author
     Lancelot de Carles was a young French clergyman attached to the French embassy who was present in 1536 when Anne fell.

Reason for Writing
     It was an account of a life in the tradition of French narrative poetry designed to provide moral instruction as well as an account of sad events. He notes the recipient was an admirer of Anne and hopes evidence of her trust in Christ throughout the worst of times will inspire him.

Viewpoint regarding Anne
     Mixed. He assumed Anne's guilt but admired her courage at the end.

Principal Stories
- the completely unexpected nature of Anne's fall
- Anne developing her musical skills in France
- Anne having beautiful eyes and being elegant in all she did
- Anne being a virgin when she married
- Elizabeth being born following an easy labour but to a sorrowful queen
- the opposition to Anne mounting after the deaths of More and the Carthusians
- a fire in Anne's apartments threatening her life
- Anne losing her baby in January 1536 when she heard of Henry's accident
- one of Anne's ladies inadvertently alerting Henry to Anne's infidelity via her brother
- George Boleyn's anger at being condemned on one woman's testimony
- Mark Smeaton confessing to adultery while in prison
- Henry offering Norris his life if he would only confess to adultery with Anne, and him refusing

---

10   Dormer p.74. Sander has: "he was the light not of England only but of Christendom." p.66
11   Circulated in manuscript prior to publication in 1545.

- the public rejoicing when Anne was arrested because they hoped Mary would be restored
- the efforts made by Weston's family to save his life
- the staunch self defence made by Anne and her brother and their bravery facing death
- Anne's active prayer life
- the scaffold speeches and addresses to the trial court of Anne and George

Reliability

He wrote the poem within two weeks of the event taking his story from things he had seen as well as those he had been told. His position meant he had access to privileged information but he was not a news reporter but a poet. Thus, the fact that he refers to maidens attending Anne to the scaffold need not be regarded as an accurate description of the women involved – whom many historians believe to have been much older – but rather artistic licence or plain chivalry.

The poem does not name the lady whose comment began the investigation into Anne nor the woman whom George Boleyn blamed. Other sources identify the former as the Countess of Worcester whilst the second could be the same or Jane Rochford.

A number of minor details are inaccurate but the work should not be judged against the standards of modern investigative journalism any more than Genesis should be assessed in relation to the understanding of present day physicists. If the author had waited longer, he may have corrected some of the mistakes. The use of dramatic tension should also be remembered. The work is valuable as an accurate report of gossip at the time: whether the gossip was true is a separate question.

Forrest

William Forrest, *The History of Grisild the Second* (1558)

Author

The author was chaplain to Queen Mary and had been witness to the disputation regarding the validity of Henry's "marriage" to Katherine in April 1530 at Oxford. He notes he was in service at the time and given he lived over forty years more, it is probable that he was then in his 'teens.

Reason for Writing

He dedicated his book to Queen Mary

Viewpoint regarding Anne

Hostile. He describes Katherine as being "lightened with grace divine" while Anne is associated with heresy, the brutal execution of priests, the destruction of crosses and the denigration of saints and the Blessed Virgin.

Principal stories
 - Katherine being discarded because she was old, ugly and sterile
 - Anne joining the court after the annulment proceedings began

Reliability
Forrest's chronology is inaccurate. He has Anne advanced to the status of Marquess before the legatine court even met – four years early – and claims that Katherine accompanied Henry on his summer progresses in Anne's train. He also states that Katherine was abused in the court at Dunstable in 1533 and that the evidence she and her lawyers presented was ignored: Katherine did not attend the court or send any representatives so this is patently untrue. It is unknown whether he ever saw Anne in person but if he did, his description is important for the debate over her age for he writes of her as being "a fresh young damsel" in 1528.

Foxe

John Foxe, *Acts and Monuments* (1563)[12]

Author
Foxe was a student at Oxford during Anne's reign and nineteen when she died. Although he never met her, he did after his graduation become tutor to the Howard family, her mother's kin. It was while with them that he started writing his history of the Church which he continued to work upon during his exile in Strasbourg in the reign of Bloody Mary. Upon his return to England, he resumed his links with the Howards. He died in 1587 aged seventy.

Reason for Writing
Foxe wished to document the Reformation, especially the persecution inflicted by Bloody Mary.

Viewpoint regarding Anne
Positive. He described Anne as a "Christian and devout Deborah" and "a most virtuous and noble lady."

Principal stories
 - Anne's generosity to the poor including giving £12 10s a week in alms

---

12 Also known as the *Book of Martyrs*. For a fuller analysis of Foxe as a source, see Thomas Freeman, 'Research, Rumour and Propaganda – Anne Boleyn in Foxe's Book of Martyrs,' *Historical Journal* vol. 38 no 4 (1995) pp.797-819.

- Anne giving Simon Fish's *Supplication* to Henry
- Henry removing Anne in order to marry Jane
- Anne assisting Thomas Patmore
- Anne having a quiet, moderate and mild nature
- Stephen Gardiner and other "wily papists" encouraging Henry to discard Anne

Reliability

Foxe's informants included Anne's silkwoman, Joan Wilkinson; one of her chaplains, Matthew Parker; her most senior Lady of the Household, the Duchess of Richmond who was also Anne's cousin; and the widow of Simon Fish. His sources were, therefore, impressive and well able to know the truth. Unlike many of the other sources listed here, they spent time with Anne and saw her both in good times and bad.

Hall, Edward

Edward Hall, *The Union of the Two Noble and Illustrious Families of Lancaster and York* (1548) reissued as *Hall's Chronicle* (1809)

Author

Hall was a lawyer and member of the Parliament which sat from 1529 to 1536. He witnessed key events in the lives of Henry and Anne and heard speeches by them.

Reason for Writing

He was continuing the tradition of the chronicle and aimed to show how the houses of York and Lancaster had been united. Dedicating his work to Edward VI, he said he wished to preserve the glorious reputation of Henry VIII and ensure the fame of his native land would shine.

Viewpoint regarding Anne

Neutral regarding Anne herself, Hall was staunchly supportive of Henry and deeply mistrustful of Wolsey and France. He strongly approved of the break with Rome.

Principal Stories
- there being talk "among the common people since the first day of his marriage" that Henry's union with Katherine was flawed because the pope could not dispense a man to marry his brother's widow

- the Spanish being the first to question Mary's legitimacy back in 1521[13]
- Longland starting the annulment crisis to strengthen the Anglo-French alliance
- Thomas Boleyn bringing back an image of Marguerite d'Alençon
- Henry's speech at Bridewell in November 1528
- Campeggio being "more learned in the papal law than in divinity."
- Henry ordering Campeggio's bags to be searched for letters to or from Rome
- huge crowds filling the streets for Anne's coronation
- Anne being crowned with St Edward's crown
- Anne wearing yellow when Katherine died
- Henry wearing white to mourn Anne Boleyn after her execution

Reliability

Almost uniquely, Hall was an actual eyewitness to many of the events he describes in this period, although ill health meant he was not at the later ones. The original publisher, Richard Grafton wrote in the preface that Hall: "perfected and wrote this history no farther then to the four and twentieth year of King Henry the eight: the rest he left noted in divers and many pamphlets and papers, which so diligently and truly as I could, I gathered the same together, and have in such wise compiled them, as may after the said years, appear in this work: but utterly without any addition of mine." Thus, Hall was a witness up to and including Anne's coronation, but after that, what we have is Grafton's compilation from Hall's notes.

Hall was a serious man. He had no interest in gossip though he did love spectacle and the records he provides of Anne's coronation and of the trip to Calais in 1532 are rich in detail, much of it unique to him. He also expounds at length on the progress of the war in Europe and on trade matters, a reminder that most people had other things on their mind than the prospects of Anne Boleyn. Unlike most other sources, he endeavours to distinguish between fact and rumour. For example, he says that people did not know why Wolsey was going to France in 1527 which is why stories spread that he was going to bring back Marguerite so that Henry could marry her that summer.[14] This was obviously untrue because Marguerite was already married but the story enables us to see what people thought, which history proves is generally more important than what was actually the case. Clearly, the proposed annulment became public knowledge almost instantly and there was no doubt amongst Londoners that it would be granted virtually by return post to Rome if a royal wedding was expected so soon. Anne Boleyn does not get a mention until after the failure of the legatine court in 1529 and Hall makes it clear that only the

---

13   The claim made by Sir Nicholas Harvey in an exchange with a Spanish marquis, pp.782-3.
14   Vergil reports the same story though he declares it to be a fact. Vergil's history is more valuable for earlier periods when he was involved at the heart of government. By this period, he was not only away from court but so filled with personal animosity toward Wolsey that his judgment was seriously impaired.

ignorant and women doubted that Henry's motivation was genuinely to obtain an undisputed heir and to save his soul. With regard her fall and execution, there is no comment at all and just a terse note of the grounds.

Aside from events which he witnessed himself, Hall had access to good sources. He states that he was able to borrow the notes which Campeggio's secretary took during an audience with Katherine and to translate them in full. Although shorthand in the modern sense had not been invented, lawyers were accomplished writers at speed so his account here is effectively a recording – and not a fanciful recreation such as would be found in other sources such as Cavendish. He also knew Henry's ambassador to the Imperial court, Sir Nicholas Harvey from whom he received information. Harvey's wife, Bridget, was a servant of Anne Boleyn.

Hall, Richard

Richard Hall, *Life of Fisher* (c.1560)

Author

The amount of detail about Fisher's appearance, voice, lifestyle and home indicate that the author was part of his household, probably a chaplain or secretary. The work is undated but he refers to one of his sources being the elderly vicar of Cuxton near Rochester, John Buttyll, whom he says was still alive.[15] The praise for Mary and lack of abuse for Elizabeth suggests the work was begun in Mary's reign and completed just afterwards as it notes the death of Cardinal Pole in 1558.

Reason for Writing

The manuscript, which was not published at the time, was a standard hagiographical work in praise of Bishop John Fisher of Rochester whom the author regarded as a martyr for the Roman church.

Viewpoint regarding Anne

Unfavourable. He compares Henry to Nero and Herod saying he was worse than both of them because as a Christian, he should have known better. He says that Henry "did not only perpetrate patricide and sacrilege but also that heinous treason of heresy all at one clap, whilst in ripping the bowels of his mother, the holy church and very spouse of Christ, he laboured to tear her in pieces and despoiling her authority (being but one of her rotten members) monstrously took upon him to be her supreme head." He describes Anne as "no better than a harlot" but does not, however, implicate her in the attempted poisoning of Bishop Fisher. He talks positively of Queen Mary and praises the execution of Archbishop Thomas Cranmer and the way in which Martin Bucer's body was dug up after death to be burnt as a heretic.

---

15   The parish register records his burial on 26th August o1576.

Principal Stories
- Anne being Henry's daughter and her mother laughing about it
- Anne asking for Fisher's head while Henry was feasting at Hanworth
- Fisher's head being sent to Anne after his execution and her scarring her hand on a projecting tooth
- an attempt being made to assassinate Fisher by someone from Anne's father's house
- Wolsey appointing Longland as Henry's confessor so that he could learn Henry's secrets and use him to sow doubts about the validity of the union with Katherine
- Katherine accusing Wolsey of starting the annulment crisis in revenge for the Emperor not making him pope
- Henry starting the annulment proceedings before falling in love with Anne
- Henry sending Convocation the bill for his annulment costs
- Henry's body bursting in the coffin and his blood being licked up by a big black dog
- an attempt being made to poison Fisher
- Henry planning to frame Katherine Parr for heresy because he was tired of her

Reliability

There is no reason to doubt the statements made by the author about Fisher's prayer life and charitable works. He says that he has heard Stephen Gardiner preach but not spoken to him. He says he has spoken to people who knew Wolsey though he gives no indication of ever having seen him himself. There is nothing to suggest that he ever saw Henry or Anne and the words he attributes to them at various points are at best hearsay or more likely fabrication. The text includes whole pages copied from Cavendish, for example the account of Katherine's speech at the legatine court and Percy's exchange with Wolsey about Anne. Hall also follows Cavendish in his error regarding the Bishop of Bayonne. Other factual errors include references to Sir Thomas Bryan (should be Francis) and the universities being polled for their views in 1527 (should be 1530). He was also evidently familiar with Harpsfield's work quoting him on Anne's appearance in Henry's life after the annulment began and Henry's body exploding in the coffin.

Harpsfield

Nicholas Harpsfield, *The Pretended Divorce of Henry VIII* (c.1557)

Author

Harpsfield trained as a canon lawyer before beoming a priest. He was Archdeacon of Canterbury under Queen Mary and examined hundreds of people during her reign with a number being sent to the flames for their beliefs.

Reason for Writing

Harpsfield saw the accession of Queen Mary as proof of God vindicating her mother and heralding a new golden age of Roman Catholic ascendancy. He sought to make the legal case for Katherine's "marriage" to Henry being valid claiming "the unlawful divorce was, and is, the very seedwoman of all the miseries and evils, of all the heavy and hateful heresies which of late have most pitifully overwhelmed the realm." Harpsfield's book is in three parts and includes an account of Bishop Fisher's Latin treatises on the subject, his own replies to books by Egidius, Wakefield and Mantua, some comments on the *Glasse of Truthe* and on the legislation which brought about religious change. He also gives an account of Henry's separation from Anne of Cleves and Kathryn Howard. He claims that God was so displeased with Henry's treatment of Katherine that he chose to "plague him with marriages"!

Viewpoint regarding Anne

Hostile. He was seventeen when Anne died and never met her. He compared her to Salome whose dancing so inflamed Herod that he gave her the head of John the Baptist (Matt.14:6-11): "By the marvellous providence and vengeance of God, this woman which at such time as with her playing, singing, and dancing, she had best opportunity, never ceased (as the other dancing damsel that craved St. John Baptist's head importunately) to crave the good bishop's and Sir Thomas More's heads, which thing at length, to their immortal glory, she compassed ere the year turned about, to her perpetual shame and ignominy, lost her head also, as did the foresaid dancing damsel."

Principal stories
- Thomas Wyatt warning Henry before he married Anne that she was a loose woman
- Henry and Anne being married at Whitehall by Rowland Lee
- Henry commencing the annulment before falling in love with Anne
- Anne's marriage being annulled due to an invalid dispensation
- Henry having a sexual relationship with Anne's mother and sister
- Henry's body bursting open in his coffin and his remains being consumed by a dog
- Warham's prediction that Thomas Cranmer would destroy the church with heresy

- Wolsey suggesting the annulment because he was upset Katherine's nephew had not wanted him to be pope
- Katherine saying Anne should be pitied and not cursed
- Anne being pre-contracted to Henry Percy

Reliability

Harpsfield claimed to have read correspondence sent by Wolsey, Cromwell and Henry VIII to their agents in Rome but does not reveal how he had access to this information. He clearly should not have been able to see it and there is no certainty that what he says he was shown was genuine. Most of his comments – such as his story about Henry and Anne's mother – are reported as hearsay, but he does occasionally give names of sources such as William Constell who he says drove away the dog from Henry's corpse and Father Elstowe who heard a sermon preached before Henry VIII against Peto. He names Anthony Bonvisi, an Italian merchant whose family had a bank in London, as the source for the story about Wyatt warning Henry against marrying Anne. For some forty years, Bonvisi was a close friend of Sir Thomas More who wrote to him from the Tower calling him the "apple of his eye." It is interesting to note how many of the negative stories about Anne came from More's friends. Harpsfield is most often quoted with regard to Henry and Anne's wedding but his account was not designed to be factual but to stress the illegality of the event and therefore the bastardy of the future Elizabeth I. To this end, the account includes multiple breaches of canon law and laughable dialogue.[16]

Latymer

William Latymer, *Cronickille of Anne Bulleyne* (c.1560)

Author

William Latymer was born in 1498 and served as a chaplain to Anne Boleyn and later to Elizabeth I. He died in 1583.

Reason for Writing

He wished to provide Elizabeth on her accession with an account of her mother's lifestyle so that Anne would "not be utterly forgotten but be commended to immortal memory" and Elizabeth inspired by her "example to embrace virtue, charity, equity and godliness." To this end, he compiled a memoir based on what he remembered, but he also spoke to other people who had served Anne in order to get their stories too. Since three of those had died

---

16   For a full discussion of Harpsfield's imaginative account, see When did Henry and Anne marry?

in or before 1550, it may be that Latymer had been working on his manuscript for some time.[17]

Viewpoint regarding Anne
    Positive

Principal Stories
 - Anne increasing the value of the Maundy money
 - Anne's ladies sewing smocks, shirts and sheets for the poor
 - Anne assisting her staff when they were in trouble
 - Anne bringing Nicholas Bourbon to England
 - Anne berating abbots for their failings of piety and obedience
 - Anne's patronage of various scholars
 - Anne distributing English prayer books to the nuns of Syon
 - Anne's encouragement of theological debates at dinner
 - Anne sending her staff to expose the blood of Hailes

Reliability
    He is the only author amongst the sources who actually knew Anne well. He was part of her household, worked for and with her and he saw the private side of her which other courtiers did not, particularly her charitable work and the way she carried out her duties as an employer. His work should be taken very seriously. Some have suggested that because the work is so positive, it must necessarily be of dubious value but that is too cynical an approach. There are, and always have been, good people in this world and there is no reason to suppose that Anne Boleyn was not one of them.

Pole

Reginald Pole, *Defence of the Unity of the Church* (1536)

Author
    He was a second cousin of Henry VIII, being the grandson of "false, fleeting, perjured Clarence" and the man who achieved infamy as the helpmate of Bloody Mary in the persecution of the 1550s. He wrote his book during the winter of 1535 to 1536 but added to it a couple of years later.[18] In 1557, he was charged with heresy by the pope but he died in 1558 before the case could be heard.[19]

---

17 Baynton d.1544, Uvedale in 1546 and Burgh in 1550. James Boleyn died in 1561.
18 He completed it in early April, less than a month before Anne fell, LP 10.659.
19 Mary refused to allow him to be extradited to Rome on grounds cases involving her subjects should be heard in England. She thus employed the argument which her father had used regarding the annulment.

Reason for Writing

Pole's friend, Starkey, had returned to England and composed a *Dialogue* which purported to record the sentiments of Pole and Lupset. In this, Pole expressed favour for restriction on appeals to Rome, for worship in English and the issuing of an English Bible. He also condemned the pope for taking the laws of God and offering to dispense from them for money and denied the pope had any authority other than to absolve sin.[20] On the basis of this, Henry asked Pole to express his thoughts on the Reformation to date. What he got was a lengthy vitriolic diatribe in which Pole told him that he had surrendered his soul to Satan, "overthrown and destroyed the laws of the kingdom and of his predecessors, the laws of the Church and finally the laws of Christ" before concluding "there is no one who can recognise the remnant of any virtue in you." Pole's claim that he wrote for Henry's benefit was not believed and he was proclaimed a traitor in May 1539, which he indisputably was under English law. He opposed the proposals of the Emperor to make peace with Henry and sought to distance England from France too because he believed that the greater isolation in which Henry found himself, and the greater the likelihood of war, the sooner Henry would return to Rome.[21] His violent language in the book, which even Cardinal Contarini thought was excessive, was deliberately employed to harden hearts.[22] He sent the volume to Henry as soon as he heard of Anne's arrest, something he regarded as a sign that God supported his own opinions. He commented that he did not think Henry would like it very much![23]

Viewpoint regarding Anne

Hostile. He described Anne as a Jezebel who had led Henry from the truth, a harlot and a prostitute.

Principal stories
 - Anne refusing to sleep with Henry unless he married her
 - Anne being a mere girl when Henry was attracted to her
 - Mary Boleyn being Henry's mistress for a long time (only added to a later edition)
 - Anne sending her chaplains to Henry to propose an annulment on the basis of divine law
 - Katherine being a virgin because Arthur died when he was only fourteen
 - Henry telling the Emperor in 1522 that Katherine was a virgin

---

20 T. F. Mayer (ed.), *Thomas Starkey's Dialogue between Pole and Lupset* (Camden Society, 1989) pp.89-91, 82-83. Whether Pole held all these opinions in 1530 is uncertain: we only have Starkey's word for it and the evidence of his support for Henry in Paris, but Starkey was a close friend. Certainly, Pole did not hold these views in later life but many people have more radical opinions in their youth.
21 LP 10.619, 626
22 LP 10.420
23 LP 10.974

Reliability

The fact that the volume begins with an account of the Donation of Constantine which was well known to be a forgery is indicative of what is to follow. Pole claims that he has been given unique access to Henry's thoughts and motivations thanks to a divine revelation of the Almighty. Such would have been very necessary given Pole was out of the country from 1519 to 1527, from 1529 to 1530 and from 1532 to 1554 meaning he had absolutely no knowledge of most of the period he was talking about. His book contains a number of lies. Arthur died at fifteen and a half not fourteen. Pole was not forced or ordered to support Henry's case at the University of Paris, the records clearly show he volunteered for the job.

Pole's selectivity with the truth extended beyond the book. He circulated absurd stories around Italy to discredit Henry, such as the imminent abolition of purgatory and every church being stripped of its treasure with it all being taken to London for Henry's personal store.[24] In February 1537, Pole told the Privy Council that he had not shown his book to the pope. This was technically true – his friend Cardinal Contarini had done that in March 1536 while Pole was checking the final proofs.[25] The pope enjoyed it so much that he appointed Pole a cardinal.

One of the most curious passages in the book is Pole's claim that should Anne acknowledge the pope, Christ "can even restore the flower of virginity to those who have been corrupted." The implication of that logic on his defence of Katherine's claim to have been left a virgin by Arthur is obvious.

An assessment of Pole's understanding of the Torah can be found in the chapter *Was Henry married when he met Anne?*

Sander

Nicolas Sander, *Rise and Growth of the Anglican Schism* (1585)

Author

Nicolas Sander was born in 1527 and trained as a canon lawyer. He left England in 1561 and travelled to Rome, Spain and Ireland where he died some twenty years later. Two of his sisters were nuns at Syon, an abbey which was particularly supportive of Katherine of Aragon.

Reason for Writing

Sander was appalled that England had broken from Rome and saw it as a land occupied by "millions of heretics" who needed to be shown that the breach was caused by Satan (who led Wolsey astray) and the Antichrist whom he named as Henry VIII. He called all those who supported Henry "impious and

---

24 LP 10.619
25 LP 12.1444; LP 10.619

ignorant." His goal was to discredit Elizabeth I as the daughter of Anne Boleyn and to foment rebellion against her. It is worth noting that Sander's works made Elizabeth I extremely angry and she employed men to refute his claims.[26] The historian Strype referred to Sander as "a most profligate fellow, a very slave to the Roman see, and a sworn enemy to his own country, caring not what he writ, if it might but throw reproach and dirt enough upon the reforming kings and princes, the reformers and the Reformation."[27]

Viewpoint regarding Anne

Hostile. Not only does he describe Anne in witch-like terms with jaundiced skin, six fingers and a projecting tooth, but he attributes malicious statements to her such as her response to Katherine's death being: "I am sorry, not because she is dead, but because her death has been so honourable." Despite this, he never suggests that Anne slept with Henry before she married him.

Principal stories
- Anne being Henry's daughter and him knowing this
- Anne sleeping with the family butler when she was fifteen before seducing the chaplain and being sent in disgrace to France as a result
- Wyatt telling Henry that he was sleeping with Anne and Henry not believing him
- Anne's sister telling Katherine all about her own affair with Henry
- Anne deciding to sleep with her brother to get a son after her January 1536 miscarriage and then opting for Brereton, Norris, Weston and Smeaton when George failed to impregnate her
- Anne being a Lutheran
- Henry "living in sin, sometimes with two, sometimes with three of the queen's maids of honour" while still married to Katherine
- Wolsey starting the annulment to punish Charles V for not making him pope
- Anne miscarrying "a shapeless mass of flesh" in January 1536
- Anne remonstrating with Henry after she caught him with Jane Seymour on his knee
- Anne celebrating Katherine's death by wearing yellow
- Henry marrying Anne on 14th November 1532

Reliability

Sander clearly did not know Anne being but a child when she died. He said that he based his book on the testimony of "men of the greatest consideration, or at least from my own knowledge and consideration." The close similarity between his book and Harpsfield's indicates that he had read

---

26 John Bruce and Thomas Perowne (eds.) *Correspondence of Matthew Parker* (Parker Society, 1853) See various letters to Burghley of late 1572, pp.409-415
27 John Strype, *Ecclesiastical Memorials* (1822), vol. 2 part 2 p.180

the latter. Not only are some of the stories the same, such as Wyatt telling Henry at the outset that Anne was his mistress and the account of Peto's sermon, but the wording is almost identical. Sander took rumours reported in Harpsfield as truths and spun sensational stories around them. For instance, Harpsfield commented that he had heard Henry had slept with Anne's mother and Sander repeated it as a fact in several places, going on to describe the scene when her mother told her husband and how Henry VIII then sent a succession of his senior nobles to beg Thomas Boleyn to bring the baby up as his own. His book is full of factual errors. It was Katherine's parents not Henry VII who proposed she marry the future Henry VIII and senior churchmen did voice doubts about the legality of the match before the dispensation was issued, including Roman cardinals. He says Arthur and Katherine never lived together which they did and maintains Arthur was sickly at time of marriage, also untrue. He claims Henry and Katherine had a son who lived nine months – untrue. His claim that England had been part of the Roman church since Joseph of Arimathea brought Christianity to the island is absurd.[28] Sander talks of the Nun of Kent as Anne Barton rather than Elizabeth and claims Cranmer was simply the Boleyn family chaplain who was made Archbishop to please them. He further claims Henry threatened to imprison every single clergyman for life when the spectre of Praemunire was raised, something never suggested. His work conflicts with accounts of the time by people much better informed. He says Anne dressed in yellow when Katherine died when Chapuys says it was Henry VIII who did so.[29] His claim that Anne took lovers after January 1536 fails to tally with the dates of her alleged adulteries given at her trial. In view of his antipathy to Anne, it is significant that he defends her virginity and makes clear that she married Henry ten months before Elizabeth was born.

Spanish Chronicle

Martin Hume (ed.) *Chronicle of King Henry VIII. of England* (1889)

Author

Anonymous. Supposed to have been written by a Spaniard living in London at the time and the references to some minor individuals such as members of the Bishop of Llandaff's staff would support this. Given his reference in chapter eight to Cranmer being alive, it is likely that the manuscript was begun around 1550 though probably finished by another hand afterwards.

---

28 Joseph of Arimathea was Jewish and there is no evidence of him ever leaving Israel. There was a legend of him coming to England invented by Robert de Boron c.1200 and assiduously repeated by the monks of Glastonbury Abbey who made considerable money from pilgrims. However, the centre of the church in Joseph's lifetime was Jerusalem not Rome as is evident from the New Testament.

29 Edward Hall also says Anne dressed in yellow.

Reason for Writing
    Given the content, one can only hope it was composed to entertain his friends and not meant to be serious. The work was not published until the nineteenth century, an era which appreciated comic novels.

Viewpoint regarding Anne
    Hostile. He refers to Katherine throughout as the "sainted" or occasionally "blessed" queen though he is careful to refer to Anne as Queen post 1533 and Princess Mary as Madam Mary after the same date.

Principal Stories
- Ferdinand of Aragon not wanting Katherine to marry Henry but Henry VII insisting
- the pope sending Campeggio to tell Henry that his union with Katherine was valid
- Henry ordering the end of the legatine court so he could be married to Anne in 1529, the celebrant being Archbishop Warham
- Anne wanting to bed Philippe de Chabot, Admiral of France
- Anne being upset people did not take their hats off at her coronation
- Smeaton first coming to court in February 1536 having been selected for his good looks
- a servant called Old Margaret hiding Mark Smeaton in a closet, naked and ready to be let into Anne's bed together with a pot of marmalade
- said Old Margaret being burnt in the Tower for her actions with Anne forced to watch
- Anne's adultery being reported by Henry Percy's brother who was jealous that Anne was showering Smeaton with expensive clothes and jewels and who wanted to pre-empt Smeaton from murdering him
- Thomas Wyatt telling Henry that he had enjoyed intimacies with her prior to her marriage. He described a romp in which Anne got bored and suddenly went upstairs to have audible sex with a groom while he waited below
- Henry sending for a swordsman from St Omer to execute Anne six days before her trial began
- Anne wearing a red damask nightgown for her execution
- Thomas Boleyn dying of grief within a week of Anne and George's executions
- Jane Seymour demanding that Elizabeth be bastardised
- all monks being wonderful landlords who charged cheap rents

Reliability
    If someone was to highlight the factual errors in red and the truths in green, they would run out of red probably before removing the lid from the green pen. The author clearly had no direct contact with the Court, never spoke to Henry or Anne and there is no sign that he spoke English. It may be

supposed that he had no contacts within More or Pole's circle either because he makes no mention of Mary Boleyn. Although he may have witnessed Anne's coronation procession, it was almost certainly from some distance. The mistakes are not only legion but extreme. For example, he has Wolsey not coming to power until 1530, Henry marrying Kathryn Howard before Anne of Cleves and Wolsey corresponding with the Emperor about the death of pope Clement VII (which took place almost four years after Wolsey died) and the Pilgrimage of Grace taking place in 1532. Nor was his Biblical knowledge any better since he talks of the five plagues of Egypt.

The chronicle is a work best left for those who take seriously headlines today such as 'Martians ate my hamster' and is only listed here because so many writers actually quote from it as though it is a serious work of reference. It does, however, make a most entertaining read for a long journey.

Spelman

J H Baker (ed.), *The Reports of Sir John Spelman,* volume 1 (1977)

Author
John Spelman was a lawyer who began his studies at Gray's Inn during the reign of Henry VII. He became a sergeant-at-law in 1521 and was appointed to the King's Bench in 1530.

Reason for Writing
Spelman was a judge and he devoted time in his later years to writing up notes of cases which he deemed of interest for the benefit of his heirs. Some of the cases were those in which he had been involved but others were simply those he knew about from the judicial circuit and reports of fellow judges. At the time Anne fell, Spelman was almost sixty.

Viewpoint regarding Anne
Neutral

Principal stories
 - Anne being accused of adultery on the basis of a deathbed statement made by Lady Wingfield
 - Anne being executed within the hall in which she was tried
 - a swordsman from Calais being selected to execute Anne
 - Anne being divorced from Henry following her condemnation on grounds of a precontract on her part
 - the judges complaining about the sentence upon Anne including an option to behead which was not according to statute

Reliability

The originals of Spelman's notebooks no longer exist. The copies which survive may be accurate or they may not: without the originals, it is impossible to say if the copyist edited the text at all.[30] What is certain is that the copyist radically transformed the original manuscript which was thematically arranged into something chronological.

A key point to remember about Spelman's reports is that they were not written at the time. Since he died in January 1546, his account of Anne's trial and execution was written within ten years of the event but the phrasing shows he was recalling a past event. It is impossible to say how far after the events took place he was writing. He certainly got key facts wrong. Anne's executioner came from St Omer not Calais;[31] she was not executed indoors but on Tower Green, and nor was she ever divorced from Henry. Spelman says he heard that she was divorced due to a pre-contract but he gives no source suggesting it was just gossip. As a judge, he would have been aware of the distinction between divorce and annulment and his use of the word divorce immediately rings considerable alarm bells. Were his faculties fading when he made the claim or did the copyist substitute the word divorce in place of annulment?

Wyatt

George Wyatt, *The Life of Queen Anne Boleigne* (c. 1590)

Author

George was the grandson of the poet, Thomas. A memorial note in Boxley parish register reveals he was born in 1544 so he never knew Anne.

Reason for writing

His expressed goal was to refute the assertion in Sander's book that his grandfather had an adulterous relationship with Anne Boleyn.

Viewpoint regarding Anne

Positive

Principal stories
 - Anne presenting Henry with Tyndale's *Obedience* after her coronation
 - a game of bowls at which Thomas Wyatt and Henry VIII clashed over Anne
 - Katherine playing cards with Anne and noting she wanted the king
 - Anne being sent a prediction that she would lose her head
 - Anne having a sixth nail

---

30   Burnet claimed to have seen the original in 1679 and his summary of the entry for Anne's trial appears in line with what exists in the copy which exists today.
31   He probably sailed to England from Calais.

- George's wife as source of accusation of incest between George and Anne
- Anne's dedication to charity and excellence as needlewoman
- the Brandons opposing Henry marrying Anne because it would affect their own children's place in the succession

Reliability

George never knew his grandfather who could have told him about Anne. His father died when he was a young boy and since he (Thomas junior) had only been in his 'teens when Anne died and quite probably never met her, it is unlikely that he was a source of information. George does, however, say that he took most of his information from two people within his own family. The first was "a lady that first attended on her both before and after she was queen, with whose house and mine there was then kindred and strict alliance" and the second "a lady of noble birth, living in those times, and well acquainted with the persons that most this concerneth, from whom I am myself descended." Neither woman was named but the first was Anne or Nan Gainsford who was second cousin to his maternal grandfather, William Haute, and whose service to Anne before she became queen is confirmed by John Foxe in his *Acts and Monuments*. Nan Gainsford married George Zouche and evidently died before 1548 because his will of that year refers to his second wife. It is therefore clear that George could not have spoken to her and that his knowledge of her time serving Anne had been passed on by other family members. This does not negate the value of the testimony but it is important to recognise that it was not given first hand. Many people can tell stories about their grandparents or other deceased relatives and this is especially the case where the ancestor was involved with a famous person or in a major incident such as fighting at the Somme or being aboard Titanic. Sometimes the stories are repeated almost word for word as the person involved originally told them, but often they get changed in the telling eventually becoming family legends rather than historical fact.

The second lady was his grandmother, Elizabeth Warner (née Brooke) who died in 1560.[32] He may well have known her, although it is impossible to know how often they might have met. Unless George had been conducting interviews for a book he planned to write in his fifties when he was in his early 'teens, it seems reasonable to suppose that most of the information from her came at least second hand and was passed on by other relatives using phrases like, "your grandmother used to say that..." How far Elizabeth either knew the King or Anne is uncertain. She separated from Thomas Wyatt and there is no reason to suppose she spent time at court in this period. Since her brother was one of the jurors at Anne's trial, it is possible she may have heard something about events from him. In 1542, Chapuys noted that Henry had paid particular

---

32 Maria Dowling has suggested that the second informer was George's aunt, Margaret Lee née Wyatt but he was not descended from her, *William Latymer's Cronickille of Anne Bulleyne* (Camden 1990) p.41

attention to Elizabeth at a banquet and this has led some writers with febrile imaginations to suggest that she was either a royal mistress or about to become one. If true, this might have made her an interesting source, but given Chapuys went on to describe her as a "pretty young creature" he was either being uncharacteristically gallant or he was looking at the wrong person.[33] Elizabeth had married over twenty years before so must have been in her forties which was old by Tudor standards.

Like all writers of the period and unlike modern academics, Wyatt gives no source for individual statements so which stories came from which lady cannot be identified. Presumably information about what Anne said to Nan Gainsford came from Nan herself but what about the physical description of Anne. Did one of her erstwhile maids really confide that she had a bad complexion and blemish on one finger? It seems more likely that George was going through Sander's account and ameliorating it to make Anne sound better and that he was doing this because neither lady had passed down a description. His reliance on printed works combined with his inability to check facts, meant he made some mistakes. For example, George describes Cardinal Wolsey taking the copy of Tyndale's book some three years after his own death! Whether or not George had heard the story from a family member as well, he had certainly read it in Foxe and repeated it under the wrong year.

Some may be aware of the tradition that Anne was accompanied on the scaffold by Margaret Wyatt but this is not stated in George's memoir. He states that she was served by virtuous ladies and it is the editor, Samuel Singer, who added a footnote recording that the Wyatt family in 1721 had a small book of psalms believed to have been given to one of their ancestors though it had changed hands a century later.[34]

Ambassadorial Reports

Summaries of reports are contained in *Letters and Papers of Henry VIII* and the *Calendar of State Papers* for Spain, Venice and Milan.

Author

Various. Throughout this period, Henry's court was home to ambassadors from the Empire, France, Venice, Milan and the pope though only the first two had continual service. The Imperialists sent the longest reports and

---

33   LP17.92. He may have confused her with her niece, Elizabeth Brooke, daughter of Lord Cobham and future wife of William Parr, the brother of Henry's last queen. She would have been in her 'teens.

34   See discussion in Cavendish, *Wolsey*, vol. 1 p.442. For a discussion on the authenticity of various prayer books said to have been given by Anne to people see Eleanor Jackson, 'A Gold Girdle Book and its connection with Anne Boleyn' on https://www.bl.uk/eblj/articles

the fact that many of those found in *Letters and Papers* are duplicated or supplemented by entries in the *Calendar of State Papers: Spain*, means that they are most accessible. The French kept a resident ambassador but, owing to the country being nearer to England than Spain, they were more inclined to work through envoys sent over on particular missions and to communicate verbally. There is no comparable volume for French reports and many have been lost or remain untranslated in French archives.

The Milanese reports have a gap from 3rd June to 28th August 1527 which covers the period when it is likely that news of the proposed annulment emerged. There are also no reports for 1528 or 1529 and a further gap from March to July 1536, the period of Anne's fall.

The Venetian reports contain a gap from the end of August 1533 to the spring of 1535 and from the summer of 1535 onwards. Reports were being sent by a secretary due to the ambassador's illness but they have not survived. The interval covers Anne's reign and fall.

The calendars only contain summaries but some full reports can be found, mostly in correspondence collections for individual authors such as Giustinian, Jean du Bellay and Fuensalida.

Reason for writing

It was their job to send news of what was happening in England to their employers who were the rulers of Europe. This meant they passed on details of events which they believed to be true but also rumours and gossip which they had heard. This fact needs to be stressed as it is common for writers to repeat a story citing some ambassador but ignoring the qualifying clause in the original where the ambassador says that this is just something they heard but have not verified.

Viewpoint regarding Anne

The Imperial ambassador, Eustace Chapuys, was universally hostile but the attitudes of the French were ordinarily supportive. The Italians were mostly neutral.

Principal stories
Milan
 - Anne's coronation being a great triumph
 - Elizabeth being born a month premature

Venice
 - Anne being very beautiful[35]
 - the pope agreeing to the annulment
 - Wolsey being afraid of Thomas Boleyn replacing him

---

35   The famous account of Anne as "not one of the handsomest women" was not written by the ambassador or any Venetian official.

- Anne being threatened by a mob of angry women and escaping over the River Thames
- huge crowds attending Anne's coronation with much cheering
- Henry's sister, Mary Brandon, speaking out against Anne Boleyn
- Anne marrying Henry on 10th January 1533
- Anne claiming God inspired Henry to marry her

Spain
(1) Mendoza (January 1527 to June 1529)
- Henry seeking an annulment because Katherine was supporting his enemy, the Emperor
- Wolsey preferring Anne to a French bride

(2) Chapuys (September 1529 onwards)
- Anne being a Lutheran
- Anne working with her father and uncle to destroy Wolsey
- Anne riding pillion on Henry's horse
- the whole country backing Katherine and longing for the Emperor to invade
- Charles Brandon telling Henry that Anne was not a virgin
- Bridget Wingfield being Anne's attendant
- Anne being upset when Henry sent fabric to Katherine to be made into shirts
- Tyndale's *Practice of Prelates* being a masterly volume of truth in support of Katherine
- Henry offering Reginald Pole the Archbishopric of York
- Thomas Cranmer marrying Henry and Anne (he later changed his mind and claimed it was George Brown)
- Anne threatening Mary and Bishop John Fisher
- Henry giving Anne a bed
- Thomas Boleyn feigning madness to prevent Henry marrying Anne
- Rhys ap Gryffydd being executed and Dacre being tried for supporting Katherine
- all those who supported Henry doing so as a result of bribery or threat
- Anne's coronation being a disaster
- Mary Boleyn being banished for her second marriage
- Henry telling Anne that Katherine was a better person, wife and queen than she was
- the French seeking Henry's daughter, Mary, as a bride in 1534 and 1535
- Henry Percy's wife alleging a pre-contract between her husband and Anne
- Anne wishing all Spaniards were at the bottom of the sea
- Henry hiding Melanchthon in one of his palaces
- Anne being healthy and young enough to bear Henry many children
- Anne accusing Brandon of a sexual relationship with his own daughter[36]

---

36 It is possible that Anne suspected Brandon intended to marry his son's fiancée. Whether Chapuys reported it incorrectly due to issues with translation or

- Jane Rochford being sent from court for seeking to help Anne rid herself of a rival
- Katherine being sent to live in hovels
- Henry's 1532 progress being halted because of female protests against Anne
- Katherine calling Anne the "scandal of Christendom"
- Anne's chamberlain taking Katherine's barge
- Anne not allowing Henry to speak to his daughter, Mary
- Henry Percy admitting that his friend Anne Boleyn sought to poison Mary
- Anne having a false pregnancy in 1534
- Katherine being murdered by Anne using poison supplied by Gregory Casale
- Henry wearing yellow when Katherine died
- Anne blaming Norfolk's news of Henry's accident for her miscarriage in January 1536
- Anne admitting that Elizabeth's legitimacy was doubtful because she was conceived during Katherine's lifetime
- Jane Seymour returning a purse of gold sent to her by Henry
- George Boleyn's failure to be elected to the Garter being a snub to Anne
- Henry discussing marriage with Jane Seymour before Anne was arrested
- George Boleyn reading out at his trial an allegation of Henry's potency problems
- Henry alleging that Anne planned to poison his daughter Mary and his son Richmond
- Thomas Boleyn wanting to serve on the jury for Anne and George
- Henry claiming that Anne had committed adultery with over a hundred men
- Anne joking she would be nicknamed Anne Lackhead
- Henry rushing to Jane's side as soon as Anne's execution was over
- Cromwell claiming to have plotted Anne's fall
- Henry telling Anne that he would not do all he had for her again
- Henry taking an interest in one of the Shelton girls, cousins to Anne Boleyn
- Anne laughing when dancing with Chabot because Henry had been distracted by another woman
- Henry vowing to send Fisher's head to Rome for his cardinal's hat
- Anne telling her aunt to box Mary's ears
- Anne being charged with poisoning Katherine
- George refusing to deny the charge that he had doubted Elizabeth's paternity
- Cranmer declaring that Elizabeth was Norris' daughter

French
- Anne being totally obedient to Henry and not politically active independently
- Henry's sincere spiritual concerns
- Wolsey's initial hopes for a marriage with Princess Renée
- Anne being sent from the court before Campeggio arrived
- Katherine and Arthur consummating their marriage

---

deliberately to make trouble is another question.

- Henry's desire to have Chapuys withdrawn
- Wolsey's belief that the Emperor would accept the annulment
- Henry and Katherine acting as if nothing was wrong until 1529
- Henry's plan to accustom the people to Anne
- Henry refusing to promote the annulment until the alliance with France was secure
- Anne being uneasy and conscious of being watched
- Mary believing she was the Dauphin's wife
- the wives of certain courtiers staging a protest in favour of Mary Tudor[37]

Reliability

Ambassadorial reports were not composed as factual accounts for the benefit of historians in later centuries but political documents intended to be private (most are in cipher) and involving variable amounts of spin depending on the mood of the author at the time and how secure he felt in his role. Regularly writing back "nothing to report" would result in rapid dismissal whilst giving the impression that he was close to leading ministers might lead to promotion. Passing on gossip would make reports memorable and could open the door to other opportunities, and a hint of involvement in uncovering major news stories or being in a position to negotiate a major trade deal might get an increase in expenses.

Although the ambassadors did attend court and have the chance to speak with Henry VIII, they were not his trusted confidants, any more than the monarch today invites the royal correspondent of the *Daily Mirror* in for intimate tête-a-têtes. The reports of ambassadors should be treated like articles composed for a particular audience. Modern readers of left wing newspapers have no wish to learn that the Prince of Wales has saved taxpayers' money by some particular change but they would love to hear of some example of waste and incompetence and many column inches might be devoted to this, even if the loss was a trifle compared to the deliberately unmentioned savings. Anne Boleyn could have spent her entire time in charitable works – and the evidence is that she did spend much of it this way – but Chapuys would never have recorded it because it did not fit his image of her or his master's agenda. Imperial policy was based on Anne being The Baddie.

Most importantly, ambassadorial reports are not independent. By definition, the French reported the news from the perspective of how it affected France, and the Spanish considered how it would affect them. This fundamental fact is often overlooked. The easy accessibility of Chapuys' comments mean he is quoted frequently but nobody would dream of writing a serious history of the British in WW2 based almost entirely on the statements of Lord Haw-Haw nor

---

37 A hand written note in the margin of the report names George Boleyn's wife as being one of those involved. Friedmann says that the writing is that of D'Inteville, the French envoy, Paul Friedmann, *Anne Boleyn*, vol. 2 (1884) p.128

an account of Jewish achievement based on Nazi sources. Chapuys was a representative of an enemy government who used his position to try and change policy. He claimed the French wanted Mary as a bride for the son of Francis I to give the impression that the French supported Katherine and Mary and would be likely to join the Emperor in a war against England when the truth is that the French sought Elizabeth as a bride: Chapuys' refusal to apply the title Princess to anyone but Mary explains his deliberate misreading of the situation. He sent reports to the Emperor and Rome implying that Katherine had been reduced to living in a hovel with barely an attendant in sight – while the Venetian and French ambassadors who saw her reported she lived in high state with hundreds of staff. Chapuys lied in an attempt to pressurise the pope into giving a verdict in Katherine's favour. Chapuys continually reported that Anne and her family were Lutherans because he knew that this was the sect which most alarmed the Emperor and pope, yet there is nothing in any of his voluminous reports over the years which suggests that he had the faintest comprehension of Luther's theology.[38]

Chapuys was highly biased and one of the world's greatest conspiracy theorists. If a pigeon had defecated on Katherine of Aragon's head, there is no doubt that Chapuys would have claimed that Anne Boleyn had trained it specially to do so. He continually claimed that people were being destroyed because they supported Katherine when there was absolutely no link between the events at all. What Chapuys never accepted was that even if Henry had tired of Anne during the course of the annulment proceedings, he would not have taken Katherine back. Henry believed he was free to marry and he intended to do just that. If it had not been Anne Boleyn, it would have been somebody else. Henry was as likely to take Katherine back as he was to declare himself a homosexual and announce he was going to marry one of the bishops. Chapuys' conviction that if Anne were out of the way, Henry would fall in love with Katherine of Aragon again and that she would conceive a son despite being a decade past her menopause indicates a marked lack of reality.

Chapuys' reports are notable for their characterisations. He recounts a number of conversations with Henry and the Duke of Norfolk all of which involve them saying something to him and him putting them right, whereupon they stand struck dumb by his brilliance. One suspects that had recording devices been available at the time, they might have told a different story. Henry is thereby portrayed as a pompous fool and Norfolk as a well meaning old duffer. Katherine, in Chapuys' eyes, is an alabaster saint while Anne is the personification of evil and deliberately drawn to invite comparisons with such luminaries as Salome, Jezebel, Locusta, Messalina and Agrippina. He uses the word 'concubine' for her to to associate her with fornication, a mortal sin, even though admitting she was a virgin until marriage.

---

38 Judging by his failure to identify Biblical quotations used by Henry during audiences, he was not an expert on Roman Catholic theology either.

For much of the time, Chapuys was kept away from court. He was no more present at most of the events he describes than the scullion turning the roasting spit in the kitchen. In 1534, it was three months before he discovered that Anne had lost her baby. He was dependent on what people told him and that meant recruiting spies, hoping to find disaffected ministers who were close enough to Henry to be able to offer him reliable information or, as he confessed, making friends with physicians who were customarily able to move between households without attracting attention. Those who spoke to him had a variety of motives. Some were devoted to Katherine and her daughter while others just wanted to sell a story – and knowing that they would get more money for a juicy bit of gossip meant fabrication and exaggeration were likely. Chapuys, for example, would not have paid good money to hear that Henry and Anne had spent a quiet evening together strumming their lutes whilst an account of Anne shouting out "You fool!" would have had him enthusiastically reaching for his purse before composing a report on grave problems in the royal relationship – even if Anne had only been expressing momentary annoyance that Henry had dropped something on her foot and he had stopped her complaints with a kiss!

It is important to remember when reading Chapuys' reports that when he quotes Anne saying something, he is only repeating what he has been told and not what he has heard. His informer may not have heard it either but only heard it from someone else. Even if they did hear the words, they did not have voice recording technology in their pockets and they probably did not hear the entire conversation. Memories are suspect and there is always the human temptation to hear what you want to hear. Historians pore over each word seeking to analyse every possible nuance and often forget the likelihood that Anne either never said the words at all or they have been taken out of context. There is also the very important point that the words have gone through a double translation process – her alleged words would have been in English, a language Chapuys did not understand, translated by informers into French for him and then translated again into English for the calendars.[39] The same applies to most of what he claims Henry said. It seems highly unlikely that just a few weeks after Anne's coronation and just as she was about to give birth to the child whom Henry confidently expected to be a prince, that he would have shouted at her saying that Katherine was her "better" in every way.[40] The choice of adjective is surely Chapuys' own.

Others spoke to Chapuys for their own ends. For example, Cromwell's boast that he had masterminded the destruction of Anne Boleyn was a way of

---

39 Given the years he resided in England, Chapuys must have picked up some English but whenever he went to court he spoke French or Latin. His statement that he did not understand English was made in 1533, LP 6.1125.

40 CSPS 4.2.1123. Writing on 3rd September, Chapuys says that Anne was so angry at Henry's words that she has not spoken to him for two to three days. Given she had taken to her chamber on 26th August to prepare for the birth, there was no possibility of them speaking, nor indeed having the argument described, LP 6.1004

stressing his own importance and convincing the ambassador that if he wanted a deal with England, he must go through him. Writers need to beware accepting everything Chapuys reports at face value without consideration of the background to the statement. A number of Chapuys' meetings with Norfolk and Cromwell involved the English deliberately feeding him misinformation for political purposes and they were entitled to do this. Their job was to defend England, not aid the Emperor. Chapuys would have known this and done the same in return.

Chapuys was a nasty, anti-Semitic man, of limited political judgement whose behaviour was considered so extreme by his contemporaries that the Emperor's Council petitioned for his dismissal. They feared his reports were unbalanced and they worried that his temper and plotting were dangerously exacerbating the international situation. The Emperor ignored these calls and indeed delighted in employing fanatics such as Garay, Ortiz and Loaysa. Why did the Emperor use such people? Neither Henry VIII nor Francis I did this. The answer was probably that the Emperor believed zealots would be less likely to complain when he failed to pay them for months on end because they saw their work as some holy crusade against evil.

Chapuys was also a deliberate trouble maker. In addition to sending reports to the Emperor, he wrote to Imperial ambassadors at other courts, such as Hannaert in the Low Countries, Mai, Cifuentes and Ortiz at Rome. Those letters have not survived but their contents can be shown by the letters written by recipients who passed on what they stated Chapuys had told them. Thus Ortiz told the Empress that Chapuys' letter to him of 9th February 1536 said that Anne had only pretended to be pregnant so her miscarriage was false.[41] The story of Henry being unconscious for two hours after his fall in January 1536 was almost certainly part of a letter to Hannaert.

Where the opportunity exists to compare more than one letter written by him on the same day, pertinent differences can be found. For example, On 29th April 1536, Chapuys told the Emperor that Carew's election to the Garter was a sign that Anne lacked influence to obtain the place for her brother (LP 10.752) while in his letter to Granvelle, he said that Carew was chosen at the request of the king of France (LP 10.753). In this case, Chapuys wanted the Emperor to believe that Anne's power had declined because that would encourage him to believe Chapuys could negotiate a new Anglo-Imperial alliance, the prospects for which had been poor. It was nothing but a politically motivated lie. On 18th March 1536, Chapuys wrote to the Emperor about the planned dissolution of smaller monasteries and a proposed meeting of Henry VIII and James V (LP 10.494), but he left out the account of Henry romancing Jane Seymour on grounds it was of no interest or importance and only shared that news with Granvelle (LP 10.495).

It seems Chapuys enjoyed spinning entertaining yarns to Granvelle and Ortiz. He told the former that Henry had walked ten miles at two in the

---

41   CSPS 5.2.38

morning carrying a two-edged sword in order to watch a play which portrayed him beheading all the clergy, adding that Henry had enjoyed the performance so much that he intended to take Anne along the next night (CSPS 5.1.179). He also told Granvelle that Anne had paid a man to say he had received a revelation from God that Anne would never conceive as long as Katherine and Anne were alive (CSPS 5.1.144). He told Ortiz that one of the executed Carthusian monks had materialised as a ghost to assure his brethren that Bishop John Fisher had been crowned in heaven and that Anne had ordered Cromwell to suppress the miracle (CSPS 5.1.217). It is tempting to laugh at such absurdities but the recipients believed him and passed on the stories as fact which did untold damage to the image of both Henry and Anne abroad and this in turn affected the prospects for European peace.

Nonetheless unlike modern historians, Chapuys actually knew Henry VIII, Katherine of Aragon, Cromwell and Anne Boleyn's father, uncle and brother and, just as the most repugnant racist today is as capable as the most tolerant person to perceive if it is raining or not, his words should be heeded lest the baby be thrown out with the bath water. Yet, it is always worth remembering the words of William Paget who wrote in June 1545, having known Chapuys for sixteen years:

> I never took him for a wise man but for one that used to speak with absolute liberty whatever came into his head without respect of honesty or truth, so it might serve his turn. Indeed he is a great practiser – with which honest term we cover untrue tales, telling, lying, dissimulating and flattering.[42]

Henry himself had thought much the same, at one point advising the Emperor that if he wanted to know the truth he should ask him and not rely on what his ambassador said.[43]

By contrast, French reports are generally shorter, not least because they could send messengers home quite quickly with confidential news, but better informed because they were in alliance with England. Prior to 1535, their ambassadors were housed in royal palaces and they spent ample time with Henry and Anne. They dined together, hunted together, played games together and generally chatted. Jean du Bellay was one of Henry's closest friends for most of this period. Sadly for later generations, many of the reports they took home were verbal. The French also made extensive use of special envoys such as the Bishop of Tarbes. Often, as in his case, these were highly experienced

---

42 SP vol. 10 p.466. The original reads "in buckam" which is from the Latin meaning cheek. It was used colloquially to mean to speak freely. I have amended it to modern English for the sake of clarity.

43 LP 7.1209

diplomats whose contacts across Europe were extensive and would prove vitally important to Henry particularly following the fall of Wolsey.

On the Italian side, Venier, Falier and Capello served in succession as Venetian ambassadors. They had very little interest in gossip and tended to confine their reports to trade matters and diplomatic travels, although they were inclined to go into detail about Henry's clothes. Perhaps the Doge regarded the King as a leading fashion symbol. The Venetians generally supported the annulment and took part in events such as Anne's coronation. They also tended to confer with their colleagues in France which gave them access to some unique stories. Scarpinello was the Milanese ambassador for most of this period and though he spoke no English, he performed his duties conscientiously. The reports of Andreasio, Milanese ambassador at Rome, are an important independent source for charting the progress of Henry's annulment.

Various papal nuncios spent time at Henry's court. At the outset of the period, there was Gambara who was a staunch supporter of the annulment and went back to Rome to argue the case for the King with the pope.[44] Borgo, who followed, was an evidently more timid man. He complained that he found audiences with Henry so intimidating that he obtained permission from the pope not to see him at all but merely communicate by letter!

Finally, it is always worth looking at the original documents wherever practical. For example, compare the differences in Anne's reported words in LP 5. 546 and CSPS 4.2.838. In LP 5.898, talking of annates, it says the pope will get a twentieth, i.e. five per cent, but in CSPS 4.2.926 it says the pope will get twenty per cent. Another radically different report exists in August 1532 where Chapuys either says that the Duke of Norfolk wishes the King of France to give him an army to lead against the Emperor (LP 5. 1256) or that he wants to join the Emperor's army (CSPS 4.2.986). Similarly, in January 1536, LP 10.141 has Chapuys saying that Thomas and George Boleyn commented when Katherine died that it was a pity that Mary had not died too – a very callous remark. Yet, the same letter in CSPS 5.2.9 has Chapuys say that he imagines the news might have caused Thomas Boleyn and his son to wish Mary had gone as well – a very different statement.

Missing sources

History has to be evidential but the gaps need to be stressed. In addition to the reports by ambassadors of other countries who were based in England, there were also reports written by English ambassadors at other courts, particularly France, the Low Countries, Venice, Rome and Spain.[45] Until the fall

---

44 Following the Emperor winning the war in Italy, he subsequently became a fierce opponent.
45 Wallop in France wrote weekly but all that remains is a list of dates received, LP 8.1179

of Wolsey, these appear to be generally complete but afterwards, there is a marked paucity. The reports were still being sent because in audiences, Henry would refer to them occasionally and some documents were described as being replies to them. The loss of these records is significant because they provide insights into what foreign governments thought of Henry and Anne as well as Henry's own policies at particular points. Although it is cannot be known exactly why all these reports disappeared, it seems likely that they were sent to Norfolk rather than Cromwell and were thrown out by the Howards. Norfolk admitted in 1535 that he regularly burnt papers he did not expect to need again (LP 8.48). It was usual at the time for ministers and ambassadors to take responsibility for papers: the concept of official government archives was many years away. Had Henry not destroyed Wolsey and Cromwell, their papers would not have been handed over to the state and our records for the period would be immeasurably smaller.[46]

Significant too is the lack of documentation regarding the fall of Anne Boleyn. Some of the material relating to Anne's trial was lost or damaged in fires but other information was deliberately removed. It is impossible to know by whom or when but the fact that even early historians did not reference items which clearly existed, suggests that the purge took place at the time. For example, there are no details of any witness interrogations and most of Kingston's daily reports are missing. Whether the destruction took place as part of a regular clearing out of papers not thought to be required further or because the government had something to hide is a matter of conjecture.

Nor is the problem unique to England. Katherine's father would have corresponded regularly with his ambassador at Rome yet the only letter to survive and make it into the official archive is the one in which he suddenly claimed she was a virgin because he was afraid the pope would not grant a dispensation for her to remarry otherwise. The odour of rodents for such a coincidence is almost overpowering..

Historians can only work on the basis of surviving material but they have to use their common sense. The fact that a burial record cannot be found for somebody born four hundred years ago does not indicate that the person remains alive, just that the information has been lost. Similarly, with the story of Anne Boleyn, it is necessary to utilise the sources to hand but always to consider what has been destroyed and to be mindful of the possible political reasons for this and the implications of that loss on how subjects are interpreted. The lack of detailed despatches from the French and Italian ambassadors in 1536, for example, has led to undue reliance being placed on the reports of Chapuys in discussions about Anne's fall. The loss of Anne's letters to Henry has made it impossible to accurately chart the development of her feelings about him.

---

46 Nonetheless, it seems surprising that copies of at least some of the reports were not sent on to the King together with replies.

Even where the documentary record appears reasonably comprehensive, it must always be remembered that considerable business was carried out verbally and never committed to paper at all. The lack of a written record is not proof of a lack of activity. It is commonly said in books that Wolsey did nothing to promote Anne's marriage to Butler despite assuring Henry that he would do so, but Wolsey had no need to write to Thomas Boleyn about the matter when he would have seen him almost daily.

Historians like to make authoritative statements about what happened but often that is just a judgment based on what has survived. In a number of areas, what is missing is like the bulk of an iceberg which is submerged under water. Nonetheless, it is important to try and so, with warnings about biassed sources and missing material, it is time to tackle the key questions relating to the life of Anne Boleyn.

When Was Anne Boleyn born?

How old are you? It is a question which we are frequently asked. When we are young, we tend to add on every passing month, e.g. "I am seven and three quarters." As we get older, we drop the months and by middle age often get to the stage of mumbling the answer or even dropping a few years. In old age, that pride we had as children often returns and is seen in responses such as "I'm eighty-seven" or "nearly ninety." Of course, we are frequently told that age does not matter and warned against it being used as a tool of discrimination, but in reality, our perceptions are affected by age. Most people would hold a door open for somebody who looked eighty when they might not do it for someone who looked thirty, even though the younger person was entitled to the same degree of respect and might be in greater physical need of assistance. Anne Boleyn never had to face the problem of old age because she was executed when she was a young woman, but how young? We know she died in 1536 but her date of birth is uncertain.

There is a practical reason for the mystery aside from the lack of any system of birth registration in this period, who knew? The obvious person to know all about Anne would be her daughter but Elizabeth was just two when her mother was executed and five and six respectively at the deaths of her maternal grandparents, Elizabeth and Thomas Boleyn. Elizabeth was ten when Anne's sister, Mary, died and nine when Anne's sister-in-law, Jane, was executed. There is no evidence that she spent time with them and given Jane Rochford has been long suspected of playing a role in the deaths of Anne and George, they might not have been friends if they did meet.[1] Two people who could have told her were the Duke of Norfolk, her great-uncle, who died when she was twenty-one, and also her aunt Shelton on her father's side who died when she was twenty-three. Others she might have asked included Henry Norris' son; her cousin, Henry Carey, and Anne's chaplain, Matthew Parker.

And of course there was her father. For all of us, Henry and Anne are simply historical figures but for Elizabeth, they were Mum and Dad. She would not have remembered her mother at all and though she would have been told of her death when she was young, the actual truth that her father had executed her mother for incest with her uncle, would not have been explained until she was much older. How did she cope with that? Did it make her more keen to ask questions about her mother or did she seek to avoid all discussion of the subject? Even in today's more liberal society, few people would wish to volunteer the fact that their mother was convicted of sleeping with her own brother. Elizabeth certainly did not grow up in a world of happy family reunions each Christmas with all her grandparents and uncles and aunts joining her parents to reminisce but she did spend time with her father. She would have

---

[1] For more on Jane's role, see Why did Anne fall? Elizabeth, as a child, would not have been in a position to investigate or make her own judgment.

sat on Henry's knee as an infant and tweaked his beard and played with his shiny buttons and the glittering jewels on his clothes. She would have held his hand when he took her for walks in the palace gardens, before probably running off to chase one of his dogs because Henry was moving too slowly for her lively little feet. Elizabeth loved music and dancing as much as her father. No doubt she twirled round to show him the latest dancing steps that she had learnt and he applauded her and gave her a treat. She probably demonstrated her early skills on the virginals and Henry may well have accompanied her. They would have sung songs together and laughed. It is well attested that Henry loved dressing up so quite possibly he donned costumes to play games with Elizabeth. However, we have no idea what the response would have been had the little princess climbed up on her father's lap and smiled sweetly and demanded "tell me about Mummy." Sadly for all historians, any such conversation would have taken place in private with no courtier or ambassador lurking behind a cupboard, pen in hand, ready to write it all down. Nor do we know if she ever asked the question.

It might be asked, does it matter when Anne was born? The answer is yes because it affects our perceptions of both Anne and Henry VIII. At the time of her death, she had been involved with the King for around a decade. If she had been born in 1507, it follows that she was only just out of her 'teens when the relationship began and Henry (born in 1491) was almost twice her age. If she was born in 1501, she was a mature woman. Rightly or wrongly, the first scenario conjures up images of a middle aged man falling for a nubile young temptress and being driven by lust, while the other suggests a conscious selection by a serious monarch of a woman whose qualities he deemed fitted her to be his consort and mother of his children.[2] Alternatively, the view that Anne was young can see her portrayed as the victim of a manipulative and ambitious family while if she was much older, she can be regarded as a scheming adventuress in her own right. Such judgments obviously reflect prejudices which are unfair but few people are totally devoid of these ideas and certainly, people in Tudor England were not moulded by ideas of political correctness and their eye-witness accounts of events are of necessity a key source in any biography of Anne Boleyn.

The question of Anne's age is also important for political reasons. If she was barely twenty when she first became involved with Henry, it can be understood why he was willing to endure such a protracted process to marry her, but if she was in her late twenties at the outset, it is difficult to explain why he was willing to wait so long and then marry her when she was almost menopausal unless one is prepared to reject all the evidence that Henry wanted

---

2   Erasmus had quoted Aristotle that in the optimum marriage a bride should be eighteen and a groom thirty-seven, Desiderius Erasmus, 'The Institution of Christian Matrimony' (1526), translated by Michael Heath in *Collected Works of Erasmus: Spiritualia and Pastoralia* vol 69 ed. John W O'Malley, Louis Perraud (Toronto, 1999) p.324

a son.[3] Equally, if Anne was in her twenties when she died, she was clearly still of child-bearing age and Henry's execution of her could not be attributed to his fear that she could not give him a son and hence other motivations would apply. If she was in her mid thirties, Henry might have argued that he needed to be rid of her in order to find another woman through whom he could secure the succession. The reasons for Anne's rise and fall will be discussed in later chapters but it is necessary at the outset to consider the evidence that does exist regarding her age.

Today, there are two main theories about Anne's date of birth. That of 1501 originated in the late twentieth century and is primarily based on the indisputable fact that Anne went to the court of Margaret, Regent of the Low Countries in 1513. Whilst there, Anne wrote a letter to her father which survives and, it is argued, this is not the work of a seven year old. Other information cited to support this theory is that Anne was said to have been born in Norfolk and given that her father inherited Hever Castle in Kent in 1505, this means she must have been born before that date. Finally, proponents of this theory quote a comment made by Anne's father that his wife gave him a child "every year" prior to his inheritance in 1505. Anne was one of five children and counting back from 1505 means that Anne must have been born around 1501.

The birth date of 1507, which was accepted for centuries, comes from two places, William Camden's *Annales* of the reign of Elizabeth I and a biography of Jane Dormer which states that Anne was twenty-eight when she died in May 1536.[4] It is also supported by some circumstantial eye-witness accounts of people who commented on her youth when they met her and an Imperial report of her returning to England when aged fifteen or sixteen.

So which is right? When was Anne born?

It is hard to regard the 1501 theory as sustainable. Although there was no such thing as marriage registers at this period, we do know when Anne's parents got married due to the existence of a jointure, which was an agreement which protected a wife from penury in the event of the sudden death of her husband by settling lands upon her and gave her some independent income during his lifetime. The jointure for Elizabeth Howard was made on 10th July 1501 by which date she was married as it refers to her as the wife of Thomas Boleyn. In it, William Boleyn (her father-in-law) gave her, by virtue of her marriage to his son, Pashley manor and other holdings in Norfolk including Holkham. On the same date, William gave his son Thomas the use of Hever, Seal and Kemsing manors in Kent for life with a stipulation that Elizabeth

---

3 Katherine of Aragon was thirty-two at the time of her last pregnancy and entered menopause when thirty-six. Henry separated from her in 1524 by which time it had been confirmed she was past child-bearing. It should be presumed that her periods became irregular before finally stopping so it is likely that the condition became evident during 1523.

4 Henry Clifford, *The Life of Jane Dormer, Duchess of Feria* (ed. Stevenson) (1887) p.80: "She was not twenty-nine years of age." William Camden, *Annales Rerum Anglicarum et Hibernicarum regnante Elizabetha (*1615) p.2.

should enjoy them after his death for the remainder of her life. These grants were confirmed four months later on 29th November 1501.[5] The interval suggests that the marriage was celebrated or agreed at the start of July with the confirmation being processed shortly afterwards once it was confirmed that the marriage had been consummated. Today, we think of marriage as a being celebrated by a single event but that was not the case at this period. Couples might take vows in the future tense ("I will") which would create a legally binding union but not take their final vows using the present tense ("I do") until later.[6] This was especially true where property was involved, be that a landed estate or something much simpler, such as a smallholding where part of the agreement involved one party building a cottage for the couple or a business where a master agreed to set up his apprentice with his own loom when he married. At the upper end of society, the initial vows might be made by proxies if the two parties lived a long distance apart. A woman would legally be the man's wife after the first vows but not be his wife in a physical sense until the second. The practice of jointures being agreed prior to consummation and confirmed afterwards was described in 1523 as the "common course" of events.[7] Thus the jointure shows that Thomas and Elizabeth married during the summer of 1501 which means that the earliest possible date for their first child being born – and there is no evidence that Anne was such – would be the late spring of 1502. If Elizabeth did not conceive immediately, the first birth would be later in the year. The idea that the jointure was made some years after the wedding which some people have suggested in their determination to argue for a 1501 birth date, simply does not make sense. Elizabeth's father, the Earl of Surrey, did not give her to Thomas Boleyn on a "try before you buy" basis. He wanted to make sure his daughter was provided for, not hand her over and hope for the best. Early death was a very common occurrence in Tudor England. By the end of the sixteenth century, jointures were being made later but this followed the radical change of marriage practices in 1549 and legal complications with dowers.[8] Anne simply could not have been born in 1501.

---

5 *Calendar of Close Rolls Henry VII* no 179. The argument that Thomas and Elizabeth must have married prior to 1498 because Henry VII would not have visited Thomas Boleyn when he was a bachelor is not credible. All the clergy whom the king visited were bachelors and some of the courtiers were widowed. Thomas Boleyn's home was visited because it was a convenient stopping place for the king's journey, not so he could pay his respects to Elizabeth, John Guy, Julia Fox, *Hunting the Falcon* (2023) p.33

6 As was said in the code of canon law: "They are truly called married after the first pledge of betrothal, although conjugal intercourse is as yet unknown to them." Gratian *Decretum* C27, q2, c6.

7 LP 3.3178, 3649. The correspondence related to Lady Maud Parr's efforts to arrange a jointure for her daughter Katherine. In Italy the same process applied: Gregory Casale was betrothed, the legal agreement made, the marriage consummated and the contract effected, Catherine Fletcher, *Our Man in Rome* (2012) pp.83, 112, 118.

The evidence for Anne being born in Norfolk stems from her chaplain, Matthew Parker, recalling in later life that she had come from the same county as him.[9] As the marriage jointure shows, Thomas Boleyn had the use of both Hever in Kent and Blickling in Norfolk from 1501, as well as other properties in both counties, and on his father's death on 10th October 1505 he inherited Blickling outright[10], a property he continued to hold as late as 1533 when he was granted the right to hold a fair there on the feast day of St John the Baptist.[11] The argument that a date of 1507 means Anne had to be born in Kent is therefore wholly false. She could have been born in either place whichever date is preferred

With regard Thomas Boleyn's comment about his wife presenting him with a child every year before his father died, this should not be taken entirely literally.[12] His wife was not an automated baby machine churning out offspring at regular twelve month intervals but a woman whose fertility would have varied and whose health would have been affected by the ease or complications of each confinement. She could have had more than one child in a single year but it is more likely her children came between twelve and eighteen months apart with intervals increasing as she got older. There is no reason to conclude that all his children were born prior to his inheritance and there may have been others who were stillborn. The context of the comment is also important. Boleyn was moaning at the time and trying to make the point that he had had a tougher time than his daughter-in-law, Jane, who was seeking money from him. He was acting like myriad numbers of old people who tell their grandchildren that examinations were more difficult when they were at school, that they thought themselves lucky to get even an orange for Christmas never mind toys, and they had to earn their pocket money, which was only a penny or two, through hard work which did not do them any harm. It does not make Boleyn's statement utterly untrue but it is clear he was exaggerating for effect – just like granny probably got more than an orange at Christmas and grandad's mathematics test did not require Einstein's levels of expertise to pass. The £50

---

8   Katherine of Aragon's jointure was made within a week of the wedding. Anne's was made on the 21st March 1533 but not ratified by Parliament until a few months later because Parliament was not sitting and it had to approve it. *Statutes of the Realm*, vol 3. pp. 14, 479. It was not until the 1549 *Book of Common Prayer* that the two separate betrothal and marriage services were combined into a single wedding ceremony, a practice which continues today. The 1536 Statute of Uses significantly altered the law regarding jointures and dowers with the result that jointures were frequently made several years into the marriage.
9   J. Brue and T Perowe, *Correspondence of Matthew Parker* (1875) p.400
10 The will of William Boleyn, made three days before his death, appears in Nicholas Nicolas (ed.) *Testamenta Vetusta* vol 2 (1826) p.465. It was proved on 27th November 1505. Hever and Seal in Kent were left to Thomas' three brothers – James, William and Edward – in equal shares, though it is obvious that Thomas continued to use the property due to its convenient location to the Court.
11 LP 6.737 grant 12 dated 15th June
12 LP 11.7 dated 2nd July 1536 i.e. two months after Anne was executed.

he complained that he had as income from his father as a young married man, equates in value to £365,000 today – hardly a pittance. He also had land in six counties held in a trust for him all of which would have generated rent.[13] Plus, he was employed by Henry VII for which he received a salary which added almost half as much again, as well as providing him with free food and lodging and the opportunity for making contacts and picking up lucrative back-handers. If Thomas' allegation about his poverty stricken early years of matrimony was so obviously false, why should we credit his claim about the annual babies? He was a man prone to hyperbole. In 1523 he claimed to have read a document to the Emperor "in my poor French" - this despite being totally fluent in the language.[14] It was like Usain Bolt admitting he could run a bit or the infamous Hollywood producer who described Fred Astaire as a man who "could dance a little." In short, his comment does not represent evidence of Elizabeth's childbearing history, but rather should be viewed as illustrative of Thomas Boleyn's character.

That Anne went to Malines some time in 1513, we can be certain from correspondence between her father and Margaret of Austria. What is not clear, is the capacity in which she travelled. If she was taken on as a maid of honour, she must have been more than seven years old. Maids were expected to sing, dance, play instruments and generally entertain their mistresses as well as run small errands and attend them at public events to make a decorative backdrop and the minimum age was ordinarily twelve though it could be older. In 1536, Anne Bassett was rejected for the role of maid-of-honour to Jane Seymour because she was barely fifteen.[15] There is, however, reason to believe that Anne did not go to Malines to work but to be educated. Margaret's letter to Thomas sent just after Anne's arrival thanks him for sending her and describes her as remarkably well spoken and pleasant for one of her "young age." If Anne was the usual age for a junior member of staff, this would seem a very strange comment. Moreover, Margaret expresses her confidence that he will be pleased with what she intends to do for her – again, a bit strange if Anne was simply a new employee. Margaret further says that she hopes that by the time Thomas returns – and there is no hint of when that might be – Anne will be able to speak French.[16] If Anne really had been twelve and going to start her first job and that in a French speaking court, it sees inconceivable that her parents would have sent her unable to speak the language, or that Margaret would have wanted to take on a maid who would not be able to understand a word she said. Anne's father was an excellent linguist and served on a number of foreign embassies. He had visited Margaret in 1512 and had been granted the customs

---

13 David Loades, *The Boleyns* (2012) p.16, HMSO *Calendar of the Fine Rolls* vol XXII 1485-1509 (1962) p.370 membrane 829 dated 11th November 1505
14 LP 3.2772
15 LP 10.1165. Kathryn Howard's maids were all aged sixteen to twenty, Gareth Russell, *Young and Damned and Fair* (2017) pp.392-394.
16 Le Glay, *Correspondance de l'Empereur Maximilien 1er et de Marguerite Autriche* (Paris, 1839) vol 2 p.461

at Calais in 1509.[17] Anne's mother had been educated for court life and would have spoken French too. Anne would have learned the language from an early age and her lack of knowledge of it at this point only makes sense if she was nearer seven than twelve.

Of note also might be Cavendish's comment that Anne went abroad when "very young", implying that she was unusually so, and Anne's father referring to her as "la petite Boleyn" when writing to Margaret.[18] The nickname could be a reference to Anne being very short but is more likely to reflect the fact that she was his youngest daughter and that Margaret had adopted the same pet name because she was younger than the other girls around her.

The fact that nobody in Anne's lifetime ever mentioned her time at Malines and all early biographies spoke only of her time in France also supports the idea that she was not employed by Margaret. Envoys from Margaret's court regularly came to England and none ever admitted to knowing her. Chapuys, who had considerable contacts there, had no idea of her presence which would be almost impossible to understand unless she had been in the schoolroom, a place he would not have visited any more than other diplomats did.

The likelihood is that Anne was sent abroad with a view to her marrying someone at the court there. It was not unusual when a spouse was from a different country to ask that they be brought up in the future country so they would get to know the language and customs before the actual wedding, which would probably not take place before the bride was sixteen. Although no evidence survives for any such arrangement, in 1527, Henry VIII sought a dispensation to marry a woman who had been betrothed before the age of seven but never consummated a marriage to the person intended.[19] Unless Henry had been thinking of marrying someone else at the time, this suggests that Thomas Boleyn had told him of some such arrangement since Anne would have been too young to remember it.

The idea of sending a very young daughter to an overseas court with the intention of her marrying and settling in that country was not unknown. Charles Brandon had sent his own daughter to the same court, possibly in December 1513, for just that reason as he admitted when he recalled her in May 1515.[20]

---

17 Ibid p.49 where Margaret on 12th October 1512 reports that Thomas Boleyn has recently left. For the Calais link see Thomas Rymer, *Foedera* (1727) vol 13 pp.258-9 dated 27th July 1509. The fact that Boleyn was to pay £30 6s 8d per annum for the privilege indicates the extent of the income which he was to expect from this grant. It was a very handsome gift from Henry VIII and some twenty years before Henry met Anne, proving Thomas did not need to rely on his daughters for favours.

18 George Cavendish, *Life of Cardinal Wolsey* ed. S W Singer (1825) vol 1 p.120; Historical Manuscripts Commission, *15th Report, Appendix part 2 The Manuscripts of J Eliot Hopkins* (1897) p.30

19 Henry Ansgar Kelly, T*he Matrimonial Trials of Henry VIII* (Oregon, 1976) p.44

20 LP 2.529, SP vol.2 p.50

Although her exact date of birth is uncertain, Brandon's daughter was definitely too young for employment being born in either early 1504 or late 1508.[21]

The letter which Anne wrote is a crucial piece of evidence. Translated into English, it reads:

> Sir, I understand from your letter that you desire that I shall be a worthy woman when I come to the court, and you inform me that the Queen will take the trouble to converse with me, which rejoices me much to think of talking with a person so wise and worthy. This will make me have greater desire to continue to speak French well and also spell, especially because you have so enjoined it on me, and with my own hand I inform you that I will observe it the best I can.
>
> Sir, I beg you to excuse me if my letter is badly written for I assure you that the orthography is from my own understanding alone, while the others were only written by my hand. Semmonet tells me the letter but waits so that I may do it myself, for fear that it shall not be known unless I acquaint you, and I pray you that the light of (?) may not be allowed to drive away the will which you say you have to help me, for it seems to me that you are sure you can. If you please, make me a declaration of your word and concerning me, be certain that there shall be neither (?) nor ingratitude which might check or efface my affection, which is determined to (?) as much unless it shall please you to order me, and I promise you that my love is based on such great strength that it will never grow less, and I will make an end to my efforts after having commended myself right humbly to your good grace.
>
> Written at Veure by your very humble and very obedient daughter
> Anna de Boullan[22]

---

21 Brandon was not married to Anne Browne at the time he got her pregnant in 1503 and he promptly married another woman. In 1508, having separated from his wife, he resumed the relationship and got her pregnant again. On this occasion, he did marry her. One pregnancy ended in miscarriage, the other in the birth of the daughter sent to Malines but which was which is unknown. S. J. Gunn, *Charles Brandon* (1988) p.28, 93,174; Retha Warnicke, *Rise and Fall of Anne Boleyn* (Cambridge, 1989) p.12,35

22 English translation from Philip Sergeant, *The Life of Anne Boleyn* (1923) pp.17-18. The gaps reflect tears and smudges in the original document, MS 119 f.21a Corpus Christi. Semmonet was the tutor employed by Margaret to teach the children of the

Margaret's court was at Veure until August 21st 1514 and given the letter concerns Anne's departure to join Mary Tudor, who had become Queen of France on August 13th, it clearly dates from this week.[23]

There is no doubt that few children today, of either seven or twelve, would compose such a document. The language is much more formal and the sentiments expressed somewhat alien. Yet this was not unusual at the time. Consider the following letter:

> In most humble wise I desire your good Grace of your daily blessing, advertising the same that I have written unto the Kings Highness, making my most humble intercession unto the same for an harness to exercise myself in arms according to my erudition in the Commentaries of Caesar. In most humble wise beseeching your said Grace to be means for me unto the King's Highness in this behalf. And my trust is that I shall, as well in this thing as in all other, my learning so do my diligence and endeavour that it shall be to the high contentation as well of the King's said Highness as of your Grace. And thus our most merciful saviour in Christ have you, my most honourable lord and loving godfather, in His most blessed and perpetual protection.
> At Pontefract, the last day of January.
>
> H. Richmond[24]

At the time of writing this, Richmond was seven and a half. Another example might be:

> Pardon my rude style in writing to you, most illustrious Queen and beloved Mother, and receive my hearty thanks for your loving kindness to me and my sister. Yet, dearest

---

household, including the future Emperor Charles V and his sisters. The French version can be found in LP 4.1. For further discussion of this document see Hugh Paget, ' The youth of Anne Boleyn', *Bulletin of the Institute of Historical Research*, vol 54 (1981) pp. 162-170 and the reply in Retha Warnicke, *The Rise and Fall of Anne Boleyn* (Cambridge, 1989) pp. 14, 260 n.27.

23 Some writers have suggested that the queen referenced was Margaret and that Anne made a mistake not realising that she was only a duchess. Given she had been working for Margaret for a year in a highly formal court, the idea that she could be so confused is unrealistic.

24 SP vol. 4 pp.407-408. The spelling has been modernised. Contentation was used in this period where we would use contentment. It is reproduced in Maria Perry, *The Sisters of Henry VIII* (1998)

> Mother, the only true consolation is from Heaven, and the only real love is the love of God.
>
> Preserve, therefore, I pray you, my dear sister Mary from all the wiles and enchantments of the evil one, and beseech her to attend no longer to foreign dances and merriments which do not become a most Christian Princess. And so, putting my trust in God for you to take this exhortation in good part, I commend you to his most gracious keeping.
>
> from Hunsdon, this 12th of May.
> Edward the Prince[25]

Edward at the time was nine. Not only did he write letters in English but in French and Latin such as the following when he was eight:

> Impertio te plurima salute, colendissime praesul, et charissime susceptor. Quia abes longe a me, vellem libenter audire te esse incolumem. Precor autem ut vivas diu, et promoveas verbum Dei. Vale.
>
> Antilae, decimo octavo Junij.
> Tuus in Christo filius,
> Edouardus Princeps

Nor was such style the prerogative of princes. In July 1528, Gregory Cromwell, aged eight, wrote to his father praising him for his "manifold benefits" and continuing "entirely desiring the continuance of the same, trusting so to accomplish and fulfil your parental commandments in the passage of mine erudition, that you my good father shall therewith be right well contented, by God's help, the which with His grace He send us. Amen."[26]

Anne was receiving her education at what was arguably the most cultured court in Europe. She was also intelligent and her daughter was to inherit this capacity being known to translate Latin and Greek from the age of five, write and translate French and Italian by the age of ten, and as an adult to speak nine languages.[27] Thus, the content alone does not prohibit the view that it was written by a seven or eight year old. Nor does the formality because

---

25 J. G. Nichols (ed.), *Literary Remains of King Edward VI* (1857)
26 LP4.4561
27 The Venetian ambassador in April 1603 noted she spoke French, Latin, Italian, Scots, Cornish, Welsh and Irish – CSPV 9.1169. She also spoke Spanish. For more on her abilities see Janel Mueller and Joshua Scodel (ed.), *Elizabeth I: Translations* (Chicago, 2009)

education manuals of the period all refer to children learning style of expression through the copying out of letters from classical antiquity.[28]

However, there is also the issue of the handwriting. The letters are very small, neat and joined up and do not appear the work of a child, neither a precocious seven or eight year old nor a twelve year old. Comparing the 1514 letter with her letters to Wolsey and writing in her prayer book it can be seen that the formation of the letters d, e, f, h, and l especially but also b, g, p, s, t and y are all different. As people mature, their writing tends to become more sloppy as they move from the rounded separate letters of early childhood to joined up script, but they rarely change the way they actually form the letters.

The letter in question was given by Anne's chaplain, Matthew Parker to Corpus Christi College, Cambridge so undoubtedly dates from Anne's lifetime, but how did Parker obtain the letter? Anne was the sender so she would not have had a copy of it. The owner of the letter was Thomas Boleyn who is not known to have had any particular connection with Parker so why would he have given him this letter? Over the years, Anne would have written a number of letters to her father so, if he did give Parker the letter, why this one only? The fact that Thomas Boleyn kept the letter is significant. He is sometimes portrayed as an ambitious man who used his daughters for his own advancement but clearly he chose to preserve this early letter from Anne for over twenty years. It was not her first letter because she referred to earlier ones in it. Nor was it her last. He must have kept it for the simple reason that he loved her and he found her earnest promises to be good, combined with her mistakes in French, sweet.   Parents today often keep drawings and cards produced by their offspring, not because they are of any value or seem to indicate a prodigious talent, but just because they love their children. The most likely scenario is that Thomas found the letter in a desk or amongst some papers one day, probably when Anne was queen, and that he smiled at the memory and had it copied out – mistakes included – to give to her as a reminder of how far she had come or how much her French had improved. He probably thought it would make her laugh. Whether it did or whether she was embarrassed – as adults often are by their parents reminding them of childhood events – we cannot know. If this is what happened, presumably either Anne gave the copy to her chaplain or her father did. Thus, although the letter is undoubtedly genuine in that it was written by Anne in 1514, the differences in letter formation from other documents written by her, strongly suggest that it is a copy.[29]

---

28 Today writing is taught alongside reading but then it was seen as a separate subject. Thus, today, children might practice writing simple words and changing a vowel or consonant but then they would start by copying out phrases they might not understand simply to improve letter formation. It was not about self expression but style.

29 Corpus Christi College, Cambridge, MS 119 f.21. Parker collected many manuscripts and his interest in this one is shown by the Latin copy of it which is appended at f.25. As Anne's chaplain he would have seen her handwriting but it is

Another plank used in the argument for Anne being born around 1500 is the letter which Thomas Boleyn sent to Archduchess Margaret on 14th August 1514 telling her that Henry's sister Mary had requested Anne join her court in France. Boleyn says he did not know how to refuse such a request.[30] Protagonists of the early birthdate argue that Mary would not have requested the services of a seven or eight year old and Ives goes so far as to suggest that Anne was needed as a translator due to her expertise in French.[31] Certainly, it is improbable that Mary would have wished to employ a seven year old as a maid, but would she have employed a twelve year old translator? Mary spoke French and so did her ladies.[32] It was a necessary qualification to get a job as part of the entourage of the new Queen of France. Before Katherine of Aragon had come to England, she had been told to learn French so she could converse with the women at court all of whom spoke it.[33] They did not need a translator, and if they had, surely would have employed an adult. A place in Mary's staff was highly sought after and it is not likely that the Boleyns would have been uniquely honoured before all the other great families of the land by having both daughters employed, and Mary Boleyn definitely was part of the team.[34] Mary Tudor had her choice of servants so why would she have demanded the attendance of a girl whom she had never met? Answer – Mary never requested Anne join her at all. Thomas Boleyn made up the story as a way of saving face. He had secured Anne the position in Margaret's household but the political situation had changed since dramatically. Back in 1513, Henry's sister had been due to marry Margaret's nephew[35] but the perfidy of Katherine's father led to Henry deciding to marry his sister instead to the King of France. Fury erupted with the Imperial ambassador to England being withdrawn and there was a series of altercations between Henry, Margaret and her father the Emperor Maximilian.[36] It was rumoured in Rome – significantly not in England – that Henry was so angry with Katherine's family that he would divorce her.[37] It is

---

unlikely that he owned any examples of it for comparison because if he had, such documents would also have been in his collection. Even if the handwriting was to be proven as Anne's, it would only serve to identify her as the copyist not to confirm that the actual ink joined the paper in 1514.

30 *Manuscripts of J Eliot Hopkins* p.30
31 Ives, *Anne Boleyn*, p34
32 She had learnt the language informally from the age of three and received instruction from a tutor from the age of seven. Walter Richardson, *Mary Tudor: The White Queen* (1970) p.23; Erin Sadlack, *The French Queen's Letters* (New York, 2011) pp.21, 24, 31
33 CSPS 1.203
34 John Leland *Antiquarii De Rebus Britannicis Collectanea* ed. Thomas Hearne (1774) vol 1 p.703. Mary's presence is attested on the payroll, Ives, *Anne Boleyn*, p.33
35 Also nephew to Katherine of Aragon who was her sister-in-law.
36 CSPV 2.503; LP 1.3174, 3253, 3264, 3282
37 CSPV 2.479. See also G. Mattingley, 'A note on Henry VIII's divorce project of 1514', *BIHR* vol xi (1934) p163

therefore not surprising that Thomas wanted to get Anne away from Margaret's court and he decided to pass the blame on to Mary Tudor.[38] Thomas' letter was written the day after the wedding at Greenwich so it seems most likely that he spoke to the new French Queen during the celebrations afterwards and persuaded her to allow his daughter Anne to join the group in France. Mary Tudor was taking a number of children with her as "enfans d'honneur" so another would not be amiss.[39] Their role was to attend her temporarily like modern brides have page boys and flower girls, a role very suitable for a seven year old. The last minute nature of the addition explains why Anne's name was not on the list of those due to go and why Mary Tudor had no opportunity to write to her new husband to seek his permission. The fact that she went as a child rather than a maid of honour also explains why the payroll records for Mary's staff while in France only include payments to one Boleyn girl – Anne's sister Mary.[40] Thomas simply saw the chance to remove Anne from a smaller court in a country with which England had strained relations to a larger court in a country which had suddenly become England's greatest ally and which offered much greater opportunities. The fact that Thomas wrote his own letter rather than using a secretary indicated in what an embarrassing situation he found himself. A hand written letter was regarded as proof of seriousness and sincerity. Even by the standard of the period, Thomas laced his letter with protestations of humility and gratitude for the "great honour" which Margaret had done him by taking Anne in the first place – an honour he was now rejecting in favour of what he hoped was a better offer.

That Anne was placed in the school at the French court explains why she did not return to England with Mary Tudor upon her widowhood but rather, as De Carles says, she grew up in France.[41] Confirmation of this was given in May 1527: the French ambassadors to England were delighted to attend a banquet at which they saw Anne whom they recognised as one "who was brought up in France with the late Queen" i.e. Claude.[42] This report, written at the time and before even Henry had any inkling that he might marry Anne, is extremely important because it was composed by those who had known her for many years. The fact that they used the verb *nourrir* rather than *servir, employer,*

---

38 In 1515, Charles Brandon employed the same tactic, Sadlack, *French Queen's Letters*, p.123
39 LP 1.3348, 3357. Those sent included offspring of Thomas Brooke whose wife was first cousin to Thomas Boleyn, of the late George Manners whose wife was first cousin to Henry VIII's mother, and of Sir John Seymour. So far as can be gauged without accurate birth records, these children were aged between six and eleven.
40 Ives, *Anne Boleyn* p.33. She is listed as Marie Boulonne. If Anne was employed as a maid of honour in 1514 as some argue, one would have to conclude that she was working on a voluntary basis which does not seem probable.
41 Lancelot de Carles, *Trial and Death of Queen Anne Boleyn* (1545) f.10
42 John Lingard, *A History of England*, (Paris, 1840) vol. 4 p.50. The detail was not in earlier editions of his work and came from a manuscript diary in French archives. This manuscript has never been translated in full or published.

travailler or any other word associated with a job is significant. If Anne had resided in France from late 1514 to the end of 1521, she would have been there from age seven to fourteen meaning that five of those years would have been spent in the schoolroom, and only two as a maid of honour.[43] This last was her role at the end as Claude's sister, Princess Renée later recalled to Elizabeth I in 1561 but the French envoys remembered her childhood.[44] Shortly after Anne's death, Henry too would state that she had grown up in France, and as her husband, his evidence should carry great weight.[45]

Another source exists to support the idea of her being born c.1506. The Imperial author is unknown which makes it impossible to determine whether they were in any position to know the truth but the document was composed in French prior to 1598 because Lord Burghley wrote comments on it. The author claims that Anne was summoned to return to England when "she was fifteen or sixteen years old."[46] Although the document is far from being an accurate account of the events of 1527-36, it does contain the earliest known account of her age, predating Camden by some twenty years, maybe nearer forty.

What then can be said about the traditional date of 1507? The source for this is Camden but how reliable is he as a source? In the introduction to his *Annales* which was published in 1615, Camden says that he wrote at the instigation of Elizabeth's leading minister, William Cecil. He describes Cecil giving him great piles of papers of all descriptions, many being dusty, and notes the many hours he spent sweating over them – literally. During the course of the project, the Queen died and he was then given access to her papers. He wrote: "From all places I procured all the helps I could to write: charters and letters patents of Kings and great personages, letters, consultations in the Council Chamber, ambassadors instructions, and epistles. I carefully turned over and over the Parliamentary diaries, Acts, and Statutes. I ran through, and read over every Edict or Proclamation." He also used notes of his own and said he had "received many things from my ancestors, and credible persons which have been present at the handling of matters." He conducted interviews. The process took him more than eighteen years.[47] The fact that Camden worked diligently does not preclude the possibility of human error. He may have come

---

43   Her return was noted in LP 4.1994 by Francis I.
44   *Calendar of State Papers; Elizabeth 1 – Foreign* 1.870. Renée was born on October 25th 1510 so was younger than Anne.
45   LP 10.1070. The verb used was again *nourrir*.
46   Nicholas Pocock, *Records of the Reformation* (Oxford, 1870) vol. 2 p.573. The document itself is vitriolic comparing Henry to Nero and Caligula and claiming he no sooner saw the young Anne – whom the author claims was Henry's daughter – than he determined to rid himself of Katherine, the woman the author maintains was Henry's legitimate wife. It also repeats De Carles' claim about Anne's adultery – which the author believes and salivates upon – being exposed by the Countess of Worcester although he makes an error in the names. The document is, therefore, untrue in key aspects but it does not follow that every statement therein is false.
47   A convenient translation of the volume can be found at
     https://philological.cal.bham.ac.uk/camden/lectorieng.html#intr

across a document with Anne Boleyn's date of birth upon it and simply copied it incorrectly. Perhaps the light was bad or it was the end of the day. Anyone familiar with Tudor handwriting will know that a four can look very much like a seven, but as it was still common to use Roman numerals, such confusion could only exist if Arabic numerals were employed. Neither MDI or MDIV look like MDVII. However, given that Camden had much better access to people and documents than later historians, his work should be taken seriously and regarded as correct unless it can be proved otherwise. So what exactly does Camden say? After a brief biography of Thomas Boleyn as a courtier and diplomat he writes:

> This Thomas, among other children, begat Anne Boleyn, who in her tender years being sent into France, attended first Mary of England, wife to Louis XII, and then on Claude of Brittany, who, with the first, favoured the Protestants' religion springing up in France. Being returned into England and admitted amongst the Queen's Maids of Honour, and being now twenty two years of age, King Henry in the thirty-eighth year of his age, did for her modesty, tempered with French pleasantness, fall deeply in love with; and when he could not overcome her chastity, he sought to make her his wife in hope of issue male.

The oft-quoted dated of 1507 is not in the text but a marginal note made by the editor who has simply calculated that if Henry was almost sixteen years older than Anne and he was unquestionably born on 28th June 1491, she must have been born in MDVII i.e.1507. In fact, Henry would have been in his thirty-eighth year from 28th June 1528 to 27th June 1529 meaning Anne, if she was twenty-two at this point, would have been born between 28th June 1506 to 27th June 1507.

Where did he get the information that Anne was twenty-two? There is no way of knowing. Was it in Cecil's papers or Elizabeth's or was he actually told by them in person? He may have known Lord Hunsdon, Anne's nephew who was ten when she died. He may also have been able to speak to Henry Norris junior who died in 1601. Henry had been eighteen when Anne died and certainly knew her because she arranged his education and was friends with both his parents.[48] Camden's dating fits in with the memoir of the Duchess of Feria who was only an infant when Anne died but who spent many years working for Bloody Mary who clearly knew Anne very well and would have known her age.[49] The author of the memoir had read Camden's book but given

---

48 E. Ives, 'A Frenchman at the court of Anne Boleyn', *History Today*, August 1998, pp.22, 25
49 Jane Dormer, later Duchess of Feria, was born on 6th January 1535 so only seventeen months old when Anne was executed. Henry Clifford, *The Life of Jane*

he did not footnote his statement to explain his source, it is a matter of speculation whether he read the date in Camden or was told by the Duchess and noted it was confirmed by the book. Many people today own volumes containing reference material such as the names of prime ministers or characteristics of certain animals, but it does not follow that because they are able to recognise a robin or Tony Blair, they had needed the book to tell them. Camden makes no comment on Anne's age at execution, just the age difference between her and Henry.

Another possible way of trying to discover when Anne was born could be if the dates of birth of her siblings were known. She had four. Two brothers died: Thomas was buried at Penshurst and Henry at Hever. Neither brass has a date on it though an expert in the styles of the period suggested around 1520.[50] At least one of them may have been born while Anne was abroad. The fact that her mother did not accompany Mary Tudor's party to France in 1514, despite her husband and two daughters being there and herself the wife of a leading diplomat and daughter of the Duke of Norfolk, is curious.[51] Her name does not appear on any list indicating that she was not taken ill at the last moment. It is possible that she did not travel because she was pregnant. Elizabeth Boleyn would have been in her late thirties at this point.

A comment about Anne's surviving brother, George, was made by Cavendish in the 1550s when he wrote that George was made a member of Henry's privy council "ere years thrice nine had passed away."[52] Cavendish is a notoriously unreliable source even though he did have the benefit of actually knowing George in person – as far as a gentleman usher or butler would know a gentleman. The fact that Cavendish seems unable to distinguish between the Privy Council – a political body – and the Privy Chamber – the domestic household – does not inspire too much confidence, though to be fair, some men were members of both. In January 1526, following the re-organisation of the royal household agreed at Eltham, George was appointed a cupbearer when the King was away from court.[53] This was a relatively lowly position though it crucially offered access to the King, but in September 1528, George was appointed an esquire of the body and part of the Privy Chamber.[54] In the autumn of 1529, he was sent on overseas missions as an ambassador, rather to the surprise of the French who thought him rather young, but an ambassadorial

---

Dormer, Duchess of Feria (ed. Joseph Stevenson, London 1887) p.xvii

50 Mill Stephenson, *A List of Monumental Brasses in the British Isles* (1926) pp.236, 251

51 Thomas Howard was created Duke of Norfolk on 1st February 1514. His son, Elizabeth's brother, had married the King's aunt so her connections were undoubtedly so close to the Tudor that she would have been included in the party if able.

52 George Cavendish, *Life of Cardinal Wolsey vol.2 Metrical Visions,* ed. S. W. Singer (1825) p.21

53 LP 4.1939

54 LP 4.4779

role suggests political involvement at Privy Council level. Which of these appointments did Cavendish have in mind and was his memory almost thirty years later that accurate? There are obviously twenty six different years which could be described as "ere years thrice nine" so it is hardly a helpful statement. If Cavendish is right, it would suggest a date of birth for George of around 1502 whereas the surprise at his youth would suggest he was born later.[55]

The question of Mary's age has been much discussed, not least because of disputes about whether she was older or younger than Anne. Evidence can be found to support either theory, even from within the Boleyn family. Mary's grandson wrote a letter in 1596 describing her as "eldest daughter" of Thomas Boleyn while his daughter's tomb has inscribed the words "second daughter,"[56] The fact that Mary married first in February 1520 would normally be regarded as clear proof of her seniority. Daughters were normally married in order of age unless there was some reason not to do so, such as one being destined for the religious life or having mental or physical capability issues. Anne was evidently able bodied and of sound mind and there is no evidence that she was planning a career as a nun and even if she had desired this, it is hard to imagine her parents consenting to the idea. Mary's date of marriage is known because Henry VIII attended the ceremony and his accounts show that he put 6s 8d in the church plate, his usual offering when he went to church.[57] It was only after that took place that discussion began regarding a match for Anne. Some have suggested that Anne must have been the elder because she had the best education, but given that nothing is known of Mary's education, this is just speculation: Anne may have shown more aptitude. In 1533, Lady Lisle sought to send her younger daughters away for an education which surpassed that given to the elder.[58] More suggestive is the grant of lands in Kent in October 1531 which named Anne as the heir after her father and her brother if George died without issue.[59] Since the law would automatically pass the land to the elder sister, or possibly to both sisters equally since Kent still accepted the validity of gavelkind[60], there was no need to specify a successor to George unless that person was not legally next in line.

---

55 Gregory Casale became an ambassador when he was around twenty-five, Fletcher, *Our Man in Rome* pp.1,4
56 Sergeant, *Life*, p.302. This could indicate the birth of a girl before Mary whose name is unknown to history because she died in infancy since second does not necessarily mean the second surviving daughter.. A possibility not normally considered is that Mary and Anne were twins which might account for the confusion!
57 LP 3 Kings Book of Payments, 1520 p.1539
58 Muriel St. Clare Byrne, *The Lisle Letters: An Abridgement* (1983) p86
59 LP 5.506.16
60 A tradition dating back to Saxon times where estates are equally divided between children rather than descending to the eldest son (primogeniture). Gavelkind continued in the county until 1925.

There is however, one piece of potential evidence for Mary's age which has been overlooked. In 1514, preparations were under way for Henry VIII's sister to travel abroad. In February 1514 when she was due to marry the future Emperor, the list of attendants did not include Mary Boleyn but in October 1514 when the same princess was about to marry Louis XII of France, she was added.[61] This could indicate that she had celebrated her twelfth birthday between these dates thereby qualifying her to become a maid-of-honour. If this is so, it would mean she was born in the summer of 1502 and thus the firstborn of the Boleyn family. A marriage around the time of her eighteenth birthday would have been entirely in line with aristocratic practices at the period.

If the scenario suggested of Anne being born in the spring of 1507 is correct, this would make her around fifteen at the time of the Percy scandal and about twenty when she first attracted the attention of Henry VIII. These are more likely than the idea of her being over twenty on the first occasion and approaching thirty on the second.[62] It may also be the source of Sanders story that Anne was sent to France when fifteen due to her misbehaviour though he names other men being involved.[63] The Percy scandal is discussed more fully in a later chapter but Anne's behaviour was undeniably immature on this occasion. The same comment might be made of her rant about wanting to see all Spaniards at the bottom of the sea and the song she wrote at the end of 1530.[64] Of course, age and maturity do not always go hand in hand but if someone behaves likes a petulant teenager, the possibility that this is because they are one, should be admitted. Also, given Henry's desire for an heir and the fact that women at that time typically entered menopause in their mid-thirties, would he really have gone to such effort to wed someone who was almost past child-bearing age?

Also supporting the 1507 date of birth is the amount of Maundy money distributed by Anne in 1536. Purses were given to as many individuals as years the queen had lived. It is possible to divide the sum spent by thirty or twenty-seven but not by anything else.[65] At the time, it was usual for somebody of twenty-nine to be described as being in their thirtieth year and the records of

---

61 LP 1.2656.6, 3348. Mary Boleyn's name appears on the payroll for the months October to December 1514 whereas Anne's name does not, further indication that Anne was present but not as an employee, Ives, *Anne Boleyn*, p.33
62 In 1526, Francis' mother objected to him marrying Eleanor on grounds she was nearly thirty and consequently likely to be little use for childbearing, LP 4.2651. One suspects the Emperor chose her in part for this reason.
63 David Lewis (ed.), Nicolas Sander, *Rise and Growth of the Anglican Schism* (1887) p.25. Sander claimed Anne has misbehaved with her father's butler and then the chaplain.
64 LP 5.24; Ives, *Anne Boleyn* pp.173-4
65 LP 10.772, 914. Attempts to divide by figures such as thirty-five result in utterly impossible fractions of a penny.

Elizabeth I show that she distributed money based on such a tradition, for example giving to thirty-nine women when she was thirty-eight.[66]

At the Royal Ontario Museum in Toronto, there is a portrait by Lucas Horenbout said to be of Anne Boleyn. The sitter is not named but her age is shown as twenty-five. Proponents of the 1501 birth date for Anne have dismissed the image on grounds that a portrait of that quality would not have been created for a maid-of-honour in 1526. Others have noted the sitter wears a gable head-dress and said Anne wore a French hood – which she did on some days but not always. The portrait medal of 1534 at the British Museum shows her with a gable hood as does the illumination of her on the twentieth page of the Black Book of the Garter created in the same year and housed at Windsor Castle. If Anne was born in 1507, the image would have been painted in 1532, possibly when she was created Marquess of Pembroke and just before her trip to France. Official publications recorded the royal visit and it may have been intended originally to use the image as a woodcut. That Henry would seek a portrait of the woman he was about to marry and make his queen is entirely likely. Whether the painting in Toronto is such is another question but it is suggestive.

Although the evidence is circumstantial, attention should be paid to the descriptions of Anne given by people who met her. Reginald Pole met Anne in 1527 and described her as a "girl."[67] Vergil used the same expression.[68] The diplomat John Casale also called her a "girl" in February 1530.[69] He had not met her himself but his brother Paul had only just returned from six weeks in England at court and his cousin Vincent met her during his visit at Christmas 1528.[70] The Imperial ambassador, Eustace Chapuys, referred to her as a "girl" – one of his more polite expressions for her – after he first saw her at the end of 1529.[71] In an age where relatively few women reached fifty and forty was well into middle age, it would seem exceptionally gallant if these men chose to refer to Anne as a girl when she was almost thirty. More significantly, in January 1534, Chapuys described her as being of an age to have many more children, a comment which only makes sense if she was in her mid to late twenties.[72] Moreover, he repeated this statement as being true in April 1536.[73]

---

66 *Archaeologia*, vol 1 (1770) pp.7-9. The Maundy was distributed on 6th April 1572, five months before Elizabeth celebrated her thirty-ninth birthday.
67 F. E. Bridgett, *Life of Blessed John Fisher* (1890) p.148
68 Polydore Vergil, *Anglica Historia* ed. D. Hay (Camden Society, 1950) p.331. It is not known if Vergil ever met Anne or saw her anywhere but he had court contacts throughout this period.
69 LP 4.6235
70 LP 4.5981, 5990, 6235; Fletcher, *Our Man*, p.55. Casale also worked with various envoys from Henry, all of whom knew her, and the subject of what she was like must have come up.
71 CSPS 4.1.232.
72 CSPS 5.7
73 SP vol. 7 p.684. Henry accepted the statement and agreed with it.

Other comments which might be suggestive include the Bishop of Bayonne, who knew Anne well, describing her in August 1528 and January 1529 as a "young lady"[74] It is a vague term and could be no more than politeness but he did not need to use the adjective. He was thirty-seven at the time. Wolsey's gentleman usher, Cavendish, described her as being a "foolish girl" in 1522 and "gorgeous lady" in 1528[75] while Father Forrest said she was a "fresh young damsel" in 1527.[76] Simon Grynaeus met her in August 1531 and described her as "young, good looking, of a rather dark complexion and likely enough to have children"[77] Her chaplain, Latymer, said that she died "ere half the race were run" implying that she was still well short of middle age which then might be considered to begin just after thirty.[78] The one common thread in all these accounts is that the authors chose to comment on her youth.

It might also be noted that the scurrilous rumour circulated by Judge William Rastell and other friends of Sir Thomas More and later reported by Sander that Anne was Henry's own daughter, would only have gained credence if she had been substantially younger than Henry.[79] Even allowing for the fact that her enemies were prepared to believe almost anything bad about her and her family, the story would have made no sense if she had been only a few years younger. Henry was not fathering children when he was nine!

In June 1532, a conversation took place between Dean John Barlow and an Imperial councillor in Brabant about Bessie Blount and Anne Boleyn with one being termed the "girl" and one the "lady." Bessie was definitely born 1500-1 so if Anne was born around the same date as some writers have claimed, there would be no reason to distinguish them by these terms but if Anne was born around 1506-7, then it would make sense for her to be the girl and this text has been used as evidence to support this birth date. However, the key to the passage lies in the conversation which preceded it. Barlow referred to Bessie having Henry's child when she was a girl and his companion, Heylwigen, assuming that the King now wishes to marry her, asks what she is like. Barlow explains that Henry wishes to marry a different lady and Heylwigen, not appreciating the fact that a dozen years have gone by, asks him how the current "lady" compares to the "girl" Bessie. In 1532, Anne was single

---

74 LP 4 5210, Appx.196
75 Cavendish, *Wolsey* vol 1. pp.122, 134
76 William Forrest, *The History of Grisild the Second* ed W. D. Macray (1875) p.53 The original text was composed in 1558 for Queen Mary by her chaplain. In the book he notes his own involvement in the annulment crisis from April 1530 onwards and says he wrote "partly by knowledge and partly by hearing say." p.22, 75-78.
77 Hastings Robinson, *Original Letters relative to the English Reformation* (1847) p.553
78 Maria Dowling (ed.), *William Latymer's Cronickille of Anne Bulleyne* (Camden, 1990) p.64
79 Nicolas Sander, *Rise and Growth of the Anglican Schism* ed. David Lewis (1877) pp.23-24

and Bessie the widowed mother of three children the eldest of whom was almost in his teens. A very courteous man might describe a lady with three such children as still a "girl" but it would be highly unusual. What is being compared is Bessie in 1519 with Anne in 1532 which means the choice of words cannot be regarded as significant in the attempt to ascertain Anne's date of birth.[80]

Not subject to gallantry or personal judgment is the evidence of Anne's skeleton. When this was examined in 1876, the eminent surgeon and professor of medicine, Dr Frederic Mouat recorded it as belonging to a "female of between twenty-five and thirty years of age."[81]

Perhaps the closing words in this debate about terminology should be left to the lady herself. In December 1530, Anne wrote: "my years be young, even as ye see."[82] If she had proclaimed this at almost thirty, the response would have been guffaws.

Yet there is one other document which could provide a clue to Anne's exact date of birth. In March 1528, Henry gave Anne twenty one diamonds and twenty one rubies set upon roses and hearts. The fact that he was giving her an expensive present was not unusual but there was clearly some significance in the number twenty one and it appears to have been the highest value item he sent her that year.[83] Could it have been a gift to mark her twenty-first birthday? If so, it would indicate Camden and Dormer were right all along and Anne was twenty when the relationship with Henry began and two months short of her twenty-ninth birthday when she died.

Arguing that a single letter is more important as evidence than all the comments made by those who actually knew Anne seems a trifle presumptuous. People could tell the difference between an eight year old girl and one of fourteen and Henry would have known if the woman he loved was twenty two or twenty nine, plus he would have heard about her childhood from both herself and her parents. For them all to be wrong and writers living almost five

---

80 Ives, *Anne Boleyn* p.51; LP 5.1114; CSPS 4.2.967.
81 Doyne C. Bell, *Notices of the Historic Persons Buried in the Chapel of St Peter ad Vincula* (1877) pp.20-21. Some have doubted that the skeleton was Anne's because of their belief that she was in her mid thirties and Mouat said she had a "somewhat square" jaw which is not evident in most of the portraits of her. However, the only two certain portraits created during her lifetime were the coronation medal, which does not show a pointed chin, and the one in the Garter roll which is too indistinct to assess. The Chequers ring was created after Anne's death and shows a more rounded face than in the more famous portrait in which she wears the "B" necklace. Paul Hentzner, who met Elizabeth I in 1598 described her as having a "face oblong" which does not appear in her portraits either, Horace Walpole (ed.) *Paul Hentzner's Travels in England during the reign of Queen Elizabeth* (1797) p.34. Artists were paid to flatter not produce photographic likenesses.
82 Ives, *Anne Boleyn,* p.174
83 LP 5.276. The account has been incorrectly calendared under 1531 but as Ives points out, the only year that Henry and Anne were at Beaulieu in early August was 1527 and hence the list covers gifts 1527 to 1528 not 1530 to 1531. Ives, *Anne Boleyn*, p.109

hundred years later to know better, seems unlikely. It is simpler to believe that there was some reason for the letter being copied than to credit that Anne's parents succeeded in convincing hundreds of people, including those who would have known them at the time of her birth and whose own children were the same age, they had misremembered the event.

Question: When was Anne born?

Answer:
Although it can never be known for certain, the likelihood would be that Mary was born in the summer of 1502, George around 1504, Anne in the spring or early summer of 1507 with Thomas and Henry following.

Was Henry married when he met Anne?

Ask anyone how many wives had Henry VIII and they will invariably give you the answer six and possibly recite to you the old rhyme:

> Divorced, beheaded, died, (Katherine of Aragon, Anne Boleyn, Jane Seymour)
> Divorced, beheaded, survived (Anne of Cleves, Catherine Howard, Katherine Parr)

In fact, he had legally only three wives – Jane Seymour (died), Catherine Howard (beheaded) and Katherine Parr (survived). He could not divorce Katherine of Aragon or Anne of Cleves because he never contracted a legitimate marriage to them and you clearly cannot divorce someone unless you are married.[1] Henry's union with Anne Boleyn was also annulled.

Nonetheless, there is no disputing the fact that in 1509, Katherine of Aragon stood before a priest alongside the eighteen year old Henry VIII, and the couple took vows to love and honour one another through good times and bad until death did them part. For fifteen years, they shared a bed and Katherine conceived at least six children but the situation then changed. From 1524 onwards, their relationship became purely platonic and in 1527 Henry VIII began his quest to have his "marriage" to Katherine declared null and void. What caused this seismic development? Did Henry allow lust to overcome reason? Was he motivated by political concerns and the need to secure the dynasty? Or was he actually right that he never had been truly married to Katherine at all? The steps leading up to Henry's change of heart are discussed in "Was Anne the cause of the break with Katherine" but here the issue is Henry's actual case.

It must be admitted at the outset that we live in a world very different to Henry VIII. A survey in 2019 found that only 38% of British adults identified as Christian with just 1% of those aged 18 to 24 claiming to be Anglican.[2] Amongst those claiming to be Christian, 84% admit that they do not attend church regularly and nor do they pray or read the Bible.[3] With barely one in

---

1 The use of the word divorce by an author implies acceptance of the belief that Henry and Katherine were actually lawfully married since nobody can get divorced unless they are married. The word was used by some in the Tudor period but that was because the first word of any annulment decree was *divortium a vinculo matrimonii* not because the writer or speaker was ignorant of the definition.
2 https://www.theguardian.com/world/2019/jul/11/uk-secularism-on-rise-as-more-than-half-say-they-have-no-religion
3 https://www.christianpost.com/news/only-6-percent-of-brits-practicing-christians-read-bible-attend-church-regularly-poll-199339. A comparison of church attendance figures with those identifying on the 2021 UK Census as Christian indicates that the 84% is an under-estimate.

twenty people having any familiarity with the Bible, and the majority of those only accepting it as an inspired text rather than the literal word of God[4] it is small wonder that modern writers have so signally failed to understand Henry's case. The following statement is fairly typical of the response to Henry's claim that his "marriage" to Katherine was forbidden by the Bible:

> Proof of this prohibition was supposedly that such a marriage would be childless. Fortunately there was a way round this invented by Henry which was to argue that only the lack of a male child was relevant.[5]

This is absolutely untrue on many levels as will be shown but it demonstrates the need to start by looking at the background to Henry's thinking and the texts in question before considering how they were interpreted at the time. All too often writers on the issue reveal more of their own attitudes to religion than they do Henry VIII's. Those who regard religion in a negative manner, seeing it as a causer of wars or the remnants of a superstitious pre-enlightenment age, tend to adopt a cynical response to Henry's claim that his soul was troubled by thoughts that his "marriage" might be displeasing to God. Other writers who see religion as largely harmless but just a case of going to church occasionally and doing good deeds like helping an elderly neighbour with their shopping, also fail to take seriously the issues and see Henry's protests as just a sideline to the main political questions. Historians and biographers do not have to share the beliefs of their subjects – indeed, it may be repugnant to do so – but they must make every effort to understand and respect them. If they do not, it is like trying to review a book or play written in a completely alien language and doomed to failure. If we want to understand Henry, we have to view the world through his eyes not the prism of the twenty-first century.

Moreover, most of those who do claim to be analysing Henry's case merely reveal their own ignorance of the matter. It is extraordinary how many writers think that after looking up a couple of verses in some modern language translation of the Bible, they know more about the subject than Henry VIII, Dr Thomas Cranmer and the countless thousands of Christian theologians and Jewish rabbis who have dedicated their lives to the study of the Scriptures. It is like a child coming home from his first ever science lesson and proudly announcing that he knows better than Einstein or a person who imagines that reading *Black Beauty* will teach them to ride a horse and win the Grand National!

Thus, in answering this question, consideration will be given to the fundamental beliefs with which Henry began his quest, the theological case and the documents on which it was based, the objections of his enemies and the case in canon law. Due to the extent of the misunderstanding about these

---

4   https://www.eauk.org/church/research-and-statistics/attitudes-to-the-bible.cfm
5   Peter Gwyn, *The King's Cardinal* (1990) p.512

matters which exists and the complexity of the issues, considerable detail is given and little or no prior understanding is assumed. Readers should be reminded of the need to suspend any ideas of modern textual criticism when it comes to the analysis of the Bible and limit themselves to what was known about it in Henry's lifetime.

What did Henry believe?

Henry believed in God. He believed God was the creator of the world, that he was all knowing and all powerful, and that he was the Father of all. He believed that God was constantly active in the world and that he answered prayer, including giving guidance to those who asked. He believed that Jesus was truly God incarnate as well as a real human being. He believed that after death, everyone would face judgment at the second coming of Jesus "according to truth and justice: and according to his holy word expressed in scripture, that is to say, according to every man's own works and deeds, done by him in his lifetime, which works and deeds shall be then examined, discussed and tried, not after men's own fantasy and invention, without authority and ground of scripture, but according to the commandment of God, and the teaching of Christ and his apostles."[6] Following the verdict, people would be consigned to the peace and glory of heaven or to hell "to be punished in body and soul eternally with fire, that never shall have end, which was prepared from the beginning of the world, unto the devil and his angels."[7]

Henry regarded Christianity as a contract between humanity and God: "For although God's promises made in Christ be immutable, yet he maketh them not to us, but with condition, so that his promise standing we may yet fail of the promise, because we keep not our promise."[8] In his annotations to the *Bishop's Book* of 1537, he wrote that people only remained children of God and heirs of eternal life as long as they "persevere in his precepts and laws."[9]

Marriage, Henry understood, to be a sacrament and as such a means of grace.[10] He provided teaching about this in his *Assertio Septem Sacramentorum*

---

6   Charles Lloyd (ed), *Formularies of Faith put forth by authority in the reign of Henry VIII* (1825) pp.238-239
7   Ibid. p.240
8   Ibid. p.225
9   See John Cox (ed.), *Miscellaneous Writings and Letters of Thomas Cranmer* (1846) p. 84 where Cranmer comments upon this statement.
10 The Latin Bible translates the original Greek word *mustérion* in Eph 5:32 as *sacramentum*, an error which Luther pointed out in his *Babylonian Captivity*. In his *Assertio*, Henry supports the Vulgate, presumably not having noticed that Erasmus himself in his revised Latin translation had used *mysterium*. The word appears twenty-eight times in the New Testament including in the famous parable of the sower where it clearly does not mean a sacrament in the sense used traditionally by the church, see Matt. 13:11, Mark 4:11, Luke 8:10. Marriage was not listed as a sacrament until 1439, less than sixty years before Henry's birth, and not officially

of 1521 and *A Necessary Doctrine* (often known as *The King's Book*) of 1543. Firstly, marriage signified the mystical union between Christ and the church, which is referred to in the Bible as the bride of Christ (Eph.5:23-7; 2 Cor 11:2). It represented too the intimacy of the Christian's relationship with God who dwelt within the hearts of his children through the gift of the Holy Spirit (Ecclus. 1:1-15, 15:1-6; Wisd. 7:14, 8:2).[11] God himself had spoken of betrothal through faith (Hos 2:20).[12] It also signified the union which existed within Christ being both man and God. Given that Christ could never give up either of his natures and would never abandon the church, it followed that marriages could not be broken or dissolved. To suggest otherwise would be blasphemy.[13]

Secondly, marriage was a necessary step toward fulfilling the commandment to "go forth, increase and multiply" (Gen.1:28) an act which united the couple with God in the act of creation. Until the *Alternative Service Book* of 1980, procreation was listed as the primary purpose of marriage which is why contraception was forbidden and why a barren wife or impotent husband were seen as obstacles to matrimony. This is in stark contrast to today where contraception is regarded as so acceptable that it is taught in schools and "family planning" is taken for granted. The rights of a woman not to be perpetually pregnant and worries about over-population and world resources, were concepts totally unknown to the Tudors.

Thirdly, marriage transformed an activity which would otherwise be sinful, into something acceptable to God. Henry described intercourse as an act of "filthy concupiscence…which of its own nature defiles to punishment" unless sanctified by marriage.[14] He argued that sex for personal enjoyment even within marriage was a sin, a view shared by Harpsfield who opined that anyone who sought "carnal pleasure" with their spouse deserved to burn in hell for all eternity.[15]

Fourthly, marriage was regulated by divine laws which began in Genesis with the instructions that the couple should cleave to one another, become one flesh, multiply, and the wife should obey and continued in the Gospels with Jesus' teaching about the indissolubility of marriage.[16] Henry wrote:

---

recognised as such until 1563.
11 Henry VIII, *Assertio Septem Sacramentorum or Defence of the Seven Sacraments*, ed. Louis O'Donovan (New York, 1908) p.392. Hugh of St Victor, one of Henry's favourite theologians, was particularly keen on this idea which also has echoes in Jewish thought. The Talmud notes that the Hebrew for husband and wife is an anagram of God and fire which represents the shecinah or presence of God and thus shows the sacred nature of marriage – Sotah 17a
12 Quoted by Aquinas
13 These three parallels appear in other texts such as Erasmus, *The Institution of Christian Matrimony* (1526) and William Harrington, *Comendacions of Matrimony* (1528).
14 Ibid. pp.382, 384.
15 Nicholas Harpsfield, *Pretended Divorce of Henry VIII* ed. Nicholas Pocock (Camden 1878) p.53
16 Gen. 2:24, 3:16, 9:1; Matt. 19:6; Mark 10:9

> It is Christ's will and commandment, that the people of God should follow and conform their doings unto the laws of matrimony then made, and should observe the same in such purity and sanctimony, as it was first ordained, without separation or divorce, and that under the pain of damnation.[17]

Key to this understanding was the belief that marriages were made by God and not by people. This was why the marriage service quoted Jesus that "those whom God hath joined together" (Matt. 19:6; Mark 10:9) and why the bride was given by the father to the priest and not the groom in the service, the priest representing God giving her then to the man as God gave Eve to Adam. At the legatine court in 1529, Bishop Fisher argued that Henry's "marriage" to Katherine had been made by God and since God was truth and could not lie, it must be valid. Wolsey replied that nobody doubted that marriages made by God were permanent unto death, but the whole question was whether God had made this particular one or not. If it was man made, it was not valid and could not be so because true marriages could only be made by God.[18]

Wolsey's intervention is important as it is a reminder that Henry's beliefs were in no way unusual and indeed, most of his views remain Christian teaching today.[19] It does, however, represent a very different world view to those who have grown up with the idea that matrimony is a legal contract between two people who are free at any time to dissolve that contract. Divorce, as Henry confirmed in his *Assertio*, could only take place where there was sexual immorality, something which he never suggested Katherine had committed. Henry's stance was entirely in line with Jesus' teaching that any man who separated from his wife for any other reason would be guilty of adultery if he remarried (Matt. 19:9) and that would be a breach of the Ten Commandments (Ex. 20:14) and mortal sin.[20] The importance of keeping God's law and consequence of breaching it was stressed by the future pope Adrian VI who told the Emperor in 1522 to take care "that God does not reject you as he rejected Saul when he failed to obey his holy commandments."[21] Erasmus told

---

17 *Formularies* p.274
18 George Cavendish, *The Life of Cardinal Wolsey* vol.1 ed. Samuel Singer (1825) p.159. In his *Assertio*, Henry had written: "Those who are lawfully married are not rashly joined together by the ceremonies of men only but by the invisible presence and insensible co-operation of God himself: and therefore is it forbidden that any should separate those whom God has joined together." p.388
19 Protestants see grace as unconditional and deny that marriage is a sacrament, not because they dispute God's involvement, but because they define sacraments as applicable to all and not everybody gets married.
20 A mortal sin killed the soul and removed all hope of eternal bliss. A venial sin could be forgiven if the sinner repented.
21 Geoffrey Parker, *Emperor* (Yale, 2019) p.32

Katherine of Aragon prior to the start of the annulment crisis that God "rewards those who observe the laws of marriage he made and punishes those who infringe them."[22]

Henry utterly abhorred the concept of divorce. His goal in 1527 was an annulment, a declaration by the pope who had allowed his "marriage" to Katherine that this union was not lawful. The best way to understand it is to think of a man who has been accused of committing a serious crime who wants his name cleared so that he can start his life again. For such a man, it is not enough for people to be left to draw their own conclusions for some will say there is no smoke without fire and still regard him with suspicion, nor does he want a pardon which implies he was guilty. The accused man needs to be publicly cleared and to have his good reputation restored. In the same way, Henry wanted everyone to know and accept that he was a man of honour. He had been accused of the sin of incestuous fornication with Katherine but he had slept with Katherine in good faith because he had been badly advised by those who told him it was lawful for him to do so. It was necessary therefore for the pope – whose dispensation had led him into sin – to declare Henry innocent to the whole world and to God himself by admitting the error. Only this absolution, Henry believed, would clear him of the mortal sin which would otherwise send him to hell, and thus make him acceptable to God thereby paving the way for his new union to be blessed. [23]

Another crucial difference between Henry's mindset and that of almost everybody today is that Henry was theocentric. In the twenty-first century, the general focus is on the individual and me in particular – my feelings, my opinions, my likes, my desires, my rights etc. For Henry and those around him, the focus was on what God wanted and thought. The change can be demonstrated by two examples. Today, many people – especially those of a secular persuasion – question the validity of the laws in the Bible by judging them against their own standards of morality. If a law appears discriminatory, it must be wrong and as God is assumed to be good (if he is thought to exist), it follows the law is not of divine origin. For Henry, and his contemporaries, this was entirely the wrong way of thinking. All laws were right because they were derived from God who was perfect. If man found them difficult or wrong, this was evidence of man's sinfulness, not any problem with the law. Secondly, the change is seen with regard to liturgy. When the church of England introduced *Common Worship* in 2000, the stated aim was to provide a myriad of choices so that people and churches could pick the style of service they liked and which they found meaningful. By contrast, when Cranmer produced the first *Book of*

---

22 Desiderius Erasmus, *The Institution of Christian Matrimony* (1526), translated by Michael Heath in *Collected Works of Erasmus: Spiritualia and Pastoralia* vol 69 ed. John W O'Malley, Louis Perraud (Toronto, 1999) p.224. It would be reasonable to suppose that Katherine showed Erasmus' book to Henry VIII.

23 Henry asked how the pope – known as His Holiness – could ever issue a dispensation to permit incest given St Peter himself had told believers to follow God's injunction to "be holy" (1 Pet 1:14-16): incest is not holy.

Common Prayer in 1549, his goal was to provide the purest and best form of service which would be most acceptable to God: there were no choices because worship was for and about God not human beings. This is not to say that Henry had no will of his own but he absolutely believed that separation from Katherine was necessary to please God and he never wavered in this opinion. Anne Boleyn came and went in his life but when Henry died in 1547, he was as sure that marriage to a brother's wife was against divine law as he was in 1527.

But how could Henry know what would please God? The answer was in the Bible which contained instructions on how to live a life which would result in God proclaiming at your death, "well done thou good and faithful servant" (Matt 25:21) and admitting you to eternal bliss. To Henry, the Bible was not the work of mere humans but contained the actual words of God. [24] It contained promises made by him that he would send his own Holy Spirit to live in his chosen so that they would have – to use a modern idiom - a hotline to God which meant they need no longer be afraid. God promised to listen to prayers and he declared that all things were possible. He promised to be faithful to those who were faithful to him, but warned that he would punish those who were not. Henry studied the Bible not as an academic exercise or in search of a loophole to escape his "marriage" – the belief he must separate from Katherine arose from his reading – but because he believed that God was speaking to him through it.[25] It is totally impossible to understand Henry's actions without accepting his fundamental belief that the Bible was the Word of God, a revelation of the mind and wishes of the Almighty with daily application to his life, and that his own response to that Word would have implications on his life on earth and in the hereafter. In 2 Tim. 3:16, Paul talks of scripture being the breath of God which was an allusion to God's breath giving life to mankind (Gen. 2:7; Ezek. 37:5) and Henry accepted this absolutely.

Over recent years, considerable attention has been paid to the canon law situation by various writers but the theological has been largely ignored even though that was the basis for the judgment in Henry's favour in 1533 and thus it is with an analysis of this that a study of the case should begin.

The Theological Case

Although we talk of the Bible as a single book, it is in fact a library of sixty-six works – or eighty-one if the Apocrypha is included – written over a

---

24 Miles Smith, who wrote the preface to the King James translation of the Bible which was also separately published as *The Translators to the Reader* (1611) p.8, noted that the text came "from heaven, not from earth, the author being God, not man."

25 This remains Christian belief. The Bible is not an encyclopedia used for consultation but the work of a living author who welcomes readers to engage with him about its meaning and application.

span of some fourteen centuries. For Christians, it is divided into Old and New Testaments. The New Testament contains the four gospels which describe the life of Jesus, a history of the acts of the apostles, twenty-one letters and the revelation or apocalypse. The Old Testament contains the psalms or prayers to God which Henry and his contemporaries used extensively in both private and public acts of worship and as a source of spiritual comfort.[26] It also contained nineteen books of prophecy, ten of history, and four guides to wisdom.[27] These sections played little part in Henry's quest to have his "marriage" to Katherine annulled. The key texts were the first five books of the Old Testament which formed the Law or Torah. The Law, or more accurately Teaching, included the Ten Commandments but considerably more detail about other aspects of daily life such as marriage, crime, relationships, caring for animals. The word Law inevitably conjures up today negative images of restrictions on individual liberties but the purpose of the Torah was to show people the nature of God and the way in which he should be honoured, one of the means of which was to live in a manner which pleased him. Not only was the Law regarded as God's own Word rather than Moses' invention, Jesus himself had promised that as long as the world existed, not a dot or letter would disappear from it and that those who set aside the Law or taught others to do it would be condemned (Matt. 5:18-19). It was no wonder that the study of the Law became central to the "marriage" question.

      Of the five books of the Law, Genesis, Exodus and Numbers contained no instruction with regard to a man taking his brother's wife as his own. The two books which did mention the subject were Leviticus and Deuteronomy. Modern textual criticism assigns different dates and authors to these works but in Tudor times, both were seen as volumes created by Moses who wrote as God dictated.[28] However, though believed to be contemporaneous, the two books were still recognised as having different purposes. Leviticus was written to describe the sacrificial system, both of animals as part of temple worship but also the sacrifice of sin to be made by all people because God required everyone to be holy. The instructions for people were contained in chapters 18, 20 and 21 and formed what remains known as the holiness code. The final chapter of the book contained promises of what would happen to those who kept the code and those who did not. Deuteronomy consisted largely of three very long speeches by Moses which included a rehearsal of the story of Israel to that point, a wide variety of laws and another set of promises and punishments for those who kept or broke the Law. The key passage relating to Henry's situation was in chapter 25. The following looks at both texts in detail.

---

26 Anne Boleyn carried a copy of the psalms to her execution and gave copies to her ladies.
27 There is some disagreement about the numbers in each category. For example, some view Daniel as a prophet, others as a writer of wisdom literature. The controversy is not relevant to Henry's theological case.
28 Ex. 24:4; Deut. 34:28; Neh. 8:1

Leviticus

The regulations defining forbidden relationships appear in the eighteenth chapter of the book of Leviticus. The chapter begins by saying that these are the words that God has spoken to Moses and which he is to convey to the people (v1). It says that people must avoid behaving like those who have lived in the land before and obeying their rules (v3) but rather "I am the Lord your God. Ye shall therefore keep my statutes and my judgments: which if a man do, he shall live" (v5). There then follows a series of proscriptions on various sexual acts which are said to make those who commit them unclean because they are abominations. God says that he has punished other nations who carried out such acts (v25) and he will do so again. Crucially, Lev. 18:26 states that the laws apply not just to the Jews but to all people.

We have Henry's understanding of the rationale behind these prohibitions in his *A Necessary Doctrine*, where he writes:

> In so much that they [the people] could not perceive nor judge, what things were of their own nature naughty and detestable in the sight of God, nor yet how far the natural honesty and reverence, which we owe unto such persons as be near of our kin, or alliance unto us, was extended: God, therefore, willing man to return from darkness, commanded his prophet Moses, to promulgate and to declare by his word unto the people of Israel, the said laws of prohibition of matrimony in certain degrees of consanguinity and affinity...Not only the Jews. but also all other the peoples of the world, were as much and as straightly bounden, to the continual observation of the same laws, as they were to the other moral laws of the ten commandments.[29]

The prohibitions refer to uncovering the nakedness of particular women (i.e. having sexual intercourse). The Vulgate at the time translated this as "thou shalt not marry" which was incorrect as the Hebrew verb here is *yikah* meaning to take not *baal* to marry. The prohibitions fall into two categories affecting women who are related to the man by family ties (consanguinity) or through marriage (affinity).[30] The prohibitions cover:

Consanguinity	Affinity
daughter (v6)[31]	father's wife (v8)

---

29 *Formularies* p.271
30 Users of the *Book of Common Prayer* will be familiar with this as the Table of Kindred and Affinity though the table does not align entirely with the Bible.
31 Literally in Hebrew, "next of flesh." but this indicates daughter as is shown by the ban on a man having sexual relations with any female whose mother he has already

Consanguinity	Affinity
mother (v7)	father's brother's wife (v14)
sister (v11)	daughter-in-law (v15)
half-sister (v9)	brother's wife (v16)
aunt (v12 paternal, v13 maternal)	wife's mother, daughter or grand-daughter (v17)
grand-daughter (v10)	own wife during her menstrual period (v19)

Note that all of the prohibitions are on the man's side. This is a vital point as will be seen as the arguments of Henry's enemies are explored and the canon law case is described. A separate prohibition covered adultery (v20) which is also included in the Ten Commandments (Ex. 20:14). It is also worth noting that in both the original Hebrew and in the Greek translation, the word which appears as wife in English and Latin, actually means either woman or wife, the assumption being that all adult females would marry.[32]

Acceptance of the prohibitions features throughout the Bible. In Ezekiel 22:9-11, God vows to pour out his wrath on those in Jerusalem who break any of these regulations, the heat of his judgement melting them like silver in a furnace (22:20-22).[33] In Paul's epistles, breach is said to lead to eternal death (Gal. 5:19,21; 1 Cor. 6:9).

The promises for obedience are expanded in Leviticus 26:3-45 where God says there will be peace in the land (v6), victory in any necessary battles (v7), full harvests (v10), an abundance of healthy offspring (v9) and he will be with them. However, if the nation is disobedient there will be no harvests (v20) but rather war (v25), plague (v25), famine (v26) and fear (v36). The very nation will be destroyed (v33) and the buildings become desolate (v31) as people are transported to foreign lands (v38). Clearly any monarch would wish to ensure that his or her country experienced the benefits rather than the problems and this is why responsible rulers like Henry were so keen to try and ensure obedience. Some writers have misunderstood later laws compelling church attendance as a form of indoctrination or denial of freedom of thought but it stems from this belief that if the people are allowed to sin, bad things will happen to the whole nation and everyone will suffer. A person who refused to attend worship was not a free thinker or champion of liberty but someone who endangered their community. A comparison might be drawn to a person who ignored blackout regulations in World War Two: such an act was not making a stand for individual human rights against government regulation but something which risked attracting the attention of enemy bombers to the area and thus the likelihood of death and destruction to neighbours. It is important to remember that the question of the legality of Henry's "marriage" to Katherine was not a

---

penetrated (v.17) and the elucidation of female next of kin in Lev. 21:2-3 which names them as a man's mother, daughter and sister.

32 Hebrew *ishshah*, Greek *gune*
33 Ezekiel lived in the sixth century BC

purely personal matter but seen as a national issue with implications for every subject from village pauper to wealthy aristocrat.

Deuteronomy 25

The text of Leviticus was clear. A man might not have sexual relations with his brother's wife because it was an abomination. However, in Deuteronomy 25:5 it says that a man should do this: the practice known as levirate marriage or yibbum. Given the belief that God was perfect, never wrong or unjust and would not issue contradictory commands or instruct anyone to commit a sin, how was this to be explained? It was a question which was hotly debated at the time and has been raised since but once again, it is important to put the passage in context before analysing it.

In Deuteronomy, after reminding the people of how God had saved them, Moses recites the law saying that each commandment has been given him by God who has ordered him to teach them to the people (6:1). As in Leviticus 26, God says that if they obey, they will have peace, prosperity, good health and abundant harvests (7:13-15). If they do not, the reverse will be true (11:17; 28:58-66). Few of the laws in this section are in the simple "thou shalt not" form of the Commandments but most give actual scenarios showing the application and Deuteronomy 25:5-10 describes what should happen if a man's brother dies without a son. Many writers then – and since – have made the mistake of assuming that all laws are the same but this is simplistic. The Bible itself speaks of different types of law, e.g. Deut 27:10, Neh 1:7, 1 Kings 8:58.[34] These include:

> (a) apodictic – commandments which apply to all people at all times. These might be positive, as in "honour thy parents", or negative as in "do not commit adultery." The prohibitions in Leviticus 18 are apodictic.
> (b) casuistic – where a law has been generated following judgment in a situation or case. Deuteronomy 25:5-10 is an example.
> (c) ordinances – laws which apply only to a particular people or time or place. These include the regulations for worship, directions for setting up the tabernacle and garments to be worn by the high priest. In Henry's time, these were often called ceremonial.

The three categories are not completely distinct and Deut 25:5-10 falls into this third category also because it is part of Moses' second discourse which contains the laws which he says that God has asked him to teach the Israelites and which they are to keep when they enter the Promised Land.

The passage in question begins by laying down the two specific conditions for the application of the law which follows: it is immediately obvious that neither of them applied to Henry. Firstly, the brothers had to live

---

34 In Hebrew, the three distinct words used are *choq, mitsvah* and *mishpat*.

together on a shared landholding (v5) and Henry had not lived with Arthur. Secondly, the brother was to marry his widowed sister-in-law in order that the family name and landholding was not blotted out of Israel (v6) and Henry did not at any time claim to have land in Israel or to be king of that land.[35] The law stemmed from the belief that God had determined which tribes should have which area of land, and Henry was not a member of the twelve tribes of Israel but an Englishman.

Since Deuteronomy was evidently inapplicable, it seems strange to spend time discussing it further but as Henry's enemies made many references to it and so do writers today, this is necessary.

The requirement related to the widow of a brother who had not born a living son. Many modern Bibles opt for the gender neutral here as did the Vulgate of the time but the Hebrew original says *ben*, i.e. son.[36] This is because inheritance in ancient Israel was through sons and a man's name was carried by his sons rather than his daughters who changed theirs when they married. If a man had left daughters, another casuistic law (Num 27:1-11, 36:1-9) applied stemming from the case of Zelophehad's five daughters. This too would feature in Henry's case as is shown by Croke's researches in Italy which are discussed in the chapter "Why did it take so long?" This law said that daughters could inherit the land provided that they married men of their own tribe. It also decreed that if a man had left neither sons nor daughters, his land should go to his brothers – no reference to the idea of any of the brothers marrying the man's widow. This covered the situation of there not being a widow but also the many instances when it would have been impossible for a man to marry his widowed sister-in-law as required by Deuteronomy 25:5. In the tractate *Yebamoth*, part of the Talmud, a long list of such cases is given including where the widow is a leper, if she is related to the brother in other prohibited ways, if she is too old to have more children or she is an idolater. The requirement might also be nullified by the brother being already married or impotent or living far away or so young that by the time he reached maturity, the widow would be past childbearing. There was also the problem of there being multiple widows given polygamy was legal: should the surviving brother marry one or all, and if one, which? In short, there were a lot more conditions to be met than the brothers living together on a shared inheritance in Israel before Deuteronomy 25:5 could be invoked.

Assuming conditions were met and the brother married the widowed sister-in-law and had a son, this child was to be regarded as the son and heir of the dead brother and not the living one (v6). Quite aside from the fact that Henry wanted a son for himself, the complications which would have ensued from this would have been enormous. The resultant son, as nominal offspring of Arthur, would have taken precedence over Henry because the son of the

---

35 Katherine's nephew, the Emperor, claimed to be King of Jerusalem due to his inheritance of Napes.
36 The Greek Septuagint used *sperma* i.e. offspring.

Prince of Wales would inherit the kingdom before the second son of the monarch. Henry was the anointed king of England and there was no precedent to un-anoint him. The idea of Henry reverting to Duke of York while Katherine became again Dowager Princess of Wales and mother of the new baby king, was never even contemplated by anyone. Not only did the law not apply to Henry or any other Christian, it was utterly impractical. This was recognised by the rabbis who quite correctly pointed out that the requirements of levirate marriage did not apply to kings.[37]

Moving on through the passage, verses 7 to 12 explain what is to happen if the brother refuses to marry his widowed sister-in-law. The very fact that there is a procedure and the text recognises that the brother has a choice is proof that it is not a commandment in the usual sense. If something is optional, it is not a law. In English translations, the actual phrase in v5 and v7 is that the man has failed to "do his duty" not that he has broken the law. Practices such as saying please and thank you might be regarded as duties but they are not laws. The Latin translation uses "not taken me in marriage" which is a case of the translator referring back to v5 as the phrase does not appear in the original Hebrew. There it simply has the word for brother-in-law – *yabam*- with a suffix to convert it to a verb, just as in English we use -ise to create verbs from nouns like departmentalise, capitalise. Literally, the Hebrew has the widow complain that the man has not "brother-in-lawed." This is obviously not good English and so a separate verb and noun have been added by translators.[38] In the Greek, there is a verb "to want" but a gap for the object, so it is clear that the brother-in-law has not wanted to do something, but not clear what because the translator did not understand and was not about to guess. This gap in itself is proof that levirate marriage was a custom unknown amongst the Alexandrian Jews who generated the Septuagint, a further proof that the custom related, as it said in the text only to Israel.[39]

The rejected widow – who has not had a choice in the matter[40] – is to go to the elders at the town gate whose role was to judge not just breaches of the law but disputes between people in general (Ex.18:21-26), report the refusal and wait for the man to be summoned. If he is found to have no good reason for his refusal and to be intent on maintaining his decision, the widow is to pull his sandal off and spit in his face (v9). Both parties then go home and get on with their lives. The sandal is removed as a sign that no contract has been made and

---

37 *Sanhedrin* 2:2
38 It is difficult for English readers to understand how a single Hebrew word can morph into an entire English phrase. Hebrew is an ancient semitic language and a number of its constructions have no parallel in English. The use of a pronominal prefix or suffix to a noun in order to express verbal action is just one example of this.
39 Some Jews have argued that wherever they live in the world, their community is a new Israel.
40 Surprisingly, Henry's team failed to make the point that under canon law, forced marriage was invalid. The same is true in Judaism.

that the widow is free to remarry outside the family.[41] The spitting was evidently a rebuke but hardly on the same level as mutilation, execution, perpetual expulsion or some of the other Torah punishments. It merely rendered the man ritually unclean for seven days.[42]

The Bible also provides us with an example of how the requirements of Deut. 25:5-10 were interpreted in practice in the story of Ruth who lived around a century or so after the time of Moses. She was to go on to be the great-grandmother of King David.[43] Following the death of her husband Mahlon and his brother, the childless Ruth returns to the land from which Mahlon had come. There she meets Boaz who is simply described as a kinsman of her late husband. Boaz expresses a desire to purchase the property which Mahlon would have inherited had he lived but acknowledges that there is a nearer kinsman and offers him first refusal. The nearer kinsman, aware that with the land comes the widow Ruth, says he does not want to take it on and marry her. He hands his sandal to Boaz as a sign that he has no desire to make a contract and Boaz simply buys the property and marries Ruth. There is no spitting or sandal tossing or protests from her. The ceremony itself is very civilised, even though the idea of purchasing a wife is clearly offensive to modern sensitivities (Ruth 4:6-7). Boaz promises that any son born will be held as heir to Mahlon in accordance with Deut 25:6 though in later genealogies, their son Obed is shown as the son of Boaz (1 Chr.2:12; Luke 3:32; Matt.1:5).

The story of Ruth, which was debated by Henry and his enemies, shows that Deut. 25:5-10 was not being taken literally even in Biblical times. It had been extended to cover kinsmen in general rather than brothers and the principle of bearing the son for the dead man was not being honoured in practice. It does, however, very clearly show that the requirement to marry the widow was regarded as optional and not a binding law. As Henry's Hebrew expert, Wakefield, pointed out, not only is the Hebrew word used for a brother's wife different in Deut 25 and Ruth than that used in Lev 18 and Lev 20, but in Ruth 3:13 the Hebrew speaks of doing the duty of a neighbour rather than a kinsman, *rehag* being the same word as used in the Ten Commandments (e.g. thou shalt not covet thy neighbour's wife) and not *kahrohv* (kinsman) which is used in 3:12. English language translations ignore this key difference which shows levirate marriage being seen as a community responsibility rather than an individual one for a blood brother.

There was another instance of levirate marriage in the Bible which would be referenced by both sides in the annulment debate and that was the case of Tamar (Gen 38:6-26). She was the daughter-in-law of Judah, one of the elder brothers of Joseph of the "technicoloured dreamcoat" fame. Given the Hebrew and Greek texts use different chronologies, it is impossible to say

---

41 Psalm 60:10 also refers to a shoe being cast as a sign of ownership.
42 Num. 12:14
43 David was believed to have lived around 1000BC and Moses some two to three centuries earlier so allowing for three generations to pass, the interval would be very approximately a hundred years.

exactly when she lived but it would have been some five hundred years before Moses and therefore the practice described relates to an older tradition than is codified in Deuteronomy. In this account, Tamar married the eldest son who displeased God in some unspecified way and was struck dead as a result. She then married the middle son who also farmed the same land together with his father and younger brother. He was an extremely reluctant bridegroom and chose to deliberately spill his seed outside her and, for thus refusing to give Tamar a child, he was struck dead too. At this point, Judah is left with just one son who is too young to marry Tamar so he sends her back to her parents and tells her to wait. The son grows up but Judah neglects to call Tamar back and so she decides to disguise herself and sleep with her father-in-law instead in order to get pregnant. When this happens, Judah opts to have her publicly proclaimed a harlot whereupon she reveals that he is the father of the child she is carrying and he admits that the fault is his for not having given her his youngest son. Key points deemed relevant to the annulment controversy were that Tamar's second marriage was certainly not consummated and that she was praised for tricking her father-in-law into having sexual intercourse with her rather than condemned to death which would have been the penalty in Lev 20:12, something held to show the primacy of the duty to raise a son for the dead man over any idea that incest was an abomination.[44] The twin sons which resulted from Tamar's trick were known as the sons of Judah rather than either of her dead husbands (Num 26:20). Given the case predated the law given in Moses by almost half a millennium, Henry was right to deem it as of far less significance than the story of Ruth, a view shared by Calvin.

The fact that levirate marriage did not apply outside Israel was confirmed in two cases from books which formed part of Henry's Bible (and that of all Roman Catholics then and today) but which were not part of the Hebrew. Judith, living near Jenin,[45] rejects suitors and chooses to remain a widow (Judith 15:22): she is not compelled to seek the hand of her dead husband's brother or near relation to continue his name.[46] In Tobit, which is set in Ecbatana in modern Iran, Sarah is constrained to marry one of her father's kin after her husband dies because she is her father's heir and her duty is to continue his name: there is no suggestion that she should wed a relation of her deceased husband or worry about preserving his name or estate (Tobit 3:14). A case in the Talmud demonstrates the same practice in Phoenicia.[47]

A final important point regarding Deuteronomy 25 is that there is no agreement about the meaning of the word brother. The Hebrew word, *ah*, is

---

[44] Calvin noted men married in order to get heirs and that wives were effectively possessions of the family which created a duty on their part to help perpetuate their new families. He denied it was a legal requirement, see Calvin *Harmony of the Law* volume 2 chapter 8.

[45] Believed to be in the West Bank area.

[46] There is some dispute about where the story is set, bur it is generally agreed today to be a work of fiction not history.

[47] Ketubot 7.10.

also used to mean a fellow Israelite (e.g. Deut. 25:3 – just three verses earlier) as well as a nephew (Gen. 13:8), a friend (2 Samuel 1:26) and an uncle (Gen 29:15). To assume the passage refers to a blood brother is simplistic and does not reflect the complexity of the original Hebrew. In the Samaritan tradition, the passage is held to relate to a son of the same father but a different mother which avoids the apparent contradiction with Leviticus 18.[48] The Samaritans were the descendants of the ten tribes which broke away from the two southern ones after the death of Solomon and as such they upheld the Torah. It is possible that their interpretation was closer to the original practice since it ties in with the expectation on Boaz as a kinsman rather than blood brother. Calvin understood the word in this section to mean kinsmen in general because the idea of God advocating incest was not only ridiculous but blasphemous.[49]

The Curse of Childlessness

Some eagle eyed readers may have noted that so far nothing has been said about the punishment for marrying a brother's wife being childlessness. Modern writers universally seem to quote this from Lev.20:21 before making sarcastic comments about how either Wicked Henry twisted the scriptures to say sons in order to avoid the inconvenience of him having a daughter or else how Foolish Henry was gulled by wicked advisers who told him childless meant sons. Some writers go further and attribute this state of affairs to Henry being a misogynist. If the said writers took the trouble to read the text in the original Hebrew instead of a gender neutral English translation, they would realise that they were chasing a mythical red herring. The Hebrew does not say childless, something which Henry – who had a rudimentary knowledge of Hebrew and Greek and a team of Christian and Jewish advisers to assist him – knew very well. Moreover, there is only one occasion on which Henry mentioned sons.[50] He based his case on Leviticus 18 not 20, not because the latter was inconvenient to his case but because a punishment cannot prove the law: a law simply exists. Treason, for example, does not cease to be a crime if nobody is prosecuted for it. He was not foolish enough to imagine that his lack of surviving sons or offspring in general either validated or invalidated the proscription in Leviticus 18. The fact that the law came from God was proof of validity in itself.

---

48 A son would not inherit land from his mother so the justification for levirate marriage would not exist.
49 *Harmony of the Law,* volume 3, chapter 5.
50 Campeggio says that Henry mentioned it to him in a private conversation. Cavendish claims that Henry spoke about it at the first main session of the legatine court at Blackfriars but Hall does not record this and nor does the Venetian ambassador nor the French. Cavendish's account of the trial is notoriously unreliable. It is not mentioned in any of the official publications of the period.

To put this ill-informed criticism finally to bed, it is necessary to look at the situation properly. In the first place, it should be noted that the Latin Vulgate of the day translated the text as "*absque filii*" which means without sons. The Vulgate was the universally accepted text across the whole of Christendom. Not one of Henry's contemporaries, from the pope downwards, ever questioned that the correct reading of Lev 20:21 was "without sons." It was not an issue for anyone until the twentieth century. Later in the sixteenth century, during a revision of the Vulgate, the Council of Trent quietly changed the verse to read "*absque liberis*" which is without children but whether this was due to Henry opening their eyes to the verse or a political attempt to support Mary Tudor, is open to debate.

In fact, the original rendering of "without sons" was rather strange because in Hebrew and Greek the same punishment is listed for the man who marries his uncle's wife and the Vulgate there did have "*absque liberis*" (Lev 20:20). Two different translations of the same word in successive verses did suggest an error on Jerome's part or that he did not understand the original.[51] Given Henry owned a copy of the Complutensian Polyglot Bible which showed the text in parallel columns of Hebrew, Greek and Latin with the Aramaic beneath, it was immediately obvious that there was a problem here. In July 1527, Richard Pace sent him a Hebrew alphabet saying that he could use it to enable him to check this for himself.[52] Produced by the Spanish humanist Cardinal Ximenes, this Bible was of unquestioned authority. Anne's uncle James Boleyn was a Hebrew scholar so it is entirely possible that he sat with Henry at some point explaining some of the words and the inaccuracies of later translations into Greek and Latin.[53]

So should it have been without sons or without children? The Hebrew original uses the word *aririm* which only appears four times in the entire Old Testament, twice in Lev 20 where it is the punishment for those who have intercourse with their brother's or uncle's wife and once each in Genesis and Jeremiah. The word means stripped or destitute or demolished and is ordinarily used in the context of children and legacy. In Genesis 15:2, Abram talks of being destitute of issue (*aririm*) by his barren (*aqar*) wife and expresses sadness that his heirs will come from his slaves. In Jeremiah 22:30, the word appears as part of a curse on King Jeconiah whose behaviour has so angered God that he is to be regarded as one who is stripped of heirs. This usage is absolutely vital to the subject because Jeconiah was not only a man with children (Jer 22:30) but he had seven sons (I Chr. 3:17-18) and numerous descendants one of whom was Joseph, husband of Mary the mother of Jesus (Matt 1:12-16). The application of the word to a man in this state proves that the word *aririm* does not mean literally childless in the usual sense of the word.

---

51 Similarly, in the Vulgate, Jerome translated *epiousios* which appears in both Matt 6:11 and Luke 11:3 as superstantial in the first and daily in the second..
52 LP 4.3233
53 Richard Rex, *The Theology of John Fisher* (Cambridge University Press, 1991) p.58.

Jeconiah had physical offspring but none of them would be able to inherit from their father. As George Joye put it in the first ever English translation of Jeremiah (1534), Jeconiah would be rather stripped or "plucked and torn in pieces and there shall none of his seed prosper to sit in the seat royal." That Henry was aware of the correct Hebrew understanding of the word as meaning stripped of accepted heirs is evident from the reference to Jeconiah's case in the 1531 *Determinations*.[54] For Henry, also a king and one who was only too aware of the fragility of the Tudor dynasty, this was a nightmarish prospect and it may well have encouraged his activity regarding the Acts of Succession. A further example of Hebrew using the word childless in a non literal sense exists in the Talmud when King Hezekiah described himself as childless because his son Manasseh was utterly depraved and devoid of worth.[55]

Moreover, this understanding was not new or an interpretation generated to please Henry. Around 1390, John Wycliffe had translated Lev 20:21 as: "He that weddeth the wife of his brother doeth an unlawful thing; he showeth the filth of his brother, he shall be without free children." In the margin, he explains this further: "if children be born of such wedlock, they shall be unlawful and shall not be heirs." He justified this interpretation by reference to St Augustine and Nicholas of Lyra.[56]

However, there is another interpretation in which the supposed curse of childlessness simply reflects the precise legal situation in a levirate union. If a man married his brother's wife, they would be technically childless as the son they had would be regarded as the child of his dead brother and not their own.

Why then do English versions use childless? For one reason, translators prefer to use single word translations rather than an entire phrase which would be needed to accurately render a rather complex expression. The other reason is because the Greek translation of the Hebrew, known as the Septuagint, uses *ateknos* in verses 20 and 21, a word which certainly does mean childless.[57] Translators such as Tyndale would have been influenced also by the fact that *ateknos* is used in Matt 22:24 when the sadducees ask Jesus about levirate marriage, though this was not really significant given neither side spoke in Greek, the language which Matthew used when he wrote.[58] There were

---

54 *Determinations*, p.21 "his children either to be destroyed or disinherited." See also p.33 "the laws of man do call them infamed persons and do put them back from their fathers heritage."

55 Berachoth 10a. Modern colloquial Hebrew uses *aririm* as childless but this differs from the Biblical Hebrew as shown, a not uncommon occurrence in a language that dates back over thousands of years.

56 Josiah Forshall (ed.), *The Holy Bible...by John Wycliffe and his followers* vol. 1 (Oxford 1850). The same appeared in the Geneva Bible which noted "They shall be cut off from their people and their children shall be taken as bastards and not counted amongst the Israelites."

57 The *teknos* means children while the *a* in front turns it into a negative.

58 We only know for certain two things which Jesus said, the ones quoted in Aramaic (Matt 27:46, Mark 5:41). All the rest of the words attributed to him appear in translation because the New Testament was written in Greek. Since then his words

many points at which the Greek Septuagint differed from the Hebrew – most famously in Isaiah 7:14 where it changed the prophecy that a young girl would bring forth a son called Emmanuel to virgin – and this was just one of them. Tyndale, whose Greek was stronger than his Hebrew, always opted for the Greek word in every single case of discrepancy.[59] Regarding the other two uses of *arimim* in Hebrew, the Greek translators used *ateknos* in Gen. 15:2 but *ekkenteó* in Jer 22:30 which means pierced. To add to the inconsistency, the Hebrew for pierced is *daqari* which the Greek translated as *katorthoma* in Zech 12:10 which means mocked, the only place it is used in the Old Testament. In Hebrew, the word for childless is *shakul* which is totally absent from Leviticus 20.

Three further questions relate to the interpretation of Lev 20:20. Firstly, what does the punishment reveal about the prohibition of Lev 18:16? It is worth noting that although Leviticus 18 lists fifteen different forbidden relationships and describes all as abominations, they do not all merit the same punishment. Leviticus 20 requires death for all adulterers and those having relations with their father's wife, daughter-in-law or mother-in-law. Those having relations with their uncle's wife or brother's wife are to be stripped of accepted heirs. Those having relations with their aunt, sister or step-sister are to do penance. This involved confession, repentance and making an offering (Lev 5:1,5-13) but given Christians believe that Jesus' death on the cross was the ultimate sacrifice, no animal offering would be involved for them. A man having relations with his own wife during her menstrual period was to be punished by excommunication for a week.[60] Curiously for us today the greatest punishments are generally for offences against affinity and not consanguinity, but this very fact was regarded by Henry as supporting his case that the prohibition of Lev 18:16 was serious.

Secondly, who is doing the stripping? Is it an act of God or an act of mankind?[61] In Abraham's case, his wife was barren and that was seen as a condition sent by God but in Jeconiah's, his sons were unable to inherit because he lost his throne and the nation was sent into exile at the hands of Nebuchadnezzar.[62] Henry certainly regarded the loss of his children as an act of

---

have been translated to almost every language.

59 A. W. Pollard (ed.) *Records of the English Bible* (1911) pp.26-53. The volume contains tables comparing verses throughout the Old Testament in the original Hebrew, the Greek, the Latin and Luther's German showing how Tyndale chose the Greek in all cases. In his translation of Lev 20:21, Tyndale added a peculiar marginal note to explain the parents being childless as meaning "they shall die immediately and not tarry the birth as Judah would have burnt Tamar being great with child." As Judah was the father and not about to die, it is clear that Tyndale really had no understanding of the verse at all.

60 The seven day period is specified in Lev 15:24.

61 In some ways this may be seen as a false distinction since the Bible shows God working through people

62 See also 2 Sam. 7:14 where God uses man to enforce his laws.

God and the idea of God as the person punishing was the usual interpretation at this period although the latter actually makes more sense. Human beings were responsible for the other punishments in Leviticus 20, putting people to death, excommunicating them and extracting atonement, and they were in a position to deny the inheritance claims of any children born to prohibited unions. At the Lateran Councils of 1123 and 1139, it was noted that civil law regarded incestuous unions as infamous and "dispossess of all hereditary rights those born of such unions."[63]

Stripping a man of heirs could mean none being born or it could mean the death of offspring before their father, as with Henry's sons. For most people today, the idea that God would kill children to punish their parents would be horrifying but there was Biblical support for that view. The Ten Commandments included God's words that He would visit the iniquity of the parents upon children to the third and fourth generations (Ex. 20:5, repeated in Num 14:18). This is generally taken today to mean that the parents' behaviour can have a negative impact on the descendants. For example a gambler who causes his family to fall into penury will affect the prospects of his children and this in turn is likely to damage the chances of his grandchildren. However, in Henry's time the verse was taken more literally and this was in line with Job 18:3,19; 27:13-15 and Dan. 6:24. It was also believed that death might not be the only means of punishment.[64] Aquinas observed, following Gregory the Great, that couples who had sexual relations despite close kinship were likely to have a defective child as a judgment. In the Wisdom of Solomon 4:3-6 it states that the children of an unlawful union might flourish temporarily but that ultimately their existence will be worthless as they will form no roots and their boughs will be snapped off half grown, a prophecy which could be fulfilled in a number of ways.

Finally, was it reasonable for the text to be interpreted as sons? Based on other texts in the Bible, a number of which Henry quoted during the case, yes. The loss of sons only as a punishment to the father appears in various stories. David was punished for his adultery with Bathsheba by the death of his son (2 Sam 12:13-18). Three kings of Israel – Jeroboam, Baasha and Ahab – all had their sons destroyed because their fathers failed to keep God's commandments (1 Kings 14: 8-10; 16:1-4,11-13; 21:20-21). King Jehoram of Judah similarly had his sons destroyed but his daughter lived and married (2 Chr. 21:12-17, 22:12). In 1 Sam 2:30-31, Eli was told that because he knew his sons were guilty of serious crimes against God but did nothing, he was considered guilty too (3:13) and that in consequence his line would be cut off, his children would either die before him or meet unfortunate ends before they were able to procreate.[65] Pharaoh is warned that his firstborn son will be taken as a

---

63 Second Lateran, canon 17
64 Job 27:14-15 speaks of offspring being killed by the sword, dying of pestilence or wasting away through famine.
65 In 1 Sam 25:22 David threatens to punish a father by killing his sons only.

punishment if he fails to let Moses lead the Israelites out of Egypt (Ex. 4:23, fulfilled Ex 12:29).

By contrast, the birth of sons was foretold in the Bible for the man who conscientiously followed God's laws. Psalm 127:3 begins by saying that a person needed to commit their actions to God in order for them to succeed. It goes on to describe the blessing which will result, namely a quiverful of sons. The Hebrew here is *banim* meaning sons, not *yeladim* which means either or both genders. Again, modern translations often opt for the word children here because they wish to appear gender neutral but that is inaccurate. Sons were seen as necessary to defend the homestead with force of arms if necessary and they were the ones who inherited the name and the land, except in extreme circumstances.[66] Psalm 128:3 – still set as the psalm for weddings in the *Book of Common Prayer* and used at Henry and Anne's wedding – also talks of a man having sons to crowd around his table and says clearly that this is the blessing in store for those who follow God's laws. It followed that those who lacked sons were not blessed because they had not obeyed God's laws.[67] This teaching is applied to kings in particular. In I Kings 2:4, God promises King David that as long as he and his descendants obey the Torah, they will have sons to sit on the throne. This promise is repeated in 2 Chr. 6:16 and 7:18 and is a key text due to the Christian belief that Jesus is the heir of David.

Nor was Henry the only person to believe that sons were a sign of divine approval. In 1533 when the future Elizabeth I was born, the Milanese ambassador at Rome summed up the feelings of many when he crowed that Anne having a daughter was a sign of God's disapproval of Henry's "unholy designs and appetites."[68] Earlier, the Duke of Buckingham alleged Henry's lack of sons was indicative of God's anger, and Katherine herself believed God's fury at her parents insistence on the execution of the innocent Warwick was the reason for Arthur's early death and her failure to bear him sons.[69]

To conclude, Henry was not fabricating some prejudice against daughters or taking advice from fools willing to tell the king what he wished to hear as many modern writers have suggested but following the actual Biblical text in front of him which specifically used the words sons and male. Nor was Lev 20:20 ever central to his case. Whilst the Bible spoke of tangible rewards and punishments for keeping the Torah, it also acknowledged that bad things

---

66 As with the daughters of Zelophehad.
67 Sterility was seen as an act of God though not necessarily as a sign of displeasure. In the case of Zachariah and Elizabeth, parents of John the Baptist, there was no suggestion that they were being punished for some sin, but rather that God had specific plans for them.
68 CSPM 1.925. One presumes, however, he gave a different significance to the birth of a daughter when the Emperor had one.
69 LP 3.1284 – Buckingham did not think God was angry at Henry's union with Katherine but rather because the Tudors were on the throne instead of himself. For Katherine's comments, see Henry Clifford, *The Life of Jane Dormer, Duchess of Feria* (ed. Joseph Stevenson, London 1887) p.77

happened to good people and vice versa. If Henry and Katherine had produced a dozen healthy sons, it would not have altered the fact that God said in Leviticus that a man must not marry his brother's wife. The allegation that Henry altered the Bible text to say sons so frequently repeated by writers today, is not only factually incorrect but irrelevant to the case. The people in error are the modern writers, not Henry.

The Case in Canon Law

Henry also had a case in canon law and since this was deemed to be the more straightforward argument, this is where the annulment proceedings began. The discussion centred around the dispensation of 1504 for him to marry Katherine and whether the document was legal.

When any couple sought to marry they had to assure the clergyman that they were (1) of age. In terms of being legally able to enter a contract, that meant boys had to be at least fourteen and girls twelve though the consent of parents or guardians was usually sought if they were below twenty-one. (2) not related by blood i.e. consanguinity. (3) not related by marriage or illicit sexual activity i.e. affinity (4) had not made vows to anyone else i.e. public honesty. These could be full marriage vows (*praesenti*) or betrothal (*futuro*) and made either before a priest or clandestinely, which simply meant outside a church and without the prior calling of banns. If any of these impediments existed, a dispensation was required before the marriage could go ahead.

Dispensations were not unusual at this period, though they were still relatively new having only started to be issued in their thousands in the fifteenth century.[70] But it is important to recognise what they were. Dispensations were a means of removing the penalties for breaking a law in certain circumstances. They were not routine documents to be obtained like a licence for a gun or television. A modern and secular example might be an ambulance driver who is required to abide by all the rules of the road in normal times but who is permitted during an emergency to break speeding limits and pass through red lights without risk of prosecution in order to save lives. Dispensations did not deny the righteousness of the law or suggest in any way that the law did not matter, was irrelevant or unimportant. This point is important because it is often forgotten today and was certainly overlooked frequently by Katherine's lawyers and supporters who often argued that marriage to the wife of a deceased brother was not forbidden anyway or certainly not a major problem.[71] In the case of matrimonial dispensations, they

---

70 D. L. D'Avray, *Papacy, Monarchy and Marriage 800-1600* (Cambridge, 2015) pp.196, 204
71 Scotus, however, had said "to dispense is revoking the precept or declaring how it is to be understood" *Ordinatio* d.41.20. This conflicts with the Bible message. In John 8:3-11, Jesus was asked whether the Law's penalty for adultery – stoning to

related to legal obstacles which might come from the Bible or they could be purely of human creation, for example laws banning marriage during Lent, and their purpose was to remove the penalty – often excommunication – which would normally apply if the couple sought to marry anyway.

Dispensations can be general, such as removing the requirement to receive Holy Communion at Easter during wartime or in a pandemic[72] but they are ordinarily issued to a named individual or group. Dispensations for future marriage are the most common but the first such dispensation was only issued at the start of the thirteenth century, just three hundred years before Henry's and over a thousand years after the time of Jesus.[73] It was not an ancient or apostolic practice but part of the development of Church power which occurred in the middle ages and an important revenue stream because dispensations were not issued free of charge. Minor dispensations such as permitting a sick person to eat meat in Lent, could be issued by parish priests, but a serious one, required a higher authority. In Henry's case, a dispensation was sought for something forbidden in the Bible. No dispensation for a man to marry his sister-in-law had ever been granted in the entire history of the church. Canon 51 of the fourth Lateran Council of 1215 said no dispensation should be granted within the first three degrees of consanguinity or affinity. In 1392, Clement VII had rejected an application by the Count of Armagnac to marry his brother's widow. As such, and because it related to a sacrament which meant it came under church law, the application had to be made directly to the pope – who was himself unsure if he had the authority when first asked.

The key points of the dispensation which was eventually issued are listed below. They have been numbered for ease of reference in the analysis which follows.

1) it was granted to Henry, son of Henry VII and to Katherine, daughter of Ferdinand and Isabella[74]
2) it was granted by the pope who claimed his authority came from God
3) it was granted in response to a petition made by unnamed petitioners on behalf of Henry and Katherine [75]
4) it says that Katherine married Arthur for the conservation of peace between Ferdinand and Isabella of Spain and Henry VII of England

---

death – should be applied to a woman caught in the act. His reply was: "let him who is without sin cast the first stone." Jesus thereby dispensed the penalty but he did not deny that the law existed or suggest it was wrong, Indeed, he told her not to repeat her sin.

72 In WW2, the Archbishop of Canterbury issued a dispensation to permit women to break the commandment in 1 Cor 11:3-15 which said that they must have their heads covered in church by veils or hats. The dispensation was intended for the duration of the war only but seems to have become permanent.
73 See article on Dispensations in the *Catholic Encyclopedia*.
74 Like other documents of the period, it calls her Elizabeth.
75 Although not explicit, it is implicit that the petitioners are their parents.

5) it notes that Katherine's marriage had been "perhaps" (Latin *forsan*) consummated
6) it claims that Henry and Katherine desire to marry
7) it says that the intention of Henry and Katherine is to make more durable the peace between their parents
8) it permits them to marry fully (*praesenti*, I do) and consummate their union without fear of excommunication
9) it describes the impediment being removed as affinity
10) it says that any children born to Henry and Katherine, including any which might already have been born, are to be regarded as legitimate unless they are the product of rape
11) it says that if Henry and Katherine have already married, they are to do penance but not be excommunicated

Before looking at Henry's arguments, it is necessary to recognise the legal situation. For a dispensation to be valid, <u>all</u> of the following conditions must be met:

- the issuing authority must have sufficient right to issue the dispensation
- the facts supplied must be true at the time of application
- the motive of the petitioners must be clearly stated and genuine[76]
- the impediment being removed must be clearly defined
- the reason for the dispensation must be verified as true at the time by the person executing it, i.e. the priest performing the wedding ceremony
- the reasons stated must be sufficient for the grant[77]

If the person to whom the dispensation is granted renounces it, the dispensation ceases to be licit. Also, if it can be shown that false information was supplied by the petitioners with a view to deceiving the issuing authority or that necessary information was deliberately withheld, that also invalidates the dispensation and any consequent marriage. However, if the information supplied is subsequently found to be false but there was no intention to deceive and the petitioners were ignorant of the matter, the dispensation is judged invalid but the marriage remains valid

What then did Henry have to say about the dispensation and was his conclusion that it was invalid justified?

---

76 This requirement also appears in Jewish law. In *Yebamoth* 109a, Abba Saul declares that a man marrying his brother's wife for any reason except to raise heirs for his dead brother is guilty of incest so the union is invalid. Examples of other reasons which would invalidate the union include love or lust for the bride, hope of financial gain and desire to avoid military service.

77 For a helpful study of these points see, John Ogutu, 'Efficacy of Dispensations granted without a just cause', *Annals of Juridical Sciences*, vol XXXIII no 4 (2023) pp.99-130

He stated that the following facts in the dispensation were false: he had not desired the marriage (6): he was a child at the time. Also, he had not been consulted about it so the petitioners were not lawfully acting on his behalf (3). Bishop Richard Foxe who was part of Henry VII's council at the time confirmed that what Henry VIII said was true. Imperialists argued that fathers can act on behalf of minors without their instruction which is reasonable but could not refute the point that the statement in the dispensation claiming Henry desired the match was a lie.

Henry averred that the pope had been encouraged to issue the dispensation by pertinent information which had been deliberately withheld. The pope had not been informed that he was a minor which was clear from the dispensation allowing him to marry immediately (8) and making provision for any children he might already have fathered on Katherine (10). It was customary for dispensations issued to minors to record that fact in the text.[78]

He said that peace had existed for over a century between England and Spain at the time and there was no likelihood of war between Ferdinand and Isabella and Henry VII. Thus, the motive of making peace more durable was insufficient and not even true (7). Henry's enemies were never able to provide any evidence to the contrary because there was none.[79] Indeed, at the time of Henry's wedding, his sister was betrothed to the future Emperor which was evidence of a firm link between the Tudors and Habsburgs.

He noted that at the time the dispensation was executed (1509), both Henry VII and Isabella were dead. Since the dispensation named them rather than their countries as the basis for peace (7), it followed that the conditions under which the dispensation had been granted had materially changed rendering it invalid.

He pointed out the use of the word 'perhaps' (5) was insufficiently precise in a legal document and said this made the definition of the impediment as affinity unclear (9), a key point since the definition of affinity and marriage differed in canon and civil law. Furthermore, many – but not all – canon lawyers regarded a marriage by vows only as creating an impediment of public honesty whilst a consummated union created an impediment of affinity. This vagueness might also indicate that the pope had not been given clear information on which to base his verdict.[80] Although Henry did not know it,

---

78 For example, to Edward II and Isabella in 1305, transcribed in full in D'Avray, *Papacy*, p.289

79 When Henry's parents had married, the justification on the dispensation given was "to end the dissensions which have prevailed between the ancestors of their respective houses or families of Lancaster and York." That was true and the dispensation was for fourth degree which meant their union was sanctioned by both the fourth Lateran Council and the Bible. *Calendar of Papal Registers relating to Great Britain and Ireland*, vol. 14 (1960) p.1

80 Most canon lawyers regarded the word 'perhaps' as indicating doubt but some saw it as confirmatory. The Bishop of Ely, Nicholas West, highlighted this confusion. For further discussion on this point, see Henry Ansgar Kelly, *The Matrimonial*

there was a precedent for the use of perhaps in a dispensation and it supported his argument. In 1453, Henry IV of Castile had secured a dispensation which covered the "impediments of consanguinity and also affinity or perhaps of public honesty deriving from this."[81] All three types of impediment were listed which was not the case in Henry's rendering it unclear.

Henry further provided evidence of how he had publicly renounced the dispensation before a notary in 1505 which invalidated it. The fact that he had done this was not disputed but he had done it the day before his fourteenth birthday when he was still technically a minor so Katherine's supporters were able to claim that his renunciation was inadmissible because it had taken place a few hours before he came of age. Obviously, he made his protest at that time because that was when he was advised to do it: the lawyers advised him incorrectly and for Katherine's supporters to argue the protest was invalid for that reason was totally unjust. However, the fact that he had made a protest was known to those about him before he solemnised his union with Katherine and they should have told him that he needed to formally renounce his protest before a notary and a bishop and then seek either a new bull or a brief revalidating the earlier one before the ceremony went ahead. There was the point that Katherine had not rejected it and as the bull had been granted to both parties, it could be argued that she still had the right to use it, although use of a document rejected by one party would have created further legal complexities.[82]

All of Henry's points were true. Dispensations do not contain expiry dates but the material change in circumstances meant that he was using an outdated document and his renouncing of it meant he needed a new one. Henry was seventeen in 1509 and could not be blamed for ignorance of the law but his bishops and advisers were culpable. By the time Henry came to seek an annulment, the pope and Imperial lawyers were happy to accept that the dispensation was invalid but as they recognised that Henry and Katherine had not knowingly misled Julius II, they saw the marriage as valid and simply in need of a new and corrected document.[83] Henry maintained that this was

---

Trials of Henry VIII (Oregon, 2004) p.72

81 D'Avray, *Papacy*, p.326. "Ac consanguinitatis necnon affinitatis seu forsan publice honestatis inde proveninentis." Henry IV had failed to consummate his previous marriage.

82 Henry's use of multiple arguments was quite usual at the time, D'Avray, *Papacy*, p.106. It could be argued that Henry had renounced the marriage rather than the dispensation but as this would still have constituted proof of him not desiring the match, his position was not weakened,

83 Harrington's *Comendacions* (1528) published at the behest of Polydore Vergil, a long standing opponent of Wolsey, said that only an impediment which occurred after a marriage had been consummated could invalidate it, such as one party being declared insane. This principle was not followed in practice by popes who routinely annulled consummated marriages after one party had suddenly remembered they were related to their partner in some forbidden decree or that they had been betrothed to someone else at the time of the wedding. The view that a precontract invalidated a subsequent marriage came from Boniface VIII *Decretals*, Book Six IV

impossible because the first condition could never be met: the pope did not have the authority to issue a dispensation against divine law. In the *Glass of Truth*, he wrote that the pope "is not exempt from the precepts of the law of God neither can exempt any other from the same: nor can give licence to sin or to do amiss...If he bid thee do one thing and God another, obey God."

Henry's argument went further by pointing out that a dispensation was meant to remove the penalties for breach of a commandment and in this case, the pope was unable to do this. Leviticus stated that the punishments for marrying a brother's wife were excommunication (18:29) and a lack of heirs (20:21). The pope claimed the power to excommunicate through his use of the keys (Matt 16:19)[84] but how could he excommunicate a king? Simply denying him the sacrament was possible but excommunication also involved cutting a person off from society. The practicalities of effectively removing a monarch to a desert island from which he would have to rule his country by some sort of telepathy because he was unable to speak to any other Christian, were non-existent. Besides, St Peter himself had said that rulers were appointed by God and must be obeyed (1 Pet. 2;13).[85] With regard to heirs, the pope had no control over whether the wife had children or not, what gender they might be and whether they were sufficiently healthy to survive to adulthood. The pope could dispense the illegitimacy which the law stipulated for the offspring of such a union, but logically only after the union had ended for otherwise he would be encouraging the sin to continue.

To claim, as some writers have, that the case in canon law should be viewed as being as important as the theological case, is to wholly miss the point. Certainly, canon lawyers of the Tudor era and since have argued this case and Katherine's supporters have upheld this position. Chapuys went so far in 1535 as to say that canon law was the "only" law which Christians had on how to conduct their lives.[86] Tyndale was told the same thing by a priest in Gloucestershire who really should have known better but asserted: "We were better to be without God's laws than the Pope's."[87] Cardinal Ancona expressed the position of Rome: "canon law must take precedence over all other laws whatsoever, even those of the kingdom itself."[88] However, canon law is simply regulations made by the church and for the church: it is not given by God. The profession of canon lawyer only arose in the twelfth century following the publication of Gratian's *Decretum* which included the forged Isidore decretals and Donation of Constantine.[89] To argue that the "marriage" was valid because

---

    tit.1 ch.1
84 In Matt. 18:18 the keys are given to the disciples as a group and not just Peter.
85 As did St Paul – Rom. 13:1, Titus 3:1
86 CSPS 5.1.178
87 John Foxe, *Acts and Monuments,* ed. Stephen Cattley, vol.5 (1846) p.117
88 Philip Hughes, *The Reformation in England*, vol. 1 (1950) p.378
89 The Donation was exposed as a forgery in the mid fifteenth century by Lorenzo Valla in Italy and Reginald Pecock in England. Allegations that they were such had

canon law said so even though the Bible said not, is like arguing that a bye law passed by the smallest parish council in England is equal – or even superior – to an Act of Parliament or that, should the bye law conflict with something like the United Nations Declaration of Human Rights, the bye law should be followed! the church is the bride of Christ and it owes obedience to God – not vice versa: it is not equal to God. As Luther wrote in his *Babylonian Captivity*: "the church has no power to make new divine promises as some rant who hold that what is decreed by the church is of no less authority than what is decreed by God since the church is under the guidance of the Holy Spirit. ... The promises of God make the church, not the church the promise of God." Whether the dispensation was or was not legal under canon law was immaterial as Henry would ultimately show by asserting the supremacy of English law, a verdict which has never been questioned since.

As well as all the above points, Henry developed his case against the dispensation during the six years that the case was being discussed. He moved on from an attack on the document itself to the person issuing it. Under canon law, anyone who obtained the office of pope through bribery or promising rewards to supporters, was automatically deemed an invalid pope.[90] There was no doubt that Julius II was a simoniac, as was Clement VII who claimed the right to sit in judgment on the case. It followed that Julius was in no position to issue any dispensations of any nature to anybody and nor could Clement judge any appeals. The fact that both popes were recognised by the church was not because their elections complied with canon law but because the cardinals were also simoniacs and unwilling to lose their own positions. Henry knew this and his response was simple. He broke with Rome.

Opposition

If the Bible passages were so clear and the truth was so obvious, why did Henry VIII have so difficult a time in proving his case? Partly it was institutionalised anti-semitism on the part of the Roman Catholic church and from Spain in particular.[91] Chapuys himself sneered at Henry employing a rabbinic advisor and he was only expressing a general attitude.[92] The fact that

---

been voiced as early as 1001 by Emperor Otto III, see Malcolm Barber, *The Two Cities* (Oxford, 1992) p.99. The Isidore decretals were not exposed until the reign of Elizabeth I.

90   Councils of Antioch (341), Chalcedon (451), Orleans (533), Rome (1074), Lateran (1179). Henry also accused Clement and Julius of being heretics because they espoused views contrary to scripture and this too invalidated their status according to many, including William of Ockham. For more on this see John Kilcullen, 'The Political Writings' in Paul V. Spade (ed.) *The Cambridge Companion to Ockham* (Cambridge,1999) pp. 302-325
91   Katherine's own parents had expelled the Jews in 1492.
92   LP 5.70, 120

Jesus was Jewish and that the Law was written in Hebrew and rabbis had centuries of experience in interpreting the text, was disregarded by them. To Chapuys and most of his contemporaries, the Jews were the people who had killed Jesus and as such were damned and the sole repository for truth was the church, and in particular its own Latin copy of the Old Testament which had been produced by Jerome centuries before.[93] They genuinely believed that medieval Christians understood the text better than the Jews in whose language it was written. Even Erasmus boasted of hating Jews abundantly and regarded such an attitude as being part of the definition of a good Christian.[94] By contrast, Henry was completely open to learning from Jews. He employed rabbis and purchased a copy of the Bomberg Talmud and the official government publications of the time such as the *Determinations* and *Glass of Truth* provided evidence of how he had taken their teaching on board.[95] When Cardinal Campeggio came to hear the annulment case in 1529, he immediately recognised Henry's wide ranging expertise on the matter exceeded his own and that of other churchmen.

Combined with this was the attitude to Biblical scholarship which existed in Henry's lifetime. the church set great store on tradition, valuing it like precedent in cases of law. What Isaiah might have meant in a passage, for example, was deemed irrelevant compared to what one of the church fathers such as Augustine or Origen said the passage meant. The whole Old Testament was interpreted using typological, figurative and allegorical methods with a strong Christological bias. For example, Isaiah noting that the angels sang "Holy, Holy, Holy" (Isa 6:3) was regarded as a prophecy of the Christian doctrine of the trinity while Balaam's prophecy about a sceptre destroying Moab (Num 24:17) was interpreted as presaging the eminence of the Virgin Mary because the Latin for sceptre was *virga*. Sometimes these methods were employed for political gain e.g. the law prohibiting muzzling an ox when trampling grain (Deut 25:4) was interpreted by the church as a divine injunction ordering that the church be free of any shackles such as civil law or taxes, the grounds for this being Jesus' reference to those spreading the Gospel as harvesters (Matt 9:37).[96] Taking verses out of context to support something which was not in the mind of the author was widespread. John Frith criticised

---

93 Jerome knew both Greek and Hebrew but generally chose to favour the Greek text where it differed which had major theological implications for the Greek fitted better with Christological interpretations of the Messiah.

94 Eric W. Gritsch, "The Jews in Reformation Theology," *Jewish-Christian Encounters over the Centuries* ed Marvin Perry and Frederick Schweitzer (NY 1994) p.197

95 For more on this topic see David S. Katz, *The Jews in the History of England 1485-1850* (1996)

96 In 1 Cor 9:9-10, Paul cites the same verse to argue that ministers are entitled to be supported in their necessities by the church. He makes no mention of exemption from taxation and indeed notes how he supported his own ministry by working as a tent maker to avoid burdening the church – Acts 18:3, 2 Thess 3:8.

Fisher for using a reference to the Israelites passing through fire and water to reach the Promised Land (Ps 66:12) as proof of the existence of purgatory and for taking a line out of the parable of the banquet (Luke 14:23) to justify the church in compelling people to believe certain things or else face the stake.[97] Henry's case arose at a time when, notwithstanding humanist ideals of returning to the original texts, people generally thought like medievalists because that was how they had been trained to think. The insignificance of studying the Bible in people's minds compared to the works of ancients was demonstrated when Rastell wrote a defence of purgatory which evinced no scriptural texts whatsoever but relied wholly on natural philosophy. The tendency amongst Christians to value the Old Testament chiefly as a prophecy of Jesus meant that the Torah was ignored because it contained arguably no messianic material. By contrast, Jews regarded the Bible as a guide on how to live a life which would please God and so the Torah was central. Although Henry was far from being an evangelical Protestant, his stress on the Word rather than tradition and on the need to read the whole Bible and not just the New Testament, highlighted one of the key differences between Roman Catholicism and Protestantism: the former valued tradition while the latter took as its motto, *sola scriptura*, i.e. the Word of God alone.

Thirdly, it was because people generally had no familiarity with the Old Testament. When they went to church, they only heard readings from the New Testament and those were in Latin which few understood.[98] There were no English translations of the Bible available and anyone seeking to obtain an illegal one from abroad was likely to be burnt at the stake if they were caught.[99] When Henry spoke of Leviticus and Deuteronomy, the majority of his subjects would have scratched their heads and asked suspiciously, "what?" As Tyndale noted in his Prologue to Leviticus: "few know the use of the old Testament, and the most part think it nothing necessary but to make allegories." Even the martyr Bilney, who gave his life for the right of people to read the Scriptures in English, expressed doubt that it was necessary to translate more than the New

---

97 John Frith, *Answer to Fisher* contained in John Daye (ed), *The Whole Workes of W. Tyndall, John Frith and Doctor Barnes* (1573) pp.56-57. Augustine had used the same parable to justify forced conversion. The Greek word is *anagkazo* which is used twice in the Gospels where it says Jesus compelled his disciples to enter a boat (Matt 14:22, Mark 6:45) but it is hard to imagine that he forced them into the boat with threats or actual violence indicating that the correct definition of the word is invite. Augustine had limited knowledge of Greek but Fisher was considered an expert so should have considered the context for definition.
98 One passage of Genesis and two from Isaiah were read at festivals but these were not part of the Sunday lectionary. No passage from Leviticus or Deuteronomy was ever read.
99 Almost all the Wycliffite English translations of the Bible which circulated illegally covered the psalms and New Testament only. Lucy Wooding, 'Encountering the Word of God in early Tudor England', *English Historical Review*, vol. CXXXVI no 581 (August 2021) p.838.

Testament.[100] The education of Henry and Katherine's daughter, Mary, excluded the Old Testament completely.[101] Men seeking ordination were not required to demonstrate that they had read even a verse of the Old.[102] Moreover, even if they had possessed Bibles, interpretation was regarded as solely the work of the church and this was based on the story in Acts when the apostle Philip saw an Ethiopian reading the scriptures. Philip asked him if he understood what he read and the eunuch replied: "How can I, except some man should guide me?" (Acts 8:31). The idea of people using their own intelligence to interpret a passage was anathema and this attitude can be seen in the twentieth century when Hughes condemned Henry as "something less than a Catholic" because he read the scriptures and used his own judgment to draw a conclusion instead of simply accepting what generations of scholastics had determined.[103]

It is time to look at the detailed arguments offered against Henry's quite simple case that Leviticus 18:16 was a prohibition by God against marrying a brother's wife and the arguments used against them. Although many volumes were written by his enemies, the main sources are *Invicta Veritas*, a volume by Katherine's chaplain Thomas Abell; the multiple works of John Fisher which are summarised in Harpsfield's *Pretended Divorce* of c.1555 alongside Harpsfield's own allegations.[104] These in turn built on works by Aquinas and Scotus and contemporary canon law experts such as Cardinal Cajetan. It is important to look at these arguments because they show the attitudes which Henry and Anne had to face and demonstrate that the problems raised by contemporaries were very different to those raised by writers today.

The prohibitions only refer to living wives as it says in Lev 18:18 (Fisher)

Verse 18 prohibits a man from taking his sister-in-law as a rival wife to his existing wife during the lifetime of the same. Fisher argued that if the union is legal after she has died, the degree of affinity cannot be an "abomination" and that the same should apply to all the other prohibitions in the chapter. This is false reasoning. The stipulation about during her lifetime is only applied to this particular union. Taking a verse and inserting it earlier in the chapter to change the meaning is simply wrong.

In 1526, Erasmus wrote a volume on Christian marriage for Katherine of Aragon in which he criticised the way popes had increased the number of prohibited relationships and advocates their reduction to those listed in

---

100 In 1527, article eighteen of the heresy charges against him asked if he believed that the Bible should be in English and he said the Gospels and Epistles should be but he was unsure about anything else being necessary. Stephen Cattley (ed.), *Acts and Monuments of John Foxe,* vol. 4 *(1837)* p.626
101 Garrett Mattingly, *Catherine of Aragon* (1942) p.141.
102 Philip Hughes, *The Reformation in England* vol 1 (1950) p. 85.
103 Ibid. pp.198, 217
104 Nicholas Harpsfield, *A Treatise on the Pretended Divorce of Henry VIII* ed. Nicholas Pocock (Camden 1878). For more on Fisher's views see Richard Rex, *The Theology of John Fisher*

Leviticus. Clearly someone at that point mentioned to him that Katherine herself was wed within a degree prohibited by Leviticus because he then hastily added in brackets that perhaps the ban only meant living brothers![105]

Leviticus only refers to the wife of a living brother not his widow (Fisher, Tyndale, Clerk)

Having sexual intercourse in such circumstances would be adultery as Wakefield pointed out and this offence is listed separately (v20). The Ten Commandments include a blanket prohibition of that (Ex. 20:13) and why would God repeat the ban but only for specific cases, such as a brother's or uncle's wife? Moreover, the punishment for adultery is death to both parties (Lev. 20:10) whilst a different punishment is shown for those having intercourse with specific family members.

Leviticus only refers to the wife of a living brother because there can be no affinity after death (Fisher, Abell, Harpsfield, Cajetan)

Based on the belief that affinity stemmed from sexual intercourse only, Fisher and Abell argued that after a man's death, his wife was no longer one body with him and thus free to marry where she liked.[106] In Rom 7:2-3 and I Cor 7:39, Paul spoke of death ending the marriage contract but he did not say widows could choose anyone. Some laws still applied and this is still the case today. For example, a man cannot marry his mother whether his father is alive to object or not and nor can a woman marry her brother or son. Paul's comments may be taken as a rejection of levirate marriage because the idea that the widow must marry her brother-in-law in order to generate an heir for her deceased husband is based on the idea that the contractual obligation to "go forth, increase and multiply" continues beyond death unless it has been met during marriage.

The use of the word abomination is an exaggeration (Fisher, Abell)

"This is to be observed that often times the Old Testament exaggerateth and exasperateth matters with words of execration and abomination ... yet the matters themselves are not ever of their own nature damnable and against the law of God." They based this argument on the fact that other things defined as abominations in the Torah were not viewed as abominations in the sixteenth century. This included eating eels and snails (Lev 11:10, 29), consuming blood (Gen 9:4) and cross-dressing (Deut 22:5). Given it was an article of Christian faith that the Bible was the true Word of God, the logical conclusion would be that either Moses had misheard what God said or that God was wilfully hyperbolizing and later changed his mind when he came to dictate Deuteronomy. If any layman had made such a suggestion, he would

---

105 Erasmus, *Institution*, pp.270, 297.
106 The idea of husband and wife being joined into one body was sometimes held to mean not their own conjugal union but the result of that in the form of offspring, see Kelly, *Matrimonial Trials* p.228.

have found himself on trial for heresy. Henry, quite rightly, insisted that the word in the text was abomination and God did not lie or make mistakes. When God labelled marriage to a brother's wife as an abomination he meant exactly that. As for the issue with eels and clothes, those laws had never applied to Christians though the consumption of blood by Gentiles had been prohibited by the Apostles (Acts 15:29) something Fisher had evidently forgotten.[107]

Other nations did not commit the "abominations" stated in Leviticus 18 (Abell)

His justification for this claim stemmed from the story of Abraham. The Bible said that when in Gerar, Abraham introduced his wife Sarah to King Abimelech as his sister for fear that Abimelech would murder him and take Sarah for himself. When Abimelech did take her, but before they had intercourse, it was revealed to him that Sarah was Abraham's wife and the king expressed his horror at thus having been put in the position of an adulterer due to the lie (Gen 20:1-12). The same scenario had also taken place in Egypt (Gen 12:14-20). From this, Abell, rather curiously, concluded that men in other countries were not in the habit of marrying their sisters "and then it followeth still that if the Egyptians and Canaanites did not use to marry their own sisters then they did not use to marry their mothers nor their aunts nor their mothers in law and so forth...This reason can no man deny." Frankly, most people would deny this leap of logic but even if they did not, as Henry stated, Lev 18:2 said that the practices of Egypt and Canaan must be rejected and that the people occupying the Promised Land before the Israelites were guilty of the prohibited unions (Lev 18:24). Gerar was part of the inheritance of Simeon in the Promised Land (Josh 19:2-8) so either God was lying when he said they were guilty or God was mistaken and needed Abell to correct him: alternatively – and most likely – Abell was wrong. Besides, whether Abimelech and Pharaoh thought such relationships were right or wrong did not matter. Christians were called to obey God not Abimelech or Pharaoh.

Leviticus 18 is not a divine law (Fisher, Harpsfield)

If you asked people what they thought was meant by a divine law, most would probably say, something ordained by God. The words in front of a law in the Bible, "and God said" or "the Lord said" would generally be taken to indicate that the following text constituted a divine law. This is the common sense definition of the term but it was not the universal definition in the sixteenth century. To people then, it was something based on reason and natural philosophy. If the Bible said God commanded something which they thought was unreasonable, they concluded it could not be a divine law because God was rational.[108] Fisher defined divine law in four ways: decrees issued by Jesus, canon law (on grounds Jesus gave the church the keys to heaven), positive

---

107 The law against blood was part of the Noahic covenant together with the positive command to multiply and regarded as apodictic.

108 The idea that their own judgment might be wrong does not seem to have occurred to them.

commandments given by Moses and natural law. Of these four, he argued the pope could dispense from all but the last. Henry, writing to Tunstall in 1531 condemned the "sinister interpretations" of "perverse persons" who would take things which were "clearly and plainly written" and "blind or colour them...for maintenance of such meaning as they would imagine." He said words should always be taken in their common meaning to "signify truth and not so to wrest them as they should maintain a lie." He added "the truth cannot be changed by words."[109]

The reason Henry's enemies spent so much time on this point was because of the widespread belief that the pope could not dispense from divine law. Harpsfield wrote that dispensations do not "give men leave to do against the law of God, but declareth only that in that case the law of God doth not bind." The reason it did not bind was because the pope said so. Should anyone think this was just hair-splitting, he added "the pope in such matters doth not change and alter the will and mind of God or of the maker of the law, but doth declare only in what manner of cases the maker of the law minded" something which was necessary because situations could be complex and "it is not possible for the lawmaker in so few words to comprise them all." A critic might recall Jesus had said that for God "all things are possible" (Matt 19:26) but what did he know? Harpsfield's theories might seem amusing until you remember that he was one of those responsible for examining hundreds of men, women and children in Mary's reign and determining which held such unorthodox views that they deserved to be burnt alive at the stake.

Until the end of the fifteenth century, nobody had doubted that the Levitical prohibitions were divine law. The first Lateran council of 1123 had stated that Lev 18 was divine law (canon 5). Yet canon lawyers generated a way round this by arguing that there was a distinction between bans and prohibitions, one being a temporary thing like a road block which God employed for a particular reason at a distinct time, the other being a permanent restriction. The fact that God speaking through Moses and later Jesus had said the law was permanent did not deter canon lawyers from declaring Leviticus 18 temporary, a move which had the considerable advantage of allowing them to charge fees to obtain dispensations which they could not otherwise have done.

---

109 Wilkins, *Consilia* vol 3 pp.762,765 where it is erroneously listed as 1533. Henry's views stemmed from the teaching of Nicholas of Lyra who is referenced in many of the official works of the period. Nicholas lived in the early fourteenth century and promoted the use of literal, common sense understanding of the Bible text backed up by a background in the geography and customs of the period. Lyra's commentary on Ruth was particularly influential to Henry's thought. Lyra, in line with Rabbi Solomon Isaac of Troyes (better known as Rashi) taught that Ruth was a book written to show the importance of obedience to God and loving concern for neighbours rather than a simple history of one of David's ancestors. This differed from the mainstream Roman tradition which interpreted the Old Testament in light of the New, valuing prophecy above law because prophecy was seen to point to Jesus and stressing the spiritual rather than practical aspects of Torah.

Henry's view that it was divine law was supported by Cardinal Cajetan. In his second commentary on Thomas Aquinas' *Summa Theologiae,* he had pondered how it had happened that Julius II had given a dispensation to Henry: "it is evident, that this is prohibited in the law divine. Thus are opposed on the one hand the divine law in precepts of this kind, on the other the authority of the Roman pontiff."[110] Cajetan was writing years before the annulment crisis. His conclusion, based on the eleventh century document known as *Dictatus Papae* which claimed that the church never had or would err and that nobody could sit in judgment on the pope or retract any of his decisions, was that evidently the pope did have authority even over divine law.[111] By the time of the actual dispute with Henry, his verdict that Leviticus was divine law was rather embarrassing to the pope so he changed his mind about that but not the extent of papal authority.[112]

Leviticus 18 is not natural law (Fisher, Harpsfield, Cajetan, Abell)

Henry's enemies were all very keen on this argument. Scholastics like Aquinas had dedicated much of their life to aligning the Bible with Greek philosophy. As part of this attempt, they had defined different types of law. Natural law was regarded as things which everybody in any part of the world and at any time period back to Adam and Eve, would agree to be right or wrong through the use of natural reason.[113] They agreed that levirate marriage would not fall into this category but what about prohibitions on things like incest, adultery, marrying in-laws? Henry, following St Paul, claimed that such things were clearly unacceptable while others thought they were legitimate.[114] Abell said that Abraham was a holy man and would not have married his half-sister had it been against natural law and Tamar would not have slept with her father-in-law if that had been against natural law, though elsewhere in his book he claimed consanguinity restrictions represented natural law but not affinity. Scotus argued that incest must be legitimate, despite Leviticus, because Adam and Eve's sons must of necessity have married their sisters because there was nobody else around. As Adam and Eve lived in paradise and this was a time of natural law, it followed this was acceptable and Leviticus simply a later restriction for the purposes of public order which the pope could overturn. In the 1531 *Determinations,* Henry quoted St Paul's words in Rom 5:13-14 that what existed before God gave the law to Moses was sin, not natural law. He

---

110 Oscar Watkins, *Holy Matrimony* (1895) p.706
111 Ernest F. Henderson, *Select Historical Documents of the Middle Ages,* (1910), pp. 366-367 nos 19,20 and 22.
112 The Second Vatican Council issued *Dei Verbum* which in paragraph 11 states: "everything asserted by the inspired authors or sacred writers must be held to be asserted by the Holy Spirit. It follows that the books of Scripture must be acknowledged as teaching solidly, faithfully and without error that truth which God wanted to put into sacred writings for the sake of salvation."
113 Wisdom 7:27, Ecclesiasticus 1:9-10, 14-15
114 Rom. 1:18-20, 27, 32.

also said: "God is not wont to punish unjustly, and against right, so he is not wont to punish but for transgression of some law." The destruction of the Egyptians and Canaanites could not have been because they transgressed God's law because it had not been given to them, so it must be because they transgressed natural law and the Bible says they were destroyed for their incestuous unions.[115]

In truth, the issue should never have been raised in the first place. The question was what God thought – not Aquinas, Aristotle, Augustine or anyone else and Henry alone seemed able to keep his focus on this point. However, owing to a belief that popes could not dispense from natural law, many felt it essential to argue the Levitical prohibitions were not against nature because otherwise, it was clear that the dispensation which had united Henry and Katherine was invalid. The topic became highly political.

Since a man can marry a woman during her period, Leviticus 18 cannot be against nature and so the pope can dispense (Abell)

If Abell had read the scriptures in Hebrew instead of Latin and had troubled to read chapters 18 and 20 in conjunction, he would not have made such a foolish claim.

Levirate marriage is natural law (Tyndale)

In an interesting take on the natural law argument, Tyndale claimed that Leviticus could not be natural law because Deuteronomy was! He argued that because Tamar was married to Er and Onan centuries before Moses was born, this showed levirate marriage was natural law and the prohibition in Leviticus must therefore be invalid because even God could not change natural law.[116]

The ban on brother's wives in Lev 18:16 must exclude widows because Deut 25:6 talks of sons being born while Lev 20:21 says such unions will be without sons (Fisher)

As Henry repeatedly said, Deuteronomy is a dispensation not a rival law.

*If the pope can allow a man to marry his dead wife's sister, it follows that a woman can marry her dead husband's brother (*Fisher, Cajetan, Abell, Tyndale)

To people today who have grown up with the idea of gender equality, this statement may seem perfectly fair. It is, however, based on two false premises.[117]

---

115 *Determinations*, p.108; Lev. 18:3,27. Peter de Palude believed all the Levitical prohibitions were natural law.
116 By the same logic, presumably Cain's murder of Abel showed killing was a natural law and so was circumcision.
117 In 1921, Parliament passed the Deceased Brother's Widow Marriage Act which legitimated such unions on the basis of equal rights, marriage to a Deceased Wife's

First and foremost, all the prohibitions are written from the man's perspective as has been stated and they are said to be the word of God. A man may not marry his aunt but he can his niece. If equality was applied, a woman could not marry her uncle but could her nephew and such laws would be in direct opposition to what the Bible text says because the relationships are identical: a woman and her nephew are the same as a man and his aunt. Canon law, fired by a desire to create a system which was in line with reason, changed the prohibitions in Leviticus to create new offences.[118] That even the clergy seemed unaware of this is seen in Abell who triumphantly notes that Othniel married his niece (Judg 1:13) and Zelophehad's daughters married their cousins (Num 36:11) citing this as proof that prohibited unions were not against the law of nature.[119] Neither union was ever prohibited by God, only by the church of Rome.[120]

The celebrated case of Manuel I of Portugal was frequently referenced by Henry's enemies but was utterly irrelevant.[121] He had married firstly his cousin's widow, then her sister and finally the niece of the said sister who happened to be also sister of the Emperor.[122] The fact that his first two wives were daughters of Ferdinand and Isabella and thus elder sisters of Katherine of Aragon and that his daughter by his second wife was the current Empress meant much of the attention was politically motivated. There was nothing in the Bible to stop him marrying the sister of his dead wife only a canon law, and since the pope had created the law, indisputably he could change or dispense from it which he did in 1500. It was not a parallel to Henry's case with Katherine at all.

Secondly, although Lev 18:18 is usually translated as relating to two sisters, the original meaning is uncertain. English Bibles show that the word sister appears in Lev 18:9,11,12,13 and 18 but in Hebrew, three different words are used, though they share a common root. Verses 9 and 11 represent the only

---

Sister having been authorised in 1907. Crucially, the Act only related to civil weddings and not those conducted in Church.

118 There was a practical reason why the laws differed between the sexes. If a man married two or more wives, the children born would all be his no matter who their mother was, unless she was guilty of adultery. If a woman married more than one man, there was no way of identifying the father and hence it was impossible for a man to ensure his goods were inherited by his own rather than somebody else's children.
119 He might also have included Solomon's son, King Rehoboam, who married his two first cousins, 2 Chr. 11:18-20.
120 There is not even a word in Biblical Hebrew for cousin.
121 It was even cited as a precedent of papal power to dispense from Leviticus by the Dean of the Rota, CSPV 4.925. An earlier case of 1410 when Margaret Beaufort (née Holland) was permitted to marry her husband's half nephew – the Duke of Clarence who wanted her fortune – was referenced later but Leviticus only prohibits aunts and blood nephews.
122 Clearly Alfonso was either very attracted to Habsburg women or deeply unimaginative in his choices. Other women were available.

usage of the word in the entire Bible while verses 12 and 13 use the most common word for sister. These two words clearly mean physical sibling. The Hebrew word used in verse 18, however, is rather different. It appears four times in Exodus in a passage about furnishings where it simply means another. The word is also used once in Judges where it means a physical sister, three times in Jeremiah where it means a country and six times in Ezekiel where on three occasions it means another and on three it means sister.[123] Forster noted that of forty-one uses of the grammatical construction in the Bible, it meant other or two in every case.[124] Thus, it is not clear whether the law in Lev 18:18 relates to marrying a wife's sister during the wife's lifetime or if it is a more general prohibition of polygamy. Even if it is interpreted as sister, the stress is on the concept of the rival wife rather than the relationship between the two women. If the sisters are willing to accept the situation as Leah and Rachel did with Jacob, there is arguably no reason why the marriages should not take place. Most significantly of all, unlike the unions which are clearly prohibited in the earlier part of Leviticus 18, there is no punishment given for anyone who makes such unions.

The idea that canon law should expand the Biblical prohibitions was fundamentally wrong. the church, as the bride of Christ, was meant to be obedient to God. As Henry reminded people, it said quite clearly in the Bible that nobody could add or take away from the Law (Deut 4:2, 12:32, Rev 22:18-19). Changing laws to make them fit human ideas of reason was tantamount to saying God had got it wrong and that was heresy.[125]

Henry would have been supported in his case by history had he known this. The ban on marrying the sister of a dead wife had been introduced to canon law because it was part of Roman civil law. Emperors Constantius and Zeno both banned levirate marriage alongside sororate and Basil of Caesarea, one of the Cappadochian fathers whom Henry did quote in the *Glass of Truth*, and Pope Siricius both did the same.[126] Basil referred to marriage to the sister of a dead wife as an "unseemly desire" and a "pollution" and said that any man

---

123 Judges 15:2; Jer 3:7,8,10 and Ezek 1:9,23; 3:13, 23:4,11,18. The Greek Septuagint translates the Hebrew of Lev. 18:18 as blood sister but the word *adelphe* is also used in the New Testament for both non-blood relatives (1 Tim. 5:1-2, Mark 3:35) as well as for the siblings of Jesus (Matt. 13:56, Mark 6:3) individuals regarded by Protestants as daughters of Mary and Joseph so full blood sisters and by Roman Catholics as daughters of Joseph only so half-sisters. Canonists regarded the word as meaning a sibling by blood relationship while the theologians interpreted it as a broader or theoretical sister due to their insistence on the perpetual virginity of Jesus' mother, Mary.
124 C. Forster, *Marriage with two Sisters contrary to the Holy Law of God and Nature*. (1850) p.32
125 The Roman church defended the practice at the Council of Trent arguing that as the church possessed the Holy Spirit, the third person of the Trinity, and it represented the earthly body of Jesus as the second person of the same, it had authority.
126 Yiffat Monnickendam, 'Biblical Law in Greco-Roman Attire: the Case of Levirate Marriage' in *Journal of Law and Religion* vol.34, no. 2 (2019) pp.140-141, 157.

who did such a thing should be excommunicated and remain so until he had separated from her.[127] Pope Julius had not seen himself as bound by Siricius' edict when he gave the ruling with regard to the King of Portugal and Fisher, Abell and Cajetan clearly chose to follow Julius' ruling too.

The severe punishment decreed for person who refuses to marry his brother's wife shows God's pleasure in levirate unions (Abell)

Abell repeats his claim that the penalty imposed by Deuteronomy was a "great pain" nineteen times in his book. Quite aside from the fact that only a person of extraordinary sensitivity would regard the removal and tossing of a sandal as being a "great pain" and sign of God's severe censure, his claim totally fails to understand the point of the ceremony. An exchange of sandals was the traditional way of demonstrating a contract had been made. Removing one meant no contract had been made and the woman was free to marry outside the family. In the New Testament, Jesus tells his disciples to shake the dust off their feet if they go to a place to preach and people do not listen (Luke 9:5; Acts 13:51). This was a way of publicly saying that an offer had been made of a place in the kingdom of heaven and not accepted, like the widow not wanted by her brother-in-law. It was not a summoning of hellfire and damnation (indeed the contrary as is shown by Jesus' condemnation of such a response in Luke 9:54-5), more an expression of sadness, like someone shrugging their shoulders and saying "I tried" when an offer of help is refused. The spitting was also a minor punishment conferring shame for a week not the lifelong ignominy which Abell, with his constant refrain of "great pain", claimed.[128] As the *Glass of Truth* observes, it was a "right small and easy punishment."

Deuteronomy cannot be a dispensation because it includes a procedure if it is not used (Fisher)

In normal circumstances, people would request a dispensation because they wanted to use it. If they then chose not to do so, that would be up to them and no penalty would apply. However, levirate marriage was not a dispensation like a couple seeking permission to marry, but rather general and it was appropriate to have a penalty in such cases. To give a biblical example, God dispensed Ahab from the commandment against killing when he went to war but he punished him afterwards for showing mercy (1 Kings 20:28,32,42).

Deuteronomy is an absolute command not a dispensation because God does not order us to do evil (Fisher)

In his *A Necessary Doctrine* of 1543, Henry gave an example of how something generally held to be evil can be commanded as a dispensation. The

---

127 Letter to Diodorus, Second Canonical Letter to Amphilochius
128 Whilst there may not be any proof of this, it is hard to believe that his contemporaries did not nickname Abell the 'Great Pain' himself. He was also a vandal. He carved a bell with an 'A' on it on the wall of the Beauchamp Tower in the Tower of London during his imprisonment there for treason and sedition.

sixth commandment said "thou shalt not kill" but yet the death penalty was imposed for a variety of activities such as murder, witchcraft and adultery. Henry explained that the exception to the law against killing was made by God so that rulers, and their representatives, could exercise justice and defend the community.[129]

Henry's case was supported by no less than an authority than Jesus here. In Matt. 19:3-9, the pharisees asked Jesus about the law regarding divorce asking him whether it was right that Moses had commanded a man to do this (Deut 24:1). Jesus corrects them saying that God's law is that marriage is for life (Gen 2:24) and that far from being a commandment, divorce was something which Moses was allowed to permit only because of the "hardness of hearts." The distinction between the types of law and the use of dispensations which may permit something evil in response to a particular situation, was just as applicable to the case of levirate marriage.

Deuteronomy is an absolute command not a dispensation because God does not order us to do evil constantly (Abell)

Abell cited Abraham being told to sacrifice Isaac (Gen 22:1-14) and the Israelites to steal goods from the Egyptians as they departed (Ex 11:1-2) as examples of God ordering evil but he said these were limited to particular individuals and occasions whilst Deuteronomy was a universal command. The idea of God advocating wrongdoing is heresy to Jews and Christians and sheds more light on the limits of Abell's theological understanding than it does Henry's case. In Hebrew, it says clearly that the Israelites were to ask for goods, not steal them: the image is of Israel as God's chosen bride being adorned for her wedding.[130] Abell must have had some qualities which encouraged Katherine to appoint him her chaplain but it cannot have been his erudition.

Levirate marriage was compulsory for all Jews at all times (Abell)

This was a simple case of taking Deut 25:5 out of context. Abell was not the first to make this mistake nor the last. It was, however, completely untrue as has been shown. Forced marriage was illegal and invalid under both Jewish and canon law.[131]

Deuteronomy shows that Leviticus excludes widows without children (Abell)

If God had meant to say this, surely he would have done so. Abell is simply trying to rewrite the text to suit his own theories. As Henry noted, people are meant to follow God's word not change it. Deut 4:2 and 12:32 as well as Rev 22:18-19 say humanity may not add or take away from the commandments given on pain of eternal damnation.

---

129 *Formularies* pp.321-322.
130 The covenant at Sinai (Ex. 24:3-8) is a binding ceremony akin to marriage. For imagery of Israel as the bride, which prefigures the idea of the church as the bride of Christ, see, for example, Isa. 62:3-5.
131 *Kiddushin* 2b

Leviticus does not apply if the first marriage was not consummated (Harrington, Pole)

This argument represented a big can of worms, but more for the canon lawyers than the theologians since it centred on what makes a marriage. Was it when the last "I do" was spoken or when the priest declared "I now pronounce you man and wife" or at the moment of first penetration? The idea that a couple were only married in a human sense before sex and divinely afterwards was based on the idea that since marriage symbolised the eternal mystic union between Christ and his church, this indissoluble union did not exist until the couple consummated the match. Before that, they were just individuals banded together like Jesus and His disciples. Afterwards they were united by the spilling of the virginal wife's blood as Jesus had united himself to the church through his blood on the cross.

As Henry's team were quick to point out, if consummation was essential to make a valid marriage, then it meant that Joseph and Mary were not married because the Roman view was that Mary remained a lifelong virgin.[132] Doubting the legitimacy of the marriage of Jesus' parents and the status of Mary was heresy. God had sent the angel Gabriel to Joseph and he had referenced Mary as his wife, not his betrothed or intended or partner etc. (Matt 1:20). Unless it was to be suggested that Gabriel was acting independently, that was conclusive proof that Mary was Joseph's wife in God's eyes.[133]

This theory of two tier marriage was not found in the Bible but a creation of canon lawyers. Their view was that without consummation, marriage was only human and could be dissolved by the pope. It followed that if Katherine's union with Arthur had not been consummated, it was not a full marriage so there was no reason for the pope not to allow her to marry Henry. Sander actually wrote that Arthur and Katherine were "not really man and wife."[134]

Such a conclusion was utterly refuted by Henry. He quoted Hugh of St Victor who said that whilst an unconsummated union might not be able to represent Christ and the church it nonetheless symbolised the spiritual union of God and soul which was a greater truth for the spirit gives life (2 Cor 3:6).[135] As further support he cited the case of Adonijah asking for the hand of his father's widow (1 Kings 2:22-25) a relationship prohibited in Lev 18:8.[136] The Bible says that the request alone was so heinous that Solomon ordered him struck

---

132 Scholastics based this on the prophet Ezekiel's vision of the Temple in which he was told that the gate would be shut as no human being could enter after God (Ezek.44:2).

133 In the Talmud, it is stated: "Wives receive a marriage contract and betrothal" (Sanhedrin 21a), Consummation is not required.

134 Nicolas Sander, *Rise and Growth of the Anglican Schism* (ed. David Lewis) (1877) p4

135 For more on this point and the Biblical references see above, What did Henry believe?

dead. This happened not only before he could so much as become betrothed to the lady but despite the fact that his father, David, had not consummated his marriage with her (1 Kings 1:4). Katherine's protests about being a virgin were hereby shown not to matter when it came to the Levitical prohibitions – a wife was the woman who had taken vows to the man and whether the union had been consummated or not did not matter a jot.[137] Also supporting Henry's case was Augustine and also Aquinas who noted that that there was no intercourse in the Garden of Eden but yet Eve was declared to be be Adam's wife by God. In addition, Innocent II had declared that full marriage existed from the point when the bride said "I do."[138]

Another argument used by Henry and his team was that Alexander III in the mid twelfth century refused to issue a dispensation to a man who wished to marry his brother's betrothed, a virgin so the only objection could be public honesty.[139]

To counter Henry's arguments, Pole conceded that Katherine may have been Arthur's true wife even without consummation but argued that if Arthur had chosen not to uncover her nakedness, it was acceptable for Arthur's brother to do so.

---

136 It is not absolutely certain that she was his wife but this had been Christian tradition for many years and Fisher did not dispute this. In the Talmud, it is said that Abishag proposed to David because the law forbade her being alone with a married man (*Sanhedrin* 21b) but he refused to marry her because he had eighteen wives already (*Sanhedrin* 22a) but the point of the legend there is as "Rav Shemen bar Abba says: Come and see how severe a matter divorce is, as they rendered it permitted for King David to be secluded with Abishag without marrying her, but they did not render it permitted for him to divorce one of his wives to enable him to marry Abishag." A study of these chapters indicates considerable disagreement between the rabbis over what rules existed, which existed in David's lifetime and their status in relation to Torah.

137 Another line of argument taken by Cranmer was that marriage had to come from vows because it was permanent as was a promise whereas intercourse was a temporary thing. A footnote on the 1534 Act of Succession nevertheless defines a marriage as a union which had been "solemnized and carnal knowledge was had" an addition clearly made by the clergy in the house of Lords because common law recognised the validity of marriages made outside a church and which were never consummated.

138 Anselm had argued that Jesus on the cross giving his mother into the care of the disciple John rather than his brothers indicated that Mary was a lifelong virgin and therefore not Joseph's true wife.

139 Kelly, *Matrimonial Trials* pp.70-71, 183-186. Fisher said it was not relevant to Henry's case because the elder brother was alive and that the man was condemned for promising to marry the girl when he was not able to do so. He argued the pope's refusal to dispense did not prove he was unable to dispense. Fisher quietly glossed over the fact that Alexander III evidently assumed the Levitical prohibitions were binding when he made his decision.

Deuteronomy is a binding commandment on all Christians (Fisher, Harpsfield)

No visitation of the period and no instructions for priests, such as those composed in the middle ages by Mirc and indeed Harpsfield's own visitations, included any questions about whether brothers were dutifully marrying their widowed sonless sisters-in-law. No man was ever prosecuted in the church courts for failing to do this, though they were routinely charged with breaches of commandments against adultery and for pre-marital sex. Fisher's argument was based on an interpretation by Augustine, who regarded Deut 25:5-10 as prefiguring Jesus' commandment to "Go into all the world and make disciples of all people"(Matt. 28:19).[140] In his *Answer to Faustus*, Augustine argued that as all Christians were brothers of Jesus (Luke 8:21; Rom 8:16-17), they all had a responsibility to raise up heirs in his name, i.e. new Christians, and that since Jesus' commandment had universal application, so did Deuteronomy.[141] In his *Glass of Truth*, Henry also quoted this interpretation but used it to show how laws which in their literal sense had no relevance for Christians might be interpreted to fulfil the lesson that all scripture is written for our learning and no word should be ignored (Rom 15:4, 1 Cor 10:11). It is absolutely certain that Moses did not have in mind proselytization when he was writing.

Deuteronomy is later and supersedes Leviticus (Fisher)

This was another theory which had its roots in the Septuagint. The name Deuteronomy means second law in Greek and hence canon lawyers argued that this meant it was later than Leviticus and showed God had changed his mind since issuing the prohibition on marrying a brother's wife. Henry's Hebrew scholar, Wakefield, pointed out that the book had a different name in the original Hebrew which was *Devarim* which simply meant words. Not only did that not have any connotations of time, it showed the texts were contemporary and of equal status.[142] That something which should have been general knowledge for two thousand years was greeted as an exciting discovery demonstrates the lack of understanding of the Torah at the time, something attributable to a lack of teaching by the Roman church and the widespread expulsion of Jews from Europe.

A positive law takes precedence over a negative

This was a generally accepted truth in both Christianity and Judaism.[143] However, Henry consistently argued that Deuteronomy was not a law but a dispensation for all the reasons stated in the analysis of the text

---

140 the church Father, not the man who brought Christianity to England in the late sixth century.
141 Book 32 q10 "what does this prefigure, but that every preacher of the gospel should so labour in the Church as to raise up seed to his deceased brother, that is, Christ, who died for us, and that this seed should bear His name?"
142 Modern Biblical criticism would suggest a more complex pattern of Torah development. See Postscript.
143 See *Yebamoth* 5a for example.

above. Moreover, the existence of a positive law does not nullify the negative. For example, Jesus gave the example of rescuing an animal whose life was in risk on the Sabbath (Luke 14:5). He did not say the Sabbath should not be kept, just that the rules could be broken to save a life.

The prohibition in Leviticus is binding but adultery is a worse sin (Luther)

It is likely that Henry thought Luther would support him because in the *Babylonian Captivity of the church*, Luther had written that the only people prohibited as marital partners were those listed in Leviticus 18, including a brother's wife. All other impediments were nothing but things "invented by men in the church" which "sprung into existence for the sole purpose of serving those grasping and robbing Nimrods as snares for taking money and as nets for catching souls, and in order that abomination might stand in the holy place."[144] Indeed, it was probable that it was reading this work which set Henry's mind in turmoil. However, Luther did acknowledge that there was one scenario in which a man could marry his brother's widow legitimately and that was if the brother was impotent. This was not to be confused with someone who did not consummate their marriage by choice. Luther argued that if a man said he was capable of consummation and proved not to be so, the marriage was null "for by his own fault he deceived the innocence of a maiden and defrauded her of the proper use of her body."[145] If a couple were physically capable and for whatever reason did not consummate their union, this was not grounds for annulment according to Luther because it was vows which made the marriage and vows were for life.[146] Luther and Melanchthon agreed that the pope should never have permitted Henry to marry Katherine because it was against divine law but Henry and Katherine had taken advantage of the dispensation to make vows to one another and in their eyes, whilst they should separate and renounce the sin, there could be no remarriage on either side because the vows had created a valid marriage and that would be adultery which was a bigger sin. He added that if the King should divorce the Queen, he would "most gravely sin against the divine law which states: 'what God has joined together, let no man put asunder.' God's joining, whether done through the law or through human action, stands higher than any man made ordinance."[147]

---

144 *Babylonian Captivity* 6.9, 6.13 referencing Matt 24:15, Lev 18:6. In I Cor 4:6, Paul says that people should abide by the rules that are written and not put the ideas of man in their place. At the time Paul was writing, only the Old Testament existed. It may be significant also that this reference came just before his condemnation of a man taking his father's wife.

145 Ibid. 6.24

146 Ibid. 6.19

147 Matt 5:32, 19:6; Luke 16:18. In September 1531, Luther warned that Henry was at risk of eternal damnation for discarding Katherine, Gottfried G. Krodel (ed.) *Luther's Works, vol. 50 Letters part 3* (Philadelphia, 1975) pp.31-40. It should be noted that at the time he wrote, he had not completed his translation of the Hebrew scriptures. Luther wrote: "this sin in past and like all other sins of the past is

The Torah has no authority since the coming of Jesus (Fisher, Luther, Erasmus)[148]

The annulment issue highlights the tension which has existed in Christianity from the time of the Apostles between law and gospel. Having denied that the Levitical prohibitions are anything but church laws (despite the words "and God said") Fisher goes on to say that marriage to a brother's wife, "if it were by Moses' law forbidden, the law was by Christ abolished." The justification for this claim depends on a literal reading of Rom 7:6 which is one of the most complex of Paul's epistles and a discussion of it is beyond the scope of this volume. Jerome had also taken this view basing it on a figurative interpretation of Deut 22:10 which forbade the yoking of different types of animals together to pull a plough.[149]

Erasmus avoided comment on Henry's case but did oppose Christians reading the Old Testament at all for fear they might start to question doctrines generated by the church and could even be tempted to become Jews. He accepted that there might be some value in reading some parts of it provided that this was done only under the accompaniment of instruction from Rome and that the interpretations were purely allegorical. Otherwise, he saw almost the entire work as having been given "only for a limited time" which ended when Jesus came.[150] The exception he made was with regard to the Levitical prohibitions

However, the idea that the Torah was entirely abolished was in direct contravention of Jesus' own teaching that "until heaven and earth pass away, not the smallest letter or part of a letter will disappear from the Law, until all things are accomplished. Therefore, whoever will break one of these least commandments, and teach others to do so, will be called least in the Kingdom of Heaven; but whoever will do and teach them will be called great in the Kingdom of Heaven" (Matt 5:18-19). As Henry and everybody else knew, earth still existed so the Torah remained. Moreover, teaching the Ten Commandments which were part of the Torah, remained part of universal church practice. In Matthew 23:3, Jesus told the multitudes to observe the Law as it was written, minus any additions. Moreover, Fisher, and everyone else in the debate, regarded the requirement to tithe, which existed only in the Torah, as binding so his argument made scant sense.[151] Given that Jesus was believed to be God Incarnate, it was hard to see why the selective reading of St Paul's epistles,

---

amended through repentance but the marriage should not be torn apart for this reason."

148 Croke noted some Lutherans of this opinion, LP 4.6713, but this conflicts with Luther's own writings.
149 John Sawyer, *The Fifth Gospel: Isaiah in the History of Christianity* (1996) p120
150 Letter to Wolfgang Capito discussed in John Barton, *A History of the Bible* (2019) pp.394-398.
151 The New Testament only speaks of the requirement of Christians to give generously to fund the work of the church.

should be considered to be more important. Paul had himself denied that the Law was void (Rom 3:31) and described the commandments as "holy and just and good" (Rom 7:12) and he had described the law as life giving.[152] Paul was a member of the Council of Jerusalem which decreed that Gentile Christians were not required to follow every detail of the Torah but only to keep the laws relating to morality as well as to abstain from eating blood and food sacrificed to idols.[153] Deuteronomy 25:5-6 did not contain a moral imperative, only an instruction relating to land tenure. As the church of England says in Article VII:

> Although the law given from God by Moses, as touching ceremonies and rites, do not bind Christian men, nor the civil precepts thereof ought of necessity to be received in any commonwealth; yet, notwithstanding, no Christian man whatsoever is free from the obedience of the commandments which are called moral.

The Hebrew is not authoritative (Fisher, Harpsfield)

After reciting the miraculous legend of how in the third century BC Ptolemy summoned seventy scholars to translate the Hebrew into Greek and they all produced exactly the same text, Augustine notes that the Greek text differs at a number of points but attributes this not to errors but the Holy Spirit taking the opportunity to effectively give an update on God's wishes. Thus changes such as sons to children were inspired. Fisher accepted this and took a similar line with the Vulgate. He accepted that over the years there might have been some errors creep in due to poor copying but he absolutely did not believe that the Hebrew original was in any way more authoritative than the Latin or Greek. In his *Reverendissimis* he argued that the question of what the Hebrew said should not even be asked because that would cast doubt on the authority of the Vulgate and the pope.[154] Harpsfield said that anyone who used the Hebrew text to point out errors in the Vulgate or the Greek Septuagint was acting "very impiously and wickedly." Henry, as a humanist, had been taught to go back to original sources and as a good scholar that is what he did. He might also have noted that Jesus used the Hebrew as is shown by his references to its divisional structure which differs from the Greek.[155] In the preface to his 1530 book on the Psalms, Cardinal Cajetan also referred to the Vulgate as an interpretation of, and no substitute for, the original Hebrew.

---

152 2 Tim 3:16.
153 Acts 15:28-29.
154 David Katz, *The Jews in the History of England* (Oxford, 1994) p.22
155 Quotations from the Old Testament in the New are often more closely aligned with the Greek than the Hebrew simply because the New Testament was written in Greek.

The Vulgate is perfect and should not be debated (Harpsfield)

Harpsfield wrote: "We must follow and embrace that sense only which the church hath from time to time universally received. And what text soever be alleged, we must reject all other interpretations that are contrary to the received understanding of the Catholic Church." Henry disagreed. God had given him a mind and gifts were to be employed in God's service (1 Cor 12:7).

God showed his approval of levirate marriages by allowing Jesus to be born to a family in which they took place (Fisher)

There are two genealogies of Jesus in the New Testament. In Matthew 1:2-16 there is the ancestry of Joseph back to Abraham whilst in Luke 3:23-38 it runs from Joseph to Adam. There are a number of differences between the two, one of which is that Joseph's own father is named as Jacob in Matthew and Heli in Luke. On the basis that scripture cannot err, the traditional resolution of this conundrum dating back to Julius Africanus' letter to Aristides in the third century, said that Jacob and Heli must have been brothers and Joseph the offspring of a levirate union.[156] Another theory is that the man had two names like Saul also known as Paul, Simon also known as Peter, Levi also known as Matthew, Jacob also known as Israel and Barjesus also known as Elymas. There is no proof that there were any levirate marriages in Jesus' ancestry and even if there were, that would not indicate God's approval, for Rahab the prostitute also appears in the same ancestry (Matt 1:5) and nobody thought that indicated God believed women should charge for their sexual favours and mate with anyone who had the cash.

Significantly, no less an authority than Nicholas of Lyra denied the assumption of a levirate match in Jesus' ancestry saying that the opinions of the Fathers should not be viewed as binding when the Bible did not offer a clear determination of a question.[157]

Jesus did not confirm Leviticus or issue any alternative regulations on marriage (the Scotists)

The Scotists claimed that because Jesus had never specifically said that he was renewing Leviticus' laws, they did not apply[158] They did not of course need to be renewed because they were as Jesus said, eternal – together

---

[156] Africanus argued that levirate marriage was only introduced because the people at the time had no belief in resurrection. He claimed that the practice therefore became obsolete following Jesus' resurrection. The same excuse of levirate marriage was used to explain why Moses' wife's father was named as Jethro in Ex 4:18, Reuel in Ex 2:18 and Num 10:29. If this were the case, it would indicate the use of levirate outside Israel. Augustine of Hippo, in *On the Harmony of the Gospels* II.iii also claimed Joseph was the son of Jacob biologically and of Levi by levirate.

[157] A. Skevington Wood, 'Nicolas of Lyra', *Evangelical Quarterly* vol. 33 part 4 (1961) p.205. Henry's team cited Lyra's *Postillae Litteralis* so evidently knew the work.

[158] Kelly, *Matrimonial Trials* p.7; Scotus iv. Disp.40, q.un. n.5

with those in Genesis, Exodus, Numbers and Deuteronomy which he also did not specifically mention.[159] It could have been argued from this logic that Jesus never ordered godparents, the creation of canon law, episcopal vestments, holy water or a host of other things which the Scotists would doubtless have claimed were essential.

Jesus did not rule on marriage laws because he wanted the pope to do it (Bonaventure)

He did not issue rules on the subject because he was not a canon lawyer and he believed that God, whom he knew as his Father, had already done so. Even for those who give preference to the keys of Matt 16:19 given to Peter over the same given to the whole church in Matt 18:18, it would be a stretch to imagine that at the moment of Peter's recognition of Jesus as the Messiah, Jesus' first concern was to lay down a principle of marriage regulation to last for millennia.

Jesus did not condemn levirate marriage (Abell)

Matt 22:23-33 describes an occasion when the sadducees (Jewish teachers who did not believe in life after death) decided to ask Jesus what would happen to a woman who had been married to seven brothers under levirate law: whose wife would she be in heaven? The question, based on a farcical situation, was evidently designed to try and trap him and Jesus did not fall into this. Indeed, Greek speakers would have spotted the pun here for the Septuagint gives the purpose of levirate marriage as being to raise up sons for the deceased, and the same root is used in the word resurrection.[160] Abell's argument was that if Jesus had disapproved of levirate marriage, he had the opportunity to condemn it and he did not do so, choosing instead to respond with teaching about eternity.[161] Had the sadducees asked a Tudor canon lawyer, the answer would have been very different and his response would have been to ask about ages, consent, whether the earlier union was consummated, if the ceremony had been performed in accordance with correct procedures, if there had been any precontracts etc. As a Christian, who by definition should be following Jesus' example, Abell should have drawn the conclusion that this sort

---

159 *Determinations* p.131: "He did not make express mention of them, because he had commanded long before, that they should forever to come continue and never fail."

160 The Apocrypha tells the story of Sarah who has seven husbands, all of whom die on the wedding night leaving her still a virgin (Tobit 3:8). There is no suggestion that the men were all brothers. The book of Tobit was probably written around two hundred years before the birth of Jesus and was never accepted as scripture by either the Pharisees or the Sadducees but it is possible that the idea of a seven times married woman was a popular image in tales of the time. The number seven is associated in the Bible with completion so it could be a way of emphasising her total loss.

161 Jesus was, of course, living in Israel before the fall of Jerusalem so the issue of tribal inheritance of land was still relevant.

of legalism was not the way to approach Henry's situation. To surmise Jesus' approval because he did not condemn was a dangerous line of argument. Jesus did not condemn slavery or drug taking or cyber bullying either but few would regard this as evidence he supported them. Abell's logic left much to be desired.

The law of love requires Deuteronomy to be given precedence (Fisher)

Fisher came to this conclusion from two directions. Firstly, the requirement to marry her brother-in-law was a way of protecting the widow from penury, loneliness and general misery and Jesus had taught that loving thy neighbour was a fulfilling of the law. Secondly, he reminded readers of the parable of Dives and Lazarus where Dives suffers mental torture in hell for fear his brothers would suffer the same fate since they too mistreated Lazarus and those like him (Luke 16:19-31). Reasoning that Dives after death was able to experience anguish, he figured that so would the brother who died and saw his wife left behind and not married by his surviving brother. In other words, Henry needed to marry Katherine to stop Arthur sobbing in his grave. Henry never saw fit to answer that one directly, possibly because he was laughing too much. What he did say in the *Determinations* was: "who so unveileth the fullness of the parts to be ashamed of, of his kinfolk be they of kin ghostly and spiritual or bodily and carnal, he is found to be a breaker and a transgressor of the whole law for the thing that he doth is contrary to love and charity which is the fulfilling and performing of the whole law." This view came directly from the Bible – James 2:10, Rom 13:10.

The New Testament shows the Levitical prohibitions were obsolete (Fisher, Abell)

Henry had pointed to two cases in the New Testament where people were apparently criticised for marrying in forbidden degrees. The first related to Herod whom John the Baptist condemned for marrying his brother's wife, Herodias (Mark 6:17-18; Matt 14:3-4). Fisher, Tyndale and Abell cited the tradition that this was different to Henry's case because brother Philip was still alive. This fact was not stated in the Bible but came from the historian Josephus in the late first century so could be held open to question.[162] By contrast, the church Father, Tertullian, said explicitly that "John reproved Herod, because he had illegally married the wife of his deceased brother."[163] Given Herodias already had a daughter, it seemed unlikely that she could claim it was a levirate marriage, though the scripture did not identify the father of the child.[164] The key point was that the Baptist's condemnation indicated that he believed the

---

162 Josephus, *Antiquities* Book 18 chapters 5 to 7. Herod's family tree is extremely complicated with Herodias also being niece to her first husband and her daughter Salome marrying successively her great-uncle and cousin. The relationship between Herodias' two husbands was half brother, both being sons of Herod the Great but by different mothers.

163 Tertillian, *Adversus Marcionem*, Book IV, Chapter 34

Levitical prohibitions to be still in force and to apply to Gentiles for Herod was not a Jew.[165]

The second case referred to a man who had taken his father's wife (1 Cor 5:1-5). Paul describes this as an abomination so heinous that even the Gentiles would not do such a thing.[166] The text does not make it clear whether the man has married the woman or is simply living with her and nor does it say whether the father is still alive, although the choice of the word *porneia* – as used in Acts 15 – rather than *moixeia*, the Greek for adultery – is strongly suggestive of the fact that he was dead. Fisher and his allies argued that Paul was condemning sex outside marriage generally and that it had nothing to do with the Levitical prohibitions: Henry said the case was singled out because it was against the said prohibitions which forbade sexual relations with a father's wife regardless of whether the couple had married or not. Since it must be assumed that there was more than this single individual in Corinth engaging in extra-marital sexual intercourse, Paul's pointed demand that the man be excommunicated does suggest Henry's interpretation was correct.[167]

The Council of Jerusalem only forbade sex outside marriage (Fisher)

The Council of Jerusalem was the most important in Church history because it involved those of Jesus' disciples who were still alive, Paul and Barnabas plus the first head of the Christian Church, James, the brother of Jesus. It addressed the question of whether Gentile converts needed to follow the entire Jewish law and it determined that they did not. Its deliberations are recorded in Acts 15. What it did rule was that Christians must abstain from all *porneia*, a Greek word translated in the Vulgate as fornication. The problem in the early modern era was that there was no agreement about what that word meant. Robert Cawdrey's dictionary of 1604 used "uncleanness between single persons." Coles' definition in 1677 was almost the same: "Whoredom between unmarried persons." Higgins in 1572 had "lechery, whoredom properly in bed, adultery." Erasmus' *Paraphrases* on Matt 5:32 and 19:9 believed the word meant adultery. Aquinas regarded it both as intercourse between people who were betrothed but who had not yet taken final vows – and thus were married in

---

164 The Baptist would have read the scriptures in Hebrew which referred to sons at Deut. 25:5, so he may have considered the question irrelevant.

165 Pointed out in the *Determinations* p.23. The Baptist was martyred for his views and Fisher controversially told the legatine court that he was prepared to suffer the same fate though he regarded John as dying for a purely political reason rather than upholding the Torah, the view of Henry and pope Gregory the Great.

166 Evidently a highly politically incorrect comment in today's terms but a reminder that most Christians at this time were Jews.

167 The woman was not excommunicated because she was not a member of the church. If she had been, the same penalty would surely have applied since Paul would have known that Jewish law required both parties in any case of sexual misbehaviour to be punished.

the eyes of the church – but also as adultery.[168] In his *A Necessary Doctrine*, Henry explained the commandment against adultery as "all manner unlawful copulation between man and woman married and unmarried, and all manner of unlawful use of those parts, which be ordained for generation, whether it be by adultery, fornication, incest, or any other mean. And in lawful matrimony a man may break this commandment, and live unchaste with his own wife, if he do immeasurably or inordinately serve his or her fleshly appetite or lust."

The definition mattered because if it only meant intercourse between single people, it followed that the Apostles were saying that all those other sexual sins mentioned in the Torah such as adultery, rape, bestiality, homosexuality, incest, prostitution, intercourse with a brother's wife or widow, were all licit unless one of the parties was married. Modern Bible translations tend to use a more general definition of *porneia* as "sexual immorality" which is more accurate and takes into account the fact that things like adultery no longer carry the death penalty which they did in biblical times and which the Apostles would have assumed.[169] Fisher's strict definition of the word fornication was not indicative of him espousing modern liberal ideas on issues such as same-sex unions but just poor scholarship. During the debate, Fisher claimed that Judah sought to have Tamar punished for adultery rather than fornication and claimed great significance for this point arguing that as Onan had died, her peers clearly saw her as married to the third son. Had he looked at the Hebrew, he would have seen that the word *zanah* was used in Gen 38:24 meaning harlotry or fornication, not adultery which is *na'aph* and used in the Ten Commandments (Ex 20:14, Deut 5:18) and in Lev 20.

The pope issued a dispensation so it was OK (Katherine)

In 2002, the government presented a report to Parliament about Iraq's weapons of mass destruction. Subsequently, key facts in this report were found to be untrue. This did not stop the report being official any more than the fact that the document was official guaranteed it was true. On a death certificate of 1901, a girl is said to have died aged fifteen of fatigue. It is more probable that the fatigue was the symptom of an underlying undiagnosed condition which caused death rather than being the cause itself but the certificate was issued by a qualified medical practitioner who should know. Just because an authority figure issues a document does not mean it is true and nor does it make it ethical. Millions of Jews died in the Holocaust on the basis of correctly completed and properly authorised paperwork. We are accustomed to popes who are models of learning, piety and moral probity and who promote peace, though they generally keep out of politics. The dispensation for Henry to marry Katherine

---

168 John Higgins, *Huloets dictionarie* (1572), Robert Cawdrey, *A Table Alphabeticall of Hard Usual English Words* (1604), E Coles, *An English Dictionary* (1677), Aquinas *Summa* q62

169 The Apostles did not specifically prohibit other capital crimes such as murder though it would be foolish to think that this meant they were condoning such acts as Christian behaviour.

was issued by the notorious Julius II, a man whom even the most devout Roman Catholic struggles to defend. He was a war-mongering, lascivious, rapacious scoundrel who disgraced his office and he was substantially rewarded financially for his compliance by Katherine's parents.[170] Of course, a document's truth does not depend on the way it is obtained. The man buying a forged driving licence down a dark alley can probably physically drive a car the same as one who passed a test. Nonetheless, trying to justify a marriage on the basis of a decision by Julius II does set alarm bells ringing. Moreover, the argument misses the fundamental point made by Henry that the pope had no authority whatsoever to issue a dispensation for a union prohibited in the Bible and that should a pope order something against God's law, he should be ignored.

The precedent of Portugal shows the pope has power to dispense (Cajetan, Fisher)

Cajetan's argument that the decision of Julius II to dispense from the non-existent prohibition in Leviticus against marrying the sister of a deceased wife proved he had the power to do so, and Hughes' approbation of him, is chilling though the conclusion was not unique.[171] Three centuries earlier, the future Archbishop of Canterbury, Stephen Langton, was astonished when Alexander III ruled that a woman could leave her husband and become a nun. He wrote: "who would not have denied that the lord pope in the light of the saying in the Gospel "whomsoever God hath joined let no man put asunder" could give dispensation in a matter of this kind? But afterwards when the decretal was issued, any man who had previously denied it would say that the pope could dispense."[172] Fisher went so far as to tell Wolsey that since the pope "by his act declared that it is lawful to dispense in this case...this alone should determine the question."[173]

Yet, not everyone was so subservient. As Turrecremata observed in the fifteenth century, the church is bound by the law and if a pope issued a dispensation against the law of God, the dispensation would not be valid or set a precedent and the pope would be guilty of sin for issuing it.[174] Pope Adrian VI also noted that the existence of a precedent did not prove the action was right.[175]

It must be wondered whether all those who blithely talk about Henry being married to Katherine of Aragon and seeking a divorce seriously share Cajetan's opinion which effectively legitimates every atrocity ordered by every dictator in history by arguing a tyrant's acts prove he has the authority to do

---

170 See How did Katherine become Queen of England.
171 Hughes, *Reformation* p.170
172 D'Avray, *Papacy* p.160
173 LP 4.3158
174 E. B. Pusey, *Evidence Given before the Commission appointed to Inquire into the State and Operation of the Laws of Marriage* (1849) p.28. This was also Luther's position. Turrecremata's judgment appears in the *Determinations p.84*
175 George Hayward Joyce, *Christian Marriage* (1948) p.444

them. Until 1500, nobody – including the popes themselves – thought they had the power to dispense from the Levitical prohibitions.[176] The *Determinations* said: "he, which is of less power, cannot dispense in those things which be ordained by Him that is of greater power.... We may not think that the pope's licence in the degrees forbidden by God's law, is just and a rightful dispensation but rather an unrightful and an unreasonable dissipation and mis-ordering of the laws of God. ... Every Christian man, that knoweth this is to cry out against it and all to bespit and bespew it and to reprove and damn it as heretical." To ram the point home, Henry also quoted Jesus' own words at the Last Supper that those who loved God kept the law.[177]

If God can dispense from the Levitical prohibitions, so could Julius II (Harpsfield)

Seeking to counter Henry's correct assertion that Deut 25:5-10 was a dispensation, something he disputed, Harpsfield wrote: "If under the old law, which was a law of rigour and severity, there was a commandment given for this marriage for the relief and ease of a few persons, much more for the ease, relief, and safeguard of two most ample realms may the pope now dispense with this (i.e. Henry and Katherine's) marriage." Henry pointed out that "as sayeth our Saviour Christ, the servant is not bigger than the master, nor he that is sent bigger than he that sent him." (John 13:16)

Julius II dispensed for the sake of peace which is a good cause (Ortiz)

The dispensation said that it was to secure peace between England and Spain and this was repeated by all of Katherine's supporters but Henry's lawyers correctly pointed out that England and Spain had been at peace for years and they enjoyed a long-standing mutually beneficial political, military and trading alliance. There was therefore no motive to grant the dispensation, pressing or otherwise.[178]

Laws can be broken for good causes (Abell)

He cited here Tamar sleeping with her father-in-law and Lot's daughters drugging him in order to have sex with him and conceive children.[179] If God approved of these things because of the important goal on the part of the

---

176 Books sometimes state that the first dispensation against the Levitical prohibitions was in 1411 but that was the year in which John XXIII – who was not accepted as a valid pontiff at Rome – issued one for the Duke of Clarence to marry the widow of his half-uncle, a relationship not prohibited in Leviticus 18.
177 *Determinations*, pp.139, 143-145.
178 Charles IV of France had argued that the cause on the dispensation for his marriage to Blanche was totally untrue but the pope in 1322 disregarded that on grounds such things were unimportant. He did, however, grant an annulment on the basis of her mother being his godmother, a fact known when they married but not covered by the dispensation, see D'Avray, *Papacy,* pp.111, 119
179 Gen. 19:30-38; 38:13-30.

women – and Abell presumed God did because the women all had sons – then it was clear that the pope could similarly dispense from laws for a good cause. Henry denied that the pope had any such power. The end did not justify the means. Incest was wrong so no pope could issue a dispensation to permit it regardless of the cause. As Henry noted, the pope's title is Holy Father and as St Peter himself said, believers are to be holy (1 Pet. 1:14-16): incest is not holy.[180]

Denying the pope can dispense is blasphemy which is punishable by death (Abell, Fisher)

Fisher wrote that the pope "may dispense even with those things which the Apostles themselves have in the church ordained and with such things as have been decreed by any general council...for the pope hath his authority not of the councils but of God" and claimed that to "our high bishop the pope, authority was given to determine and decide all hard, dubious and litigious questions insurging upon Moses' law, yea with commandment that those persons should suffer death that showed themselves refractory and disobedient to his sentence." Abell agreed. Their loyalty to the queen and pope might be laudable but Katherine never suggested Henry should be executed for questioning the validity of the dispensation. It is an argument which highlights the extremes to which Henry's enemies would go and why they were regarded as dangerous men and why the death penalty was used to silence them.[181]

Henry's response to Fisher's reference to "Moses' law" was a reminder that the Torah "be not Moses' precepts but the commandments of God" as it states quite clearly throughout the scriptures and in Neh 10:29.[182]

Marriage to a brother's wife cannot be a mortal sin because Gregory the Great allowed people in such unions to receive Holy Communion (Fisher, Abell)

When the evangelist Augustine came to England in 597 to bring the Roman form of Christianity, he found Saxons who had married their brother's wives and he asked the pope what he should do about this.[183] He was told not to dissolve the unions and to welcome the new converts into the church as full

---

180 In 1481, Felino Sandeo, papal auditor, had claimed: "The pope for a reason can interpret and delimit divine law...He cannot entirely abrogate it because divine law is immutable." Quoted in Kelly, *Matrimonial Trials*, p.13
181 Henry's views on papal authority are discussed in the chapter "Was Anne a Protestant?"
182 In the Tanakh, the verse is Neh 10:30. Tyndale shared this error with Fisher, invariably referring to the Torah as if it was the work of Moses, in the *Practice of Prelates* explaining: "Moses in all his laws sought the glory of God and the pureness of his people."
183 Henry Gee and William Hardy, *Documents Illustrative of English Church History* (1896) pp.5-7. It was in answering this question that the pope established the rule that cousins should not marry which he derived from the general injunction in Lev 18:6 against sexual relations with those "near of kin."

members, which meant allowing them to receive the sacrament. In 1 Cor 11:29 it says that those who receive unworthily are consuming their own damnation so Fisher reasoned that marriage to a brother's wife could not be an abomination (Lev 18:16,29) because the pope would not have allowed people to eat and drink their own damnation. Henry observed that the pope did not support the unions, indeed Gregory said it was: "prohibited to marry with a sister-in-law because by the former union she is become the brother's flesh" describing such marriages as "heinous", "execrable" and "a grievous sin" because they were forbidden by God. If Christians should make such marriages "they are to be excluded from the communion of the Body and Blood of the Lord, although the offence is, in some measure, to be tolerated in those who have done it in ignorance."[184]

Marriage to a brother's wife was allowed by Innocent III (Cajetan)

This allegation related to a case in 1201 when some pagans in what is now Latvia were converted to Christianity having already married their brother's wives. Innocent ruled that the unions should not be dissolved provided that those affected had entered into the unions solely to raise up heirs for their deceased brothers. If they had married to raise up children for themselves, the unions were invalid. This precedent was the subject of vast amounts of debate during the annulment crisis with Henry's enemies claiming it was relevant because it demonstrated the pope's authority to rule on the matter and Henry pointing out that the situation was totally irrelevant because he and Katherine had not been pagans. Innocent's decision had been criticised by the Fourth Lateran Council of 1215 which ruled (canon 52): "it is more tolerable that some who have been united contrary to the laws of men be separated than that those who have been legitimately united separate in violation of the laws of God."[185] Innocent himself had been clear that his ruling only applied in the circumstances described and had no bearing on those who were Christian at the time they married.

First degree affinity is only a church law and the pope can change church law (Abell)

Affinity was regarded as first, second or third degree according to the relationship between the individuals and the shared ancestor. If they were on the same level, such as siblings or cousins, it was first degree, if lower down, second or third or more. The distinction was a creation of canon lawyers but the prohibitions are in Leviticus. Nobody disputed that the pope could dispense from laws made by the church but laws made by God were another issue.

---

184 This was not the line taken in the Bible which demanded the dissolution of marriages contracted against the law even where children had been born, Ezra 10: 11,19,44

185 H. J. Shroeder, *Disciplinary Decrees of the General Councils* (New York, 1917) pp.281-282. Innocent's bull was *Deus qui ecclesiam*.

Without consummation, there can be no affinity (Fisher, Abell, Katherine)

This was a highly controversial subject at the time. As the Jesuit historian, Henry Kelly has affirmed, the church's original position that affinity was based on vows not consummation was entirely in line with Leviticus: it was over a thousand years before the idea that any act of intercourse created it emerged.[186] Throughout the middle ages when Thomism dominated, affinity continued to be defined as beginning with vows but by around 1500, this belief was on the wane and affinity was generally seen as stemming only from sexual contact with public honesty being regarded as a separate impediment which stemmed from vows alone.[187] This was the Scotist view and that given in Gratian's *Decretum*.[188] The dispensation for Henry and Katherine was written at the time when legal views were changing and the use of the word 'perhaps' makes it impossible to know for certain which definition of the word affinity Julius had in mind. In either case, the distinction between affinity and public honesty was an invention of lawyers and only existed in canon law. As Cranmer noted in his 1533 verdict, English civil law defined affinity as "a propinquity arising from nuptials"[189] i.e. vows. The Bible had no concept of public honesty.

Both parties in the dispute did, nonetheless, cite the Bible. Those who favoured the idea of affinity stemming from intercourse, quoted Paul's statement that because Christians have the Holy Spirit within them, it is blasphemous to indulge in any form of sexual activity outside marriage as that would couple God to harlots (1 Cor 6:15-17). Those who accepted vows as the definition of affinity argued that the law which required a single man to marry a woman if he had sexual intercourse with her outside of marriage (Deut 22:28-29) indicated that the Torah did not regard the two as the same. It was also the case that adultery had never been regarded as creating bigamous marriages.[190] Generally, canon lawyers tried to avoid the use of a book which they found

---

186 Kelly, *Matrimonial Trials*, pp.33-34. Kelly notes that the "common sense reading" of Leviticus shows the prohibition on marrying a brother's wife relates to "the fact of the marriage not the fact of carnal knowledge." He observes the change of definition was primarily due to pressure from Germanic Christians who wanted to see church law brought into line with their own civil law, not because the cardinals of the time had received some new divine revelation

187 Further clouding the issue, in his *Commentary on Sentences of Peter Lombard*, IV, dist Xli, q.i, Aquinas defined affinity as being the result of cohabitation following vows. This only required the couple to live under the same roof: they did not need to have any form of sexual contact. Arthur and Katherine had shared a home for almost six months and shared a bed, as Katherine confirmed. The assumption in canon law was that they would have had intercourse regardless of what either party testified.

188 *Decretum*, p.2 cause 35 q.10 ch.1

189 The full verdict *Articuli Duodecim* is given in Nicholas Pocock, *Records of the Reformation* (1870) vol 1 pp.334-399 and discussed in Kelly, *Matrimonial Trials* pp.222-238

190 The Roman Catholic church only amended canon law to say that affinity came from vows in 1917.

worryingly imprecise, the word "wife" being used where they would insist upon betrothed or widow e.g. with regard to the Virgin Mary and to Tamar.

The reason for so much focus on this point was Katherine's claim to have been left a virgin by Arthur. Henry disputed that – and as her husband he was in a good position to know – but retorted that if she was a virgin, the dispensation was certainly invalid because it only covered affinity and not public honesty.[191]

The issue of Katherine's virginity was much discussed at the time and has been the subject of attention since. If Arthur said he had consummated it and Katherine said he had not, surely one of them was lying but which? In fact, they might both have been telling the truth. Definitions of what constituted consummation varied from lawyer to lawyer and over the centuries, considerable prurient debate had been held between popes and canonists – all committed celibates – on this. Some believed it was consummated if the woman had an orgasm even if there was no penetration. Others thought it was enough for the man to ejaculate even if it was not inside the bride – which led to discussions on how far away he could be! Then there were other problems such as if it could be consummated if they were standing up or if the woman did not have an orgasm, something believed at the time to be essential for procreation. More disagreements existed over the status of the union if the man penetrated but did not ejaculate. Erasmus admitted that "there is some doubt about incomplete or unnatural sexual acts" adding that being "known by only one man" was a form of virginity.[192] From today's perspective, it is all rather comical and it is likely that the topic proved fascinating for medieval students who may have found the other lectures on the canon law course a trifle soporific. In 1514, Henry's sister Mary married the French King, Louis XII. He was not present at the ceremony so his representative that evening, got into Mary's bed and rolled up one leg of his red hose and laid his naked thigh briefly against her own. This momentary contact by a third party was deemed full legal consummation of the union by the canon lawyers who witnessed it.[193]

Such debates serve to potentially explain why there was a disagreement about whether the match had been consummated or not. If Arthur and Katherine had both been told different things about what constituted consummation, both could answer the question in good faith while coming to alternative answers. We should not automatically assume that either of them, or Henry, were liars.

---

191 It also featured in the argument about Henry and Mary Boleyn, the canonists claiming this created affinity the same as marriage. It was not until 1861 that it was accepted in England that vows were needed to establish a marriage before intercourse could create affinity.
192 Erasmus, *Institution*, pp.270, 235.
193 LP 1.5337

The council of Neocaesarea did not condemn marriage to a brother's wife (Abell)

The council which took place in 315 decreed that a woman who had married two brothers should be denied the sacrament for life. It said that "at the hour of death she may, as an act of mercy, be received to penance, provided she declare that she will break the marriage, should she recover" but added that unless this happened, penance for herself and the man would be "very difficult," which Abell interpreted as meaning both would be damned.[194] Ordinary people, including Henry's supporters and every single scholar since, saw this as a clear condemnation of levirate marriage but Abell claimed the decree was issued not because of any concern about the ethics of the union or Leviticus but because the council was angry that the couple (he presumes it was a single case) had married without applying for a papal dispensation first. He went on to say that anyone who married without proper church authority should be punished and the union be declared null and void. On this last point at least Henry was in agreement. He argued all along that the dispensation of 1504 was invalid and hence his "marriage" to Katherine was invalid. Abell's claim about the motives of the delegates is totally without foundation. The decree was one of fifteen which sought to regularise clergy behaviour, including provision of Holy Communion. It had absolutely nothing to do with papal dispensations which did not even exist at the time and would not do so for centuries.[195]

Augustine accepted levirate marriage as lawful (Harpsfield)

Harpsfield argued because Augustine did not say marriage to a brother's wife was unlawful, it must be lawful. Henry did not reply to this point directly but would have argued this was a false assumption and poor logic. He might also have quoted Augustine's preface to the remark where he said that if a command prohibits something (as in Leviticus) it should be taken literally but if it commands something otherwise seen as a sin (as in Deuteronomy) it should be viewed as figurative e.g. "except ye eat the flesh and drink the blood" (John 6:53).

Only marriage to women of a higher generation are forbidden (Tyndale)

His conclusion was based on the Biblical teaching that a wife must obey her husband (Eph 5:22-23; 1 Pet 3:1; Col 3:18) and the commandment to honour thy parents (Ex 20:12). He reasoned that a man could not marry his mother, aunt or grandmother because he owed them respect as his seniors but

---

194 Canon 2. Abell mistakenly refers to it as the Council of Nicosia. The verdict was confirmed at the Council of Chalcedon in 451.
195 The first individual grant was to William the Conqueror in 1059 but this came eight years after he had married Matilda of Flanders, a union deemed illegal by the church because they were third cousins though the relationship was not prohibited in the Bible. Dispensations only started to become common in the later thirteenth century and then only amongst royalty and the nobility, the only people who could afford them.

he could marry his niece or daughter-in-law because they naturally owed him obedience as a man in a higher generation.[196] This did not apply with a sister or sister-in-law and hence Henry was free to marry Katherine. Tyndale says marriage within families was so beneficial that the ban on it was a sign of heathen ignorance.

It must be said that this is an argument which has not found much acceptance, either in his own time or today. The twenty-first century may be vastly more liberal than Tudor times and not base its laws on the Bible but there has yet to be a mass campaign for the legalisation of incest. Tyndale's comment "my reasons may not be good" may be one of the great under-statements of the age.

The law is different for princes (Abell)

The idea that popes would and should offer dispensations for princes which they would not do for ordinary people went in the face of Bible teaching that judges should not be influenced by the status or wealth of those before them (Ex 23:6-8, Lev 19:15; Deut 1:17, 16:18-20). The law was "thou shalt not uncover the nakedness of thy brother's wife" not "thou shalt not uncover the nakedness of thy brother's wife unless thou art a prince and thou art only doing it to promote peace between nations."

Both Leviticus and Deuteronomy are obsolete because celibacy is God's ideal (Harpsfield)

He justified this from a teaching by Tertullian that Deuteronomy was written at a time when people were required to go forth and multiply while Paul was writing when it was believed that the second coming of Jesus and end of the world was nigh and hence there was no time to enter into new unions (1 Cor 7;1,8,29). Harpsfield talks of the thousands of "most happy and blessed" monks and nuns across the country and describes this as a fulfilment of Isaiah 56:3 "Let not the eunuch say "behold, I am a dry tree." Henry would have agreed that celibacy was highly regarded by God but also have noted that Paul says that marriage is not a sin (1 Cor 7:36) and rules must therefore apply. Paul himself created a new rule that Christians must only marry other Christians (1 Cor 7:39) though this could be seen as an extension of the Old Testament law regarding marriage within the tribe.

the church only adopted the Levitical prohibitions to encourage Church growth (Abell)

"Those holy fathers and prelates did see and manifestly perceive that the charitable love and kindness that was wont to be among Christian people did sore diminish and decay. Wherefore, these holy fathers and prelates ... did limit our certain degrees of affinity and kindred in the which they supposed that

---

196 Henry repeats this theory about generations in his *A Necessary Doctrine*.

love would continue without the help of marriage...to the intent to spread abroad and sow love and charity by marriage."

Imaginative – and neglects to mention the Bible at all.

If Ferdinand of Aragon had proposed something evil with the union of Henry and Katherine, God would not have rewarded him (Fisher)

Fisher's argument here was that the New World had brought countless riches to Ferdinand of Aragon "the which great benefit, I suppose, God would never have employed upon him if he had so grievously offended his law and the law of nature" with his suggestion that Katherine marry Henry. As any historian would confirm, the New World was discovered in 1492, ten years before the idea of Henry and Katherine's union was mooted. Fisher did not take this theory to its logical conclusion that Henry was richer than he was himself so God must favour Henry's argument over his. In 1526, the pope had claimed that Henry abounded in money because God had seen his piety and goodness and wished to reward him.[197]

Ferdinand and Henry VII were wise princes and would not have suggested something evil (Katherine)

It is good that Katherine honoured her father and her father-in-law and thought they were perfect in wisdom but this was an argument based on sentiment alone not fact. Doubtless they did not propose the union from any desire to destroy her immortal soul by encouraging her to commit a mortal sin, but they were human beings. They made mistakes.

The fact that Henry has even had the idea of annulling the union means he has been possessed by a devil (Fisher). *He is Antichrist (*Sander*). Anne is the conduit of Satan* (Ortiz).[198]

This calumnious idea does not even merit rebuttal.

These therefore were the arguments thrown at Henry's case from different sides. Some might be viewed as having a modicum of merit while others just demonstrate new depths in scraping the barrel. With regard to canon law, Henry considered it as of less status than divine. With regard Bible interpretation, not only did he demonstrate the true behaviour of a humanist scholar in having the text analysed in Greek and Hebrew, he eschewed some of

---

197 LP 4.2315, see also 2290.
198 Nicolas Sander, *Rise and Growth* p.106. The word Antichrist appears in 2 John 7 and 1 John 2:22 and 4:3 which discuss the end of the world. Although some have associated the word with the beast in Revelation 13, the true definition can be found in 2 Thessalonians 2:3-11 where it describes a man who usurps the authority of God and who believes, and causes others to believe, that what is false comes from God. CSPS 4.2.960

the fanciful ideas of his enemies to follow the example of Jesus himself. In the Sermon on the Mount (Matt. 5-7), Jesus takes a variety of laws direct from the Torah and proceeds to explain them in line with conventional rabbinic practice. At no point did he launch into an aside about the definition of natural law or stop to clarify whether adultery could occur if a marriage was unconsummated, any more than at the Last Supper when he said "this is my body" he entered into some teaching about inner and outer signs and the precise means of grace.[199] These were concerns of canon lawyers and theologians. Henry upheld the common sense interpretation of the Bible and showed himself the true Defender of Faith. As Bishop Stephen Gardiner wrote: "he both obeyed God and obeyed truly."[200]

Conclusion

Henry's case was not weak and those who suggest that it was are not only barking up the wrong tree but located in a different forest. Both theologically and legally, his case was totally sound and vastly better than many other cases which were accepted by Rome. The reason for its non-acceptance at the time was a combination of politics and ignorance. The reason for its non-acceptance by many today is also chiefly ignorance, writers lacking an understanding of the Bible and canon law themselves and preferring either to draw quick and unsafe conclusions from their reading of two verses taken out of context from a modern English translation of the Bible, or else solemnly and uncritically citing the opinions of authors who are unashamedly partisan and selective in their accounts, such as Henry Ansgar Kelly and Herbert Thurston (Jesuit canon lawyers), as if they are expressing unquestionable truths.[201] The above analysis of the texts and the various arguments demonstrates the complexity of the case and inadequacy of these approaches. The other factor behind its frequent non-acceptance is sentiment: people feel sorry for Katherine and assume that Henry was wrong. That Katherine was a victim of what happened is undeniable but so was Henry and emotion should not be allowed to cloud judgment. As it says in the *Glass of Truth*, many "follow more affections and respects than God's Word only" but, as Henry quotes St Peter, "we must obey God rather than man." (Acts 5:29).[202] The more difficult question is not what grounds Henry possessed to secure an annulment but what grounds Julius

---

199 The catechism in the *Book of Common Prayer*, as memorised by all Anglicans until recently, defines a sacrament as: "an outward and visible sign of an inward and spiritual grace given unto us, ordained by Christ Himself, as a means whereby we receive the same, and as a pledge to assure us thereof."
200 Stephen Gardiner, *De vera obedientia. An Oration Made in Latine... Touching True Obedience (1553)* f.46. The original work was written in 1536.
201 Other notably partisan works include those by Parmiter and Hughes.
202 Also in the *Determinations*, p.150 "if God forbiddeth that which man commandeth, shall I hear man and be deaf and not hear God?"

had to issue the dispensation in the first place. It was Julius who had the weak case, not Henry. It was the issuing of the dispensation which was a novelty, not Henry's interpretation of the Bible.

Question – Was Henry married when he met Anne?

Answer
No. It follows that Anne Boleyn was not a scarlet woman and he could never have committed adultery with Mary Boleyn – or anyone else prior to 1532. The fact that Katherine had been wrongly accepted as his wife for many years does not mean that she was, any more than people believing slavery was right for years made that acceptable or that those who thought the earth was flat were correct. Katherine was simply the anointed queen.

Postscript

It must be remembered that Henry lived over two hundred years before Jean Astruc first questioned the Mosaic authorship of the Torah,[203] more than three hundred before archaeologists uncovered evidence of Canaanite religion separate from the Bible and over four hundred before the discovery of the Dead Sea Scrolls. Nobody at the time, whether they supported Henry or Katherine, doubted that both Leviticus and Deuteronomy were by Moses and written by him at the dictation of the Almighty. Today, many experts suggest Deuteronomy dates from the time of King Josiah (mid seventh century BC) while the holiness code in Leviticus may have been compiled during the exile (late sixth century BC), though in both cases these dates are speculative and only relate to the written form and not the oral tradition which is older by many centuries.[204] Thus, modern Biblical criticism sees Leviticus as later than Deuteronomy which resolves the conflict between Lev 18:16 and Deut 25:5 by showing that levirate marriage had died out very quickly as it was viewed as inconsistent with godliness. Henry was right all along!

---

203 Jean Anstruc, *Conjectures sur les memoires originaux dont il paroit que Moyse s'est servi pour composer le livre de la Genese* (Bruxelles 1753)
204 It should be remembered that there remain Jews and Christians today who continue to accept this. The differing opinions of modern Biblical critics are far from universally accepted and subject to continual revision as new evidence comes to light.

Was Anne the cause of the breakdown of Henry's 'marriage' to Katherine?

Henry beamed as he held his infant son up to the window.

"Look," he said. "See how busy everyone is getting things ready for the tournament."

His baby gurgled as Henry pointed out the brightly coloured tents, the horses being exercised, the workmen painting the pavilions.

"This is all for you," Henry assured him. "Everything I have will be yours one day. I'll teach you to ride and hunt and we will have such a wonderful time together."

The infant opened his blue eyes and Henry grinned even more broadly, tears of joy in his eyes. He was certain that his son could understand every word. He was so beautiful, surely no child had ever been so perfect. He laughed as the baby's fingers reached toward one of the jewels on Henry's coat.

"Not yet, my son."

The little prince seemed to share his father's good humour as he reached for Henry's finger and gripped it tightly.

"Oh yes, I promise you the best life ever that a prince could have," Henry whispered as he kissed his son. "Just you wait and see."

Ten days later, the little prince's body, still wrapped in his christening gown, was carried out for burial. He was fifty-four days old.

There are a number of readers at this point who will be tutting at the inclusion of the above. Surely such material belongs in a novel and not in a serious academic work. Historians are meant to be objective and analytical and adhere strictly to the evidence. This is entirely true, but historians are also meant to use their common sense. The fact that we have no evidence for Henry cradling his son in his arms or being devastated by his death, does not mean that such things did not happen. As anyone who has lost a child will know, it is not an experience which lends itself to objectivity. In Henry's case, months of waiting for the child to be born, of making plans, of dreaming dreams had been followed by unsurpassed joy and relief when the new arrival appeared strong and healthy. Those first two months passed happily with no sign of any problem – and then, suddenly, the prince died. Even in the twenty-first century, infant cot deaths occur and doctors are unable to explain why the child who was tucked in happily one evening simply never wakes up again. The cavalier attitude adopted by some writers that people in Tudor times were used to high levels of infant mortality so did not experience pain, is both offensive and wrong. Cancer is common today but do those who lose somebody to it not feel the loss? And yet virtually no writer when they draw out their family tree for the Tudors even includes this prince. He has been airbrushed from history as if he did not exist. If they had lost a child, would they want it treated this way? One of the most common complaints made by people today who lose a child is about those who studiously avoid mentioning the child's existence or make some comment about having another one as if the life of a child can be compared to replacing an empty packet of biscuits. Katherine had carried the prince for nine months in her body, did she forget so easily? No, the death of the infant Prince Henry in February 1511 was a watershed moment for both King and Queen and the fictionalised account of Henry and his son at the window has been included for a serious reason: history is about people and if we want to understand Henry's behaviour, we need to start by accepting he was a human being and that like everybody else, his actions and beliefs were shaped by his experiences of life.

When Henry made his vows to Katherine in 1509, he would have anticipated having children. He had been one of eight and she one of at least six.[1] Henry and Katherine went on to have six of their own. The first pregnancy ended with a stillborn daughter. The second, was the prince who lived for two months. A further son was born two and a half years later but he died very soon after birth and the lack of any known name, suggests he did not survive even long enough for the midwife to baptise him. A year later came another son who seems to have either been born dead or lived for only minutes. The fifth child came three years later and grew up to become the infamous Bloody Mary. Finally, in November 1518, a month short of her thirty-third birthday, Katherine delivered a stillborn daughter of eight months gestation.

Even today, in a secular age, any couple who lost five children in ten years – and there may have been other miscarriages along the way which occurred too early to be recorded – would be screaming out for answers. If the doctors could not provide them, which they certainly could not in Tudor times, they might be prompted to think "someone up there has got it in for me." Although Henry was initially supportive of Katherine with these losses, inevitably they put a strain on the relationship. As Katherine buried her grief in more prayers, fasting and pilgrimages, Henry railed against God with the passion of Job. Why was this happening? Moreover, other countries watching this pattern of death started to wonder too. Just days after Katherine lost her third child in the autumn of 1513, Emperor Maximilian requested a change to the matrimonial agreement between his grandson and Henry's sister to provide for their succession if Henry died without issue.[2] A year later, a Venetian at

---

1 Ferdinand and Isabella had five children who survived infancy– Isabella, Juana, Maria and Katherine plus a son Juan. Maria's twin did not survive and the seven year gap between the first two children may indicate that there had been other unsuccessful pregnancies. Four of Henry and Elizabeth's children reached maturity – Arthur and Henry plus Margaret (later Queen of Scotland) and Mary (Queen of France then Duchess of Suffolk).

2 François Foppins (ed.), *Lettres du Roy Louis XII* vol.4 (1712) p.239

Rome reported that the French believed Henry was about to annul his union with Katherine because he was unable to have living children by her.³

The loss of these children, combined with what was probably a very difficult atmosphere at home, resulted in Henry losing control in the autumn of 1518. Henry's two year old daughter Mary was married to the seven month old Dauphin, heir to the French throne, on 5th October. Katherine was seven months into her final pregnancy at the time and although she did not openly oppose the union, the Imperialists were actively seeking to prevent it.⁴ The only cheering thought for them was that Katherine might have a son which would make Mary's marriage less politically important as the son would replace her as heir to the English throne. However, as the Venetian ambassador noted, there was considerable concern about the pregnancy.⁵ It is possible, that Katherine herself had noticed a lack of movement in the child. Certainly, her condition gave her every excuse to avoid most of the celebrations laid on for the event. Henry, however, entered into them wholeheartedly and it was at this time that he committed adultery, not once but twice.

Bessie Blount was born between 1499 when her parents married and autumn 1500, presuming she was twelve when she first appeared at court.⁶ Henry had therefore known her for some years. At Christmas 1514 she danced with Henry VIII, an event which has caused some writers with febrile imaginations to describe this as evidence of him having an affair with her for at least five years. Yet, there is no reason to draw such a conclusion.⁷ In the first place, Henry would have danced with many ladies instead of Katherine that evening as she was still recovering from the birth of a child a month before and hence unable to participate. Ordinarily, Henry led the dancing with his sister, Mary, but she was in France. The Christmas Day masque was a major court event with hundreds of people present.⁸ It is likely that people remembered Henry and Bessie's dance because it was put on to amuse the guests. Henry was

---

3   CSPV 2.479. The letter from France referenced was dated 15th August. At the time, Anglo-Spanish relationships were strained with the Spanish ambassador leaving London a month later, CSPV 2.503. Katherine was actually around five to six months pregnant at the time but the unnamed author of the letter clearly did not know that.
4   LP 2.4479. The prospect of a united England and France would have been a direct threat to both Spain and the Low Countries, both of whom were under Habsburg control.
5   CSPV 2.1093. Cardinal Campeggio was in England at the time and attended Mary's wedding. Sebastian Giustinian, *Four years at the Court of Henry VIII* trans. Rawdon Brown vol. 2 (1854) p.237
6   Beverley Murphy, *Bastard Prince* (2001) pp.17-18. In May 1513, Bessie first appeared on the payroll when she received wages for the period from 8th May 1512. LP 2. King's Book of Payments, 1513 p.1461
7   In 1985, Diana, Princess of Wales famously danced with John Travolta but nobody interpreted that as a sign of them having a sexual relationship.
8   LP 2 Revels Accounts no 7, 25th December 1514 p.1501. Anne Boleyn's father and brother (then a child) both appeared in the same masque.

a grown man over six feet tall and Bessie was a child of fourteen and probably about four feet in height. It was memorable in the same way that Shirley Temple dancing with Bill 'Bojangles' Robinson or Buddy Ebsen was memorable, not because there was anything sexual involved but because it was funny.[9] Although the legal age of consent for women was twelve, it was accepted that this related to an ability to enter into the contract of marriage and was not indicative of them being ready for a sexual relationship. There is absolutely no evidence that at any time of his life, Henry indulged in sexual activities with young teenagers and indeed he opposed the practice believing that it put the girl's health at risk.[10] However, in the autumn of 1518, Henry did get carried away and the result was a conception.

We do not know for certain how Henry reacted to Bessie's pregnancy. The chances are that he was horrified. He had been a faithful husband and took the sin of adultery seriously.[11] In his *Assertio*, he wrote: "all generation out of wedlock is damnable."[12] There is no doubt that he loved the company of women and that he was a flirt. He was also a generous man who enjoyed to give gifts and see the pleasure that resulted. It does not follow that he jumped into bed with every woman that he met. Sex was not a leisure activity designed for the enjoyment of the participants to Henry or his contemporaries but a work of procreation which is why it only belonged within marriage. Lust for women was sinful. Henry wrote that God had forbidden men to "thirst after stolen waters of other men's cisterns but also not to inebriate ourselves with our own."[13] In this he was following the teaching of Jesus who had said that a man looking on a woman lustfully was as guilty of adultery as the one who actually committed the sin (Matt 5:28). Getting Bessie pregnant would have caused

---

9 In 1472, a visiting ambassador similarly commented when Edward IV at 6'3" led the dancing with his six year old daughter, Elizabeth, the future mother of Henry VIII, Amy Licence, *Edward IV* (2016) p.182.

10 LP 4.2974, 2981. Henry's grandmother, Margaret Beaufort, had been damaged by giving birth at just thirteen and she would have influenced his opinion,

11 The story sometimes repeated of Henry's relationship with the one of Duke of Buckingham's sisters, Lady Anne Stafford, a married lady, rests solely on the report of the Spanish ambassador who claimed that this sister was "said to be" a favourite of the King while the other was the favourite of the queen. An argument had ensued which the ambassador admitted he did not understand due to his unfamiliarity with the language. LP 1.474, CSPS Supplement no 474.

12 Henry VIII, *Assertio Septem Sacramentorum or Defence of the Seven Sacraments*, ed. Louis O'Donovan (New York, 1908) p.384. In 1535, John Hale – a renowned enemy of the King – reported that he had heard a story two years earlier that Henry had kept women at Farnham for his entertainment when visiting Richard Foxe, Bishop of Winchester, LP8.567. Henry did indeed have a hunting lodge there but the records show he visited it only in the autumn of 1514 and 1517 when he was accompanied by Katherine of Aragon, LP 2 Book of Payments pp. 1465, 1476. The Queen's presence does not preclude the rumour being true but surely makes it rather improbable..

13 *Assertio* p.384.

Henry to seek absolution and separate from her, though he supported her and her child for the rest of their lives.[14]

Yet, a part of him was also pleased as it assuaged the sorrow at the death of another child and at Christmas, by which time he would have known about the baby on the way, it appears he got rather drunk and wound up in bed with Mary Boleyn. There has been much speculation over the years about the timing of this event but Reginald Pole, writing in 1538, observed that Mary had been Henry's mistress and given that he left England in February 1519 and did not return until the spring of 1527, it follows that the relationship had to have begun before he left or he would not have known anything about it.[15] How long it lasted is another question. Given that Katherine was probably cold shouldering Henry for getting her maid-of-honour pregnant and was still mourning the loss of what would turn out to be her last baby, it may have continued through the Christmas season but there is no reason to suppose that it extended much beyond that. Writers who have claimed that it continued through her marriage to William Carey, which took place in February 1520, and that she even had Henry's child, are way off the mark. Henry would not have cuckolded his own cousin and he himself admitted to having only ever fathered the one bastard.[16] In 1529, Darcy noted that Henry had only had one mistress and the chronicler Hall, who knew many at the court well, concurred.[17] Neither Katherine of Aragon nor members of Henry's own bodyguards appear to have been aware of the relationship so it was clearly neither serious nor long lasting.[18] Chroniclers such as Hall and Cavendish were either similarly in the dark or thought it totally insignificant and nor did any overseas ambassador

---

14 Dean John Barlow confirmed in his recollections of 1532 that the relationship did not extend into Bessie's marriage, LP 5.1114; CSPS 4.2.967. It may be implied from his reaction to the idea that Henry would never have entered into a relationship with a married woman.
15 F E Bridgett, *Life of the Blessed John Fisher* (New York, 1890) p.148. Pole's statement that Henry kept Mary as his mistress for a long time can be discounted as he was not in the country so knew nothing about it. Pole's date of departure is sometimes stated to be later than this but in April 1519, he wrote to Henry VIII to advise him of his safe arrival in Padua, a journey which would have taken around six weeks, or longer if he had stopped to visit Paris en route – LP 3.198
16 Murphy, *Bastard Prince* p.5. The fact that Henry gave gifts to Carey's children was undoubtedly because they were part of his family, Carey being his cousin as well as his friend. Mary had a son in 1525 and a daughter whose date of birth is uncertain. There may have been miscarriages or other children who died in infancy: history only tends to record survivors. If she only had two children in eight years, it would not suggest she was particularly fertile.
17 LP 4.5570. H. Ellis (ed.), *Hall's Chronicle* (1809) p.703.
18 Throckmorton, esquire of the body to Henry from 1511 onwards and sometime servant of Wolsey, was told about Mary Boleyn by Friar Peto years later, LP 11.952. This raises the question of how Peto knew and the disturbing thought that he was guilty of revealing something learnt in the confessional.

ever mention her.[19] Also unaware of the existence of this relationship was the author of the 1531 Determinations who spent seven pages highlighting the prohibition on a man having sexual relations with two sisters – something he would not have dared write had he known.[20] It is worth noting that Henry's privy purse expenses show no gifts to either Bessie or Mary, a stark contrast to his later relationship with Anne whom he showered with presents.

For Wolsey, Henry's behaviour was indicative of the fact that he was being led astray by a coterie of young friends who were over familiar and more interested in encouraging him in wild behaviour than in serious matters of state. Henry obviously accepted this judgment and repented because he agreed to have the said gentlemen who were deemed to be bad influences, sent abroad.[21] Wolsey drew up a list of issues which needed to be addressed and together with the King, began to tackle them. The list included the government of Ireland.[22]

Meanwhile, in June 1519, Bessie Blount had a son, a healthy one, and one who with every passing year seemed more sturdy and princely than ever.[23] For Henry, this was a cataclysmic moment of awakening because it proved that the failure to father a healthy son on Katherine was not his fault. Modern medical understanding would obviously question this but that was what Henry and everyone around him believed. Having a healthy son was a sign of macho pride, a proof of virility. Moreover, the fact that God had apparently rewarded him for a relationship which Henry would have presumed at the time was adulterous and sinful, meant he must have made a mistake somewhere. God did not punish virtue and reward wickedness, so it followed that his relationship with Katherine itself must be wrong.

It took time for the repercussions of this to sink in. It must be assumed that Henry had experienced periods of doubt as his children by Katherine died but he would have stoically put that down to God's will and carried on. Indeed, after his son's birth, he returned to Katherine and by his own deposition, continued to sleep with her until 1524 in the hope of having another child.[24] At

---

19 Given Cavendish's hatred of Anne Boleyn, he would surely have mentioned it had he known. Ambassadors were famed for their gossip so the omission is significant.
20 Edward Fox, *The determinations of the moste famous and mooste excellent vniuersities* (London: 1531) pp. 42-49. The author worked with the King who approved the text.
21 LP 3.246. The King of France found it all rather comical and gleefully reported the comments made to him by the gentlemen that Henry had "an old deformed wife, while he himself is young and handsome." CSPV 2.1230. Francis had not met Katherine himself at this point.
22 LP 3.576
23 Alfred Suckling, *Antiquities and Architecture of the County of Essex* (1845) p.27 says he was born on the 15th.
24 Letter of Grinaeus to Bucer dated 10th September 1531, quoted in Gilbert Burnet, *History of the Reformation of the Church of England* with introduction by Nicholas Pocock (Oxford, 1865) vol 1 p78. Grinaeus had visited England that summer and met both Henry and Anne and he obtained his information directly from the King. When Campeggio mentioned this long cessation of marital relations to Katherine in

this point, Katherine's menopause began and he separated from her although he continued to live under the same roof.[25] There is nothing to suggest that at this time, he planned to actually leave her. No man decides to leave the woman to whom he has been attached for some two decades overnight, particularly when he is a devout Roman Catholic.

The years 1519 and 1520 saw the country plunged into severe trouble with two failed harvests and exceptionally high rates of mortality due to the sweating sickness. It is possible that Henry pondered if this was a sign of God's displeasure because Lev. 26:14-32 said that a failure to keep God's law would result in the land being punished by drought, disease and death. What is certain is that in 1522 or 1523, Henry discussed his doubts about the legality of the union with his confessor, Longland, who in turn sought advice from Dean John Barlow. Longland told Barlow that Henry was in a very distressed state because he still loved Katherine.[26] After due thought and study, Longland, a noted scholar, confirmed the King's suspicions. According to Harpsfield, he later told his chaplain that "he did sore forethink himself and repented afterward" because "there was never any one thing that did so much and so grievously nip his heart as did that his consent and doing toward the divorce" but this seems improbable.[27] Longland remained until his death in 1547, a supporter of Henry's supremacy, of the dissolution of the monasteries, the rights of the future Elizabeth I and the introduction of an English Bible. In January 1534, Chapuys had reported that Longland had said he wished he had never been a royal confessor or councillor but he claimed that the comments had been made in reaction to Henry's daughter, Mary, being given poor lodgings.[28] It is almost certain that Harpsfield deliberately took a comment out of context for polemical purposes. Henry's upset at this point would be labelled today cognitive dissonance, a period of extreme psychological stress due to holding simultaneously conflicting beliefs. i.e. that God was just and punishing him and Katherine for their "marriage", and also that God's representative in the form of the pope had blessed the said "marriage" and required it to continue until death.

1529, she did not deny it.

25 By July 1525, English diplomats were aware of this fact and they told the Emperor of it– LP 4.1484. Henry himself declared that he would have no more children in March 1525 – LP 4.1212. The Emperor's awareness of her sterility was a prime motivating factor for his behaviour during the annulment crisis. He was less interested in Katherine's well being than in ensuring Mary was the heir, a woman whom he would have hoped to marry to one of his kin with a view to absorbing England into the Habsburg empire.

26 LP 5.1114. As the original conversation was probably held in confessional, there would have been no documentation. There may have been earlier discussions with someone in 1520 or 1521 when Henry was preparing his response to Luther who had written his opposition to unions contracted against the Levitical prohibitions.

27 Nicholas Harpsfield, *The Life and Death of Sir Thomas More, Knight* (1557) ed. Katherine Stearns and Alexander Taylor (Dallas, 2020) p.15

28 LP 7.14

Yet Henry was no ordinary man but a king and so issues related to his "marriage" inevitably had a political implication. His uncle, Edward V, had been deposed due to a scurrilous rumour that his parents' marriage was invalid, a rumour spread by Richard III who usurped the throne. Edward V had then been murdered in the Tower – not a fate Henry would have wished on his daughter. Previous to that, unfounded rumours about the legitimacy of the marriage of the "Black Prince" to Joan of Kent had been spread by those who wanted John of Gaunt to succeed Edward III rather than the son of that union. In 1370, the pope had threatened to annul the "Black Prince's" marriage – despite it being confirmed by Urban V and Innocent VI – and declare the son illegitimate simply because the pope was French and England was at war with France.[29] Clarity of Henry's situation was vital.

The fact that Henry only had a daughter was perceived to be at best a risk, at worst a problem. The Venetian ambassador noted how everybody wanted a prince.[30] For all those who have grown up in the successful reign of Elizabeth II and who are aware of the similarly successful reigns of Elizabeth I (1558-1603) and Victoria (1837-1901)[31], this may seem misogynistic but the desire was universal at the time. Monarchs of this period were not constitutional but had full personal rule. They were expected to lead their troops into battle, devise and conduct foreign and economic policy, be a fountain of justice, get involved in inheritance disputes and the prosecution of heretics and rebels. Back in England's history, when Matilda had been the sole surviving child of her father Henry I, the result had been a bloody civil war which lasted thirteen years and ended when said Matilda ceded her claim to her son who in turn became Henry II in 1154. In 1455 a second civil war began in England which lasted until 1485 causing thousands of deaths across the country: this was less than forty years ago so well within living memory and nobody wanted a repeat of that. Significantly, at the end, neither Margaret Beaufort nor Elizabeth of York had been felt to have viable claims on the throne and so Henry Tudor being Margaret's son and Elizabeth's husband had become king.[32]

---

29 Penny Lawne, *Joan of Kent* (2015) pp. 135-138,182. The "Black Prince" was Edward, Prince of Wales, eldest son of Edward III and elder brother of John of Gaunt. He died before his father leaving his young son to become Richard II.
30 Giustinian, *Four Years*, vol 2 p.237
31 Also Queen Anne (1701-14) though she is less famous.
32 Much has been written about the Tudor claim to the throne. The childless Richard II had been the undisputed king when he was usurped by his cousin in 1399. Henry VI, grandson of the usurper left no son so the throne passed to Edward IV who was descended from two of Edward III's sons, the second and fourth. In 1485, Elizabeth of York was his eldest surviving child. Margaret Beaufort was a descendant of Edward III's third son. The Beauforts were legitimised by the pope in 1396, *Calendar of Papal Registers*, vol. 4 no 545. Parliament accepted this and Richard II confirmed their rights to inherit on 6th February 1398. Henry IV decided to exclude them from the succession because he had three sons of his own at the time and wished to protect their interests. He did not seek Parliamentary approval for this,

Although Henry was born after the war ended, he still had experience of the dangers of civil disturbance. In 1497, when a child of almost six, he had been forced to flee for his life with his mother to the Tower. Having lived through such a traumatic event, he understood the situation differently to those who had not. Today, historians spend hours studying memoirs, film footage, records and sometimes even engage in reconstructions of war, but whilst in factual terms they are likely to know more about an event than the soldier going over the top or the mother in a dugout clutching her screaming baby as enemy planes swoop overhead, no amount of dedicated research will ever generate the understanding produced by personal experience. Knowing from hindsight that the area where the mother sheltered would not be hit might give rise to a conclusion that she was in a low risk area but she did not know that and her fears would have had a huge impact on her day to day existence and her relationship with her baby. Whilst we cannot know exactly how Henry was affected by his experience, we can be certain that the memory of it, together with the accounts told him by his parents and others of that generation, gave him a very real horror of civil war and the implications of a disputed succession. When he spoke about the risk being a factor in his need to have a son, he was being utterly genuine, not making an excuse. The concern of Henry and his advisers that a female heir would not be accepted was not unreasonable at the time. In 1376, Edward III had ruled out both female heirs and females passing on their claims to the throne.[33]

If Henry turned to France, he saw a country which employed Salic law to prevent the accession of a female ruler.[34] His brother-in-law, Louis XII, had left two daughters named Claude and Renée but neither had been permitted the throne.[35] Claude de Seyssel had argued that such a law was vital to prevent the kingdom falling into the hands of "a man from a foreign nation which is both pernicious and dangerous: for a foreigner has been brought up differently, has other habits, another language and a way of life that that of the country which he has come to rule."[36] It was not simply a question of cultural clash, a wife had to obey her husband which meant that her own country would become subservient to his rather than an independent country and this could lead to asset stripping or being drawn into expensive wars. There was also the possibility of her leaving to live in her husband's country and thus creating a dangerous power vacuum.[37]

---

simply wrote by hand a marginal note in 1407 *excepta dignitate regali* against the original Act. For more detail and discussion on the legitimacy of such a note see William Stubbs, *The Constitutional History of England* vol.3 (Oxford, 1878) pp.56-60.

33 Ian Mortimer, *The Reign of Henry IV* (2008) pp.31-32.
34 England had tried this but rejected it *sexum excludendo femininum, ibid.* p.56
35 Francis I had married Claude to enhance his own claim to the crown.
36 Claude de Seyssel, *La Monarchie de France* (Paris, 1515) pp.112-113.
37 When Princess Elizabeth married Prince Philip in 1947, she promised to obey him even though she was heir presumptive. Upon her coronation, he promised to obey

In Spain, Katherine's father had declared his own daughter Juana insane when she became Queen of Castile so that he could continue to rule in her stead.[38] After Ferdinand's death, Katherine's nephew, the future Emperor, continued to keep his mother shut away telling her that Ferdinand was still alive, meanwhile having himself proclaimed King of Aragon as well as Castile.[39] Henry's own father had protested that Juana seemed totally sane and capable to him[40] but the Habsburg family combined to say otherwise and so ensure male succession. It was hardly the sort of behaviour to convince Henry that if his daughter Mary did become queen, her rights would be honoured. Indeed, in the marriage negotiations for her with the Emperor and then with the Duke of Orleans, it was admitted that any man she married would automatically become King of England.[41] It would be an understatement to say that this was not an attractive prospect to people. The English were not internationalists and they wanted to be ruled by an English person, not a Frenchman or a Spaniard. The rebellion when Mary did become queen and marry Philip would not have surprised her father and if Philip had actually stayed in England and pursued his role as king instead of hurrying overseas to escape his unloved wife, it may be supposed that there would have been further unrest and quite possibly civil war.

Moreover, if Henry had sought for examples of successful female rulers, he would have had some difficulty. Katherine's mother had been the fearsome Isabella of Castile who had introduced the famous Spanish Inquisition as well as passed the Alhambra decree which led to the persecution, deportation and forced conversion of thousands of Jews, plus spearheaded the conquest of Granada which led to the deaths of thousands of Moslems as well as sought the destruction of native people in the New World. Contemporaries saw her as a champion for Christian evangelism but as later events would show, the English had no desire for tyrants on their throne. The Low Countries were governed by Margaret of Savoy, but her powers were restricted with her ministers being appointed by the Emperor who retained control of foreign policy, finance, war and patronage.[42] Henry's sister was Queen of Scotland and had authority there because her son, the King, was a minor, but the chaos and bloodshed which ensued was not liable to encourage anyone to defend female rulers. How far the

---

her as his monarch, though it is said he continued to rule in the home.
38 Geoffrey Parker, *Emperor* (Yale, 2019) p.52
39 Parker, *Emperor* pp.79-80
40 Berwick y Alba, *Correspondencia de Gutierre Gomez de Fuensalida, embajador en Alemania, Flandes e Inglaterra 1496-1509* (Madrid 1907) pp.461-2
41 LP 3.1150; LP 4.2651. The same sentiments would be expressed during the talks about Elizabeth marrying Angoulême by the Imperialist envoy to France in August 1534 and by Cromwell, writing on behalf of Henry, in May 1535 when he spoke of the likelihood of "the said Duke of Angoulême shall succeed the King's Highness in the Imperial Crown of this Realm in the right and title of the said Lady Princess." See LP 8.793 SP vol.7 p.612 "in case "; C. Weiss (ed.), *Papiers d'Etat du Cardinal de Granvelle (Paris, 1841)* vol. 2 p.146
42 Parker, *Emperor* p.23

problems were due to her mismanagement and how far the behaviour of the lords contributed is an issue for later historians to discuss but Henry certainly had no confidence in Margaret's abilities and nobody in England thought otherwise.

For people today, accustomed to a clear line of succession, the existence of confusion about the identity of the heir seems strange. Surely it was Mary, Henry's only child? Not necessarily. In October 1518, the Venetian ambassador, Sebastian Giustinian, wrote that if Henry died without a son, it was thought that the Duke of Buckingham would succeed and that failing him, Charles Brandon "has great hopes of the crown in right of his wife."[43] In May 1521 it was revealed that Buckingham believed he would become king because a prophecy had said "the King would have no issue male of his body." [44] Today, we would assume that following Henry and Mary it would be Henry's elder sister, Margaret, and her children, and only in event of that line becoming extinct would the crown pass to his younger sister, Mary and her children by Brandon. Then, it was not so simple. Princesses who married foreign rulers usually gave up their rights to the succession but unusually Margaret did not do so when she married James IV of Scotland.[45] When Mary married Charles of Burgundy, her rights to the English throne were explicitly included in the treaty and in a supplementary agreement which Henry made with Emperor Maximilian and Margaret of Burgundy in October 1513, it was stated that if Henry died without heirs, the crown would pass to his sister Mary and her children.[46] Even without this, the idea that the English would wish to be ruled by a king from an enemy country – and in Henry's lifetime, Scotland was an enemy – would have been viewed as unacceptable. It was a case of political practicality. Had a major incident wiped out George V and his heirs in 1916, nobody would have wanted to welcome the Kaiser as next King of England regardless of any blood right.

Henry, therefore, was in a difficult situation. His 'wife' was past childbearing and it was questionable whether his daughter would be accepted as

---

43   Giustinian, *Four Years*, vol. 2 p.315-316.
44   LP 3.1284. The prophecy was made in 1514 but only became known to Henry at Buckingham's trial. Another which emerged at the trial was made in 1520 "that neither the King nor his heirs should prosper."
45   The marriage contract was signed in January 1502 when Henry VII had two sons living, Arthur and Henry. See Rymer, *Foedera* (1725), vol. 12 pp.790-797.
46   François Foppins (ed.), *Lettres du Roy Louis XII* vol.4 (1712) p.239. Rymer, *Foedera*, vol 13, pp.236-239. CSPS 1.558. The agreement came just days after Henry received news that Katherine had miscarried their third child, a boy. This promise was why toward the end of his life, Henry specified that Mary's heirs should follow his own, a decision followed by his son Edward VI and which is why Lady Jane Grey, who was Mary's grand-daughter, came to the throne. Jane's mother, Frances, was still alive but had been excluded by both Henry VIII and Edward VI for some reason. Nobody challenged this, including Frances herself and her husband, so it would seem likely that she had some disability which was obvious to all who knew her but never recorded in any documentary source for later generations.

his heir. Even if the English accepted her, there was likely to be war as European rulers probably would not. An incident on 10th March 1524 must have highlighted the risk. On that date, Henry was placed in "great jeopardy of death" when his brother-in-law's spear hit him in the face shattering his helmet, an accident blamed on the Marquess of Dorset for allowing Henry to ride out with his visor up. Henry made light of it and was not seriously injured but it was a reminder to everyone of how the fate of the kingdom rested on this one man surviving until he had an heir who was adult and capable of ruling. An eight year old girl was nobody's idea of a suitable heir.[47]

It is necessary to give an overview of the political situation leading up to the annulment crisis which began in 1527 before looking at Anne's entry to the situation and the timing of the final breach with Katherine.

The Political Route to Annulment

When the teenage Henry had come to the throne, his first desire had been to go to France and secure a great victory like his hero Henry V. There had been an invasion of France but the victories were on a much smaller scale and in 1518, a peace treaty was signed. In 1519, Katherine's nephew, who had previously been king of Spain and ruler of the Low Countries, became Holy Roman Emperor and with that gained territory in Germany and Italy. This was perceived as a threat by France and war broke out. Henry allied with the Emperor and in 1522 agreed to marry his heir and daughter to him when she was of age and to join him in a military expedition against France. That led by Brandon in 1523 got within seventy miles of Paris but had to turn back due to a failure of Imperial support. The defection of the Duke of Bourbon from France led to renewed efforts but the Emperor continued to let Henry down which unsurprisingly made the King very angry. War was very expensive and considerable sums were being spent for no gain. In the spring of 1524, secret peace negotiations were opened with France (LP 4.170) but progress was slow and the fact that Francis led his army into northern Italy into land claimed by the Emperor in the autumn, did not help. Henry was legally bound by treaty to support the Emperor and in early 1525 he was still sending money to the Imperial army (LP 4.1017, 1102, 1237). In February, the situation changed dramatically. As the pope was seeking to create a league of Italian states to unite behind Francis, whom he expected to be victorious, and against the Emperor, the tables were turned by the Imperial army at Pavia, in which battle the King of France was taken captive and most of his able bodied nobility were either killed or taken prisoner. (LP 4.994, 1002, 1036, 1072, 1102, 1139).

---

47 *Hall's Chronicle* p.674

Henry was incredulous and his reaction is supposed to have been to tell the messenger who brought the news that he was as welcome as the Angel Gabriel.[48] This story only dates from 1765 so is probably fictitious but contemporaries did describe him as joyful and bonfires were lit across England.[49]

Such a momentous event required all the European players to re-think their strategy. The Emperor's initial demand was that Francis not only renounce his claims to Milan and Naples if he wanted his freedom but that he cede Artois, Picardy, Flanders, Burgundy, Provence and Languedoc to him and Gascony, Normandy and Guyenne to Henry.[50] Knowing that no king of France would ever agree to such terms, Henry was fired with an enthusiasm to invade envisaging an English army entering from the north, an Imperial from the south and a Dutch from the east.

In June 1525, Henry sent his daughter Mary, aged nine, to Ludlow which was the traditional seat of the Prince of Wales, though he did not create her as such but rather sent her as nominal head of the Council of the West Marshes. He ennobled his bastard son as Duke of Richmond and Duke of Somerset. The Somerset title was part of the Beaufort inheritance – Henry's grandmother had been daughter of the Duke of Somerset. His father, Henry VII had been Earl of Richmond prior to becoming king so this was also a family title, the status raised to a dukedom in line with Somerset and the six year old boy being son of a king rather than a great-great-grandson of one as his father had been. Both titles were public indicators of the King's paternity and his bestowing on him of the titles of Lord Admiral of England, Wales and Ireland as well as – rather optimistically – Normandy, Aquitaine and Gascony was a clear sign that he anticipated him growing up to take a full role in government when older. Richmond would be sent north a few weeks later as Warden General of the Marches toward Scotland.[51] A third child ennobled at this ceremony was the three year old son of Henry's sister Mary by her husband Charles Brandon, Duke of Suffolk: young Henry Brandon was created Earl of Lincoln. Alongside them, Henry created his maternal cousin, Henry Courtenay, Marquess of Exeter.

At the time when the event had been planned, Henry had been anticipating that he might be about to leave for France and his purpose was to leave behind a show of family strength in different parts of his kingdom.[52] However, it rapidly became obvious that despite treaty obligations, the Emperor

---

48 As Scarisbrick notes, this tale originated from a French author who provided no details on his source, something which makes it highly suspect, J.J. Scarisbrick, *Henry VIII* (1968), p.136.

49 CSPS 3.1.33. Henry was told on 9th March by a courier sent by the Duke of Milan. The battle had taken place on 24th February. The defeat was a surprise to everyone except Gregory Casale who predicted the outcome, LP 4.1064. Casale and Ghinucci were the two most perspicacious of Henry's ambassadors.

50 LP 4.1208; CSPS 3.1.27, 46

51 LP 4.1510

had no interest in supporting Henry's claim to the French throne but was only in favour of an invasion as a diversionary tactic if it became necessary to put pressure on Francis to agree to his terms, and even then he expected Henry to foot the bill for all the armies plus pay the huge arrears which the Emperor had allowed to build up with his own army in Italy. The Emperor argued that he could not afford to contribute a penny but commented that Henry had plenty of money.[53] He also noted that he still had to win the war in Italy and pacify his rebellious subjects in Germany.[54] To add to Henry's fury, he suggested that given Henry was the richest prince in Europe, he was justified in not repaying any of the thousands of pounds which he owed Henry, most of which had been owing for four years. He thought that maybe if things went well he might be able to pay back a little in four years' time?[55]

Henry was unhappy. At home, his subjects showed no inclination to pay for war and there was the prospect of the Scots invading should he attack their ally France. Ireland was in turmoil. Relations with the Emperor had been strained by a diplomatic incident at the start of the year and now things deteriorated further.[56] The Emperor claimed his own lack of heir meant that unless Henry was prepared to send his nine year old daughter to him immediately (three years ahead of the scheduled marriage) complete with her full dowry in advance, he would be forced to break the betrothal. The fact that the King of Portugal had promised the Emperor almost a million ducats to marry his own daughter, Isabella, was undoubtedly a contributory factor though the fact that she was of child bearing age helped.[57] This rejection of his daughter was taken as a slight by Henry and may have contributed to his rejection of Katherine two years later as a tit for tat. The Imperial ambassador, Mendoza, suggested that this event, combined with the Emperor's failure to pay his debts to Henry, were the principal causes of the royal fury which was being

---

52 Thomas Boleyn, whose son-in-law was Henry's cousin, became Viscount Rochford on the same occasion. Lincoln died in March 1534, LP 7.337.
53 LP 4.1213, 1237, 1282, 1378; CSPS 3.1.8. Henry's claim to France dated back to when Philippe IV of France died in 1314 leaving three sons and one daughter. The sons in turn became king but all had died by 1328 without issue. The daughter was married to Edward II of England and was mother of Edward III who claimed the crown on her behalf, arguing even if she could not rule, her claim was still valid and passed to her son. Faced with the prospect of an English king, the French quickly selected Isabella's male cousin instead citing ancient Salic law which, in its political convenience, suddenly seemed very important to them. Under English law, there was no doubt that Henry's claim was totally justified.
54 This was the summer of the Peasants' War in Germany.
55 LP 4.1409. Given the gold which the Emperor was receiving from the New World, his claim to poverty is hard to credit.
56 CSPS 3.1.20, 28, 31, 32, 33, 38, 50, 51, 55
57 LP 4.1378. The idea of him marrying her had been proposed some years before as the English ambassador to Spain had advised Wolsey in July 1519, LP 3.385. Isabella was then twenty-two.

taken out on Katherine.[58] Henry had said in September 1525 that it was the Emperor's betrothal to Mary in 1521 which had been the chief grounds for the alliance and if there was no marriage, there was no grounds to continue it.[59] Katherine herself had made a similar observation in 1523 telling the papal nuncio and Imperial ambassador that "as long as our nephew keeps his promise to marry our daughter, the alliance will remain unbroken. As long as the marriage treaty stands, he may be sure of England."[60]

Meanwhile in Italy, Imperial demands for large sums of money combined with fears that the Emperor had ordered Francis to be brought to Spain so that a deal could be done which would lead to the complete subjection of all the Italian states, saw the princes there unite against him. The Emperor responded by besieging Sforza, the Duke of Milan whom he claimed was his vassal and therefore should not be conniving with his enemies. In response, Milan, Venice and the pope turned to Henry for support.

The breakdown in relations between Henry and the Emperor, combined with widespread distrust of the latter across Italy, encouraged renewed efforts toward peace with France. England made peace in August 1525 and the pope orchestrated a league of Italian states whose objective was to drive the Emperor out of Italy and then force him to release Francis. The pope boasted that whilst the presence of Imperial troops might force him to deal with the Emperor, he would have no hesitation about breaking his promises as soon as he could because the Emperor had done that to him.[61] At the end of the year, the serious illness of the French king made the situation even more precarious.

The uncertainty continued into 1526. Francis recovered and was released following his acceptance of the Treaty of Madrid by which he agreed to yield Burgundy and his Italian territories to the Emperor, to marry the Emperor's sister, and to abandon the King of Navarre. Francis' two eldest sons were accepted as hostages by the Emperor until Francis fulfilled the terms of the treaty. As soon as he escaped, Francis predictably refused to do so saying that agreements made under coercion were invalid, an argument the pope had used before the treaty had even been signed.[62] Wolsey said the treaty was unreasonable and that the princes of Europe should unite to resist the tyranny and ambition of the Emperor who sought to rule the world and did not fear God.[63] In June, much encouraged by Henry and Wolsey, a league was set up to defend Italy which included France and the pope. Henry did not provoke the Emperor by joining it – much to the annoyance of its members. He was offered the role of its protector and it was believed that he had accepted it, but he

---

58   CSPS 3.2.252
59   LP 4.1628
60   CSPS 3.1.108
61   LP 4.1608, 1719
62   LP 4.1868.
63   LP 4.2036

denied this arguing that he would not be in a position to negotiate peace if he was seen to be allied with either side.[64]

It is easy to understand why in such a political situation, having a queen who was the Emperor's aunt was a major embarrassment and nobody needs documentary evidence to realise that the atmosphere in the palace must have been strained to breaking point. Katherine was, first and foremost, a Habsburg. At the end of the year, Henry even stopped the annual performance of the morris dancers at court on grounds they were Spanish.[65]

The importance of the breach with the Emperor and the new alliance with France cannot be overstated. Without it, the break with Katherine would never have happened regardless of Anne Boleyn's existence. Henry would have continued to have doubts about the "marriage" but endured for the sake of international peace and hoped to outlive her and get a son at some time in the future. With the security of French support, he was enabled to think what many would have called the unthinkable. French lawyers and theologians not only agreed that the "marriage" to Katherine was invalid but, together with their king, they petitioned the pope about it and they offered private advice to Henry which led to the final break with Rome taking the format which it did. Yet, there is nothing to suggest that as 1526 drew to a close, Henry had any intention of discarding his queen.

Anne Boleyn's route to 1527

In a famous television interview of 1995, Mrs Merton asked Debbie McGee: "So what first attracted you to the millionaire, Paul Daniels?" The question was meant as a joke and Debbie took it as such even though it was deeply offensive being based on the premise that no beautiful young woman would choose to marry an older man unless she was in it for the money.

Writers about Anne Boleyn asking themselves the same question have tended to produce different responses depending on their conceptions of Anne and Henry. For those who view Henry as a wicked tyrant, it is inconceivable that their heroine could possibly have fallen in love with him and so they tend to blame the relationship on her parents or uncle suggesting she was the victim of their ambition. Writers who regard Henry as some easily led fool, the pawn of first Wolsey and then Cromwell, have inclined to see Anne as a manipulative temptress, another individual able to govern his behaviour. Meanwhile feminists have seen Anne as an independent minded career woman with her

---

64 LP 4.2398, 2638.
65 Ronald Hutton, *Stations of the Sun* (Oxford, 1996) p.265. Whether morris dancing originated in Spain is open to debate but Henry believed it had,

eyes fixed firmly on the crown while romantics have preferred to stress the passionate love that existed between her and Henry.

Ultimately, the question of why is impossible to answer. Nobody knows exactly what one person sees in another and everybody can think of couples they know who seem to be utterly mismatched but yet live happily together for years whilst other pairs, who seem so well suited, barely have time for one another. In Anne and Henry's case, they appeared well matched on the surface with shared interests in music, the outdoor life, dogs, dancing, Bible study, fashion, building and horses. In temperament too, both were emotional and fond of children. Yet, despite these positive indicators their marriage ended in tragedy. Why it went wrong is the subject of a later chapter. For now, it is necessary to try to understand how and when Henry and Anne came together.

It is not known when Henry and Anne first met. As the daughter of a diplomat, it is not impossible that she was taken to court at Christmas for the festivities or invited to see some tournament spectacular, when she was a very small child. Only a deeply incurable romantic would argue that Henry would have taken one look at a toddling Anne and vowed, "this is the one!"

Most of Anne's childhood and youth was spent overseas and probably her first memorable encounter with the King would have been in June 1520 at the Field of the Cloth of Gold. As an attendant on Queen Claude, she would have been present when Henry entered the room. Whether she had any chance to speak to him is less certain. Claude was seven months into her pregnancy and no doubt occupied considerable attention from her staff. Most likely, Anne would have been caught up in the spectacle and excitement of the occasion just as people are today when a senior member of the royal family visits. She would have witnessed – perhaps close up, perhaps from a distance – a tall, handsome prince clad in dazzling jewels who veritably oozed charm and good manners, and it is fairly safe to speculate that this vision would have been a subject of considerable discussion and giggling amongst the young ladies for some time afterwards.

It was Mary Boleyn's marriage in February 1520 which showed that the time had come to think about a match for Anne and the first evidence for that being discussed dates from 6th October that year when Anne's uncle wrote to Wolsey from Ireland referring to a conversation which had taken place before his departure:

> And where at our being with Your Grace, divers of us moved you to cause a marriage to be solemnised between the Earl of Ormond's son being with Your Grace and Sir Thomas Boleyn's daughter; we think if your Grace caused that to be done and also a final end to be made between them for the title of lands depending in variance, it should cause the said Earl to be the better willed to see this land brought to good order.[66]

Anne's uncle had arrived in Ireland in May of that year indicating that the discussion must have taken place prior to Easter.[67] Moreover, Wolsey had discussed the matter with the King because Henry had written to Anne's uncle just a few days earlier, their letters crossing to say:

> As ye desire us to endeavour ourself that a marriage may be had betwixt the Earl of Ormond's son and the daughter of Thomas Boleyn, knight, Comptroller of our Household; so we will ye be means to the said earl for his agreeable consent and mind thereunto and to advertise us by your next letters of what towardness ye shall find the said earl in that behalf. Signifying unto you that in the meantime, we shall advance the said matter with our Comptroller and certify you how we shall find him inclined thereunto accordingly.[68]

The proposal is of interest at several levels. Firstly, it is a reminder of how different things were in the sixteenth century. Neither Anne Boleyn nor James Butler, Ormond's son, were to be consulted: they were not even named. Secondly, it is indicative of Anne's uncle seeking to exert his authority as head of the family over his brother-in-law. The fact that he had not spoken to Thomas Boleyn himself before he left is instructive. He claims credit for the idea and it is easy to see why he thought it would appeal to the King. Thomas Butler, Earl of Ormond, had died in 1515 leaving two daughters, one of whom was Thomas Boleyn's mother. Thomas Boleyn claimed the title but so did Piers Butler who was his mother's cousin.[69] The legal dispute had been ongoing since then, partly because of the prestige of the title – Boleyn clearly liked the idea of being an earl rather than a knight – but also because it was a very valuable estate. Moreover, it was of great political and strategic importance comprising modern day Tipperary and Kilkenny plus parts of Leix and Limerick. The Earldom of Ormond lay between the territory controlled by Desmond in the

---

66 SP 2 p.50
67 LP 3.669
68 SP 2 p.57
69 The family tree appears in the Appendix 6: Key Relationships.

south and Kildare in the north, the two key powers of the time. To the north and west, the territory was in the hands of the native Irish while to the east, MacMurough was in control, a subject of particular concern to Anne's uncle who had inherited castles there from his Brotherton forebears which he was unable to occupy together with land "commodious and fertile." He knew that if he could secure the support of Butler through this marriage, he had every chance of persuading Butler to help him take them.[70] Thus, his promotion of the proposal was not entirely disinterested.

For Henry, if the marriage could be agreed, it would end a long standing legal dispute and if Butler would agree to take over the government of Ireland as a sweetener to the deal, should mean that he could withdraw English troops and thus save money, as well as gain extra income from taxes coming from a peaceful land. Being realistic, Thomas Boleyn was not about to move to Ireland to take up the government himself or to learn the language so he could deal with the natives, hence a compromise which safeguarded everyone's honour seemed the most appropriate answer. If Anne married James Butler, the Ormond title would descend through her children thus keeping it in the family. Thomas would not get his earldom but Henry could always find him something else.

There is no documentary evidence of what happened next. Anne's uncle would have spoken to Piers Butler in person and Henry and Wolsey would have spoken to Boleyn. In November 1521, Wolsey wrote a note to Henry promising "I'll talk to you on return how to bring match about" and clearly this happened because a month later, Anne returned to England.[71] The King of France noted her departure in a letter written at the start of 1522 along with English students at Paris and expressed his disquiet at what he saw as a sign of England preparing for war against him. Wolsey reassured him that she had been recalled so that she could be married and thus end litigation between nobles.[72]

Exactly when she arrived is unknown but in March 1522, Anne appeared in a court masque put on for the benefit of Imperial envoys. It was a standard piece of entertainment involving beautiful maidens playing the part of virtues, fighting off negative characters such as Scorn and Envy before being rescued by a bunch of gallant knights representing chivalric characteristics such as Loyalty.[73] A number of writers over the years have proclaimed great significance in the names of Anne and Mary's characters assuming the former

---

[70] LP 4. 2405. Brotherton had been the fifth son of Edward I. In 1347, Edward III granted Brotherton the lands of Catherlough with all its castles including Ferns and Rathvilly and O'Drone. MacMurough was normally the ally of Kildare who was the enemy of Butler. Desmond was said to be at war with Butler in 1526, LP 4.1352. For Butler's side of the dispute, see LP 4.1278.

[71] LP 3.1762

[72] LP 3.1994; CSPS FS p.30 dated 17th January. This document states that at the time of her recall, Anne was working for Queen Claude.

[73] *Hall's Chronicle* p.631; LP 3 Revels 1522 account, pp.1558-1559. See also CSPS Further Supplement 69-73.

played Perseverance and the latter Kindness but the original record does not reveal who played which part.[74] We have no idea of how the masque came into being. The leading lady was Henry's sister but were the other roles played by her own staff or did she pick her attendants from amongst Katherine's staff? The masque was performed at Wolsey's home not one of Henry's palaces so was the cardinal involved in selecting the players or did he simply ask the King's sister to arrange something and leave it to her? Who wrote the masque and how many rehearsals were involved? It would have taken time to make the scenery and all the costumes. Records show that the carpenters began work on the set on 20th February, twelve days before the performance, and the materials must have been ordered before that.[75] The lack of this information means we are unable to say how either Anne or Mary came to be selected. Was it because they were especially good dancers or did they just happen to be the right size and colouring for the roles? Many casting directors today are more interested in finding a group of girls who look good and are the same height: an expert dancer who happens to be extraordinarily tall with buck teeth and a squint would not get chosen. Masques were a regular feature of special occasions so it could be that those involved were those who ordinarily took part and that Anne was added because somebody else had dropped out. The names of the performers at masques were not generally recorded but survive in the accounts in this instance because the head-dresses were kept by the ladies rather than returned to the Wardrobe. Inevitably, the masque would have meant that Anne met Henry, probably for the first time as an adult in her own right, but there is nothing to suggest that the event was especially memorable for either of them. Henry's principal dancing partner that evening was his sister and whilst he may have danced briefly with Anne as partners were changed just as he would have done the other players, it was likely a passing thing.

In the same month as the masque, Piers Butler was appointed Deputy of Ireland, the documentation all referring to him as Earl of Ormond indicating Henry's tacit recognition of his right to the title.[76] This appointment slowed the negotiations down for Anne's marriage. Wolsey advised that it was best to wait and see how Butler did in the job before hastening to send his son over, a journey on which Anne would have accompanied him had they wed. Wolsey argued that keeping James Butler in England was a good way of ensuring Piers' loyalty until he had demonstrated his abilities.[77] By this point, Anne would have met James but what she thought of him is not known.

---

74 It seems to have been Retha Warnicke who first made this claim which was achieved by putting the names of the characters mentioned by Hall in parallel with the names of players in the Revels accounts. There is no reason to suppose, however, that the clerk and chronicler happened to use the same order.
75 LP 3 Revels p.1559. Other participants in the masque included Jane Parker who would marry George Boleyn in 1524 and the wife of the King's cousin, Gertrude Courtenay.
76 LP 3.2086
77 LP 3.1762

The early summer of 1522 must have passed in a whirl of excitement for Anne due to the visit of the Emperor which occasioned multiple masques, banquets, parties, tournaments and various sporting events. However, it seems likely that she started to feel bored in the autumn when the court returned to the serious business of government and all the talk was of war. Her uncle departed for France and her father to Spain. She was young and unsupervised. She got into trouble. Although neither Cavendish nor Wyatt give a date for her involvement with Henry Percy, it must have occurred at some point between September 1522 and the spring of 1523 because that is when both men were away, and the assumption must be that it was in the earlier part of the period because in October 1522, it was announced that Percy was being sent north.[78] Had her father and uncle been at court, they would have nipped the burgeoning romance in the bud and if they had arrived back while it was still active, they would have faced summons from Wolsey about the matter. Evidently, therefore, the supposed great romance was of very brief duration.

Cavendish's tale of how a young Anne Boleyn fell in love with Henry Percy has been repeated frequently, even in his own century by Wyatt. Cavendish claimed that the couple made promises of some description to one another and that Henry ordered the separation via Cardinal Wolsey because he was secretly in love with Anne himself, a step which Cavendish claims led to Anne's lifelong enmity and determination to destroy him.

Is Cavendish reliable? He worked for Wolsey so was in a position to at least hear gossip within the household but he was a gentleman usher, effectively a butler, not a confidential secretary and he had not long joined the Cardinal's service. Cavendish describes how Wolsey summoned all his staff to hear him berate Percy before handing him over to his father.[79] The scene is regularly re-enacted in dramas but is it credible that Wolsey would have done any such thing? Why would he have wanted his butler or cook to witness him telling Percy off? Not only are we to believe he did so but that said butler was able to remember it word for word thirty years later! And how would Cavendish have found out Anne's thoughts on the subject? He never spoke to her. The truth is that the relationship was severed because both parties were due to marry someone else. Anne was a pawn in the ongoing quest for peace in Ireland. Percy had been promised to Shrewsbury's daughter prior to May 1516 and his father was engaged in talks with Shrewsbury in September 1522 about the details.[80] The Percy match was deemed vital for the good government of the north. In September 1523, Wolsey assured Anne's uncle that it was about to go ahead and that this would mean Shrewsbury had his two daughters wed to the greatest magnates in the area, Lord Dacre of Gilsland and Henry Percy, heir to

---

78   LP 3.2636, 2654. He did continue to appear at court on occasion as part of his governmental role.
79   George Cavendish, *The Life of Cardinal Wolsey*, ed. Samuel Singer (1827) pp.121-125. Cavendish does not use the first person for any event prior to 1522 indicating he was not a member of the household before this date.
80   LP 2.1935; LP 3.2523.

the Earldom of Northumberland, something which would commit him to giving them armed support.[81] As a gentleman usher, Cavendish would have had no idea about such things. He was simply writing with the benefit of hindsight and considerable venom because even twenty years after the event, he blamed Anne for the fall of his beloved Cardinal. He fabricated the exchanges and existence of promises to support his characterisation of Anne as evil.

What was the extent of the relationship between Anne and Percy?

In July 1532, Percy's estranged wife claimed promises had been made but she was trying to get her marriage with Percy annulled and could only do so if she could prove he had been contracted previously. Percy denied it under oath.[82] In 1536, when Anne fell, Percy was asked again and he once more denied it.[83] It may also be assumed that Henry asked Anne about it while they were courting and she denied any wrongdoing too. He would not have considered a woman who was not a virgin or widow to be suitable as his consort or mother of his children. Ordinarily, the fact that the two people who were in a position to know what had happened told the same story should be regarded as better evidence than the claims of later gossip mongers but the story has lived on for two reasons. Firstly, romantics have allowed themselves to get carried away by thoughts of Anne being taken away from her true love only to end her life on the block.[84] Secondly, in 1528 Henry obtained a dispensation to marry a woman who had previously contracted a clandestine union with someone else.[85] Some writers such as Kelly have seized on this as evidence of Anne being a loose woman but it was just part of a general dispensation prepared to enable Henry to marry almost any woman in the country, not Anne in particular. The issuing of such general dispensations for princes was not unusual. The Emperor had one and this may have been what gave Henry the idea of seeking one for himself.[86] It does not prove anything about Anne's relationship with Percy which was almost certainly, entirely innocent. She may or may not have been filled with some brief romantic fancies but she was not an idiot. Girls of her class had arranged marriages and they did not risk their futures or the reputations of their families by cavorting with young men.

We only have Cavendish's word for Anne being sent from court but it is likely that her behaviour would have led to a suspension. However, the court

---

81 LP 3.3321, 3322. David Starkey, *Six Wives* (2004) pp.276-277 suggests that Percy married on 23rd August 1525 on the basis of a ledger of the couple's accounts beginning on that date.
82 Paul Friedmann, *Anne Boleyn*, vol. 1 (1884) pp.159-161
83 LP 10.864
84 The extent of Percy's gifts to his male favourites has led to some speculation that he was homosexual. See Gwyn, *Wolsey* p.233 for a discussion of this theory.
85 Clandestine meant a union entered into by free consent of the parties involved but without formal taking of vows before a priest.
86 Geoffrey Parker, *Emperor*, p.159. Henry Ansgar Kelly, *The Matrimonial Trials of Henry VIII* (Oregon, 1976) pp.50-51.

was full of young ladies and gentlemen and such incidents cannot have been that uncommon. Being sent home in disgrace to grow up and face parental discipline was probably not unusual but it is unlikely that the punishment would have been permanent. After a due interval, maybe three months, the recalcitrant member of staff would have been expected to make their apology and promise never to repeat their mistake. There is no sign of this happening with Anne. Her name does not feature on payrolls, New Year gift lists or in any accounts of masques or revels. A reasonable person would assume this indicates her absence from the court rather than a concerted plot to expunge her name from all records.[87] So where was she? This question has received almost no attention in the vast literature about Anne and no doubt this is because writers are meant to focus on evidence and there is none. Nonetheless, it is a significant point. The five missing years represent almost a third of her adult life and impact upon the crucial question of when Anne's relationship with Henry began.

There are several possibilities. She could have stayed at Hever with her mother all this time but that seems highly unlikely as her parents would have wanted to see her earning money and making a good match. She could have spent time with her sister and her young family, but there is little sign that they were close enough to justify a visit lasting years. She could have returned to France. Sander claims she went to Brie in France at fifteen and there is a tradition dating back to at least 1654 of her being at a castle owned by a cup-bearer of Francis I.[88] She could have spent some time with the Norris family. Mary Fiennes, who had been at the French court with her, was her cousin and had married Henry Norris in 1520 and started a family. We do not know whether they were close friends but Henry Norris would end his life with Anne in 1536 and Elizabeth I went on to maintain a close friendship with Norris' descendants which suggests that there may have been a link there. It is possible that Anne was godmother to at least one of Norris' children which would account for her interest in them and Elizabeth regarding them as her spiritual siblings.

Another possibility is that Anne was despatched to the household of Thomas Boleyn's friend and fellow ambassador, Sir Richard Wingfield. Anne would later briefly employ his widow, Bridget as one of her gentlewomen. Lady Wingfield had accompanied her husband on some high profile visits such as the Field of the Cloth of Gold in 1520 where she may have had the opportunity to spend time with Anne, but for the most part, she had been busy since 1513 having children, not spending time at court. If this is the case, Anne would have been living mostly at Kimbolton Castle in Huntingdonshire with occasional visits to London. Wingfield was very well established in court

---

87 She could have left court for another reason such as having an accident which left her unable to work for some period.
88 Alison Weir, *Mary Boleyn* (2011) p.85. Weir presumes the story relates to Mary. Professor John Guy has dismissed the legend as "pure invention", *Hunting the Falcon* (2023) p.65.

circles. His first wife had been the aunt of Henry VIII's mother and the godparents to his eight children included the Emperor, Cardinal Wolsey, the dowager Queen of France and Margaret, Regent of the Netherlands. His cousin was Charles Brandon, Duke of Suffolk. For Anne to spend time there would not have harmed her marriage prospects but rather strengthened them due to the high regard in which he was held. Sadly, Wingfield died in the summer of 1525, the news reaching England on 12th September.[89] His widow, who was much younger than him being probably in her mid thirties, chose to remarry. The date is unknown but the fact that she had at least five further children by her second husband who died in August 1532 would suggest that she married in the spring or summer of 1526. It is likely that this would have been the occasion for Anne to leave the household and seek a new place at court and a husband. The Butler scheme had evidently died, either because of lack of activity with the principal parties all being otherwise occupied in different parts of Europe or because Butler's tenure as Deputy had been less than successful and he had been replaced by Kildare in the summer of 1524. The only possible reference to any marriage arrangements being contemplated on her behalf is in a 1523 letter by Maud Parr which notes that the Lord Treasurer, then Anne's uncle, had made enquiries about the heir of Lord Scrope for one of his own family. Whether he had in mind his niece or his own daughter is unknown though Anne would seem more likely given she was closer in age while his own child was aged just three. Either way, nothing came of the enquiry.[90]

Also possible, is that Anne spent some time in the household of Humphrey Wingfield. Anne would later write a letter to his wife telling her that "next mine own mother, I know no woman alive whom I love better." It is difficult to imagine how Anne could have become so close to this woman unless she had spent considerable time with her.[91]

An incident often referenced in histories of Anne is when Henry wore an outfit at a joust with an embroidered burning heart and the motto "Declare, I dare not." A number of writers have seen this as a sign of Henry's secret love for Anne but was it? The outfit was worn at a joust on Shrove Tuesday 1526. At this event, two teams of twelve men led by the King and the Marquis of Exeter respectively, competed in a display of horsemanship and chivalric honour in front of a large crowd. Today, we think of Shrove Tuesday principally as pancake day but then it was a much bigger festival, a final opportunity for feasting, music, dancing and sexual activity before the abstinence of Lent began. Henry was not the only man on the field to be wearing a heart and motto: every member of his team was wearing exactly the same outfit,

---

89   LP 4.1655. He had died on July 22nd at Toledo.
90   Letter of Maud Parr dated 23rd August 1523 in Thomas Dunham Whitaker, *An History of Richmondshire* (1823) vol. 1 p.386. Scrope's heir was his son John born c. 1509-10 so would have been closer in age to Anne.
91   M A Wood, *Letters of Royal and Illustrious Ladies* (1846) vol 2. p.74-5, LP 5.12. Humphrey's wife was a kinswoman of Elizabeth Boleyn, Anne's mother, see Appendix 6: Key Relationships.

complete with "Declare, I dare not." Exeter's team all wore hearts too but they also had an embroidered lady's hand grasping a ewer on their outfits. Jousts tended to have a theme and here each of the twelve men on Henry's team competed against their opposite number on Exeter's. If Henry's man won, the ewer represented the grace of love being poured as balm over the burning heart of the suitor, but if Exeter's man won, the ewer represented water extinguishing the hopes of the suitor. In short, the outfit and motto had absolutely nothing to do with Anne Boleyn – unless one is to adopt the nonsensical idea that all twelve men on Henry's team were in love with her – and was simply part of the play. Probably at the end, however many damsels Henry's team had "won" came on to the field with garlands and a kiss for the victors, but this is not stated in the account. Being a routine form of entertainment, Hall never thought it necessary to add such details because he assumed his readers would know. The idea that Henry's costume had some coded romantic significance is bizarre. At various times in his life he dressed as a Turk and Robin Hood but nobody thought he was signalling an intention of converting to Islam or overhauling the tax system for the benefit of the poor. Henry was King of England and behaved in a courtly manner. He was as likely to emblazon his romantic attachments at a public event – which Anne almost certainly did not even attend – as Queen Elizabeth II was to arrive at a jubilee event wearing an "I love Philip" T-shirt.

The reference on the costume was political. A month before the joust, as the costumes were being made, Wolsey noted that the pope had just confirmed an alliance with the Emperor, something for which the pope had sent an apology though the letter was yet in transit. Rumours were also rife about what sort of settlement Francis – still in captivity – might make with him. Wolsey said this had caused Henry to ponder the dangers which might result and the outcome was his support for a league between France and Venice with himself as protector. This news, he felt sure, would strengthen the pope's resolve to stand up to the Emperor and pursue the liberation of Italy from the Spaniards. However, owing to the extent of trade between England and the Low Countries, a declaration of intentions would be damaging. Wolsey advised that if the Emperor remained in doubt about what Henry would do, he would be more likely to accept the King's arbitration and this should hopefully avoid much bloodshed.[92] With this in mind, the message "Declare I dare not" had clear significance.

Moreover, indirect evidence also argues against any early relationship between Henry and Anne. In July 1526, Anne's aunt, the Countess of Oxford, was widowed. She had a number of problems as a result, particularly with regard to disputes over her rights to parts of the estate. The person she turned to for help later that year was Wolsey claiming she had nobody else. If Anne had been at court and Henry's great love at this point, as some romantic writers have suggested, she surely would have sought her help. Not only did she not do this but the legal disputes continued for a very long time with Cromwell

---

92 LP 4.1902

becoming involved in 1530.⁹³ If Anne's own family were unaware of any relationship between Henry and Anne in the summer of 1526, it seems extraordinary that writers almost five centuries later can claim to know better.

The evidence suggests that Anne did not return to court until the end of 1526. An entry in her father's account book for November to December that year shows an expenditure on her of £3 12s 6d, equivalent to over £25,000 in today's terms.⁹⁴ Such a huge sum would only be consistent with two things – a wedding trousseau or taking up a position at court. This supposition is supported by evidence from Katherine's earliest biographer who stated that in 1527, Anne was "in the Court new entered."⁹⁵ It would also make sense for Henry to be bowled over by a new arrival at court rather than imagine he had only suddenly realised the attractions of somebody he had been seeing every day for years, though this seems to have been what happened with Jane Seymour.

How did she get the job? She had experience of the English court from 1522 and of working in the French court previously but positions at court were not advertised with the Queen and her senior attendants carrying out interviews to see which candidates matched their desired skills profile or personality specification. Clearly, the ability to do the job was important but the crucial factor in obtaining a position was having the right contacts. Her uncle, the Duke of Norfolk, had married Henry's aunt, a daughter of Edward IV. Anne's mother had served the Queen at the start of the reign. Her father had been a jousting partner of the King in his younger days, a Knight of the Body performing not only the duties of the role but taking part in such sad events as the funeral of Henry's son in 1511. Thomas Boleyn had served on diplomatic missions across Europe, become a senior member of the Privy Council, was deemed sufficiently important to receive a pension from the Emperor and he had held key appointments within the royal household such as comptroller. In 1515, he had expressed his desire to spend his entire career at court.⁹⁶ Anne's brother had been Henry's page, a junior position but still within the Privy Chamber, that charmed circle of people closest to the King. Her brother-in-law, William Carey, was the King's cousin and in charge of two of his favourite palaces, Beaulieu and Greenwich.⁹⁷ Some authors have suggested that these favours to the Boleyn family owed something to Mary Boleyn's sexual favours but this is not only historically indefensible but astonishingly patronising. Why would anyone imagine that Henry would appoint people to jobs just because he had once slept with Mary Boleyn? Thomas Boleyn and William Carey were granted

---

93 Wood, *Letters,* pp. 10-14, 67-68
94 LP 4 Appendix 1524 to 1527 no 99
95 William Forrest, *The History of Grisild the Second,* ed. W. D. Macray (London 1875) p.53. Forrest knew many of the people about Katherine and served her daughter so would not have made a mistake on such a key point. The fact that Forrest might be termed a hostile source makes his evidence the more compelling.
96 LP 3.223
97 LP 3.2074.5, LP 4.2218.12

honours and responsibilities because they were capable and professional men. It was not a case of them benefiting from the attractions of Mary and Anne but of Mary and Anne benefiting from their access to the King and the favour they earned through their own skills.[98]

What did Henry see in Anne? There are a few descriptions of her.[99] George Cavendish, one of Wolsey's gentlemen ushers, saw Anne frequently when she accompanied Henry to Wolsey's home. Despite his disapproval of her for coming – as he saw it – between Henry and Katherine, he described her as a "**gorgeous lady**."[100] Cardinal Wolsey himself wrote of her that she was a most virtuous gentlewoman, a virgin who demonstrated "chasteness, meekness, humility, wisdom and laudable qualities and manners" together with an "apparent aptness to the procreation of children."[101] Grynaeus described her as "good looking" after their meeting in 1531.[102] A French writer told the Venetians in February 1528 that she was "very beautiful."[103]

By contrast, Venetian archives contain an account of Henry and Anne's visit to France on 31st October 1532 which begins:

> Madam Anne is not one of the handsomest women in the world; she is of middling stature, swarthy complexion, long neck, wide mouth, bosom not much raised, and in fact has nothing but the English King's great appetite, and her eyes, which are black and beautiful, and take great effect.[104]

The document itself is very strange which renders it suspect. The section appears to have been added at the start of a report with no preamble and is in a

---

98 Grants in 1527 and 1528 show no favouritism to Anne or her family despite her being the acknowledged intended of the King so it is unclear why anyone would think that grants in the earlier period proved a relationship with Mary.
99 Interestingly, Campeggio never described her which is strange given that it might be assumed that the recipients of his letters would love to know more about the siren who had allegedly enticed the King of England from his duty. This could be because he never met her. Henry had planned to introduce them (LP 4.4894) but may have been dissuaded. The French ambassadors had no need to describe her because Francis and others knew her from her years at the French court. The Emperor almost certainly met her in 1522 when he visited England, though probably just in passing when she was noted to be the daughter of Thomas Boleyn.
100 George Cavendish, *The Life of Cardinal Wolsey* (ed. Samuel Singer, 1827) vol.1 p.134
101 LP 4.3641 dated 5th December 1527.
102 Hastings Robinson, *Original Letters relative to the English Reformation* (1847) p.553
103 CSPV 4.236. The information was passed on by an unnamed spy so it cannot be known whether he was reporting from first hand experience or just passing on gossip.
104 CSPV 4.824

totally different style of language. It is unclear who wrote it and how close they were standing when they saw Anne. The occasion described was formal and the author was not an invited guest so was clearly unlikely to be very near. Nor is it obvious for whom he is writing since he finds it necessary to explain that Henry and Francis are unhappy with the pope, a fact which it might have been thought almost everyone in Europe knew.[105] It is questionable therefore whether it should be taken seriously at all especially given the author had an agenda. It was believed that a beautiful woman added honour to a man while an ugly one showed him in a poor light, an attitude sadly still evident today with the appallingly sexist concept of 'trophy wives'. To have described Anne in glowing colours would have suggested she was a fitting spouse for a monarch because kings should have beautiful wives, their looks reflecting the wonders of the country as well as being symbolic of virtue. If it had been reported that Henry had secured the affections of some talented goddess type creature, that would have paid tribute to Henry's virility and – because Henry represented England – to have implied that England was strong. By contrast, criticising Anne suggested that Henry was losing his grip and was weak and that the country might be vulnerable, a reassuring message for the Doge and one which also flattered him by implying his moral superiority.[106]

It is also worth reflecting that the account is often quoted as being negative but ideals of beauty differ. A French manual called *La louange et Beaute des dames* defined the ideal woman as having the following:

> three things white: skin, teeth and hands
> three things black: eyes, eyebrows and eyelids
> three things long: body, hair and hands
> three things broad: bosom, brow and space between eyebrows
> three things narrow: mouth, waist and ankles
> three things small: breasts, nose and head.[107]

On the basis of this, Anne would have been considered attractive.

Another peculiar description comes from Sander who wrote the notorious description of her having six fingers, a large wen on her neck and a

---

[105] The author refers to having been in Calais and Boulogne both of which were out of bounds for officials from other European countries. He may have been a merchant who was acting as a spy. He includes two details which do not appear in the official accounts – the loss of fifteen hundred crowns by the Cardinal of Lorraine when gambling with the Duke of Suffolk and the Bishop of Bayonne's intention to marry Henry and Anne on Sunday. The latter was nothing more than a rumour suggesting the author was obtaining his information from tavern gossip rather than anyone closely involved in the meeting.

[106] In the same way, Francis I described Katherine of Aragon as "old and deformed" in 1519 (CSPV 2.547). He had not met her but wished to highlight the superiority of his own wife which he saw by extension as validating his own superior virility.

[107] Quoted in Walter Richardson, *Mary Tudor; the White Queen* (1970) p.105

projecting tooth, but also says of her: "She was handsome to look at with a pretty mouth, amusing in her ways, playing on the lute, and was a good dancer. ...She was always well dressed and every day made some change in the fashion of her garments."[108] Given his earlier comments, it is obvious that this account was the one he had been given and which he had amended due to the contemporary belief that a person of evil character (and Sander saw Anne as to blame for the break from his beloved Rome) must have that wickedness embodied in physical form.[109] The witchlike hag of his invention was clearly not handsome and it is impossible to believe that Henry VIII, who had his choice of beautiful women, would have selected such a creature. Sander never knew Anne and nor did George Wyatt though he claimed to have heard anecdotes handed down from two people who did. Wyatt described Anne as possessing a "rare and admirable beauty...the graces of nature graced by gracious education.. her favour passing sweet and cheerful ... increased by noble presence of shape and fashion" before trying to incorporate Sander's references to moles and extra nails and "not so whitely" skin which he then gallantly, and rather unconvincingly, tried to claim added to her beauty.[110]

The reference to swarthiness or darkness of complexion can be read in one of two ways. To many Englishmen, it associated Anne with foreigners – and traditionally in English history, that was not a positive thing. Alternatively, and probably in Wyatt's case, it suggested that owing to her love of outdoor pursuits such as riding, hunting and falconry, she had developed a tan which was not seen as desirable in an age which prized lily white skin. Tans were associated with common women like milkmaids, not court ladies or potential consorts of the King. They could also be associated with wantonness, the idea being in humoral theory that the pale skin of the archetypal English rose represented chastity.[111]

The Frenchman Lancelot de Carles who saw Anne in 1536 and possibly before wrote:

---

108 Nicolas Sander, *Rise and Growth of the Anglican Schism* ed. David Lewis (1877) p.25. This description is in the same paragraph as the witchlike features but much less frequently quoted.
109 This same belief is memorably seen in Shakespeare's characterisation of the hunchbacked Richard III. In 1535, the Imperialist Dr Ortiz, who had never seen Anne, advised the Empress that she was "very ugly" for the same reason, LP 9.249.
110 Wyatt's "Life of the Virtuous Christian and renowned Queen Anne Boleigne" appears as an appendix to volume one of George Cavendish, *The Life of Cardinal Wolsey* (ed. Samuel Singer, 1827) pp.423-424.
111 Ruth Goodman, *How to be a Tudor* (2016) p.267.

Nobody would have considered her to be English but rather a native Frenchwoman. She knew how to sing, and dance and grew in wisdom. She played the lute and other instruments to banish sad thoughts, enlarging her talents and many exquisite graces which she had happily acquired in France. She was beautiful and of elegant stature and had most attractive eyes which she knew well how to use. [112]

John Russell, one of the senior gentlemen of the privy Chamber who had served Henry since 1507, compared Anne with Jane Seymour saying that Anne was naturally better looking but "the richer Queen Jane was in clothes, the fairer she appeared but that the other (Anne) the richer she was apparelled the worse she looked."[113]

William Thomas, writing in 1546, shortly before his appointment as Clerk of the Privy Council, said Anne was a wise woman "endued with as many outward good qualities in playing on instruments, singing, and such other courtly graces, as few women were of her time; with such a certain outward profession of gravity as was to be marvelled at."[114] It is uncertain that he saw her, as the date of him entering royal administration is unknown, but he would have worked with those who did serve her.

William Forrest, was a young man in 1530 so heard about her though he may not have seen her, described her as fresh-faced, an excellent French speaker, possessed of a stately bearing and able to sing and dance "passing excellent."[115]

Her musical abilities were clearly an attraction to Henry who was a skilled musician himself. In 1538, when seeking a wife to replace Jane Seymour, he said that he wanted to hear the ladies whom the French ambassador thought might be suitable, sing to him several times before he made his choice [116]

Some evidence of Anne's appearance can also be drawn from her skeletal remains. These were examined in 1876 and Dr Mouat observed that she was a woman of just over five feet tall, making her a foot shorter than Henry and indicating she would have reached up to his shoulder. He wrote: "The form of the head appears to have been round, and the face of an oval shape; the forehead straight and ample, and denoting considerable intelligence. The lower part of the face, judging from the form of the jaw, must have been moderately

---

112 Lancelot de Carles, *Trial and Death of Queen Anne Boleyn* (1545) f.5 lines 52-63
113 Edward Herbert, *Life and Reign of Henry VIII* (1741) p.335. Russell added that Katherine of Aragon in her youth had been prettier than either Jane or Anne.
114 William Thomas, *The Pilgrim*, ed. James Froude (1861) p.56
115 William Forrest, *The History of Grisild the Second*, ed. W, Macray, (1875) pp.53, 55
116 "I will have them sing to me a few times before I settle.' Chastillon to Francis I, 12th August 1538, quoted in William Thomas, *The Pilgrim*, p.119

full, with a somewhat square chin." He added that she had "large eyes" and good teeth except for slight decay on one molar on her left. He noted she had an upright carriage with limbs "in due proportion to the rest of her body." Her neck was "short and slender" and her legs "singularly delicate and well formed." He went on: "The ribs show depth and roundness of chest. The hand and feet bones indicate delicate and well-shaped hands and feet, with tapering fingers and a narrow foot." Mouat specifically noted the lack of any malformation of either hand.[117]

The idea of Anne being petite is confirmed in a verse composed at her coronation which refers to her "body small" and another composed just after her execution which compares her to a "small bird."[118] Another verse at the former proclaimed "your beauty dazzles us" and describes her complexion as "fairer than Thames' swans, than milk, than snow."[119]

That Henry fell in love is clear and he admitted in an undated letter that he had been "struck with the dart of love" but was it a case of:

> Their eyes met across the room. He swayed as his legs suddenly seemed to collapse beneath him. His heart pounded and rockets exploded in his head before being replaced by angelic music. He blinked and looked again. The vision of perfection was still there and looking at him, her eyes inviting, her body tantalising. "I must have her," he mumbled as he stumbled across to the siren.

According to virtually every novelist, film maker and even quite a few historians, this is what happened and Henry immediately decided to discard Katherine. Contrary to these flights of romantic fancy, the evidence is clear that this was not the case. In the letter referenced, Henry spoke of having been affected for a year but still being "in great agony... whether I shall fail or find a place in your heart and affection."[120]

---

117 Doyne C. Bell, *Notices of the Historic Persons Buried in the Chapel of St Peter ad Vincula* (1877) pp.26-28. Some devotees of the 1501 birth date have attempted to deny that the skeleton belonged to Anne Boleyn but it was located on the precise spot which ancient records said, was observed not to have been disturbed for over three hundred years (which means since she was laid to rest) and was the only female burial in the area. Katheryn Howard's remains had been lost to lime within a century of her death, ibid. p.24.
118 Frederick Furnivall (ed.), *Ballads on the Condition of England in Henry VIII's and Edward VI's reigns* (1868-1872) pp.390, 411.
119 Ibid. pp.371-372. This could be dismissed as flattery but it was an eyewitness account so should be taken seriously. Not every queen over the centuries has received like tributes.
120 Jasper Ridley, *The Love Letters of Henry VIII* (1988) p.41. It is letter IV in the series and calendared at LP 4.3218

Anne was evidently unsettled by the situation. She had been brought up to believe that Henry was lawfully married to Katherine, the lady who was also her employer. How many girls would credit a would be lover saying that they weren't really married so it was all right to have a relationship? She must have taken some convincing and even then faced divided loyalties notwithstanding her attraction to Henry. The famous portrait of him by Holbein which shows him as an overweight man with an enormous codpiece and small hard eyes conjures up a great sense of power but not the idea of a tender lover. Yet, Henry was a real human being. He smiled and laughed and danced and sang and Anne would have seen him in this way. She would have observed him as a majestic king but also in private, seeing him lose his temper, burst into tears, making himself ill with worry and playing with his dogs. She saw his romantic gestures such as sudden gifts and treasured his ardent love letters and undoubtedly found such adoration and cosseting extremely enjoyable. Later, having married him, she saw him in his most intimate moments, a privilege not granted to historians nor contemporary chroniclers. It is essential to remember this key limitation. To paraphrase Tyndale's translation of 1 Cor. 13:12, we see Henry through a glass darkly while she saw him face to face.

An interesting description was given by Giustinian, the Venetian ambassador who not only saw Henry at close quarters on a frequent basis but also met other monarchs to whom he could compare him. Giustinian wrote that Henry was "extremely handsome; nature could not have done more for him; … very fair and his whole frame admirably proportioned…. He has now got a beard which looks like gold. He is very accomplished; a good musician; composes well; is a most capital horseman; a fine jouster; speaks good French, Latin and Spanish; is very religious; … is very fond indeed of hunting and … is extremely fond of tennis. … He is affable, gracious … very rich indeed… He is the best dressed sovereign in the world; his robes are the richest and most superb that can be imagined."[121] William Thomas, a member of his Privy Council, said of Henry after his death: "he was most amiable, courteous and benign in gesture unto all persons, and specially unto strangers; seldom or never offended with anything, and of so constant a nature in himself, that I believe few can say that ever he changed his cheer for any novelty how contrary or sudden soever it were. Prudent he was in council and forecasting; most liberal in rewarding his faithful servants, and ever unto his enemies as it behoveth a Prince to be: he was learned in all sciences, and had the gift of many tongues; he was a perfect theologian, a good philosopher, and a strong man at arms; a jeweller, a perfect builder as well of fortresses as of pleasant palaces… all his doings were open to the whole world, wherein he governed himself with so much reason, prudence, courage, and circumspection, that I wot not where in all the histories I have read, to find one private king equal to him."[122]

---

121 Giustinian, *Four years* vol. 2, pp.312-313
122 Thomas, *Pilgrim*, pp.78-79

Small wonder perhaps that Anne was in awe of Henry, falling in love but yet scared of what would happen. We cannot know the exact date on which she decided that she was willing to become his queen and it is likely that her resolve waxed and waned as more and more obstacles were thrown in her path, but certainly she was being courted by Henry throughout the summer of 1527 and she was aware of Henry's efforts to extricate himself from Katherine.

Timing of the annulment quest

The key question remains though, which came first, did Henry decide to seek his freedom and then propose to Anne or did he secure her consent before starting the process?

The story told by Henry and Wolsey was that the crisis began in March 1527 when the French asked for evidence about Henry's marriage. At the time, negotiations were in process for Henry's daughter Mary to marry either Francis I himself or one of his sons. Wolsey explained that the English had asked for clarification over whether Francis was free to marry Mary given it was said that he had married the Emperor's sister in Spain though not consummated it. If this was true, a papal annulment would be necessary before Francis could marry Mary. The French took the perfectly reasonable question the wrong way and effectively said, we'll show you our papers if you show us yours. Wolsey duly ordered the dispensation for Henry's wedding to be dusted off the shelf and handed it over. Probably to his surprise and embarrassment, the Bishop of Tarbes, frowned and started to highlight all the errors in the document. The bishop was an experienced diplomat and expert in canon law so not intending to start a major crisis. It is likely he was just commenting on how such an amateur document could ever have been issued and saying that it would not happen that way today, rather like some people today enjoy circling grammatical and spelling errors in letters they receive from their local council. Henry immediately ordered an enquiry into the matter and the rest as they say is history.

In November 1528, Henry summoned members of Parliament and his Privy Council together with the Lord Mayor of London and various other leading officials, to tell them how the issue had originated. At this juncture, Campeggio had just arrived from Rome and plans were under way for the legatine court to open. Henry's actual notes for the speech have not survived but the French ambassador, Jean du Bellay gave one account and the chronicler Edward Hall another: both were eyewitnesses. Mendoza, the Imperial ambassador also wrote a report but his information was provided by spies.[123] Given the lack of recording devices in the period and the absence of an efficient system of shorthand, it is not surprising that the three accounts of what he said

---

123 LP 4.4942, *Hall's Chronicle* pp.754-5, Joachim Le Grand *Histoire du Divorce* (Paris, 1688) vol 3 pp.217-218; CSPS 3.2.586

differ in crucial points. Du Bellay, who was best informed, said that Henry admitted to have long had doubts about the legality of his marriage which had been brought to the fore when the Bishop of Tarbes raised the matter. In view of the importance of ensuring there could be no question about the succession, Henry felt it necessary to check.[124] Mendoza reported that Henry had claimed Francis himself had demanded to know if Mary was legitimate before he would enter into negotiations about her marrying his second son. This was evidently a case of lost in translation because Wolsey admitted to Henry on 16th August 1527 – more than three months after the union of Mary and Orleans had been agreed – that he had yet to advise Francis of Henry's "marriage" being questioned.[125] Hall says that a French counsellor asked about Mary's legitimacy during the negotiations but reckons the talks took place in France which they certainly did not. Otherwise, his account bears close parallels to du Bellay's. There is a fourth account by Cavendish who was not there and who was writing some thirty years later. Cavendish blames the Bishop of Bayonne (Jean du Bellay) whom he says asked outright if Mary was legitimate during the negotiations for her to wed Orleans.[126] Not only does he get the bishop's name wrong but Cavendish says that Henry gave the speech at the legatine court in 1529 rather than in 1528. Modern writers who have checked the minutes of the French visit and not found any such question have been quick to dismiss these accounts but that is unwise. What is crucial to remember is that in canon law, even where a marriage is subsequently found to be invalid, the children are not automatically bastardised. If Henry had thought for one moment that the Bishop of Tarbes – who did understand canon law much better than the likes of Cavendish or Hall – was suggesting Mary was illegitimate, he would have had his head there and then and Francis would have agreed with his action. [127]

Although there are some minor differences between the accounts, they agree that that Henry already had doubts when the matter was raised by the French prompting him to demand a formal but private investigation of the situation. The fact that one of the accounts was written by du Bellay is of vital importance because he does not contradict what Henry says and he knew both Henry and the Bishop of Tarbes extremely well. If Henry had publicly blamed the French for trying to break up his "marriage" and it had not been true, this would have resulted in a major diplomatic incident and nobody from the French side ever queried it. In August 1528, du Bellay noted that the annulment began before Henry committed his heart to Anne.[128] Credibility for this pattern of events is also provided by the French report of the negotiations in March 1527 which highlight the acrimonious discussions which took place on the 3rd, 7th and

---

124 Le Grand, *Histoire,* vol 3 pp.317-318
125 LP 4.3080, 3350. If Francis had openly told Henry he was an incestuous adulterer with a bastard for a daughter, he could have expected a declaration of war. The idea was ridiculous.
126 Cavendish, *Wolsey* p.219
127 SP vol.1 pp.196-201.
128 LP 4.4649.

8th over the issue of whether Francis was or was not free to marry Mary.[129] This was a month before the interview with the Bishop of Winchester which marks the first written evidence of the annulment process in England – though clearly the plans for the interview would have been drawn up a few days before.[130] The report also reveals that the Bishop of Tarbes did ask if Mary was really the heir, not from any doubt about her legitimacy but as a gentlemanly way of enquiring if Katherine was likely to have any more children, something he was told was not a possibility. As the chapter 'Why did it take so long for Henry and Anne to marry' with its month by month account of events from January 1527 onwards shows, there was absolutely no sign that Henry was proposing to unleash such a political grenade as annulling his "marriage" and nor did it make sense at that juncture given what was happening in Europe. A cynic might claim that Tarbes was acting under directions from Wolsey or Henry but there is nothing whatsoever to support such an idea. Tarbes was there to represent Francis' interests not theirs. Certainly Francis had no idea about the problems with the dispensation and Tarbes, having made his comments about the document, evidently thought no more about it until he was told that further investigation had confirmed there was a problem.[131] Although many writers today are keen to suggest Henry started the annulment process purely for love of Anne Boleyn, there is independent confirmation of Tarbes' involvement. On the 19th of May 1527, the Milanese ambassador at the French court reported that the Bishop, who had returned with Poyntz a fortnight earlier ready to travel to Spain, had suddenly dropped everything and rushed back to England alone, travelling post, on some "secret matter" of Henry VIII.[132] The ambassador had no idea of the reason for this unexpected event but the fact that Wolsey opened his own court on the 17th to investigate the legality of Henry's "marriage" to Katherine cannot be considered coincidental.

Many contemporaries, including Katherine and the Emperor, tended to regard Wolsey as the instigator of the annulment. Katherine thought it was revenge for her criticising his ostentatious lifestyle while the Emperor thought Wolsey was upset because he had not made him pope.[133] William Tyndale, by

---

129 LP 4.3105. The report makes no mention of the Bishop of Tarbes asking to see Henry's dispensation but the secretary who wrote it did not attend every conversation which the bishop had with Wolsey and it does talk of similar tit-for-tat demands being made for ratification of articles by the parliaments of each country when negotiations were going badly.
130 LP 4.5791.
131 The briefing note for the English ambassador in Spain made no mention of the French and attributed the enquiry solely due to Henry's Bible study, LP 4.3327. The reason for the different account was political. If the Spanish thought that the French were behind the plan, they would automatically oppose it and interpret it as a hostile move. At the time, delicate negotiations were in process to end the war in Europe so England had no wish to upset them.
132 CSPM 805.
133 Polydore Vergil, *Anglica Historia*, ed. Denys Hay (Camden Society, 1950) p.331; LP 4.3312, 3844; CSPS 3.2.69

then living in the Low Countries under Imperial rule, repeated this accusation in 1530. Describing Wolsey as a "mis-shapen monster sprung out of a dunghill" he wrote:

> He waxed furious mad and sought all means to displease the Emperor and imagined this divorcement between the King and the Queen, and wrote sharply unto the Emperor with menacing letters, that if he would not make him pope, he would make such ruffling between Christian princes as was not this hundred year, to make the Emperor repent.[134]

Tyndale was not in any position to know and was merely repeating gossip he heard overseas. In March 1528, the Emperor had ordered a propaganda campaign in the Low Countries which promulgated just this view.[135]

Curiously, Sir Gregory Casale, Henry's ambassador in Italy and a man who knew Wolsey well and reported directly to him, asked in June 1526 whether Wolsey's goal was the ruin of the Emperor.[136] He thought Wolsey's plan might be to get the pope to orchestrate war in Italy to achieve this end. Wolsey's reply does not survive but it is interesting that Casale suspected Wolsey of anti-Imperial sentiments ten months before the annulment crisis began.

Sander, Camden and Harpsfield all suggested that Wolsey had wanted Katherine out of the way so that Henry could marry a French princess. Harpsfield named Wolsey as "the first author and incensor" of the annulment claiming that it was an act of revenge for the Emperor not ensuring he was elected pope in 1521 and that he, "to bring about his ungodly intent, devised to allure the King to cast his fantasy unto one of the French king's sisters, the Duchess d'Alençon." Harpsfield says that "not long after", Wolsey went to France to arrange this only to be stopped by Henry sending a messenger in pursuit to say that he had decided to marry Anne Boleyn instead.[137] This would have seemed conceivable to them because in 1514, English policy had shown a similar volte face when the Imperial alliance was thrown over for one with France this being sealed by a royal marriage, on that occasion, Henry's sister to Louis XII. Wolsey had been blamed then so observers may have thought he was repeating the practice. In fact, their surmises were totally off the mark. Francis only had one sister and Marguerite was not widowed until Easter 1525 by

---

134 William Tyndale, *The Practice of Prelates*, (Parker Society, 1849), pp.331-2. Tyndale had been out of the country since 1524.
135 LP 4.4112. William Camden would also write that the idea of separating from Katherine stemmed from the "cunning dealing of Thomas Wolsey" and his grudge against the Emperor, *Annales* (1616) p.2
136 LP 4.2273
137 Sander, *Schism*, pp.15-16, Harpsfield. *More*, p.15. Wolsey went to France in 1527 which was five years and eight months after he failed to be elected, not a period most would define as "not long after."

which time she was thirty-three and had been married for sixteen years without having children – hardly a fertility record likely to attract Henry. Within days of her widowhood, Marguerite's mother, who was then Regent of France, had spoken of the strategic need for an alliance with Navarre to aid an attack on the Emperor through northern Spain. Conveniently, Navarre happened to have a bachelor king but as Henri II was an Imperial prisoner at the time this seemed impossible and there was brief talk of marrying her to Bourbon.[138] However, Navarre's escape led to her marrying him at the start of 1527 – four months before the annulment process began.[139] The agreement for this would have been discussed in April 1526 when the newly released Francis went straight to Navarre's home, an event which Wolsey knew all about.[140] Vergil's claim that Marguerite rejected an offer from Henry in 1528 because Katherine was being upset by the proposed annulment is utter nonsense and a reminder of the need for writers to verify statements before they quote them.[141]

Francis did, however, have a sister-in-law, Renée who had been born in October 1510.[142] In August 1528, Jean du Bellay said that he believed Wolsey had hoped Henry would marry her when the annulment was granted.[143] Du Bellay was a confidante of both Wolsey and Henry so in a good position to know. In January 1526, Renée had been suggested as a match for Bourbon but at the start of March 1527, her hand was offered to the Duke of Ferrara's son, a match Wolsey knew about and supported because he sent John Casale to the Duke to encourage him to accept.[144] This was just before the annulment crisis began. If Wolsey had been plotting to marry Henry and Renée, sending Casale in this way would make no sense. However, it was far from certain that Ferrara would accept her and on March 18th Wolsey had proposed a marriage alliance between Renée and Henry's son, the Duke of Richmond. Although there is no evidence this idea was taken seriously, rumours of it could have spread and, in the way that so often happens, the story changed with the telling so that with hindsight people thought the proposal was for Renée and Henry himself, not his son.

Or, it could be that having begun the annulment, Henry and Wolsey did have a private discussion of this nature. The prospect of Mary, whom Henry had confirmed was his only heir, marrying a Frenchman was so unpopular that in May 1527 the celebrations of the treaty agreed to that effect had to downplay

---

138 LP 4.1283.
139 LP 4.1365.
140 LP 4.2068. At this period, Joachim was regularly crossing the Channel with messages between Francis and Wolsey.
141 Vergil, *Anglica*, p.329. Given Vergil refers to her as Duchess d'Alençon, he evidently had not noticed her marriage to the King of Navarre.
142 Francis also had two daughters, Madeleine aged seven and Margaret aged four but these were too young to be considered as brides.
143 LP 4.4649
144 LP 4.1875; CSPV 4.54, 59

that aspect.[145] If the annulment could be quickly arranged, as seemed feasible at the outset, the idea of a different or second Anglo-French alliance of Henry with Renée which would hopefully generate a son and so make the nationality of Mary's husband irrelevant, would have seemed quite attractive. Evidence that such an idea may have been discussed with Henry is strongly suggested because in July 1527, while on his way to France, Wolsey met the Hungarian ambassador, Lasco, who told him that "when he saw the personage of Madame Renée not meet to bring forth fruit as it appears by the lineation of her body he forbear" from requesting her hand for his master.[146] Wolsey immediately reported this to Henry which he surely would not have done unless he had reason to believe the information would be of interest to him. The choice of wife for a Hungarian prince was not something which Henry was likely to care much about and certainly would not have necessitated a report sent by special courier: it could have waited until Wolsey got home. If Renée was not considered good enough for a Hungarian or capable of having children, she certainly would not have been considered suitable for a King of England, particularly one desperate for a male heir. This despatch is of key importance because Henry would have received it around the 10th July which is six weeks before he decided to send Knight to Rome seeking a dispensation to marry.[147]

William Forrest also blamed Wolsey but he suggested that an astrologer told the cardinal that he would be destroyed by a woman and he, assuming that could only mean Katherine, decided to get in a pre-emptive strike by destroying her. Forrest says that Wolsey took advantage of a trip to France on state business to seek to negotiate a match for Henry with a French princess but "at time of canvassing this matter so, in the court new entered there did frequent a fresh young damsel" named Anne Boleyn and Henry's passion for her scuppered the French marriage proposal but caused him to favour Wolsey's plot to oust Katherine.[148]

As to the allegation that Wolsey was angry with the Emperor for not making him pope, if that was his concern, he could have been equally angry with Francis who also made him the same offer.[149] Both monarchs would have welcomed Wolsey as pope - if they could not get one of their own into the job first.

The major reason for Wolsey getting the blame was because he was a hated figure and people are always prone to blame those whom they dislike when something they perceive as bad happens. Often this behaviour is totally unreasonable but it happens and history is full of examples of it, from Nero blaming the Christians to Hitler blaming the Jews. Had there been a major outbreak of plague in the early 1530s or another great fire of London, Chapuys

---

145 *Hall's Chronicle* pp.720-724; CSPS 3.2.37, 66; CSPM 1.803
146 SP vol.1 p.203. LP 4.3231. In fact, she went on to have five healthy children who all lived into old age.
147 LP 4.3400.
148 Forrest, *Grisild,* p.53
149 LP 3.122, 728.

would undoubtedly have claimed Anne Boleyn was responsible for it. In 1529, Roy and Barlow claimed "none is faulty but the butcher" alleging that Wolsey had maliciously invented the story that Katherine was past child-bearing.[150] This was not a lie: she was but they blamed Wolsey from personal animosity.

Partly too, it was a reflection of the tradition of deference which said that the monarch was never wrong and any mistakes made must be the result of evil or incompetent advisers. At the legatine court in 1529, Wolsey asked Henry if he had been the instigator of the scruple and Henry said he had nor, but rather that Wolsey had opposed him. This exchange was clearly intended as a bit of political theatre, a means of publicly proclaiming Wolsey to be an independent judge in the case, but this does not mean the statement was untrue.[151] Cavendish, ever loyal to his master, depicts Wolsey going down on his knees to beg Henry not to seek the annulment, but this is probably fictitious and coloured by hindsight and Cavendish's own hatred of Anne.[152]

That it was so widely believed was also because Wolsey was so powerful. The Venetian ambassador had observed: "this cardinal is king, nor does his majesty depart in the least from the opinion and counsel of his lordship." He said that all state affairs "are managed by him, let their nature be what it may. ...He is in very great repute, seven times more so than if he were pope."[153] Mendoza, the Imperial ambassador, observed in July 1527 that Wolsey could lead Henry whichever way he pleased.[154] Roy and Barlow, in no position to know the truth but reflecting popular opinion, wrote of the King: "by the cardinal ruled he is."[155]

However, there was one occasion in mid October 1528 when Wolsey did claim some credit for having started the process. He told Jean du Bellay that he had said to Francis' mother at Compiègne in September 1527 that within a year, there would be a permanent disjunction between England and the Emperor adding the "divorce" had been begun "in order to put perpetual separation between the Houses of England and Burgundy."[156] Wolsey's claim has been quoted in various books but it needs to be seen in context. Wolsey's meeting with Du Bellay was arranged so that Wolsey could complain about Francis' failure to support Henry in urging Venice to return Ravenna and Cervia to the pope and also his late payment of the League's troops which Wolsey argued

---

150 William Roy and Jerome Barlow, *Rede me and be not wroth* (1529) line 628. The reference to a butcher reflected Wolsey's family background. Neither man was involved in government or court circles or even living in England so they were not in any position to know what they were talking about. They would also have been influenced by the Emperor's propaganda.
151 Cavendish, *Wolsey* p.219
152 Ibid. p.204
153 Giustinian, *Four Years*, vol. 2, p.294, 314.
154 CSPS 3.2.113
155 Roy and Barlow, *Rede me,* line 500
156 Le Grand, *Histoire*, vol.3 pp.185-186; LP 4.4865. Wolsey evidently expected the annulment to be granted by summer 1528

was the cause of Imperial advances. Wolsey said that Francis' behaviour had embarrassed Henry internationally because he had boasted that Francis would support him and it had made the pope doubt the strength of the Anglo-French alliance causing him to delay granting Henry's annulment, something which meant Henry was being prevented from marrying and having another heir. Wolsey's aim, in this conversation, was therefore to stress his pivotal role in maintaining the alliance between the two countries. He said that he had been the first to speak of the annulment but this is not the same as saying that he started it. Wolsey had been the first to take news of the plan to Francis and his mother and he could have meant this. That Wolsey had encouraged the breach between Henry and the Emperor was widely recognised and in December 1527, Wolsey told Sir Gregory Casale that it had been a very difficult task because Henry was by nature very loyal and he had clung tenaciously to the Emperor despite all the evidence of this support not being mutual.[157] But the breach had begun almost two years before the annulment process started and Henry had left Katherine's bed three years before. The timing of events shows the Imperial alliance was already broken and, as Wolsey said, the annulment was designed to cement the fact.

The truth is most likely that Wolsey poured all his efforts into achieving the annulment because he wished to obey the King, his very commitment leading to suspicion it was his idea. At the start, he may have seen it as an opportunity to enhance relations with France through marriage but it became clear quite early on that this was not going to happen. Had Renée appeared fit and fertile things might have been different. When Wolsey realised Henry wished to marry an Englishwoman, he may have cautioned him against it, not least because the last time an English king had done this, it had caused dangerous divisions amongst the nobility, but, seeing the King was determined, he devoted himself to Anne's cause.[158]

There were other theories about what started the annulment ball rolling. Reginald Pole, who was not in England when the process began, stated nine years later that Anne Boleyn had sent her chaplains to advise Henry that marriage to a brother's wife was illegal, a claim so fantastical it is only worth repeating to show the degree of credence in which his comments should be held. At the time, Anne was a maid-of-honour and as such did not employ chaplains.[159]

---

157 LP 4.3644.
158 Edward IV's marriage to Elizabeth Woodville had caused divisions in his lifetime and was a major contributory factor to the usurpation of Richard III and the murder of the princes in the Tower after his death. Henry was alert to the danger writing in the *Glass of Truth* that it would be hard to find any subject "whom the whole realm would and could be contented to have." Nicholas Pocock (ed.), *Records of the Reformation* (Oxford, 1870) vol. 2. p.387.
159 He may have been thinking about Cranmer who did spend some time living in her father's house in 1529-30 while working on the annulment. Pole certainly blamed Cranmer for much of what happened which is why, together with Bloody Mary, he

Eustace Chapuys, the Imperial ambassador to England from 1529, reported rumours that the pope himself had started the annulment in order to revenge himself on the Emperor for the attacks of 1526.[160] A sixty-one page work of 1533 entitled *A religious and political rhapsody* also alleged that the pope had instigated it in order to break the Anglo-Imperial alliance.[161] Chapuys himself blamed the Bishop of Tarbes.[162]

Miguel Mai, the Imperial ambassador at Rome, thought the idea of annulment came from Staffileo, member of the Rota, the legal arm of the Vatican.[163] Wolsey did not meet him until September 1527, five months after the annulment started, so this was untrue.

The chronicler Edward Hall blamed Henry's confessor, John Longland, for putting the scruple into Henry's head.[164] Certainly Henry discussed his doubts with Longland but Henry had been reading the Bible all his life and would have known about the prohibition in Leviticus for many years. Indeed, Luther's 1520 book on the *Babylonian Captivity of the Church* which Henry had answered in 1521 had included a section highlighting the passage and noting that the pope had no authority to dispense with it. Significantly, Henry had not responded to that particular section but rather brooded on it.[165]

John Foxe claimed the Spanish first questioned Mary's legitimacy in 1523 because they did not want the Emperor to marry her and that Henry simply followed up on their scruple.[166] If this had been the case, it might be supposed that Henry would have used this in his case. Nonetheless, this was also the claim made by Sir Nicholas Harvey, ambassador to the Imperial court who told them all had been well until "you of Spain moved first the question and put the marriage in ambiguity."[167]

Wolsey and William Thomas simply claimed that the Holy Spirit had intervened to open Henry's eyes.[168] Since God cannot be called as a witness, this argument is irrefutable.

The Duke of Norfolk, Anne Boleyn's uncle, reportedly thought that Satan had instigated the annulment.[169] He was evidently having a bad day at the time.

---

    had him burned at the stake in 1556. Or he may have had Barlow in mind.
160 CSPS 4.1.160
161 LP 6.416.
162 CSPS 4.1.373
163 LP 4.5827
164 *Hall's Chronicle* p.728
165 If anyone was to blame for putting the scruple in Henry's head, it was arguably Luther.
166 John Foxe, *Acts and Monuments*, ed. George Townsend (1846) vol.5 p.46
167 *Hall's Chronicle* pp.782-783
168 LP 4.3913; Thomas, *Pilgrim*, p.17
169 CSPS 4.2.720.

What none of these people knew, and what historians generally choose to ignore, is that Henry had expressed his doubts about the legality of a union to Katherine back in 1509. This is confirmed by the Spanish ambassador of the time who reports the issue was discussed in the Privy Council and he called upon Katherine's father to offer reassurance.[170] Having been advised it would be acceptable, Henry went ahead but experience kept his doubts alive. In reality, what happened in 1527 was not a case of Henry being consumed by lust and inventing some scruple but him seizing upon a question raised, finding that it confirmed a long held opinion of his own, and deciding that this was the time to go ahead. War with the Emperor looked likely to erupt, the pope was firmly allied to England, and he was advised that annulment should be a straightforward exercise.[171] Sadly, he was wrong.

Conclusion

Although we can never know for sure and emotional experiences such as falling in love can rarely be pinpointed to a single moment, the evidence shows that Henry had doubts before his "marriage" and most significantly from at least 1521 about its validity due to it being solemnised in contradiction to Bible teaching. He was persuaded that the dispensation meant he was all right but a nagging suspicion remained which led to him consulting seven other bishops about it.[172] In 1524, he separated from Katherine in a sexual sense but he remained on good terms with her. Toward the end of 1526, he met Anne and fell under her spell, probably over the Christmas festivities which would have seen plenty of opportunities for her to sing, dress up, dance and generally catch his attention. The flirtation continued into 1527 through the long, cold and dark winter days but Anne did not take it seriously, though she was flattered. At this stage, she still believed Henry and Katherine were married and she had no wish to get involved. Whether she knew about her sister's very brief fling with Henry cannot be known: she was out of the country at the time it happened. In

---

170 See How did Katherine become Queen of England?
171 Reginald Pole claimed in 1539 that Henry told someone else that he had received an assurance as to the project's simplicity from a person whom he did not name. Pole did not reveal his source so it is only third hand hearsay. In the same *Apologia*, Pole blamed Cromwell for what he saw as the disaster and given Cromwell at the time was only a clerk in Wolsey's office handling property affairs, this indicates the recollection is not to be trusted. See discussion in Geoffrey Parmiter, *The King's Great Matter* (1967) p.143; Arthur Ogle, *The Tragedy of the Lollards' Tower* (1949) pp.205-208.
172 LP 4.5751. The bishops were Warham (Archbishop of Canterbury), Fisher (Rochester), Tunstall (London), Clerk (Bath and Wells), West (Ely), Standish (St Asaph) and Carlisle (Kite).

the spring, the Bishop of Tarbes drew attention to the deficiencies of the dispensation. Henry had no choice in the circumstances but to launch an enquiry and as more evidence was found to support his case, told Wolsey to resolve the matter. Wolsey's initial response would have been to apply for a new dispensation which corrected the errors in the original but Henry believed that his original fears had been proved right and the dispensation could not be corrected because the pope had no authority to overturn the Bible. To Henry, the situation represented a light at the end of the tunnel: he could now go and get himself a male heir. From being a victim of repeated and otherwise inexplicable bereavement, Henry now had an answer and some action he could take to regain control. In May 1526, Wolsey had spoken if the need for a "just ground and cause reasonable" to totally break with the Emperor and the annulment presented just such an opportunity.[173] Yet at the time proceedings began in April 1527, there was no plan to marry Anne, simply to obtain his freedom.

The summer of 1527 was a crucial period. Wolsey went to France and the possibility of a French alliance may well have been on the agenda. It is inconceivable that Wolsey and Henry would not have discussed the King's future at the outset. The report of Renée's apparent inability to have children may have convinced Henry to take his current flirtation with Anne more seriously. Certainly he showered her with gifts that summer and in September – five months after the process began – he amended what was almost certainly a document which had been discussed prior to Wolsey's departure, to express his intention of at least asking her to be his wife.

The document in question was the proposed dispensation for Henry to marry. The original request has been lost so we only have the pope's actual dispensation of December 1527 but it is reasonable to suppose that this was drawn up along the lines requested, though the clause relating to legal kinship was likely part of a general grant.[174] Before it was issued, Henry and Wolsey drew up new instructions but this information arrived in Rome too late so it was not until early 1528 that the final version was issued. The fact that the terms were changed between August and December 1527 is significant.

The first dispensation covered anyone to whom he was related due to licit or illicit intercourse, even in the first degree, a very specific and unusual clause which surely stemmed from Henry's request.[175] First degree affinity meant sisters-in-law. It may be assumed that Henry was not intending to marry Katherine's widowed sister, Juana who was the Emperor's mother, so the intercourse involved must have been illicit. By his own admission, Henry had slept with Mary Boleyn on at least one occasion – and in canon law it need only have been once – and that put Anne into first degree affinity. This request therefore, which may have been made as early as September 1527, appears

---

173 LP 4.2148
174 This permitted Henry to marry anyone who was his ward. The clause was later dropped suggesting it had not been part of the original request.
175 Pocock, *Records* vol. 1 pp.22-27

proof that Henry wanted to marry Anne. Her opinions on this point are not known because the request was made in his name only: he may have been expressing his hope at this stage and still awaiting her agreement or she may have already agreed. The dispensation also covered anyone to whom Henry had affinity due to an unconsummated marriage or to whom he was related from first cousin level down to third. This meant virtually any woman who shared one of his great-grandparents or great-great-grandparents. Anne did not fit into this category. Renée was his third cousin once removed (same as Katherine of Aragon) so would not have needed a dispensation, though there may have been some confusion over this point.[176] The question of her match to Ferrara's son had yet to be finalised so this clause could indicate that she had been considered as a bride when the draft was first made.[177]

Finally the dispensation covered spiritual kinship so Henry could marry any of his god-daughters or the mothers of any of his god-children or of his daughter Mary. There is no reason to imagine that Anne could have been covered in either of these definitions but it is impossible to identify all the women who would have been. It is quite likely that Bessie Blount would have been covered since Henry may have been godfather to Richmond. Bessie was still married but sudden death was not unusual in Tudor England and Henry may have contemplated marrying her if she became available and legitimating his son by that means.

The spiritual kinship clause would also have included anyone who shared a godparent with the King either spiritually or physically. The name of only one of Henry's three godparents is known and none of Anne's so it is impossible to verify if there was an impediment here or the clause was simply added to cover all bases.[178] Although Anne's grandfather was a courtier at the time of Henry's birth, it seems improbable that he would have been selected to be one of his godfathers as a prince of the realm would ordinarily have much higher ranking godparents.[179] Anne's parents both had court connections and monarchs did sometimes graciously agree to serve as godparents to the children of their favourite courtiers so it is just possible that Henry's father was Anne's

---

176 Renée was the daughter of Charles VIII's wife by a separate husband so not actually a blood relation even allowing for the concept of Anne of Brittany being made one body with Charles VIII due to intercourse. Anne Boleyn was Henry's third cousin twice removed, see Appendix 6: Key Relationships.

177 Henry Percy was also Henry's third cousin and Kelly – whose genealogy for him is incorrect – surmises that this clause proved he and Anne had married but this assumption stems from the fact that Kelly refuses to believe Henry ever considered anyone else as a bride and that Henry began the annulment for this reason, which is evidently untrue. *Matrimonial Trials* pp.45,46

178 CSPS 4.1.224. The godfather was Philip of Burgundy, son of Emperor Maximilian and husband of Katherine's sister, Juana.

179 Anne's grandmother was godmother to Henry's elder sister, Princess Margaret. Gareth Russell, *Young and Damned and Fair* (2017) p.27

her godfather, though it seems unlikely.[180] If there was a link, the most probable candidate is Anne Plantagenet who was aunt to both Henry and Anne. She was the sister of Queen Elizabeth so could have been invited to be godmother to the prince and she later married Thomas Howard, the future Duke of Norfolk. It is not impossible that Anne's mother would have selected her sister-in-law to be one of Anne's godmothers. If this was the case, Henry and Anne would count as spiritual siblings and so require a dispensation to marry.

Whatever the thought process behind the original draft, by the end of 1527, the situation had changed and this meant the dispensation had to be amended. Henry now removed affinity from an unconsummated marriage but left in consanguinity to third cousin level extending it to second cousins. He wanted a generic dispensation against anyone related at any level to any woman with whom he had ever slept. Also added was anyone who might have been informally betrothed before their seventh birthday and anyone who had made an unconsummated marriage. The clauses were not exclusive so the same person could be covered by both.

The reference to a marriage in childhood would cover Anne if she had been sent to the Low Countries with a view to marrying a Flemish nobleman. Under canon law, a marriage contracted before the age of seven was invalid so did not require dispensation unless the vows were either confirmed in the present tense after that age or the couple lived under the same roof, referred to one another as husband or wife or exchanged gifts. If they did so, the impediment of public honesty existed and required dispensation.[181] The reference to an unconsummated marriage could be considered to cover Anne if she had ever entered into some binding vows with Percy – though both denied this and the malicious allegation that she had was investigated thoroughly in July 1532 and April 1536 – but it also included many other women both in England and abroad.[182]

As regards the change in blood relationships, Anne was certainly not the King's second cousin so why did Henry insist on this change if he was exclusively committed to marrying her?

In April 1528, the pope issued the revised bull which covered second and third cousins, god-daughters and mothers of god-children, anyone who had married privately but not consummated their union, the close relations of anyone Henry had ever slept with and anyone privately betrothed but who had not proceeded to actual marriage.[183] Henry pronounced himself happy. The document allowed him to marry Anne – but crucially, hundreds of other women as well.

---

180 Henry's mother died in 1502 so could not have been Anne's godmother unless the early date for her birth is accepted. Even then, there is no reason to imagine the Boleyns were is such high favour as to be thus honoured at the time.
181 Decretals Gregory IX Book 4, T1,c3
182 LP 10.864. See July 1532 in Why did it take so long?
183 Stephan Ehses, *Römische dokumente,* (Paderborn, 1893) pp. 33-36

It would seem that the person wavering in their commitment to the great marriage plan was Anne. Given Henry continued to live with Katherine and honour her as his queen, it is easy to imagine she would have felt insecure in her position. In the summer of 1528, Anne was ill and Henry stayed miles away. That was the responsible thing to do because his responsibilities as king required him not to take unnecessary risks, but the long period of Anne's absence from him suggests that she did not see it quite that way. One of Henry's letters to her from this period note that he was still uncertain of her feelings, describing himself confused by her responses which seemed positive on some days and negative on others.[184]

Those romantics who like to claim that Henry broke with Katherine to marry Anne need to recognise that if Anne had died in 1528, he would have been upset but carried on with the annulment process. He was never going to return to Katherine. It was a matter of principle and constitutional need, not romance. They also need to pay more attention to dates. The "marriage" to Katherine was over years before Henry became involved with Anne and the annulment process began before Henry decided to ask Anne to marry him, not after.

Question: Was Anne the cause of the breakdown of Henry's 'marriage' to Katherine?

Answer
No, but she was the beneficiary of it. If she had not appeared in his life, it would have been someone else.

---

184 See Appendix 2 – The Love Letters. LP 4.3218

Why did it take so long for Henry and Anne to marry?

The usual story runs along the following lines.

> Dastardly Villain Henry falls for Feisty Temptress Anne and decides to divorce his wife Saintly Victim Katherine. Given he has No Case and the pope is a prisoner, this represents an Impossible Task for Wolsey. When Wolsey suffers inevitable failure, Dastardly Villain Henry destroys him before spending almost three years sitting around waiting for Clever Clogs Cromwell to come along and sort the mess all out for him.

It is a familiar tale and writers often employ carefully selected texts to try and justify it, whilst keeping quiet about all the contradictory evidence. Henry's case was excellent as has been shown and Wolsey almost achieved the reasonable task he was set. The annulment crisis lasted six years and the pope was only a prisoner for seven months of this. The period from the collapse of the legatine court in the summer of 1529 to the spring of 1532 was full of activity and Henry was totally proactive and in control. Not only is the conventional story wrong in many key respects, it is based on simplistic characterisation which pays little if any attention to the wider context. Readers could be forgiven after completing most biographies of Anne if they were unaware of a European war going on for much of the time: a bizarre omission. Nobody would write a biography of Clementine Churchill and fail to mention the Second World War yet books about Anne or the annulment often give the impression that the only thing happening in the world was this affair, as if the people involved all lived in little bubbles. This is not how it was. In the first three months of 1528, barely five per cent of official documents as recorded in the *Letters and Papers of Henry VIII*, related to the "Great Matter." It might have been the most important issue on Henry's mind but the daily business of government went on and so did life in general for Henry and Anne. They did not spend all their time poring over legal documents: they hunted, they played music, they went to look at a new lion, they laughed. We can be sure they worried about what to wear, if their hair was greying or their girth expanding, and other such things. This must be remembered for it is the story of real people not events associated with flat portraits in various galleries.

In order to answer the question of why it took so long for Henry to marry Anne, it is necessary to follow the advice of David Starkey and employ "a due attention to contemporary judgment and description; a rejection of broad based developmental or teleological interpretation, and emphasis instead on circumstance and personality; a return to narrative and a willingness to take the long view."[1] Hence the decision to plot the story here month by month. Readers may at times feel frustrated that issues are raised repeatedly and that there are months when not much seems to happen, but this is important. If we are to understand the problems and opportunities and the characters of those involved, we have to go on the journey with Henry and Anne not jump from the legatine court to the Act of Succession. Along the way, we will learn a lot about them as individuals, about European history and about the people who made it. Some issues will come up over and over again. Questions which should have been resolved in minutes were protracted over years by lawyers who had no interest in a quick solution. With a king on one side and an emperor on the other, the opportunities to make a fortune were evident. The struggle involved people who were forced to react to a wide range of events. Sometimes, the news they heard was incorrect but they did not have the benefit of centuries of hindsight or one-click access to all the European archives or satellite television allowing them to see what was going on in another part of the world. They did the best they could. As the situation unfolded, their own attitudes changed and developed: only a fool fails to mature in life. Some of the things which happened had an immediate and obvious impact, others were more subtle. This 'saga' approach also ensures that evidence so frequently repressed by historians is brought to the fore, such as the amount of money the Emperor spent on securing the support of cardinals and scholars, the vicious mentalities of some of Henry's enemies and some of Katherine's questionable behaviour. It allows for a more accurate assessment of sources for the period. For example, Chapuys is frequently quoted in books about the period but when all his despatches are considered rather than just the odd one or two, a more nuanced view of his reliability is possible. Going through the events in detail should also help to correct the sense of inevitability which so often exists in books written about a familiar event. Everyone knows that Henry married Anne Boleyn, just as they know she lost her head, but it is important to try and step back to see the world before these things happened.[2] Such things are vital if we want to see the "big picture."

Throughout this diary of events, references are made to people who will feature later in Anne's story. Some such as William Brereton who was executed as one of her lovers in 1536, are well known while others will be less familiar and people will need to read on to discover the relevance of them, e.g. the Marquis of Mantua. A number of people changed their names and titles during the period under discussion. Anne's father, for example, became Viscount Rochford and then Earl of Wiltshire at which point his son became Viscount Rochford. To avoid confusion amongst readers, names are kept the same throughout. Thus, Thomas Boleyn is always listed as that rather than as Rochford or Wiltshire, his son always as George Boleyn and so forth. Job titles

---

1   David Starkey (ed.) *The English Court* (1987) p.24
2   As Conrad Russell once observed, the "historian is like a man who sits down to read a detective story after beginning with the last chapter." 'Parliamentary History in Perspective', *History*, vol. 61 (1976) p.1

are repeated relatively often which may irritate those who are totally familiar with the names of all the different ambassadors across Europe and their dates of service, but will hopefully assist everyone else in keeping track.[3] To avoid excessive footnoting, in the summaries below, calendared documents are referenced in brackets whilst references to documents from other sources are noted in the usual manner.

Following the narrative, there is a conventional analytical summary.

Introduction

In 1527, Western Europe was dominated by two men, Francis I and Emperor Charles V. Francis was thirty-three (three years younger than Henry) and ruled what should have been the richest country in Europe, France. Charles was twenty-seven. He had inherited Burgundy from his father, Spain from his mother[4] and in June 1519 had been elected Holy Roman Emperor following the death of his grandfather. The empire included areas which are today incorporated within Germany, Belgium and the Netherlands. These territories meant that Charles controlled almost all the lands around France. Through his Habsburg relations, he also had links to Denmark and Hungary: in October 1526 his brother Ferdinand had been elected King of Bohemia.[5] This naturally worried France and this is why it was so keen to have friendly rulers in Northern Italy. At this time, Italy was a collection of independent states, though in practice most of the rulers were supported by either Francis or Charles who expressed various claims to territories in their own right. Although alliances continually changed, at the start of this period Venice, Florence, Milan and Genoa were pro-France whilst Naples and Sardinia were Imperialist.[6] The pope was a prince in his own right who controlled considerable lands and maintained armies to defend them. In 1527, the pope was Clement VII, a member of the Medici family which ruled Florence.

---

3   The word ambassador is generally used for clarity even though some foreign representatives were special envoys sent on short term missions not resident.
4   His mother Juana was alive but had been incarcerated for insanity.
5   His claim to Hungary was disputed by the Vayvod, John Zápolya, known in documents of the period usually as Zapolski. Ferdinand's wife had been the only daughter of King Vladislaus and following the death of her brother in August, would have succeeded in an hereditary monarchy but Bohemia was elective and the Hungarian nobility were divided about whom they wished to rule, a situation Francis, the pope and Henry would exploit.
6   Milan and Naples were both claimed by the French and the Spanish. Naples had been ruled by Aragon from 1442 before being conquered by the French. The Spanish took it back in 1504 and now France wanted it returned. Milan was French until 1521 and then became Spanish. When its Duke, Francesco Sforza II was ousted by Charles V, Milan itself remained Imperial while the Duke joined the French as he sought to regain his territory.

England's main trading partner was the Low Countries ruled also by Charles and it had dynastic links to Spain and Portugal going back to the fourteenth century: Katherine was Henry's third cousin once removed. Defeat in the Hundred Years' War followed by thirty years of civil war had weakened England on the international scene but the accession of the Tudors and decades of stability had led to it being on the rise at this time. Although he could not compete with Charles or Francis when it came to resources, Henry was wealthy and he had an internationally respected statesman in Wolsey at his side. The majority in England were Imperialist in sympathy. The aristocracy still resented the defeats inflicted on their grandparents in France while the common people wanted to preserve trade. A general and deep seated mistrust of the French had existed for centuries but encouraged by Wolsey, Henry had decided to pursue a pro-French policy. Almost twenty years of being continually let down by the Spanish and Imperialists had upset him and he does seem to have preferred Francis as a person – despite their rivalry – to Katherine's nephew, Charles. The policy also made good strategic sense. France had long maintained close links with Scotland – ruled presently by Henry's fifteen year old nephew James V - and Henry did not want to risk invasion from the north. Similarly, it was more likely that France rather than Spain would mount an invasion bid of England in event of hostilities because it was much nearer. Amity with France gave England security and prevented it facing a continent which was under the dominion of one man – a prospect as unattractive in 1527 as it was in 1939. That Charles could achieve this domination was a very real fear. In 1525 he had captured Francis and held him hostage for a year, only releasing him after he had agreed to the Treaty of Madrid which required him to cede Burgundy, renounce his claims to Italy, marry the Emperor's sister and send his sons – the Dauphin aged nine and the Duke of Orleans age eight – to Spain as hostages. The king's ransom had depleted French coffers and with his heirs in Spain, there was a concern that if Francis died, Charles could install a puppet ruler in France and destroy England. Fearful of this, Henry had committed himself to helping Francis get his sons back. In the summer of 1526, a League had been formed involving the pope, France, Venice, Florence and the Duke of Milan in opposition to Charles.[7] The stated aims of this were to:

1. persuade the Emperor to release Francis' sons for a reasonable ransom instead of ceding land
2. have Francesco Sforza reinstated as Duke of Milan
3. see all Italian states return to their pre-war boundaries
4. ensure that the Emperor repaid his debt to Henry VIII in full
5. limit the size of the entourage which the Emperor brought to Italy for his coronation to a number to be agreed by the pope and Venice.

---

[7] It was variously known as the League of Cognac, the Holy League or the Clementine league.

If the Emperor refused these terms the League would seek to seize Milan, Genoa and Naples and so force him into compliance.[8] He had refused and war had broken out with Imperial troops attacking the papal palace in Rome and desecrating St Peter's – an act which had horrified Henry. England was not a member of the League of 1526 though Henry had been invited to be its protector, but at the start of 1527, it was considering its position.

So in the year the annulment crisis began, the policies of the leading players can be summed up as follows:

> Francis – win the war in Italy, develop links with England to prevent being encircled by Emperor Charles V and his allies, get his sons back
> Charles – win the war in Italy, maintain links with England to keep France under pressure and weak
> Henry – mediate between Charles and Francis to bring peace to Europe, get Francis' sons back
> Pope Clement – get both French and Imperial troops out of Italy

1527

January 1527

Events

- the Milanese ambassador suggests Henry marry his daughter to the Imperial commander, Bourbon[9] or his son so that the Emperor will make peace in return for having his kinsman as the next king of England and thereby be inclined to restore Sforza as duke of Milan (CSPM 1.760).
- Francis' sister Marguerite d'Alençon marries Henri II, King of Navarre (LP 4.2774; CSPV 4.6).
- Albert of Brandenburg praises Henry as a theologian and pillar of orthodoxy and orders a print run of his book against Luther, the *Assertio* (LP 4.2776)
- Francis's mother praises Wolsey and attributes the prosperity of England to his wisdom, and seeks his advice (LP 4.2805)
- the Emperor assures Wolsey of his love and confidence in a rare handwritten note writing "I have perfect faith in you. ...You will always find me to be

---

8 Geoffrey Parker, *Emperor* (Yale, 2019) p.165.
9 Bourbon was a leading French nobleman who had traitorously turned to support the Emperor following a dispute about the inheritance of property owned by his late wife. He had previously suggested that he would be happy to make Henry King of France – provided Henry was willing to fund the conquest (LP 4.365, 996, 997, 1175).

your good friend" (LP 4.2825). He also determines to reward Wolsey's secretary, Brian Tuke, for his loyalty to the Imperial cause (CSPS 3.2.15).
- Francis appoints three envoys to negotiate a marriage treaty with Henry's ten year old daughter, Mary (LP 4.2771, 2773, 2774, 2790). Venice expresses delight at the prospect believing it will encourage Henry to join the League. Milan is pleased also thinking a united England and France will strengthen papal resolve in the war (CSPM 1.758, 760; CSPV 4.20).
- Wolsey summons the ambassadors and asks them to obtain powers from their sovereigns so that peace talks can begin (CSPM 1.759).
- meanwhile, at Valladolid in Spain, the Emperor's chancellor, Gattinara, opens his own peace conference demanding that ambassadors there obtain and present powers from their sovereigns. Assisting him is the Emperor's confessor, Loaysa. The Milanese ambassador attends along with the Venetian but they are convinced that the process is just a sham given the Emperor's success in the war gives him no motive to make peace (CSPV 4.17, 19). Ghinucci, the Bishop of Worcester who arrives there on the 15th to assist the resident English ambassador Lee, says he believes the talks are just to convince the Spanish parliament to vote more money to the Emperor so he can continue the war (LP 4.2812).
- Imperial troops attack churches, monks and nuns and desecrate crucifixes in a rampage at Fiorenzuola. They threaten Florence leaving the pope much afraid (LP 4.2763, 2779). Rumours fly that the troops will remain unpaid to encourage them to attack Rome and make their own money through pillage and hostage taking (CSPS 3.2.3,9,11).
- the papal nuncio in England, Gambara, receives a letter from the Datary, Giberti describing the desperate situation in Rome: "We are on the brink of ruin. Fate has let loose upon us every kind of evil so that it is impossible to add to our misery. It seems to me as if sentence of death has been passed upon us and that we are only awaiting its execution which cannot be long delayed."[10]
- Henry despatches Sir John Russell to Rome with 30,000 ducats for the pope's use in defending Rome (CSPV 4.3; LP 4.2770).
- the pope declares himself dependent on Henry and Wolsey's aid and he authorises them to negotiate peace, suggesting also that Henry be arbiter of the fate of Milan (LP 4.2763, 2782, 2826, 2827).
- a new Spanish ambassador arrives in England, Don Inigo de Mendoza, and has acrimonious encounters with Wolsey and Henry, the latter observing: "the Emperor is not my friend." The English favour a truce while peace is negotiated whilst the Spanish want an outline peace to be agreed first. The English complain about the money the Emperor owes and his renunciation of his betrothal to Henry's daughter, Mary. They refuse to

---

10 Ludwig von Pastor (trans. Frederick Antrobus), *History of the Popes* (1908) vol. 7 p.347

consider negotiating a new Anglo-Imperial alliance until peace is made in Europe and debts are paid (CSPS 3.2.8).
- the pope issues a letter warning Naples that it will be excommunicated if it does not cease its rebellion against him – this despite papal lawyers being uncertain whether the territory belonged to the pope or the Emperor (CSPS 3.2.9). It is reported that the pope has ordered a bull to be drawn up depriving the Emperor of the Holy Roman Empire itself (CSPS 3.2.3).
- William Brereton's brother, Urian, is made constable of Chirke Castle (LP 4.2839.19)

Comments

From 1521 until the summer of 1525, Henry's daughter Mary had been due to marry the Emperor. The then pope had been very keen on the match as he saw it as a means of punishing France for invading his territory.[11] The Emperor was sixteen years older than Mary and in 1525 he decided that his need for an heir was too great for him to wait for Mary to grow up, so he would marry Isabella of Portugal. Pope Clement, aware that the Emperor's behaviour would create an irreparable breach between the Emperor and Henry, hastened to encourage a marriage between Mary and Francis hoping that a united France and England would challenge the dominance of the Emperor in Europe.[12] Henry's offer of his daughter to Francis was indeed motivated by this goal but the main objective was to stop Francis going through with the marriage to the Emperor's sister which he had been forced to accept as one of the conditions for his release in 1526.[13] The prospect of France and the Emperor being united against England was a serious threat.

The proposal of the Milanese ambassador was never taken seriously and is of interest only for what it shows about attitudes of the time. People did not expect Henry to have more children and they assumed that whoever married Mary would go on to rule England rather than her. Writers today often give the impression that Henry was being unreasonable in saying he needed a son as his heir but the opinion expressed by this diplomat and others, plus the experience of history, showed he was right to doubt anyone would accept Mary as queen in her own right. Henry himself spoke of Mary's future husband becoming king of England after his death which is why the choice of groom was so important.[14]

Thirty thousand ducats would be worth around fifty million pounds today so Henry's donation was considerable, albeit according to the pope a drop in the ocean given the cost of waging war was one hundred thousand ducats a

---

11   LP 3.1402, 1802.
12   LP 4.1523
13   Henry had declared the frustration of the Francis-Eleanor match a key English strategy in September 1525, LP 4.1628. See also LP 4.1705 which lists the arguments the ambassadors are to use.
14   LP 4.1150, 1212. See also the *Glasse of Truthe* which is contained in Nicholas Pocock, *Records of the Reformation*, vol. 2 (1870) pp.385-421

month to him (LP 4.2827). The Emperor's secretary believed the pope exaggerated his poverty and noted that his profiteering on wheat prices was more than sufficient to fund his army and navy.[15]

According to Henry – and the Emperor did not dispute this – he was owed £139,835. 15s, the equivalent of some £978 million today.[16] The money had been owing for various lengths of time covering many years, and the Emperor's excuse was that he could not afford it because of the costs of the war. Henry retorted that he should not have been waging war in the first place. The Emperor had offered to send letters of credit but Henry pointed out that he had lent him cash, actual gold coins, and he wanted the same back. Following the Emperor's recent marriage and his receipt of an enormous dowry plus a large sum voted by the Spanish parliament, neither Henry nor Wolsey could believe the Emperor was unable to pay up, rather they believed he was deliberately refusing to pay and took this as a hostile act. Given the sums involved, it is easy to see why Henry was upset.

The English played no part in the Spanish peace talks because England was officially neutral. This was why Wolsey was attempting to lead his own talks at Henry's direction and with the pope's backing. Wolsey's previous efforts, such as the Treaty of London, show he was a very experienced negotiator. The tributes he received from world leaders were undoubtedly politically motivated exercises in flattery but they were not void of truth. The cardinal might be unpopular with many in England but he was highly respected on the European stage and that reflected glory on England. [17]

Giberti was one of the pope's leading advisors and one of the architects of the League of Cognac and staunchly pro-French.

The rumours about the attack on Rome are important. After the sack of May 1527, the Emperor was to claim that it occurred without his authorisation and he was unable to prevent it but letters from his own envoys to him show that he was aware of what was happening well in advance. The Emperor did nothing suggesting he did not oppose the plan.[18]

The Emperor's gift to Tuke should be noted. Over the years, Katherine's supporters have made much of Henry's alleged payments to people he hoped would favour him. As will be shown, the Emperor did this all the time and gave a lot more to many more people.

---

15 CSPS 3.2.9
16 CSPS 3.2.2. This sum probably represented a year of Henry's income.
17 The Emperor had agreed to accept Henry's mediation at the end of 1526, LP 4.Appx 95.
18 For more detail see June 1527 Comments

February 1527

Events

- Francis's envoys depart for England amid rumours picked up by English ambassadors in Spain that Francis is not serious about marrying Mary (LP 4.2785, 2859, 2862, 2867).
- Cardinals in Rome pass a unanimous declaration of admiration for Wolsey's dedication to the pope which is held all the more remarkable because he lives in the "very corner of Christendom" (LP 4.2866). The pope agrees and orders a reprint of Henry's *Assertio* claiming Henry is a blessing from God, the true defender of Italy and a man who supports Christianity by his money, arms and genius (LP 4.2857). The pope says he is more bound to Henry than any other ruler (LP 4.2875) and calls him his saviour (LP 4.2919). He promises to make Ghinucci and Giberti cardinals to please Henry (CSPM 1.768).
- the ambassadors from the pope, Emperor, Francis and Venice gather in London for peace talks with other representatives expected from Germany and other Italian states. Preparations are made in London amid rumours that Francis himself will attend (LP 4.2878).
- Francis notes the great respect paid in Italy to Henry's authority and to Wolsey's advice (LP 4.2895). He tells the Venetian ambassador that Wolsey has as much authority as Henry and is the man "on whom the greatest reliance might be placed on earth." (CSPV 4.44)
- a marriage between the pope's "niece", Catherine de Medici, and Henry's illegitimate son, the Duke of Richmond, is proposed (LP 4.2875). It is also reported that the pope has offered her to the Duke of Ferrara as a bride for his son if only the Duke will cease his support for the Emperor and join the League (CSPS 3.2.30).
- the pope remains desperate for funds to pay his army as Francis's payments are over four months in arrears. He threatens to make peace with the Emperor if Francis does not marry Mary (LP 4.2875, 2912) and worries about the fate of Florence (LP 4.2910). Venice sends him cash and an army to help defend Florence on condition that he rejects any terms offered by the Emperor (CSPS 3.2.31).
- it is reported that the Navarre marriage has been consummated (CSPV 4.21).
- the Valladolid peace conference is disbanded without any progress being made. The Emperor blames the pope for the war and increases restrictions on Francis' sons whom he has in captivity (CSPV 4.41). The Emperor says that Francis' insistence on any terms being approved by Henry is unreasonable while the pope's demand that he pay his debts to Henry is irrelevant. He accuses Francis of fuelling war not peace by joining the League. He does, however, claim that his love for Henry is so great that nothing could ever come between them (CSPS 3.2.24).

- Wolsey unveils his peace plan. Francis pays half the ransom for his sons and the first prince is released and sent to England to be cared for by Henry until the full ransom is paid. Francis marries Henry's daughter Mary and the Emperor's sister marries Bourbon and is given Naples. Sforza is restored as Duke of Milan (CSPV 4.48, 49). The Milanese think this is too favourable to Bourbon who also claims Milan as his own (CSPM 1.777). The pope says it is too late and he has no choice but to make some sort of peace with the Emperor (CSPM 1.776). Scenting victory, the Emperor wants war not peace (CSPM 1.778).
- the Emperor's ambassadors and his military commanders send further letters to him demanding urgent payment for his troops many of whom have not been paid for over a year (CSPS 3.2.26, 27).

Comments

Catherine de Medici is routinely referred to as the pope's niece in correspondence of the period but she was actually the grand-daughter of his first cousin. Aged eight at the time, she was a considerable heiress and there was great competition for her hand. She would be sought during this period by the Duke of Milan, the Marquis of Mantua, James V of Scotland, Francis I of France (for his sons) and the Duke of Ferrara.[19]

There is no evidence that Francis ever planned to come to England for the peace talks but the rumour that he was going to do so indicates the importance placed on this high level diplomacy and the confidence in Wolsey's powers of persuasion.

The pope's eulogy for Henry was not empty rhetoric. The money sent from England had just arrived and must have seemed a lifeline to a man facing Imperial armies threatening to march on Rome from every direction, his own troops deserting fast due to a lack of pay and starvation and still the damage from the assault in September 1526 to repair. Henry's Italian ambassador at Rome, Gregory Casale, says that the pope told him that he felt safer knowing that he could rely on Henry's support (LP 4.2891). The pope's concern for Florence was because he was a member of the ruling Medici family himself. In the treaty of November 1524, the pope had made an alliance with Francis and Venice on behalf of both the Papal States and Florence.

Ghinucci was the Italian Bishop of Worcester. He had been a papal employee for more than twenty years and was a scholar and a diplomat serving Leo X and Clement VII as well as Henry. His nephew was Wolsey's physician. Henry would make repeated efforts to obtain a cardinal's hat for him and one was granted in 1535 by which stage the Reformation had begun. Although Henry eventually removed him as Bishop of Worcester – he had never carried

---

19 For the relationship between Catherine and her brother Alessandro and their cousin Hippolito and the pope, see Appendix 6– Key Relationships

out any duties in the diocese – he showed his continued respect and affection for him by granting him a pension for life.

Nothing seems to have come of the proposal to marry Richmond to Catherine de Medici, but if it had gone ahead, it might have made Henry's quest for an annulment a great deal easier.

It seems strange to us today that marriage consummation was an item of news. Nobody could imagine someone being sent to ask Prince Philip in 1947 if he had done his duty to Princess Elizabeth so that a report could be transmitted to all the ambassadors of the British Empire. Yet, it was common behaviour in the medieval and Tudor period. Grooms would publicly proclaim their prowess to their courtiers and in some countries, blood stained sheets were exhibited. This was why when questions were asked about the consummation of Katherine and Arthur's marriage, nobody demurred at the interrogation of witnesses.

March 1527

Events

- the Emperor tells the English ambassadors in Spain that he refuses to allow Francis to break the Treaty of Madrid which Francis signed in January 1526 (LP 4.2948). He wants Milan to be given to Bourbon (LP 4.2952).
- the *Assertio* is sold in Bohemia. The Duke of Saxony orders a German translation of it (LP 4.2960, 2968).
- Francis offers Renée, the younger sister of his late wife, as a spouse to the Duke of Ferrara's son in a bid to persuade the Duke to join the League. John Casale, the English ambassador in Venice, is sent to Ferrara to encourage him to accept the proposal (CSPV 4.54, 59) but the Duke refuses to join as he mistrusts the pope (CSPV 4.63). Instead, Ferrara confirms a proposal for his son to marry the Emperor's bastard daughter (CSPS 3.2.45).
- suspicion mounts that the pope is ready to do a deal with the Emperor (LP 4.2962) and this does indeed happen to the fury of the League with an armistice agreed for eight months (CSPS 3.2.38). Henry and Wolsey complain that this has ruined all hope of peace and accuse him of breaking his promises to them (LP 4.2971, 3001; CSPV 4.83). Wolsey tells the Milanese ambassador: "I cannot but blame his holiness' counsel and regret having promised my king so much with regard to the pope's good faith." (CSPV 4.74) John Casale explains that the pope's expenses for the war are 100,000 ducats a month and he simply does not have the money to continue (CSPV 4.53).
- Gregory Casale and John Russell in Rome report that the pope is a weak man and susceptible to pressure and too concerned about Florence and say many cardinals wish that Wolsey was pope as he would be stronger and stand up to the Emperor (LP 4.2971, 3001, 3003).

- Francis's envoys arrive in England to negotiate the marriage. An issue arises over whether Francis is free to marry Mary with Henry saying "I am unwilling to separate man and wife" (CSPS 3.2.39). The French query if Henry and Katherine are likely to have more children and Wolsey says not and that Mary is the heir. Henry himself confirms this when he says he will not "give his heiress to a man about whose capacity to marry there might be doubts." This pleases the French whose king observes that this means that whoever marries her will inherit England. There is also disagreement about whether the marriage should be settled before or after peace is made. Wolsey suspects Francis of using the negotiations as a means of pressurising the Emperor into giving him Eleanor as a wife in person and not just in name. Katherine, meanwhile, takes the opportunity of telling the French envoys that she disapproves of the plan because it will upset the Emperor which prompts an embarrassed Henry to say it will help peace. Another area of concern is that Francis wants Mary immediately. His mother says she is old enough to consummate marriage at eleven and promises Francis will be gentle but Henry refuses to allow Mary to consummate any marriage until she is fourteen. Wolsey suggests that perhaps Mary should marry Francis's son the Duke of Orleans instead. Thomas Boleyn plays an active part in all the negotiations. At a dinner, Henry impresses the French with his great learning and theological understanding (LP 4.2974, 2981, 2988, 3105; CSPM 1.788; CSPV 4.62).
- Mendoza admits to feigning illness as he struggles to carry out the Emperor's orders which include not speaking about the money the Emperor owes Henry and effectively preventing peace negotiations by delaying tactics such as waiting for a lawyer whom the Emperor refuses to send. Mendoza admits that Wolsey is angry about the 45,000 ducats which the Emperor owes him too and expresses his fears that a breach between the Emperor and England is inevitable. Wolsey tells him: "the King of England would certainly have much liked to see peace concluded here through his mediation but as the Emperor seems not to desire this, there is no need for further discussion. The King therefore withdraws from the negotiations and will now act independently and as best suits his interests." Henry himself tells Mendoza that "The Emperor ought to be content with his present dominions" and warns that the Emperor's pursuit of universal monarchy will meet fierce resistance. Mendoza advises the Emperor of the need to invest in substantial payments to Henry, Wolsey and various councillors and government officials if the situation is to be saved (CSPS 3.2.32, 37).
- an evaluation prepared for taxation shows Thomas Boleyn to be one of the wealthiest men at court and that Anne's brother-in-law William Carey is very comfortably off too (LP 4.2972).

Comments

The Duke of Ferrara had agreed that his son would marry the Emperor's bastard daughter in September 1526 (LP 4.2737). Francis' offer of Renée to him was clearly made at the start of 1527 and with Wolsey's approval to allow time for the latter to send instructions to John Casale to support the plan. Messages took, on average, a month to reach Italy from England. Casale left Venice just after March 2nd and was back by the 11th. This is relevant because a number of people at the time alleged that Wolsey sought an annulment for Henry to marry a French princess yet Marguerite was already married and Renée's union was being planned. The reason that the support of the Duke of Ferrara was so keenly sought by both the Emperor and the League was that he was extremely rich, very influential and regarded as a skilled military strategist plus his territory was believed to be key to holding Milan and thus the League's military campaign. Francis had previously offered Renée to the Duke of Bourbon when it was thought that the Emperor might agree to give Milan to him. [20]

Henry employed Sir Gregory Casale as his ambassador at Rome and his brother John Casale at Venice. The former was a layman, the latter a cleric. Other members of the family also served both the pope and Henry on a less formal or permanent basis. Gregory had been introduced to Henry when he came to England in 1519 as part of Campeggio's staff and had impressed him so much that he knighted him and offered him employment and a generous income.[21] As well as serving as ambassador, Gregory was involved in purchasing horses for the King. At this time, Gregory was around twenty-seven.[22]

The taxation list for the royal household gives some indicator of where the Boleyn family fitted into society at this point by enabling comparisons of wealth. Top of the list was the earl of Northumberland, father of Henry Percy, who was assessed on £2920. The Earl of Worcester, whose wife became a friend of Anne's, on £2000. The King's brother-in-law, Charles Brandon, the Duke of Suffolk, was valued at £1000. The King's uncle, whose wife Honour was also a friend of Anne's, on £900. After Thomas Boleyn rated on £800 came Fitzwilliam the treasurer on £666, Carew the Master of Horse on £400 and Sir Thomas More who was valued at £340 with William Carey at £333. Lower down the list came Henry Norris at £104 and Thomas Cromwell at £50. In real terms, a pound in this period would have the spending power of £7000 today so it is abundantly clear that the Boleyns were doing very well for themselves with Thomas' value being some £5.6 million excluding income received from pensions and fees and Carey's £2.3 million.[23]

---

20 LP 4.1875.
21 LP 3.421. The starting salary was set at 200 crowns.
22 Catherine Fletcher, *Our Man in Rome* (2012) p.1
23 Prior to 1522, Boleyn had lent Compton a thousand marks so his wealth was not recent but long standing, LP 4.4442.

The French query about whether Mary would inherit was couched in a gallant comment that Katherine appeared young enough to have more children. They knew she was forty-two and this was impossible and the remark was made both to flatter her and to elicit confirmation from the English to this effect. Katherine's open criticism of the plan – her comments were recorded by the French who heard them – show her great concern for her Spanish family and that she regarded their interests as above those of England and her husband. It was a foretaste of things to come.

Francis had been forced to marry the Emperor's sister, Eleanor, as part of the Treaty of Madrid. At the time, Francis was the Emperor's prisoner and he was told that he must agree to the marriage if he wanted to be released. Francis later commented that he would have married the Emperor's mule at that point just to escape. The union was regarded as of questionable legitimacy because bride and groom were related in fourth degree consanguinity and no dispensation had been issued at the time of the marriage and because Francis was forced into it. Following the service, Francis was released but his bride was kept in Spain with the Emperor saying he would only send her when Francis had fulfilled all the terms of the Treaty. Given the conditions and because the marriage was unconsummated, Francis should have been able to secure an annulment from the pope if he wished although he would have faced the same problem as Henry did in the pope not wishing to offend the Emperor.

The idea of Mary marrying the Duke of Orleans had been suggested by Francis' mother in November 1526.[24] She had suggested the young Duke could, on his release from captivity, be brought up in England which would accustom him to the language and people and they to him meaning that he would be readily accepted as king after Henry. The English had been less than enthusiastic about this but it was indicative of a general attitude that Mary would not be able to rule in her own right and need a husband to do the job for her. Regardless of the issue of misogynistic prejudice here, this proposal shows the clear danger to England that would arise if European powers would not recognise Mary as ruler in her own right. Wolsey's revival of the idea was more of a negotiating ploy than expression of serious intention. The Duke was Henry's godson and so in first degree spiritual affinity with Mary making him a prohibited groom unless a dispensation was obtained from the pope. Such a document could no doubt have been purchased but there is no evidence that anyone ever even enquired about doing so which tends to prove the lack of real intention toward the match.

The Anglo-French marriage alliance, whether to be formed by Francis or his son, was very important politically. Francis wanted to oblige Henry to do more to help get his sons out of captivity. The pope and Venice wanted it to go ahead so they could secure English arms and money for the war in Italy. For Henry, it would be a prestigious match for Mary either way and help him to

---

24 LP 4.2651.

enact revenge on the Emperor for reneging on his promises to marry her and repay his debts.

The anger over the armistice was unsurprising. The League had taken most of Naples and the Abruzzo and had a victory over the Imperial army at Frosinone. The pope claimed he had no choice because he had no money but the Imperialists suspected – as had Casale – that the pope's chief concern was the fate of Florence (CSPS 3.2.59). His decision to make an agreement without the prior consent of his allies seriously upset France and Venice. Wolsey had been open in saying that the prime reason for the Anglo-French marriage was to prevent the pope abandoning the League so when the news came that he had done so anyway, the dynamic of the talks shifted slightly.

Mendoza's comments about the risk of a complete breach between England and the Emperor were to be proved right a month later as the annulment crisis began.

April 1527

Events

- Thomas Wyatt is captured by the Spanish while on an embassy to Italy and held for ransom but released (LP 4.3011).
- the pope and viceroy of Naples (Lannoy) confirm the truce but the Emperor's military commander, Bourbon, refuses to accept it (LP 4.3023). Imperial troops continue on their rampage and commit scores of atrocities (LP 4.3046, 3065, 3066). Wolsey urges the pope to excommunicate the Emperor in response (LP 4.3046).
- Bourbon sends a representative to tell the pope that unless he immediately pays 150,000 ducats, his army will march on Florence and Rome (CSPS 3.2.47). The pope refuses so the troops continue to advance. Two weeks later, the demand is for 300,000 ducats (CSPS 3.2.56). Having disbanded his army in accordance with the terms of the armistice, the angry pope begins recruiting fresh troops. Venice and France offer him asylum should he choose to flee (CSPS 3.2.58).
- Francis orders the Bishop of Tarbes to treat for a marriage between his second son the Duke of Orleans (still captive in Spain) and Mary (LP 4.3059). Following Henry's comment that he wants to visit France to plan war against the Emperor, he extends an invitation for Wolsey to come ahead in May for private talks about the European situation (LP 4.3105, Appx.108).
- Henry asks Francis to refrain from helping his sister Margaret, Queen of Scotland, get an annulment saying he is ashamed of her behaviour (LP 4.3070, 3088).
- the Emperor expresses distrust of Francis and the pope and threatens to withdraw allegiance from the pope and call a General Council (LP 4.3047-9).

- the pope admits his efforts to appease the enemy with money are not working (LP 4.3046) and revokes the truce (LP 4.3063). He rejoins the League of Cognac on the 25th.[25]
- the Emperor is told that an attack on Rome is "very desirable" and the "best solution" given the pope's behaviour (CSPS 3.2.59).
- France and England agree a treaty on the 30th which says that Mary will marry either Francis or his son and that the two countries will jointly declare war on the Emperor to get Francis's sons back unless they are released promptly. Francis will pay Henry's costs. If Mary is not Henry's sole heir, the treaty is void. Thomas Boleyn is one of the five commissioners for England who has negotiated this treaty. (LP 4.3080). The treaty is publicly celebrated on 4th May although Hall reports that special watches were held in London for fear of riots given the unpopularity of the match as people said "they would have no Frenchman to be king of England."[26] Mendoza confirms that the French marriage is deeply unpopular (CSPS 3.2.37). Henry tells the French of his desire to humble the Emperor and invade the Low Countries and asks Brandon to lead the army (LP 4.3105).
- William Carey, husband of Mary Boleyn, is granted four manors (LP 4.3087.18) and William Brereton two hundred acres (LP 4.3087.26).
- the aged Bishop of Winchester, Richard Foxe, is questioned on the 5th and 6th about the circumstances leading up to Henry's "marriage" to Katherine (LP 4.5791).
- Wolsey is taken ill but recovers in time to start planning a trip to France in early June in order to make plans for an Anglo-French assault on the Emperor's forces if he does not respond favourably to the peace proposal (CSPV 4.90,97,98; CSPM 1.800; LP 4.3081,3088; CSPS 3.2.55).
- Ghinucci says that he does not believe that the Emperor is interested in peace and warns that his colleague, Lee, is too trusting of the Emperor, an opinion shared by the Venetian ambassador (CSPV 4.19, 92; LP 4.3057)
- in an effort to make peace, Henry offers his son, Richmond, to the Emperor as a groom to any Imperial princess of appropriate age. He describes Richmond as living in "the state of a great prince" and says that he has the power to easily exalt him "to higher things" (LP 4.3051). Mendoza suspects this is a bluff and that what England wants is to see the proposed marriage between the Portuguese Infanta and the Dauphin of France abandoned so that the Dauphin can marry Mary.[27] He suggests the Emperor arrange for James V of Scotland to marry an Imperial princess to upset Henry (CSPS 3.2.39, 55).

---

25 Pastor, *History*, vol 7 p.383
26 H. Ellis (ed.) *Hall's Chronicle* (1809) p.721-722
27 The match had been agreed as part of the Treaty of Madrid.

Comments

Some confusion exists about what happened to Thomas Wyatt. He had gone to Italy as an assistant to Sir John Russell who had been sent by Henry to assist the pope in the war. Following an accident to Russell, Wyatt went on to Ferrara where Spanish troops captured him and demanded 3000 ducats for his release. Gregory Casale reports that he escaped (LP 4.3011) while his brother John Casale, ambassador in Venice, says that the Duke of Ferrara negotiated his release (LP 4.2982). Wyatt had been travelling under a safe conduct issued by the Duke so it is not improbable that the Duke did intervene. Henry and Francis were keen to recruit Ferrara to join the League

What did Henry have in mind when he spoke of exalting Richmond? It is unlikely that he had considered legitimising him and placing him before Mary in the succession but he could have contemplated sending him to rule Ireland. Was he even serious given the preparations for war?

Hall was extremely anti-French in his sentiments but some support for his comments can be found in the report of the Milanese ambassador who noted that the celebrations made much of the Anglo-French peace and scarcely any mention of the proposed marriage (CSPM 1.803).

The interview with Foxe is the first written evidence which exists of the annulment crisis. A further report on the interview appears in LP 4.4149 where it has been misdated as taking place in 1528 but the official records of the legatine court confirm that the testimony was taken in 1527. Foxe had been Wolsey's patron at the start of his career so the two men knew each other well, though there is no reason to suppose the subject would have been raised during those years. As the interview took place at the start of April, it must be assumed that the questions were drawn up toward the end of March.[28]

Was Wolsey ill or was he analysing Foxe's response and preparing for the annulment hearing which began in May? It is impossible to say although the fact that he had to depute the Bishop of London to sing mass when the prestigious Anglo-French treaty was celebrated on 4th May because he was too weak to do it himself, suggests that he may have been sick. Wolsey's health was not good and there are multiple references to problems he had throughout the *Letters and Papers* of previous years. He was fifty-five when the annulment crisis began which meant he was an old man by Tudor standards.

Henry's bellicose comments about waging war on the Emperor are significant, not because any physical attack took place but because they were made in the month the annulment crisis began. Romantics might like to imagine that it was all about Anne but the truth is that the process emerged from the context of international conflict.

---

28 Foxe was one of several bishops who had served Henry's father and who were still alive. Blythe of Coventry and Warham of Canterbury had been appointed in 1503, Fisher of Rochester in 1504 and Nix of Norwich in 1501. Of these, Foxe had been the only one involved in the debates immediately following Arthur's death though Warham had come on the scene after the decision to seek a dispensation was made.

The Emperor's threat to withdraw allegiance from the pope and call a General Council of the church is very important. He did not do it because just three weeks later, his troops took the pope captive. When Henry not only made such a threat but carried it out in 1533, the Emperor denounced this as an act of unparalleled wickedness, a view shared by his ambassador, Chapuys, and repeated by a large number of writers since without thinking. The hypocrisy is startling. It is a pity that nobody reminded Henry of this at the time as he would have enjoyed telling the Emperor that he was merely following his own advice on how to protect his country's interests!

May 1527

Events

- Thomas Wyatt and John Russell arrive at Savona. The pope sends two courtesans to them to entertain them after their long journey, together with a dispensation for the sins he expects them to commit with them.[29]
- the Emperor tells Wolsey that his wife will shortly give birth but as her health is poor, he expects her to die. He says that he would like to marry Mary and offers his sister Eleanor's daughter as a bride to Richmond. An aghast Wolsey says that making overtures for Mary during the Empress' lifetime is totally dishonourable and Henry would rather see her married to a commoner than to him (LP 4.3105).
- during the celebrations at court for the Anglo-French alliance, Henry dances with Anne Boleyn.[30]
- Rome is sacked on the 6th by Bourbon's troops. Many atrocities are committed over the ten days including the murder of a bishop in his eighties, the tossing of young children out of windows to persuade their parents to hand over valuables, the execution of a priest in his church for refusing to give Holy Communion to an ass dressed in the robes of a cardinal, the gang-raping of nuns, the torture of Venetian citizens, the desecration of churches and tombs. Gumpenberg wrote: "All were doomed to certain death who were found in the streets of the city; the same fate was meted out to all, young or old, woman or man, priest or monk. Everywhere rang the cry: 'Empire! Spain! Victory'"[31] Bourbon is killed. The pope and a few cardinals including Campeggio, plus the English and French ambassadors, escape to the Castle of San Angelo (LP 4.3114, 3116, 3136, 3200). News reaches Florence on the 12th May,

---

29 Susan Brigden, *Thomas Wyatt: the heart's forest* (2012) p.118
30 John Lingard, *A History of England*, (Paris, 1840) vol. 4 p.50.
31 Pastor *History,* vol. 7, pp394-418

France on 21ˢᵗ May and London on 2ⁿᵈ June ³²(LP 4.3136, 3147; CSPV 4.110,114).
- the Imperialists rejoice in the sack. Describing the murder of more than thirty men on the altar of St Peter's itself, Najera (an abbot) tells the Emperor: "it was the sentence of God; may those who executed it be counted not unworthy before Him." Secretary Soria claims it shows God using the Emperor as a tool of divine vengeance against the wicked pope. They hope that the pope will remain permanently under the control of the Emperor and advise him that stripping the pope of all temporal power and rights would be a meritorious act pleasing to God (CSPS 3.2.76, 78).
- the Emperor's brother, Ferdinand, congratulates him saying "the pope is currently in your hands, or at least in a condition where you can do what you like with him" and recommends maintaining him in captivity.³³
- the Florentine ambassador, who witnessed the Emperor being told the news, writes: "he laughed and joked so much while talking to his entourage that he scarcely found time to eat" adding "His Imperial Majesty has already begun to imagine himself as an absolute monarch with everyone forced to accept his decisions." Indeed, the entire entourage were suffused with "excess of joy and immoderate happiness." ³⁴
- Thomas Boleyn is sent to France to take Francis's oath regarding war plans (LP 4.3124).
- on the 17ᵗʰ, Wolsey opens the first hearing into the validity of Henry's "marriage" to Katherine. It meets on the 20ᵗʰ, 23ʳᵈ and 31ˢᵗ. In support of the alleged invalidity of the dispensation, and citing Torquemada and the ruling of Innocent III, the following points are made: (i) Henry was a minor at the time (ii) Henry repudiated Katherine in 1505 which rendered the bull invalid for use in 1509 (iii) England and Spain were at peace so the pope granted the bull in 1504 based on false information that it was necessary for peace and to save lives (iv) the bull did not explicitly cover public honesty – the impediment created by the taking of marriage vows even when no consummation followed³⁵ (v) the bull was not in the correct legal format. The Bishop of Tarbes returns for the hearing (CSPM 805).
- on the 18ᵗʰ, Mendoza, the Imperial ambassador in England, reports that an investigation into the "marriage" has begun with the intention being that it is ended. He reports the problem of Katherine being the wife of Henry's brother but says the real motivation is the way Katherine totally identifies herself with the Emperor's interests rather than England's (CSPS 3.2.69).
- William Brereton as a Page of the Privy Chamber is granted five manors and an annuity of £5 (LP 4.3142)

---

32 Mendoza knew on 25ᵗʰ May that an attack had been made and Bourbon killed but had not been advised of the extent of what had happened (CSPS 3.2.75).
33 Letter dated 31ˢᵗ May 1527, quoted in Geoffrey Parker, *Emperor* (Yale, 2019) p.172
34 Letter dated 31ˢᵗ May 1527 to the Eight, Ibid. p172
35 The bull had said Katherine and Arthur's marriage had been "perhaps consummated"

- Florence takes the opportunity of confusion in Italy to cast off Medici rule and declare itself a republic. Catherine de Medici is taken captive (CSPS 3.2.78).

Comments

Most histories of Anne Boleyn only include a stray sentence about the Sack of Rome so it might be wondered why more detail is given here. The answer is because it made the sort of impact on contemporaries that the 9/11 attacks made on people in 2001. By leaving the pope a captive of the Imperialists, it altered the political map of Europe. It soured relations between the Emperor and both Henry and Francis. It raised questions about the nature and location of the papacy which would encourage the Reformation. The extent of the revulsion felt in England can be seen in Hall's chronicle which details the event fully. The revolt in Florence which followed the Sack would arguably have an even greater long term impact on Henry's case. The pope was a Medici by birth and determined to secure his family's return to power there and he would allow this personal objective to interfere with his mission as pope. Florence not only wanted independence for its own sake but to give it some freedom in the war which was then raging around it, giving it a chance to choose whether to side with the Empire or France.

The story of the courtesans is shocking, but the provenance of it is exemplary having come from Wyatt himself. It shows a lot about the morals of the age and the cavalier attitude to sexual sin at Rome. One could not imagine Pope Francis acting in this way.

This is the only reference to Brereton as a Page. In all other cases he is listed as a Groom which is a higher rank. It must be suspected that the clerk made an error in the entry unless Brereton was covering the role temporarily for some reason.

Modern historians have made much of the fact that the first trial of Henry's "marriage" was held in secret and used this to conjure up an image of Henry which only requires a swirling cloak and some sinister moustache twirling to turn him into the archetypal baddie of a Victorian melodrama whose entry to the stage invites the audience to boo and hiss. Such a view stems from a belief that Henry was only concerned about his love life, which is clearly untrue. The trial began within a few days of the French ambassadors going home and a herald being sent tasked with declaring war on the Emperor if he failed to return Francis' sons. As the outcome of this trip was necessarily unknown, it was essential that the trial be held in secret. Publicly attacking the position of the Spanish queen would not be conducive to peace talks and this would mean thousands more people being killed or maimed in war, and it would also prevent the issue being used as a bargaining tool in the future. There was also no reason whatsoever to inform Katherine at this point as Mendoza admitted. The legal format required that Wolsey as legate accuse the

King of living incestuously with his brother's wife: Henry was the defendant. If the allegation was proved, Wolsey would then inform Katherine and commence discussions about how the situation might be resolved – either by annulment or by seeking a new bull to ratify the "marriage." As it was, the sack of Rome meant the case could not continue as planned.

The return of the Bishop of Tarbes for the trial is of huge significance though rarely mentioned. The story told at the time was that the Bishop had raised the matter originally, a view rejected by many modern writers in their desire to put all the blame on Henry, yet why would the Bishop have attended the trial if he was not involved?

It is worth noting that Mendoza mentions the subject only as a minor item of news at the end of a long report about the state of European relations and prospects for peace. He says that he thinks the pope would agree to an application for an annulment so the Emperor should take steps to stop this, though he warns that it is likely that Wolsey has the power to grant it anyway. At the time he wrote, Mendoza had no idea that the Imperial troops had just sacked Rome, a move hardly likely to have won the pope's favour. Mendoza added that Katherine wanted the proposal kept quiet but notes reassuringly that he cannot see the idea will progress as the people love her and hate Wolsey, whom he blames for raising the subject, because they fear Wolsey wants a war against the Emperor which will be costly in terms of taxes and lost trade.

The significance of Henry dancing with Anne should not be over emphasised. The news featured in a report by a Frenchman who named her simply because he recognised her from Queen Claude's court and he knew that the recipient of his report would be glad to hear news of her. Henry danced with many ladies during the course of the evening. Turenne did not know the others and had no reason to suppose his reader would want to know any details. There was no suggestion that Anne had been singled out for special honour or that Henry danced with her in a manner which was somehow different to the way he conducted himself with his other dancing companions.

June 1527

Events

- Wolsey sends Bishop John Fisher's response to Henry which claims the pope has power to dispense and interpret all scripture with a comment that "his said opinion proceedeth rather of affection than of sincerity of his learning or scripture" (LP 4.3147; SP vol. 1 p.189).
- Thomas Boleyn spends the month in France. He meets Francis and Renée (LP 4.3171, 3185, 3193). It is said that he has carried a portrait of Francis' sister back to England.[36]

---

36 *Hall's Chronicle* p.728

- the Emperor says he regrets the events in Rome but suggests they would not have happened had his enemies not refused to accede to his peace demands (LP 4.3201). Wolsey does not believe him as those responsible have not been punished and says that unless the Emperor takes action, the attack on Rome will be grounds for war (LP 4.3179).
- the pope is forced to surrender to the Imperial army. He is ordered to pay them 400,000 ducats, a quarter of which must be paid immediately. Papal tiaras and vessels used at mass are melted down to try and raise cash.[37] The pope and cardinals write to Henry begging for money (LP 4.3155, 3156, 3157, 3160-5). To add to their woes, plague breaks out (LP 4.3206). An eyewitness account of Rome describes the scene: "no bells ring, no churches are open, no masses are said, Sundays and feast days have ceased. The rich shops of the merchants are turned into stables, the most splendid palaces are stripped bare; many houses are burnt to the ground; in others the doors and windows are broken and carried away; the streets are changed into dunghills. The stench of dead bodies is terrible; men and beasts have a common grave and in the churches I have seen corpses that dogs have gnawn. ...In Rome all sins are openly committed, sodomy, simony, idolatry, hypocrisy, fraud. Well may we believe then that what has come to pass has not been by chance but by the judgment of God."[38] Perez, the Emperor's representative in Rome, confirms the account and comments that he wishes the pope had more faith in Campeggio who is loyal to the Emperor (CSPS 3.2.94).
- Mendoza, Imperial ambassador in England, loyally denies that the Sack took place and claims reports of atrocities are lies dreamt up by the English (CSPS 3.2.83).
- Gregory Casale travels round Italy trying to drum up effective resistance to the Imperialists (LP 4.3206, CSPS 3.2.96) and help for the pope.[39]
- Wolsey warns Henry that "if the pope's holiness fortune either to be slain or taken, as God forbid, it shall not a little hinder Your Grace's affairs, which I have now in hand, wherein such good and substantial order and process hath hitherto been made and used." (LP 4.3147; SP vol. 1 p.189)
- Henry Norris, Squire for the Body, obtains a lease and Henry Percy inherits the lands and title of Earl of Northumberland (LP 4.3213. 5, 18, 19).
- Henry Wingfield fails to obtain an office he seeks despite the support of the Dukes of Norfolk and of Suffolk, Thomas Boleyn and Henry Norris.[40]
- the Emperor complains to the Duke of Ferrara that he feels betrayed by the pope claiming that since he chose to have Clement elected, surely Clement's first loyalty should be to him (CSPS 3.2.99)

---

37 Pastor *History* vol. 7, p430
38 Ibid. p.427. The writer was a Spaniard who regarded the devastation as a sign that God was punishing the pope for his opposition to the Emperor.
39 Ibid. p.426
40 S. J. Gunn, *Charles Brandon* (Oxford, 1988) p.99

- a Greek known as John Negro, employed to lead the forces of Ferdinand (the Emperor's brother) against the Vayvod in Hungary, opts to demonstrate his loyalty by having his leading Russian henchman beheaded at dinner for rape. He then sends a message to Ferdinand assuring him that he will "always find me ready to execute his orders and that he may consider me as his most faithful servant and subject." (CSPS 3.2.101)
- on the 22nd, Henry tells Katherine that the pope had no authority to grant the dispensation which permitted their union and that as a result, he is separating himself from her. He asks her where she would like to live but she bursts into tears and does not answer (CSPS 3.2.113).

Comments

The Henry Wingfield incident is interesting as much for what did happen as what did not. The controller of the customs as Ipswich was dying and Wingfield wanted the job. He contacted his cousin, the Duke of Suffolk plus he visited the Duke of Norfolk who asked Thomas Boleyn to speak to the King about it. Henry Norris also petitioned the King. This was a conventional approach to obtaining an office at the time. There was no such thing as fair recruitment processes to fill vacancies! However, Wingfield's aunt was Anne Boleyn's friend, Bridget, and there is no evidence that he contacted her which suggests that he had no idea that Anne was close to the King and potentially able to help.[41] Given his contacts, this is worthy of note. With the benefit of hindsight, it is easy to assume that Anne was in the ascendant in the early summer of 1527 but her contemporaries were not aware of this. It is likely that they were not aware because it was not the case.

Fisher's comments were very general. It was not until the following month that he would meet with Wolsey and be told of the problems in full.

The chronicler Hall claimed that Boleyn brought back the portrait of Marguerite, Duchess d'Alençon because Henry was seeking a new wife and wanted to see what she looked like. Hall was clearly unaware that Marguerite had married the King of Navarre six months earlier. The confusion was because Marguerite was Francis' actual sister while Renée was his sister-in-law. Given Anne had been friends with the latter, it is more likely that Boleyn brought back an image of her for Anne as a remembrance rather than as some pick-a-bride portrait for Henry who would have known what both ladies looked like anyway from meeting them at the Field of the Cloth of Gold.[42]

Campeggio would be selected to try the annulment case in 1529 so Perez' comment about his loyalties is worthy of note.

---

41 Bridget undoubtedly became an employee of Anne's in 1530 so it is reasonable to assume that they knew one another before this date.

42 Renée had been ten at the time she met Henry so it could be argued that she had changed substantially. If Henry had sought to marry her, the image may have been brought back for him rather than Anne.

It is interesting that Henry told Katherine the problem was that the pope could not dispense from divine law. The case which Wolsey had been hearing related to canon law technicalities. This is a reminder that Henry's biblical argument was there from the start, not a later idea introduced when the former seemed unlikely to result in a quick response, a suggestion made by a number of modern writers.

Wolsey was quite right not to believe the Emperor's protestation of innocence. In June 1526, the Emperor had told Moncada to negotiate with Cardinal Colonna over the expulsion of the pope from Rome while in his congratulatory letter to Bourbon just after the Sack – written before he knew that Bourbon had died from his wounds – he said "I do not know for sure what you will have done with the pope after you entered Rome" and spoke of the advantages to be gained from bringing him to Spain, a plan which had clearly been discussed with his chancellor.[43]

The behaviour of John Negro is a salutary reminder that the Tudor world was not like ours.

July 1527

Events

- Wolsey promises Henry with regard his Great Matter "there is nothing earthly, that I covet so much, as the advancing thereof….In this matter, and in all other things that may touch your honour and surety, I shall be as constant as any living creature; not letting for any danger, obloquy, displeasure, or persecution; yea, and if all did fail and swerve, Your Highness shall find me fast and constant, according to my most bounden duty." (LP 4.3217, SP vol. 1 pp.194-5)
- after a stay at the home of the late Sir John Wiltshire, Wolsey meets with Archbishop William Warham of Canterbury and Bishop John Fisher of Rochester. Wolsey tells them that the investigation into the 1504 dispensation began due to an incident at the negotiations for the marriage of Francis I to Princess Mary. The English had asked if Francis was free to proceed with the match given that it was reported that Francis had married the Emperor's sister in order to be released from his captivity in Spain. The French took offence at this question and the Bishop of Tarbes said that in order to defend the honour of his master, he must make a reciprocal demand and ask to see the dispensation which Henry received "for taking away the impediment of that marriage whereof my Lady Princess cometh." Henry ordered the bull to be shown to the Bishop who read it, frowned, and declared it insufficient because "this impediment

---

43 Parker, *Emperor*, p.166, 172-3, 621. The pope had initially been taken hostage in September 1526 in accordance with these instructions.

was against divine law wherewith the pope could not dispense except for an urgent cause." Wolsey then points out other flaws in the bull and Fisher says he "misliked it much" and that dispensations were null and void if they were raised in response to lies or deliberate omissions of fact. Fisher expresses his surprise that a new bull was not sought in 1509 and he condemns the royal advisors of the time for their negligence. Although he says he cannot give a definitive verdict on the bull, he calls it "slender" and notes "great difficulty in it" and adds that Henry is right to press for answers on the matter. Fisher volunteers to go and tell Katherine this. Warham's response is "howsoever displeasantly the Queen takes this matter, yet the truth and judgement of the law must have place, and be followed." (LP 4.3231, SP vol. 1 pp. 196-201)
- England's ambassador in Spain suspects the French of going behind their backs (LP 4.3270, 3290-1, 3321).
- the Bishop of Tarbes arrives in Spain with the Anglo-French peace proposals. The Emperor rejects terms offered and continues to press for adherence to the Treaty of Madrid. Wolsey says that the Emperor's unreasonable behaviour means there is currently "little appearance" of peace in the offing (LP 4.3270, 3285, 3286, 3287, SP vol. 1 p.220).
- Katherine sends a messenger to tell the Emperor in Spain about the proposed annulment. Henry urges Wolsey – who reaches France on the 11th – to stop him. Wolsey tells the King that he needs to have ports watched as the messenger may travel by sea not land and advises Henry to treat her gently until he discovers what the pope will do and how far Francis will support him. He warns Henry that if the Emperor finds out, it will not only "be no little hindrance" to his plans but ruin the talks in progress for an end to the war in Europe (LP 4.3217, 3278, 3283, SP vol. 1 p.230).
- with Francis' backing, Wolsey seeks to summon cardinals to France to make plans for the church while the pope is held captive (LP 4.3243).
- Robert Wakefield, Hebrew scholar, offers to show Henry the errors in the Greek and Latin translations of the Torah (LP 4.3233, 3234).
- in accordance with Katherine's request, the Emperor asks the pope to revoke Wolsey's legatine powers to prevent him annulling Henry's "marriage" with Katherine, an idea he describes as beyond belief, scandalous and motivated by anti-Imperial sympathies. He says that even if Henry is right and the dispensation was procured by lies and the pope had no authority to issue it, the matter should be kept secret to avoid scandal (LP 4.3312, CSPS 3.2.113).
- Margaret, regent in the Low Countries and the Emperor's aunt, also hears rumours of the annulment and asks if they are true (LP 4.3313).
- Bologna takes advantage of the war to throw off papal government but Cardinal Cibo arrives to retake the town (CSPS 3.2.119, 125).
- the Emperor writes to the cardinals denying all responsibility for the Sack and laying the blame entirely on the pope's machinations against himself.

He claims the Sack was an expression of God's just judgment (CSPS 3.2.126, 136, 137).
- Mendoza expresses the belief that Wolsey is off to France to try and get Francis to cede Boulogne to England in return for armed assistance in the war, though he doubts Francis will agree. He advises the Emperor that since he now has the office of pope at his disposal, he should offer it to Wolsey and so win England back to the Imperial cause. Mendoza claims that Henry is always led by Wolsey and this would end the war. Mendoza also says that he sees little prospect of Henry proceeding with the annulment due to the political situation and that even if he did, although people might complain, they would accept it (CSPS 3.2.113).
- the Emperor decides to send Quinones, the General of the Franciscans, to Rome to talk to the pope. He tells Mendoza that the objective will be to get a decision about the legitimacy of the disputed dispensation before Henry or Wolsey can take further action. He repeats his belief that Katherine is a good woman and does not deserve to be dishonoured (CSPS 3.2.131).
- Venice seizes Ravenna. The newly independent Florence joins the League but continues to negotiate with the Emperor in a bid to cover its options as the outcome of the war is uncertain (CSPS 3.2.119).
- Gregory Casale joins Wolsey in France and sends back news to Italy that Henry will fund ten thousand soldiers for the war against the Emperor (CSPS 3.2.148).
- Sampson sends Wolsey a letter saying that Henry is at Beaulieu and "the merry visage is returned" noting there is "less suspicion, or little" meaning "the great matter is in very good train." Sampson adds "The other party, as your Grace knoweth, lacketh no wit, and so sheweth highly in this matter." (LP 4.3302).
- Wolsey tells Henry of a report saying that Princess Renée is unable to have children (LP 4.3231).

Comments

Mendoza's suggestion that the Emperor make Wolsey pope in place of Clement is interesting. Clearly, Mendoza assumed that because the Emperor held the pope prisoner, he was in a position to dismiss him from the job, though most others would have questioned the legality of such a move. If the Emperor had followed the advice of his ambassador, it would have played into Henry's hands and Wolsey could promptly have ruled against Katherine. Either Mendoza did not think the proposed annulment was a serious threat or he felt that she should be sacrificed in order to secure European peace. If Wolsey had been made pope, Henry would have broken from France leaving Francis no choice but to sue for peace.

That Katherine's first step upon being officially advised of the proposed annulment was to send a message to the very people with whom England were likely to be at war in a few weeks' time, showed her lack of concern for the country which had been her home for over a quarter of a century. It is easy to sympathise with her distress but could one imagine in a similar situation, Queen Mary appealing to the Kaiser in 1914? It is a measure of the success of Katherine's supporters both then and now that her image remains that of the virtuous wronged wife rather than a traitor and fifth columnist. Katherine's messenger was her cup bearer, Francis Phillips (CSPS 3.2.113, 224) who had been in her service since at least 1519 (LP 3.491). The Emperor admits that he spoke with him before sending his request to the pope about removing Wolsey's legatine authority. The pope rejected the idea, indicating that despite his captivity, he was not a slave.

The Regent Margaret was also the sister-in-law of Louise of Savoy, who was mother of Francis I.

The mentality of the Emperor is exposed by the letters written by him in this month. His refusal to accept responsibility for the behaviour of his own troops who went on a murderous and destructive rampage due to his refusal to pay them for months is heinous. His belief that a potentially illegal dispensation should be covered up rather than investigated simply because Katherine was a nice lady and should be treated as such, demonstrates an extraordinary lack of interest in justice which is the more reprehensible because he was a prince and in a position of authority.

The issue of Ravenna would prove a long standing thorn in the annulment case, an example of what might appear a minor event in Italian politics having a bearing on Anne Boleyn's future.

Sir John Wiltshire had been a long standing and high ranking employee of Henry VIII. He had spent many years in Calais as comptroller where he also organised the spy network.[44] His daughter, Bridget, was wed to Sir Nicholas Harvey. Sir John's home, near Dartford, was a convenient resting place for any journey from London to the Kent coast and Henry and Anne would stay there in 1532.

Wakefield's involvement at this early stage of the annulment crisis is significant. Henry based his case on the Bible and as a good humanist and any responsible scholar would today, that meant he wanted to know what the original text said rather than rely on a translation.

Ravenna had become Venetian in 1441 with the Treaty of Cremona but was captured by pope Julius II in 1509 along with Cervia. Venice saw its capture as a restoration of its territory, the pope as an act of war.

Sampson's letter of the 25th is important but obscure. Who is the "other party"? He could mean Wolman, the King's canon law adviser, who may have

---

44 LP 3.390, 426. For more on the spy system see Ian Arthurson, 'Espionage and Intelligence from the Wars of the Roses to the Reformation', *Nottingham Medieval Studies* vol.35 (1991) pp.134-154

been taking advantage of Wolsey's absence to try and convince Henry that he would be better able to secure the annulment than the cardinal. Someone had certainly been suggesting to Henry that Wolsey lacked enthusiasm for the project because Wolsey had written to assure the King this was untrue on July 1st (LP 4.3217).[45] Or he could have meant Katherine who was then with Henry. Did he believe she was now less suspicious of what was happening and that despite not being a stupid woman, she had failed to find out the purpose of Wolsey's trip? Or was Sampson referring to Anne Boleyn? If this is the case, it would be proof that Wolsey knew Henry wanted to marry Anne before he left England and if that is so, the idea of him seeking Renée as a bride would be unlikely. If this meaning is attached, the implication would be that Henry is less suspicious of Wolsey because Anne has been working on his behalf, an idea which would show she was not working for his destruction (despite the hysterical conspiracy claims of Cavendish) but rather with and for him. Given the impossibility of asking Sampson what he meant, it cannot be known which of these three people was the "other party." It is a reminder that whilst writers may select an interpretation and use that to bolster their own view of events in this period, much remains uncertain.

August 1527

Events

- Wolsey tells English envoys in Spain that Henry's "marriage" is being investigated to please the French and not to obtain a separation and says they must not let stories to the contrary harm the peace talks (LP 4.3327). He summons Ghinucci to join him in France (LP 4.3340).
- the Treaty of Amiens is agreed on the 18th. Wolsey promises to tell Francis of Henry's Great Matter "in such a cloudy and dark sort that he shall not know Your Grace's utter determination and intent." (LP 4.3350, SP vol. 1. 260) Francis' response is carried back to Henry verbally by the Bishop of Bath and Wells, John Clerk (LP 4.3382).
- in England, Mendoza discovers the "general" belief that Henry intends to marry Anne Boleyn. He says that Henry is basing his case on two points: firstly, the pope having no authority to permit that which God had forbidden and secondly, that the application being based on the false claim that England and Spain were at risk of war renders the dispensation

---

45 The day after Sampson wrote, Wolman wrote to Wolsey saying how he had discussed with the King Wolsey's claim to present to benefices in Calais which now the King disputed. Wolman said Wolsey was welcome to provide evidence to back up his claims if he could but warned that Henry was upset at what he saw as an act against his prerogative (LP 4.3304).

granted in response null and void. Mendoza talks to Gardiner who suggests that a new dispensation is sought but Mendoza advises Katherine that this is not a good idea as it would mean accepting Henry's argument that the original was flawed (CSPS 3.2.152).
- the Emperor tells Henry that whilst he did not order the Sack of Rome, he believes it is God's judgment on the pope for taking Naples away from him (LP 4.3332). He seeks to bring the pope to Spain (LP 4.3374). In a similar letter to the King of Portugal, the Emperor complains that the pope had been "forgetful of favours granted by us to the Christian church in general and to him in particular" and had chosen to unite with "malignant parties" to attack Naples which meant the Imperial army was entitled to attack Rome in revenge. He claims the Sack "was more owing to a visitation of the Almighty than to the power and will of man, and God – on whom we place all our trust – permitted that the injuries we had received should be avenged. It befits us all to thank Him for His favours." (CSPS 3.2.143)
- the Emperor also writes to Wolsey saying he considers him to be his best friend in the whole wide world and that Wolsey can name anything he likes within the Emperor's dominions and the Emperor will be only too pleased to give it to him. He adds that he is praying daily for Wolsey to have success in all his doings (CSPS 3.2.176).
- clearly in the mood for catching up with correspondence, the Emperor sends a letter to Katherine of Aragon telling her not to make herself ill with worry about the proposed separation as all will be well (CSPS 3.2.166).
- the Duke of Ferrara refuses to take on the command of Imperial forces claiming that they are ungovernable since they have not been paid for so long. He asks the Emperor to confirm his holding of Modena and Rezzo which he claims were granted to him by the Emperor's grandfather, Maximilian and promises Francis that he will not aid the Emperor further provided that he too recognises his right to these two places (CSPS 3.2.172, 173).
- Genoa falls to the League on the 18th and Boscho and Portofino soon follow. With Alessandria likely to be taken next, the Venetians arming galleys to attack Sicily and confusion about the loyalties of the Duke of Ferrara, the pope expresses his optimism of a full victory. Meanwhile, the Imperialists despair and send a barrage of letters to the Emperor warning him that they are likely to lose the war and urging him to make the best peace he can. Such advice is given by his ambassador in Venice (Sanchez), in Rome (Perez), his Viceroy in Naples (Lannoy) and the commander of his army (Leyva) (CSPS 3.2.147, 148, 155, 158, 169).
- the latest English peace plan has Francis stay married to Charles' sister Eleanor, Henry's daughter Mary marry the Duke of Orleans and Henry's son, Richmond marry Eleanor's daughter who will present him with Milan as a dowry. This is conditional on the Emperor releasing Francis' sons and the pope (LP 4.3353, 3361, 3362, 3363, 3364).

- Henry Percy is revealed to have debts of £1,761 6s 1½d mostly inherited from his father (LP 4.3379).
- the cardinals in Italy are divided over whether to accept Francis' offer to go to Avignon (CSPS 3.2.175, LP 4.).
- Venice invites the Marquis of Mantua to take command of its armies (CSPS 3.2.163).
- an acrimonious exchange takes place between Henry and the Imperial ambassador, Mendoza. Henry expresses frustration that the Emperor has not repaid the debt he owes him and only seems willing to offer securities and promises of payment at some unspecified date in the future. He rages: "I am tired of hearing about treaties and securities; deeds not words are wanted." (CSPS 3.2.152).
- Henry gives Anne a ring set with emeralds to signify his faithful love for her (LP 5.276).[46]
- Knight tells Wolsey that Henry agrees it is "necessary and requisite for approbation of the process" for either the pope or college of cardinals to approve Wolsey's planned annulment (LP 4.3363). On the 29th, he tells Wolsey that Henry is sending him to Rome about the matter.[47]

Comments

There is no evidence that Henry replied to the Emperor's self justifying letter. Wolsey did not reply to the Emperor either, perhaps because his letter left him prostrate with laughter. Given that the Emperor knew that Wolsey was working on the annulment, it is interesting to ponder if he really was asking God to give Wolsey success. Just as well, Katherine never saw the missive.

Mendoza's naming of Anne Boleyn is the first time she appears formally as Henry's intended in Imperial sources. His comment about it being a "general" belief is interesting. Mendoza did not mix with ordinary people in England. The Venetian ambassador, who spent considerable time at court, though moving in different circles because he represented the League, had no inkling of there being any talk of separation. As late as the end of November 1527, the Venetian ambassador was happily reporting home that nothing was happening of any significance and the Signory only learnt of the plan via a letter from France in February 1528 (CSPV 4.236). Some writers, such as Vergil, have suggested that even Wolsey was unaware of Anne's importance at this date so the "general" can only relate to the tight knit group of Imperial supporters around Katherine herself. The idea that Mendoza knew better than Wolsey is not credible. What gave Mendoza the idea that Henry had such an

---

46 This entry has been calendared under 1531 but belongs to 1527.
47 This letter has not survived so we do not know how much Knight told him about his mission. We only know of the letter because Wolsey wrote on 5th September to Henry VIII referring to Knight's letter to him on this date, LP 4.3400.

idea? Perhaps he saw the ring or heard about it. Although it is easy to conclude with the benefit of hindsight that this was an engagement ring, this is quite unlikely, certainly in the way in which we would understand the term today. Henry may have believed he was free morally but he knew that legally he was still tied so he could not enter into a betrothal. What may have happened is that Henry had admitted his feelings for Anne and confirmed that with a valuable gift in order to show her he was serious.

Too little attention is given to the very real likelihood which existed at this point that the League would win the war. With such an expectation, Henry had every reason to believe that his annulment would be speedily granted.

It is a great pity that Francis sent back a verbal rather than written response to Henry's announced intention of replacing Katherine which was the news Wolsey told him: he already knew of the investigation into the validity of the dispensation because the Bishop of Tarbes would have had to tell him in order to get permission for his attendance at the trial in May. What did he really think? The next six years were to see him provide very high levels of support for Henry: in modern terms, he went the extra mile. He would have seen the political advantages to him of England becoming increasingly alienated from the Emperor but there was a strong tradition of anti-papal feeling in France which went back for centuries. Some of the legal expertise which underpinned conciliarism would be employed on Henry's behalf and it is evident that French advice was being given freely when the eventual break with Rome came because elements of the English Reformation bear such resemblance to the Pragmatic Sanction of Bourges, which abolished annates and appeals to Rome. The justification for the royal supremacy would include elements taken from Claude de Seyssel's *Le Grand Monarchie* of 1518. There was also a history of French kings receiving annulments in line with political need. In 1599, the French jurist, Guesle, listed a number of cases of rulers having unions annulled due to childlessness, amongst them Charlemagne, Charles IV and Louis XII. He observed that in the case of Louis VII, it was because only daughters had been born.[48] It is impossible to know how much Wolsey told Francis in his "cloudy" way on this occasion. It is extremely unlikely that any mention was made of Anne whom Francis would have known well due to the years she spent in the service of his wife. Wolsey had to tread a fine line because the pope was a founder member of the League and Francis may have been concerned that a rift between Henry and the pope would reduce papal support for his own claims to parts of Italy.

---

48 D'Avray, *Papacy, Monarchy and Marriage, 800-1600* (Cambridge, 2015) pp.10-20 notes that archival research has shown Guesle was mistaken in some of his allegations but the key point was that this was what people believed which meant Francis would not have thought Henry's request unusual or unreasonable..

September 1527

Events

- Henry confers the Order of the Garter on Francis who responds by conferring the Order of St Michael on Henry (LP 4.3409, 3466).
- troubles continue on the English-Scottish border (LP 4.3404, 3407, 3421, 3508, 3516).
- upset that Katherine has managed to get a messenger through to the Emperor and worried she might do the same with the pope, Henry decides to send his own envoy to Rome hoping to get there ahead of her. Wolsey warns it will be difficult for Knight to obtain access and suggests the use of the two Italians whom Henry employs – Ghinucci and Gregory Casale. Having discussed the case with the newly arrived Ghinucci, he says there is "no man in my opinion so meet, nor propice for obtaining of anything" from Rome. He also believes that the papal nuncio, Gambara, will be willing and able to assist (LP 4.3400, 3419, 3422; SP vol. 1 pp.271, 273).
- Henry invites the humanist scholar Desiderius Erasmus to retire to England saying that he has long desired to reform the church and would appreciate his input (LP 4.4348)
- in France, Wolsey meets Staffileo who assures him that the bull of dispensation issued by Julius II is "clearly void and naught for that the impediment of affinity is of divine law as that the pope cannot dispense the same." and because there was no great cause. He offers to support Henry's case. Wolsey regards this as a very major step forward and tells Henry that if he would only show "a little patience suffering such things to be experimented and done" he shall "honourably and lawfully" have the desired annulment "which to bring to pass is my continual study and ardent desire, ready to expose my body, life and blood for the achieving of the same." Indeed Wolsey says he has "nothing so much in my heart, daily study and thought, as the bringing of Your Grace's intended purpose to honourable fruit and effect." (LP 4.3400, SP vol 1 pp.271-3).
- Wolsey remains deeply distrustful of the Emperor and advises Henry "it is now manifest and explorate to all the world, not only by the Emperor's actions and proceedings, but also by letters intercepted, that whatsoever exterior visage or demonstration he doth make, his intent drift and compass is to be the ruler and monarch of the world" (LP 4.3411, SP vol. 6 p.603). He also notes that the Emperor has no interest in finding a bride for Richmond from amongst his family and giving them Milan as a dowry because the Emperor has decided he wants it for himself. He warns that the Emperor wishes to take the pope to Spain for his own "execrable" and "detestable purposes." (SP vol. 1 p.269,275)
- the Emperor orders his ambassador to try and recruit Wolsey to his service with bribes of over 60,000 ducats (LP 4.3464).

- in peace negotiations, the Emperor demands Francis withdraw his army from Italy first: Francis says he will not do that until terms are agreed. The Emperor says he will release Francis' sons in return for fifteen high ranking hostages, all of whom are members of Francis' council: Francis said he would rather get his sons back by war than surrender his advisors. The Emperor demands that France, Venice and Florence pay the expenses he has incurred in wars in Italy since 1525 and suggests the 800,000 crowns which he owes Henry could be a bargaining tool: Francis considers the idea unworthy even of a response (LP 4.3430, 3431, 3443, 3453).
- Wolsey sends Gregory Casale to apply for a commission allowing him to rule the church while the pope is held captive (LP 4.3420). He assures Henry that his best chance of a speedy solution to the annulment crisis is if the pope will grant him full authority to hear the case (LP 4.3400). Meanwhile, Wolsey, Cardinal Salviati and the three French cardinals meet at Lorraine and agree a joint letter to be sent to the pope promising they will not recognise any grants or appointments which he is coerced into making during his captivity, that if he is killed they will arrange a fresh election in non-Imperial territory and urging the appointment of a regent to rule during his captivity. They further urge that monies due to Rome be with-held to prevent them falling into the hands of the Imperialists (CSPS 3.2.195).
- the Emperor's ambassadors and advisers in Italy together with the commander of his army, Leyva, continue to urge him to make peace because they do not believe they can win the war. They say they have pawned all their possessions, even their clothes but they simply cannot pay, feed or equip the men. Leyva complains that he has received no word from the Emperor for three months. (CSPS 3.2. 184, 196, 204). Alessandria falls to the League on the 12th who go on to threaten Pavia. German troops employed by the Emperor vow: "we shall go to Rome and set fire to it and then sell it to the Venetians or the League for we would rather make our peace with the pope and become his friends than consent to the Emperor profiting by our conquests." (CSPS 3.2.200) The Emperor's newly arrived envoy, De Veyre, reports that Florence has not paid any of the money it promised in return for safety from Imperial assault and the pope only a fraction of his debt. De Veyre suggests the pope could afford to pay but is vacillating because he believes the French army will shortly be able to rescue him. He warns that whether the French do this or the mutinous Germans kidnap the pope themselves, the result will be the Emperor's defeat and the pope left free to plot his ruin. (CSPS 3.2.212).
- the pope issues a brief detailing arrangements for a new election should he die in captivity and placing all Imperial territories under interdict if his death should not be by natural causes (CSPS 3.2.184, 196).

- Knight arrives in France to see Wolsey en route to Rome, Whilst there, he receives further instructions from Henry "to me only committed" regarding Henry's desire for a dispensation to marry while the annulment case is in process. Knight admits he thinks this is doubtful due to anticipated difficulties reaching the captive pope but assures the King "having any possibility of access, I shall soon obtain it." (LP 4.3422; SP vol. 7 p.3)
- Mendoza tells the Emperor that Henry is extremely anxious to have his debt repaid and he advises the Emperor to do so if he wants to renew his treaties with England and weaken the Anglo-French alliance. He says that if the annulment goes ahead, objections at home will keep Henry too busy to cause the Emperor problems in Europe (CSPS 3.2.189).
- the Imperial ambassador in Venice remarks that the pope is upset about Venice seizing Ravenna and Cervia, towns which he claims are his by right. Nonetheless, he notes that the papal nuncio is spending considerable time with the French ambassador and senators in Venice which lends him to suppose that the pope is still intriguing with the League (CSPS 3.2.196).
- Wolsey returns from France at the end of the month and finds Anne with Henry at Richmond. She is reputed to say: "where else is the Cardinal to come? Tell him that he may come here where the King is." (CSPS 3.2.224).
- Henry pays for a book of Anne's to be covered in silver and gilt work (LP 5.276).

Comments

Staffileo was a significant find for Wolsey as he was a senior canon lawyer in the Rota, the judicial arm of the papacy. As such he had influence over both pope and cardinals and was in a position to greatly advance Henry's cause. Staffileo tried to do this by writing on Henry's behalf, debating with Fisher and advising the pope on the matter. His death in July 1528 was a serious blow. His support for Henry is important to note because it indicates acceptance of Henry's case at the highest level in Rome – before political considerations replaced justice.

Sixty thousand ducats was worth around £13,500 at the time or £94.5 million today. The extent of the money offered by the Emperor shows how important he thought it was to secure Wolsey's support. The sum was made up of a pension of 15,000 ducats a year plus property in Milan of the same value plus 45,000 ducats which the Emperor already owed him. Given the Emperor's record of paying his debts and the fact that Milan was claimed by France, it is probable that Wolsey had his doubts that he would ever get the promised sum should he choose to accept the offer, which he never did.

Wolsey's contention that Ghinucci and Casale would have a better chance of reaching the pope who was still in captivity than an Englishman was wise advice. Ghinucci was a bishop and papal auditor and close friend of the pope while Casale was also much respected by him, not least because of the support Casale had provided during the Sack of Rome. Unfortunately, as Henry was to point out in his letter of response, Ghinucci was en route to Spain and Casale had yet to be fully acquainted with the issues. Henry explained his motivation for sending Knight without taking time to discuss it with Wolsey first: "because as yet since the pope's captivity we never sent to salute him, nor have no resident there to advertise us of the affairs there; and also lest the Queen should prevent us by the Emperor's means in our great matter; we think it meet to send this bearer thither, of whose truth and sincerity we have had long proof, praying you to give him such instructions and commissions as shall be for our affairs there requisite."[49]

Knight was being sent for a lot more than simply reporting the situation in Rome. Henry's letter to him refers to "the secret bull I sent you for" and about the need to prevent Wolsey suspecting that Knight is being "sent, as ye be indeed, for things that I would not that he should know."[50] Previously, the King and cardinal had always worked very closely so this seems strange. Was it a case of Henry mistrusting Wolsey's commitment to the project as had happened earlier in the summer? Was it because Henry suspected that Wolsey would advise against making such a request either at all or at this time? Or was it because Henry had made changes to something which he had discussed with Wolsey before? Henry's letter does note that Wolsey is aware of the request and he adds "we are of the opinion that the cardinal is." Historians can only speculate using their gift of hindsight because the first and second drafts of the requested dispensation no longer exist. All that survives is the dispensation of December 1527 (LP 4.3686), Wolsey and Henry's notes on changes they wanted made (LP 4.3643.1) and the pope's revised bull.[51] Given that the annulment was being sought so Henry could remarry and have a male heir, he and Wolsey must have discussed the subject of remarriage and the likelihood of needing a dispensation. Princes often sought rather generic dispensations before a bride was chosen so they could select a bride in line with political need. Charles V had done this and given that document was expected to be used when he married Henry's daughter, Henry knew all about such things and may have seen it and discussed obtaining similar for himself with Wolsey prior to his

---

49 Gilbert Burnet, *The History of the Reformation*, ed. Nicholas Pocock (1855) vol. 6 p. 22; LP 4.3419.
50 James Gairdner, 'New Lights on the Divorce of Henry VIII', *EHR* vol. 11 (1896) p.685
51 The revisions were drawn up on the 6th December before the first bull was issued on 23rd December but they would not have reached Rome in time to be incorporated. They were therefore revisions of the first and second drafts which have not survived. The final bull is in Stephan Ehses, *Romische Dokumente* (Paderborn, 1893) pp.33-36.

departure to France. The secret was not the bull *per se* but the contents of it. Given Henry went on in his letter that "he and I shall jointly devise another" he clearly intended to work with Wolsey on the subject in future, so perhaps not too much stress should be made of this point. Henry was not a canon lawyer so could not have drawn up any draft bulls on his own so whatever he sent was probably the work of Wolman.

A lot of misunderstanding is expressed with regard to Henry's request for a dispensation to marry with a number of writers almost having a fit of the vapours as they express their horror at him contemplating bigamy. Henry was doing nothing of the sort. In the first place, it was not uncommon for people to remarry while a suit was being held. Provided that the annulment was agreed, the marriage contracted during the suit would be regarded as lawful from the date of celebration and any children of it as legitimate. Contemporaries – including the pope – saw nothing wrong with the idea.[52] Louis XII of France had obtained a dispensation to marry while his annulment case was in progress and nobody suggested he was planning bigamy. Given the length of time it often took to obtain a dispensation, the practice made sense. An analogy might be made with heirs to an estate being allowed use of the property while probate is awaited. Dispensations could be granted in one of two formats – *constante* allowing marriage while a case was heard or *soluto* which permitted it only after a verdict in the petitioner's favour. Even the Jesuit canon law expert Henry Ansgar Kelly, whose opinions on Henry's matrimonial suit rival the vitriolic Sander, admits this – albeit in small print in a footnote![53] Secondly, and most importantly, Henry considered himself a bachelor because his union with Katherine was unlawful. Bigamy is only possible if someone is already married.

The pope's precautions regarding an election might be seen as a snub to Wolsey but at the time he made his plans, he had no knowledge of Wolsey's proposals. They are significant because during the annulment crisis, the pope would protest that he had no power to alter decisions issued by his predecessors but here he is doing just that.

Although it is clear that Wolsey wanted papal authority for himself, he would probably not have been too worried if it had been granted to Salviati or Du Prat. The idea of appointing a regent while the pope was captive was perfectly reasonable. In England, a regent or protector had been appointed when Richard the Lionheart was in captivity and when Henry VI was ill. The church as an institution held vast amounts of property across Europe, was responsible for all legal issues relating to wills and marriages, as well as employing thousands of staff which meant issues of discipline, resignation, pensions and recruitment abounded. To leave everything in limbo due to the war in Italy would cause considerable distress to many people. Whatever their motives, the cardinals were entirely correct to urge the pope to do the

---

52 The pope recommended this course of action in January 1528. LP 4.3802.
53 Henry Ansgar Kelly, T*he Matrimonial Trials of Henry VIII* (Oregon, 1976) p.40. .

responsible thing and make contingency plans to allow the church's work to continue during not only his enforced absence but the scattering of its regular administrative functionaries.

Mendoza notes that Wolsey was annoyed by Anne's imperious tone when he returned and that is probably true. However, the shock registered by Wolsey and others was not that she was with Henry, as some writers have suggested, but that she presumed to give an instruction which related to royal security. The only person who could authorise somebody to approach the King was the King himself. Small wonder that the report says nobody moved until Henry repeated the instruction. It was an error on Anne's part which her long familiarity with court etiquette meant she should not have made. Neither Katherine of Aragon nor Queen Claude in France would have behaved in this way. Whether Henry spoke to her privately afterwards is not known. He may have dismissed the incident in the belief that Anne was simply very excited and impatient to hear Wolsey's news and she spoke without thinking. Others interpreted it as a sign that she was an unsuitable bride. Women were to be obedient and docile, especially in public. A woman who sought to give orders to her king was dangerous indeed.

October 1527

Events

- German soldiers take some cardinals hostage until the pope gives them money (LP 4.3473)
- the Emperor promises to release the pope if he pays him 600,000 crowns, gives more hostages and surrenders six cities in Bologna. The pope appeals to the League for rescue (LP 4.3476) but the Swiss mercenaries hired by Francis are falling away and Gregory Casale expresses his concern that he will not be able to hire new troops in time (LP 4.3497, 3498).
- in an audience with the Imperial ambassador, Henry rebukes the Emperor (LP 4.3485) before having an anti-Imperial play performed (LP 4.3518)
- Grand Master of France, Anne de Montmorency, arrives in England as Francis' special envoy (LP 4.3494). He is greeted by Henry and Katherine and dances with their daughter, Mary at an entertainment which includes performance of a play which shows the two young French princes and the pope appealing to Henry and Wolsey for rescue from the tyrant Emperor and his barbarian Spaniards (CSPS 3.2.240). He is warned by an unnamed source that certain courtiers are plotting against Henry and Wolsey and that their plan is to kill Henry and marry Katherine or Mary to a Spanish prince or anyone who will re-unite them with the Empire and permanently break the Anglo-French alliance (LP 4.3509).

- the Emperor is sent yet more letters by his ambassadors and commanders urging him to make peace as the war cannot be won. German troops refuse to leave Rome unless they are paid and Perez suspects that the pope is deliberately refusing to pay them because all the time they are in Rome, it means the troops are unable to go and assist Leyva, and a weak Imperial army is less threat to the League (CSPS 3.2.213, 214, 215, 218, 222)
- Mendoza seeks to discover if Henry has any interest in having his bastard son, Richmond, married to one of the Emperor's nieces in the hope that a new marriage alliance might reduce tension (CSPS 3.2.220). He claims that Anne Boleyn has no love for Wolsey because he once deprived her father of high office and she has heard that during his recent visit to France he sought a French bride for Henry. He claims Anne's father and uncle tried to discredit Wolsey during his absence in France but that Henry would not listen (CSPS 3.2.224).
- Pavia falls to the League and Gambara, who had been papal nuncio in England and travelled to France with Wolsey, reaches Rome with personal messages for the pope from Henry (CSPS 3.2.214).
- Lautrec, commander-in-chief of the League's army in Italy sets up camp awaiting instructions on what he is to do next. Henry and the Venetians want him to go to Rome and rescue the pope and then go on to take Naples but Francis and Sforza want him to proceed to Milan (CSPS 3.2.215).
- Gregory Casale, with Cardinal Cibo and the ambassadors of France and Venice, goes to visit the Duke of Ferrara to try to persuade him to join the League (CSPS 3.2.225).
- Henry dismisses Francis Phillips, Katherine's cup-bearer (CSPS 3.2.224).
- Wolsey tells Henry about the bribes which the Emperor has offered him saying that this is proof of "how bad the Emperor's cause is." (CSPS 3.2.224).
- following the third consecutive year of drought, the harvest in England fails resulting in the price of bread doubling and peas and beans increasing by a third. This causes widespread hardship and unrest.[54]
- Henry gives Anne some gold buttons and a brooch (LP 5.276).

Comments

Obviously the plot which Montmorency reports, if it existed at a serious level, did not materialise but the strength of anti-French feeling existed at all levels of society. Anne's association with France did her little favour in the public mind. When people spoke of her French ways, they were not admiring her sense of style but rather associating her with the French reputation for acting dishonourably and being inveterate liars and cheats.

---

54 Peter Gwyn, *The King's Cardinal* (1990) p.456

The nieces who were suggested as potential brides for the eight-year old Richmond were the daughters of the deposed king Christian II of Denmark whose wife had been the Emperor's sister and Katherine of Aragon's niece. One of the daughters, Christina, would in 1538 became famous for allegedly refusing to consider Henry VIII as a husband on grounds she did not have a spare head which given his record, she thought she might need.[55]

Francis Phillips was the man Katherine had sent to the Emperor so it is hardly surprising that Henry did not trust him or wish his employment to continue.

Mendoza was a much more astute judge of the political situation in England than his successor, Chapuys. His report of 26th October notes the rumours that Wolsey wants a French bride for Henry before saying that in his opinion, this is the very thing which Wolsey does not want because a French princess would be in a position to threaten his position unlike Katherine who has no political influence whatsoever. He concludes, therefore, that no matter what Anne might think, Wolsey is actually totally committed to her cause as being his best option. Mendoza makes no comment about who has been spreading the rumours. The story may have come from the large anti-French faction at court who would have thought the prospect of a French queen would encourage opposition to any talk of an annulment. The reference to Wolsey depriving Thomas Boleyn of high office probably relates to the occasion in 1519 when the Treasurer of the Household retired and Boleyn, having been told by Henry that he would become Comptroller to the replacement, was passed over. At first, Boleyn was upset but then it was explained to him that the reason was that Henry wanted to appoint him to the senior role, something which clearly delighted him and the incident ended with Boleyn thanking Wolsey for his recommendation.[56] Neither Anne nor Mendoza had been in the country at the time and it is difficult to regard this as grounds for any grudge though clearly somebody must have remembered it and told the ambassador at least part of the story.

Montmorency was one of the highest ranking figures at the French court. Married to the King's cousin, he had become Grand Master in March 1527. His visit was indicative of the close relations between England and France. One can only wonder at the fixed expressions which Katherine and Mary must have worn during the play but given the atrocities of the Sack of

---

[55] This story is almost certainly apocryphal. The reason the idea of her marrying Henry was dropped was because being Katherine of Aragon's great-niece, she had a third degree affinity with Henry, leading Imperial canon lawyers to claim that meant a papal dispensation would be needed. Given Henry did not recognise the pope's authority, and no doubt knew that Leviticus did not prohibit a man from marrying such a relative, negotiations did not progress and Henry married Anne of Cleves instead. For a full account of the story, see Julia Cartwright, *Christina of Denmark* (New York, 1913) pp.144-206

[56] LP 3.223, 446.

Rome and the treatment of the young princes, they could hardly have expected less.

The harvest failure was important. Bread was the main constituent of the diet for most people and there was no flexible job market enabling them to go elsewhere and earn more money. When the crops failed, it impacted farmers who lacked feed for their livestock and their reduced incomes meant they were unable to contribute cash for the relief of the poor. It also affected other industries such as thatching which in turn affected the wider business of building. In an era when harvest failure was seen as a sign of God's displeasure, it meant people were likely to ask for reasons and this encouraged a seeking for scapegoats. The popularity of Katherine was real but the fact that Anne came to prominence at a time of economic struggle meant she was destined to be particularly associated with things being wrong. Obviously, neither Henry not Anne were responsible for the failed harvest and its repercussions but that would not have stopped people shaking their heads and observing that life was better in the past before all this annulment talk began.

November 1527

Events

- rumours from Italy claiming or denying the pope has made an alliance with the Imperialists are received throughout the month leading to much confusion (LP 4.3550, 3557, 3584, 3599, 3601, 3604). The League' commander, Lautrec, asks if he is to lead his troops to Rome or not ((LP 4.3599).
- having also heard rumours that the pope has escaped, the Emperor sends him a letter congratulating him on his freedom whilst denying all responsibility for the Imperial troops which had held him captive (LP 4.3596).
- meanwhile, on the 15th, France, England, Milan, Venice, Ferrara and the College of cardinals sign an agreement to work together for the release of the pope using force if necessary.[57]
- amid fears of mass starvation in England. Wolsey sends commissioners to visit every barn across the country and to report on what food is available with orders that surplus grain is to be sold to prevent hoarding which would otherwise increase prices (LP 4.3544, 3553, 3572, 3587, 3625, 3664, 3665, 3713)
- secretary Knight arrives in Rome but is unable to secure an audience with the pope (LP 4.3553).

---

57 The full text can be found in Lodovico Muratori, *Delle antichità Estense ed Italiane*, vol 2 (Modena 1740) pp 341-352

- the Emperor is so certain that Henry will not wage war on him that he offers a bet on the matter to the Bishop of Tarbes (LP 4.3597).
- the Bishop of Verona advises Wolsey that Henry's gift of 25,000 ducats to the pope to help him in captivity encouraged him to grant the requested bulls for Wolsey's college (LP 4.3562).
- in Spain, the Bishop of Tarbes expresses suspicion about what is being said in secret meetings between the papal nuncio and the Emperor's chancellor (LP 4.3597).
- Francis makes payment of the pensions he owes. After the King, Wolsey, Norfolk and the Suffolks, Thomas Boleyn receives the highest amount of 262 crowns, almost double the 150 crowns received by Thomas Cheyney and Thomas More (LP 4.3619).
- efforts are made to get the Marquis of Mantua and Duke of Ferrara to join the League (LP 4.3578, 3599). The latter agrees and is rewarded with a marriage between his son Ercole and Francis' ex-sister-in-law Renée (LP 4.3585; CSPS 3.2.239).
- William Brereton is awarded eight stewardships worth £46.6s.8d while Henry Norris is granted custody of Hunsdon. Brereton's brother, Urian, gets an annuity of £13 6s 8d (LP 4.3622.8,15,27)
- the Emperor rules on a case involving Don Pedro de Castro who had been arrested for assaulting a woman he claimed was his wife and therefore his property to discipline. Pedro wants to be tried in a church court where the punishments are notoriously less severe and where the bull he obtained from the pope allowing him to marry whilst retaining his clergy rights will be appreciated. The Emperor has opposed this and Pedro now wants to appeal direct to the pope. The Emperor orders that no such appeal be permitted because such a move would be against "our royal jurisdiction." (CSPS 3.2.238)
- amid mutinies and ongoing destruction in Rome, the pope signs an agreement with the Imperialists on the 26th promising to pay them 250,000 ducats from a tax on Naples and 60,000 in cash which he will raise by offering three people the chance to become a cardinal at 20,000 apiece. (CSPS 3.2.249).
- Henry has two of Anne's books covered in velvet and another which she brought back from France repaired (LP 5.276).

Comments

Wolsey's plan to ensure the supply of food across the country is extraordinary. Although not all the returns for every county have survived, many have and it is probable that the others were simply destroyed after the work was done and the crisis passed. To have been able to orchestrate such a mass inspection demonstrates the calibre of the Tudor administrative machine – and they did it all without telephones, computers or masses of sub-committees sitting around arguing about terms of reference. It is an achievement which should be taken as a lesson to the twenty-first century.

By contrast, the problems of waging war in Italy from England are made apparent. It would typically take a month to get a letter from one country to another and given most were in cipher, additional time would then be required to decode it. Sometimes, a skilled courier could do the journey in less but war created a host of other difficulties and dangers. By the time an item of news had reached England for which a response was required, the situation had almost certainly passed.

The Emperor's letter to the pope of 22nd November is one of the most remarkable which he ever wrote, firstly for his straight faced denial of responsibility for the actions of his own troops but also because it suggests that even he had no idea of what was happening in Rome, though his meetings with the nuncio may hint otherwise. It is possible that the Emperor was just a little over eager in his desire to be the first to congratulate the pope and he sent the letter before the actual agreement was confirmed.

Urian Brereton is listed as a Page of the Privy Chamber, William a Groom of the same and Norris as Squire of the Body. Urian is lowest in rank, Norris highest. Hunsdon was significant because revenue from there would be granted to Anne Boleyn in 1532 (LP 5.1370.3).

The pension received by Thomas Boleyn would be worth around £450,000 today. The high rate reflects his status as an ambassador and key role in the Field of the Cloth of Gold and was agreed years before Henry's relationship with Anne. It is a reminder to those who seek to argue that Thomas Boleyn only shot to prominence because of his daughters that this was simply not the case. Anne benefited from her father's position at court, not vice versa.

What does the case of Pedro de Castro have to do with Anne Boleyn? It demonstrates the two faced hypocrisy of the Emperor who happily denies appeals to Rome from his own subjects because he believes his law should be final in Spain, yet when Henry expresses the same belief that his law should be supreme in England, throws a fit and calls it heresy.

The records do not say which books were covered or mended at this time. Books were precious items and Anne was clearly a keen reader. At least nine of her books have survived and there would have been many more. Most would have been religious works, copies of sections of the Bible such as the Book of Psalms or the Gospels, commentaries on them and aids to prayer. [58]

---

58   For more details, see James Carley, *The Books of King Henry VIII and his wives* (2004) pp.124-133

December 1527

Events

- Gregory Casale is appointed to deal with Henry's secret matter in Rome. Wolsey tells him that he has absolute confidence in him because he knows he never refuses any "toil, danger or trouble" in his diligent service to the King. Wolsey says that there is no matter which Henry holds closer to his heart, which is of greater importance or which is more ardently desired. The issue involves "most of all the King's conscience, the salvation of his soul, and the preservation of his life and safety, also the continuation of the royal line, and the peace of the commonwealth and welfare of all subjects, both those who live in his kingdom now and those who will live in it in the future." Wolsey explains that Henry has "for a long time" felt God was punishing him by taking the lives of his sons. Henry has employed "constant study and learning" as well as consulted "the wisest doctors, men of most mature and sound judgment, theologians and jurists from both this kingdom and living elsewhere, in order to know clearly and truly whether the dispensation previously granted for himself and the queen" is valid. Of their response Wolsey says: "It is asserted by many and various of these doctors, that the pope cannot dispense in the first degree of affinity, as it is by divine law, morally and naturally prohibited." The canon lawyers meantime have stated that the reasons given for the dispensation being granted are untrue: there was no prospect of war between England and Spain and Henry did not request any dispensation being a minor. As a result, Henry seeks an annulment "to remove this inmost pain" and so he can "take another wife, and, God willing, have from her a son who may secure the succession." If this does not happen, there will be civil war when Henry dies and "more serious evils in this kingdom that have ever been heard of before." Casale is to do all he can to obtain a private audience with the pope as Henry wants a commission granted for Wolsey to "legitimately and sufficiently proceed to the investigation of the insufficiency of the dispensation" of 1504 "without any doubt, difficulty, contradiction or delay thrown in at all." If news of the plan comes to the ears of those "who are likely to be disturbed", they "may wish or be able to hinder or slow it down." Casale should remind the pope of "how many and how grave evils could result from propagation of this business." In order to ensure that the pope has no need to involve advisers or secretaries, Wolsey has drawn up a letter which the pope needs only to sign and seal. If the pope says he is too scared of the Emperor to do so, Casale is to point out that by granting the commission "he would be exonerated from every part" because the verdict would be given by Wolsey. If the pope suggests Wolsey is not impartial, Casale is to deny this and assure him that Wolsey believes his first duty is "the

profession I have made towards Christ and that I will never deviate from the right, true and just path." If the pope is not convinced, Casale should seek Staffileo as judge but accept no other foreigner. Casale is to remind the pope of Henry's loyalty and compare that to the untrustworthy Emperor and if necessary, to remind the pope of his blatantly political and unjustified dispensation granted to the Emperor to break his promise to marry the Princess Mary: "If the pope was pleased to show the Emperor such gratitude who was an enemy, how much more inclined should His Holiness be to help this prince who had always demonstrated true faith and filial obedience." (LP 4.3641)
- in follow up letters, Wolsey tells Gregory Casale that the pope risks losing English obedience if he fails to act because Henry regards acting in accordance with his conscience and God's will as more important than politics. He says that he had to work hard to wrest Henry from his "tenacious" attachment to the Emperor and that he was only able to do so by promising him that the pope would be a more faithful ally due to his "perpetual love and indissoluble friendship." Wolsey says that if the pope does not grant Henry's reasonable request which he is sure will be "acceptable in heaven", the result will be war in England and loss of life (including possibly his own) with the immediate result that the pope will lose English aid for the war in Italy. He makes clear that Henry will never sleep with Katherine again citing her unspecified but incurable health problems (LP 4.3644).[59] Casale is assured that Henry's life and safety depend on this matter (LP 4.3662). He also proposes other cardinals who might serve with him on a commission naming Campeggio, Trani or Farnese, or if none of them are available, Monte, Cesi or Sienna. Under no circumstances is he to allow the pope to appoint an Imperialist (LP 4.3693).
- Henry sends a letter to the pope stressing the urgency of the issue with a handwritten postscript. He includes a draft commission for the case to be heard in England with the instruction that his daughter Mary should remain legitimate (LP 4.3647).
- the Emperor writes to the pope telling him not to grant Henry's annulment. This news is received from Jernyngham, an Englishman serving with Lautrec's army and who had not been told of Henry's "secret matter" thus indicating that the plan is no longer secret (LP 4.3687)
- Lautrec is urged to advance (LP 4.3661). The pope – who had previously told Lautrec not to do so because his presence at Parma effectively deterred the Imperialists from taking him to Gaeta - expresses doubt that he will (LP 4.3715, Appx. 131).

---

59 This letter was sent almost in duplicate to Gregory's brother John at Venice (LP 4.3645) but Wolsey did not reveal to John the contents of the other letter to Gregory (LP 4.3641) which meant John had very little idea of Henry's case, something which may have affected John's later dedication to the cause.

- secretary Knight is able to get a letter to the captive pope who agrees to issue a dispensation so Henry can marry (LP 4.3638). A week later, on the 8[th,] the pope is released and goes to Orviento. News reaches England on the 20th (LP 4.3691). One of his first actions is to send for Gregory Casale (CSPS 3.2.278) who finds him miserable and alone. Casale tells Wolsey that if Lautrec advances, the pope will annul but if not, he will do nothing though his intentions are good, something Casale attributes to Gambara's efforts on Henry's behalf (LP 4.3682). On the 23rd, the pope grants the dispensation for Henry to marry (LP 4.3686).[60]
- on the last day of the year, the pope agrees to grant Wolsey the commission to investigate the truth of Henry's "marriage" but predicts the Emperor will kill him when he finds out. He says his life depends on Henry's help as he does not trust Francis (LP 4.3715).
- the Emperor's ambassadors and military advisers across Italy all send him further letters advising him to make peace as the war cannot be won. They predict the pope will join the League and wage war and report that the Marquis of Mantua has accepted a commission in the League's army (CSPS 3.2.251, 257). Advice from Mendoza in England is that the Emperor must break the Anglo-French alliance and he recommends making peace and that the Emperor bribe the cardinals with Spanish bishoprics so they will urge the pope to adopt an Imperialist policy. (CSPS 3.2.252).
- the pope accepts 25,000 ducats from the twenty-two year old Ercole Gonzaga (brother of the Marquis of Mantua) to make him a cardinal plus 20,000 apiece from the two Neapolitan Archbishops, Carafa and Palmieri (CSPS 3.2.259, 276). Gonzaga is a friend of the Casale family and a layman. San Severino, another layman from Naples, buys his hat for 20,000 also (CSPS 3.2.345).
- the pope sends Cardinal Farnese to the Emperor to complain about his treatment which he believes is unfair given that he gave the Emperor a dispensation so he could marry a rich heiress to ensure his succession when he was actually promised to Mary of England. The pope confirms that he has been in receipt of the 10,000 ducat pension which the Emperor gave him but notes that the promises of land in Naples and a rich wife for his nephew have yet to materialise. The cardinal is to remind the Emperor that the pope is waiting (CSPS 3.2.280).
- the Emperor tells Mendoza that he will be sending Miguel Mai, a canon lawyer and regent of the chancery in Aragon, to join him in England so that he can assist Katherine. Mai will be bringing with him an attested copy of the 1504 dispensation which the Emperor believes is "ample" (CSPS 3.2.279).

---

60 David Wilkins, *Consilia Magnae Britanniae et Hiberniae*, Vol. 3 (1737) p.707; Nicholas Pocock, *Records of the Reformation*, vol. 1 (1870) p.22-27

- in Italy, Quinones, a relative, councillor and confessor of the Emperor, rejects all requests to go and see the pope about Katherine's case saying that the time is not right (CSPS 3.2.259, 272).
- Henry gives Anne a brooch of the Virgin Mary containing a diamond which could be worn as a pendant on a red ribbon (LP 5.276).
- Henry Percy is appointed bailiff of Northumberland and Tynedale at a salary of £1000 per annum (LP 4.3628).
- Thomas Boleyn settles his lawsuit with Butler over the Earldom of Ormond, a dispute which has raged for twelve years. The agreement is negotiated by Wolsey, approved by Henry and signed in February (LP 4.3728, 3937).

Comments

Different stories of how the pope regained his freedom circulated for some years. In 1531, Dr Mai reported that the Imperial captain, de Scalengues, had allowed him out in disguise upon payment of 10,000 ducats.[61] Edward Hall reported that the pope had fled by climbing up a chimney – despite being almost fifty at the time and leaving at a season when chimneys were likely to be in use.[62] The truth was more prosaic. The pope made a deal with his captors and gave them money. The Emperor knew all about it and saw it as the best way of him saving face.[63]

Henry's handwritten postscript would have been interpreted by the pope as a special mark of favour: as today, monarchs generally employed secretaries to write their letters rather than pick up pen and paper themselves. Henry's desire to see his daughter retain her legitimate status is also important to note. His concern was Deut 23:2 which said that no bastard might enter the assembly of the Lord and no heir either down to the tenth generation. He reasoned that this meant she would not be admitted to heaven and could not be consecrated as monarch if bastardised, a view which might seem strange to people today who view the monarch as simply a human being who is in the role due to an accident of birth, but to those who view the monarch as chosen by God, it makes sense.[64] Popes were not allowed to be illegitimate either and given the circumstances of Clement's birth, Henry may have expected him to understand the issue very well. Writers frequently assume that questioning the status of the dispensation was the same as questioning Mary's legitimacy: they were not.

Percy's advance was expected. As Earl of Northumberland, he was required to keep order in the north. It had nothing to do with Anne Boleyn.

Mendoza's memorandum is interesting because he continues to regard Henry's opposition to the Emperor as being a response to the money which the

---

61 CSPS 4.2.699.
62 *Hall's Chronicle*, p.727
63 The agreement made appears in Joachim Le Grand, *Histoire du Divorce*, vol. 3 (Paris, 1688) pp.48-57. The Emperor's acknowledgement of his involvement was given in an audience with the French and English ambassadors, LP 4.3844.
64 Jer 1:5; Isa. 49:1; Gal 1:15; Ps. 139:13-16.

Emperor owes him and his anger at the Emperor reneging on the Treaty of Windsor by which he had promised to marry Mary. The annulment issue he sees as a side issue, possibly a product of the opposition but certainly not a cause. Amongst other interesting comments he makes in it is the suspicion that Mary might be sent to France to make room for Richmond to become king and a recommendation that Chapuys be sent to foment disputes between Henry and Francis.

Mai never came to England. He was eventually sent to Rome where he would maintain a staunch defence of Katherine's case. The Emperor's comment that he is sending Mai with a copy of the original dispensation is interesting because Mai would spend months at Rome complaining that he had never seen it and needed a copy of it. The allegation that the document was "ample" indicates the Emperor's belief that the pope had the power to issue dispensations to break God's law – something Henry disputed.

The pope's instructions to Cardinal Farnese demonstrate his devious and duplicitous mind.[65] His simultaneous promise of a commission to Henry and angling for rewards from the Emperor show him sitting on the fence ready to jump down on whatever side was most beneficial to himself. In the 1960s, T-shirts and bangles bearing the words "what would Jesus do" became popular. It is safe to answer, not act like Clement VII who was meant to be Jesus' representative on earth. The pope was not a weakling, just a crook.

Quinones refusal to proceed with Katherine's case is significant. It was his relationship to the Emperor which meant he felt safe to reject the order but it also shows that he did not believe there was any urgency about the matter.

The traditional season for gift giving was not Christmas but New Year. The brooch was as much a devotional item as a decorative one. The Christmas story puts the model of Christian womanhood as personified by the Virgin Mary, centre stage. The diamond, symbolic of constancy, indicated the reliability which could be placed in her intercessions. Anne would have been expected to wear the pendant and trust that the Blessed Virgin would help her – also a virgin – in her time of trial.

Wolsey's revelation that Henry had consulted canon lawyers and theologians in England and overseas is interesting. Cranmer is generally credited with the idea of seeking judgments from European universities but some consultation had already taken place.[66]

The timing of events in December is important. When Wolsey wrote to Gregory Casale on the 5th (LP 4.3641), he had no idea that Knight had already been able to make contact with the pope.[67] He told Casale that Knight was believed to be near Rome and had similar instructions because the King was unclear whether Casale would be able to obtain an audience in person. Wolsey suggested that Casale might have to use the excuse of trying to improve

---

65 Had Henry known the pope was in receipt of a large pension from the Emperor, he might have altered his policy sooner.
66 He may have meant his own consultation of Staffileo on Henry's behalf.
67 The full despatch is in SP vol. 7 pp.18-33.

relations with the Duke of Ferrara or disguise himself to get into the pope's prison and he sent him ten thousand ducats which could be used as bribes to get past the guards. On the 5th, Wolsey was adamant that the commission should be to himself or Staffileo only but on the 27th, after news of the pope's release was received, a list of alternative cardinals was drawn up (LP 4.3693). Campeggio held an English bishopric and was Cardinal Protector for England so should have been involved in any case relating to the country but there is no evidence of Wolsey or Henry writing to seek his help. Trani was a man renowned for his scholarship and piety. Cesi was a canon lawyer who had joined the papal secretariat in 1502 straight after college. Farnese, at this stage of his career, was anti-Imperial and backed limited reform of the church.[68] Monte was another anti Imperial canon lawyer and would go on to be very active on Henry's behalf at Rome. Little is known about Piccolomini of Sienna so Wolsey's choice of him is a mystery. The comment that Casale should ensure an Imperialist was not appointed to the commission suggests that neither Henry nor Wolsey believed Campeggio to be such at this time.

The dispensation issued for the marriage allowed Henry to marry anyone related to himself in the third or fourth degree or who had been married but not consummated that union or who had incurred affinity to him through illicit coitus. In April, a revised dispensation allowed him to marry anyone to whom he had no spiritual ties. Anne was not named in either document. Some writers have seen this general dispensation as being evidence of Henry and Wolsey trying to pull the wool over the pope's eyes by not identifying the intended bride while others have assumed that the document was designed wholly with Anne in mind and argued this proves that she had already been married at least once when she wed Henry as well as being possibly his daughter![69] Neither theory is justified. General dispensations to marry were routinely issued to princes to facilitate the negotiation of treaties. The Emperor had obtained one which similarly allowed him to wed any woman other than first degree consanguinity (i.e. a sister) in 1521.[70] Significantly, the dispensation was granted before the commission which suggests that the pope was confident of the result, though he did say it would only be operative after the annulment had been granted.

---

68 He succeeded Clement VII as pope by which time he had become an Imperialist. In October 1530, Henry said that he hoped for support from Farnese and Trani (LP 4.6667).

69 See Kelly, *Matrimonial Trials* pp.43-53. The use of the word clandestine for a union does not mean secret, which would be the modern understanding of the word, but simply that the union was agreed without banns being read.

70 Parker, *Emperor*, p.159. As the Emperor had obtained this in order to marry Henry's daughter, it is reasonable to suppose that Henry and Wolsey may have seen the document and based their own request on it. D'Avray, *Papacy* provides a number of examples of princes with similar generic dispensations, e.g. Charles IV in 1307, p.106

The pope issued a general commission for the case to be tried in England: Henry and Wolsey sought a decretal. The difference between the two is best explained with a modern analogy. A manager sends a traffic warden out to record what cars are parked on what road markings and report back – that is a general commission, it simply authorises someone to gather facts for someone else to judge. Another manager sends the same traffic warden out to record what cars are parked on what road markings with instructions to prosecute those marked on double yellow lines because that is an offence – that is like a decretal commission in that the verdict already exists: if a particular point is proved then he is authorised to carry out a certain action. Quite aside from wanting a quick resolution of the matter rather than months of discussion, the fact that a war was raging in Italy meant there was no certainty about what the political situation might be when the commission completed its report, so Henry's request was not unreasonable as it might have been regarded if Europe was at peace.

1528

January 1528

Events

- Thomas Boleyn and his wife, Henry Norris and his wife, plus George Boleyn's wife Jane, all receive New Year gifts from Henry VIII (LP 4.3478). Anne receives two bracelets set with ten diamonds and eight pearls plus a book garnished with gold (LP 5.276).
- in Italy, Spanish troops break into Knight's house and search his belongings in an attempt to discover Henry's intentions and what the pope might have promised (LP 4.3749).
- Jean du Bellay, the Bishop of Bayonne, suggests to Wolsey that the pope should depose the Emperor for his role in the Sack of Rome and holding the pope captive for months. Wolsey agrees (LP 4.3757).
- from Scotland, James V asks his uncle Henry to prevent the return of the Duke of Albany (LP 4.3773).
- Francis praises the efforts of Ghinucci in Spain in seeking the release of the French princes from captivity (LP 4. Appx.141)
- Wolsey's surveys into grain continue amid fears that with no surplus, there will not be enough to sow next season. Cattle murrain devastates livestock and continued low rainfall reduces freshwater fish stocks to a dangerously low level (LP 4.3761, 3819).

-the pope reveals that while he was held captive, the Emperor sent him a demand that Henry's annulment be not heard in England. Nonetheless, he tells Knight and Casale that while he could not grant the commission as Wolsey requested, he will re-issue it at a later date in stronger terms if Lautrec advances and then tell the Emperor he was forced to grant it out of fear. Until Lautrec comes, Henry is not to use the commission as that would endanger the pope's life and those of the five cardinals still held hostage (LP 4.3751, 3788). Two days later, the pope tells Casale that he has consulted San Quatuor and Simonetta who have advised that Wolsey should hear the case using the commission provided and give his verdict. Henry should then marry Anne using the dispensation already granted and only after that apply to Rome for a legate to come to confirm it. They advise against citing Katherine to appear because she is sure to appeal and the Imperialists will then demand the pope prohibit Henry from marrying Anne. If, however, he presents the world with a *fait accompli*, the pope can declare any offspring they have legitimate (LP 4.3802)
- Lautrec finally moves and the League's campaign goes well. Imola and Sardinia are taken. The pope employs spies to record enemy troop movements and take the information to Lautrec (LP 4.3802, 3855). The Imperialists cause much bloodshed in the Papal States (LP 4.3758).
- in Spain, negotiations are at a stalemate with the Emperor demanding that Francis withdraw his army first and Francis demanding that his sons are released first. Unconvinced England will fight and concerned Henry's annulment will harden the Emperor's mind further, the Bishop of Tarbes has the declaration of war read to the Emperor on the 22nd due to take effect in forty days if the Emperor fails to (i) release the pope, (ii) release the French princes (iii) pay Henry the 1.4 million ducats he owes him (LP 4.3826, 3827; CSPS 3.2.298).[71] The Emperor responds by pointing out that the challenges had been written in November and the pope was already free. He notes that as Francis has failed to abide by the Treaty of Madrid, he is in no position to challenge him, and claims that the Sack of Rome was "without our consent or approval but entirely against our will." He says he holds Francis "in contempt" and vows to "destroy him and all those who espouse his cause." He then orders the imprisonment of the French, Venetian and Florentine ambassadors and house arrest of the English (CSPS 3.2.298, 317).
- the Emperor sends a direct response to Henry saying that Francis started the war and announcing that he has no intention of paying the money he owes which he defines as a "trifling sum." He claims that Henry's doubts about his 'marriage' to Katherine impugn the pope which gives him more grounds for war against Henry than Henry does against him. He suggests

---

71 This sum comprised the 400,000 ducats referenced in January 1527 (CSPS 3.2.2) plus three years of arrears on the bond of indemnity and "the remainder as forfeit for not fulfilling these sacred obligations at various times. "

Wolsey has sought to bastardise Mary in revenge for not being made pope (LP 4.3844). He tells Mendoza to go to France and promises to release Henry's ambassadors – Ghinucci and Lee – only when Mendoza reaches Fuentarrabia (CSPS 3.2.308).
- meanwhile, the Emperor is visited by the sons of De Puebla who had been ambassador to England at the time of Katherine's marriage to Arthur. Ruiz hands the Emperor an original brief or letter from Pope Julius giving consent for Katherine to marry Henry together with a copy of the bull which was issued. Both documents have the same date (CSPS 4.1.571).
- Staffileo is appointed Anglo-French ambassador to the pope and Henry's chief proctor in the annulment case (LP 4.3766, 3777). He discusses the case with the Bishop of Rochester (LP 4.3820).
- Leyva, in charge of the Emperor's army in Italy, complains to him that the Spanish troops have not been paid for three years which is why they are mutinous and impossible to control. He reminds him that the men earn 4 ducats a month each and the cost of the army is 32,500 per month – meaning arrears are now over a million ducats excluding the money owed to the German troops (CSPS 3.2.286).
- the pope writes to Venice demanding the return of Ravenna and Cervia. He also demands Reggio and Modena from the Duke of Ferrara and suggests that until all these towns are returned to him, he will not re-join the League, sending Gambara back to tell Henry and Francis (CSPS 3.2.287, 294; LP 4. Appx.145, 147).

Comments

Henry's gifts to his courtiers were generally gilded bowls and cups of various weights according to the status of the recipient. They were distributed in public when gifts to him were also received. The gifts to Anne would have been delivered in private and were in addition to nineteen diamonds given to her for her hood. It must be wondered what she did with all these gifts. At the time, she was still employed by Katherine of Aragon and surely she did not present herself for work in the morning wearing gold buttons and diamond and pearl bracelets? And where did she keep them? Ordinarily the maids-of-honour shared a dormitory. Leaving such items in a box would have been to invite theft.

It has already been observed that the idea that Henry might marry before his case with Katherine was settled at Rome, was not a proposal for bigamy. Here we have none other than the pope advising Henry to do just that. It is tempting to wonder if Henry ever regretted not following this course of action but he was determined that there should be no grounds for question about his union with Anne and he was probably already thinking about a grand coronation for her. He would not have expected the process to drag on for years to come. If Katherine had heard the pope's recommendation, she would have been horrified. The pope certainly expressed his sorrow that Henry had not taken his advice and two years later, he still wished Henry would simply marry Anne.[72] Henry was right not to trust the pope's promise to issue another commission later and then tell the Emperor that he had only done so through fear. As the pope had already proclaimed, promises made under duress were without value so any such commission would be meaningless.

The letter handed over by Ruiz de Puebla was to achieve notoriety as the Spanish brief. Questions about its authenticity would abound for years.

It is impossible not to feel sorry for Mendoza, given the job of reading the Emperor's response to Henry. The Emperor had known of the proposed Sack in advance and his failure to pay his troops was a direct cause of it, so his claim now that it was his sacred duty to defend the pope's position by waging war on Henry should he reject Katherine was laughable – though one suspects that Henry's reaction was couched in language that would have made the ambassador blush. The Emperor's debt was over two thousand million pounds, hardly what anyone else would call a "trifling sum."

February 1528

Events

- learning of the Emperor's treatment of his ambassadors, Francis promptly imprisons the Imperial ambassador to France (LP 4.3876, 3882). Henry places Mendoza under house arrest (CSPS 3.2.340).[73]
- French ships attack Spanish ships off the Sussex coast (LP 4.3887). Thomas Boleyn expresses Henry's anger to Wolsey with instructions to convey this to the French ambassador (LP 4.3993).
- Henry and Wolsey seek the support of four cardinals (Campeggio, Ancona, San Quatuor and Monte) and two Italian bishops (Verona and Tortona) (LP 4.3904-3905, 3908-3911).
- Henry tells France's ambassador, Jean du Bellay, that he trusts the pope's word (LP 4. Appx.147)
- the pope asks his nuncio in England to find out who suggested Henry separate from Katherine (LP 4.3889).
- Wolsey sends Stephen Gardiner and Edward Foxe to the pope complete with sixty five pages of instructions. They are to demand a revised dispensation and decretal commission. They are to assure the pope that God has enlightened Henry with true doctrine so he now understands that his "marriage" is against divine law as well as human, and to hand the pope a book which proves this. Whilst stressing that this is his motive and

---

72 LP 4.6290
73 *Hall's Chronicle* p.742. Mendoza was removed on the twelfth from his home on St Swithin's Lane to the home of a trusted courtier in Mark Lane.

not love for another, if pressed, they are to admit that Henry has an unnamed bride in mind who is virtuous and godly: "the purity of her life, her constant virginity, her maidenly and womanly pudicity[74], her soberness, chasteness, meekness, humility, wisdom, descent of right noble and high regal blood, education in all good and laudable [qualities] and manners, apparent aptness to procreation of children" all making her a suitable consort. They should urge the Emperor's excommunication and get the pope to put his verdict in writing and to tell Katherine to submit so she can live out her life in a state of honour being loved as Henry's sister (LP 4.3913).
- Francis Phillips and Juan Vives are banned from court or leaving England (LP 4.3943).
- Lautrec returns Rimini to the pope and captures Aquila and the whole Abruzzo turning toward Naples (LP 4.3934, 3949). This territory is rich with provisions to feed their men and, being on the coast, offers plentiful custom dues (CSPS 3.2.365). The Spanish troops leave Rome (thereby freeing Campeggio) and go to meet Lautrec's army (LP 4.3949).
- the pope continues to protest about Venice holding Ravenna and Cervia which he says are his, Wolsey and Henry tell the Venetians to return them in order that the pope cannot use this as an excuse to join the Emperor (LP 4.3989, 3996).
- Francis writes to the pope in support of Henry's annulment which he terms a just request (LP 4.3977).
- the Emperor launches an enquiry into vulnerable points on the English coast with a view to attacking them from the Low Countries (CSPS 3.2.323). He also sends an ambassador to James V saying he is "greatly to exaggerate" all wrongs to try and provoke James to declare war on Henry (CSPS 3.2.326).
- the pope declines to pay the Emperor the money he promised as part of the terms for his release arousing suspicion that he wants to keep Imperial troops unpaid and mutinous so they will not impede the progress of the League (CSPS 3.2.335, 359).
- Anne receives gold buttons set with diamonds and pearls for the sleeves of her gown from Henry plus two diamonds on hearts for her hood as a Valentine (LP 5.276).

Comments

Vives was the humanist scholar responsible for Mary's education. Phillips was the member of Katherine's staff who had been dismissed back in October 1527 but he had clearly either made or was seeking a return.

The account of Anne's virtues is interesting in light of modern representations of her. Today, she is often portrayed as independent, even to the

---

74 Modesty or chastity

point of being a feminist, but here she is praised for her obedience and humility. Today too, authors and film makers have no problem with the idea that she might have had sex before marriage, indeed they tend to assume it, but here she is praised for her virginity and innocence. Obedience and virginity are traditional Christian virtues rather than modern ones and the stress on childbearing ability also seems alien to generations who have grown up with the idea of contraception. Was Wolsey exaggerating Anne's perfections or was she such an ideal bride? There is no reason to suppose he lied despite tales told years later by her enemies trying to imply she had enjoyed relationships with Percy or gentlemen in France. Later on, occasions would arise when Anne would demonstrate a certain argumentative streak but at this point she probably was on her best behaviour because a crown was at stake. Besides, people change as they grow older, partly from maturity and partly as a result of their experiences of life. Anne would go through a lot before she died. Wolsey's letter was apparently very convincing for the pope told Edward Foxe a month later that he had heard the King wanted to marry a woman who was carrying his child but this missive showed this was not the case but rather Henry's intended was a lady worthy of him.[75] It is likely that the rumour which had reached the pope was a case of mistaken identity with someone assuming that Henry wanted to marry Bessie Blount and legitimise his son by her, Henry Fitzroy. That was never a proposal, no doubt to the relief of Bessie's husband.

The arguments over Ravenna and Cervia would continue for months with the pope bringing them up at virtually every audience and in almost every letter.

The four cardinals on whose support Henry felt confident were all canon lawyers. At this point, Wolsey and Henry were seeking to work through the legal system rather than pursue the theological case because they hoped it would be quicker. The Bishop of Tortona was Gambara who had been papal nuncio to England in 1527.[76] The Bishop of Verona, Henry trusted as a "fast and assured friend.". In April 1529. he advised his ambassadors to seek his help to overcome the Archbishop of Capua's "falsities, crafts and abuses set forth to the hindrance of our causes" and to petition for his election as cardinal.[77]

Cardinal Ancona was an expert canon lawyer which is why Wolsey sought his help, though the fact that he was currently handling the annulment for Henry's elder sister may have helped.[78] The editor of the *Calendar of State Papers: Venice*, claimed that Ancona was secretary to Pope Julius as the time the dispensation for Henry and Katherine was raised and hence he never wavered in his opposition to Henry's case.[79] Although Ancona was employed at the Vatican at the time, there is no evidence that he was involved in the grant: after all, the Vatican employed hundreds of people, the vast majority of which

---

75 LP 4.4251
76 Created a cardinal in 1549
77 Burnet, *History of the Reformation*, ed. Pocock vol. 4 pp.116-117
78 LP 4.4091
79 CSPV vol. 4 p. x, 397

had no connection to the case. Ancona, himself, never gave any hint of prior knowledge and neither the pope nor any of the cardinals, or even the Imperialists, ever suggested he had such. Henry Kelly credits Ancona with composing the English Articles of 1532, a rebuttal of Katherine's case but the pope said it was Ancona who convinced him to threaten Henry with excommunication if he did not return to Katherine.[80] Whether this last was true or not is open to question. The pope was a liar and Cardinal Ancona was dead at that point so unable to comment.

Although it is generally said that Gardiner and Foxe went to Rome purely to deal with the issue of Henry's annulment, this was not the case. They travelled with Gambara planning to go via France where they would urge Francis to put pressure on Venice to return Ravenna and Cervia to the pope as well as discuss financial arrangements for the proposed war against the Emperor in Flanders (LP 4. Appx.149).

The book which Gardiner and Foxe gave the pope to prove the prohibition on marrying a brother's wife was a divine law does not survive. A cynic might query if they gave him a Bible?

March 1528

Events

- Erasmus advises Katherine to be grateful in adversity and take Jesus as her true spouse (LP 4.4000).
- Gambara returns to Italy and tells the pope that while Henry believes Venice should return Ravenna and Cervia, Francis utterly rejects the idea (CSPS 3.2.364).
- Henry arrests Spanish ships and merchants so the Low Countries do the same to the English (LP 4.4018, 4071). The Low Countries also raise troops and repair defences ready for war (LP 4.4026, 4112). England similarly prepares for a war at land and sea (LP 4. Appx.153, 156).
- Francis challenges the Emperor to a man-to-man duel (CSPV 4.257).
- in Scotland, Queen Margaret gets her annulment from the Earl of Angus together with a bill for legal costs and advice on how much the granting cardinal expects for the favour (LP 4.4113).
- Anne urges the restoration of Wolsey's favour for her kinsman Thomas Cheyney. She also expresses a longing for shrimps or carp from his fish pond (LP 4.4005, 4081).

---

80 Kelly, *Matrimonial Trials*, pp.160-163; CSPV 4.877. Ancona also drafted a reply for the pope to a letter sent by Henry in December 1530 (LP 4.6759) but it was never used, see Philip Hughes, *The Reformation in England*, vol. 1 (1950) pp.378-82.

- the Emperor orders his aunt Margaret, regent of the Low Countries, to commence a propaganda campaign to convince the English that he is the good guy and Wolsey the villain who seeks war and Katherine's downfall (LP 4.4112).
- Gardiner and Foxe reach Orvieto on the 23rd and, together with Gregory Casale and Gambara, spend nine days with the pope and his advisors. They present Henry's book justifying his case and answering possible objections which the pope declares impressive and learned. They complain that the commission and dispensation which was sent "be in some material points altered from the minute and form by the King's Highness required and desired, and by reason thereof cannot fully serve for the achieving of the King's desire and intent." They remind the pope of his promise to address any issues which the pope admits but he says that he must do so secretly until the war in Italy is over. He tells them that the honour of Henry and of the papacy are "so conjoined in this cause, as what toucheth the one must needs touch and pertain to the other." He asks about Katherine and they tell him that she is aware of proceedings and "content to stand to the judgment of the church." The pope queries if Wolsey is impartial and is reminded that in a decretal commission, responsibility for defining the law remains with the pope and Wolsey's role would simply be to verify the facts on his behalf. The pope is content with this but Cardinal San Quatuor and Simonetta, Dean of the Rota, note that this format has not been used for some years. The fear is expressed that the Emperor would regard the issuing of a decretal as an act of war and it becomes clear "only fear of victory of the Spaniards letteth this cause." The pope is impressed with Henry's learned justification for his case but warns that the Emperor will "cause diverse Universities to write." Campeggio writes to the pope advising him to "give faith to the King's writings and reasons in this matter." The English are pressed to agree to a general commission with a promise that the pope will support them in three months or so when the war in Italy is over but the English protest "that which is promised to be done after the sentence, we require it to be in effect done before." Eventually the pope promises to issue a decretal but only as a secret document, not under lead, so that "the see apostolic be not slandered." If the Emperor dislikes his decision to annul provided the facts are as stated, "he cared not therefore." His words are witnessed by Gardiner, Foxe and Casale on the English side, the papal employees Gambara and Simonetta, plus Cardinals San Quatuor, Monte, Cesarino, Orsini and Cesi. The idea is that the secret decretal would "remain with the King's Highness for justification of his matter. In the event, that the confirmation by some chance cannot be obtained, the same to be kept secret, and to be shown to no man, but only the King's counsellors." The English are nervous about this because they know secret documents can be denied but the war is not going well. As they seek Wolsey's advice on whether to accept a public general commission

and secret private decretal, the pope summons Gregory Casale to tell him that Rimini has fallen again to the Emperor and that the Imperial army is about to go into action to capture Viterbo, part of the Papal States. Reminding him that Venice has not returned Ravenna and Cervia, the pope warns that if Henry cannot remedy his problems in Italy, he will join the Emperor, a prospect Casale says will be "to the total ruin of all Italy and hindrance of the common affairs." (LP 4.4120)[81]

- in accordance with the terms of his release, the pope send orders to Parma and Piacenza to surrender to the Spanish troops. He also sends secret instructions for them to disregard his orders (CSPS 3.2.363).
- Wolsey proposes a new peace plan which involves Francis evacuating Genoa and Asti and paying his debt to the Emperor as a ransom whereupon the eldest prince will be released. As soon as he is back home, Francis will withdraw his army from Italy and when that happens, the younger prince will be released also. Mendoza promises to present it to the Emperor (CSPS 3.2.367, 386; LP 4. Appx. 153, 158, 162).
- the Emperor appoints Mendoza as Bishop of Burgos (CSPS 3.2.370).
- King Juan of Portugal rejects pressure to send an ambassador to England to protest to Henry on Katherine's behalf, despite being warned that if he delays, Wolsey will probably issue the annulment anyway and Henry re-marry (CSPS 3.2.371, 379).
- Loaysa is removed from the Emperor's Council of State (CSPS 3.2.380).
- Henry gives Anne twenty-one diamonds and twenty-one rubies set upon roses and hearts (LP 5.276).

Comments

In his 1530 *Practice of Prelates,* Tyndale refers to a book issued by the Emperor which openly blamed Wolsey for creating the annulment crisis and alleging this was in revenge for him not supporting Wolsey's candidature for the papacy. Tyndale had links to the Low Countries so had presumably seen this text although his lack of familiarity with the language means he had misunderstood it for he claims that Wolsey's campaign to separate Henry and Katherine began after the Sack of Rome during the autumn when the pope was in captivity which is clearly wrong. [82]

Margaret's annulment is significant because it was, as Henry observed totally indefensible.[83] Angus had left her for another woman which obviously annoyed Margaret but it did not render her marriage to him invalid. It had after all been celebrated before a priest and witnesses with both parties making their vows of their own free will and promising to maintain them until death. With divorce being forbidden, Margaret initially tried to claim her union with Angus

---

81 The full report is in John Strype, *Ecclesiastical Memorials* (1822) vol. 1 part 2 pp.66-91.
82 William Tyndale, *The Practice of Prelates*, (Parker Society, 1849) p.322
83 LP 4.4131

was bigamous because there had been reports that her first husband, James IV, was alive at the time. Given James had been slain on a battlefield and his body seen by hundreds before being sent to London, these reports must have been the product of individuals with either intense spectral sensitivity or else excessive alcoholic consumption. As Angus had no desire to return to Margaret, he then had a highly convenient moment of recovered memory and recalled that he had been engaged at the time he married her and hence not free to make vows, and he persuaded a lady to duly sign a letter to that effect. It was an example of the practices used at Rome to break the bonds of holy matrimony when it suited both parties. Margaret's annulment was also significant because it was granted despite the marriage having produced a daughter: as part of the sentence, the pope declared young Margaret Douglas, legitimate. Henry sought the same protection for his daughter, Mary, and it is one of the great mysteries why he did not publicise this goal more widely because concern at the disinheriting of Mary encouraged many into his enemy's camp and strengthened the Emperor's resolve to oppose the annulment.

Cardinal San Quatuor is an interesting figure. Aged seventy at this point, he had been professor of canon law at Pisa. He worked hard to support Henry and he was offered a reward of two thousand crowns as a thank you (LP 4.3751) which he refused (LP 4.4120). In December 1530, the Emperor offered him two thousand ducats which he also refused, to the pope's dismay (LP 4.6758). A number of historians have highlighted this as a sign of his strong ethical beliefs. This might have been his motivation or it could have been because rewards were usually made more discreetly, but only five years earlier, he had been investigated for profiteering from indulgences and suffered demotion at the hands of the previous pope. Perhaps he had learnt his lesson, but given his reputation at Rome for shady financial practices and "convenient" legal interpretations it was reasonable for both sides to make the offer.[84]

Also interesting is the pope's prediction about the Emperor seeking university opinions. It is normally said in books that Henry got the idea from Cranmer but maybe it was the pope himself!

As the most famous and prestigious humanist in Europe, both Henry and Katherine would have welcomed Erasmus' support. He knew both of them and wisely kept his own counsel which makes his letter at this point fascinating.[85] The idea that Jesus was the "spouse of all pious souls and nearer to each than the nearest tie" was not unusual. Henry, himself, used it in his explanation of the sacrament of marriage in his *Assertio*. It stemmed from passages in the Apocrypha which spoke of wisdom as a bride living in the heart of the godly soul, passages interpreted by Christians as the Holy Spirit or the Word.[86] Nonetheless, bringing this up at the time her "marriage" was in question and

---

84 For fuller details see https://cardinals.fiu.edu
85 In his 1526 work dedicated to Katherine, he had expressed the belief that the Levitical prohibitions were divine law.
86 Ecclus. 1:1-15, 15:1-6; Wisd. 7:14, 8:2

reminding her of the need to take up her cross was hardly the resounding endorsement she would have wanted.

In an era before supermarkets, wealthy men and inland monasteries would often have a fish pond to provide them with a regular supply of fresh fish. Given meat was forbidden during Advent, Lent, on Fridays and various other occasions, people consumed a great deal more fish than they do today. This was a boon for the fishing industry but designed as a spiritual benefit. The symbol of the early church, during the days of its prosecution by the Roman emperors, was a fish, partly because the initials of Jesus Christ, Son of God, Saviour in Greek spelt *Ichthus* or fish but also as a reminder that four of the twelve disciples were fishermen and that Jesus had gone fishing with them. Anne's request indicates that she was accustomed to dine at Wolsey's and to receive gifts from him, a sign that her relationship with him at this time remained warm.

Wolsey's negotiations with Mendoza indicate that the latter remained under house arrest but still in contact with the court. He was not imprisoned in the Tower. A draft peace treaty based on these proposals was prepared by Margaret, Regent of the Netherlands, for the Emperor in April but it crucially omitted the requirement for the Emperor to pay his debts (CSPS 3.2.393). Mendoza continued to send letters to the Emperor as is shown by the Emperor acknowledging receipt but none of the letters survive, a loss which impacts upon our understanding of the period.[87]

Portugal's response to Katherine's plight is instructive. Juan III was another of her nephews as well as being married to one of the Emperor's sisters. Throughout the long running annulment crisis, he dithered and found excuses for inaction. Given England's long history of alliance with Portugal and trading links, he was more interested in upholding the good of his country than her position, arguably entirely the right response of any monarch.

The question of a duel had been discussed for some time. The Emperor challenged Francis to one in September 1526, something which he later denied but which all three ambassadors who were present at the time recorded in their despatches written the same or next day. He repeated the challenge in March 1528 which elicited a similar challenge from Francis.[88] Cheyney's argument with Wolsey was over a wardship. The case continued for months and is detailed under January 1529.

The pope's threat that he will join the Emperor unless Henry secure his lands in Italy, with the implication that this means he will support Katherine instead, is worthy of comment. It is a reminder that the pope's motive was self interest and not justice. Those who like to quote the eventual verdict from Rome regarding it as proof Henry was wrong, are guilty of crediting integrity to a man who was devoid of such.

---

87 On 5th July, the Emperor noted letters dated February 12th, 19th and 21st, March 24th, April 18th and 27th as well as other correspondence from December and January (CSPS 3.2.483). The last one in the archives is November 15th

88 Parker, E*mperor*, pp.169, 178. For Lee's account see LP 4.2470.

The gift to Anne was noteworthy. Not only was it the most valuable gift Henry ever gave her but he had been planning it for some time as the delivery of twenty-one rubies on roses of crown gold back in January affirms. The Tudors did not celebrate birthdays as a rule except for coming of age. The likelihood is that Anne celebrated her twenty-first birthday in March 1528.

April 1528

Events

- George Throckmorton seeks a senior position in Princess Mary's household (LP 4.4136).
- the Abbess of Wilton dies. There are two candidates to succeed her, the Prioress Isabel Jordan, and Dame Eleanor Carey who is the sister of Anne's brother-in-law, William Carey (LP 4.4197)
- Gardiner and Gregory Casale continue meetings with the pope. Staffileo joins them and represents Henry in a formal debate about Henry's case before the pope. He reveals that Henry told him at the More that he felt Wolsey should not be judge because Katherine "might and would refuse" his decision and says he personally sees no problem with a general commission only which leads to a row with Gardiner. The pope accepts Henry's case but continues to dither about issuing the promised decretal commission Wolsey and Henry want saying he does not believe they can protect him from the Emperor. Gardiner says if this impasse continues, the King "would do it without him." The pope complains he is not learned and God has not given him wisdom. Casale urges him to issue the required bull in secret. Trying to be helpful, the pope offers to send a brief to Katherine which will "show her what he thinketh" and stop her objecting to the commission. Meanwhile, in a private meeting, Simonetta admits that having reviewed the King's case fully, it is "in his opinion great and just." (LP 4.4167).[89]
- the French ambassador in England, Jean du Bellay, the Bishop of Bayonne, notes how Henry seems to hear every conversation inside and outside the court (LP 4.4206).
- Lautrec takes Melfi for the League and camps just fourteen miles from the Imperial forces under Orange in Naples. The pope says he will wait to see the outcome of what happens there before he makes his decision about Henry's annulment (CSPS 3.2.395). The Imperialist ambassador at Genoa says that the pope has asked Henry for "a large sum" in order to grant it and later in the month reports that it has been agreed. Meanwhile, Lautrec and the League move ever closer to Naples capturing all in their wake (CSPS 3.2.396, 399). A major battle at Salerno sees heavy Imperial losses

---

89 The full report is in Pocock, *Records*, vol. 1. pp.120-135

including the death of the Viceroy of Naples. (CSPS 3.2.413). Venice is alarmed by reports of advancing Germans and seeks help from Francis and Henry (LP 4.4171, 4207, 4212, 4224)
- the Emperor refuses to consider Wolsey's latest peace plan (CSPS 3.2.409). He tells Quinones to go to the pope and tell him to hear Henry's case himself rather than allow a commission to do so and argue that Henry's dispensation must be declared valid or all those in similar cases would be invalid also (CSPS 3.2.411).
- Francis also expresses his disinterest in the peace plan feeling that the progress made in Italy means the Emperor will be forced to surrender his sons soon anyway (LP 4. Appx.163).
- Renée, the sister of Francis' late wife, marries Ercole d'Este, the son and heir of the Duke of Ferrara (CSPS 3.2.461)
- the Brandons prepare to visit London. Henry's sister, Mary, sends him a letter saying how she is looking forward to seeing him and ending "I pray God send you your heart's desire."[90]
- at Henry's request, the pope issues the revised dispensation for him to marry Anne.[91]
- William Roy and Jerome Barlowe publish *Rede me and be not Wroth* which blames Wolsey for instigating the annulment crisis and brands the pope "antichrist."

Comments

Du Bellay's remarks may be seen either as a testimony to the loyalty of Henry's staff or else the efficiency of his network of informers. In 1541, Queen Kathryn Howard was impressed by the same phenomenon but she suggested that the principal informer was none other than the Almighty, perhaps reasoning that Henry, as Supreme Head, was so close to God that he passed on things he believed the King should know direct![92]

It is often commented that Henry's sister opposed his relationship with Anne. Her comment about hoping he obtained his heart's desire suggests otherwise. It is possible that she knew he was trying to buy a particular horse or something and she meant that but surely it is more likely that she knew his great desire was for the annulment. Whether she thought Anne was a good

---

90 Erin Sadlack, *The French Queen's Letters*, (New York, 2011) p.194. The actual letter is undated but an early hand has written on the original 1528 and she did visit London that year, most likely in line with legal matters relating to the death of Margaret Downes. See note ibid. p.240.
91 Kelly, *Matrimonial Trials* pp.52-3. Ehses, *Romische* pp.33-36. The changes were the addition of clauses permitting Henry to marry anyone to whom he had spiritual kinship, who had taken marriage vows but not solemnised them in a church or contracted clandestine spousals.
92 Quoted in David Starkey, *Six Wives* (2003) p.680. In the Bible, Ecc. 10:20 says that privately spoken criticisms of a king might be taken to him by the birds of the air working as God's messengers.

choice as bride was another issue but both Mary and her husband appeared always loyal to the King, even though if he had a male heir, it would put their own children further down in the line of succession.

Was the Emperor showing his ignorance of Henry's case or just being cunning in his claim that a verdict for Henry would invalidate similar cases? There were no similar cases. Henry was the only man given a dispensation to marry his brother's wife. Marriage to a dead wife's sister was not similar because it was permitted in the Bible. As regards the demand for the pope to hear the case in person, he had indeed done that – Clement had just not told the Emperor about it.

Roy and Barlowe's book was a vitriolic attack on Wolsey and the mass written in Strasbourg. The annulment occupied only a dozen lines in a poem of over three thousand three hundred. They were not in England to know what was happening, which could explain why there was no reference to Anne in it.

Simonetta's support for Henry's case is worth noting given his later change of opinion.

The English should have taken the pope up on his offer to write to Katherine and tell her his decision to annul and to stop her objecting to the legatine court. It would have prevented lots of problems.

The dispensation for Henry's marriage was a long document but is worth quoting because it will feature in Anne's fall. It begins by noting that Henry had wed Katherine "having no sufficient canonical dispensation" which means he "cannot without sin live in the said marriage." This means he needs absolution and that "the marriage itself should be declared to have been, and still to be null and invalid, and that it is and may be lawful for you to marry any other woman, any canon to the contrary notwithstanding … provided she be not the widow of your said brother." It ends by pronouncing "the threat of divine vengeance" on any person who "shall presume or attempt to allege, propose or object either in open court or private discourse, any impediment in the marriage which by the tenor of these presents you shall contract, or to speak or act or attempt anything in word or deed against the legitimacy of the said marriage, or the children which shall be born of it on any insinuation or pretence of marriage precontracted" or any other allegation of affinity, consanguinity or spiritual kinship.[93] Given it would eventually be the pope who condemned Henry's marriage to Anne, it can be argued he was damned by his own dispensation.

---

93 Reproduced in *Cobbett's Complete Collection of State Trials* vol. 1 (1809) pp.334-336. It is to apply after the annulment has taken place.

May 1528

Events

- aware that the Privy Council do not support war in Flanders and concerned at the cost of waging it and of compensating people in England to prevent civil disturbance, Henry asks Wolsey to negotiate a truce with the Low Countries and France to preserve English trade and jobs (LP 4.4285; Appx.163).
- Wolsey sends Sylvester Darius as a new peace envoy to the Emperor in Spain (LP 4.Appendix 162, 166).
- Thomas Boleyn spends time in Kent putting down rebellious artisans whose poverty has caused them to attack property (LP 4.4300, 4310).
- outbreaks of smallpox appear and the sweating sickness (LP 4.4305). Cases of smallpox amongst the Queen's ladies cause Henry to separate Anne from them into a room above the tiltyard gallery at Greenwich (LP 4.4251).
- Campeggio says his gout prevents him leaving Italy. Wolsey suspects the pope is delaying him to see the outcome of the war (LP 4.4288, 4290).
- Gregory Casale reports that the pope will not help until he gets Ravenna and Cervia back (LP 4.4255). His brother, John Casale, petitions the Signory in Venice daily for this to happen but they refuse to listen and say they do not care if the pope does excommunicate them as a result (CSPS 3.2.421, 427)
- Wolsey and Henry urge the need for the decretal commission. Wolsey promises that if the pope will issue it secretly, he will only show it to Henry (LP 4.4246)
- Henry's sister and her husband, Charles Brandon, the Duke of Suffolk, obtain a bull from the pope confirming the legality of their marriage and children and of the sentence passed previously which annulled the Duke's earlier marriage due to an invalid dispensation (LP 4.5859).
- a new French ambassador arrives in Venice (CSPS 3.2.421). The Imperial ambassador describes him as being very opposed to the Emperor's interests (CSPS 3.2.428).
- in Italy, both sides experience mixed fortunes. The Imperialists take Pavia and Brescia and seize a French galley taking 50,000 crowns to pay the League's troops but they fail to stop grain ships getting through from Sicily to the League and the pope raising men. Lautrec's army is hit by plague which costs thousands of lives. Francis sends the Count de St Pol with reinforcements (CSPS 3.2. 421, 427, 434, 438).
- the Emperor's envoy to Scotland reports that there is no indication that Henry is planning to wage war on the Emperor so the plan to encourage James V to invade is being shelved (CSPS 3.2.431).

- Mendoza, Imperial ambassador in England, threatens to hit Jean du Bellay, the French ambassador, who expresses his willingness to go outside and engage in a battle of croziers and mitres. Wolsey intervenes and peace is restored between the two bishops by Mendoza claiming his French was poor and he had only meant to wage a war of words! (LP 4. Appx.168)
- Cardinal San Quatuor rules that a bull of dispensation granted to an individual cannot be revoked while the person is alive but it can be modified. This comes in response to the case of Don Pedro de Castro which opens the way to the man's prosecution (CSPS 3.2.433).
- Edward Foxe arrives back from Rome on the 2nd and is sent by Henry to reassure Anne of Stephen Gardiner's abilities. Anne then leaves before Foxe makes his report to Henry alone. Only when Henry is sure the news is good and the pope is willing to send a written promise to confirm the verdict of the legatine court, does he bring Anne back into the room. Wolsey is less convinced when he gets his report and says that a decretal commission is essential because it is not safe to rely on the pope. Wolsey says he thinks that Henry's strongest case is the fact that he did not request any bull to marry Katherine but he asks Staffileo to advise on whether the bull's failure to mention public honesty would invalidate the union if Katherine persists in saying there was no consummation so no affinity (LP 4.4251).
- Henry loses patience with the pope and asks why he should "further employ our study, travail, wit or counsel" or "spend our treasure to the impoverishing of ourself, our realm and subjects" for someone who "by crafty means and under the face and visage of entire amity caused his learned men there to pretend ignorance and doubt in the justness of our cause" neglecting to exercise due care for the "public weal and the quiet of our realm" and his own "tranquillity of conscience." He describes the commission granted by the pope as useless because "he might revoke [it] again and inhibit at his pleasure; leaving in the same such remedies of appellations and other delays to the adversary, as though he seemed nothing else to intend but to involve and cast us so in the briars and shackles of those laws, that we should hang always under his yoke and bondage, and not to be delivered thereto." He rails against the "great difficulties pretended and contrived delays" and Foxe reports that Henry's and Wolsey's hopes in Campeggio's "favour and inclination" and even departure are now "almost extinct" and both are in "total despair." Gardiner is warned that unless he is able to obtain rapid remedy from the pope for the situation, he need not bother coming back to England (LP 4.4290).[94]
- Wolsey tells Henry that he is willing to brave his "high indignation, yea, and his body jointly to be torn in pieces, than he would do anything in this cause otherwise than justice requireth, nay that his Highness should look

---

94 Pocock, *Records*, vol. 1 pp.156-159.

after any other favour to be ministered unto him in this cause on his Grace's party, than the justice of the cause would bear; but if the bull were sufficient he would so pronounce it." (LP 4.4251)
- Wolsey confides his worries about the war in Europe and Venice's continued refusal to return Ravenna and Cervia to the pope to Jean du Bellay who says he had to rely on God giving him the necessary words to succour him (LP 4. Appx.163).

Comments

Henry's concern for Anne's health and his invitation to her to join him when the returned ambassador gave his report is a sign of Anne's increasing importance to him. If anybody had possessed any doubt that she was the intended new queen, this would have ended it. Anne's move into her own apartment away from those she would have shared with Katherine's other attendants seems to have marked the end of her employment there. The fact that this took place a full year after the annulment process began should be noted: she was not in a privileged position at the start. However, it is significant that Henry only allowed Anne to hear a small part of the report and only the part which contained good news. She was being deliberately shielded from the difficulties.

It is not known when the Suffolks decided to apply for the bull confirming their marriage which is unfortunate as it would be most interesting. Even if the suit was not contested, the legal process would have taken some weeks.[95] There is no evidence of anyone questioning their marriage so it seems likely the application for a bull confirming it was made for political motives relating to the succession. If they assumed Henry's marriage to Katherine was about to be annulled, they would have wanted their sons recognised as heirs to the throne either before or after Mary. Alternatively, it could have been because Brandon's daughters were approaching marriageable age. The other interesting point about the bull granted to the Suffolks by the pope is the statement that the grounds for annulling the Duke's previous union with Margaret Mortimer were that an invalid dispensation was used for the wedding – exactly the same case Henry was making regarding his own "marriage" to Katherine. It is certain that Henry would have taken note of this point.

There are several accounts of the sweating sickness. Jean du Bellay reported that it began with headaches and chest pains and then a great sweat followed which could prove fatal in as little as two hours. He noted that in the last visitation a dozen years before, ten thousand died in London in just ten days (LP 4.4391): such a figure would represent probably a sixth of the population. Sir William Parr (uncle of Henry's final wife, Katherine) said that

---

95 Of Brandon's previous wives, Anne had died in 1510. Margaret had remarried Robert Downes and died during 1528 but the exact date is unknown. Her death may have prompted the Brandons' action. She and Brandon had no children.

great cold and shivering were followed by a fervent heat and then delirium (LP 4.4305). The Duchess of Norfolk told Wolsey that the most dangerous period was the first sixteen hours: if one survived that, prospects of a full recovery were good. She recommended fasting and bed rest until all symptoms had passed and the use of a folded linen cloth soaked in vinegar and rosewater and stuffed with brown breadcrumbs and wormwood to hold against the nose. She believed that people who had been ill remained infectious for at least a week after recovery and urged the need for their total isolation. As this could not be guaranteed, people should close their doors and avoid contact with anyone until the scourge passed (LP 4.4710). The universal horror of the illness meant its arrival in England would have engendered great panic at all levels of society.

The San Quatuor ruling is pertinent because of Henry's case that his bull of dispensation should be revoked. The cardinal was not a disinterested judge in the case of Don Pedro because he had been the man who advised the pope to grant the original dispensation and he was therefore covering his own back. This ruling explains why San Quatuor favoured issuing a revised dispensation for Henry and Katherine rather than an annulment.

June 1528

Events

- an eight month truce is agreed between England, France and the Low Countries to protect trade, fishing rights, foreign nationals and travel (LP 4.4376-4378, 4625).
- Francis's mother, Louise of Savoy, vows to go to Rome herself to demand the pope grant Henry's annulment if it is not sorted soon (LP 4.4319). Francis writes to the pope about it and Henry expresses his pleasure at the firmness of the letter (LP 4. Appx.180).
- the pope issues a general commission to Wolsey and Campeggio with no right of appeal (LP 4.4345). He gives Campeggio a secret decretal commission to safeguard the sentence (LP 4.4355, 4380). Campeggio's departure is delayed due to the war and outbreaks of plague which make it impossible to obtain a galley to Marseilles (LP 4.4368, 4380).
- the pope sends a letter to the Emperor telling him of the commission and of the promise he has made not to recall the legates or forbid their proceeding. He says that the legates are authorised to pronounce judgment but only after asking and obtaining his approval (CSPS 3.2.444).
- Venice ignores letters from Francis and Henry to return Ravenna and Cervia to the pope. Wolsey decides to send Gardiner to the Doge and Signory. The pope refuses to re-join the League until the cities are returned. The French report rumours of the Emperor trying to woo Venice (LP 4.4368, 4372, 4430, 4440).

- the pope asks the Duke of Brunswick, who is bringing German reinforcements for the Imperial forces, to retake Florence for the Medici family but his messenger is intercepted by the Venetians. The Imperialists intercept a letter from Lautrec to Francis I reporting a loss of six thousand men to plague and skirmishes and another saying that Francis blames the Venetians for the pope's failure to support the League (CSPS 3.2.445, 448). Encouraged by this news, they seek to entice Genoa away from France (CSPS 3.2.456) and promise the pope the restoration of Ravenna, Cervia, Modena, Reggio, Civita Vecchia, Florence and Ostia plus the wealthy heiress of Vespasiano Colonna as a bride for his "nephew", if only he will join them. The pope cheerfully tells the Venetians of this offer saying he will accept it unless they comply with his wishes (CSPS 3.2.468).
- Anne thanks Wolsey for all his hard work on the annulment and declares that next to Henry, she loves him more than anyone. She says she knows "the great pains and troubles you have taken for me is never like to be recompensed on my part" but hopes that "daily proofs of my deeds shall manifestly declare and affirm" her affection. She adds that she is confident that he longs for Campeggio's arrival as much as she does and signs off "your humble servant" (LP 4.4360).[96] Anne also admits to Heneage that she misses Wolsey when he is away (LP 4.4335).
- Henry flees the epidemic and makes a new will as does Henry Percy (LP 4.4404).[97] Wolsey also leaves London (LP 4.4391).
- William Carey asks Wolsey to keep his promise and favour his sister at Wilton (LP 4.4408). Hours later, Carey is dead of the sweating sickness. Others taken ill are Anne, her father and brother, Henry Norris, Nicholas Carew, Thomas Cheyney, Urian Brereton and William Kingston but all of these recover. (LP 4.4422, 4408, 4440).
- in a series of letters to Anne, Henry tells her that he will intervene if her father refuses to support her newly widowed sister (LP 4.4410).
- the French note the intensity of Henry's love for Anne and wonder whether the forced separation caused by her illness will affect it (LP 4.4391).
- letters from Gardiner go missing creating a massive, but unsuccessful, hunt amid fears that they have fallen into Imperial hands (LP 4.4358, 4359, 4361, 4390).
- Henry continues to send large sums to Italy – 35,000 ducats a month, almost £8000 – in pursuit of the war and defence of the pope (CSPS 3.2.249, 461).
- Bessie Blount and her husband receive a gift of land worth £100 from his mother. (LP 4.4357).

---

96   James Halliwell-Phillipps, *Letters of the Kings of England*, vol. 1 (1848) p.321
97   E. B. Fonblanque, *Annals of the House of Percy*, vol. 2 (1887) p. 384

- Perez, the Emperor's ambassador at Rome, reports to him that all England has risen in Katherine's favour and that Wolsey has been arrested (CSPS 3.2.475).
- still hopeful that Francis may agree to a duel, the Emperor orders a new suit of armour modestly monogrammed Charles the Divine.[98]

Comments

Henry's famous love letters to Anne are all undated but some clearly belong to this period since they refer to Anne's illness. The sequence begins with Henry hoping that their time apart will be short and sending her a hart so that she can eat it and think of his lonely heart.[99] Anne's replies have not survived but presumably she expressed some degree of fear that he had gone and she was left behind with reports of sickness coming ever closer. His next letter therefore expresses his concern for her and his recommendation that she return to Kent which he thinks may be safer. He writes:

> "I beg you, my entirely beloved not to be afraid… few or no women have caught this illness and what is more, no one at our court and few elsewhere have died of it… Comfort yourself and take courage and keep clear of the disease as far as you can and I hope shortly to make you sing for joy at your recall… I wish you were in my arms that I might a little dispel your unreasonable thoughts."[100]

Whether Anne was totally reassured or not is impossible to know. The same letter also informed her that the King had been forced to move from Waltham to Hunsdon owing to two of his ushers, two Grooms of the Privy Chamber, Anne's brother and the Treasurer all falling ill. They had recovered but the fact that so many people who were so close to the King had been ill, must have been alarming not just to her but the whole government. She may not have had much time to speculate for on Tuesday 16th she was taken ill herself. Henry wrote to her immediately: "There came suddenly to me in the night the most unpleasant news that I could have received… because I heard of the illness of my mistress whom I esteem more than all the world."[101] He sent her his physician telling her

---

98 Parker, *Emperor,* p.179
99 LP 4.4410. Letter IX
100 LP 4.4403. Letter III
101 Mistress is not used in the modern sense of indicating a sexual partner but in the courtly sense. Superiors and employers were known as Mistress, a tradition which survives in female teachers invariably being called "Miss" by pupils regardless of their marital status. The word "missus" or "mrs" is a contraction of this form of address. Henry was politely ascribing to Anne superior qualities and virtues which

to follow his orders: "if you do, I hope to see you again soon which will be a greater cordial for me than all the precious stones in the world." [102] By the 23rd June she was reported to be out of danger at which point someone presumably broke the news to her of her brother-in-law's demise.[103]

Henry's promise to support Mary is both interesting and curious. His phrase is "I trust that Eve shall not have the power to deceive Adam," the meaning of which is obscure, though it has been suggested that Carey had expressed his suspicions to the King that Mary was cheating on him while he was away at court. He describes her as being in "extreme necessity" and says of Thomas Boleyn "surely, whatsoever is said, it cannot stand with his honour" if he does not take pity on her. Why was Mary in dire need? Being suddenly widowed and left with two children under four would be hard on any woman but Carey was a Gentleman of the Privy Chamber, considerably better off than most of his contemporaries and possessed of a home which presumably was very comfortable so Mary should not have needed urgent financial support from her father. Was he in debt? Perhaps there had been some family dispute in which Mary had sided with her husband against her father. Also odd is Henry's reference to Mary as Thomas' "natural daughter." In the fourteenth century, the word simply meant legitimate but by the seventeenth century, it meant bastard or mentally deficient.[104] There is no evidence that Mary was illegitimate and her selection as a maid to Henry's sister in 1514 would seem to indicate she was not retarded, so was Henry simply using the word to suggest she had been foolish in some way? Or was it a French usage? In 1532, Francis introduced his sons to Henry describing himself as their "natural father."[105]

The argument over whether Carey's sister should become Abbess of Wilton would continue for some time. Carey addressed his request to Wolsey because the Cardinal had responsibility for such appointments. Given Carey died before the matter was resolved, it is impossible to know whether he would have involved Anne or simply gone direct to Henry himself had Wolsey not favoured his suit. He was the King's cousin and high in his favour so probably would not have thought he needed an intermediary. If he had lived and chosen to involve Anne, that would have been a clear indicator of her perceived influence on patronage at this stage, just as his non-involvement of her would have indicated the opposite, but his death means we cannot know.

Years later, Cavendish was to record that Anne hated Wolsey from the early 1520s. Her letter to Wolsey proves this was not the case. Unless one is to argue that she was an inveterate liar and skilled actress, the letter shows that at this stage, she admired and trusted Wolsey and probably liked him: it was only

---
were deemed to belong to the fairer sex.
102 LP 4.4383. Letter XII
103 LP 4.4408
104 See James Halliwell, *Dictionary of Archaisms and Provincialism from the Fourteenth Century* (1852), E. Coles, *An English Dictionary* (1677).
105 *Hall's Chronicle* p.791. Henry referred to Mary as his "natural daughter" in April 1536, SP vol. 7 p.685.

after the failure of the legatine court that she turned against him. Also worth noting is the style of the letter which is informal and positively girlish, both in its expressions and manner of composition, complete with a postscript written by Henry who says that Anne refused to seal it until he had added something. It is unwise to make generalisations about behaviour based on age because age and maturity do not always go hand in hand, but most people would regard it as a letter composed by an excited young woman rather than a woman of nearly thirty which the protagonists of the early birthdate for Anne would claim.

The grant of the decretal commission was a major step forward for Henry. It required the legates to investigate just three points. Firstly, was the marriage of Henry and Katherine necessary to preserve peace between England and Spain as the bull claimed? Secondly, did the young Prince Henry request the bull for this reason? Thirdly, were Ferdinand, Isabella and Henry VII alive at the time the bull was used? If any one of these points could be found to be true, the legates were required by the pope to annul the "marriage."[106] These were simple questions. Henry had only been eleven at the time and clearly not had an opinion on the matter. The bull had been granted to Henry VII of England and Isabella of Castile and Ferdinand of Aragon, and the first two were incontrovertibly dead in June 1509. Given that by then, Henry's sister Mary was espoused to the Spanish heir, Charles (Emperor from 1519), there was no need for a second matrimonial alliance. Since there was no question whatsoever about these points, the annulment was effectively agreed and the pope's dispensation for Henry to marry again confirmed this. This is why Henry was so angry when the pope withdrew the document and broke his well witnessed promise to allow Henry to keep written confirmation of it.

The fact that the secret decretal commission was granted at this particular time was due to Gregory Casale telling the pope on one hand that Campeggio was willing to take it while telling Campeggio that Henry had been promised he would take it. As the two men evidently did not communicate directly, the pope was encouraged to grant it because a leading cardinal approved and promised to keep it safe while Campeggio could hardly refuse to accept it without offending Henry. The written promise of accepting whatever decision he made just afterwards also offered Campeggio much needed protection. Wolsey expressed his admiration for Casale's work.[107]

Perez was clearly misinformed but it is a sign of the rumours which were flying round at this time. By contrast, the Imperial ambassador to Venice told the Emperor that Campeggio had gone for the sole purpose of pronouncing the pope's annulment of Henry's "marriage" (CSPS 3.2.427).

---

106 Herbert Thurston, 'The Canon Law of the Divorce', *English Historical Review*, vol. 19 (1904) p.642; 'The Divorce of Henry VIII' *Studies: An Irish Quarterly Review*, Vol. 21, No. 81 (Mar., 1932) p.63
107 Catherine Fletcher, *Our Man in Rome* (London, 2012) p.42

July 1528

Events

- Wolsey is taken ill. Anne Boleyn writes to him during his sickness and assures him that he is in her prayers. She thanks him for the "rich and goodly present" which he had sent her while she was ill at Hever and says he should not doubt "as long as any breath is in my body" that she will be loyal to him. She expresses her hope that Campeggio will arrive soon and bring "this matter shortly to a good end" whereupon she will be in a position "to recompense part of your great pains." After attributing Wolsey's preservation to God "for great causes known only to His wisdom," she signs off as "your humble and obedient servant" (LP 4.4480).
- a dispute breaks out over the wardship of Russell's step-daughters between Wallop and Thomas Boleyn's cousin, Thomas Cheyney (LP 4.4456, 4597)
- trouble is reported in Ireland (LP 4.4459, 4541), Scotland (LP 4.4457, 4531) and Wales where Irish immigrants are said to be overwhelming the local population (LP 4.4485).
- an investigation reveals that Carey's sister, Eleanor, has two bastards and is mistress of a priest despite being a nun (LP 4.4477). Henry's instructions that an outsider be appointed Abbess of Wilton instead are lost causing Wolsey to give the role to the Prioress, much to Henry's annoyance (LP 4.4488, 4497, 4507). Realising the problem arose when Wolsey was ill and when his regular servants were sick also, Henry forgives him describing it as "no great matter" (LP 4.4468, 4509).
- panic breaks out in Calais due to the sweating sickness and rumours of war (LP 4.4492-4494).
- the Imperial ambassador presents a petition from Katherine to the pope on the 20th demanding the revocation of the commission, that her case be heard at Rome and saying her marriage to Henry was contracted in line with papal decree and warning any dissolution of it would weaken papal power and provoke war (LP 4.4535).
- the pope continues to harangue ambassadors and send letters to Francis and Henry complaining about Ravenna and Cervia (LP 4.4458, 4487). Venice again refuses to return them (LP 4.4553). The pope threatens to ruin the Venetian republic (CSPV 4.324).
- the pope makes a written promise to Henry in a document known as the pollicitation in which he promises to confirm the decision to be made by Campeggio and Wolsey's legatine court and to allow nobody to interfere with it at any stage (LP 4.4550).[108]

---

108 A pollicitation is a promise made by one party which has yet to be accepted by the other. Such documents were legally binding under canon law, see Randall Lesaffer, 'Medieval Canon Law and Early Modern Treaty Law', *Journal of the History of*

- the English ambassadors in Spain, Ghinucci and Lee, report the Emperor is refusing to do anything for Henry owing to his anger about Katherine. They are, however, released from house arrest but ordered to stay in the country at the Emperor's pleasure (LP 4.4564).
- France intercepts letters indicating that the pope is using Campeggio as a delaying tactic at the request of the Emperor. Wolsey warns Henry (LP 4.4540, 4553, 4565, Appx.181).
- Nicholas Carew, Henry's Master of Horse and who is married to Anne's second cousin, receives offices worth £41 17s 9d a year (LP 4.4583.)
- George Throckmorton offers to contribute to Wolsey's college at Oxford if he will persuade Henry to appoint him Under-Treasurer of England (LP 4.4483).
- the Emperor tells Mendoza that he has not seen Wolsey's peace proposal in full and he suspects the French of intercepting the couriers. He comments that Henry is making too much fuss about the money owed which is a "trifling cause." He vows to defend Katherine because "her cause is ours and we shall hold it as such." He says that he knows Henry never acts without Wolsey's advice and urges Mendoza to promise Wolsey rewards should he abandon the French (CSPS 3.2.483).
- the German reinforcements bound for Naples desert in droves due to not being paid. The harassed Imperial envoy complains to the Emperor that the money drafts which he has sent have been for banks in Venice, Florence and Genoa, none of whom are willing to hand over cash to help (CSPS 3.2.485).
- the Emperor announces that Mai is to travel to Rome (CSPS 3.2.487).
- an offer of a rich Imperial heiress as bride is made to the Marquis of Mantua to try to recruit him to the Imperial cause (CSPS 3.2.487).
- the situation in Naples remains on a knife edge. The League hold almost all the land around and are effectively stopping supplies reaching the city but plague in their camp is depleting their ranks and at the end of the month, their commander, Lautrec, is infected. Meanwhile, in the north, an Imperial assault on Lodi fails (CSPS 3.2. 485, 489, 494, 495, 500). Unaware of the plague, Francis confidently predicts victory "in a very few days" and tells Montmorency that things "could not possibly feel better."[109] Henry contributes 30,000 crowns toward Francis' army (LP 4. Appx.186)
- Doria, the Genoese admiral, decides to switch his support from the League to the Emperor thereby allowing Imperial aid through to the besieged city of Naples (CSPS 3.2.496, 526; LP 4.4712, 4626, 4663).[110]

International Law, vol. 2 part 2 (2000), pp.178-198. Wolsey had drafted one for the pope to sign but Gardiner reported in April 1528 they had yet to hand it over because the debates remained ongoing about the format of the commission (LP 4.4167).

109 Parker, *Emperor*, p.180
110 The terms of the agreement are in LP 4.4626.

Comments

It is not clear whether Wolsey actually had the sweat but some of his household did which inevitably created confusion and panic. Certainly, he was not seriously ill with it so he may have had a simple viral infection. Anne's letter to him is again rather childlike in its expressions. She says she has prayed for just two people to be preserved, those she loves most, i.e. Wolsey and Henry. Evidently she was not concerned about her own family! She is clearly optimistic that the legatine court will settle the annulment and this hope has been fostered by Henry and Wolsey. It is only a bit later on, when Campeggio arrives, that the hopes start to fade. How far Anne was informed of this is unknown but her rapid change of heart toward Wolsey later on was a product of the great hopes she was given at the outset and their failure to materialise. If she had been given a more nuanced picture of the complexities of the situation, she would probably have been more forgiving. That this did not happen suggests that Henry kept her in the dark about it, perhaps from a loving wish not to upset her, perhaps from fear she would leave him if she knew, perhaps because he associated his success with his own virility which he did not want questioned, perhaps because he held the typical male attitude of the time that women should not trouble themselves with difficult matters like politics, maybe for all these reasons and more.

The pollicitation was a very important document. It said that the commission was being established to investigate Henry's union with Katherine which was "contrary to the laws both of God and man." It defined the purpose of the legatine court as "speedily administering justice, and freeing him [Henry] by our immediate sentence; from that tediousness and vexation wherewith the most just causes (by the corruption of the present times) are so far embarrassed, as scarce to be finished, and finally determined in an age." It said that the court would be "firm, valid and irreversible" and went on: "we do engage, and, upon the word of a pope, promise, that we will never by the entreaty, request or instance of any person, or from our own mere motion, or otherwise, at any time grant any letters, breves, bulls or writs of any sort, either under show of justice, as acts of grace, or on any other pretence whatever, to inhibit or revoke the matter of the commissions" but rather "we will preserve entire, ratify, confirm and defend to all purposes with our utmost power and authority, most effectually the commissions and...we will effectually make valid, and without refusal, delay, or any difficulty whatever, grant all such letters, breves, bulls or writs, which may serve any ways to strengthen or confirm the execution of the said commissions, commission or aforementioned process, or to ratify and establish any things by virtue thereof, by our aforesaid delegates decreed, determined, or adjudged" and "will support and preserve all and every one of them firm, valid, fixed and inviolable." The final promise was that "if (which God forbid) we should act or attempt any thing in any wise against the premises...every such act and attempt shall be null and void; and it is hereby made null and void, and is declared, pronounced and adjudged to be of no force and efficacy." [111]

Katherine's denial of the commission was unreasonable. She claimed to be loyal to the pope but he had granted the commission so her protest was an act of disloyalty to him. The pope would later claim precedent for acceding to her request based on the guidelines drawn up by Innocent III in 1202 which stated that judges should be from neutral countries to the parties in the case and that if one party objected to the verdict being given in the said country, it must come from Rome. The papal lawyers knew about those when the commission was drawn up and regarded them as irrelevant, only changing their mind to please the Emperor.[112] At this juncture, the pope simply ignored her complaint and permitted the promised commission to continue.

The Under Treasurership was granted to Sir Richard Weston, father of Francis, rather than to Throckmorton.[113]

The pope's continued focus on territory and his threats to Venice demonstrate him acting as a prince rather than as a man of God.[114] Many of Henry's problems stemmed from his naive belief that Clement was a Christian first and a prince second, whereas the reality was the reverse.

August 1528

Events

- Anne returns to court (LP 4.4649). She thanks Wolsey for granting the parish of Sundridge, six miles north of Hever, to John Barlow but says the clerk has inadvertently written Tonbridge so he is unable to claim it. She goes on: "I reckon myself much bound to your grace for all these that hath taken pain in the King's Matter. It shall be my daily study to imagine all the ways that I can devise to do them service and pleasure." In a postscript, she asks him to remember the parson of Honey Lane shortly for her sake (LP 4. Appx.197).[115]
- Piers Butler – father of James whom Anne had returned to England to marry – is appointed Deputy in Ireland (LP 4.4609).
- Katherine's almoner, Robert Shorton, tells Wolsey she has two bulls in Spain which will show that all impediments were removed and advises that

---

111 Herbert, *History*, pp.352-354, also in Cobbett, *State Trials* pp.304-6. The original Latin is in Burnet, *Reformation* vol. 6 pp.26-7
112 D'Avray, *Papacy* p.81. The guidelines were generated for the annulment suit of Philip II of France and Ingeborg of Denmark.
113 Gwyn, *The King's Cardinal*, p.200. Weston had previously been Treasurer of Calais.
114 When offered the Kingdoms of the world, Jesus had responded "Thou shall worship the Lord thy God and Him only shalt thou serve." (Luke 4:8)
115 Richard Fiddes, *Life of Cardinal Wolsey* (1724) Collection pp.255-6. Her father had requested the grant to Barlow a month before, LP 4.4647.

Katherine will not respect the court to be convened by Campeggio and himself because they are biassed judges. Wolsey tells the almoner that Katherine is disobeying the pope and that she will "incur the indignation of the Apostolic See, deserve the obloquy of all good chosen people and ingenerate in their hearts a perpetual hate and enmity against her." He notes that the commission has been set up by the pope from a sense of pastoral duty and is to investigate the facts not set her and Henry against each other. He describes her demand for Spanish lawyers as "frivolous" because Scotland (England's enemy) is "now either confederate or in thraldom and captivity to the Emperor's tyranny" and involving an enemy's allies is not consistent with her role as Queen of England. Besides, she already has a team of expert canon lawyers and advisers and to suggest that "this realm is marvellously destitute of men of sincere learning and conscience" slanders both the men involved and England itself. Wolsey says that her continued claim not to have consummated her marriage to Arthur is not credible noting the length of time they lived together and that Prince Arthur frequently boasted of having "been the night before in the midst of Spain in so much that commonly his so premature death was attributed only to too much sex." He adds that those "most privy and secret about" her when Arthur died thought she might be pregnant which is why there was a delay in Henry succeeding as Prince of Wales (LP 4.4685).[116]

- angry letters are exchanged about Ravenna and Cervia. Venice admits it does not trust the pope and fears he would let the two cities pass into Imperial hands. As they have strategic importance, this would seriously hamper the war (LP 4.4680, 4682-4684). Wolsey blames Venice for the pope's ill will toward England (LP 4. Appx.196).
- the Emperor urges the pope to delay Campeggio reaching England until a European peace is concluded, the prospects for which seem bad (LP 4.4637).
- the French ambassador in England, Jean du Bellay, confides in a letter home that Wolsey is worried about the war and the annulment. Bellay says Henry has committed himself so far now that he cannot go back and thinks that pressure caused him to accuse Wolsey in the late spring of being negative about the process when Wolsey said the pope would not consent to the annulment at the present time. Bellay predicts that the Emperor will ignore peace proposals from Henry on principle unless he maintains Katherine as queen which is why England is so dependent on French support. Unfortunately, the whole council oppose the French alliance being "by natural inclination" Imperial and because they hate Wolsey. Bellay says Wolsey's greatest problem is convincing Henry that the pro-French policy will benefit him and warns that if Wolsey were to stumble there are many watching to pick up the pieces. As France benefits

---

116 Fiddes, *Wolsey* Collection pp.213-214

by the Anglo-French alliance, this represents a risk to Francis. He says Wolsey has spoken of retiring once the annulment is settled and Anne has produced a son but he suspects that if Anne's family come to power, Wolsey would lose influence anyway so this idea is just to save him losing face. In passing, he also comments that he thinks that Wolsey originally hoped Henry would marry Renée if the annulment was granted. (LP 4.4649)
- Campeggio reaches France where he tells the Venetian ambassador that his intention is not to grant the annulment but to change Henry's mind (CSPV 4.340).
- Francis Bryan is sent to France to escort Campeggio to England and to express Wolsey's opinion that Doria in Genoa would be more loyal if Francis paid him more. He warns that if Doria turns, all will be lost (LP 4. Appx.196).
- the pope raises almost nine thousand men but gives no clear sign whether he intends them to fight for the League or Imperial side (CSPS 3.2.529).
- the plague in the League camp rages and two thirds of French troops are lost (LP 4.4663). Their commander Lautrec dies on the 15th. His demise leads to a collapse and Naples is taken by Imperial forces on the 28th(CSPS 3.2.533, 536).

Comments

The problems of waging war across a continent are seen here. John Clerk, English ambassador in France, had sent the news of Genoa's defection home on 7th August but the letter evidently took more than two weeks to reach London from Paris for on 21st August Wolsey sent Sir Francis Bryan to France with instructions to urge him to get Francis to prevent this happening (LP 4.4656, Appx.196). The Genoese commander, Doria, accepted a promise of 5000 ducats a month and a dukedom in Naples from the Emperor with a benefice worth 3000 ducats a year for his kinsman (LP 4.4626; CSPS 3.2.526).[117]

Jean du Bellay, Bishop of Bayonne, was a friend of Wolsey's and one of the few to stand by him when he fell from favour. Wolsey's comments to him about how he had secured the Anglo-French alliance against considerable opposition could be seen as a means of putting pressure on France to support Henry more but the antipathy to France was well rooted in all levels of English society, even amongst Henry's councillors many of whom received a pension from France as well as the Emperor.

It is not known when Anne returned to court after her illness. Du Bellay did not mention her in his letter of 21st July (LP 4.4542) but included it as news in his letter of 20th August (LP 4.4649). She must have been apart from Henry, therefore, for between two and three months. Presumably she was more ill than she let Henry know or else she was in no hurry to return to him, savouring the

---

117 The agreement was signed on 11th August but back dated to July 1st.

chance to consider her position. Many of the famous love letters from Henry to her date from this period of separation and they indicate that despite all that had happened and the gifts made to her, Henry remained unsure of whether she was fully committed.

The two men mentioned in Anne's letter were John Barlow, who was involved in the annulment from the start having been consulted by the King's confessor, John Longland, about the legality of the "marriage" to Katherine around 1522-23, long before Anne came on the scene (LP 5.1114). Late in 1527, Barlow was carrying messages from the King to Knight and he then went on to Italy (LP 4.3749, 3784, 3787, 3789). In autumn 1532, he was said to be one of Anne's staff – presumably a chaplain (LP 5.1366). Barlow was the man who would famously compare Anne to Bessie Blount (CSPS 4.2.967).[118] The second man mentioned was the parson of Honey Lane was Thomas Forman who had been suspended for possessing heretical books in April. He died in October 1528 but it is unclear if any action had been taken with regard to his case by this time in response to Anne's letter.[119]

The conversation with the almoner was the first time that Wolsey had heard of the existence of another document in Spain and it must have alarmed him. Following huge effort and expense, the legatine court was due to open soon and Wolsey would have believed that all the necessary papers were to hand and had been reviewed and analysed. The mystery document would turn out not to be an actual bull but rather a letter or brief written by Pope Julius to Katherine's mother. Under the terms of the Anglo-Spanish agreement entered into by her parents and Henry VII back in 1503, all documents relating to the effort to obtain a dispensation should have been shared.[120] The conversation is worthy of note for two other reasons. Wolsey recites the evidence which would be given when the court convened about the words spoken by Prince Arthur, showing it was not concocted on the day. Also, Wolsey said that the Spanish ambassadors in 1501 "did send the sheets they lay in spotted with blood" back to Katherine's parents, an event which does not seem to have happened although it is impossible to know what packages might have been sent back by courier and the Emperor would not have admitted their existence anyway.[121] It is more likely that Wolsey assumed that this had happened than that he was deliberately lying. He never mentioned it again so presumably somebody corrected him.

---

118 Although Thomas Boleyn had sought the living of Sundridge for him, there is no evidence for the claim so often repeated that Barlow was the family chaplain. He had evidently been in the royal service for years by this point.

119 Retha Warnicke, *The Rise and Fall of Anne Boleyn* (Cambridge, 1989) pp.111, 279

120 In fact, it had been sent to England but passed by the English directly to the Spanish ambassador as requested. There is no evidence that they had opened it before handing it over. The ambassador had shown Katherine.

121 The fact that her parents expressed confusion over the matter in June 1502 indicates that if any such package had been sent, it had not been received, CSPS 1.325.

September 1528

Events

- in Scotland, Queen Margaret's ex-husband, the Earl of Angus, is condemned. He appeals to Henry as his brother-in-law for help (LP 4.4701, 4709, 4716-4720, 4728-4731). Henry Percy reports that James V is raising an army against Angus and fears it will cross the border and invade England (LP 4.4764).
- Wolsey expresses his regret that nobody seems to trust the pope. Jean du Bellay responds that given the way the pope has behaved since his election, this is not surprising (LP 4. Appx.199)
- a priest who supports Eleanor Carey is reported for stalking the court and seeking to contact Henry Norris. An order is given for his arrest (LP 4.4703).
- Henry is reported to have settled the Russell wardship dispute by giving one daughter to Thomas Cheyney and the other to Wallop (LP 4.4710).[122]
- news is received of the fall of Naples, a disaster described as more series than the Sack of Rome for the League. Over seven thousand die with more dying every day due to a lack of water and food. It is said that not ten horses are left alive. (LP 4.4713, 4723). Wolsey is made ill by the shock (LP 4. Appx.203)
- the pope's secretary tells Campeggio in Paris to delay Henry's "great matter" as long as possible. He says that the pope personally and without hesitation supports Henry's case but the recent loss of Naples and Genoa by the League mean that the Emperor is on the verge of destroying Christendom and it is necessary not to anger him further in case he turns on Rome. Ideally, Campeggio should delay matters until peace is restored (LP 4.4737).
- the French learn that Campeggio plans to return home via Spain after the court case. Concerned that this is not something he would be likely to do if he had just given a verdict against Katherine, they warn Wolsey of their suspicions that Campeggio is not coming to grant the annulment as Henry believes (LP 4.4750).
- George Boleyn, as Squire of the Body, receives an annuity of fifty marks (LP 4.4779).
- the Emperor sends a letter to Katherine telling her not to consent to any separation from Henry because that would dishonour the Habsburg family name. He attributes Henry's desire to declare the Princess of Wales illegitimate to evil advisers and says he is astounded to learn that Henry "doubts and contests the authority of the pope as Vicar of Christ over this world." He says that Katherine should not be condemned without being

---

122 It appears that Katherine Broughton may have been made the ward of Wolsey rather than Wallop.

heard but reassures her that Campeggio will simply tell Henry to do his duty by her and refer all to Rome. Telling her that he is enclosing attested copies of the bull and dispensation issued to permit her "marriage", he concludes: "I place all trust in the pope's sanctity and virtue." (CSPS 3.2.537)

- Anne Boleyn is sent to Hever as soon as news is received that Campeggio has reached Paris to avoid her coming into contact with him. Mendoza says she has been encouraged to depart by the start of preparations for her wedding with Henry though he believes that the pope will avoid giving a sentence in order to keep Henry in his power and that Wolsey and Campeggio will collude in this because the longer they delay, the more they will be able to make in money (CSPS 3.2.541, 550).
- the League take Pavia and France and Venice make plans for a new spring offensive but Florence, the Duke of Ferrara and the Marquis of Mantua remain concerned about the long term prospects of the League and they make enquiries about joining the Imperialists. Soria assures the Emperor that the pope will pay a lot to get Florence back and Florence will pay even more for this not to happen which means the Imperial coffers will be replenished and the pope weakened which will improve the prospects for peace in Italy (CSPS 3.2.555, 559)
- the Emperor formally rejects Wolsey's peace plan saying that he is unwilling to talk until a new Anglo-Imperial alliance is formed and Francis honours all terms of the Treaty of Madrid (CSPS 3.2.561).
- Katherine demands that the Emperor and the Kings of Hungary and Portugal all tell the pope that if he allows Henry to cast her off, there will be war across Christendom (CSPS 3.2.562).
- Mendoza advises the Emperor that the papal brief in Spain will be without value unless an attested copy can be sent from Rome (CSPS 3.2.550).

Comments

Fifty marks was £33 6s 8d. Squire of the Body was the second level down in the Privy Chamber, above page and groom but below gentleman. It was a position which provided George Boleyn with close and regular contact with the monarch but not as a boon companion.

The Emperor's letter is extraordinary. Mary was not the Princess of Wales and nor had Henry ever expressed any intention of having her declared illegitimate: indeed, he had stipulated the opposite. The idea that Katherine had a right to be heard is highly questionable. What was under investigation was not her but the validity of the "marriage" and she was neither a qualified canon lawyer nor a theologian. As for the expression of faith in the pope's "sanctity and virtue", the Emperor's nose must have been scraping the paper as he wrote – unless he was laughing so hard he had fallen off the chair.

Katherine's claim that there would be war across Europe if the annulment was granted was not only untrue but an attempt to bully the pope into submission. The Spanish had lied about the prospects of war before in order to help persuade Julius to grant the dispensation and now lied again to persuade Clement to maintain the match.

The reports from French spies about Campeggio's plans, combined with news of defeats in Italy, must have left Henry and Wolsey in a deeply worried state. Henry's love letters to Anne betray no concern showing he was deliberately shielding her from the truth.

October 1528

Events

- Tyndale publishes his *Obedience of a Christian Man*
- Wolsey sends Gregory Casale to try and secure Genoa's return to the Allied cause saying Henry will fund them (LP 4.4813).
- Bishop Richard Foxe, a key witness in Henry's case, dies of old age (LP 4.4824). Wolsey is appointed Bishop of Winchester in his place (LP 4.4864).
- Campeggio reaches London. He spends the first night with Henry's sister Mary and her husband, the Duke of Suffolk then goes to reside in a house owned by Clerk, one of Katherine's supporters. At his first audience with Henry and Jean du Bellay, the French ambassador, he brings up the subject of Ravenna and Cervia (LP 4.4851, 4857). Henry says that he and Francis will press the Venetians after the pope shows good faith in resolving his "great matter." (LP 4.4857).
- the fact that the copy of a letter from Julius II produced by Katherine is not recorded in papal records leads to it being suspected of being a forgery. Katherine is requested to petition the Emperor to send the original to England. A belief that she will not do this means that the Queen has to make her promise under oath upon the Gospel and before notaries and bishops. She vows that she will not "use any frivolous delay, but with all diligence and to the best of her ability, without guile, fraud, or evil ingenuity, as soon as she can, procure that the original brief be delivered into the King's hands" and that if the Emperor refuses to hand it over promptly, she will complain to the pope about the "damage and injuries" which her case will suffer as a result (LP 4.4841, 4842).[123]
- Campeggio offers Henry a new dispensation to cover flaws in the original but finds that he does not want one because the "marriage" is against divine law. He notes Henry is an expert theologian who is more learned than most professionals and that he has studied the canon law of the case

---

123 Pocock, *Records*, vol. 1 pp.180-181.

carefully as well. Campeggio concludes that not even an angel could dissuade Henry of his belief that his union is forbidden by God (LP 4.4858).
- Campeggio and Wolsey seek to persuade Katherine to enter a nunnery. She is reminded that she has not had sexual intercourse with Henry for many years, is past childbearing and told her compliance would maintain her honour and Mary's place in the succession as well as prevent bloodshed. In addition, it would please the pope who is keen for her to do this. Katherine refuses saying God has called her to be a wife and she will maintain that status if she is torn limb from limb (LP 4.4858, 4875, 4881). Campeggio describes her as obstinate and expresses his anger at her disobedience to the pope (LP 4.4875).
- a commission is appointed to negotiate with Scotland (LP 4.4592-93).
- the pope refuses to let the papal fleet sail with the French. Nor will he encourage the Emperor to enter peace talks until Francis sends him 100,000 crowns (LP 4.4871).
- the Emperor reiterates that he will not get involved in European wide peace talks until he has negotiated a new alliance with England (LP 4.4849).
- Katherine offers to use her influence with the Emperor to encourage peace (LP 4.4875).
- Thomas Cheyney is appointed Chief Steward of Beaulieu, a post previously held by William Carey (LP 4.4896.14).
- Dr Miguel Mai is instructed to go to England taking with him copies of the bull of dispensation and the brief. The Emperor says he has the original of the brief but only a copy of the bull. A few days later, the Emperor changes his mind and decides to send Mai direct to Rome as per his original plan (CSPS 3.2.487, 563).
- the Emperor tells Mendoza that he must stop the Campeggio and Wolsey trial. Mendoza is to start by trying to persuade Campeggio to disobey the pope and just go home. If that fails, he could challenge Wolsey as a judge on grounds Wolsey is known to be Katherine's enemy. Alternatively, he could hand the protest which the Emperor has had drawn up to Katherine for her to use at the start of any trial in which she renounces the validity of any hearing outside Rome (CSPS 3.2.566).
- Katherine tells Mendoza that she plans to defend herself by saying she was a virgin when she wed Henry. Mendoza seeks to discourage her saying it cannot be proved and the issue is covered by the brief. Katherine writes to the Emperor to tell him that Henry plans to have lawyers give their verdicts so he can send them to the pope. She wants the Emperor to warn the pope and discredit any such verdicts which are against her claiming that "to win the pope over to our side" is "doing God's service." She adds that any annulment would "bring grave discredit to the Apostolic See" saying, "Were the pope to waver now, in this particular case, many might be led astray into thinking that we were not in the right."(CSPS 3.2.570, 571)

- the Faculty of Theology in Paris vote that the pope is unable to dispense in difficult questions which involve the law of God and note that Julius granted the dispensation for financial gain acting freely and not under coercion. The Spanish doctors who had argued against the motion demand a recount which takes place in the presence of the President who confirms the result. They then demand to see the names of those who voted for the motion and are told this is not allowed as voting is in private. Moscoso assures Katherine: "let me and my colleague (Garay) count the votes and we shall easily come to a different conclusion!" The Spanish believe the motion was only passed because it was badly worded and that those who voted in favour really were voting for Katherine because the pope's power of dispensation was unlimited. Fra Ambrosio claims that the Madame d'Alençon, princess of France, described the verdict as "completely erroneous and false." The Bishop of Lisieux is so angered by the behaviour of the Spaniards that he institutes proceedings against them for slander (CSPS 3.2.578).

Comments

The Emperor's insistence on a new alliance with England was simply a way of saying that he had no interest in peace. He was winning the war in Italy so had no need to make concessions. His terms would have involved Henry giving up the annulment and the Anglo-French alliance, neither of which Henry was prepared to consider as the Emperor well knew. Katherine's offer to use her influence to broker peace was equally meaningless because she had no influence with the Emperor. Her utter lack of political importance is evident from the manner in which the Emperor had ignored her over the years. His sudden concern for her honour was rooted in his desire to separate Henry and Francis for if he could win England to his side, France would be encircled and weakened.

The situation in Italy was dire and the pope was in need of money. Francis had promised it before and not sent it, so it is not surprising that the pope made payment a stipulation for his support. However, it does not sit well with the image of a religious leader to place financial demands before seeking to bring about the end of a war. He had evidently forgotten the text: "blessed are the peacemakers."

Many people today, especially those of secular persuasion, might view the prospect of someone being shut away in a nunnery in a negative light but at the time, the chance to devote one's entire life to God's service was seen as a huge privilege and a means of special grace. Henry's two grandmothers, Margaret Beaufort and Queen Elizabeth Woodville, had taken a vow of chastity and entered Bermondsey Nunnery respectively. It was one of the few vocations open to women in which they were able to pursue a leadership role if they wished. Katherine was not being offered some inferior form of life but the chance to find a new form of fulfilment. Her refusal, with characteristic histrionic flair – nobody was proposing to tear her limb from limb so saying she was willing to endure this fate was unnecessary and probably untrue - must have worried Campeggio deeply. He had been led to believe that Katherine was a deeply pious woman who would accept the advice and instructions of the pope, but clearly she was only prepared to do that if the pope's wishes happened to coincide with her own. By rejecting the proposed solution outright, she was expressing her willingness to see the country descend into civil war and her daughter be bastardised, something Henry did not want and had persuaded the pope to agree to in the terms of the commission.[124] All this was explained to Katherine but she was adamant: she intended to remain Henry's wife. Was she an admirably strong woman refusing to be victimised as she is often portrayed or a stubborn and selfish one prepared to let thousands of innocent people die in bloody warfare just to maintain her position? Views may vary but it was undeniably an extraordinary response from somebody who had been crowned Queen of England and who had pledged to work for its welfare. It is a sign of how badly she was regarded that she was required to make her promise to obtain the 'Spanish brief' before a notary and three bishops. Ordinarily, a queen's word would not be questioned but contemporaries, even those who may have had some sympathy with her position, thought she was a liar.

Why did the Emperor change his mind about sending Mai whom both Katherine and Mendoza were keenly awaiting? No reason was given but it was probably part of his strategy for sabotaging the papal commission to Campeggio and Wolsey by ensuring Katherine did not have Mai's legal advice.

The vote at the Faculty of Theology would remain in dispute for some time but it does smack of desperation to claim that those who voted for the motion really thought they were supporting Katherine. The voters were experienced canon lawyers who could read and understand a motion. As for the denouncing of the verdict by Madame d'Alençon, that was clearly total fabrication. Not only would Francis' sister not have made such an ill-judged remark which would have been seen as criticising the King, she was the Queen of Navarre not Madame d'Alençon and had been for almost two years.

The emergence of the "Spanish brief" seemed suspiciously providential to Henry and his advisors. This was an age which believed in signs in the sky and one may suspect that some of them at this point craned their heads out of windows to see if there were any pigs flying past.

---

124 Quoted under May 1529 Comments.

November 1528

Events

- the Emperor offers James V of Scotland an Imperial bride (LP 4.4978).
- Wolsey complains that Campeggio refuses to give him a copy of the secret decretal commission. He says he fears the pope does not trust him and warns Henry is already muttering that he feels deceived (LP 4.4897).
- back in Rome, the pope continues to complain to every ambassador about Ravenna and Cervia and says that if Henry and Francis cannot get them back, he will find someone who can. He vows that he is prepared to ally himself to this end with anyone except the actual Devil (LP 4.4900, 4920, 4956).
- the Emperor promptly sends an envoy to the pope offering him 150,000 gold pieces, the return of Florence and war to recapture Ravenna and Cervia if he will only join him (LP 4.4929).
- an Irish rebel, the Earl of Desmond, sends to the Emperor offering to lead an uprising against Henry in Ireland if the Emperor will only fund it (LP 4.4911, 4919).
- Wolsey is awarded a papal bull allowing him to suppress monasteries and nunneries with less than twelve inmates as part of his design to reform monasticism and re-organise dioceses and cathedrals, a plan the pope praises (LP 4.4900, 4921).
- Henry summons representatives from London and elsewhere and tells them that the investigation into the validity of his "marriage" resulted from a long held scruple which was increased by an unnamed French bishop. He warns that if anyone doubts the integrity of his motives, he will behead them regardless of status (LP 4.4942).[125] In a report of the same meeting which spies passed on to Mendoza, Henry said that investigations began when the French questioned the legitimacy of the Princess Mary as part of the negotiations for her to marry Francis or one of his sons (CSPS 3.2.586).[126]
- Campeggio tells the French ambassador that whilst his view of the annulment is "invincible," other views could and must be argued because the pope will never accept any limits to his power to dispense (LP 4.4942).
- in Spain, preparations increase for a spring offensive in Italy (LP 4.4909, 4948).
- the Spaniard, Lodovico Vives, reports that Katherine is upset that Henry wishes to remarry (LP 4.4990).
- the Emperor's Chancellor tells Wolsey's peace envoy, Darius, that the Emperor has God on his side and all he wants is for Francis to abide by

---

[125] *Hall's Chronicle,* pp.754-5
[126] For more on this, see Was Anne Boleyn the cause of the breakdown of Henry's 'marriage' to Katherine?

the Treaty of Madrid and apologise for challenging him to a duel. Boasting Imperial forces could drive Henry out of England within three months by fomenting rebellion, he then sends Darius home saying there is nothing further to discuss (LP 4.4909). Undaunted, Wolsey requests a commission from the pope to negotiate a European wide peace deal on his behalf (LP 4.4897).

- Katherine gives Campeggio a copy of the papal brief of dispensation. A shocked Henry, sends the Archbishop to ask why she had not produced this document earlier. She tells him that she received it from the ambassador Mendoza six months before and did not realise its significance. She then sends an urgent message to Mendoza who promises that if asked: "I shall so shape my answer that it may not disagree with the Queen's declaration nor make it appear as if she had stated an untruth." Campeggio sends an urgent letter to the pope seeking further instructions (CSPS 3.2.586).

- brandishing the said brief, Katherine then summons the Archbishop of Canterbury (Warham) plus the bishops of Rochester (Fisher), St Asaph (Standish), London (Tunstall), Bath and Wells (Clerk) to tell them that although it states clearly that her marriage to Arthur was consummated, this is not true and that those who sought the brief (her parents) did so "following rather the presumption of law than the truth of the matter" and not at her own instruction. She vows not to use the brief in court as evidence of the match being consummated (LP 4. Appx.211).[127]

- Sir Francis Bryan and Peter Vannes are sent to the pope to discuss peace and to offer him a personal bodyguard of up to two thousand men to be funded by Francis and Henry.[128] While there they are to secretly obtain legal opinion about whether Henry could remarry if Katherine became a nun. They should assure the pope that Henry is "utterly resolved and determined" never to sleep with her again. They are to work with Gregory Casale to investigate papal records to furnish proof that the brief is not genuine. They are to remind the pope of all that Henry has done to support him and that he deserves a "thank reward" commensurate. They are to make clear to the pope that Henry will not be frustrated in his purpose or "restrained or minced with the quiddities and discrepant opinions of the laws" but that if the pope prefers to side with the Emperor, the result will be that Henry and "many other princes" will withdraw their allegiance (LP 4.4977).

- in further instructions, Henry asserts his belief that the brief, which he describes as a "vain and frivolous writing", has been forged due to the "deliberate avarice of learned men" and says that if it is admitted as

---

127 Pocock, *Records*, vol. 2 pp.431-433

128 Wolsey says that he has used the excuse of expediting his bulls at Rome as a means of sending his own money to the pope as a contribution toward funding this (LP 4. Appx.219).

evidence in the case, the verdict will be unsound and "there is no place to be given henceforth to truth and authority." He wants the brief sent to him on grounds that it rightly belongs to himself and Katherine and not the Emperor but is prepared to have it sent direct to the pope so that he can rule on it. Henry asks Vannes and Bryan to request that Francis send a letter in support of this. Henry lists his reasons for believing the brief to be false – it bearing the same date as the bull but a different text, the fact that nobody knew of its existence until it appeared just in time for the court hearing, the mistakes in it of grammar and address, the form of the seal, the fact that there was no reason to issue a brief when a bull had just been produced. Henry warns that if the pope advokes the case to Rome as Katherine wants, it "would be a great inquietation to the King's mind putting His Grace for that season in marvellous perplexity whereof might arise danger of his health and most royal person and consequently most high and perilous inconveniences to his succession and realm." He reiterates that "knowing the frailty and uncertainty of all earthly things and how much dangerous and perilous to the soul...he hath in this doubt and matter of matrimony whereupon depend so high and manifold consequences of greatest importance, always abjected and cast from his conceit the darkness and blundering confusion of falsity and specially hath put before his eyes the light and shining brightness of truth; upon which foundation is a most sure base and perpetual tranquillity of conscience." They are to tell the pope that as the case is "in point of process of judgment, the cause almost expedite and finished" any efforts to interfere "shall be vain and frustratory" (LP 4.4978; SP vol 7 pp.117-140)

- threats to the life of Henry and Wolsey are reported. A protest to Katherine, who is believed to be inciting them indirectly, is prepared though not formally delivered (LP 4.4981).[129] Mendoza notes that Katherine dismisses such an idea when Warham and Tunstall put it to her and he suggests that the idea has been raised because if it could be shown that Katherine was a threat to Henry's life, it would justify her dismissal from court and an immediate annulment (CSPS 3.2.586).

- George Boleyn and Henry Norris, both Squires of the Body, are made keepers of Beaulieu and East Greenwich respectively, Boleyn succeeds William Carey and gets £14 11s 3d per annum in the role (LP 4.4993.6, 4993.15, 5248).

- Wolsey asks the French ambassador, Jean du Bellay, Bishop of Bayonne, a man who is a reputed theologian, if he believes the Bible gives the pope the power to dispense from God's word saying that Henry's case is built on this more than canon law. The Bishop upholds the supremacy of the

---

129 Had the protest to Katherine, which included criticism of her deliberate efforts to win the war for public opinion, been delivered we might expect Campeggio to have noted it in his reports to Rome.

Bible but declines to put his opinion in writing without permission from Francis (LP 4.4915). In his letter to the French king, du Bellay expresses his belief that Katherine slept with Arthur and says that no human authority could make Henry's "marriage" valid "for God has long ago Himself passed sentence on it" (LP 4.4897).
- the Emperor complains that Francis has not accepted his suggested date and location for a duel (CSPS 3.2.579)
- Muxetula, Imperial ambassador at Rome, reports that despite considerable enquiry, no trace of the bull or brief can be found at Rome (CSPS 3.2.585).
- Henry tells Katherine to appoint a Flemish legal adviser and he appoints to be her counsel, the Archbishop of Canterbury (Warham), the Bishop of London (Tunstall) and the Bishop of Rochester (Fisher) (CSPS 3.2.586).
- Mendoza secures a copy of Wolsey and Campeggio's commission which he passes on to the Emperor, though he expresses a belief that there is a secret commission also which Campeggio has shared with Henry. He reports that rumours are rife around the court. Some say that Henry has given Campeggio extensive presents but Mendoza doubts this. Some say Wolsey is trying to get out of being a judge because he would rather be Henry's advocate, this either because he hates and fears Anne Boleyn and wants to see the case fail or because he has a close alliance with the Boleyns and this is their preferred plan for success. Mendoza says the only thing which is clear is that the annulment is not popular but because there is no focus to the opposition, nothing much will happen, "all will end in smoke." (CSPS 3.2.586)
- Katherine sends the Emperor another letter, this time demanding that he get the pope to order parliament not to proceed against her (CSPS 3.2.593).
- Francis' sister, Marguerite, Queen of Navarre, gives birth to a daughter, Jeanne

Comments

The question of whether a person could remarry if their spouse became a monk or nun was one which divided opinion. Everybody agreed that a husband or wife needed the consent of their partner before they could make any sort of vow (1 Cor 7:4-5) and that entering a religious community meant dying to the world: Aquinas had said "the religious life is a kind of spiritual death." There was also acceptance of Alexander III's ruling that an unconsummated marriage could be dissolved for this reason. Less clear was whether this spiritual death could terminate a physical marriage which the church taught was "till death do us part." Could the would-be monk or nun take full vows to Christ while their spouse was still alive? Could the person left behind remarry immediately or must they wait until their spouse was dead?[130] In 1533, Cranmer referred to the

---

130 D-Avray, *Papacy* p.53 notes there was some conciliar support for the view that immediate remarriage was legitimate. For further discussion on this see George

legal opinion which argued that as marriages could be dissolved if a partner was an infidel (I Cor 7:15) so this Pauline privilege could be claimed if one entered religious life.[131] This was just the sort of question on which a pope was expected to give an answer which would then become binding on future generations but Clement VII was no expert in canon law or theology and by his own admission, unable to give a verdict, though his recommendation of Katherine entering a nunnery as a solution to Henry's problems should be taken as proof of his opinion. His honesty about his shortcomings is praiseworthy but does raise questions about his suitability for such an important role. Indeed, any student today faced with the question: "list the achievements of Clement VII" as pope would be entitled to expect a pass if they returned a blank sheet of paper. Clement's marked lack of ability – a sharp contrast to, for example, such scholars as Benedict XVI in the twenty-first century– created a major problem for Henry, quite aside from his personal failings and love of vacillation. Wolsey had already warned Henry that even if Katherine became a nun, he would need to apply for a new dispensation to marry and such a dispensation could not be guaranteed for the reasons given above (LP 4.4897). Annulment was the safest option.

Bellay's verdict regarding Henry's case is important. His comment about God having already given his verdict is not a reference to Henry's lack of sons but confirmation that the prohibition on marrying a brother's widow came direct from God. It is also worth noting that on the eve of the legatine court opening which was primarily concerned with canon law, Wolsey was stressing the theological case. This is not because he had concluded the canon law case was weak but because the appearance of the 'Spanish brief' had complicated the matter. The commission had only been issued to investigate the bull, not the brief which was unknown at the time. The emergence of a document which was significantly different but allegedly issued by the same man on the same day not only complicated the case but it raised questions of whether Julius II was incompetent or someone in high places was guilty of forgery, neither being options the present pope would be willing to acknowledge. This major development necessitated delay dashing Henry's hopes of a quick verdict and was political dynamite.

The importance of Henry's "great matter" meant that he kept more than one ambassador at the papal court. Gregory Casale was the permanent ambassador. A native of Bologna, he had a home in Rome and was well regarded there. His connections were invaluable to Henry and as a fellow Italian, he was sometimes able to open doors and find out information which the English could not. He had visited England twice – in 1518, when he travelled with Campeggio, and in 1523 – plus he had also spent time with Wolsey in France during the summer of 1527, but he was naturally unable to keep up with the changing politics at Henry's court due to distance and his lack

---

Hayward Joyce, *Christian Marriage* (1948) pp.341-59.
131 Kelly, *Matrimonial Trials*, p232

of English.[132] The two men sent in November knew Henry very well. Vannes was the King's secretary, Italian but multi-lingual. Bryan was a Gentleman of the Privy Chamber and Anne Boleyn's cousin and he had assisted Wolsey on diplomatic missions in 1521 and 1527.[133] They were trusted and senior figures and their selection was a sign of Henry's close involvement. He knew that they would report directly to him while Casale tended to deal with Wolsey. Their appointment should not be taken as a sign that Henry was losing confidence in Wolsey, just keeping his eyes open.

For writers with the benefit of hindsight, it may seem strange that Katherine had apparently only just become aware of Henry wishing to marry, despite Mendoza suggesting everyone else knew in August 1527 (CSPS 3.2.152). Many modern historians have claimed Henry's infatuation with Anne was evident from at least 1526 but Katherine – who was actually there – evidently knew nothing about it.[134] What is not clear is whether she was upset by this in principle or because Henry had chosen a chosen a younger and prettier model to replace her. Millions of middle aged women the world over have experienced this humiliation and can feel for her distress. However, it does not excuse her blatant lie about the brief and her enlisting of Mendoza to cover for her.[135] She had not had it for six months and it is also hard to believe that the document was new or surprising to her given that the Spanish ambassador said he had shown it to her in August 1504 when she made no objection to its contents.[136]

Wolsey's plans for monastic reform were never completed due to his fall from power but the assistant whom he employed to carry them out did go on to mastermind the great Dissolution of 1536 and 1539 – Thomas Cromwell. Henry is often criticised for this event but the closure of small and non-viable monasteries was an act which met with full papal approval.

Although parliaments in this period were not democratically elected on the basis of one person, one vote, in the way we would expect today, parliament was the supreme legislative and representative authority in the country. The idea that the pope should have any say whatsoever about what it discussed is

---

132 He may have visited England briefly on other occasions as he regularly bought horses on Henry's behalf in Italy.
133 Bryan's mother was first cousin to Anne's mother. His brother-in-law was Sir Nicholas Carew, while his cousin Mary was married to Henry Norris. His mother would later serve as governess to Henry and Anne's daughter, Elizabeth. He was appointed a Gentleman of the Privy Chamber in 1518
134 Anne does not seem to have been aware either. Hindsight has been known to produce miraculous insights.
135 Mendoza's first reference to the brief was in September 1528 (CSPS 3.2.550), two months before, not six. The Emperor himself only received the document eight months before and would have passed it to his legal advisers before sending a copy to England, a journey taking at least a month.
136 CSPS 1.398. It would strain credulity to believe that the document described as a brief of dispensation from Spain was anything but the same as that produced in 1528.

utterly horrifying. Members of parliament exist to represent their constituents and to advise the King, not to carry out the diktats of the pope or have their freedom of debate curtailed by him.[137]   That the idea was promulgated by the Queen of England who was supposed to uphold the laws and traditions of the said England is almost unbelievable. Katherine's lack of respect for parliamentary democracy and freedom was absolute and remains one of her least attractive characteristics. Fortunately, the pope declined to do as bid.

To us, the idea of a prince saying his cause should be favoured because of his past services to the church is quite immoral but the pope would not have thought this unreasonable. Dispensations and annulments were often granted with that stated to be the reason.

December 1528

Events

- a proclamation is issued banning private individuals in London from keeping crossbows or handguns (LP 4.4998, 5016).
- Imperial legal advisers for Katherine arrive from Flanders (LP 4.5016). With no sign of the case being heard in England in the near future, they return home (LP 4.5471).
- a five year peace is agreed between England and Scotland in the Treaty of Berwick (LP 4.5030).
- a Spanish plot to kidnap Renée and her husband Ercole de Ferrara is foiled (LP 4.5035).
- Wolsey's new peace proposal is for the pope to go to Avignon to meet with himself, Francis's mother and either the Emperor or his chancellor (Gattinara) plus representatives of the Italian states to agree terms. If the Emperor refuses peace, Spain will be invaded from France next summer. Freed from fear of the Emperor, he believes the pope will hasten to grant the annulment (LP 4.5050). Jean du Bellay doubts this will happen, not least because it depends on Venice returning Ravenna and Cervia first (LP 4. Appx.224).
- the pope expresses anger at Wolsey's desire for a copy of the decretal commission and letter promising to ratify whatever sentence he and Campeggio pass. He says that he issued the documents privately on the condition that they would be shown to Henry and then burnt. He says he wishes that Wolsey had annulled the "marriage" himself and not involved the papacy. He suggests that if Henry will give up the idea of separating from Katherine, he will issue a dispensation to allow Mary to marry Richmond, her half brother so they can rule together. (LP 4.5038, 5072).

---

137 D'Avray, *Papacy*, pp.225

- the pope reminds Francis and Henry that the terms of the League mean that if one member attacks another, force should be used to repel this and effect restitution if negotiation fails. As Venice has attacked him by seizing Ravenna and Cervia, they are bound to get them back for him (LP 4.5038).
- Francis tries to placate the pope by writing to Florence urging them to release Catherine de Medici (LP 4. Appx.225)
- Henry suggests that Francis' delays in paying troops is a key reason why the war is going so badly (LP 4.5053).
- it is reported that the papal prothonotary, Gambara, has made an attempt on the life of the Duke of Ferrara (LP 4. Appx.226).
- Anne Boleyn returns to court for Christmas but is housed separately. Du Bellay notes that great court is paid to her as part of Henry's plan to accustom the people to her (LP 4.5016, 5063).
- discussing the annulment with the Venetian ambassador, the pope says he fears that if Henry remarried his new wife's family would supplant Wolsey thereby weakening the influence of the Roman Church in England. He suggests that the Emperor might urge Katherine to agree to the annulment on condition Henry abandon his alliance with France (CSPV 4.383).
- Henry tells Katherine that he will no longer live with her because he fears for his safety in the hands of her Spanish servants. Nonetheless, he continues to visit her at Greenwich, dining with her and spending the night (CSPS 3.2.600).
- Katherine tells Mendoza that she took an oath before Campeggio that she was still a virgin when Arthur died (CSPS 3.2.600).
- keen to see his "nephew" Hippolito marry the wealthy heiress of Vespasiano Colonna, the pope urges that all the lands be given to her now and the lawsuit – necessary because other family members are contesting the will – be held later (CSPS 3.2.604, 607).
- Mendoza claims that Henry wants to send a petition to the pope signed by all his nobility to show they all support the annulment. He gleefully reports that so far, only Anne's father, brother and uncle have signed it (CSPS 3.2.600).
- Henry Carey becomes the ward of Anne Boleyn (LP 5.11).[138]

Comments

The pope was a founder member of the League of Cognac which was primarily set up to oppose the Emperor in Italy. The pope's behaviour indicated that he was inclined to forget this fact which made his demand that Henry act to get Ravenna and Cervia back for him rather ironic. Henry was not actually a member of the League of Cognac though he supported it financially.

---

138 Exchequer files suggest this happened a few months earlier, see John Guy, Julia Fox, *Hunting the Falcon* (2023) p.166

The suggestion that Henry permit his daughter to marry his illegitimate son is shocking and demonstrates the pope's absolute disdain for Leviticus which stated quite clearly that a man could not marry the daughter of his father or mother (Lev. 18:9).

Those who doubt whether the pope could ever have suggested that Henry marry Anne before the annulment case was heard on grounds that no holy man would ever show such disrespect for the law, should note well the Colonna case. Clement was not holy and he did not respect legal process. He respected money.

Du Bellay's comment about Henry wanting to accustom people to Anne as his consort before they wed invites parallels with the behaviour of Prince Charles and Camilla. Anne was reviled for seeking to replace a popular queen just as Camilla was for seeking to replace the immensely popular, Diana, Princess of Wales. Commentators in both cases tended to portray the cases in simplistic, black and white terms. Eventually, following the death of Diana, Camilla was able to marry her prince but it took many years for her to earn public respect and she has yet to receive the love and adoration accorded her predecessor. Anne married Henry in Katherine's lifetime and there is no reason to doubt that given time, she would also have been able to earn public acceptance for her new position but she was executed only three years later. Of course, the cases were different in one key respect. Charles and Camilla were both unquestionably validly married whereas Henry and Anne were single, though Henry's enemies tried to allege otherwise.

The exact date of Mary Carey's children becoming wards of Anne Boleyn is not known and may have taken place in late 1528 or 1529. To modern eyes, it would seem strange to make such an arrangement given their mother was still alive but it was entirely usual at the time for children who lost their father to be placed as wards if an inheritance was involved. The assumption would have been that the mother would remarry and this would mean the stepfather obtaining rights over the inheritance which could easily be exploited to the extent that when the child came of age, nothing was left. Wardships allowed individuals to take the profits from the inheritance and use them to maintain the estates on the child's behalf and also for the care and education of the child. What is interesting is that the wardship was given to Anne rather than to Thomas or George Boleyn. It was more common to give wards to a man than a woman because women were prone to marry at which point all their property became that of their husband. Evidently, Henry felt safe in his assumption that Anne would marry nobody but himself.

1529

January 1529

Events

- the pope is taken ill and reported dead creating consternation at the impact his demise will have upon the annulment (LP 4.5147, 5161, 5162, 5187, 5194). In fact he recovers but remains too ill to attend to business further delaying the process (LP 4.5225).
- the papal prothonotary, Gambara, predicts two hundred thousand people would die in a civil war if Henry died without a male heir and recommends Henry give large bribes to the cardinals to expedite matters (LP 4.5152).
- the Imperial ambassador, Mendoza, claims Henry told someone it was Wolsey's idea to try and frighten Katherine into becoming a nun and that the King is unhappy that Wolsey has not managed to secure this (CSPS 3.2.614). Mendoza predicts that if Katherine refuses there will be no trial of the "marriage" and recommends the Emperor expel English ambassadors in Spain as a means of further upsetting the cardinal (LP 4.5177).
- no trace of the brief is found in the official registers in Rome nor in the secretary's books. Suspicion falls on the Archbishop of Capua, an ardent Imperialist, and legal advice is sought regarding its potential status as evidence (LP 4.5179, 5213, 5230).
- Sir Thomas Cheyney has another altercation with Wolsey and is expelled from court. Anne Boleyn intervenes to get him back (LP 4.5210).
- from his sickbed, the pope says he will go to Narbonne to broker peace but only if Wolsey will go with him. Gregory Casale comments that Wolsey will easily dominate the pope and Wolsey agrees to go wherever and whenever required (LP 4.5139, 5230).
- Wolsey receives a demand for 13,000 ducats (about £3000) for an official bull confirming him as Bishop of Winchester (LP 4.5225).
- a note for ambassadors in Spain is prepared which says that Henry believes the loss of his sons is a divine punishment in line with Lev. 20. It states that the prohibition in Leviticus refers to the widows of brothers as well as wives and that the pope has no authority to dispense from God's commandments. They are to point out to the Emperor the sincerity of Henry's motives noting that he would not have gone to all this trouble and expense if his only objective was lust (LP 4.5156).
- Katherine finally sends a letter to the Emperor requesting the original of the brief be sent to England but sends a second one telling him to ignore her request (LP 4.5154). She does this at Mendoza's urging because he tells

her that the brief contains "the whole of the Queen's right" which is why it should be kept in Spain and not given to Henry who might lose or destroy it (LP 4.5211).
- Campeggio writes to Rome that he thinks Wolsey does not favour the annulment but is being forced to promote it because he is the King's loyal servant. Campeggio claims Wolsey has told him "the only course open is somehow to satisfy the King, whatever the consequences, since in time some remedy will be found."[139]

Comments

The English ambassadors in Spain were trying to negotiate a European peace settlement, not there to enjoy the weather. The idea of withdrawing them to annoy Wolsey shows the lack of interest which the Imperialists had in making peace.

The arguments sent to the ambassadors were only to be used if the Emperor should raise the subject himself with them. The reference to Leviticus 20 is unusual.

The story about Anne intervening to secure Cheyney's return to court is sometimes taken as a sign of her political influence and hatred of Wolsey. The report was made by the French ambassador, Jean du Bellay, who probably knew Cheyney well since he had been involved in the negotiations for the Anglo-French alliance after the capture of Francis I. Cheyney was a kinsman of Anne's but he had been a courtier and diplomat for more than fifteen years including serving as ambassador to France. This meant he had worked for Wolsey but he was primarily a Gentleman of the Privy Chamber and thus Henry's employee. In March 1526, he was described as one of those most trusted by the King with his secrets.[140] The grounds of the dispute followed the death of Russell's stepson, John Broughton who left two sisters as heirs, the younger of whom was under age and a ward of Wolsey's.[141] Given both were heiresses, Cheyney sought the wardship of both girls as did Sir John Wallop. The dispute raged for some months with Anne urging Wolsey in March 1528 to favour Cheyney's suit. In July, after an angry altercation, Henry sent Cheyney from court to cool down saying that he would only be re-admitted when he was prepared to make a humble apology to both himself and Russell. Presumably he did this but six months later, there was evidently a similar incident and Bellay says that Anne had angry words with Wolsey over the matter. Nonetheless, the only person who could expel Cheyney was Henry and he was also the only man who could restore him. Anne might plead his case but she could not authorise his return. In the end, Henry sought to be fair by awarding the elder sister to Cheyney who went on to marry her, although she must have been at least

---
139 Gwyn, *The King's Cardinal*, p.517
140 LP 4.2039
141 Sir John Russell was also a Gentleman of the Privy Chamber.

twenty years his junior. The younger sister, after Wolsey's fall, was made a ward of Anne's grandmother, the Dowager Duchess of Norfolk (LP 4.6072.21) and went on to marry her uncle William Howard. The story shows a long running legal dispute in which Anne – and presumably her father and uncle – sided with Cheyney against Wolsey but it is far from certain that Henry would not have supported his employee without her intervention or that he was not moved by a recommendation from the Duke of Norfolk as his councillor, or from Thomas Boleyn rather than Anne. A key question and one which we have no way of answering, is whether Anne's involvement was her own idea or something she did at the prompting of her father or uncle. Cheyney was the son of her father's uncle by his second wife and roughly his contemporary so much more likely to have been his friend than hers.[142] Either way, it was not the sort of issue to engender a deep seated hatred and desire on Anne's part to destroy Wolsey – unless she was unbalanced.

Mendoza's use of the word "frighten" is curious. Being a nun was not a punishment.

The fee being demanded for the bull to confirm Wolsey as Bishop of Winchester was around twenty-one million pounds in today's money. Even allowing for all the couriers and clerks involved, the price represented profiteering at an extraordinary level. It is small wonder that Henry's later abolition of fees to Rome was extremely popular.

It is interesting to see the papal representative, Gambara, brazenly advising that the way to obtain a verdict was to offer bribes. There was not even the pretence that the cardinals would study the case objectively or seek to do justice.

February 1529

Events

- in Spain, the Emperor reduces the household of the two French princes to just three or four people and bans all visitors (CSPS 3.2.619, 620).
- the pope's health continues to wax and wane. New reports of his death are received leading to French and English courts making plans to elect Wolsey. Francis vows to send ten thousand troops to Rome to guard the conclave. If Imperial troops arrive first, the French cardinals and their Italian supporters are to remove themselves and hold their own election. Eventually the pope rallies and the plans come to nothing (LP 4.5250, 5270, CSPV 4.409).
- Mendoza reports that Norfolk, Suffolk and the Boleyns are seeking to undermine Wolsey in Henry's eyes but he will hear nothing against him though he is frustrated by the delays. Mendoza says that he does not trust Campeggio to support Katherine (LP 4.5255). He describes Anne as "the

---

142 See Appendix 6: Key Relationships

cause of the King's misconduct" and adds "the King is so blind with passion that there is nothing he will not do or promise to attain his object." (CSPS 3.2.621)
- the English ambassadors in Spain say that they have yet to see the brief and express doubts that it exists. They note it only appeared when Katherine's envoy, Francis Phillips, came to see the Emperor (LP 4.5284, 5307).
- the Emperor reiterates that Katherine's "marriage" is valid because it was made following permission from the pope. He claims the annulment "emanates not from the King's own free will, but solely from the sinister persuasions and intrigues of some persons who, for the sake of their own private interests and wicked purposes, and from their lust of power, have deceived him" and admits the case is about papal authority which compels him to do all he can to "hinder" it (LP 4.6266, 5301; CSPS 3.2.623).
- Sir Gregory Casale, England's resident ambassador in Rome, writes to his cousin Vincent whom he has sent to London to advise Henry and Wolsey to "make other arrangements" as he has no confidence in the pope whom he says is willing to please but not to do. He criticises Vincent for giving them false hope by suggesting that the pope is simply afraid of the Emperor. Gregory says that an armed guard will not help and even the liberation of Italy, which is not an immediate prospect, may not be enough because the pope will argue that his hands are tied by canon law and claim he is unable to comment or rule on any document – be that a bull or brief – issued by his predecessors. (LP 4.5302).
- Henry continues to believe that he needs papal approval for the verdict to be universally accepted so continues his campaign (LP 4.5270).
- an envoy is sent by the Emperor to treat with the Earl of Desmond in Ireland (LP 4.5322).
- Henry Norris receives two manors (LP 4.5336.10) and Gilbert Tallboys – Bessie Blount's husband – a wardship LP 4.5336.27).
- the French and English prepare to raise an army for Italy of 30,000 foot and 3,000 cavalry with Henry funding a third of the men (CSPV 4.409).

Comments

The reference to a plot being hatched by Norfolk, Suffolk and Thomas Boleyn is most likely to have been wishful thinking on the part of Mendoza. Norfolk was pro-Spain and would later be a conduit of stories to Chapuys – some leaked at official request – but all three men received pensions from the Emperor. They were, however, working to secure the same goal as Wolsey. All the parties involved – Henry, Anne, Norfolk, Suffolk and Thomas Boleyn – were frustrated by the delays and it is to be expected that this resulted in short tempers and harsh words on occasion, but whatever their personal feelings toward Wolsey might have been, they all knew that he had more influence and contacts with the pope than they did.

Was it likely that Wolsey would have been elected if the pope had died? Probably not. The cardinals would have wanted someone they knew rather than a stranger from overseas whom they only knew by reputation. For centuries, popes had been Italian, the only exception being Clement's predecessor and that had not been a positive experience for most. The French and English both drew up lists of which cardinals they believed would attend an election and marked those they believed were favourable to their cause. The lists varied slightly but generally showed thirteen Imperialists, fourteen Anglo-French with eight neutral.[143] The Imperialists also drew up a list but reckoned only three could be relied upon to support them with Cardinal San Croce being described as especially "doubtful" because he was "much given to God" something they attributed to "mania." They believed the most likely successor was Cesi who was thought to be pro-French and likely to support Henry's annulment.[144] Although the question became irrelevant when Clement recovered, the issue did put Wolsey and Campeggio in a difficult situation. Should they go ahead with the trial before a new pope was elected and hope a successor would honour the commission and pollicitation they held or wait and see who came next?

As usual, Sir Gregory Casale was the ambassador passing on the truth to Henry. It was a pity that his words of wisdom were not taken seriously.

The Emperor's argument that the "marriage" was valid because the pope said so was the line taken by Katherine. Whenever Henry or anyone else sought to explain the Bible to her, she simply replied that she knew she was Henry's wife and closed her ears.

March 1529

Events

- Dr Mai, new Imperial ambassador in Rome, finds the pope cold and worries that if he dies, they will not be able to secure the majority needed to see an Imperialist elected. He writes: "The truth is that the cardinals attached to the Empire are but few and do not serve with the zeal and ardour of those of the opposite party." He believes that between twelve and fifteen cardinals are ready to depart Rome and go to Avignon if the pope dies and blames preachers who are continually reminding people of the Sack of Rome for the marked lack of love for the Emperor. He draws up plans for the invasion of territories held by enemy cardinals and their removal from office should there be an election which does not produce the desired result (CSPS 3.2.657). Meanwhile, 12,000 Imperial troops are brought to

---

143 Pocock, *Records*, vol. 2 pp.605-6; Le Grand, *Histoire* vol. 3 pp.299-302. The English thought Campeggio was on their side but the French labelled him as Imperial. See Appendix 8: The Cardinals Involved

144 CSPS 4.1.17. The remark is especially interesting given the cardinal was the Emperor's confessor.

within sixty miles of Rome ready to take whatever action might be deemed necessary (LP 4.5344).
- the League lose Aquila and Labrucio (LP 4.5344, 5348). Over 9,000 Imperial troops begin their march on Florence (CSPS 3.2.639).
- in Ireland, Butler continues to wage war against Desmond and Kildare and requests urgent additional assistance from Henry (LP 4.5349).
- the Imperial ambassador in England, Mendoza, presents Katherine with a fresh copy of the brief. She hands it to Henry whose council discuss it and draw up a list of errors in it. Wolsey sends a copy of both to the English ambassadors at Rome and urges them to remind the pope that if he fails to rule against what is clearly a forgery, God will punish him (LP 4.5375-7)
- Dr Mai tells the Emperor that there is no record of the brief in the registers at Rome. He reports that he has received a hand-written letter from Katherine smuggled out of England appealing for the case to be heard in Rome and promises to give it to the pope as soon as the latter is fit to return to his duties (LP 4.5356, 5357). The Emperor also demands that the commission to hear the case in England be revoked in favour of Rome (LP 4.5346).
- Dr Mai warns the pope that the Emperor has thousands of troops in Naples ready to invade the Papal States. He comments that his threat has made the desired impression: "once detached from his confederates, His Holiness will accustom himself to the alliance of His Imperial majesty whose power and virtue, both of mind and person, he is known to admire." (CSPS 3.2.643, 647).
- Francis asks Henry to fund another 14,000 mercenaries for the war (CSPV 4.426).
- the English ambassador, Vannes, is told by the pope that he has made his decision for Henry and will order Simonetta and Cardinal San Quatuor to find a way to effect this using means to which the Emperor will not be able to object. Vannes observes that this promise was made to him separately and warns "I do not want to judge anything without due thought, but unless the performance follows I conceive no hope of them."(LP 4.5401, SP vol.7 p.157)
- Anne gives Henry a copy of Tyndale's *Obedience*. He says "this book is for me and all kings to read."[145]
- Henry Norris is granted an advowson for a church in Lincolnshire and the office of collector of tonnage and poundage in London (LP 4.5406.1 and 25). Jane Seymour's brother Edward gets two manors (LP 4.5406.5).
- canon lawyers in Rome advise that should Katherine become a nun, Henry will not be allowed to marry until after her death (LP 4.5344).

---

145 Ives, *Anne Boleyn*, pp.162-163. The tale was told in Wyatt's "Life of the Virtuous Christian and renowned Queen Anne Boleigne" which appears as an appendix to volume one of George Cavendish, *The Life of Cardinal Wolsey* (ed. Samuel Singer, 1827) pp 438-441. The exact date of the event is not known but took place in the spring of 1529 just before the legatine court opened.

- Henry tells the Venetian ambassador that "if the pope will not annul it, I will annul it myself. I have a weight on my conscience. The pope who gave me a dispensation to take my brother's wife who had consummated the marriage was not authorised to do so." (CSPV 4.437)

Comments

Historical research can involve many hours poring over documents which are not likely to raise a titter. Mai's indignation at preachers reminding people of what they had suffered at the hands of his fellow Spaniards is, however, quite amusing. What perversity on the part of the cardinals in not wanting to be dominated by someone whose army had destroyed their homes and incomes, threatened their lives and killed so many of their colleagues!

The pope's statement to Vannes that he has decided in Henry's favour is significant, not just because it shows him supporting the King, but because he made the announcement three weeks after Mai had threatened to use Imperial troops to invade the Papal States. Evidently Mai was as mistaken in his belief that the pope was cowed as he was in the idea that Clement was a fan of the Emperor.

Throughout the annulment crisis, Henry maintained that Katherine consummated her marriage with Arthur. Although it is fashionable to dismiss this out of hand, his view should be treated seriously. Her behaviour on their wedding night in 1509 clearly convinced him that she was not a virgin. Katherine said otherwise. Clearly, there would have been no witnesses in the bedroom she shared with Arthur so nobody then, and nobody today, can say for sure what happened. It may be that either Henry or Katherine lied or the difference of opinion could represent genuine confusion about what constituted consummation.[146] It could be that Katherine was advised to say it had not and repeated it so often that she came to believe it.

The attested copy of the brief had been sent to Mendoza by the Emperor in December 1528 (CSPS 3.2.602) so it is unclear why it had taken so long for it to be handed over. Whether the courier had travelled by sea or land, it would not have taken three months to reach England. Henry had clearly seen a copy of the brief before as his list of errors in it referenced in November 1528 shows. Looking at the new copy aroused fresh suspicions as more faults were found.

The fact that Anne had a copy of Tyndale's book and had clearly read it because she had marked passages in it, is significant. We do not know if she bought it or if it was a gift. Tyndale was on the government's most wanted list as a heretic so Wolsey would have been alarmed to discover that the future Queen of England was reading his work. At one level, the book itself was not harmful. It urged people to obey their rulers, women to obey their husbands and servants their masters. This was traditional and biblical. More controversial was the case it put for the Bible being made available in English. Tyndale noted that the various authors of the Bible had used their native tongues so people

---

146 For more on this point, see Was Henry married when he met Anne?

understood them, that Anglo-Saxon kings had allowed English translations, and he queried why it was that people were allowed to read stories of Robin Hood and Hercules in English but not of Jesus. His answer was to blame the church: "pervert they the whole scripture and all doctors; wresting them unto their abominable purpose, clean contrary to the meaning of the text, and to the circumstances that go before and after. Which devilish falsehood, lest the laymen should perceive, is the very cause why that they will not suffer the scripture to be had in the English tongue; neither any work to be made that should bring the people to knowledge of the truth." Tyndale poured out special criticism of how John Fisher, Bishop of Rochester, twisted and misquoted the Bible to generate false doctrine yet his greatest venom was directed at the pope:

> O how sore differeth the doctrine of Christ and His apostles from the doctrine of the pope and of his apostles! For if any man will obey neither father nor mother, neither lord nor master, neither king nor prince, the same needeth but only to take the mark of the beast, that is, to shave himself a monk, a friar, or a priest, and is then immediately free and exempted from all service and obedience due unto man. ... They have robbed all realms, not of God's word only, but also of all wealth and prosperity; and have driven peace out of all lands, and withdrawn themselves from all obedience to princes, and have separated themselves from the laymen, counting them viler than dogs; and have set up that great idol, the whore of Babylon, Antichrist of Rome, whom they call Pope.

Small wonder that Wolsey, as a Cardinal, found the book objectionable. Quoting the story of David's refusal to take the life of Saul and the teaching of saints Peter and Paul, Tyndale concludes:

> God hath made the King in every realm judge over all, and over him is there no judge. He that judgeth the King judgeth God; and he that layeth hands on the King layeth hand on God; and he that resisteth the King resisteth God, and damneth God's law and ordinance. If the subjects sin, they must be brought to the King's judgment. If the King sin, he must be reserved unto the judgment, wrath, and vengeance of God.[147]

---

[147] See 1 Sam. 24: 1-6; Rom.13:1-6; 1 Pet. 2:13-15. William Tyndale, *Obedience of a Christian Man* (1528) pp. lxii(b), xxix, xxxii.

With the legatine court about to open, Anne was right that this was just the sort of book to please Henry, though it was to remain prohibited. Around the same time she is also thought to have given Henry a copy of Simon Fish's *Supplication of the Beggars* following the recommendation of her brother. Ives suggests that this second gift did not exist and the story just demonstrated confusion with the Tyndale work, but the account came from Fish's own widow which is a strong indicator of its veracity. The fact that Henry also got a copy of Fish's work from another source does not make the story that he received a copy from Anne untrue.[148] Many people have had to smile and express surprise at a gift to avoid hurting the feelings of the giver by revealing they already have the item in question. As an inflammatory work liable to generate civil unrest, it may be presumed that Henry was told about Fish's work by multiple people because it would have been their duty as loyal subjects to do so.

April 1529

Events

- Henry complains to Mendoza about the Emperor's interference and claim to be representing Katherine's legal interests at Rome. Mendoza says the Emperor is just following Henry's example of providing Katherine with expert advisors for her defence and his efforts to see Henry and Katherine live happily together until death is an act of love. Henry's response was recorded as being "great wrath" (LP 4.5687).
- Desiderius Erasmus praises Henry as a "genius" and confirms that the theological works which bear the King's name are indeed Henry's own compositions (LP 4.5412).
- Calais and Guisnes are fortified amid fears of Imperial attack (LP 4.5420, 5466).
- Francis says that if the Emperor goes into Italy, he will follow with 10,000 men (LP 4.5421). He tells Henry he has waited long enough for the Emperor to agree peace and will raise 40,000 men otherwise to invade Spain (LP 4.5482).
- Anne Boleyn tells Stephen Gardiner that she hopes his latest mission will be successful and thus "more pleasant to me than your first." She comments that the hopes raised last time were such that they led to "more pain" when they were not fulfilled but adds: "I trust that this hard beginning

---

[148] Ives, *Anne Boleyn*, pp.162-163; John Foxe, *Acts and Monuments*, ed. Stephen Cattley, vol.4 (1846) pp. 657-658. For more on Fish's work see Was Anne a Protestant?

shall make the better ending." She sends some cramp rings to Gregory Casale and Peter Vannes (LP 4.5422).[149]
- Henry tells Cardinal Campeggio that the Roman church has broken divine law. Campeggio disagrees (LP 4.5416). Nonetheless, Henry assures his ambassadors in Rome that he finds the Cardinal "not having such affection toward the Emperor as in him was suspected" adding "if ever he had been of other mind, we have said somewhat to him as might soon change that intention."[150]
- in Spain, the Emperor admits to being worried that there is no trace of the brief at Rome, He says he is keen for peace with Henry but not with Francis. He says that he will be sad if the pope issues a verdict in Henry's favour but he will accept it and not employ any reprisals (LP 4.5423).
- in Rome, the pope also expresses disquiet that the brief is not in the registers and sends an envoy to Spain to bring the original back for inspection (LP 4.5475). He tells Campeggio that he cannot rule on its authenticity without seeing it (LP 4.5477).
- Mai recruits spies in the houses of the French, English and Italian ambassadors who report to him on their activities and decode despatches (CSPS 3.2.645).
- the Chancellor of Spain allows the English ambassadors and Katherine's chaplain, Thomas Abell, to examine and copy the brief, He tells them that its survival is a miraculous work of the Holy Spirit showing God's support for Katherine. He claims it was found by De Puebla's nephew.[151] Having seen the document, the English are even more convinced it is a forgery and send a detailed report to Wolsey (LP 4.5470, 5471).
- Flanders prepares for war with France and attacks on French citizens are made in Tournai and Valenciennes (LP 4.5494, 5495).
- the Emperor's representatives meet with Desmond to discuss his offer of 16,500 foot and 1,500 horse to wage war on France and England. Desmond says his motives are hatred of Piers Butler and of Wolsey for making an alliance with France (LP 4.5500, 5501).
- Henry Percy expresses his loyalty to Wolsey and gratitude for the care Wolsey showed in bringing him up. He is like a father to him (LP 4.5497, 5498).
- an informer tells Wolsey that he knows where William Tyndale is hiding and how to take him (LP 4.5462)
- Francis's younger son, the Duke of Orleans, is reported to be very ill in his captivity and close to death (LP 4.5470, 5701).
- Dr Mai says that the pope is unfriendly and trying to interest him in Katherine's plight is like "breaking stones." He says the pope's favoured solution is for Katherine to become a nun (LP 4.5440).

---

149 Burnet, *History of the Reformation*, ed. Pocock vol. 5 p.444
150 Burnet, *History of the Reformation*, ed. Pocock vol. 4 pp.115-116
151 The footnote in CSPS 4.1.571 states it was Puebla's son.

- the English ambassadors in Rome advise Henry to start the trial in England as soon as possible as they foresee only delays and excuses. Sir Francis Bryan admits that he dare not write a true report to his cousin Anne Boleyn of what is happening and leaves it to Henry to tell her what he thinks best. He writes bluntly of the pope to Henry: "He will do nothing for Your Grace. If I should write otherwise then I should put Your Grace in a hope of recovery where none is to be had. There is not one of us but that hath assayed him both by fair means and foul but nothing will serve. And whosoever hath made Your Grace believe that he would do for you in this cause hath not, as I think, done Your Grace the best service. Always Your Grace hath done for him in deeds and he hath recompensed you with fair words and fair writings, of which both I think Your Grace shall lack none; but as for the deeds, I never believe to see and specially at this time." He recommends that Henry cast the pope and his cardinals aside: "I trust Your Grace will quit them and be no more fed with their flattering words." (LP 4.5476, 5478, 5479, 5481; SP vol. 7 pp.166-8)
- the pope publicly announces that Wolsey will accompany him for the peace talks, to the dismay of the Imperialists. However, aware that Wolsey will not be allowed by Henry to do so unless the annulment is settled, he suffers torment privately. He admits that without Wolsey the peace talks will fail as he will be left like a man with no right hand (LP 4.5480, CSPS 3.2.653).
- at the Diet of Speyer, the Lutherans protest against the revocation of the Edict of Worms. The word Protestant is born.
- Florence falls to the opponents of the Medici family. Gregory Casale warns Wolsey that this makes it likely that the pope will now join the Emperor in order to get it back (LP 4.5478).
- on the 27th, the Imperial ambassador in Rome makes an official appeal to the pope demanding the case be advoked there and that he also prohibit parliament and all universities from discussing it or giving opinions. He further demands that the pope order Henry to send Anne from court and that the papal nuncio in England be instructed to send the names of all of Henry's supporters to Rome so they can be punished (CSPS 3.2.667, 674, 676, 677). Ferdinand's ambassador joins with him (LP 4.5604; CSPV 4.452).
- Mendoza says that Katherine's prospects will be improved if the Emperor gives his sister to James V of Scotland as wife because this will make Henry afraid (CSPS 3.2.668).
- Dr Mai deliberately and maliciously chooses to interpret the English vow to use other means if the pope refuses to grant the annulment as indicating a plan to poison Katherine. Alleging this is proof her life is in danger, he pressurises the pope into promising of the annulment "I will never authorise it." In a calmer mood, Mai admits that it is common practice for briefs to be sent when a bull is found wanting and he suspects that the 'Spanish brief' may have been raised precisely because the original bull

was deficient. Mai notes that he has found in the papal archives a copy of a letter sent by Pope Julius saying he was sending the brief to Spain in a hurry because Queen Isabella was dying. Mai observes that a promise was given that it should be kept secret which is why the English did not know about it and why there was no record in the papal registers (LP 4.5440; CSPS 3.2.664).
- Ghinucci complains about the Imperial use of the word 'divorce' saying "there needeth none for that which is not cannot be dissolved." He also queries why Katherine's conscience is not troubled. He seeks to reassure the Spanish that the legatine court will be fair because Campeggio is one of the judges and he is totally devoted to the Emperor. The Imperial Council maintain that if the "marriage" is declared null, Katherine will have been publicly shamed as no more than a concubine. Ghinucci denies this on grounds she entered the union in good faith (LP 4.5471).
- the Emperor refuses to send the brief to England but says he will send it to Rome – but only if the case is advoked there (LP 4.5471).
- Wolsey instructs Gregory Casale, Francis Bryan, Stephen Gardiner and Peter Vannes in Rome to seek a new commission which allows himself and Campeggio in the pope's name "to make out compulsories to any princes, or persons of what pre-eminence, dignity, state, or condition soever they be and in what countries and places soever they be, to exhibit and produce any manner witness, record, original rescript or other thing, in what place, or time we, or the one of us shall require them, or any of them in this behalf, with all and singular the circumstances requisite and necessary to such a commission." He asks them to check if the pollicitation will need strengthening too if the commission is amended. He warns them "always note, remember, and regard, that this the King's cause admitteth nor suffereth any manner negative, tract, or delay." He reassures them that a French bishop will soon be joining them because Francis treats this case as his own. He suggests that as the pope is too sick to travel, he grant himself and Campeggio a commission to negotiate peace in Europe on his behalf and says that he is willing to set off just as soon as the pope approves the annulment. He warns that failure on the pope's part will cause him to "lose him (Henry) and this realm, the French king and his realm, with many other their confederates." He prays, however, that the pope will "bring us out of this perplexity, that this virtuous prince may have his thing sped to the purpose desired, which shall be the most joyous thing that this day in earth may chance and succeed to my heart." He tells them that Henry is unhappy and mistrustful of the pope and that the decision has been made to open the legatine court very soon using the existing commission while they continue to seek a new one. They are not to tell the pope that this is happening for fear it will cause more delay. Wolsey asks Bryan and Gardiner to hurry home (LP 4.5428, 5429).[152]

---

152 Burnet, *History of the Reformation,* ed. Pocock, vol. 4 pp.79-102.

Comments

Historians sometimes express doubts about the reports of ambassadors but Mendoza's comment that Henry was in "great wrath" at his words is something nobody is ever likely to question.

Wolsey's demand for a new commission and comment that the court will open using the old one is of vital importance. He and Henry recognised the difficulties they faced. The impression often given that Henry expected the case to proceed smoothly and rapidly to his desired end is wrong. They were worried and knew time was not on their side. If France and the Emperor made peace with each other and the pope, it would leave Henry isolated.

Despite being part of the Habsburg family which ruled most of Europe, Katherine obtained little support from them. Ferdinand's ambassador did on occasion accompany Mai at the papal court but this was really the extent of his activity. Unless we are to assume that all the European archives, including the English, all systematically destroyed all traces of communication with Katherine – and there is no reason why that should have happened – it is clear that virtually nobody bothered to send her any letters of support nor any gifts and nor did they protest on her behalf to the pope or make much attempt to secure expert legal advice for her. Later generations of strangers have expressed much more concern for her than her own family.

The pope told Mai that he would not authorise the annulment, not that he did not support it.

Casale's prediction about how the pope would act in order to get Florence back was prescient. Florence was not part of the Papal States but territory which had long belonged to his family, the Medicis. The Medici had lost power in May 1527 but the new ruling party had been willing to enter into dialogue which was not the case with those who took over now.

Ghinucci's report into the brief (LP 4.5471) raised the following concerns:[153]

1. the date is 26th December 1503 in the first year of Julius' reign which is "almost a year before Julius II was pope"[154]
2. the subscription was written in a different hand to the rest of the document
3. the handwriting is not that of the usual papal clerk
4. errors in the text suggest that the writer was an apprentice. In Lee's report, he described it as the work of "some learner and not of one exercised in writing of such things"
5. the word dispensamus appeared to have been erased in two places
6. the wax rose in the middle as though something were underneath
7. the name of the prince was mis-spelt Artherus instead of Arthurus

---

[153] These points are also listed in Edward Herbert, *History of England under Henry VIII* (1719), pp. 359-362, 377-378. See also LP4.5376.

[154] This was indisputable. For an explanation of the issue see Appendix 1: the Bull and the Brief

8. the word charmorum was mis-spelt and abbreviated as charmmo
9. the word consumavit was mis-spelt consummavit
10. the word propterea was written as pprea
11. the brief has the same date at the bull but the contents differ. The fullest document should be the bull which is the more formal and usual documentary form of a dispensation and in any dispute, a bull should be followed rather than a brief. Given that Henry and Katherine were not due to marry for some years, there was no hurry. Two documents suggests two suits at Rome yet Henry VII and Ferdinand and Isabella were said to be working together, thus if another agent was there requesting the brief, it was not with their consent
12. if Katherine had sworn she had not consumated her union with Arthur, the issuing of a brief saying she had must have been done without her consent or show it was a forgery[155]
13. the brief is said to have been requested by Katherine and Henry but neither knew anything about it and Henry was only twelve.
14. if it had been requested by Henry and Katherine, it should have been sent to them not Ferdinand
15. Chancellor Gattinara and Perrinot say it was found among De Puebla's papers but why would he have had it in England if it was sent to Ferdinand? De Puebla lived in England for more than five years after the brief was issued so he had ample time to give it or a copy to both Katherine and to Henry VII.[156] Surely Ferdinand would have wanted it back meanwhile.
16. Katherine would have been asked when Arthur died if her marriage had been consummated. If she had said "yes" then the bull would have been worded to dispense that: if not, there was no reason for a brief
17. the brief as shown is in parchment but should be in lead
18. Et was abbreviated as &
19. Gattinara and Perenot admit that De Puebla left considerable correspondence about Katherine's marriage to Arthur and union with Henry and that there is no reference in any of the documents to the request or need for a brief nor to the existence of one

With such a large number of concerns, it is easy to see why Henry and Wolsey thought it was a forgery. The fact that there was no record of it at Rome also left the pope and Emperor unconvinced of its validity. Eventually, in the nineteenth century, it was proved to be genuine. However, it was clearly sent without being checked and with a deliberately false date upon it. In July 1504, the pope had admitted the dispensation had yet to be raised.[157] Unbeknown to Henry, Katherine's father had forged a papal dispensation to marry her mother

---

155 The third option that Katherine was a liar was something Ghinucci did not dare suggest
156 Puebla died in England just before Henry VII, LP 5470.
157 CSPS 1.396

so the possibility of this brief being another of his creations was quite conceivable.[158]

May 1529

Events

- the pope says that he wishes Katherine were dead: "He would, for the wealth of Christendom, the Queen were in her grave; and, as he thought, the Emperor would be thereof most glad of all; saying also that he thought, like as the Emperor hath destroyed the temporalities of the church, so shall she be the cause of the destruction of the spiritualities." He expresses despair over "that family" (LP 4.5518).
- Henry's brother-in-law, the Duke of Suffolk, goes to France to discuss military tactics to be employed against the Emperor (LP 4.5523, 5535, 5579, CSPV 4.464).
- the League make progress in Sicily and Naples and make preparations for an assault on Milan (LP 4.5545, 5579).
- the pope sends the Bishop of Vaison to Spain to negotiate a marriage between his "nephew" and the Emperor's illegitimate daughter (CSPS 4.1.2).
- at Rome, the English and Imperial ambassadors continue to make demands and protests even disputing angrily with one another while the harassed pope looks on. Dr Mai proclaims that the behaviour of the English team is making the pope ill. (LP 4.5529, 5534, 5591). Mai confides to the Emperor: "I fear the weakness of the pope more than anything" (LP 4.5529). Henry concurs with this assessment and notes "fear causes men to do things which they had no intention whatever of doing" (LP 4.5572). Mai describes the pope as a "very low minded man, easily bribable." (CSPS 4.1.6)
- the Emperor declares that if any attempt is made to decide Henry's case in England, he will appeal to a General Council (LP 4.5572). He tells the pope that Katherine refuses to act herself because as Henry's wife she is obedient to him – hence he has decided to prosecute the case for her (LP 4.5518).
- from London, a beleaguered Campeggio complains of a lack of support from Rome and says Henry and Wolsey refuse to listen to him but rather blame him for the delays (LP 4.5535, 5572, 5584). Wolsey tells Campeggio confidently that "on the dissolution of this 'marriage' we shall easily find some means of agreeing with the Emperor." Campeggio alleges that the plan that Wolsey and Henry have in mind is that Katherine be allowed to remain Queen with all her existing status except any right to share the King's bed and that a new Anglo-Imperial marriage alliance is made

---

158 Nancy Rubin Stuart, *Isabella of Castile,* (Lincoln Nebraska, 2004) p.86

through arranging a marriage between Henry's illegitimate son Richmond and the Emperor's bastard daughter (LP 4.5535).
- Thomas Boleyn goes to France. He reports Francis has sent another envoy to Rome to support Henry's annulment (LP 4.5583).
- Jean du Bellay, French ambassador to England, expresses deep concern about Wolsey's position and health: "He is so concerned at seeing his master, whom he loves more than himself, in his present trouble that I wonder he does not die of vexation." (LP 4.5610) He acknowledges that Suffolk and Norfolk are whispering in Henry's ear that Wolsey is not trying hard enough and he urges Montmorency, Grand Master of France, to assure Suffolk when he sees him that this is untrue. He describes the situation as "extremely urgent" and notes that France has a lot to lose if Wolsey falls (LP 4.5581, 5582, 5601).
- reports are received that the Turks are planning to invade Germany. As urgent preparations are made for its defence, Wolsey reflects that it will stop the Emperor going to Italy and meeting the pope which is good (LP 4.5544, 5595). From France, Suffolk writes to Henry in agreement saying that anything which means the Emperor cannot "embusy himself with hindrance or impeachment of your great matter" is to be welcomed (LP 4.5675).
- a peace congress is planned for Cambrai between Francis' mother, Louise of Savoy and his and the Emperor's aunt, Margaret, Regent of the Low Countries.[159] Doubts are expressed that it will achieve anything and war continues to rage amid deep distrust on all sides. Campeggio declares that such weighty matters as peace are beyond the capabilities of women to negotiate (LP 4.5572). Margaret tells the Emperor that she will not invade France as he has ordered until the talks have taken place and the outcome is known (LP 4.5599).
- the date is set for the legatine court to open. Katherine requests the return of her two Flemish lawyers, Giles de la Blekerie and Luis Van Scoere. This puts Margaret, Regent of the Low Countries, into an awkward position because she wants to help her but is aware that the Emperor does not wish this (LP 4.5599). Wolsey urges speed fearing that if the brief is sent to Rome, the pope will use that as an excuse to advoke the case there (LP 4.5576, 5599, 5613). Henry predicts the case will last two months but Jean du Bellay believes it will take at least twice that long (LP 4.5581).
- Francis says that if the pope will not sort the annulment, he will make another pope who will. He urges Poland and Denmark to join France and England in any new schism (LP 4.5572, 5601).
- the pope continues to pressurise Francis about Ravenna and Cervia reiterating his threat to him and Henry that if they cannot get them back, he will take other steps (LP 4.5543).

---

159 Margaret had been married to Louise's brother making her an aunt by marriage to Francis and by blood to the Emperor whose father was her brother.

- a formal report is sent from Rome following an investigation by the cardinals to confirm that there is no record of Katherine's "Spanish brief" in the papal records. It also confirms that the year for briefs begins on December 25th and for bulls on 25th March (LP 4.5615).[160]
- Henry Norris is granted lands in Greenwich, Eltham, Deptford and Woolwish (LP 4.5624.1)
- Spanish troops seek to ambush the French cardinal Triulzio as he enters Venice on Francis' behalf to plead for the return of Ravenna and Cervia. Triulzio escapes. Venice is excommunicated by the pope (CSPS 4.1.5).
- Henry and Wolsey row with Campeggio at Windsor over whether the pope promised to give his legates plenitudinary power. Campeggio and his secretary deny this. Henry urges the two cardinals, "be good friends to me and have pity on me." (LP 4.5572)
- Francis Bryan describes the efforts of the English to get a resolution from the pope as "We be like men that hope to gather fruit on a rotten stalk." He warns Henry that Campeggio cannot be trusted: "Your Grace writes unto us that the Cardinal Campeggio says he is your servant and that he will do for Your Grace in all things; Sir, his fair words that he says to Your Grace is because he would have the Bishopric of Durham." He says that the pope has shown them the letters Campeggio has written to Rome and they conflict sharply with Henry's words. (LP 4.5519; SP vol.7 pp.169-170)
- Bennet is sent to Rome to assist Casale and Vannes in the struggle against the "sinister pursuits and solicitations of the Imperials." He is to continue to ask for a new commission "with some more full pregnant and effectual causes than the other hath." Meanwhile the legatine court will open in England and try to complete its business before the Imperials have time to frustrate it or get the pope to advoke it. Bennet is to tell the pope that Henry is glad that he intends to satisfy his requests and is now "very desirous to know and understand the same." (LP 5575; SP vol. 7 pp.171-177)
- Sanga sends a copy of the official Imperial appeal against the case being heard in England to Campeggio noting that the pope has refused to accept it. He tells Campeggio to continue the good work of procrastination, avoid taking any decisions and make sure that the pope is portrayed in a good light. He is reminded that the Apostolic See is in peril and assured the pope will advoke the case to Rome as he has recommended just as soon as Campeggio advises that it is safe to do so without creating a scandal, although he does not really wish to do so as this is likely to force him into making a decision which might offend Henry. Sanga says the pope is keen to satisfy Henry and will do so as soon as peace has been agreed and he can see a way of doing so without causing great outrage. However, the pope's definition of satisfying Henry does not involve ever giving a sentence. He is sure that Campeggio will be able to find at least a

---

[160] Rymer, *Foedera*, vol. 14 p.296

thousand pretexts for making sure the legatine court makes no progress at all and comments that the 'Spanish brief' will be a good excuse for raising difficulties and delays. Sanga further requests Campeggio to liaise with Wolsey and see if they can persuade Henry to write another book against Luther, a project which will "renew the glory he has already acquired" by writing the *Assertio*, help keep England free from heresy and (a motive not stated but no doubt on the pope's mind) distract Henry from the annulment (LP 4.5604).

- unbeknown to Henry, Katherine appoints Cardinal San Croce and the Imperial ambassador as her proctors at Rome, thereby indicating her lack of intention of recognising the legatine court in England. In her statement she denies that her marriage to Arthur was consummated, confirms that the bull of dispensation was read at her wedding to Henry and says that it is not her wish to separate from Henry whom she references as "my most beloved husband" for any reason, including becoming a nun. She acknowledges that "many" have questioned the validity of the union and wish it to be dissolved.[161]

Comments

On 6th June, Gregory Casale helpfully sent Henry copies of letters by Campeggio and his secretary confirming the papal promise of absolute power (LP 4.5649).

The commission read out at the start of the legatine court is worth quoting. It notes the controversy over the validity of Henry and Katherine's union and says it is "necessary to proceed to some quick and speedy determination herein, to avoid that danger which must unavoidably ensue upon deferring it. But since we, whom God has appointed Servant of his Servants to administer to all men impartial justice in judgment and truth, are not able in our person to inquire into the truth of the fact and examine this cause ourselves...we do hereby give and grant a plenary authority and most ample power and commission to your eminences (Wolsey and Campeggio) in our own stead either both jointly or in case of unwillingness or any other impediment, to either of you singly; that being subject to the authority and jurisdiction of no court or person whatever, nor liable to any appeal or question concerning your jurisdiction; you do hear and examine all and everything which may relate to the validity or invalidity of the said marriage or of any apostolic dispensation whatever to be exhibited and produced before you...that you proceed judicially... and if it shall this appear that the dispensation is invalid and the marriage null, that you do judicially, deliberately, summarily and clearly pronounce a sentence of divorce and grant a faculty and licence in the Lord to the aforesaid King Henry and Queen Katherine to marry again...and publish if

---

161 D'Avray, *Dissolving Royal Marriages* (2014) pp.231-235 (English), pp.288-93 (Latin).

it shall to you seem convenient that the children by the first marriage as well as by the second are legitimate."[162]

The official report from Rome regarding the brief was not sent until May 31st so would not have been available to the legatine court when it opened. It is important to note its existence. The authenticity of the brief was not proved until the nineteenth century when it was discovered that the document had been deliberately backdated which is why there was no trace of it in the registers under the date shown. Most of Henry's contemporaries, including the pope, suspected it was a forgery and who could blame them. If a document was produced today signed by Queen Elizabeth II and dated 6th May 1951, it would be branded fraudulent because she did not come to the throne until 1952. It might be found that a secretary had simply mistyped 1951 instead of 1957, or had deliberately backdated it for nefarious purposes, or it might be an outright forgery, but it would certainly raise legitimate questions just as did the Spanish brief in 1529. Those who suggest that Henry and his team were being unreasonable in demanding that the brief be excluded are themselves being unreasonable. The aroma of a very large rodent unsurprisingly filled rooms whenever the document was mentioned.

The writs for the court were issued by Henry on the 30th May. On the following day, the commission was read out and legal teams appointed with the first session booked for the 18th June.

Many writers have claimed Anne was firmly in the ascendant by this point and a person of political significance. If Henry and Wolsey were united in their plan to leave Katherine as Queen after the annulment, this suggests otherwise. Would Anne be willing to marry Henry and then retire into the shadows while Katherine attended functions with him and greeted visitors? It does not sound feasible. It may be supposed that Henry had not shared this "solution" with her. Either his desire to marry her was not yet matched by a desire to make her his consort or Campeggio was lying.

Katherine's acknowledgement of "many" wanting the annulment to go ahead should be stressed. Too many writers take their lead from Chapuys who regarded it as so unbelievable that anyone could wish such a thing, he simply denied that such people existed – other than the Boleyns themselves. Henry could not have achieved all that he did if it had not been for a substantial level of popular support.

---

162 Cobbett, *State Trials*, pp.318-319

June 1529

Events

- at Henry's request, and following a suggestion from Anne's cousin Francis Bryan, Suffolk asks the French king privately at the start of the month for his view on the legates. Francis says that Campeggio told him on his way to England that the annulment "shall not take effect... I trust I shall show unto the King of England such reasons as he shall be contented to leave that matter," words which he immediately passed on to John Clerk, the Bishop of Bath to tell Henry. He said that in his view Campeggio intended "only to use dissimulation with Your Grace, for he is entire imperial." Regarding Wolsey, Francis says "as far as I could perceive in him, he would the divorce should go forth and take effect, for he loved not the Queen." Nonetheless, noting how close Wolsey was to the pope and Campeggio, he says that Henry should avoid putting too much trust in one man but rather "look substantially upon his matters himself, as I hear say he doeth, which I am not a little glad of."(LP 4.5635; SP vol.7 pp.182-184)
- Mai, Imperial ambassador at Rome, laments that the majority of cardinals are pro-French. When one reminds Mai of the sack of Rome two years before and Imperial depredations since and suggests that they would live more safely under Turkish rule than the Emperor's, Mai vows to have him beheaded or burnt alive in his apartment should he repeat these sentiments (CSPS 4.1.29).
- Cardinal Ancona and his nephew, Cardinal Ravenna, offer their services to support the English ambassadors in Rome (LP 4.5656, 5657).
- Francis sends the Bishop of Tarbes to Rome to petition the pope to grant the annulment quickly adding that he has chosen him because of his diplomatic experience and his deep knowledge of the case. Francis also sends his own letter to the pope supporting Henry (LP 4.5688-89).
- news is received from Rome about there being no trace of the brief there and that the date indicates that it is false. Campeggio is said to be "half conquered" by this news (LP 4.5742).
- Le Sauch, ambassador of Margaret in the Low Countries, tells her that Katherine's brief has not been found valid at Rome (CSPS 4.1.50).
- the Imperial assault on the French fleet at Marseilles fails but French troops mutiny at Apulia due to lack of pay (LP 4.5633).
- the pope expresses fury at the French capture of Perugia which is part of the Papal States. He refuses to believe the French are holding it temporarily for strategic purposes and raises three thousand troops to go to its aid. The pope declares he would rather work in the Emperor's stables cleaning out horses than endure these insults and loss of territory. He notes the Emperor has offered to help get Perugia back and to rescue his "niece"

who is being held in Florence. Gregory Casale warns Henry and Wolsey that the pope is close to joining the Emperor because these offers are attractive to him and the pope now believes the Emperor will win the war LP 4.5640, 5641, 5649, 5676).
- the pope tells the Archbishop of Capua "I have quite made up my mind to become an Imperialist" but refuses to announce this publicly (CSPS 4.1.36, 38). Mai hopes this is true but says that the pope is "prone to change his opinions." (CSPS 4.1.41)
- Eustace Chapuys is appointed Imperial ambassador to England (CSPS 4.1.43, 54, 57).
- Gregory Casale notes that Mai's complaints have resulted in himself and Peter Vannes receiving instructions not to say anything to the pope which might upset him and make him ill again (LP 4.5649)
- the Emperor repeats his refusal to allow the Flemish lawyers to return to Katherine despite the recommendations of his ambassador. Katherine is upset (LP 4.5681, 5687).
- the legatine court opens on the 18th. Katherine appears to lodge an official protest which is disallowed (LP 4.5685, 5707). She returns on the 21st when Henry is there and falls to her knees before him urging him to consider the reputation of herself and their daughter Mary and threatens him with the fury of Spain. Henry says he has had his doubts about the marriage from the start and can no longer live in mortal sin and when Katherine asks why he has kept quiet all these years, he tells her it is because he loves her. Katherine walks out and refuses to return to court which results in her being declared in contempt of court. The French ambassador reports the presence of women cheering Katherine on and her employing "Spanish tricks" to encourage them (LP 4.5702, 5707; CSPV 4.482).
- Katherine's team continue work in her absence arguing that any separation would be damaging to England's international relations and that "continuance of so long space had made the marriage good." These arguments failing to win over those who maintained that the union was against God's law "they left that ground and fell to pleading, that the Court of Rome had dispensed with that marriage" only to be reminded "no earthly person is able to dispense with the positive Law of God."[163]
- Stephen Gardiner returns from Rome on the 22nd. He reports that the pope has said the "Spanish brief" is a forgery but does not have this in writing (LP 4.5733, 5742).
- on the 25th, Bishop John Fisher of Rochester appears at the legatine court claiming that the "marriage" is solid. He references John the Baptist who was executed following criticism made of King Herod that he married his brother's wife. Wolsey retorts that nobody disputes the fact that no human agency can dissolve a marriage made by God but the question is whether

---

163 *Hall's Chronicle* p.758

Henry's union with Katherine was made by God at all and to remind him that the pope did not appoint him a judge in the case.[164]
- the pope goes into a rage that the commission he sent to hold the trial is actually being used and restraint is needed to stop him immediately advoking the case to Rome. Wolsey is told to consider the advocation as something postponed not prevented (LP 4.5725). Meanwhile the lawyers at the papal court speculate happily on the money they will be able to make when the case comes to Rome (LP 5.5722).
- three days after the trial opens, the French and Venetians suffer a catastrophic defeat by the Imperial army at Landriano. The French commander, St Pol, is taken (LP 4.5705). A week later, the pope allies himself to the Emperor (LP 4.5737). The Treaty of Barcelona is ratified on 29th June in Spain and 8th July at Rome (CSPS 4.1.45, 56).
- William Brereton marries Elizabeth Savage and is granted wardship of her son and of her estate. Elizabeth is a widow and the sister of the Earl of Worcester.[165]
- Henry Norris obtains a wardship and Richard Page is appointed Head Trencherman (LP 4.5748.5).
- in order to reduce the chance of Ghinucci returning to England in order to give evidence at the legatine trial regarding the authenticity of the "Spanish brief", the Emperor insists that the ambassadorial exchange – Ghinucci (Henry's ambassador in Spain) for Mendoza (Imperial ambassador in England) – take place at a location three hundred miles away (LP 4.5485, 5670, 5687).
- plans for the peace summit at Cambrai continue. Henry is angry that it is due to be held while the legatine court is in session meaning Wolsey cannot attend. He feels snubbed as does the pope who has not been invited to send an envoy. Casale describes the pope as "the most suspicious of men" (LP 4.5640, 5649, 5679, 5713, 5742). It is feared in England that a quick peace between Francis and the Emperor with Francis paying a ransom for the return of his sons would give the Emperor the money he needs to complete the conquest of Italy (LP 4.5675, 5702, 5713). Venice shares these fears (CSPV 4.473).
- Jean du Bellay, Bishop of Bayonne, continues to worry about Wolsey (LP 4.5679, 5701, 5702).
- the papal prothonotary, Gambara, tells Wolsey that if the pope has not granted the annulment already, it must be the fault of foolish advisers who have not understood the matter or need for it. He tells him to be of good cheer (LP 4.5653).
- the cardinals demand three thousand gold pieces before they will issue a bull to erect a new cathedral, part of Wolsey's planned diocesan re-

---

[164] Reports of Fisher's speech appear in LP 4.5732, 5741; Cavendish, *Wolsey*, p.224; Ehses, *Romische Dokumente* pp.116-7

[165] E. Ives, *Letters and Accounts of William Brereton*, Transactions of the Lancashire and Cheshire Record Society vol CXVI (1976) p.59

organisation. After some negotiation, Cardinal San Quatuor gets the price down to three hundred (LP 4.5638).

Comments

The Herod referenced by Fisher is not the one of the Christmas story who ordered the massacre of the infants but rather his son. The Bible does not say whether Herod's brother was alive at the time that he married his wife but Josephus' *Antiquities,* written around sixty years after the death of Jesus, says he was not. Whether widow or wife, Herodias was not childless for she had a daughter Salome, which meant that her union with Herod was forbidden in the Torah. Seeking to draw a parallel between Henry and Herod was deliberately provocative as well as ill informed.[166]

Henry asking Suffolk to get Francis' private opinion of Wolsey's behaviour is extraordinary. It demonstrates Henry's trust of Francis at this point and his doubts about Wolsey, but the fact that he admitted those doubts to Francis shows the extent of disturbance in Henry's mental state. Kings did not routinely ask the heads of state of foreign powers for a review of their own employee's performance. This was not Henry introducing the idea of 360° appraisal centuries before any employment guru dreamt it up, just paranoia. The fact that the suggestion came from Bryan has led some to suggest that this shows his cousin, Anne Boleyn, was behind it and trying to stir up trouble for Wolsey, but that is improbable. Bryan was in Rome and his letters home show that he did not dare to write to Anne because the situation was so bleak and he thought it safer to let Henry decide what she should be told (LP 4.5481, 5519). As a Gentleman of the Privy Chamber, Bryan was loyal to Henry and did not require Anne to urge him to such things. They may have communicated but it is entirely probable that they had not done so. The incident also demonstrates Brandon's unique position. He was not a man who relished political intrigue or attending meetings but he was the person Henry trusted most as a friend. Nobody else would have had the necessary authority to have such a conversation with the King of France.

At three thousand gold pieces, a bull for a cathedral was one of the most expensive pieces of paper ever. The extreme nature of the demand and the way it was open to negotiation – no doubt through payments on the side – demonstrates what we would today regard as endemic corruption, though they would have seen it as part of the routine reward system.

Katherine's appearance at the legatine court has become famous over the years due to Cavendish's dramatic account which was incorporated into Shakespeare's play. In this, a weeping Katherine kneels before Henry and reminds him that she came to him a "true maid". There are six contemporary accounts of what happened by Henry VIII, Edward Hall (English chronicler), Jean du Bellay (French ambassador), Lodovico Falier (Venetian ambassador),

---

166 See Was Henry married? Footnotes 36 and 159

Campeggio and the official court record.¹⁶⁷ In none of these does Katherine mention her virginity or marriage to Arthur. The fact that not one of these individuals, all of whom were in the room, mentioned such a challenging statement, combined with other major inaccuracies in Cavendish's account, means it is certain that he made it up, either deliberately to fulfil his political agenda or accidentally because he was writing decades later when he was an old man and possibly genuinely confused about events. The reliability of eye-witness accounts written by people who were closely involved in the process is clearly greater than the comments of Wolsey's butler made years afterwards. Katherine had used the same drama of publicly throwing herself at Henry's feet back in 1520 (LP 3.689).

Gambara had been papal nuncio in England at the start of the annulment crisis and was closely involved in it, working with Wolsey. His attitude in September 1530 was to be rather different.

The Emperor's insistence on Ghinucci being sent hundreds of miles out of his way was what is popularly known as a "dirty trick" and suggests he was afraid of what Ghinucci would say.¹⁶⁸

Brereton's wife was what might be termed a "good catch." The Earl of Worcester was Henry's cousin on the Beaufort side.

The terms of the Treaty of Barcelona were: The Emperor would compel Venice and Ferrara to return papal territories; make Florence accept Alessandro de Medici as ruler with the Emperor's own illegitimate daughter Margarita (currently aged 7) as his betrothed; confirm papal rule over Parma and Piacenza; restore Francesco Sforza as Duke of Milan provided that he begged forgiveness for his treason in joining League of Cognac and paid a large fine. If Sforza refused, Milan would be partitioned amongst its neighbours. The pope would re-invest the Emperor as King of Naples, make Gattinara a cardinal, pardon all those who took part in the Sack of Rome and permit the Emperor and his brother to with-hold a quarter of the revenue from benefices in the hope they would use those sums to fight the Turk. The crucial clause for the English was that the pope was to advoke Henry's annulment case to Rome.¹⁶⁹ Unsurprisingly, the pope was in no hurry to make this public. Given that he had signed a promise not to do this, it is easy to see why. As Wolsey observed, his behaviour was impossible to justify in light of clear Gospel teaching (Matt. 5:33,37) (LP 4.5428).

---

167 A detailed summary of the official court record appears in English in Herbert, *History*, pp.366-396.
168 Mendoza was in the Low Countries. He had been allowed to travel there on account of his ill health having volunteered himself as a prisoner or hostage until Ghinucci and Lee were back in France (CSPS 4.1.44)
169 Parker, *Emperor*, p.184

July 1529

Events

- news of the defeat at Landriano reaches England on 2nd July (LP 4.5775).
- the Emperor seeks permission to sell all immoveable church property to raise funds (CSPS 4.1.58).
- Katherine is upset that her appeal to Rome has made Henry angry with her (CSPS 4.1.83).
- the Emperor issues an edict legitimising his bastard daughter prior to her marriage to the pope's "nephew", Alessandro (CSPS 4.1.51, 62).
- in order to get a majority in the college of cardinals, the Emperor is told he will need to spend 20,000 ducats a year in pensions and provide benefices worth 35,000 ducats a year, plus make extra rewards for key figures such as Cardinal Farnese (CSPS 4.1.87).
- Mendoza, ex-Imperial ambassador to London, advises delaying Chapuys as a lack of Imperial representation in England will show Henry he is insignificant in Europe without the Emperor's friendship (CSPS 4.1.83).
- the pope says he feels caught between a hammer and an anvil and wishes he were dead. He claims he wants to support Henry but says that now Katherine has appealed, he must advoke. Cardinal Ancona refuses to assent to this saying that having given the decision to allow the trial in England, the pope should allow the process to continue. The Imperial ambassador says the proposed annulment is an insult to the Emperor's family honour. Gregory Casale, the English ambassador, reminds the pope that his duty is to do what is right, not judge on the basis of political expediency (LP 4.5762).
- Dr Mai, Imperial ambassador in Rome, urges the pope to write to Henry offering a new bull to supply the defects in the original dispensation so that Henry can remain wed to Katherine (LP 4.5827).
- at the trial, witnesses give evidence regarding Katherine's marriage to Prince Arthur including seeing them in bed together (LP 4.5774, 5778). Wolsey and Campeggio plan to give sentence but having heard from Rome and in light of the impending Franco-Imperial peace, Campeggio prorogues the court for two months on the 23rd (LP 4.5775, 5789). The Duke of Suffolk rises in fury and shouts "there was never Legate nor Cardinal, that did good in England" to which Wolsey retorts that "if I, simple cardinal, had not been, you should have had at this present no head upon your shoulders wherein you should have a tongue to make any such report."[170]
- news of the alliance between the pope and Emperor emerges in Rome on the 15th. The pope advokes the annulment case on the 16th, the day before the

---

170 Cavendish, *Wolsey*, p.233. Also in *Hall's Chronicle* p.758. Wolsey had saved Brandon's life by interceding for him when he married Henry's sister without permission.

Treaty of Barcelona is officially proclaimed. He writes to Wolsey on the 17th about the Treaty and on the 18th sends him a letter apologising for the advocation, saying he hopes Wolsey will have no hard feelings and telling him to ensure that Henry remains well disposed towards the papacy (LP 4.5779, 5780, 5785).
- Wolsey says that if the pope intends to summon Henry to Rome, he can think again. Henry is a king and will not be summoned like some lackey and nobody in England will either "tolerate nor suffer" that any such summons be obeyed. If Henry goes to Rome, it will be at the head of a great army "as should be formidable to the pope and all Italy." (LP 4.5797; SP vol.7 p.195)
- George Boleyn is appointed Governor of Bedlam (LP 4.5815.27). William Boleyn is appointed vicar of a church in Durham (LP 4.5815.3) while Anne's father and two others obtain presentation rights to All Hallows in London (LP 4.5815.28). Henry stays with Thomas Boleyn at Durham Place from July 15th to 27th (LP 4.5965)
- the Emperor claims that if Henry is allowed to separate from Katherine it will be a massive dishonour to his family and that preventing this is more important to him than all the lands he has inherited and conquered (LP 4.5762).
- at Rome, Katherine's lawyers claim the bull and brief cover affinity and public honesty.[171]

Comments

Historians have been known to suggest that Wolsey was given an unreasonable task by Henry when told to obtain an annulment. That is open to debate but the pope's instruction that Wolsey should make sure Henry only felt loving feelings towards Rome when the pope was reneging on his promise, really was an absolutely impossible job.

Mai's suggestion of a new bull is important to note. The pope had also offered the same.[172] If the original dispensation was perfect, there was no need of any new bull. The fact that the offer was made by both pope and the Imperial lawyers is proof that Henry was right and the original dispensation was flawed, though whether to such a degree that it invalidated the marriage contracted on the basis of it was another question.

Katherine's lawyers were deliberately seeking to mislead in the articles they drew up. They referred to the dispensation (singular) which was read out at Henry and Katherine's wedding (the bull) and also to the dispensation (singular) which covered public honesty and affinity. The bull only referenced

---

171 D'Avray, *Dissolving* p. 236.
172 LP 4.4858. Mendoza had advised Katherine to refuse the offer because accepting a new bull would prove the original was flawed.

affinity. The brief – the authenticity of which was still in doubt – does not specify affinity or public honesty.[173]

Exchange rates varied but a ducat was between 4s 5d and 5s in English money so the sum Charles was being asked to spend to get his majority in the college of cardinals was at minimum £12,150 in contemporary terms or around eighty-five million pounds today.

The Emperor's comments about the annulment being a point of family honour demonstrate his utter contempt for justice and God's word. Whether the "marriage" was valid or not was a point of law. Canon and divine law might disagree on the verdict but neither regarded individuals as above them.

Evidence presented to the legatine court included four witnesses to Prince Arthur saying at breakfast on the morning after his marriage, that he was thirsty having been in Spain that night. The witnesses were the Duke of Norfolk, the Duke of Suffolk, Lord Fitzwalter, and Anthony Willoughby.[174] Thomas Boleyn testified that though he was not in the room at the time, he heard the comments the same morning because they were the talk of the palace – something easy to credit. Suffolk also noted that Maurice St John, who was in the room serving breakfast and who accompanied Arthur and Katherine to Ludlow, said that Arthur was fit and well until Shrovetide in 1502 and that it was said that his illness then was made worse by the exhaustion he was suffering because of his over-exertions in the marital bed with Katherine. This was hearsay evidence as St John was dead and unable to confirm it, but he was Arthur's cousin and closer to him than the average servant so it is quite likely that this speculation existed in 1502, even though no medical authority today would regard it as a clinical diagnosis![175] Amongst other witnesses were a Spaniard who had served at the papal court for thirty years as a doctor of canon law and who confirmed what Ghinucci had said about the erroneous dating on the brief. Archbishop William Warham described how he had told Henry VII that for Prince Henry to marry his brother's widow was against divine law and would incur God's displeasure. Warham said that he had recommended the young Prince enter a protest against it when he reached puberty. Asked why, in this case, he had gone along with the "marriage" when Henry VIII came to the throne, he said he was persuaded by Bishop Richard Foxe and the fact that the pope had issued a dispensation.

What is interesting is that they were discussing the consummation at all. The decretal commission had required three aspects of the bull only to be

---

173 D'Avray notes that the Latin for dispensation regarding public honesty could be construed as plural and should be given the existence of the brief but it is singular in the rest of the clause and this is the usual understanding of the word. At this date, it was far from certain whether the brief would be accepted as evidence.

174 In 1501, when this incident took place, neither Norfolk nor Suffolk were Dukes, but waiting gentlemen of Arthur's Privy Chamber.

175 The same claim was made by Sir Davy Philips, Vice Chamberlain to Arthur from 1495 onwards and who was at Ludlow throughout the marriage. LP7.128.

investigated.[176] If the trial had been conducted in line with the decretal commission, Henry should have had his verdict within a couple of days. What had prevented that happening was the presentation of the brief which meant that even if the bull was ruled invalid, another case would need to be started to establish whether that was sufficient to validate the "marriage."

Why was the trial prorogued on the 23rd when it was anticipated that a judgment would be given? According to Cavendish, Campeggio used the excuse of the Roman legal holidays to halt the trial saying: "I will give no judgement herein until I have made relation unto the pope of all our proceedings whose counsel and commandment in this high case I will observe."[177] Regarding the discussion of Katherine's virginity, he said "the truth in this case is very doubtful to be known." He said he was unsettled by Katherine's refusal to participate and her determination to appeal if the verdict did not go her way and that the only reasonable way forward was to get further direction before "we proceed to judgment definitive." It must be wondered whether he was able to look anyone in the eye as he said this given he did not expect the court to re-convene in the autumn.

A letter from Wolsey provides the true answer. He notes that at eight in the evening of the 22nd, a packet of letters arrived from Gregory Casale and his colleagues in Rome dated the 9th.[178] They told him that Katherine's appeal of May 10th had just been received at Rome having been sent via Margaret in the Low Countries and that the pope had been advised he had no option but to accept it and advoke. There was no point in Henry allowing a verdict to be issued in London if it was to be overturned at Rome because there would be no rescuing of the situation thereafter. Wolsey and Campeggio had discussed this and, it should be assumed, had an urgent meeting with Henry. Wolsey wrote: "such discrepancy and contrariety of opinions hath here ensued in the said cause, that no manner of hope is the same opinions can be in any brief time groundly trutinate, weighed, and every part to the point pondered, but that it must require more long demur and tract of time for the profound digesting of the same." Therefore, it had been agreed to prorogue in order "to study and excogitate some other ways and means here for remedy of the Kings cause" and since the matter was urgent, this prorogation should be immediate for "the sooner it come, the better it shall be for the experimenting of other things." [179] Thus when the announcement was made, Henry was not in the least surprised and it must be assumed that he had already arranged for Suffolk to make his protest aware that witnesses would spread the story. Cavendish, being merely a gentleman usher, was not privy to the correspondence so was surprised.

In canon law a bastard could be legitimised by his or her parents marrying (provided that conception had not taken place in an adulterous union) or by the father acknowledging them in a public document signed by three

---

176 See March 1528 Comments
177 Cavendish, *Wolsey*, p. 229
178 LP 4.5761 to 5767
179 SP vol. 7 pp.193-197

witnesses (provided that the father would not by so doing disinherit legitimate progeny).[180] The Emperor was not placing his illegitimate daughter in line of succession and she had been born before he married Isabella of Portugal so he was entitled to act as he did.

There was no expectation that George Boleyn would install himself at the Bedlam hospital for the mentally ill. He was not a doctor or an administrator. It was a position which paid a salary and he was expected to appoint somebody to do the work on his behalf using that money and pocket the difference. Such a use of offices was widespread in Tudor times.

August 1529

Events

- a peace treaty is signed at Cambrai on the 5th (LP 4.5829, 5832, 5833). At Henry's direction, Wolsey spends considerable time analysing the clauses in various treaties (LP 4.5875, 5881-5885, 5890, 5891, 5893, 5894).
- parliament is summoned to meet in November, the first time in six years (LP 4.5837). The French ambassador predicts that it will do what the pope has not (LP 4.5862).
- Imperial forces enter the Papal States and the pope is forced to pay large sums to get them to leave (LP 4.5848). Cardinal San Croce is captured. Imperial troops prepare to do battle for Florence (CSPS 4.1.191). The pope expresses sorrow that peace has not come despite his agreement to the Treaty of Barcelona (LP 4.5841).
- in Rome, the English press the pope to give sentence in Henry's case directly and not pass the matter to the cardinals. The Imperial ambassador notes this would be legal but opposes it because he fears the pope still favours the English. He blames the recently arrived Bishop of Tarbes for the idea (LP 4.5854, 5877, 5909).
- the bishops of London and Bath, Katherine's advisers, despair of her "wilful behaviour" and refusal to listen to legal advice (LP 4.5845, 5868).
- Thomas Boleyn obtains a wardship (LP 4.5906.4) and William Brereton is given Merseley Park with an annuity of £3 (LP 4.5906.20).
- Katherine is sent a legal bill for her defence in Rome by the Emperor (CSPS 4.1.100).
- the Duke and Duchess of Suffolk publicly display the bull they obtained over a year before regarding the legality of their marriage and children (LP 4.5859).
- the pope writes to Henry on the 29th suspending further action until at least Christmas telling him this this is to give him "time duly and carefully to

---

180 The pope could also legitimise children regardless of circumstances. In 1396, Gaunt's children were legitimised as the Beauforts despite being born in adultery.

consider an affair of so great moment and importance as this is and thereby settle it without the vexation and trouble which suits of law engender and produce." He admits that he had previously granted the commission to have the case heard in England by two cardinals but says "since which at the instance of our most dear son in Christ, Charles most Catholic King of Spain, and elected emperor" he has changed his mind. He notes "we whose intention it never was, nor is it to subject Your Highness's person, who have so well deserved of us, and of the apostolical see, to any censures or penalties whatsoever.. hereby rescind, declaring them to be null, of no power, efficacy, or validity."[181]

- at Waltham, a Cambridge don by the name of Thomas Cranmer meets up with two of his old colleagues, Stephen Gardiner and Edward Foxe. Their discussion of the annulment results in Cranmer being introduced to the King and him being taken into royal service.[182]

Comments

The timing of the Suffolks' action was deliberate. Although the legatine court had in theory only been prorogued for the summer, there was clearly a fear that it would not re-open and that meant there was some doubt whether Henry would get his annulment, at least in the near future. Brandon was very close to Henry as his brother-in-law so his actions would have been discussed with him in advance. Authors often like to claim that the Suffolks disapproved of Anne because they loved Katherine but whatever their feelings on the subject might have been, the principal point for them was that their son was next in line to the crown after Henry and Katherine's daughter, Mary, a girl noted to be small for her age and often unwell so not certain to survive to maturity. Their objection to Henry marrying Anne – if it existed – was most likely because the prospect of Henry having more children reduced the chances of their own son becoming king. In the event, their son died in 1534.[183]

Over the years, the Imperialists came up with all manner of stories about Cranmer, a number of which still appear in books today such as him being the Boleyn family chaplain or even one of Anne's relatives. The true account of how he became involved with Henry was written by his secretary of more than twenty years, Ralph Morice, for Archbishop Parker. Morice had the account from Cranmer himself and knew both Henry and Anne, and since Parker had been Anne's chaplain, any false claims would have been spotted. Morice tells how Cranmer said to Gardiner and Foxe that in the "common process and

---

181 Herbert, *History*, p.398
182 John Nichols, *Narratives of the Days of the Reformation* (1859). Henry was at Waltham from August 2nd to 10^{h}, LP 4.6965.
183 For more details of the bull refer to May 1528. Had it not been for the ongoing war with Scotland, some might have held that the son of Henry's elder sister had a better claim but that line had been excluded in 1513, see Was Anne the cause of the breakdown of Henry's 'marriage' to Katherine?

frustratory delays of these your courts the matter will linger long enough and peradventure in the end come unto small effect." Instead they should have the subject discussed by the divines or theologians who were not only better positioned than canon lawyers to interpret the scriptures but had a pastoral duty to resolve the doubts which assailed the King's conscience. Two days later, Foxe passed on this advice to Henry who asked to meet Cranmer. Whether the idea of asking foreign universities was mentioned at this point is unknown: it may simply have been the plan to seek a verdict from English divines. The theologians would have included both those who were supposedly active in ministry such as bishops and those who were academics. Given that at this period the universities were religious foundations rather than secular institutions, Cranmer's suggestion can be seen as a way of undermining the pope by obtaining opinions from those who had pledged loyalty to him. What is certain is that Henry offered Cranmer – a doctor of divinity and lecturer at Jesus College, Cambridge - a job studying the annulment case and writing a report, providing him with lodgings while he worked at Durham Place, the house occupied by Anne's father though owned by the Bishop of Durham.[184] Henry asked Thomas to "let Dr Cranmer have entertainment in your house at Durham Place for a time, to the intent he may be there quiet to accomplish my request and let him lack neither books, nay anything requisite for his studies."[185] Some three months later, Cranmer accompanied Thomas Boleyn on a mission to the Emperor, probably in the hope that he would have the opportunity of arguing Henry's case and convincing doubters, though, he most likely assisted as a chaplain on the trip. Cranmer's introduction to Henry was one of the turning points of English history and Cranmer would go on to lead the English Reformation, playing a key role in the provision of the Bible of English to the masses, to the introduction of worship in English and in the establishment of Protestant theology. At this stage, however, he was a minor figure – a scholar and a trainee diplomat.

The peace of Cambrai was one of the most notable achievements by women during the century. Henry's reaction to it was mixed. He would have preferred the honour of being peacemaker in Europe to fall to Wolsey and himself and their exclusion from the talks was humiliating. At this point, the

---

184 Until 1529, this was Wolsey and from February 1530, Tunstall. Exactly when Wolsey gave up the see is unclear. There was talk of him exchanging it for Winchester, the bulls for which he received in March 1529 (LP 4.5429 but also of him holding both (LP 4.5313). In July 1529 Henry gave the revenues of the see to Thomas Boleyn but as he had to ask Wolsey to get his staff to collect the money, it appears Wolsey was still in post or at least responsible for maintaining the administration of the see until a new bishop was appointed (LP 4.5816). Boleyn reckoned the revenues to be £2400 per annum which was less than the figure of £3023 quoted in the *Valor Ecclesiasticus* of 1535. Boleyn's involvement in the diocese explains why his kinsman received a parish there the month before.
185 Foxe, *Acts and Monuments,* vol. 5 p.541; Lauren Mackay, *Among the Wolves of Court* (2018) p.134

exact terms were unknown but it was believed to have been based on the Treaty of Madrid and be highly favourable to the Emperor. That Henry was consulting Wolsey about this through to the end of the month – albeit through his secretary Gardiner rather than face to face – indicates he had not given up all faith in him. Wolsey was involved in advising about payment schedules, risks of Francis being compelled to join the Emperor in any future war against England and about the situation in Italy, Hungary and Scotland.

September 1529

Events

- suspicion mounts in England against the French, especially since Francis delays over a month before sending Henry a final copy of the Treaty of Cambrai (LP 4.5912, 5931, 5942).[186]
- Florence dismisses Renée's husband who had been commander of their forces (CSPS 4.1.134).
- Henry Percy and his wife hurl accusations at each other. Percy refuses to live with her (LP 4.5920).
- Katherine's announces her intention of serving Henry with the summons to Rome in person. Wolsey steps in to persuade her otherwise and she swears before Wolsey and Campeggio that she has no wish to see Henry cited. Henry congratulates Wolsey on obtaining this promise and hopes it will prevent further action at Rome (LP 4.5936).
- Wolsey's influence declines sharply as the month progresses. Jean du Bellay, Bishop of Bayonne is upset that Wolsey's trust is being betrayed by his servants labelling them turncoats (LP 4.5945).
- Katherine warns Chapuys, the new Imperial ambassador to England, not to call on Wolsey saying: "The Cardinal's affairs are at this moment rather embroiled." She tells him that Henry's motivation for the annulment is not conscience or lust but malice (CSPS 4.1.160).
- the Emperor arrives in Italy and the pope sets off to meet him. Imperial forces besiege Alessandria and threaten Florence and Ravenna (LP 4.5963).
- Henry writes to the pope accusing him of breaking his promise and says if he can relax divine law at will, there is no reason that he cannot do the same with human (LP 4.5966).
- Jean du Bellay prepares to leave England to visit his sick father. Wolsey, who is still working on the annulment, asks him to speak to Francis about obtaining opinions from the French divines (LP 4.5945).
- Campeggio travels with Wolsey to take his leave of Henry at Grafton (LP 4.5953). Cavendish records that a disgruntled Anne intervenes to prevent

---

186 It was sent on the 9th and received on the 13th, LP 4.5931, 5942.

Henry and Wolsey spending time together.[187] At Wolsey's advice, Henry treats Campeggio kindly on grounds that the Emperor may yet upset the pope which will incline the latter to help him (LP 4.5945).

Comments

Cavendish's account of Wolsey's meeting with Henry at Grafton is often repeated by writers on Anne Boleyn. Recording a report from a waiter, Cavendish alleges that over dinner, Anne criticises the cardinal and says that if any other man had behaved as he had done, he would have lost his head. Henry replies in surprise, "ye are not the cardinal's friend?" Next morning, Anne arranges a picnic to keep Henry away from Wolsey and the King never sees the cardinal again. It is a dramatic story of a vindictive and scheming woman, but is it true? Cavendish detested Anne and saw her malign influence everywhere. He was at Grafton but not at the dinner where Henry and Anne would have been attended by trusted staff from Henry's Privy Chamber. They would have been on hand to carve meat, refill goblets, offer finger bowls and towels for hand washing, move dishes. This would have involved some noise but probably not a huge amount. Cavendish does not give any indication of the number of people dining, whether it was just Anne and Henry or a group. The nearest servants would have been maybe six feet from the King. Could they have heard every word spoken? Is it likely that if they could, they would have run out to regale Wolsey's gentleman usher (a.k.a. butler) with the conversation? The Privy Chamber staff were a highly privileged, tightly knit group not prone to such behaviour: indeed, this episode is unique. Moreover, according to Cavendish, Anne had been nursing a vendetta against Wolsey for years. He claims she hated him. Yet, Henry, in love with her for at least two years and who had spent considerable time with her, apparently had no idea of her feelings! Was Henry utterly stupid or Anne the greatest actress who has ever lived – or could it be this whole episode is a fabrication by Cavendish? As for his statement that Anne kept Henry from Wolsey, the record shows quite clearly that Henry spent the entire morning with his Privy Council including Thomas Wolsey. Whether Cavendish, who wrote his account when an old man years after the event, was genuinely confused about what happened or whether he was seeking to blacken Anne's name, is unknown. Either way, the story is untrue.

Nicholas Harpsfield, biographer of Thomas More, writing in 1557 offered an alternative explanation for Wolsey's fall. He claimed that Stokesley, the Bishop of London, was so angry at being rebuked by the cardinal that "to incense the King's displeasure toward him, busily travailed to invent some colourable device" and did so by suggesting that Wolsey was not really supporting Henry's policy of annulment.[188]

---

187 Cavendish, *Wolsey*, p.133
188 Nicholas Harpsfield, *The Life and Death of Sir Thomas More, Knight* (1557) ed. Katherine Stearns and Alexander Taylor (Dallas, 2020) p.17

October 1529

Events

- Jean du Bellay urges Francis to write to Henry on Wolsey's behalf. He says the French are so hated in London that he is mocked whenever he goes out (LP 4.5983, 6003, 6011). He reports Anne has made Henry promise not to see Wolsey again because she believes that if he did, he would feel sorry for him and regret his action (LP 4.6011).[189]
- Campeggio departs. His baggage is searched at Dover. Henry supports the custom officials and tells Campeggio that he should not be surprised his subjects are so angry given the way he has behaved (LP 4.5995, 6016).
- on the 9th, Wolsey is accused of breaching the Statutes of Provisors and Praemunire. On the 22nd, Wolsey surrenders his pensions and property to Henry and confesses to the offence (LP 4.6017, 6035).
- the pope tells Henry that marriage to a brother's wife is not against divine law and cites Innocent III in support. He claims popes can dispense for good causes and that if Katherine was a virgin, Henry's conscience should be clear (LP 4.5994).
- Anne's uncle, the Duke of Norfolk, replaces Wolsey as chief of the Council with Charles Brandon, Duke of Suffolk, taking over on any occasion when he is absent (LP 4.6019). Thomas More becomes Lord Chancellor (LP 4.6018, 6025). Chapuys tells Norfolk that the Emperor will be glad to see Henry served by a man of noble birth which will guarantee his competency (LP 4.6026). Jean du Bellay jokes that closer than either Norfolk or Brandon is Anne Boleyn who is above all (LP 4.6019).
- Henry takes Anne, her mother and Henry Norris to view Wolsey's treasure. He admits that he expected more (LP 4.6028, 6026).
- Henry sends Wolsey a ring via Henry Norris. Jean du Bellay wonders if Wolsey will be reprieved and allowed to retire (LP 4.6030).
- Ghinucci, the Italian Bishop of Worcester, returns from Spain where he has been ambassador to tell Henry the Spanish brief appears to be forged. Ghinucci then departs for Rome (LP 4.5987, CSPS 4.1.182).
- Chapuys claims that Henry "often confessed" to witnesses that Katherine was a virgin when he married her (CSPS 4.1.182). He claims Henry is the richest prince in Christendom (CSPS 4.1.196).
- Katherine says that she is not interested in evidence from the Bible or in legal opinions, she simply "knows she is Henry's wife." (CSPS 4.1.182).
- Florence comes under siege. The artist Michaelangelo Buonarotti becomes engineer in charge of defences.

---

189 Le Grand, *Histoire*, vol. 3 p.375

Comments

At the time, it was suspected that Campeggio's bags were searched for property that it was thought Wolsey might be sending overseas for safe keeping as the penalty for breaking Praemunire was forfeiture of goods. Later historians have suggested that the officials were seeking Henry's love letters to Anne Boleyn which went missing and turned up in the Vatican. This is unlikely. It is unknown when they were stolen and if Henry had believed that such personal correspondence was in the bags, he would have sent one of his own Privy Chamber to retrieve it and not left the job to customs officials. A more probable explanation is that they were seeking the brief which the pope had sent with Campeggio which promised a resolution in Henry's favour, something they would not find because Campeggio had burned it on the pope's instructions. Henry said that searching the baggage of foreigners leaving the country was usual which was true in theory, though ambassadors were normally exempt. Searching Campeggio's baggage could be considered indicative of a lack of respect being paid to the pope though it had happened to him before.[190]

Katherine's retort that she did not care what the Bible said sums up her attitude to the whole annulment affair. Her response was always that if the pope said it was all right, that was it. A strange response for a pious woman.

Chapuys' claim that Henry often told people that Katherine was virgin when he married her should be taken with a hefty pinch of salt. What sort of conversation might have been in process for Henry to chip in with this piece of information? Are we to credit that Henry walked round the court collaring people to tell them, "she was a virgin, you know." Did he come out of his bridal chamber shouting "I was the first!" For Katherine to have known about it, the supposition must be that she was there which would suggest he launched into the topic of her sexual history as she was standing next to him. It is hard enough to believe that Henry would have discussed this highly personal fact with anyone but absolutely impossible to believe that he did it "often" with multiple "people." In 1531, Chapuys asked Katherine to name some of those who might have heard him say this and she struggled to do so, eventually suggesting that there might be possibly some merchants (CSPS 4.2.754). Did Henry drop it into conversation while shopping? On the plausibility scale, the event is surely sub zero.[191] The other two people she suggested were Philippe de Bregilles, who had served as the head of Margaret, Regent of the Low Countries', household in the 1510s and visited England briefly on her behalf in February 1514 (LP 1.4726) and Hernando Lopez de Escoriaza who was Katherine's doctor from 1515 to 1529. Quite how the subject of her virginity could have come up in a conversation with the former is a mystery, and it would only be hearsay evidence anyway. The latter would have been more

---

190 Campeggio's bags had also been opened and searched in 1520, see *Hall's Chronicle* pp.592-593, 759

191 Henry did admit to Chapuys that he had once made a joke about the matter at a men's drinking party (LP 6.351)

likely to have heard from Katherine herself. Neither man had any knowledge of the events of 1501-2 when she was married to Arthur and significantly, neither was willing to testify to the story that they had heard Henry make any such comment. Given that both were loyal Imperialists with Doctor Escoriaza being still employed as the Emperor's personal physician, their refusal to support Katherine's assertion is significant. She either lied deliberately and then got caught out, or she exaggerated in the hope it would help her case.

The pope's reference to Innocent III is bizarre. The case in question relates to 1201 when Innocent III permitted the newly converted Latvians who had married their brother's wives before they became Christians, to keep them because he feared that refusal would cause the new converts to turn from Christ.[192] This was very different to Julius II's dispensation issued to a Christian man to deliberately marry a brother's wife. Innocent also required that the children of such unions be considered heirs to the deceased not living brothers in line with Deuteronomy, a requirement not mentioned by Julius. Innocent's acceptance of the situation, as with Gregory's when Augustine asked the same question in the sixth century, did not imply that this form of marriage was right or acceptable: indeed, the Fourth Lateran Council condemned it in 1215. Rather, it was an expression of the principle given by Jesus on the cross: "Father, forgive them for they know not what they do."[193] Inncoent wrote: "we concede that they enjoy marriages they contracted with their brother's widows, provided they contracted with them to raise up seed to the dead brother in accord with the Mosaic law [Deut. 25:5], when their brothers died without offspring. But we forbid such marriages after they have come to the Faith." Either the pope was appallingly ill informed about the facts or he lied to Henry in the vain hope that the King would not know any better.

There were two statutes of Praemunire, one in 1357 and another in 1393, as well as two statutes of Provisors passed in 1351 and 1390.[194] All would feature in the annulment crisis, particularly the later two. Their purpose was to prevent English subjects being summoned out of the country to answer for matters which should be handled by English courts; to stop judgments reached overseas being applied in England in prejudice of the Crown and English legal system and to ensure that appointments to English bishoprics and abbacies be subject to free election by English patrons and churchmen and not the whim of the pope whereby they might fall into the hands of non-resident aliens. The 1393 Act included the famous statement that "the crown of England has been so free at all times that it has been in no earthly subjection but only immediately subject to God" going on to say that "the laws and statutes of the realm" were not to be "defeated and avoided" by the pope or any other foreign usurper. It

---

192 The full text of the bull appears in Book 4 of the Decretals of Gregory IX, Title XIX C.9. For an English translation see John T Noonan, *Marriage Canons from the Decretum of Gratian and The Decretals, Sext, Clementines And Extravagantes* (1993)
193 Luke 23:34
194 Praemunire is Latin for protecting or safeguarding.

made the purchase, pursuance or implementation of bulls, excommunications or processes from Rome without royal assent illegal.[195] From the late fifteenth century, Praemunire cases were increasingly being raised by laymen seeking to protect themselves against church courts. However, they were also used for political purposes as with Cardinal Beaufort in 1431 and Bishop Pecock in 1457.

The Praemunire accusations against Wolsey relate to two appointments to vicarages he made on 27th July 1529 and 2nd December 1523 respectively when others were the patrons and to his obtaining bulls to be legate for life in 1524, which was said to have infringed the royal prerogative.[196] The charges were nonsense and simply an excuse to make a public example of Wolsey by destroying his power and taking his goods. It was a sign that Henry would not be thwarted and the action was aimed more at the pope than Wolsey himself. Wolsey, after all, was the representative of papal power in England and after the debacle of the legatine court, respect for that institution was at a nadir. That Henry still cared for and respected Wolsey is shown by Cavendish's story about the ring. According to him, Norris told Wolsey that Henry had said his treatment was "for no displeasure that he beareth you but only to satisfy more the minds of some whom he knoweth be not your friends" and urged him to "take patience" and expect to be restored to "a better state than ever ye were." The wording given may have been coloured by Cavendish's hatred of Anne but the joy of Wolsey on receiving the ring was no doubt genuine. It was a gold ring which Wolsey "knew very well for it was always the private token between the King and him whensoever the King would have any special matter dispatched at his hands." Cavendish, a witness to the event, noted that Wolsey sent back to Henry his fool as that was all he had to give.[197] The fool was known as Patch, probably because of the clothes he wore, and was evidently a large man and one who was extremely loyal to Wolsey. Cavendish reports that it took a team of armed men to drag him away from Wolsey's side. Patch remained with Henry until July 1535. The significance of Henry sending the head of his Privy Chamber and his closest personal servant, Norris, would not have been lost on Wolsey or bystanders either.

The belief that Henry was the richest prince in Europe was widely held and not lost on the lawyers who were debating the annulment and working out their bills.

---

195 For more on these acts and the texts, see Henry Gee and William Hardy, *Documents Illustrative of English Church History* (1896) pp.103-125; Arthur Ogle, *The Tragedy of the Lollards' Tower* (1949) pp.228-230.
196 Clement VII granted Wolsey the legateship for life in thanksgiving for his support in the recent papal election, LP 3.3549, LP 4.15. Neither Wolsey nor Henry had requested it.
197 Cavendish, *Wolsey*, pp.105-107. For more on Patch see John Southworth, *Fools and Jesters at the English Court* (1998) pp.65-69.

Wolsey's departure left Henry – to use a thoroughly non-academic expression – up the creek. He was not entirely without a paddle but was stuck in the mud.

The question of Anne's political influence has been much debated over the years, particularly in and since the twentieth century due to a greater interest in powerful women. However, whilst her influence no doubt waxed and waned over the years and in relation to different subjects, it is worth considering the comments of the Duke of Norfolk in 1540 who expressed total astonishment at the idea that any monarch would accept advice from a woman and that suitors would be advised to seek the assistance of a royal mistress.[198] He had been witness to Anne's rise and fall and was at the heart of Henry's court. If Anne had been all powerful, would he not have regarded such a situation as being feasible, even if he had private reservations about the wisdom of it?

November 1529

Events

- the Emperor and pope meet at Bologna. Sforza, the dispossessed Duke of Milan, is restored and reconciled to Charles V (CSPV 4.524, 570; LP 4.6065; CSPS 4.1.235, 242).
- Parliament opens in London. The chronicler and M.P., Edward Hall, says it was "for reformation of certain exactions done by the clergy to the lay people."[199]
- Francis makes the first payment of £10,657.7s.4d toward the debt of £426,315.12s.0d which he owes Henry (LP 4.6040).
- Dr Mai, the Imperial ambassador in Rome, reports that Henry is seeking advice from Jews (LP 4.6068). Richard Croke is sent to Italy to obtain such as well as information from other libraries.
- the pope sends a nuncio to Henry asking him to fund a crusade against the Turk. The nuncio chosen is Paul Casale, younger brother of Henry's Italian ambassador in Rome, Gregory (LP 4.6069). Henry declines to contribute saying he would not trust the Emperor not to use the money to wage war in Italy instead and notes the Turk is in retreat anyway. He says it is the Emperor's responsibility to assist his brother Ferdinand fighting the Turk and not his. Henry comments that the church in England has sent considerable sums to Rome for the purpose of defeating the infidel over the years and suggests that if the pope wants money, he use that (CSPS 4.1.224).

---

198 SP vol. 8 p.258
199 *Hall's Chronicle*, p.760

- Henry horrifies Chapuys by saying that Luther had brought "many truths" to light and expresses his intention of reforming the church in England to abolish pluralities and annates. He says the pope and cardinals should live their lives on the basis of the Gospel and not "inordinate ambition" and declares that the only power possessed by the clergy is absolution. If the pope refuses to follow Bible teaching, Henry will denounce him as a heretic (CSPS 4.1.224).
- Katherine reiterates her claim that as her first marriage was not consummated, there was no affinity so there is no issue with the validity of her union with Henry (CSPS 4.1.224).
- ever suspicious, Chapuys claims Katherine is being sent to reside at Richmond because there is plague there (CSPS 4.1.211). He complains to the Emperor that he has not been given enough money to bribe Henry's Privy Councillors (CSPS 4.1.216).
- Mai reports that although some cardinals have now changed sides due to Imperial gifts, others are angry they have not received pensions from the Emperor (CSPS 4.1.215).
- Cardinal Farnese offers to try to persuade the Emperor to urge Katherine to accept reality and become a nun (LP 4.6069).
- Henry Norris obtains a number of manors, stewardships and offices to boost his annual income by £76.16s.6d (LP 4.6072.24). William Boleyn is granted a parish surrendered by Wolsey's son (LP 4.6072.24). Richard Page, Gentleman of the Privy Chamber, is made solicitor for subsidies in kersies in survivorship with Fitzwilliam (LP 4.6072.18). Norfolk's mother gets the wardship of Katherine Broughton, the younger of the two Broughton sisters (LP 4.6072.21).
- Carew and Sampson are sent to ratify the Treaty of Cambrai on Henry's behalf. They are warned not to raise the subject of the annulment with the Emperor but if he should mention it, they should advise him that it would not be in Imperial interests to try and thwart Henry (LP 4. Appx.240).
- Jean du Bellay comments that Norfolk is not finding it so easy to do Wolsey's job because Henry "is not so easy to manage as is supposed" (LP 4.6041).[200]
- Henry returns Wolsey to his protection and has More tell Parliament that "according to his desert he hath had a gentle correction" (LP 4.6059).[201]

Comments

Annates – effectively the first year's income of new bishops – were originally introduced to fund the crusades so Henry was right in his statement that the pope had presumably misappropriated the money raised if he needed more at this point. It is, however, common for charges to be introduced for a reason and then to become permanent. Income tax was introduced in England

---

200 Le Grand, *Histoire,* vol. 3 p.384.
201 *Hall's Chronicle,* p.764

in 1798 to fund the war against Napoleon and it continues to be charged, despite the war ending in 1815.

Even if Katherine's first marriage had not been consummated – and only she and Arthur knew and both told different stories – it was against canon law for a widow to marry her husband's brother which is why a dispensation was needed. The bull dispensed for affinity so, if there was none as she said – and many argued affinity began with vows not intercourse – the dispensation was invalid and her "marriage" to Henry was null and void. No affinity did not mean no problem.

The idea of consulting rabbis was attributed to John Stokesley, at this time Archdeacon of Dorset but set to become Bishop of London in 1530 (LP 4.6105). He was a very learned man and a leading Greek and Hebrew scholar.

The Duke of Norfolk does not appear to have been an original thinker or a dynamic individual. That he found it hard to step into Wolsey's shoes is not surprising. Wolsey had worked a prodigious number of hours. Not only did Norfolk have problems keeping up, it should be recalled that he had only a fraction of the workload for Wolsey had also been deeply involved in legal and church affairs.

Cardinal Farnese's view is worth noting because he would go on to succeed Clement VII as Pope.

Richmond was one of the premier Tudor palaces. Katherine had stayed there on many occasions. Being sent there was not a punishment.

December 1529

Events

- George Boleyn and John Stokesley are sent to France to obtain learned opinions regarding the annulment (LP 4.6073)
- Thomas Boleyn is created Earl of Wiltshire in England and Earl of Ormond in Ireland (LP 4.6085). At the celebration dinner, Anne sits next to Henry which breaches rules of precedence as Henry's sister is present who outranks her both as a Dowager Queen of France and a Duchess as well as being of the blood royal (CSPS 4.1.232).
- a list of articles is drawn up against Wolsey by various lords including Anne's father (LP 4.6075).
- Chapuys reports that the pope is hated in England and that there is much anger in England at the advocation. He predicts that papal dispensations will be outlawed (CSPS 4.1.228, 232).
- Venice agrees to restore Ravenna and Cervia to the pope and to make peace with the Emperor (LP 4.6101).
- the pope admits that Julius II's failure to investigate whether any urgent cause existed before he issued the dispensation in 1504 was a "serious mistake" and warns the Emperor that if this is proved, he may not be able to help Katherine – a comment which leave the Emperor open mouthed with

horror. The pope continues to express sorrow that the Emperor will not let him grant the annulment (LP 4.6103).
- Wolsey grants George Boleyn an annuity of £333 8s from the revenues of Winchester and St Albans where he remains bishop and abbot respectively (LP 4.6115). He asks Anne to intercede for him in a letter sent via Thomas Cromwell and carried to her by Richard Page. Wolsey tells Cromwell "All possible means must be used for attaining of her favour" and assuaging her "displeasure." He says "this is the only help and remedy." (LP 4.6076, 6114)
- Norfolk admits that nothing will stop Henry obtaining his annulment (CSPS 4.1.232).
- Henry proposes to marry his illegitimate son, the Duke of Richmond, to Norfolk's daughter (CSPS 4.1.228).
- Chapuys sends the opinions of Fisher and Tunstall to the Emperor recommending they be forwarded to the pope and cardinals who can thereby save time discussing the case and simply pronounce in Katherine's favour on the basis of what those two have written. He says the only way to stop Henry marrying Anne is for the Emperor to "interfere actively to prevent it." (CSPS 4.1.232, 241)
- Chapuys proposes trying to get Norfolk on side by seeking to arrange a match between his son and Princess Mary. He admits that Katherine would not sanction such a match because she hates Norfolk and wants to injure him (CSPS 4.1.232).
- the Milanese ambassador opines that the cause of the annulment crisis was Katherine's reproductive history and says that if it had been known in advance, the "marriage" would never have been allowed because having children is the principal purpose of matrimony. He therefore supports the annulment (CSPS 4.1.241).
- Anne Boleyn complains that her youth is being wasted: "I have been waiting long and might in the meanwhile have contracted some advantageous marriage out of which I might have had issue which is the greatest consolation in this world; but alas, farewell to my time and youth spent to no purpose at all." (CSPS 4.1.224) She then leaves court for Christmas (CSPS 4.1.241).
- Katherine asks that the Emperor's wife write to Henry in her support (CSPS 4.1.224).
- a rumour is spread amongst Henry's enemies that he is seeking to marry one to whom he is in closer affinity that he was with Katherine (CSPS 4.1.232).
- Chapuys predicts Wolsey will be restored because he is so gifted and Henry admires him so much. He claims Henry has only acted against Wolsey to please Anne Boleyn. Chapuys hopes Wolsey will be restored because he thinks this would mean Katherine's restoration and Anne's death (CSPS 4.1.232).

- the pope refuses Henry's request to make Ghinucci and John Casale cardinals (LP 4.6095).
- Wolsey is taken ill at Christmas. Henry sends his own physician, Doctor Butts, to him together with a ruby ring. Anne sends a tablet of gold from her waist to him also. Henry says "I would not lose him for twenty thousand pounds" and tells Butts to "tell him, that I am not offended with him in my heart nothing at all" and to reassure him of his favour.[202]

Comments

There is no evidence that the Emperor's wife ever wrote to either Katherine or Henry in either English or Imperial archives.

It must be presumed that Anne's decision to go home to Hever for Christmas was her attempt to put some emotional pressure on Henry: he did not send her away. If she was unhappy that the situation was not resolved at this point, it was probably as well that she did not know that she would have more than three years to wait. Her comment about wanting children is interesting and suggests this was her goal rather than power. If the story about Henry's warm words about Wolsey are true – and Cavendish was not there to hear them so was only reporting what the doctor said – it might be that she found this irritating and this influenced her decision to depart.[203]

Anne's reply to Wolsey's request for support came five months later and consisted of kind words but no promise of action. Was this because she hated him or because she did not know Henry's wishes on the subject? Her correspondence with Wolsey prior to the legatine court appears warm and friendly and she was a frequent visitor to his home so the image of her as a vengeful Valkyrie is hard to justify. It is likely that she was upset by the failure of Campeggio and Wolsey to pronounce the annulment but this was not their fault. Henry had led Anne to expect a swift solution. His letters had spoken of "this well willing legate" (LP 4.4894) and "shortly you and I shall have our desired end" (LP 4.3990) and just prior to Campeggio's arrival he had allowed her to make wedding plans (CSPS 3.2.550). Bryan acknowledged that her confidence in her situation was high which was why he was not prepared to risk Henry's wrath by telling her otherwise. It seems that Henry deliberately let her continue in this frame of mind which must have made her displeasure all the greater. Did he ever explain the facts to her? We simply do not know.

The affinity rumour related to Henry's relationship with Mary Boleyn and is the first reference to this. Canon law said that fornication produced ties

---

202 Cavendish, *Wolsey*, vol. 1 pp.287-288.
203 Cavendish declines to repeat Anne's "very gentle and comfortable words and commendations" to Wolsey during his sickness. It is strange how his memory for what Henry said was crystal clear some three decades later and utterly befogged when it came to Anne.

of affinity in the same way as marriage.[204] Thus, for Henry to seek to marry the sister of a woman he had once slept with was the equivalent of him wanting to marry his wife's sister. Chapuys did not give any source for the story.

Thomas Boleyn was given an earldom because he was about to go on a major embassy and Henry wished him to be able to converse with people of similar rank more easily. His elevation meant that his son became Viscount Rochford and Anne Boleyn, the Lady Anne Rochford.

The articles against Wolsey were presented to the Commons but not discussed. Henry had no wish to allow them to debate the matter which might make it impossible for him to restore Wolsey in future.[205] Other people who fell went to the Tower and then the block but Wolsey would be pardoned, given a handsome settlement which he negotiated and allowed to continue as the second most senior churchman in the land, all clear proof of Henry's continued love and regard for him.

Chapuys inhabited another dimension when it came to politics. As Anne's uncle, Norfolk had a vested interest in the annulment and neither Chapuys nor the Emperor were in any position to determine whom Mary might marry. The idea was absurd. The point most worthy of note is that it represents a rare occasion of Chapuys portraying Katherine in a bad light. Hating someone as a result of a squabble over precedence and wanting to injure them is hardly the behaviour of a pious saint, his usual description of her. As for his belief that a returned Wolsey would somehow order the execution of Anne Boleyn and cause Henry to fall in love with Katherine again, he must have been seeing pink pigs floating past his window. What did he think Wolsey had been trying to do for the last two years?

---

204 Theologically, this was based on Basil of Caesarea's comment in his Letter to Diodorus that the prophet Amos condemned a man and his son for sharing a woman (Amos 2:7). On the basis that she could not have married both men, Basil reasoned that the Levitical prohibitions must apply to concubines. Croke reported he had located this letter in March 1530 (LP 4.6250).

205 *Hall's Chronicle*, p.768. Cavendish's claim that they were and Cromwell defended Wolsey was totally untrue.

1530

January 1530

Events

- Anne sends Henry a New Year's gift of a ship containing a damsel being tossed about with a diamond.[206]
- following the end of the twelve days of Christmas, Katherine and Henry separate not seeing one another until March (CSPS 4.1.265, 270).
- the Emperor tells his brother that he suspects Henry will commit the "folly" of marrying Anne regardless of what he or the pope says. He expresses mistrust of the pope's friendship with Francis whom he believes is encouraging Henry in the annulment simply to spite him. He says that if Henry does marry Anne without papal consent, it will be grounds for war but predicts any conflict will be waged in Italy with Venice, Milan, Ferrara and Florence being recruited by Francis and Henry to attack the Emperor via Naples (CSPS 4.1.245, LP 4.6142).
- Ghinucci and Croke spend the month searching libraries in Italy and consulting rabbis, including Marc Raphael (LP 4,6140, 6145, 6149, 6150, 6153, 6156, 6173, 6174).
- the House of Commons presents a list of grievances against the clergy. These include excessive probate and mortuary fees, parishes being left without a resident priest and the fact that anyone who criticises these practices is liable to prosecution for heresy (LP 4.6183).[207]
- in a four hour long heart-to-heart, Henry tells Jean du Bellay, Bishop of Bayonne, that extreme perplexity is ruining his life (LP 4.6169).
- Wolsey grants Henry Norris an annuity of £200 from his estates (LP 4.6182-6183).
- Thomas Boleyn obtains the wardship of Robert Knyvet and becomes Keeper of the Privy Seal at a salary of £365 per annum (LP 4.6163. He departs

---

[206] Jasper Ridley, *The Love Letters of Henry VIII* (1988) p.42-3. It is letter V in the series and calendared at LP 4.3325. The letter is undated but Anne would not have had the money to purchase such an object in 1527 and she spent the New Year of 1528 and 1529 with Henry so it must be assumed that he would have thanked her in person for any gift rather than by letter. The letter was written in French and Ridley notes that the word "estrene" applies only to a gift sent at New Year although he is inclined to believe it was sent in 1528. Authors who have thought the love letters were stolen before Campeggio left have naturally tended to favour an earlier date but there is no evidence whatsoever when the theft took place. Given no use of them was made in the annulment case by the Imperialists, they may not have been taken until after her death.

[207] *Hall's Chronicle* pp.765-766. For further discussion on the grievances and their relation to other petitions, see Stanford Lehmberg, *The Reformation Parliament* (Cambridge, 1970) pp.81-86; Ogle, *Tragedy*, pp.297-330.

with Cranmer and Stokesley on an embassy to the Emperor with instructions to explain Henry's position (LP 4.6111). The Duke of Norfolk, Boleyn's brother-in-law, requests that as Boleyn is of a very timid rather than warlike disposition, extra security is provided for his journey (CSPS 4.1.255). Toward the expenses of the trip, Boleyn is given £1,743 8s (PP p.19).
- Norfolk says of the annulment: "the King is so bent upon it that I do not think anyone but God could turn him aside." Anne's father adds: "I cannot persuade myself that the Emperor wishes to hinder a plan which would be so beneficial to this kingdom." (CSPS 4.1.249)
- Anne Boleyn returns to court mid month and receives gifts of jewellery from the French and lays on an entertainment for their ambassadors (CSPS 4.1.250, 252).
- Chapuys expresses the hope that Campeggio and Mendoza[208] will be able, together with other cardinals, to convince Cranmer, Stokesley and Lee that Henry is wrong and Katherine right. If not, fear of Katherine's relations will be needed to support her position (CSPS 4.1.252).
- Henry tells Chapuys that he is "marvellously pleased at being relieved of the very close alliance with the French into which the cardinal had dragged me." He adds that as soon as Francis' sons are returned "I am released from all bonds." (CSPS 4.1.250) He adds that he is worried about getting all the money back which France owes him but this does not stop him surrendering half his annual pension from France as his contribution to the ransom which Francis is due to pay the Emperor (CSPS 4.1.252).
- representatives of the Duke of Saxony arrive at court. Unable to discover their business, Chapuys initially reports that they have come to offer German support for the annulment (CSPS 4.1.241). A week later, he has changed his opinion and tells the Emperor he thinks they have come to propose a marriage for Mary which means they will have to support Katherine for fear of Mary being declared illegitimate (CSPS 4.1.252). Another week passes and this time Chapuys tells the Emperor that they have come to intercede for Wolsey (CSPS 4.1.255).
- Henry enjoys a party on Twelfth Night being entertained by the Duke of Suffolk's minstrels and gambling. His expenditure – or losses – during the month on cards, dice games, shovelboard, bowls and such come to £787 10s. He does not forget the poor entirely giving money and clothes to three blind men at a cost of £5 6s plus £1 10s to four people who came to him in need at York Place. Mark Smeaton, Francis Weston are amongst the staff granted new hose (PP pp.15-21).

Comments

Thomas Boleyn's trip represented a major investment by Henry. The £1,743 8s was almost two per cent of his annual income and in today's money

---

208 His predecessor as ambassador and now Bishop of Burgos.

around £12.2 million. It is no wonder that Henry was angry when it failed. Chapuys said Boleyn was sent because his French was better than Norfolk's though his greater diplomatic experience no doubt helped (CSPS 4.1.250). Whether he needed extra security or it was requested in order to give prominence to his entourage cannot be known,

The office of Lord Privy Seal was one of the four great offices of state because it provided frequent access to the King.[209] Thomas Boleyn replaced Tunstall, the Bishop of London, who was moving on to become Bishop of Durham. Aside from Henry Marney holding the position briefly in 1523, it was a role which traditionally was given to a churchman so Boleyn's appointment marked a shift in Henry's practices. After Boleyn, the position would remain in the hands of the laity. It is likely that the appointment confirmed practice rather than was wholly new because Thomas Boleyn was residing at Durham Place – the home traditionally of the Lord Privy Seal – from the summer of 1529, the time at which Tunstall was sent to France.

The extent of Henry's gambling is extraordinary. It was Christmas and entertainment was inevitably largely indoors due to the weather, but it was a huge amount. He was either extremely unskilled or desperately unlucky or he lost deliberately as a means of treating his staff. Of course, it should be remembered that the accounts only note expenditure not income so we do not know how much Henry won.

Writers who like to quote Chapuys should always remember that his information was often inaccurate and based on sheer guesswork. In March, he was forced to admit to the Emperor that he had got the information about Henry's contribution to the ransom wrong. Henry had generously donated a full year's pension – 100,000 crowns, i.e. £21, 315. 12s (CSPS 4.1.270). Many more examples will be given in the months that follow. Historians beware!

The grievances of the Commons against the clergy were strongly felt. Henry Guildford revealed that a fee of 1000 marks (£666 13s 4d) had been demanded to process probate when William Compton (Henry Norris' predecessor as Groom of the Stool) died in 1528. As his estate was valued at £1689, this represented a fee of forty per cent. At this time, all inheritance came under church courts not civil. Mortuaries were payments required for a burial and where cash was not forthcoming, clergy would take goods to the value in lieu even from poor families whose survival might be put at risk by loss of livestock or food. In 1511, Richard Hunne had refused to give the bearing sheet in which his child had died on grounds it was the property of the deceased and so not his to give. He was promptly charged with heresy and in 1514 died in prison, the coroner recording a verdict of murder.[210] Popular opinion believed

---

209 For more on court organisation, see David Starkey, *The Reign of Henry VIII* (1985) pp.7-10.
210 In 1504, Bishop Nix had recommended to Archbishop Warham that anyone who threatened the church with Praemunire should be prosecuted as a heretic: Hunne had done just this. Daniel Gosling, *Church State and Reformation* (PhD thesis 2016) p.181

Hunne had been persecuted and killed by the church. Hall devoted eight pages of his chronicle to the case and Foxe, who regarded Hunne as a martyr, twenty-two. Whether this was the case or not, it was widely believed and it generated immense anger which lasted for years culminating in this complaint and subsequent passage of Acts to establish a sliding scale of fees for both mortuaries and probate based on ability to pay.[211]

The Emperor's comments about war show that he had no desire for conflict with England or any intention of waging war in defence of his aunt. Given his mistrust of Francis keeping the peace, he was in no hurry to risk turning England completely against himself. He wanted to keep his options open.

Henry's discussion with Jean du Bellay is important to note. Although a diplomat, Du Bellay was a sincere churchman and he chose to maintain the King's confidences – something which might be disappointing for later historians but which indicated Du Bellay's respect for the privacy of pastoral conversations whether they took place in or outside a formal confessional. It cannot be known if Henry had similar lengthy talks with English clergy but certainly his behaviour shows a great degree of trust, even friendship, with the Frenchman and the depth of Henry's upset at this point. Cynics today might laugh at the idea of Henry having a conscience but Henry's faith was real and he was prepared to humble himself and seek guidance from a bishop as he grappled with the age old problem or why those who sought to do God's will did not find the path easy.[212] It also demonstrates Henry's commitment to personal growth. Muhammad Ali once said that a man who thought the same at fifty as he did at twenty had wasted thirty years of his life. Henry was not afraid of asking questions and wrestling with the answers. He developed. This is in complete contrast to Katherine who showed no inclination to open her mind at any point. She typified the "as it was in the beginning, is now and ever shall be" attitude.

Anne's gift reflects the doubts she had experienced since the collapse of the legatine court but also her resolution to carry on. Henry describes it as "so beautiful that nothing could exceed it" and thanks her for the submission she has made in the letter sent with it. "The demonstrations of your affection are such, and the beautiful words of your letter are so cordially phrased that they

---

211 For a succinct appraisal of the Hunne case, see Gwyn, *The King's Cardinal*, pp.34-41; for a thorough one see Ogle, *Tragedy* pp.11-169. The acts may be found in *Statutes of the Realm* vol. 3 (1817) pp. 285-289. The probate fees were: 6d if the value was below £5, 3s 6d if between £5 and £40 and 5s if over £40. Mortuary payments were 3s 4d for any testator with moveables worth from £6 13s 4d to £30, 6s 8d if they were worth between £30 and £40 and 10s if over £40. Children, non-householders and wayfarers were exempt from mortuary fees which meant that a situation such as Hunne's case could never happen again.
212 Jean du Bellay was almost the same age as Henry and had trained in civil and canon law though he was best known as a theologian. He also had lengthy heart-to-hearts with Wolsey indicating the trust in which he was held.

oblige me to honour, love and serve you for ever, imploring you to agree in this same firm and constant purpose… Beseeching you also that if I have in any way offended you, you will give me the same absolution for which you ask." Clearly they had not parted on the best of terms. It is unfortunate that we do not have Anne's letter or know the whereabouts of the diamond. If on the damsel, it would have signified her constancy in the sea of difficulties whereas if on the ship, it would have signified her confidence that Henry would rescue her from all her trials. If hanging as a pendant beneath the ship, the diamond would have represented the strength of their relationship against all that might assail it.

February 1530

Events

- Ghinucci and Croke continue their researches. They obtain the support of the learned Franciscan and Venetian senator, Francesco Georgius, who writes a book on Henry's behalf (LP 4.6192, 6193, 6197, 6205, 6209, 6229)
- Wolsey is granted an official pardon and awarded a handsome settlement. Chapuys says Henry bears Wolsey no ill will and would reinstate him but for Anne (LP 4.6199, 6202, 6213, 6214, 6220).
- the Bishop of Tarbes witnesses the Emperor's coronation by the pope. He says the pope looked very doleful and signed so much that his cope shook! Afterwards the pope confides to the Bishop that the more time he spends with the Emperor, the less he likes or trusts him (LP 6244).
- Carew and Sampson report that the pope has told them that he granted things he should not have done because he was afraid of Henry (LP 4. Appx.253).
- George Boleyn writes to Dr Bennet in Rome asking for news of what is happening with the annulment "I would hear the truth of everything as it is, without any manner covering. ...They of this country say nothing, whether it is because they cannot or else they will not, I cannot tell." (LP 4.6539).[213]
- Chapuys employs bribery and spies to try to find out the reason for the Germans being at court. He announces there are two separate groups and neither is from the Duke of Saxony. He thinks one may have come to seek money from Henry but reckons that not enough had been given to arm the Germans against the Emperor (CSPS 4.1.257, 265). He suspects the other has come to intercede for Wolsey, a motive he attributes to the newly arrived French envoy. He suggests that the Emperor have the Germans

---

213 The document has been mistakenly calendared as July but George returned to England in the last week of February. In his letter, he talks of hoping to be home soon.

- searched when they pass through the Low Countries to see if that will reveal the truth (CSPS 4.1.257).
- Henry Norris obtains the wardship of his wife's fourth cousin once removed, Richard Fiennes, age eight and heir to the barony of Saye and Sele (LP 4.6248.24).
- George Boleyn returns from France saying Francis appears less friendly since the Treaty of Cambrai (CSPS 4.1.265).
- Wolsey is taken ill. Anne is reported to have sent him her best wishes for a speedy recovery, Chapuys says he does not believe this and suspects it was some trick for she is "an accomplished mistress" of intrigue (LP 4.6199).
- Fisher composes another book on Katherine's behalf which Chapuys dutifully sends to the Emperor to pass to the pope. He says that given Fisher is English and supports the Queen, his opinion is more worthy of attention. Other works by Englishmen have been written at Henry's request so are obviously unfair and erroneous (CSPS 4.1.257).
- Henry says he intends to pursue his annulment through theologians not jurists (LP 4.6205).
- the Countess of Worcester is safely delivered of a child and her nurse and midwife are rewarded by Henry (PP p.22).
- Chapuys tells Henry that his letters to the Emperor never contain "anything that is not absolutely true." He does not record Henry's response (CSPS 4.1.265).

Comments

The Countess of Worcester was a friend of Anne Boleyn's but it is likely that Henry paid the bill for the nurse and midwife because he had agreed to be godfather to the child. He would do the same for Bridget Harvey in March 1532 for the same reason.

George Boleyn's request to Dr Bennet indicates the confusion which he and Anne both felt about what was happening. They had probably thought that with Wolsey out of the way, all would be well and it was not. George had been in France for some three months and would have been corresponding with Anne so it is clear she was starting to wonder if fair words were being used to keep her sweet while he was frustrated at the lack of news from Rome. It exhibits a situation at odds with Chapuys' portrait of a manipulative and politically active Anne who was pulling all the strings.

The wardship of Richard Fiennes is a reminder of the wide kinship network which operated in this period. Today, few people could name their fourth cousin once removed but then it was usual to record such links. Partly this was because of the need to ensure marriages did not occur within prohibited degrees but also it was because any relative, however remote, was worth pursuing if they had an inheritance or were influential in some area, particularly the court. Richard Fiennes' prospects would have seemed assured when he became the ward of the King's closest personal attendant.

Georgius was one of the most respected scholars in Italy and his support for Henry's case was of great importance in persuading other theologians and lawyers to take the case seriously. Many recent writers have tended to dismiss the opinions gained by Henry's men in Italy because they have followed Chapuys' frequent claims that the only people who supported Henry were threatened or bribed to do it. This is demonstrably untrue and reflects Chapuys' personal belief that anybody who was sane must back Katherine. The great Jesuit scholar, Edward Surtz, who studied the Italian opinions admitted that he began with this assumption too but found "the academic stature and the professional integrity of Henry VIII's adherents were almost unimpeachable."[214]

March 1530

Events

- Croke continues his researches despite being hampered by Imperial agents buying up books he needs (LP 4 6250, 6266, 6287).
- Reginald Pole is praised by Henry for his stout, and unsolicited, defence of the annulment in France. Henry is delighted by "the fact that you are acting so energetically there on behalf of the royal cause" and that Pole, whose learning he admires, has now become "patron of his cause" (LP 4.6252, 6253).
- Thomas Boleyn arrives at Bologna on the 14th and meets the pope and Emperor. The latter refuses to listen to the case and says he will only accept the pope's decision, whatever that is. A delay in proceedings until September is agreed (LP 4.6285, 6293).
- the pope threatens those who speak or write against Henry's "marriage" with excommunication. He follows this with a letter to the Emperor asking him what he wants him to do next (LP 4.6279, 6284).
- the Bishop of Tarbes spends considerable time with Thomas Boleyn who tells him that if Anne becomes Queen, she will be loyal to Francis. The Bishop says that the pope has told him three times that he wishes Henry would simply resolve the situation through the English church, marry Anne and leave him out of it, provided that the verdict does not question papal authority (LP 4.6290).
- the university of Cambridge votes in support of Henry (LP 4.6259) but at Oxford, women pelt the royal commissioners with stones. The women are jailed (CSPS 4.1.270). Archbishop Warham steps in to urge Oxford to answer the King's question promptly (LP 4. Appx.254).

---

214 Edward Surtz, *Henry VIII's Great Matter in Italy* (Xerox University Microfilms, 1974) p.iii

- the pope creates the Emperor's confessor, Loaysa, and Mendoza, ex-ambassador to England, cardinals. Henry requests that Ghinucci be made a cardinal, something the pope had promised to do in February 1527 (LP 4.6292).
- Henry Norris is granted seven manors (LP 4.6301. 22).
- the new French ambassador, Jean Joachim, visits Wolsey who is preparing to move to York where he remains Archbishop. He admits that Francis has set him the task of brokering a solution to the annulment impasse which is acceptable to both Henry and the pope. So far he has not had any ideas (CSPS 4.1.279).
- an investigation into paperwork regarding the marriage of Francis and the Emperor's sister, Eleanor, raises concerns that a false statement in a letter of 7th February regarding exhibition of a document might invalidate the papal bull of dispensation, and hence the marriage, itself. The same Imperial lawyers express their concern about mistakes and erasures in the paperwork generally (CSPS 4.1.280).
- Henry loses over £60 in dice games with the Duke of Norfolk and the sergeant of the cellar (PP p.32).
- Thomas Boleyn asks Lord Lisle to either return the ewer he sent him to review or to pay for it saying he is but a "poor man" and cannot afford the loss (LP 6.589.12).
- the pope passes the annulment case to the Auditor of the Rota, Paul Capisucio, giving him authority to cite anyone – including Henry – and fine those who do not attend Rome when asked 10,000 ducats (£2250). He further warns that if Henry marries again, he will be excommunicated and all England placed under interdict (LP 4.6256).

Comments

Henry's efforts to uncover documents relating to his union with Katherine had clearly made the Emperor nervous. He had earlier asked his own ambassador in Rome to check the registers for a copy of the dispensation issued for his own marriage. When he learnt that it could not be found, he ordered a copy to be made and sent (CSPS 4.1.98).

In his 1539 *Pro ecclesiasticae unitatis defensione*, Pole claimed that Henry had ordered him to support the annulment in Paris and that he had immediately written back asking Henry to send somebody else because "any kind of death would have been easier for me than to undertake this task."[215] The records prove this was not the case.[216] Pole altered his view as Henry's position against the papacy hardened. The fact that in 1535, Henry requested

---

215 Joseph G Dwyer (trans), *Pole's Defence of the Unity of the Church* (Maryland, 1965) p.192
216 LP 4.6252 says *non rogatus* i.e. unsolicited or without being asked.

Pole's opinion indicated that he was unaware of any deep seated opposition from him. Pole either lied in his book in order to present himself as a papal champion or he composed it while afflicted with amnesia.

The fine for refusing the citation to Rome was equal to about sixteen million pounds in today's money. One can only hope that there were no ladies present when someone told Henry. They might have needed ear defenders.

The dice games took place on separate days. That the King would sit down and play a game with the Duke of Norfolk is perhaps unsurprising but that he was also happy to sit down with a servant is revealing. Henry was a proud king but he was not a snob.

It is easy to forget just how huge a task Henry had set Croke. We are used to being able to obtain copies of ancient documents at a click of a button, generally in modern English with footnotes to explain difficult words or highlight variations between manuscripts and often with links to related texts. Croke had none of this. He had to root through libraries with limited catalogues, copy out documents in very bad light which might be in poor condition, translate them – without an array of printed dictionaries to hand – and copy them out again several times so that couriers could convey them to ambassadors and to England. Croke was an argumentative, moaning old man with a persecution complex, but his achievements and dedication were extraordinary. His health was not good and his funding was totally inadequate and most of those he met were deliberately obstructive, yet he soldiered on and obtained vast amounts of relevant evidence for Henry's case. He studied Greek and Hebrew texts, documents by the better known Church fathers such as Tertullian as well as by the Cappodocians. The breadth of learning was phenomenal encompassing both Roman Catholic sources and Orthodox. In modern times, Croke would have earned a knighthood.[217]

That Clement VII was not a man of integrity is indisputable. Here we have him urging Henry to marry Anne in one breath and then threatening him with excommunication if he does.

Thomas Boleyn thought he was a poor man? To quote a certain modern retired tennis player, he could not be serious. Lord Lisle's jaw must have dropped.

April 1530

Events

- Katherine says that she fears the pope will let the case drift on forever (LP 4.6337).
- Thomas Boleyn advises that the Emperor is "stiffly set" in his opposition to the annulment and blames Chancellor Gattinara and Chapuys for this

---

217 For more on his work, see Surtz, *Henry VIII's Great Matter in Italy*

intransigence. He claims "the pope is led by the Emperor so that he neither will nor dare displease him" and says the cardinals and most of the canon lawyers in Italy "be much set to maintain the pope's authority." The only hope he can see is that the Emperor is unpopular in Italy and that his Spanish and German subjects hate one another. Boleyn comments "if this hatred increase as it daily doth... and specially, if any thing shall be attempted in Italy by the French King, I suppose the pope would soon revoke from the Emperor." Whatever happens, he thinks Henry could benefit, either from the Emperor needing his friendship and so becoming more tractable over the annulment or else the pope no longer being too afraid to grant it (LP 4.6355; SP vol. 7 pp.234-5).

- a list of cardinals is prepared for Henry. It reveals 32 Italian, 5 French, 4 Flemish, 3 Spanish, 4 German and 1 English (LP 4.6362).
- Henry has a furious exchange with Chapuys about the Emperor's interference in English efforts to obtain learned opinions and his refusal to listen to Boleyn and Stokesley. Chapuys retorts that only four or five people in England support Henry and says the Emperor could hardly be expected to take seriously a man who had a vested interest in the annulment. Henry predicts that the pope will never give a decision in his favour as long as the Emperor's army remains in Italy. Norfolk asks if the Emperor would wage war if Henry married Anne. Chapuys says there would be no need as the English would rise up and depose Henry themselves (CSPS 4.1.290).
- Henry establishes a new household for Katherine. Suspicious, Chapuys suggests that the additional staff are to help him spy on her (CSPS 4.1.290).
- Henry invites his son Richmond to court where he makes an excellent impression on everyone appearing "very handsome and well dressed, learned for his age, charming and well mannered" as well as athletic like his father (LP 4.6307).[218]
- Joachim who – to Chapuys' intense annoyance – spends much time at court, reports that Henry is considering withdrawing his ambassador from the Imperial court knowing the Emperor would then make a tit-for-tat withdrawal of his from England. Henry thinks this is his best chance of getting rid of the objectionable Chapuys (LP 4.6307).
- an impassioned Spaniard, Dr Garay, sends the Emperor an account of what he calls Henry's "diabolical device" which involves Jean du Bellay's brother, William de Langais, inviting doctors of the University of Paris to dinner, explaining Henry's case and then giving them a financial reward for signing their agreement. He describes this as pure "wickedness and malice... this increasing and scandalous evil ... these iniquitous practices to which the infidel Turk himself, the bitterest enemy of Christianity

---

218 Le Grand, *Histoire*, vol. 3 p.412

would not resort." He reveals that the bribe provoking this support is one crown per head (CSPS 4.1.285).
- Henry plays tennis with Francis Weston and loses four matches. He also experiences a musical mood having five pairs of virginals delivered to different palaces. (PP p.37).
- the Marquis of Mantua marries Julia of Naples, the second cousin once removed of the Emperor. The bride does not attend the ceremony. The Emperor gives them 50,000 crowns as a wedding present (just over £11,000) and elevates the Marquis to Duke of Mantua (CSPS 4.1.283, 284).
- two servants of the Marquis of Mantua arrive in England. Henry welcomes them and rewards them. He also purchases two mules from George Boleyn (LP 5 p.749).
- Bessie Blount's husband, Gilbert Tallboys, dies.[219]
- Henry denounces the pope as simoniacal (LP 4.6307).
- Croke obtains a verdict in Henry's favour from the influential and respected Prior Thomas Omnibonus (LP 4. Appx.265).
- whilst staying with Fitzwilliam, Wolsey tells Cavendish that he only confessed to breaching the Statute of Praemunire because "there was a continual serpentine enemy about the King that would, I am well assured, if I had been found stiff necked, [have] called continually upon the King in his ear (I mean the night-crow) with such a vehemency that I should with the help of her assistance [have] obtained sooner the King's indignation than his lawful favour: and his favour once lost (which I trust at this present I have) would never have been by me recovered. Therefore I thought it better for me to keep still his loving favour, with loss of my goods and dignities, than to win my goods and substance with the loss of his love and princely favour, which is but only death."[220]

Comments

The one crown bribe – worth between 4s 8d and 5s – was probably less than the cost of the dinner. At this time, a skilled carpenter earned 6d a day, his assistant 4d, so this bribe which Garay claimed was so offensive amounted to around two weeks wages for a working man. In purchasing terms, it would buy a bottle of ink, a ream of paper, a shirt and a bucket.[221] Garay's protest is therefore hard to take seriously. By contrast, in Italy, Imperial agents were offering from 500 to 3000 ducats to people for opinions, equivalent to between twenty and a hundred years' wages for a working man.[222] If Katherine's case was so certain, one can only wonder why they felt the need to pay so much more. Croke's average payment for opinions for Henry across Italy was 7s and

---
219 Beverley Murphy, *Bastard Prince* (2001) p.110
220 Cavendish, *Wolsey,* p.316
221 LP 4.6788
222 For example, LP 4.6581, 6669.

this covered the cost of the parchment, ink and the scrivener's wages.[223] Writers today who like to highlight examples of Henry's team making payments using similar terms of disapproval might like to ponder how much real difference there is between paying a scholar for his opinion and paying a celebrity today to endorse a product.

The fact that England had only one cardinal (Wolsey) who lived almost a month's journey from Rome, was a reminder to Henry of what an uphill struggle he faced trying to obtain anything from the papal court. The Spanish, German and Flemish cardinals were obviously Imperial and over half of the Italians lived under Imperial rule, which meant that the Emperor could expect a majority of almost two thirds on any vote. Even if Henry had succeeded in obtaining hats for Ghinucci and John Casale as he repeatedly tried to do, the situation would not have changed.

The privy purse records show that Henry used his tennis courts at Windsor and The More for eleven days during the month. The court at The More may have been recently built since a payment of £60 was made in the same period for building works and there is no evidence that Wolsey, who previously held the property, enjoyed the sport.[224] Weston was playing having been hired by George Boleyn but no reason is given for this. Clearly George made a bet with Henry about the matches but whether George chose to employ Weston because he himself was injured or simply not a very good player is unknown.

Although it is unclear why the Marquis of Mantua had sent members of his staff to England at this time, it is likely that they were bringing one or more horses.[225] The Marquis was reputed to have one of the finest studs in Europe and Henry used to purchase animals from him via his agent Gregory Casale.

Tallboys' death gave Henry the opportunity to marry Bessie and legitimate Richmond by getting the Archbishop to declare the bull used to unite him to Katherine invalid due to one of the many legal technicalities that flawed it. Such a course of action would not have involved denying papal power to dispense and could have been grounds for a compromise agreement with the pope. Why did he not do this? It was not just love for Anne or fear of Katherine having the verdict overturned in Rome or concern that his own subjects would not accept the idea. Henry genuinely believed that God's law could not be changed by anyone: it was a matter of faith. As Hall observed, although Katherine's supporters "largely spake and said that she [Anne] so enticed the King, and brought him in such amours, that only for her sake and occasion, he would be divorced from his Queen, this was the foolish communication of people, contrary to the truth."[226]

---

223 LP 4.6502, 6521, 6567, 6670, 6702, 6728.
224 A further £60 toward building work at The More was spent in June 1530, PP p.40
225 A payment for three horses appears in June 1530, PP p.54. It may be that the payment on the last day of April signalled their arrival and that on June 22nd the actual purchase.

Richmond was approaching his eleventh birthday when he came to court. Aside from Henry's deep love for his son which meant he desired his company, his presence signified to contemporaries that the King was capable of fathering healthy sons – if he had the right woman.

Henry's denouncing of the pope as a simoniac was significant. It was a claim he would make frequently in the years to come and have proclaimed in print. Chapuys pronounced himself appalled by such impiety but even the most devout Roman historians have been unable to provide any evidence to contradict Henry's statement. Clement VII bought his way into the papacy – like most of his predecessors and quite a few of his successors. The importance of the claim rests in a decree of the Council of Constance and the papal bull, *Cum tam divino*, which specifically states that any man who obtains the papacy through simony is not to be regarded as a valid pope. As Jenkins wrote of the bull: "It would be difficult to establish the legitimacy of any of the popes from Alexander VI. down to much later times if its searching tests were applied, while all the cardinals who derived their appointment from them would be equally illegitimate."[227] Moreover, the problem was recognised in Rome. Around 1525, Petrus Gammarus, wrote a commentary on the bull for Clement VII, stating that he had done so following a discussion with a cardinal who had observed that the bull provided any man "a handle for effecting a schism."[228] Gammarus told the pope bluntly that his own election was indeed simoniacal, an opinion which prompted Clement to seek the bull's abrogation though it remains in force today. Henry was not, therefore, just engaging in a bit of name calling but denying the legitimacy of Clement VII, both as head of the church and as a judge of himself or anyone else. Particularly notorious as a simoniac was Julius II, the man who had granted the dispensation for Henry and Katherine in the first place. It was a justification for the break with Rome.[229] Not only was the dispensation *ultra vires*, it was the work of an invalid pope.

Joachim's comment about Henry considering means to rid himself of Chapuys is worthy of note. Chapuys, arguably, was the cause of most of the delays and acrimony relating to the annulment affair. Not expelling him may be considered Henry's greatest mistake.

---

226 *Hall's Chronicle*, p.757. Bessie's would be suitor, Leonard Grey, in May 1532 took care to verify that Henry had no such intentions before seeking her hand (LP 5.1049).
227 R. C. Jenkins, 'The Pre Reformation Theory of the Papacy', *The Churchman*, May 1893 p.394.
228 Ibid.
229 Session 43 of the Council of Constance in 1418 declared that all simoniacal elections and promotions were "rendered null by the law itself and nobody acquires any rights through them. ...We decree, moreover, that both those who give and those who receive money in this matter of simony automatically incur the sentence of excommunication, even though their rank be pontifical or cardinalatial."

May 1530

Events

- Roderigo Niño, Imperial ambassador at Venice, discovers the English have a letter from the Bishop of Verona – a man close to the pope – which they are using to encourage experts to give their opinion on the annulment issue. He dismisses the views of those with whom they have spoken as unimportant saying that it would only matter if the University of Padua decided for Henry because that was a renowned institution whose verdict would have great authority and force. He regards such an eventuality as impossible (CSPS 4.1.311, 312).
- following pressure from Imperial agents and mindful of the trade they do with England, Venice votes not to allow its subjects to write in support of either Henry or Katherine (CSPV 4.578-580).
- Henry convenes a gathering of theologians to examine heretical books and to list translation errors and concerns with Tyndale's New Testament. He advises that an approved English New Testament is needed but not until the people abandon heresy. Amongst the books banned are Tyndale's *Obedience of a Christian Man* and the *Parable of Wicked Mammon*. (LP 4.6367, 6377, 6391, 6401-6402, 6487, CSPS 4.1 302, Hall *Chronicle* p.771).
- from Norwich, the bishop reports that people were clamouring for an English New Testament (LP 4.6385).
- Imperial agents seek to prevent Henry's men from obtaining opinions in Italy, France and England (LP 4.6360, 6369, 6378, 6392, 6399, 6408). Cardinal Salviati – cousin of the pope – tells Gregory Casale that the pope has no wish to hinder Henry's cause but it is essential that people are not allowed to discuss papal authority, a matter on which there has been agreement for centuries (LP 4.6412).
- the pope issues a brief saying people may only write or speak about the legitimacy of Henry's "marriage" as their conscience dictates and in accordance with canon law, advising those who accept money or other favours to do so that they face excommunication (LP 4 6396, CSPS 4.1.364). This is done at Katherine's request, forwarded by the Imperial ambassador, who believes this means all opinions will favour her (LP 4.6379). In August, the pope re-issues this ban saying people must not be "led by hatred or fear or favour, to allege or advise, in writing or verbally, nor to presume to attempt anything else by word or deed..to misinterpret the canon law or Holy Scriptures in favour of one of the said parties."[230]
- efforts are made by the Emperor's agents to persuade the Bishop of Chieti to travel to England to convince Henry that Katherine does not deserve this treatment for she is a good woman (LP 4.6378).

---

230 Pocock, *Records* vol. 2 pp.644-645.

WHY IT TOOK SO LONG 331

- Ghinucci tells Henry that the pope has never seen the Spanish brief and has no idea where it is. Apparently, nobody will send it to him for examination (LP 4.6387).
- in Italy, a list of names of people who support Henry, together with thirty learned opinions, is snatched from the home of Father Francis by papal and Imperial agents. The documents are burnt. The leading perpetrator tells the pope and Emperor that force was not used and the information was willingly handed over (LP 4.6405). Croke and Father Francis start again and by the end of the month, fifty-four doctors of theology and canon law plus fourteen senior Observant Friars have resubscribed their statements which are safely on their way to Henry (LP 4.6407, 6413).
- Thomas Wyatt is replaced as clerk of the King's jewels (LP 4.6418.8).
- Florence continues to hold out against Imperial forces. The Prince of Orange brings eleven thousand more men to the city. The pope, who is funding the exercise, expresses his dissatisfaction that Florence has not yet fallen (CS{S 4.1.296, 320).
- Katherine tells Chapuys that she thinks fear of the Emperor will stop Henry marrying Anne but that even if he does, he is sure to regret it and will soon come back to her. She claims Wolsey was of the same opinion (CSPS 4.1.302).
- Chapuys claims that he knows many who can provide incontrovertible proof that Arthur did not consummate his marriage with Katherine, but says they are all too scared to come forward (CSPS 4.1.302).
- Francis offers one of his sons to the pope as husband for his niece, Catherine de Medici (CSPS 4.1.306).
- Charles Brandon, Duke of Suffolk, absents himself from court. Chapuys reports a rumour that he rowed with Henry about Anne accusing her of having had sexual relations with an unnamed courtier. Chapuys admits that others doubt this is the reason and promises to reveal all in a separate coded despatch as it is politically sensitive (CSPS 4.1.302).
- Francis Weston marries Anne Pickering. Henry gives the couple £6 13s 4d (PP p.46).
- Henry's spaniel escapes and is retrieved by one of Katherine's servants. Henry rewards him with 10s. Three days later, another of Henry's dogs gets lost in Waltham Forest. It is returned to him and a grateful and relieved Henry rewards the person with 5s. (PP p.43)
- Henry buys Anne various items of equipment for shooting. She evidently enjoys the pastime as additional bows and arrows follow (PP p.47).

Comments

It is interesting that Henry thought heresy needed to be eliminated before he would allow people to read the Word of God in English. Some might have thought that reading this would cure people of their heresies. Nonetheless, it did show that Anne's encouragement to him to read Tyndale's *Obedience* had been productive. One can only wonder whether Henry had kept her copy for himself to prevent her being accused of owning a forbidden work.[231]

The brief requiring people to conform their views to canon law was a gagging order on Henry because canon law had its roots in Roman civil law rather than the Bible. For example, Leviticus 18 prohibits thirteen unions, canon law banned any relationship created by blood or marriage between people across four generations as well as godparents and god-siblings. The pope's message was that canon law was of equal status with the Word of God.

Who were the "many" whom Chapuys claimed could provide "incontrovertible" evidence that Arthur had not consummated his marriage to Katherine? Were they with the couple twenty four hours of every day for the six months they were wed? Of course not. It was an empty boast.

Chapuys never did reveal all about Brandon's argument with Henry – probably because as usual he was mistaken and there had been no row. Gunn's authoritative biography of Charles Brandon points out that he had been failing to attend Privy Council meetings for some time and had lost power by January 1530, suggesting that this was mainly because he preferred hunting to politics and was content to let Norfolk do the work.

The fact that Thomas Wyatt went overseas a month after Chapuys wrote has led some to suspect that if Brandon did speak out, it was about him but Wyatt had served abroad before and he would not have seen his position in the Jewel House as a permanent role. [232] The nature of his relationship with Anne has engendered some speculation but there is no evidence for there being one other than friendship. Wyatt's home at Allington was about twenty-five miles from Hever and he was married to her second cousin, Elizabeth. They shared an interest in music and poetry and were both fluent French speakers. As a devout Christian, Anne would have had no interest in pursuing an adulterous relationship with Wyatt either before or after she became involved with Henry. Wyatt was probably closer to George Boleyn who was nearer his age than to her. When George married in 1524, Wyatt's gift to him was a translated satire on the evils of women, not the sort of present anyone would give to a casual acquaintance. Wyatt's views on the annulment are not known but he was employed by Katherine and his cousin was her ward. The two pieces of "evidence" usually brought out to suggest a link between the two are Wyatt's famous poem *Noli me tangere* which was based on Petrarch's *Una Candida Cerva* and not autobiographical and the story of the lost locket which his grandson said related to Francis Bryan and another woman. [233]

---

231 The first papal list of prohibited books dates from 1557,
232 Friedmann, *Anne Boleyn* vol 1 p.121. Wyatt had been sent to France in 1526, Italy and France in 1527 and Spain in 1529.
233 Susan Brigden, *Thomas Wyatt: the heart's forest* (2012) pp.99, 132, 139, 144, 146-9, 155, 188, 284.

June 1530

Events

- the Bishop of Tarbes becomes a cardinal (LP 4.6441).
- Cardinal Ravenna promises to support Katherine when the case comes to consistory (CSPS 4.1.340, 372).
- the universities of Bourges and Bologna vote in Henry's favour (LP 4.6448).[234] The fact that Bologna was founded by a Spaniard and the vote was unanimous with many Spaniards supporting Henry leaves the Imperial ambassador in Venice spluttering. He concludes that those who did so evidently lacked learning but comments that they should have defended Katherine's case with their swords if they could not do so with their minds (CSPS 4.1.365).
- the university of Paris begins discussions. The Emperor is told that only ten of eighty doctors there support Katherine and urgent efforts are made by Imperialists to get the pope to stop the discussion, or declare any vote against her invalid and to deprive anyone who votes for Henry of their livelihoods (LP 4.6449, 6454). In the heated atmosphere, the Imperialists liken Francis and Henry to idols of Baal (LP 4.6455). Norfolk observes that within a week support for Henry has diminished by a fifth saying it is "not without cause that this has given rise to suspicion." (LP 4.6461)[235]
- Francis suggests a treaty in which he will undertake to supply Henry with six thousand men if the Emperor attacks England over the annulment (LP 4.5790).[236]
- the pope learns from intercepted letters that Francis and Henry are encouraging Florence in its rebellion (LP 4.6450, 6452, CSPS 4.1.357). An attempt to poison the pope by a disaffected Florentine is discovered (LP 4.6476).
- Henry gathers his leading subjects to write a letter to the pope urging the annulment. Those unable to attend are visited at home (CSPS 4.1.354, 368).
- William Brereton, after spending much time riding north and east carrying the said letter for the King, replaces his father Ranulph as chamberlain of Chester (LP 4.6489, 6490.11).
- Thomas Wyatt, squire of the body, becomes Marshall of Calais (LP 4.6490.23).
- Praemunire charges are brought against six senior churchmen and eight bishops including Fisher, Clerk and Standish who support Katherine (LP 4.6458).

---

234 In the *Determinations*, Bourges is listed as Biturs.
235 Le Grand, *Histoire*, vol. 3 p.472
236 Incorrectly calendared under 1529 as is observed in Starkey, *Six Wives*, p.411.

- Katherine says that if Anne could only be kept from court for a month, she is sure Henry would return to her. She steadfastly maintains that Henry is acting because his conscience is troubled and not from lust (CSPV 4.584). At her request, the Emperor tells the pope to order Anne from court and Henry to return to Katherine's bed (CSPS 4.1.345, 360).
- in Rome, Imperial lawyers seek to have the annulment case heard immediately and Henry charged with contempt if he does not arrive or send proctors. The pope says that following Campeggio's precedent of a summer recess, nothing can happen until the autumn. Cardinal Ancona supports this. Ghinucci's discussion with cardinals leads him to believe that most support Henry. Mai, the Imperial ambassador at Rome, names Egidius and Cajetan as being amongst them and urges the Emperor to write to them persuasively and meantime send him money to buy support. He admits that most cardinals are "very cold" toward the Emperor because the promised remuneration for their support has not been forthcoming (CSPS 4.1.358, 364).
- Chapuys reports that Henry sent some fabric to Katherine to be made up into shirts for himself and that Anne lost her temper with the hapless bearer of the material (CSPS 4.1.354).
- Wolsey settles into his position as Archbishop of York where his reforming zeal and charity earn him new respect (CSPS 4.1.366, CSPV 4.584, 601). He writes to Chapuys commenting that Anne's friends believe that the longer the case is delayed at Rome, the more likely it is that the Emperor and Katherine will give up the fight (CSPS 4.1.366).
- the Mayor of London sends Anne a gift of cherries (PP p.48).
- faced with continued papal efforts to restrict free speech the English observe that the pope must "wish to lose the obedience of our island." (CSPS 4.1.342).
- Henry tells Chapuys that his job is to promote peace and not division (CSPS 4.1.366).
- Georgius is summoned by the pope to explain Henry's case (LP 4.6465).
- Anne takes Bridget Harvey into her service (CSPS 4.1.535)

Comments

Katherine's confidence that Henry would restore her and forget Anne if only Anne could be removed is very sad. Henry and Anne had spent weeks apart in 1528 with the sweat and it had not dampened his ardour. Even if Anne had died, he would not have returned to Katherine.

The importance of receiving news on how things were progressing can be seen in the Privy Purse expenses which show a reward of £1 paid to a courier who travelled post from Venice, that is, barely stopping except to change horses.

Wolsey's comment about Anne's supporters welcoming delays as furthering their cause suggests that his absence from court had meant he was less able to gauge the situation. Anne wanted to get married, not wait for ever.

Cardinal Ravenna was one of the least scrupulous men in the Curia. He would continually pledge his support to both sides and seek reward from them. He threatened to kill John Casale and in 1535 was tried for murder, blasphemy, corruption and perverting the course of justice.[237]

Mai's reference to Cardinals Egidius and Cajetan as being supporters of Henry is very interesting. Egidius was the only cardinal to be a Hebrew scholar and Cajetan was a Thomist. When the English and French drew up their lists of which cardinals they believed to be politically Imperial or Anglo-French, both thought Cajetan an Imperialist. The French thought Egidius an Imperialist while the English thought he was neutral.[238] Cajetan was the man who had expressed astonishment when Pope Julius permitted Manuel of Portugal to marry his sister-in-law, finding only his oath of obedience to the papacy led him to believe that Julius had the authority to do so.[239]

The behaviour of the Imperialists was appalling. The principles of free speech which we take for granted were not part of their vocabulary. If Katherine's case was so obviously right as they persistently claimed, why did they feel the need to go to these lengths?

The saga of the shirts might be viewed as slightly comical. It demonstrates jealousy on Anne's part and some unreasonableness since the messenger was only following orders. It is, however, interesting that Henry still thought it was acceptable to ask Katherine to make his shirts. It is likely that she had been doing this without complaint for the last three years despite the ongoing annulment crisis and that it was only by accident that Anne found out at this point. Anne must have wondered if Henry ever would leave Katherine and Katherine must have regarded such continued domestic duties as a sign that he was not yet committed to Anne. Six months later, the Privy Purse accounts record Anne purchasing linen – at Henry's expense – to be made into shirts, though it does not say whether they were to be for him or herself or anyone else.[240]

The authorisation of Francis to Jean du Bellay to promise Henry that France would offer military support in event of conflict arising from his repudiation of Katherine and anticipated marriage to Anne Boleyn was highly significant. It showed Henry was not alone and must have strengthened his resolve.

Bridget Harvey had previously been Lady Wingfield, but following her husband's death in 1525, she had remarried. In the payment records, she is

---

237 Catherine Fletcher, *Our Man in Rome* (2012) pp.170-171.
238 Pocock, *Records*, vol. 2 pp.605-6; Le Grand, *Histoire*, vol. 3 pp.299-302. The lists were drawn up in February 1529 when there were rumours that the pope was likely to die.
239 For more on this see Was Henry married when he met Anne?
240 PP p.97.

always referenced as Lady Harvey, the name which Chapuys associates with her also. Although her date of birth is unknown, her first marriage took place around 1513 and she went on to have eighteen children so it is likely she was born in the early 1490s making her closer in age to Henry than Anne.

July 1530

Events

- the theology faculty at Padua votes unanimously in Henry's favour (LP 4.6491, 6493, 6494). The Imperialists are furious (LP 4.6514). The theologians at Paris similarly vote for Henry the following day (LP 4.6497). Garay says Paris has voted against God and the Emperor and that it has consigned Henry to hell (LP 4.6503). Reginald Pole, who has worked for the Paris verdict, expresses his pleasure in it (LP 4.6505).
- on 1st July, the French princes finally return home. Bonfires and celebrations are held in London, Rome and Ferrara (LP 4.6528, CSPS 4.1.373, 374). Henry rewards the messenger who brought the news to him on the 9th with £23 6s 8d (PP p.59).
- investigations begin into Wolsey's landholdings in England. Anne's uncle, Sir James Boleyn, is involved in Norfolk, Sir George Throckmorton in Warwickshire. The total value is found to be £3205 6s. Grants from these are made including lands worth £88 5s 4 ½d to Anne's cousin Sir Francis Bryan, £30 to the Earl of Worcester and £53 6s 8d to Sir Richard Page (LP 4.6515, 6516).
- the letter signed by twenty-eight senior ecclesiastics including Wolsey, twenty-two nobles including George Boleyn, twenty-two leading gentlemen and eleven parliamentarians including Sir William Kingston is sent to the pope demanding an immediate decision in Henry's favour for the good of the realm (LP 4.6513). Thomas Boleyn does not sign the document as he is in France (LP 4.6522).
- the Imperial ambassador in Venice sneers at Henry for employing Jewish experts (CSPS 4.1.384). Henry pays ex-rabbi Marc Raphael £40 to come to England (LP 4.6541).
- the King's secretary, Peter Vannes, tells Wolsey to keep out of politics if he wishes to retain Henry's favour (LP 4.6496).
- Thomas Cranmer reports from Rome that people are too afraid to give opinions on whether dispensations from Leviticus are beyond papal authority (LP 4.6531).
- Henry Norris is robbed of 11s 8d (LP 4.6541).
- George Brooke, brother-in-law of Thomas Wyatt, comes into his inheritance (LP 4.6542.8).
- Henry departs on a three month hunting holiday – with Katherine (CSPS 4.1.373).

- Chapuys tells Henry that although he cannot have sons by Katherine, he can have grandsons when Mary marries (CSPS 4.1.373).
- Norfolk expresses a wish that Katherine and Anne were both dead so that Henry could remarry freely and have sons. Meanwhile, he suggests two French cardinals judge Henry's case – Liège and Tarbes. Chapuys says that the Emperor would never agree to them as they would not be neutral, particularly given that Tarbes gave Henry the idea in the first place (CSPS 4.1.373).
- Anne Boleyn allegedly presses Henry to marry her claiming her family could raise and fund ten thousand soldiers if necessary to defend the country should the Emperor make war as a result. She reports a prophecy that a queen would die and assures Henry "It matters not...even if I were to suffer a thousand deaths, my love for you will not abate one jot." (CSPS 4.1.373).
- Mai, Imperial ambassador at Rome, warns the Emperor that if Henry's case was decided on divine law, he would win, which is why they must act to ensure that the case is restricted to canon law (CSPS 4.1.382).
- Norfolk says that he has never seen a worse conducted mission than Thomas Boleyn's to the Emperor nor has he ever seen Henry so angry (CSPS 4.1.373).

Comments

Marc Raphael was around seventy at the time and recognised by Cardinal Egidius as one of only two Hebrew experts in Italy (LP 4.6499). He had invented a form of invisible ink some years earlier for which he received a pension from the authorities in Venice.

It is unclear whether Anne ever really thought her family could muster an army to defend England and given the source is Chapuys, it is unlikely she ever said they could. If she did think that, it suggests she was either desperate or not too well versed in reality.

Norfolk had known Henry many years and seen him in various tempers. It was probably as well for Boleyn that his daughter was so beloved by Henry or he might not have had a head on his shoulders with which to excuse his performance. The curious thing is that Norfolk told Chapuys this. Was he trying to minimise damage to Anglo-Imperial relations which were already deep in the mire by making Boleyn the scapegoat? Or was he trying to keep Chapuys on side so that the pension he received from the Emperor was likely to be paid?[241]

---

241 For an alternative view that Thomas Boleyn's mission had been successful in that it showed Henry the futility of finding a solution via the pope, see Starkey, *Six Wives*, pp.405-410.

The letter of the lords to the pope was quite lengthy but is worth quoting in part. It refers to the "very vain expectations" which have been their experience when looking for help from him and reminds him of all the universities and learned individuals which have declared in Henry's favour. It continues:

> Since your holiness is not to be prevailed upon, either by the justice of the cause, the remembrance of the good services you have always found, or by the earnest and continued requests of the best of princes, to do that which might be expected from your paternal love and affection alone, our grief is by the remembrance of our miseries and calamities increased to that immense degree that it overspreads the whole body of the realm. ... Cannot a confirmation of this so acknowledged a truth be obtained from the holy apostolical see by that prince, by whose support and assistance that see still keeps and preserves its authority, which has been shaken and undermined by so many and so powerful adversaries, till he withstood and opposed their designs, partly by his sword, partly by his pen, at other times by his commands and authority? We see that from hence a flood of miseries is flowing in upon the commonwealth and a sort of deluge of calamities overwhelming us from the disputes about succession which will soon overtake us, never to be settled without infinite slaughter and effusion of blood....[unless] he leaves a son to succeed him from lawful and true matrimony."

It makes the point that if peace was considered reason enough to grant the original dispensation, so it should be grounds to grant the annulment now. It goes on to say that if the pope refuses to help "we can make no other construction of it but that the care of ourselves is committed to our own hands and that we are left to seek our remedy elsewhere."[242]

Those who continually dismiss Henry's theological case as weak should pay attention to Mai's admission. He was the Imperial expert in charge of Katherine's case. He knew Henry was right.

It is interesting to speculate on the sentiments of Katherine and Anne as they set off on their summer break with Henry. It may be presumed they did not fraternise but did they acknowledge one another even by a glance? Henry must have been quite a man to inspire such devotion in both ladies that they would endure this situation. A thought should also be spared for the servants caught in the middle. It is easy to imagine the arguments which might have arisen as both

---

[242] Herbert, *History,* pp.448-451; Rymer, *Foedera,* vol 14 pp 405-7

parties suspiciously eyed the other for proof they were getting better food, rooms, horses etc.

August 1530

Events

- rows about the Paris verdict rage on (LP 4.6562-6565, CSPS 4.1.398, 412). Jean du Bellay, Bishop of Bayonne, calls Imperial protests a farce and wonders if he is living in fairyland. Francis orders an investigation into the behaviour of Imperial agents (LP 4.6563).
- Wolsey writes to Henry and a number of senior lords begging that his college at Oxford be maintained and his scholars there not allowed to suffer on his account. He declares: "as God be my judge, I never used the said authority contemptuously or maliciously, intending to do thereby anything that should be either to the derogation of the King's dignity, majesty royal, jurisdiction, or laws." (LP 4.6574-6578)
- in Venice, the Emperor rewards a friar for writing in Katherine's favour with a benefice worth 500 ducats per annum (about £112 10s). The efforts of his agents to get the verdict from Padua overturned fail (LP 4.6581).
- the universities of Poitiers and Alcala vote for Katherine (LP 4.6548, 6591).
- Fisher writes another book in defence of Katherine (LP 4.6596).
- William Brereton and his wife obtain the manor of Longdendale in Chester for a penny rent per annum (LP 4.6600.2).
- in the belief that the only reason Parliament will meet in the autumn is to remove Katherine as queen, Chapuys circulates to MPs a warning from the pope that supporting Henry against Katherine will result in their excommunication (CSPS 4.1.396).
- Henry interrupts his hunting holiday for a week long meeting with his Privy Councillors and the French ambassadors at Hampton Court. Chapuys, who has not seen the King for some weeks, is frustrated that nobody will tell him what it was about (CSPS 4.1.411).
- negotiations begin regarding the surrender of Florence (CSPS 4.1.463).
- Katherine's chaplain, Thomas Abell, calls Henry's Privy Councillors a bunch of traitors. Henry dismisses him from court and demands Katherine punish him. She refuses on grounds that he spoke the truth (CSPS 4.1.396).
- the Milanese ambassador reports that since the fall of Wolsey, Henry "chooses to know and superintend everything himself." (CSPM 818)
- from the gardens of Hampton Court, Henry enjoys pears and damsons. He also goes fishing there and takes delivery of some more greyhounds and a new clock as well as having the palace clocks repaired. On the last day of the month, he continues his investment in a lead mine in Glamorganshire (PP pp.65-66, 68).

- the Dutch scholar Desiderius Erasmus sends Thomas Boleyn a commentary on the psalm "The Lord is my Shepherd", the accompanying letter showing they are good friends and that Thomas is a man of learning (LP 4.3345).[243]
- Henry composes a reply to the pope's letter from October 1529 (LP 4.5994) saying that although the pope's promises betoken "zeal, love and piety", his actions have indicated the opposite with the result that Henry has been made ill. He accuses the pope of seeking to protract the cause with infinite vain hopes "to lead us whither ye will" and of acting "inconstantly and deceivably." He says that if the pope will accept the judgments of the learned men which he has presented to him, he will forgive the past and attribute it to the pope being ill advised. He says it is evident that Rome is "destitute" of learning and condemns the idea that avoiding scandal should be considered a motive for dispensing with God's law. He says it was never his wish to question papal authority but asks "What should we do in so great and so many perplexities? For truly if we should obey the letters of your holiness, in that they do affirm that we know to be otherwise, we should offend God." He concludes by saying his cause "toucheth not worldly things but divine, not frail but eternal: in which things no feigned, false or painted reasons but only the truth shall take place. And God is the truth whom we are bound to obey rather than men." (LP 4. Appx.260)[244]

Comments

Thomas Abell would write *Invicta Veritas* in early 1532 a work of lamentable theology and unintentional humour. He was executed for treason in 1540.

Wolsey's Cardinal College would be formally dissolved but re-established temporarily by Henry in 1532 then permanently in 1546 as Christ Church College, Oxford.

Parliament did not meet until the start of 1531 due to plague.

---

243 In Roman Catholic Bibles, this was psalm 22 but Protestant Bibles use the original Hebrew numbering so it is psalm 23. The difference was because the Vulgate followed the Septuagint and saw psalms 9 and 10 as one. The letter is incorrectly calendared under 1527 but the work was commissioned at the end of 1529 and written during the spring of 1530, see Dominic Baker-Smith (ed.), *Collected Works of Erasmus* vol. 64 Expositions of the Psalms (Toronto, 2005) p.120.

244 Burnet, *History of the Reformation*, ed. Pocock, vol. 4 pp.169-173

September 1530

Events

- Henry requests that the Duke of Orleans be sent to England in accordance with the marriage contract with Princess Mary. Aware that Henry might then be able to hold him hostage until he pays the huge debt he owes him, Francis refuses (CSPV 4.618,621,626; CSPS 4.1.425). Meanwhile Francis sends the Duke of Albany to the pope proposing Orleans as a husband for Catherine de Medici. The pope thinks this must be a hoax (CSPS 4.1.420, 423).
- the papal prothonotary Gambara, ruler of Bologna, arrests Dr Pallavicini who supports Henry and demands the names of his similarly minded colleagues. On Henry's behalf, Croke protests (LP 4.6608, 6609, 6619, 6622-4). Croke is encouraged by the doctors refusing to accept any rewards for their verdict saying that they were led by the Holy Spirit to pronounce Julius' dispensation worthless (LP 4.6033).
- the universities of Toulouse and Ferrara vote in support of Henry, that of Salamanca in Spain for Katherine. The Chancellor at Ferrara is Cardinal Salviati which delights the English (he is the pope's cousin) and upsets the Imperialists. Cardinal Campeggio's secretary, who lives in Ferrara, tries to prevent the verdict being issued (LP 4.6625, 6628, 6636, 6639, 6641).
- Dr Mai tries to collect documents for Katherine's defence at Rome. He confides to the Emperor that if they cannot prove she was a virgin when Arthur died, the case could go either way (CSPS 4.2.428).
- a papal nuncio arrives in England. He is met by George Boleyn and escorted to London. Henry expresses considerable anger at the pope's behaviour saying that Clement wrote to him from Orvieto saying that the annulment was necessary and he would support it (CSPV 4.421; CSPS 4.1.433).
- Cardinal Trani asks permission from the pope to give his opinion on Henry's case and is refused (LP 4.6626).
- Gregory Casale forwards the pope's latest idea for a solution which he thinks the Imperialists would support, that Henry have two wives. He warns Henry that the idea came from them "but what their aim and design herein should be, I dare not certainly affirm" (LP 4.6627).[245] Casale describes Cardinal Ancona as a valued friend who has observed that he has never known a case in which more doubt existed than Henry's. Ancona counsels Henry to wait until the pope's dependence on the Emperor lessens (LP 4.6626). The pope also tells Ghinucci that it would be less scandalous for Henry to have two wives than to allow him to leave Katherine. Ghinucci says the "marriage" is invalid and must be annulled properly.[246]

---

245 Herbert, *History*, pp.445
246 Pocock, *Records*, vol. 2 pp.5-11.

- Florence falls (CSPS 4.1.424).
- Chapuys says that since Wolsey departed from power, France obtains favours through Anne and her family. He tells the Emperor that the pope needs to issue a letter prohibiting Parliament from discussing the annulment before it meets again in October. He further claims that Anne Boleyn has replaced the gentlemen who used to visit Katherine to spy on her with women who will do the same all day (CSPS 4.1.422, 450).
- the Duke of Milan sends agents to England to try to secure the 50,000 ducat loan which Thomas Boleyn promised the Duke he would be able to secure from Henry (CSPV4.614-617).
- a proclamation is issued preventing the obtaining or publishing of any papal bull prejudicial to the interests of Henry or England (LP 4.6615).
- the pope replies to the letter from the English nobility saying that the delay is Henry's fault and not his. He is ready to hear the case as soon as Henry either appears in person at his court or sends proctors. He acknowledges that Henry "has deserved all that your letter mentions, nay even much more. … In our private person, we owe so much to His Highness's affection as we shall scarce ever be able sufficiently to recompense." He claims that he remains "unbiased inclined to favour neither side" but notes that a divorce would cause "great scandal." He adds "we are truly willing to gratify His Highness in all things wherein we are able by our authority, but then our ability cannot extend to those things which will destroy that authority." (LP 4.6638).[247]
- Edward Seymour, Jane's brother and a Squire of the Body, is granted an annuity of 50 marks (LP 4.6654 [20]).
- the Emperor's commander-in-chief of forces in Italy, the Duke of Mantua, announces that he wants to dissolve the marriage he contracted in April and return to his first wife, despite having had that marriage annulled previously, something he now claims that the pope should not have done although he had himself requested this! (CSPS 4.1.440)
- George Boleyn wins £5 12s shooting at Hunsdon with the King (PP p.72).
- a cow is killed by greyhounds belonging to Anne Boleyn and Urian Brereton. The owner is compensated by 10s (PP p.74).
- Henry suggests that Katherine's enjoyment of wealth and status is fuelling her efforts to delay the inevitable (CSPS 4.1.433).
- Henry tightens up security around his Privy Council leaving Chapuys complaining that he cannot find anything out (CSPS 4.1.433).
- Henry gives his daughter Mary £10 "to make pastime withal" and spends the same amount on purchasing linen for Anne Boleyn. He also dines on artichokes, cucumbers and herbs grown at Beaulieu and on exotic delicacies brought to him at some expense – oranges and lemons (PP pp.70-72)

---

247 Ibid. pp.454, 457

- the Milanese ambassador reports that Thomas Boleyn is not in favour with Henry because he has failed to follow instructions (CSPV 4.621).
- Ghinucci sends Henry a verdict in his favour by Decio, noting that he wrote it despite threats from Cardinal Piccolomini. He says that Gallatinus began writing in his favour too but Cardinal Egidio threatened him with death so now Gallatinus will only write if the pope says he can, adding that he hopes Henry can persuade the pope to permit this. Ghinucci also reports that the pope remains interested in the idea of dispensing Henry to have two wives though he does not think the Emperor would agree. Ghinucci points out that it is not up to the Emperor to sit in judgment on what dispensations are granted or refused saying that it would set a precedent for him to block marriage alliances which were perfectly legitimate but not in his political interest. Ghinucci says that neither the pope nor the cardinals seem to realise the danger they face (LP 4. Appx.261).
- Dr Mai calls the annulment "the greatest piece of rascality that was ever seen among princes" (CSPS Supplement 587).
- Stokesley claims the pope is convinced marriage to a brother's wife is against divine law but says he will never yield on the principle that as God's representative on earth, the pope can dispense even this for a good cause. He adds that the pope agrees that the cause given in Julius' bull was not sufficient for the case (LP 4.6637; SP vol.7 p.260)
- Casale and Stokesley send Henry copies of bulls issued by Julius II against simony and appeals to General Councils. They say doctors in Rome do not believe that arguing Clement is not a valid Pope because he is illegitimate would work – despite it being illegal - because so many of his predecessors have been the same (LP 4. Appx.262).

Comments

The letter from Orvieto to which Henry refers was that written by the pope and brought by Campeggio which said that Henry's case was valid and he would confirm the annulment. Under orders issued by the pope when the political situation changed, Campeggio burnt this after showing Henry. The King was, therefore, unable to provide documentary proof of the pope's initial decision and subsequent hypocrisy, a situation which understandably made him angry.[248]

Urian Brereton was the younger brother of William and a groom of the Privy Chamber. In a hunting party, it would be usual for the dogs of different owners to mix.

Judges are meant to be motivated by truth and justice, not fear of a verdict causing a scandal. Henry's conclusion that the pope was an unfit judge was totally fair.

---

248 The pope was at Orvieto from December 1527 to mid June 1528. LP 4.3658, 4352, 4365.

It is unknown if the idea of challenging the pope's validity, first expressed in April, was Henry's own or suggested to him by an adviser.

October 1530

Events

- Mai's teacher, Decio of Sienna, whose verdict that the cause of peace given by Julius II was indeed insufficient to justify issuing the bull of dispensation allowing Henry to marry Katherine and that therefore Henry is right and the union is null and void, promises Mai that he "will write the very contrary of what he has written if we only pay him for it." Cardinal Tortona (Gambara), meanwhile, says that the opportunity to make money is too good to miss and he is ready to write for either Henry or Katherine depending on who offers him most (LP 4.6661).
- Wolsey's college at Oxford is dissolved. He sends letters to Henry VIII via Henry Norris and William Brereton reminding the latter of all the favours and rewards he has received at his hands over the years (LP 4.6666, 6668).
- severe floods in Rome leave a third of homes either collapsed or uninhabitable and cause over a million ducats worth of damage (CSPS 4.1.452, 461).
- Henry says he sees no reason for the church of Rome having authority over other churches and that if princes were foolish enough to allow it in the past, that is no argument for the future. He reiterates that marriage to a brother's wife is against both natural and divine law and whilst he thanks Decio for the verdict in his favour, he corrects him with the reminder that canon law should derive from and support divine law and not set itself up as interpreter of it or – even worse – in contradiction. He says that the law does not permit a case to be outside the diocese in which it originated and voices his anger at the idea that a case which "concerns the discharge of our conscience, but also touches the succession of the Kingdom" should be determined by the pope "as if the Kingdom were in his hands to determine the succession, so that his opinion on our marriage might define the title of royal dignity, which he could confer on this or that one at his discretion." He describes the advocation as "a great wrong done to us" and complains that the pope "passes over our petitions in such a manner as shows contempt, either answering nothing, or carelessly and lightly." He says that it is as if the pope "does not know what to answer." Henry continues: "Since the Pontiff has already admitted to you and to others that our marriage is forbidden by divine law, if he wishes to be considered the vicar of God, his first care should be that the divine precepts are observed, and that the order established by God should be kept safe and sound. He should take care not to dispense haphazardly, as

is the case, nor spend time considering what has been done, but consider what ought to have been done." Henry warns that if the pope does not act, he will find "a serpent in his lap." Asking that the case be deferred until at least the end of January, Henry asks Ghinucci and Casale to seek legal advice on "how to decline the judgment of the pope, by what means we might escape judgment, what we might propose, what we might allege, or say, as the case may be, so that we might be able to anticipate the weapons of our adversaries with premeditation, and the more easily avoid them" adding that English lawyers are working on the same (LP 4.6667).[249]

- the Bishop of Tarbes actively promotes Henry's case in Rome and his recall to France disappoints the English who say that unless Ghinucci obtains a cardinal's hat, they will not have anyone of such authority in the papal court nor anyone with such close and continued access to the pope. To the delight of the English, the pope promises to create Ghinucci a cardinal in December.[250] Tarbes tries to conciliate the Imperial ambassadors by telling them that delays favour Katherine because "the King is principally stirred on to action by amours which come and go." Unconvinced, Mai continues to press for immediate action, though he admits privately that given he has been waiting for over two years to obtain the necessary documents from Spain, the pope's continual delays are actually helpful (LP 4.6697, 6705; CSPS 4.1.452, 471).

- in Italy, Croke bewails Imperialist money taking opinions away from Henry. Raphael Comensis of Padua wrote for Henry and then accepted money from the Emperor to write for Katherine alleging his previous work was merely an academic "exercise of ingenuity." Croke extends rewards to three crowns but notes the Emperor pays six hundred (LP 4.6669, 6670, 6672, 6702).

- the Duke of Mantua's first wife dies. This creates a problem as he was using her existence to claim that his second marriage to Julia of Naples was invalid – even though the first union was annulled and his ex-wife was engaged to someone else when she died. He now claims that the marriage to Julia should be dissolved on grounds that he was misled into thinking she was thirty-two when in fact she was thirty-eight. The pope asks the Emperor for advice (CSPS 4.1.452, 457, 461, 476).

- in France, Dr Garay continues to tell the Emperor how he thinks the "designs of the enemy" should be overcome and says that if it was not for his status as a clergyman, he would fight Henry's supporters with his bare fists. He notes that although authorities of the past said that marriage to a brother's wife was unlawful, they did not say existing unions should be dissolved and he reminds the pope that in 1526 he had permitted Luce to marry the wife of his dead sister. This, Garay claims, shows how strong the case was

---
249 SP vol. 7 pp.261-265
250 Pocock, *Records*, vol. 1 p.459

for Luce was a poor man and unable to pay the full fee. He recommends Anne Boleyn be sent to a convent and Henry be forced to do penance and fast on bread and water. He urges the pope to deprive of their livelihoods anyone who supports Henry and to excommunicate them, and goes further to say that these prohibitions should apply to all who support Henry in the future (LP 4.6692; CSPS 4.1.450, 463).
- keen to secure a majority in the college of cardinals before the annulment case comes to trial, the Emperor asks the pope to create four more Spaniards as cardinals (CSPS 4.1.479).
- Bennet tells Henry that the pope's suggestion that he have two wives was a test and that if Henry had agreed, the pope would have concluded that Henry accepted his authority and therefore there was no reason for him not to accept the authority of the dispensation of Julius II. He adds that the pope is unsure if he could permit bigamy but that a "great divine" had advised him "for avoiding of a greater inconvenience, his holiness might dispense" though other cardinals had "showed him plainly that he could not do it." (LP 4.6705)[251]
- Anne's cousin, Sir Francis Bryan, is sent to France as the new resident ambassador (LP 4.6665).
- Chapuys grumbles that the French ambassador has magnificent apartments in Hampton Court palace as well as a house in Dover while he and the papal nuncio have much smaller lodgings away from the court (CSPS 4.1.460).
- the papal nuncio goes to complain about Henry's proclamation against papal bulls. Henry tells him it was issued to prevent the pope interfering with the programme of church reform on which he is embarking, a necessary step given that the pope has failed to reform it himself. Henry claims that he would not wish to be prevented in his work by the pope alleging some point of law, such as the excuse about holidays in the Roman law courts which was used to stop the Blackfriars trial. He also warns the nuncio about spending too much time with Chapuys whose views are too one sided and complains that the pope routinely reveals details of confidential conversations with the English ambassadors to Mai (CSPS 4.1.445).
- Norfolk, Suffolk and Thomas Boleyn fulminate against popes. Boleyn's language is so violent that Chapuys claims he had to leave the room in horror (CSPS 4.1. 445, 481). Despite this, Norfolk seeks a papal dispensation to allow his step-sister to marry his son-in-law (CSPS 4.1.460).[252]

---

251 Pocock, *Records*, vol. 1 p.459. It has been plausibly suggested that the "great divine" was Cajetan which seems probable, John Alfred Faulkner 'Luther and the Bigamous Marriage of Philip of Hesse', *American Journal of Theology*, vol. 17 no 2 (April 1913) p.219

252 Norfolk's daughter Katherine died of plague in March 1530 not long after her marriage to Edward Stanley, Earl of Derby who was her father's ward. Rather than risk the Derby inheritance being lost to the family, Norfolk gave Stanley his step-sister Dorothy. Roman canon law required a dispensation as Dorothy was aunt to

- Mai jubilantly reports that a Jew in Rome has been forced to marry his dead brother's wife showing the law in Deuteronomy is still valid (LP 4.6661). He receives a letter from Chapuys reporting that Henry has found a rabbi to support his case. Chapuys asks the pope to detain the said rabbi and prevent him crossing to England (CSPS 4.1.460.
- the pope agrees to contribute 10,000 ducats a month toward the Imperial army in Italy (CSPS 4.1.470).
- Norfolk says that Henry's lack of sons is a sign of God's displeasure (CSPS 4.1.481).
- Katherine writes to her niece, Eleanor, now queen of France for help. Garay predicts the request will be ignored because Eleanor is a loyal wife and will support Francis rather than her brother, the Emperor (CSPS 4.1.450).
- Henry tells his Privy Council that Wolsey was a better minister than any of them, a much more able administrator, and says he misses him every day (LP 4.6738; CSPV 4.637).
- Thomas Boleyn is tasked with negotiating a change to the 1527 agreement with France commuting the salt into cash (LP 4.6755, 6775)

Comments

Although Wolsey writes to Henry, it is unclear if the letters are received by him. Norfolk talks of reading Wolsey's covering letter to Brereton but it is unclear if that is because Brereton passed it to Norfolk instead of Henry for fear it might be treasonable or whether Henry passed it to Norfolk after reading it himself.

The passion shown by the Emperor's representatives in supporting Katherine is quite extreme. The idea that the pope – or any foreign leader – should have the right to tell the English Parliament what it can and cannot discuss, is preposterous. Not even the King of England has – or had – the authority to ride roughshod over the liberties of English subjects in that way. As for Garay, an ordained clergyman supposedly committing to sharing the Gospel of Christ and the message of loving our enemies, seriously recommending that everybody, including those alive today, who supported Henry's assertion that the pope cannot overrule the word of God should be condemned to hell, it is symptomatic of fanaticism not reason. People sometimes wonder why people in the sixteenth and seventeenth century feared Roman Catholicism so much but these examples provide a clue. The Roman Church then was not like it is today. Garay was right about one thing though – Eleanor did not support Katherine.

Another interesting point in Garay's report is his reference to papal authority existing for a thousand years. Historically, he was being fair but he was also – and it would have pained him to know this – supporting Henry one of whose arguments against such authority was that it was not biblical and only emerged some five hundred years after the life of St Peter!

Stanley's first wife.

Mai's claim that the Roman Jew was forced to marry his dead brother's childless widow is untrue and demonstrates his complete lack of understanding of the situation. Jews did not require a rabbi to perform a marriage or to approve it, though custom meant that the vast majority of weddings were conducted by a rabbi. Forced marriages were prohibited for men and women and Levirate marriage was banned by Ashkenazi Jews and frowned upon, though permitted, by Sephardi. Judaism was not structured like the church. There was no pope and no system of dispensations. It is likely that the rabbi, upon being asked by the couple concerned, had a beth din summoned to discuss the case. However, it is entirely possible that the wedding was arranged by Mantino on behalf of the Imperialists. As Katz comments, the timing of the marriage and location "makes the event more than a little suspicious."[253]

There was no prohibition in scripture against a man marrying the wife of his dead sister. This was a rule that existed only in canon law: it had no relevance to Henry's case whatsoever. Similarly, Garay's comment about past authorities not ordering that illegal unions be dissolved was also irrelevant for they had been discussing unions made by pagans prior to conversion, e.g. Pope Gregory's response to St Augustine (*Registrum Epistolarum* Book XI, Letter 64, Question 7). Henry and Katherine were both baptised Christians when they "married".

The pope's decision to ask the Emperor's advice regarding the Duke of Mantua's marital status might seem curious given that the Emperor was not a canon lawyer and it was the pope's job to deal with such questions. However, the Duke was the Emperor's employee, his vassal, and his wife was the Emperor's cousin. The pope could also cite a precedent in his asking him about what to do about Henry and Katherine! If Henry had known about the pope's actions, he could have exploited the situation. The pope argued his own authority was absolute but here he was requesting instruction from a lay prince. Did this not show the supreme authority in matrimonial questions rested with rulers and their parliaments?

Henry's letter to Ghinucci and Casale noting the laws and custom of England require that cases be settled in England and not overseas, is interesting as being an early example of Henry referring to the pope as the Bishop of Rome, an accurate title and one which would be enforced in England from 1534.[254] Henry's belief that as king he was the fountain of law and had no earthly superior was in line with his coronation oath and the 1393 Statute of Praemunire.

---

253 David S Katz, *The Jews in the History of England* (OUP 1994) p.41. Katz presumes that Croke had spoken to Ashkenazi or European Jews while Mai had spoken to Sephardi or African.

254 Pope Francis replaced the long list of papal titles on yearbooks with a simple Bishop of Rome on his succession. He added: "The bishop of Rome is a pastor and a disciple, not a powerful man of this world." Pope Francis, *Hope* (2025) pp.195, 206

The idea of Chapuys as some delicate flower unable to remain in a room when bad language was employed is comical. He was not some Victorian maiden aunt liable to an attack of the vapours but a grown man, albeit not a nice one.

November 1530

Events

- Chapuys tells the Emperor that Anne bewailed her lost time and reputation waiting for Henry and threatened to leave him unless he destroy Wolsey. Henry, with tears in his eyes, begged her to stay and promised to do just that (LP 4.6738; CSPS 4.1.509).
- Wolsey is arrested on the 4th by Walter Walsh, Gentleman of the Privy Chamber and by Henry Percy, Earl of Northumberland. He commences his journey to London to face treason charges.
- Henry writes to the Earl of Shrewsbury with whom Wolsey stays almost three weeks telling him to treat the cardinal with all honour "as one whom he loves and favours" and promises that he himself will sit in judgment on Wolsey, not parliament or a court of his enemies. Wolsey, however, is taken ill and on his deathbed opines that if he had served God as diligently as he had Henry, he would not be in trouble. He says people must think he has lost his wits if they believe they would conspire against a king who has treated him so well despite his failures to obtain the annulment: "I pray God that this sacrament may be the damnation of my soul if ever I thought to do disservice to my King." He dies on the 29th [255]
- the lack of information about Wolsey's offences from the government leaves ambassadors confused and worried. The French ambassador, Joachim, two of whose friends have been arrested, expresses concern for the "poor cardinal" but says Henry has assured him that he himself is safe. Chapuys tells the Emperor that he believes his own correspondence with the cardinal was not treasonous and nobody has questioned him yet. The Venetian ambassador reports that Wolsey's physician, Dr Agostini, was arrested with him but says he does not know why (LP 4.6720, 6738; CSPV 4.631, 632; CSPS 4.1.492).[256]
- further confusion exists when it is revealed that the physician, rather than being held in the Tower, is living at Norfolk's house where he is treated "like a prince" (LP 4.6735, CSPV 4.637).
- Henry writes to Anne's cousin in France alleging that Wolsey sought a return to power as papal legate. Bryan takes the news to the French king who

---

255 Cavendish, *Wolsey*, pp.363-4.
256 The French reported news of the arrest on the 10th, the Imperialist and the Venetian ambassadors on the 13th and the Milanese on the 17th.

says he trusts Henry's sense of justice and that Wolsey had "so pompous and ambitious a heart, sprung out of so vile a stock" it was inevitable that he "would once show forth the baseness of his nature, and most commonly against him that hath raised him from low degree to high dignity." Francis goes on to say that in his opinion, "by his outrageous misbehaviours he [Wolsey] had well merited a life worse than death, or else of all deaths the most cruel." He adds that he is glad his ambassador was able to help expose the plot. At the same meeting, Francis tells Bryan to inform Henry that in his view "the pope will do, in your said matter, no other wise then the Emperor would have him." (LP 4.6733)[257]
- the Imperialists, fearing an alliance between the pope and Francis, do all they can to dissuade him from considering the offer of the Duke of Orleans for his "niece" Catherine (CSPS 4.1.493).
- hearing that Henry plans to have the university opinions in his favour circulated to MPs, Chapuys sends a manuscript of Fisher's works to Mai in Rome asking him to have copies printed so he can distribute them to M.P.s too. He admits that he has not asked Fisher's permission but says he does not expect he will mind. He alleges that Henry told Thomas Boleyn to have Cranmer (then employed in Rome) translate the university opinions into English but to embellish them as he went to make them more favourable (LP 4.6738).
- Thomas Boleyn is forced to backtrack on his promise to the Duke of Milan and tell him that Henry is unwilling to give him a penny. The Milanese ambassador describes Boleyn's efforts as feeble (LP 4.6738; CSPV 4.642).
- Mai sends orders to ports and and governors to arrest Marc Raphael, the ex-rabbi whom Henry wants to come to England as an advisor (CSPS 4.1.513).
- Margaret, Regent of the Low Countries, is taken seriously ill (LP 4.6743).
- Henry tells the papal nuncio that God has shown his displeasure at the pope's behaviour with the recent floods in Rome. He asks why the nuncio repeats every word he says to Chapuys and Joachim (CSPS 4.1.492).
- Katherine appeals for witnesses to the non-consummation of her marriage to Arthur. Even the ever loyal Chapuys doubts that she will be able to prove the point (CSPS 4.1.492).
- Geneva rejects the pope and becomes Lutheran (CSPS 4.1.496).
- Cueva, the Emperor's new Spanish envoy at the papal court expresses alarm when the pope recommends Ghinucci and John Casale for cardinal's hats, but is reassured when the pope says it will never happen. Cueva is unimpressed with Rome describing the cardinals as "the greatest knaves in the whole world" and saying, "I have little faith in Roman truth." (CSPS 4.1.503, 511)

---

257 SP vol.7 pp.211-215.

- the Emperor decides to have his brother elected King of the Romans. The pope obligingly issues letters to allow the election to go ahead and produces them in two radically different and contradictory forms so that the Emperor can use whichever version suits him in any particular circumstance (CSPS 4.1.518)
- the pope's response to the death of the Archbishop of Saragossa is to turn to his nineteen year old nephew, whom he created a cardinal in 1529, and say "now the Emperor might give you something good." (CSPS 4.1.503)
- the Emperor urges the pope to agree to the calling of a General Council to sort out affairs in Germany and elsewhere. The gloomy pope predicts that if it goes ahead, there will be as many new popes elected as there are countries represented at it. He agrees to call one, but hopes that Francis will find excuses to delay it indefinitely (CSPS 4.1.512).
- Anne Boleyn is given £20 to redeem a jewel from her sister and £15 worth of crimson satin, enough to make a gown. Francis Weston and Mark Smeaton get new hose for their service at court. Henry purchases two sackbuts, three tenor shawms and three treble shawms though judging by the number of books he has delivered to him at Hampton Court, he spends much of the month reading (PP pp.86-89).[258]
- Norfolk assures Chapuys that if the pope will only grant the annulment, he will ensure Henry does not attack the church in England (CSPS 4.1.492).
- Chapuys complains he is underpaid and requests a benefice to boost his income. He also complains that Anne was allowed to stand at a window so she could overhear his exchange with Henry. (CSPS 4.1.492).

Comments

There is no doubt that Chapuys was a conspiracy theorist. His account of Anne threatening to leave Henry unless he destroyed Wolsey is simply an attempt to portray her as Salome, the wicked temptress whose lascivious dancing so aroused Herod that he agreed to give her the head of John the Baptist (Mark 6:17-28). It is also an example of a story which should not be taken at face value. If Henry and Anne were having such a squabble, would they really have been doing it in front of people who were evidently close enough to see the tears in Henry's eyes? Chapuys was not there and is only reporting what he has been told second or third hand and had translated along the way. It is more likely that somebody overheard shouting behind a closed door with Anne saying something on the lines of, "I'm tired of waiting. I'm off" and Henry replying "Darling, please don't" and all the rest is embellishment either by Chapuys for the sake of the Emperor or by the servant who overheard it in order to spice up the story and hopefully get a bit more money for it.

---

258 Sackbuts were a form of trombone, shawms like an early oboe.

The idea that Percy was chosen to make the arrest because Anne wanted her revenge on Wolsey was first suggested by Herbert writing in 1649 and has been repeated often. It is a theory which can easily be disregarded. Wolsey was arrested at Southwell which was at the southern most end of the northern province and Percy was the premier lord in the north and as such, would have been sent to arrest any high ranking person. In April 1530, he had welcomed Wolsey to the north (LP 4.6345). Shrewsbury was his father-in-law and alleged to be a supporter of Katherine (LP 5.120) which further makes it unlikely that Anne was pulling the strings.[259]

Francis' response to Wolsey's arrest is chilling. Wolsey had worked tirelessly for Francis' release when he was held prisoner and also for the release of his sons. He had negotiated peace settlements that benefited both countries and strengthened France in the face of Imperial aggrandisement. Francis' response reflected his desire to disassociate himself with Wolsey and protect his alliance with Henry, particularly given how close he came to implication through his ambassador. He would treat Anne Boleyn in just the same disparaging way when she was in trouble in 1536. As Wolsey might have quoted, "put not your trust in princes" (Ps. 146.3).

There are three interpretations of Wolsey's arrest. The first sees Norfolk as acting to protect his own position following Henry's comments about missing Wolsey. In this view, Norfolk, with the assistance of Anne Boleyn and her father, plotted Wolsey's downfall whilst claiming to act proactively to protect Henry from a traitor. Between them, they then concocted evidence and duped Henry into believing them. There are some obvious problems with this. It implies a degree of initiative which is not normally associated with Norfolk's government – although that does not mean they did not make an exception here. It suggests that Anne was active politically when the only evidence for such a theory rests on Chapuys who saw her as a combined Eve, Jezebel and Salome, an image he used for contrast against Katherine whom he regarded as the personification of saintliness. It does, however, explain why Wolsey's physician was so well treated and why no documents were actually produced in support of the supposed plot. Agostini's evidence consisted of a claim that Wolsey had told him to write to Francis via Joachim in order to encourage him to make war on the pope and Emperor. This would incite rebellion in England which the Scots would exploit by invading from the north, at which point Henry would be forced to restore Wolsey to bring back order. Agostini admitted that the letter had never been written.[260] As evidence for a treason trial, it was obviously inadequate and the entire story is

---

259 It was Chapuys who made this claim but there is nothing else to indicate Shrewsbury's views on the annulment. He testified for Henry at the legatine court but he missed Anne's coronation, whether on principle or because of sickness, is uncertain. He did not serve on the jury that condemned Anne in 1536. Shrewsbury died in 1538.
260 Agostini was the nephew of Ghinucci, the Italian Bishop of Worcester and key advisor and ambassador for Henry VIII.

too ridiculous to credit, though Henry described it to Francis Bryan, his ambassador in France.[261] The English were not likely to rebel if Francis waged another war on the Emperor and there is no evidence to suggest that Wolsey was so popular that there would be demands for his re-instatement if they did.

The second view is that Henry was the man who masterminded the whole scheme, planned to have Wolsey arrested on deliberately fake grounds with the intention of scaring him into compliance with his wishes. If Henry was planning to hold a tribunal on his "marriage" to Katherine, he would have needed the two senior churchmen in England to sit in judgment, namely the Archbishops of Canterbury (Warham) and York (Wolsey). If he harboured doubts that Wolsey would vote in his favour, what better way to focus his mind than the prospect of a charge of treason to be followed by the ignominious and painful death of a traitor – hanging by the neck, being cut down while still alive, disembowelled and then quartered? Having publicly cleared Wolsey of the treason charge, Henry could then let Wolsey sit in judgment and return to government – if his health permitted. This view makes sense of the leisurely journey which Wolsey was invited to make south, the comfort in which he travelled, the letters and assurances he received.

The third view is that Wolsey was actually guilty and that either Joachim let something slip or some correspondence was intercepted. If this was the case, it might have been expected that there would be some record of this. Whilst it is clear that Wolsey had written to the pope to complain about his treatment and this would be construed as "contrarious to his faith, truth and duty of allegiance"[262] he had received no response so it would have been hard to convict him of high treason on the basis of it. The fact that the pope, who should have shown support for a man who was his loyal friend and a senior cardinal, did nothing is a further indicator that he was not a man of any sort of integrity. The pope should have sent a letter to Henry demanding an explanation for his treatment of Cardinal Wolsey and threatening him with excommunication. As it is, the pope washed his hands of Wolsey like Pilate did with Jesus.[263]

It might be asked why this matters in a book about Anne Boleyn. Firstly, the case either shows or disproves the political influence of Anne in the autumn of 1530. Secondly, it either portrays Henry as being led by his scheming councillors, probably against his will, or as being a machiavellian of the first degree. If Henry was duped in 1530 to destroy Wolsey, it follows that he was likely to have been duped by Cromwell and the Seymour faction in 1536 to destroy Anne: if Henry was the mastermind of the Wolsey debacle, it is

---

261 L. R. Gardiner, 'Further News of Wolsey's End, November December 1530', *Bulletin of the Institute of Historical Research,* vol. LVII, (November 1984), pp.103-4
262 Ibid. p.101. Letter of Henry VIII to Francis Bryan dated 11th November 1530.
263 Matt. 27:24. Hand washing in this context was seen as a way of saying effectively "it is nothing to do with me" - Deut. 21:6-7.

clear he could have planned Anne's fall as well on equally trumped up and unsubstantiated charges.

The idea that MPs would want to read Fisher's works is rather curious and begs the question of whether Chapuys had read them himself or was just totally out of touch with reality. Many of the MPs would not have understood the Latin in which they were written, let alone been able (or willing) to plough through lengthy theological treatises. If he had wanted to circulate Fisher's views, he should have created a brief summary and had it translated into English.

Henry's refusal to support the Duke of Milan is not surprising. The sum requested was fifty thousand ducats, worth £11,250 at the time (almost eighty million today). There is evidence that the Duke was keen to marry Princess Mary and Boleyn may have encouraged this on grounds Milan was a good distance away, but Henry was not about to see his beloved daughter married to an aged invalid with a precarious hold on power. In July 1531, Henry was to describe the Duke as "so vexed with disease and sickness, debilitated and extenuated...impotent and like to die" that he was "neither meet to join with such youth nor able to continue any years with her."[264]

The regent of the Netherlands was the same Margaret to whom Anne was sent as a child. She died shortly after the letter advising of her illness was written.

It is interesting to ponder whether Norfolk's boast that he could govern the King was an ill-judged act of bravado designed to impress Chapuys or indicative that he was delusional. Nobody had the power to restrain Henry or dictate policy to him.

Chapuys was a layman and not a priest so the belief that he should have a benefice indicates his view that the church should serve the state, even though publicly he would have argued the reverse. The Emperor had no objection to this in theory: he would obtain a cardinal's hat for his chancellor who was also a layman. It was rather a long way from the ideal of ministry described by Peter and Paul in the New Testament who saw clergy as ministering to their flocks and being rewarded by them for their labour, not people accepting the money while living elsewhere and doing nothing for them whatsoever. The income for a benefice was derived from the people living in it, either through tithes or rent or through labour. Asking Christians to contribute toward maintaining a pastor, toward the upkeep of a building which might have emotional significance as the burial place of beloved family members, toward aiding those who had fallen on hard times through sickness or age, toward evangelism and worship, was entirely reasonable and scriptural. Expecting the said people to work to raise money so that an ambassador could have furs and wine, was not. A priest might be provided at a pittance by the recipient of the benefice but he was likely to have as little interest in the welfare of the people in the said benefice as the person drawing the money. Chapuys was not being

---

264 SP vol. 7 p.315

unusually wicked or cynical in his request but it does demonstrate powerfully the utter hypocrisy of the man when he later criticised Henry for what he regarded as taking church income for inappropriate purposes. As Henry noted in his *A Necessary Doctrine*, accepting such money without doing the work was a blatant breach of the commandment "Thou shalt not steal."

Chapuys was shocked by Anne being allowed to watch and hear his audience with Henry from the gallery. It was a significant sign of her importance, though she was only there for the section of the conversation relating to the annulment. In France, Queen Claude had been permitted to eavesdrop of meetings between her husband and ambassadors too from behind a screen.[265]

Henry's reading probably reflects his engagement in preparing the *Glass of Truth* but may also show him doing some follow up research to texts shown to him in the *Collectanea Satis Copiosa* which was being prepared by Foxe at this date.

December 1530

Events

- the Dukes of Mantua and Ferrara seize the seals of their universities to prevent them giving official verdicts in Henry's favour. The pope allows Bologna and Padua to debate the annulment issue but the Imperialists decide not to ask them for fear they will again uphold Henry's case (LP 4.6758). Henry meanwhile obtains another verdict from Sienna (LP 4.6781).
- Bennet and Casale warn Henry that the pope is planning to issue a brief at Katherine's request forbidding him from marrying while the suit is pending and ordering him to dismiss Anne from court. Norfolk asks the nuncio why such news comes from the English ambassadors in Rome and not him and the nuncio admits that he finds audiences with Henry alarming because the King uses such violent and threatening language about the issue. The nuncio says the pope has given him permission to communicate in writing to avoid confrontation (LP 4.6757).
- the cardinals – by a majority rather than unanimous vote – approve the pope sending a letter to Henry forbidding any new marriage but refuse to order Anne's dismissal from court because there is no evidence that any adultery has taken place. Mai, the Imperial lawyer, himself admits that all the evidence shows that Anne is a virtuous woman (CSPS 4.1.588).
- Henry sends an angry letter to the pope complaining about the way he has had Henry's supporters threatened, has denied liberty of speech to people, intercepted confidential letters between himself and his ambassadors, lied

---

265 LP 2.4661

about him to Francis I and has failed to honour the promise made to him in 1529 and confirmed in the letter which Campeggio exhibited and then burnt. He demands the case be heard in England (LP 4.6759).
- Katherine also sends a letter to the pope complaining about his refusal to issue a verdict and saying this has left her in a living hell. She claims Henry is a loyal son of the Rome at heart and is being led astray by the "inventors and abettors of this cause." She demands that the pope order Anne Boleyn from Henry's court for two months because she is sure she could win her husband back in this time (CSPS 4.1.548).
- Wolsey's physician remains at Norfolk's home after signing an agreement never to disclose any details of Wolsey's plot on pain of paying Henry £100 (LP 4.6763).
- Chapuys says that Henry offered Reginald Pole the position of Archbishop of York but Pole refused saying that he had sinned by following Henry's orders in supporting the annulment in Paris (CSPS 4.1.547).
- Imperial representatives at Rome work hard to defeat Henry's requests for cardinal's hats for Ghinucci and Casale. The pope asks the Emperor to suggest a plausible excuse he can give Henry for refusing. Meanwhile the pope grants two hats to the Emperor's nominees, including the Archbishop of Seville whom he has been led to believe will grant a substantial financial reward to his nephew Cardinal Medici (CSPS 4.1.535, 537, 538, 540, 543, 544). This gives the Emperor 12 cardinals, Francis 5 and Henry 0.
- tensions rise between England and Scotland as Henry continues to support the exiled Earl of Angus, his erstwhile brother-in-law. Henry orders fortresses along the border to be repaired and provisioned (LP 4.6779, CSPS 4.1.539).
- another French ambassador arrives. He is granted apartments in Bridewell Palace and together with Joachim enjoys three days of feasting and celebrations at Christmas with Henry and Anne. Chapuys is not invited but tells the Emperor that he stayed away to deprive Henry of the honour of his company (CSPS 4.1.555, 584).
- Anne's brother and her cousin Nicholas Carew are sent to France as Henry's representatives to witness the coronation of the new French queen, Eleanor, the sister of the Emperor (CSPS 4.1.547).
- the Emperor tells his wife that he needs to sail to the Low Countries following the death of the regent Margaret. He says the prospect worries him because in event of a storm, he might be forced to land in France or England and "the King of England is ill disposed toward me and I am not over sure of France either." (CSPS 4.1.527)
- Ferdinand of Austria is elected King of the Romans. His brother, the Emperor, admits to spending 200,000 gold crowns to effect this but six German princes refuse to recognise the result (LP 4.6773, CSPS 4.1.547).
- Henry tells his ambassadors in Rome to avoid any "act, appearance or allegation" which would "tacitly or expressly, obliquely or directly,

implicitly or explicitly, consent, allow or approve the pope's jurisdiction… authority and laws, as We should thereby preclude Ourself from such remedies as We may attain here at home." He admits he is loath to see the matter delayed but this is an important matter of principle. He tells them to be "entire Englishmen" rather than "Englishmen papisticate" (LP 4.6760; SP vol.7 pp.269-71). Chapuys reports Henry's latest idea is to gather six doctors supporting his case and six supporting Katherine and let them argue it out before the Archbishops of Canterbury and York. Chapuys tells Fisher to have no part in this (CSPS 4.1.547).
- Sir Richard Page, knight of the body, is granted the abbey lands of St Leonard's in Essex previously held by Wolsey (LP 4.6803 (24)) William Brereton meanwhile appears on a list of people who owe Henry money (LP 4.6792).
- despite having people watching the ports and roads Imperial agents are unable to apprehend Henry's rabbinic advisor (CSPS 4.1.535).
- both Chapuys and the Milanese ambassador report that three thousand copies of Tyndale's *Practice of Prelates* have been distributed across London. Henry orders the arrest of the author's brother who arranged this and has him paraded through the streets in a pasteboard mitre before being forced to burn copies of the work. Chapuys described the book as a defence of Katherine written in a "masterly and most complete manner" and says that it "tells the truth too plainly to please the King." (CSPS 4.1.539; CSPV 4.642).
- Anne Boleyn is given £100 for Christmas by Henry: he gives his daughter Mary £20. Henry also spends £80 having fur added to Anne's gowns to keep her warm (PP pp.98, 101). Anne spends some of the money having a motto embroidered on the liveries of her servants (CSPS 4.1.547). The motto is referenced in the love song she composes for Henry that Christmas.[266]
- Chapuys advises the Emperor to get the pope to excommunicate Henry if he fails to take Katherine back and to put the whole of England under interdict. He claims this measure would cause "great suffering" among the people and foment rebellion. It would also justify the Emperor in declaring war (CSPS 4.1.547).

Comments

The idea of the twelve doctors meeting is only found in Chapuys' reports. He gives a date for this meeting of January 12th which is the day convocation – the parliament of the church – opened. Most likely he misunderstood the nature of the meeting. Convocation always met alongside parliament but in a separate building. Mostly composed of bishops, abbots and archdeacons, it was divided into two chambers, an upper and lower house, like

---

266 Ives, *Anne Boleyn*, pp.173-174

parliament. The convocation of the southern province was presided over by the Archbishop of Canterbury while that of the smaller northern province was presided over by the Archbishop of York, at this point vacant following the recent death of Wolsey. In 1970, general synod with its houses of laity and clergy, replaced both convocations.

Although the Emperor did not remove Chapuys from his position, it must be wondered why he did not. As Henry had correctly observed, ambassadors were meant to foster good relations not encourage war. Chapuys' direct recommendation that the Emperor have England put under interdict and then invade is reprehensible. An interdict was a papal measure which meant that churches were closed and no services could be held. Couples could not marry. Babies could not be baptised – a serious threat when many believed (wrongly) that baptism was necessary to a place in heaven. Funerals could not be held. No foreign national could trade with England, and as Chapuys recognised, the result would be widespread starvation and homelessness. His obsession with Katherine meant he was prepared to countenance the death of hundreds of thousands of innocent English subjects just to uphold the validity of a papal bull of 1504. The Emperor did not follow Chapuys' advice but nor did he rebuke him.

The recognition that Anne was not an adulteress by the Imperialists and cardinals is worthy of note. The former especially must have hated saying it and one can only imagine the efforts which they employed to try and prove Anne was not a virgin, but all failed. It speaks volumes not just for the behaviour of Henry and Anne and the care they obviously took with regard to chaperones but of the loyalty possessed by the royal staff. If a servant had been willing to tell a different tale, it is certain that a healthy financial reward and passage out of the country into Imperial territory would have awaited them.

The question is sometimes asked whether Chapuys understood English. It is clearly relevant to any study of the period because things can get lost in translation and it means that conversations he records may be third or fourth hand rather than direct. His comments about Tyndale's tract seem to provide conclusive evidence that he did not understand the language well. The *Practice of Prelates* is a work of some hundred and sixty pages which contends that bishops should have no role in government but rather stick to ministry. The bulk of the work relates to the papacy. Tyndale cites evidence from the New Testament that neither Rome nor Peter had any primacy in the early church, nor indeed for over six hundred years after Jesus's death (Acts 8:14, 11:1-4, 12:17, 15:4-22, 21:18; Gal. 1:19, 2:9). He identifies the keys of the Kingdom with the preaching of the Gospel rather than the powers to absolve, dispense and excommunicate and says that authority was given to the church as a whole and not Peter individually (John 20:21-23; Matt. 18:1-18). He describes the pope as a blind guide, as the whore of Babylon and the antichrist. He writes: "The pope is a cruel and merciless tyrant", a "foul and mis-shapen monster" who has prevented people studying the Bible "and corrupted it with false expositions." Instead of feeding the sheep of Christ's flock and leading them in green pastures, the pope has "poisoneth their pasture with the venomous leaven of his traditions and with wresting the text unto a contrary sense." In fact, the pope has "perverted the order of the world and turned the roots of the trees upward and hath put down the Kingdom of Christ, and set up the Kingdom of the devil whose vicar he is, and hath put down the Ministers of Christ, and hath set up the Ministers of Satan." He denies the pope's authority to overturn God's laws and condemns the way the papacy has become involved in politics. In particular, he criticises the interdict imposed on King John and the church's sanction of the deposition of Richard II and he notes how this worldly power is not only in contrast to the life of Jesus and his disciples but is based on the forged Donation of Constantine. He accuses Fisher of responsibility for the murder of Thomas Hitton at Maidstone.[267]

Throughout the work, Tyndale offers various praises for Luther and sharp criticism of Thomas More and Bishop Fisher for their efforts to suppress the Gospel. The last quarter is devoted to an attack on Wolsey for failing to promote English interests with his pro-French policy, something Tyndale regards as motivated by a desire to weaken the Emperor "that the pope might reign a god alone." In a brief section at the end, Tyndale claims Wolsey "imagined the divorcement between the King and the Queen" as an act of revenge for not being elected pope and because Katherine stood in the way of a French alliance. He says that if she had supported this, her union with Henry would not have been challenged even if it was illegal. He offers some comments on the Leviticus and Deuteronomy texts which he mistranslates (given he was working on a translation of the Torah at the time this must be deliberate) and suggests that marrying a brother's wife is permissible, but he also admits that he is uncertain and "my reasons may not be good" and is aware that critics might accuse him of adding to scripture to draw this conclusion. He hopes the King will publish his reasons for thinking otherwise in English for review and says that if Henry's interpretation is valid, then it is entirely right that he should separate from Katherine and that he should allow no opposition to prevent him. Tyndale's interest is not defending Katherine but his fear of civil war. He says that because "the lords and commons not knowing who hath most right to enjoy the crown: the realm could not but stand in great danger" and proposes that the King should define the succession for the next three places and have adults take an oath accepting this order. This then is the volume which Chapuys, an ardent advocate of the papacy and Fisher, claims is a masterly volume of great truth and unwaveringly supportive of Katherine!

The mystery around Wolsey's arrest was destined never to be cleared up due to the non-disclosure agreement made with Dr Agostini who went on to work for Norfolk, Cromwell and Henry VIII for the next sixteen years, travelling on embassies to the Low Countries, Germany and Italy.[268] Ordinarily,

---

267 Foxe, *Acts and Monuments*, vol. 4 p.619
268 E. A. Hammond, 'Doctor Augustine, Physician to Cardinal Wolsey and Henry VIII', *Medical History* (1975) pp.215 – 249

the government would have been only too keen to expose the behaviour of a traitor, particularly one associated with the pope by being a cardinal. They even quelled the publication of Tyndale's tract against him, although that was more because it was critical of the French who were Henry's ally. The silence suggests that they were far from sure they had any case against him at all. If Henry had been hoping to at least have the benefit of his advice, he may have been disappointed by his death rather than exultant.

It is usually said that Anne's adoption of the motto *Ainsi sera, groigne qui groigne* (it will be, grumble who will) was an aggressive act on her part or certainly an ill advised bit of social climbing because it was so closely based on that of Margaret of Austria, Regent of the Low Countries, *Groigne qui groigne et vive Bourgoigne (grumble who will and live Burgundy)*. It is possible, however, that she adapted it as a tribute to her first employer who had recently died. The text itself stems from the incident of the Israelites in the wilderness who grumbled that they had been led out of Egypt on false promises of a good life. God intervenes to show his faithfulness and Anne may have been trying to suggest that her becoming queen would be a means of succouring England and helping it toward the Promised Land.[269]

Although it is not certain that Anne wrote the love song for Henry entirely herself rather than either commissioning it or collaborating with someone, it is clear that the intention was to reflect her state of mind. In the song, she says that people may grudge on all they like but she will be Henry's wife when she will "well appease the chiefest cause of his mis-ease." She notes her youth but says she is mature in faith. She calls Henry her master sent by God and says her only desire is to serve him. She says that in Henry she has found

> A friend which giveth to no man place
> But makes me happiest that ever was

And goes on

> A heart I have besides all this
> That hath my heart and I have his
> If he doth will, it is my bliss
> And when we meet, no lack there is.

With a refrain that dolefully laments the existence of an unspecified obstacle to her joy – one can imagine her looking at a portrait of Katherine or the Imperial

---

[269] Chapuys never showed any indication of knowing that Anne had ever been in the Low Countries, and nor did Sander or Cavendish. The story of the Israelites is in Ex. 16:1-12. Another possible reference is in James 5:9 where people are told to be patient and grudge not as they await the coming of the Lord.

arms at this point – her song concludes that when she does achieve her end, "my mirth should double once or twice."²⁷⁰

When the annulment process began back in 1527, Henry wanted things to proceed as fast as possible. By this point, he wants things to slow down. This is not because he has realised he has no case as some have suggested and nor is it because was lost without Wolsey and was just drifting around in some sort of fog waiting for Cromwell to come along and sort the mess out. Henry had two clear goals, extricate himself from Katherine by legal means and to uphold the sovereignty of England. He knew this last was incompatible with papal claims and his studying of the subject had led him to realise that the New Testament made no mention of popes or the primacy of Rome. Casting off the beliefs he had held for almost forty years was not easy but Henry was being consistent rather than altering the rules to suit his purpose. He genuinely believed that the Bible was the Word of God and that as such it must be obeyed. Just as Leviticus told him that marriage to a brother's wife was wrong, so the New Testament told him that churches were independent, regional structures obedient to civil rulers. If Henry was to be criticised at all, it should be for failing to realise this earlier. Having identified his path, all he had to do was to find his way along it and he knew that would take time, hence the need for a delay. He was not the lovestruck fool of romantic fiction but a statesman whose primary objective was not bedding Anne Boleyn but upholding England. Her feelings on the continued delay are not known for certain but the song she wrote may reflect a determined effort on her part to try and smile and carry on as the prospect of a wedding must have seemed further away than ever. To wait all this time for Henry indicated devotion and determination on her part and considerable strength of character since she would have been aware of the calumnies against her.

1531

January 1531

Events

- Chapuys reports that an exasperated Anne has wished all Spaniards were at the bottom of the sea and vowed never to acknowledge Katherine as her mistress. He says she has the courage of a lion (LP 5.24).
- at Katherine's request and following a meeting of the cardinals on 23ʳᵈ December, the pope writes to Henry telling him that he may not marry while the suit is pending and that if he does, the issue of such a union will be illegitimate. He adds that because the case is to be heard in the papal

---
270 Ives, *Anne Boleyn*, p.174

court, no other court may rule on it – civil, ecclesiastical or parliament. (LP 5.27). The pope also sends a private letter to Henry two days later admitting that Katherine has no grounds for saying that England is an unsafe place to hear the case but reiterating that unless he is willing to accept an alternative place, the fact that she has appealed to Rome means that the case must be heard there to ensure the verdict is accepted as valid. He reassures Henry that he is genuinely impartial and not at the Emperor's beck and call (LP 5.31).

- Dr Mai, Imperial ambassador at Rome and responsible for preparing Katherine's case, urges the Emperor to arrange a meeting with Henry while he is in Flanders and sort the issue face to face. He warns that there is no guarantee of victory in Rome because the law is not clear cut and he has still not obtained the documents which he needs, including the reports of the legatine court held at Blackfriars against which proceedings he is meant to be appealing. He notes that Decio has said that while some aspects of canon law favour Katherine, the fact that Henry was under age and Julius had no grounds to grant the bull render the dispensation invalid and hence the "marriage" null and void. Mai continues to feel a defence based on the Portuguese case is the best route forward (CSPS 4.2.588, LP 5.57).

- Anne's father invites the French ambassador to dinner at his home where a farce is performed showing Wolsey going to hell. The ambassador is appalled but a happy Norfolk has the play printed (LP 5.62).

- an offer is made to William Tyndale to return to England but he rejects it (LP 5.65).

- Sir Edward Boleyn, Anne's uncle, is granted the wardship of John Appleyard (LP 5.80.29).

- Chapuys claims that Henry is preparing a house for Anne ready for when the papal brief arrives ordering her from court. He says confidently, "God and the Queen will guard against her return." (LP 5.70)

- Marc Raphael, the ex-rabbi, evades Imperial agents and arrives in England. He confirms the Deuteronomic reference to marrying a brother's wife is so that an heir can be raised for the dead brother and says it does not prevent Henry taking a wife of his own to raise up children for himself. Chapuys finds what he terms this "judaising" distasteful (LP 5.70).

- Henry sends an excusator to Rome, Edward Carne, to say that he cannot appear in person because his responsibilities as king prohibit him leaving the realm and English history is proof that when a king left "revolts, disturbances, scandals, disputes, conflicts and dissensions arose which led to complete ruin and grave loss." Nor, he says, can he appoint a proctor because the personal nature of the case means that he would need to have regular contact with such which is impractical from England. The faculty

of canon lawyers in Paris agree and urge the pope to appoint two judges to a neutral country (LP 5.75).[271]
- Cardinal Monte, a pro-French Florentine, proposes that the Emperor appoint Katherine as regent in the Low Countries. He says this would enable her to leave Henry with honour and keep her well away from the English court. The Emperor, however, has already given the job to his sister, Mary, widow of Lewis of Hungary (LP 5.60, CSPS 4.2.586).
- the Duke of Milan is advised by his ambassador to send an envoy with "some trifles brave and novel" to Anne Boleyn if he wants to secure Henry's support. These gifts should be worth around 1250 crowns a year (about £300). The only other person whom Henry trusts is said to be Joachim, the French ambassador (CSPM 843).
- the Duke of Mantua has Henry's ambassador in Venice – the papal prothonotary John Casale – stopped and the verdicts gained in Henry's favour from Mantuan citizens seized. His own complex matrimonial situation remains unresolved and the pope reckons the case will take at least a year in the papal court (CSPS 4.2.558, 623).
- the papal nuncio in England attempts to enter the convocation of Canterbury but the horrified members shoo him out. (LP 5.62).
- Francis writes to the cardinals urging their support for Henry's case (CSPV 4.649).
- Imperial lawyers draw up questions to be asked in Spain of servants who worked for Katherine at the time of her marriage to Arthur. These include, (3) Did Arthur look impotent? (5) Was Katherine ill after Arthur died? (8) Did Henry defy his grandmother, Margaret Beaufort, to marry Katherine? (CSPS 4.1.572, 4.2.601).

Comments

Cardinal Monte's proposal was an interesting idea which could have solved the annulment crisis with the Emperor not losing face, Katherine getting a new role with increased authority, and Henry being assured of a friendly ruler in the area with which England did most trade. Henry and Anne could have married and had a family. The Low Countries were near enough to enable Mary to visit her mother. It could have worked very well had Katherine not been so intent on maintaining her claim to be Henry's wife.

The questions drawn up by the Imperial lawyers were carefully composed to prevent any information being given which might damage their case. For example, nobody was to be asked if there had been blood on the sheets after the wedding night, nor why the staff had waited three months when Arthur died to see if Katherine was pregnant, something clearly superfluous if everyone knew she was a virgin. An explanation was provided for the fifth question about Katherine's state of health when Arthur died. This said that at

---

[271] D'Avray, *Papacy*, p.180

that time, Katherine was "very ill, a cripple, emitting many bad humours from the mouth." Spanish physicians had apparently claimed that the cause of her condition was her virginity and said that if she was to remarry she would speedily recover her health.[272] The Imperialists in 1531 sought further information about her illness with a view to arguing those doctors were right because after marrying Henry and getting regular sex, Katherine became stouter and looked healthier.

There was evidence that Katherine had been ill when Arthur died, almost certainly because she had caught the same infection which was rife in Ludlow at the time, probably some form of the sweating sickness or a respiratory ailment.[273] Her mother-in-law, Queen Elizabeth had sent her own litter to bring Katherine to Croydon because she was too weak to travel in any other way.[274] Yet what the Imperialists were implying was that she was suffering from an ailment known then as suffocation of the mother or green sickness but from 1615 as chlorosis. In 1652, Fontanus described the symptoms of a sufferer:

> Her pulse is sometimes weak, various, and obscure: she hath inward discontents and anxieties, and is most commonly invaded by, at least very subject unto, convulsion fits: she lies, as if she were astonished and void of sense: and from her belly you may hear rumbling, and murmuring noises; she breatheth so weakly, that it is scarce discernable, and indeed she is so sad an object, that the by-standers may easily mistake her to be dead.[275]

Lange in 1554 added that victims tended to be nauseous and "sadly pallid." Jorden in 1603 described:

> They make many strange faces and mouths sometimes as though they laughed or wept, sometimes holding their mouths open or awry, their eyes staring, &c. Sometimes the hands, arms, legs, fingers, toes, &c. are contracted, sometimes particular muscles in the sides, back, arms, legs, &c. one or more at once, as in cramps.[276]

---

272 There is no evidence of any such medical report from 1502 so the source of the Imperial claims is unclear.
273 G. Mattingly, *Catherine of Aragon* (1963) p.44
274 H. Nicolas (ed), *Privy Purse Expenses of Elizabeth of York*, (1830) pp. xc, 14, 103
275 Nicholas Fontanus, *The Womans Doctour*, (1652) p.53. A tendency to masturbate was also observed.
276 Edward Jorden, *A Briefe Discourse of a disease called the Suffocation of the Mother* (1603) unpaginated

The cause of the problem was universally agreed to be a failure to menstruate and chlorosis was used interchangeably with amenorrhoea. Why this happened was attributed variously to an imbalance of humours (specifically excess blood) due to a rich or otherwise inadequate diet, "perturbations of the mind" or a lack of semen in the womb to summon down the blood and female seed. Lange recommended that affected women get themselves pregnant because that seemed to offer the best and most permanent cure. Quite aside from the limited gynaecological knowledge of 1502 affecting diagnosis, there was a political element to the issue. Katherine's value to her parents was as a diplomatic pawn and nobody would want their son to marry an infertile princess, no matter the quality of her parentage or the amount of her dowry: the primary role of a consort was to provide a healthy heir and spare. If Katherine was not menstruating, for whatever reason, she clearly could not do her duty and that created a major problem for Ferdinand and Isabella. It was in their interests to see that she did so as soon as possible. Interestingly, in 1505, Henry himself noted that Katherine was taking her religious fasting to excess causing her to become very thin and cease menstruating and he had to get the pope to order her to stop.[277] No suggestion was made by English or Spanish doctors at the time that virginity was the reason for her amenorrhoea.

Whether a court would be convinced that Katherine's illness in 1502 was chlorosis on the basis of such medical knowledge of the time is open to debate but the Imperial argument had three major weaknesses. Firstly, over seven years passed between Arthur's death and Katherine entering a sexual relationship with Henry and she was not ill for that entire period. Given their determination to claim she was a virgin in 1509, her recovery by mid 1502 made no sense if they were to allege that the cure was intercourse. Secondly, if she had been well prior to her marriage, enemies might query if that showed she had not been a virgin when she left Spain. Their third problem was that doctors were agreed that the ailment did not just affect virgins but "lecherous women and lusty widows" and those who were "apt to venery" i.e. in colloquial terms, sex maniacs.[278] It also affected godly married women. Anne Boleyn was said to have suffered from it when in the Tower, though the cause was attributed not to lack of intercourse but stress and hysteria, and Queen Mary, Regent of the Low Countries too.[279] Thus, even if they did show Katherine as being affected, it would not have proved her virginity but could have been taken to prove the opposite.[280]

---

277 Ehses, *Romische Dokumente*, pp.xliii-xliv.
278 Fontanus, *Womans Doctour*, p.55. It could also affect boys, the young Charles I being said to be a sufferer, TNA SP14/89/35.
279 LP 6.155; Burnet, *History of the Reformation*, ed. Pocock vol. 1 (1865) p.317
280 For further discussion of the development of clinical understanding see I S L Loudoin, 'Chlorosis, anaemia and anorexia nervosa', *British Medical Journal* vol. 281, 20-27 Dec 1980 pp 1669-1676. For a consideration of the issue in the nineteenth century, see Rose E Frisch, 'Population, Food Intake and Fertility', *Science* vol. 199 (January 1978) pp.22-30.

The quotation from Anne regarding Spaniards and the sea may be genuine but it is worth noting that Chapuys heard the story from a gentleman who had it from a lady who waited on Katherine who must have heard it from someone else, so it is at least fourth hand and has been translated in the telling. His comment about her having more courage than a lion was not meant as a compliment, which is how most women might regard it today. Women were meant to be meek and mild: lions were associated with masculinity and violence.

The brief forbidding Henry from remarrying while the case was pending in Rome and saying that any issue from such a union would be illegitimate is the reason why Roman Catholics refused to accept Elizabeth I as their legitimate queen. The ban was unusual and of dubious legality.[281] Chapuys clearly did not realise when he wrote that the cardinals had refused to demand Anne's exclusion from the court. Aside from Chapuys and Katherine, it is unlikely that anyone would have agreed that the pope had the right to say who Henry could and could not have in his palace.

It is interesting that modern writers frequently suggest that Henry's case was doomed and weak but Imperial lawyers at the time were far from certain that they would win. The efforts to increase the number of Spanish cardinals reflects this as does the continual recourse to the Portuguese situation. The Emperor's wife was the daughter of King Manuel who had married two sisters and then the niece of the same.[282] These unions were not forbidden in the Bible, just in canon law, and had no bearing on Henry's case.

There is nothing to suggest that Henry was present when the farce about Wolsey was performed and it is unlikely that Anne or her brother were present either since Chapuys would have been quick to highlight their attendance. That Thomas Boleyn thought this was suitable entertainment and his brother-in-law, the Duke of Norfolk, clearly agreed, shows a want of political acumen as well as a fundamentally unkind nature. No copies of the play have survived so it is impossible to assess it. In 1529, a poem had appeared called *An Impeachment of Wolsey* which spoke of how those who followed Lucifer in their life would follow him down to hell and this may have been the inspiration for the play.[283]

Edward Carne would play a prominent role in Henry's case at Rome for some time and achieve considerable success. His efforts were the more remarkable because he was barely thirty years old.

---

281 See comments September 1527
282 She was the daughter of Manuel's second marriage.
283 Neville Williams, *The Cardinal and the Secretary* (1975) p.76

February 1531

Events

- Dr Ortiz arrives in Rome from the University of Salamanca to assist Mai in prosecuting Katherine's appeal. He admits that neither of them understand Henry's theological case (despite Ortiz being a theologian) but says that Katherine is so obviously in the right, the pope should decide in her favour without even holding a trial. He justifies this by saying a court case will disturb consciences and lead to scandal (LP 5.91).
- the cardinals refuse to admit Henry's excusator on grounds he does not have the correct signed paper from the King appointing him to this role (CSPS 4.2.630).
- Henry receives two camels from the Emperor's brother who is seeking financial aid for his wars against heresy in Germany and the Turk in Hungary. The strange animals attract considerable attention. (LP 5.105).
- Katherine is disappointed to learn that the pope has not issued a letter ordering Henry to dismiss Anne from court (LP 5.112).
- the pope suggests suspending proceedings in Rome for two years in the hope that the situation will resolve itself either by Henry tiring of Anne or the death of one of the parties. He cites other matrimonial cases which have been held in limbo at Rome for up to twenty years. The Emperor refuses to agree to so much as a day's delay (CSPS 4.2.634).
- Chapuys suggests that the request for the legatine court papers is just another delaying tactic and argues that the pope should decide against Henry on grounds he has refused to go to Rome and is thus in contempt of court. He says that if it could be proved that Katherine and Arthur did not consummate their marriage, Henry would lose much support but admits that it is improbable that this could ever happen. In law, where husband and wife live together and share a bed as Katherine and Arthur did, the presumption is that they had sexual intercourse (LP 5.112).
- Henry tells the assembled clergy of Canterbury province that his costs so far in obtaining the annulment have exceeded £100,000 and given the problem has been caused by the church, he requires them to reimburse this sum. The clergy submit in return for a pardon of their infringement of the statutes of Praemunire and agree to pay the money over a five year period. They acknowledge Henry as the supreme head of the church of England as far as the law of Christ allows. Chapuys, who dismisses England as nothing but a "tributary of the Apostolic See" is horrified and blames Anne, reporting that she shows such enthusiasm for the measure that anyone would think she had entered paradise (LP 5.105, 112, 149).
- Cardinal Trani advises the pope that he does not have the authority to dispense from scripture and that therefore Julius' dispensation for Henry

- and Katherine is invalid. The pope sends him to the Imperial lawyers to be re-educated (CSPS 4.2.634, 642).
- Thomas Boleyn obtains a manor in Kent (LP 5.119.34). Anne's uncle is one of a group of six trustees appointed to care for Bessie Blount's father-in-law who has been regarded as a lunatic for some years. They replace Wolsey who took on the role in 1517 (LP 5.119.67).
- a farm at Greenwich is purchased for Anne Boleyn at a cost of £86 13s 4d. She also receives almost £50 as a gift (PP pp.111, 113).
- the French ambassador, Joachim, continues to be welcomed at court, attending mass with the King, being taken to see parliament at work, dining with Henry and Anne, and generally being entertained (LP 5.105).
- Bishop Fisher's household are made ill by a purgative added to some pottage as a jest. Unfortunately it turns out to be poisonous and two people die. Henry visits parliament to demand an act against poisoners be passed. Chapuys expresses a belief that Anne was responsible (LP 5.120, CSPS 4.2.646, CSPV 4.668).[284] A few days later, it is alleged that an attempt is made to assassinate the bishop using a weapon fired across the River Thames by someone in Thomas Boleyn's house.[285]
- German Lutheran princes and free towns form the League of Schmalkalden
- the convocation of Canterbury examines the will of William Tracy and declares him to have been a heretic (LP 5.928).
- Henry's court is entranced by the arrival of a Brazilian chief complete with bones through his cheeks and a jewel in his lower lip.[286]

Comments

It is only Richard Hall's biography of Fisher which claims that the fine levied on the clergy represented the costs of Henry's annulment case to date.[287] Other sources say that it was simply the price paid by the clergy in order to avoid being charged with Praemunire. The fact that the original demand was for £100, 044 8s 8d from Canterbury province and £18,840 0s 10d from York, both very precise amounts, gives credence to Hall's story. Like his father, Henry kept a very keen eye on his account books.[288] By the time the actual

---

284 *Hall's Chronicle* pp.780-781
285 Richard Hall, *Life of Fisher* (1921) pp.72-73
286 Richard Hakluyt, *The principal navigations, voyages, traffiques and discoveries of the English nation* vol. 14 (1890 edition) pp.250-251. The account was written by the son of William Hawkins of Plymouth who brought the chief back late in 1530 and presented him to Henry and his court when they were at Whitehall. An exact date is not given but records show Henry was there during this month. The chief came of his own free will and spent a year being feted by various dignitaries before setting sail for home. Sadly, he died on the journey home. Henry had no interest in overseas exploration and was never involved in slavery or the exploitation of native peoples.
287 Richard Hall, *Life of Fisher*, p.75
288 Lacey Baldwin Smith, *Henry VIII* (1973) p.61

payment plan was agreed in March, the sum had been rounded down for Canterbury to £100,000. If the £118, 888 9s 6d does represent Henry's costs, it does indicate his determination to obtain his annulment for that amount was equivalent to over a year of his revenue and is equivalent to around £832.25 million today. The case still had another two years to go so the final cost is unknown. If Henry did suggest that the clergy were to blame for the annulment crisis, his charge would be more fair than that of Praemunire. Certain clergy had failed to warn Henry VII against allowing the match with Katherine, they had accepted young Henry's renunciation of the dispensation on the wrong day, and they had allowed him to wed Katherine without advising him to seek prior revalidation of the bull due to the change in circumstances since its issue.

     Richard Hall is also the only source for the assassination story. Even with a modern weapon, shooting somebody across the Thames and managing to hit the area just above where Fisher's head would have been had he been in his study at the time, would be an impressive feat of accuracy. To do it in 1531, and for someone to be able to pinpoint the location of the assailant, is literally beyond belief. The story shows the longevity of the hysteria created by the annulment crisis. Interestingly, Richard Hall makes no mention of any suggestion that Anne had anything to do with Fisher being poisoned despite his antipathy toward her.

    The case of William Tracy attracted considerable anger at the time with William Tyndale and John Frith writing about it as well as the chronicler Edward Hall. Tracy was a Gloucestershire man who made his will on October 10th 1530. As was usual at the time, he began by expressing confidence that God would have mercy on his soul but he also said that he believed his faith was sufficient without works, that Jesus was the only mediator between humanity and God and that "therefore will I bestow no part of my goods for the intent that any man should say or do to help my soul for I trust only to the promise of God." He expressly denied that anything he could do would obtain God's favour and pointed to his only merit being from Jesus, a statement he supported with quotations from Romans 14, Matthew 25, Job 19 and Mark 16. He finished by leaving all he had to his wife and son.[289] Such a will might seem uncontroversial today but at the time, the expectation was that a man would ask for prayers for his soul from the Virgin Mary and other saints, that he would give money to his local church so that the vicar would say a prescribed number of masses for him and this in the belief that such acts were necessary and efficacious because faith alone could not save and good works were needed to merit release from purgatory. Tracy's vicar was obviously angry not to have received the anticipated bequest and when the will went to the church court for probate, it was rejected even though there was no civil or church law which said that a man had to leave money to the church, let alone that it was a mortal sin not to do so. Convocation supported this verdict and damned Tracy

---

289 The will is given in full by John Day (ed.) *The Whole Works of W. Tyndale, John Frith and Dr Barnes* (1573) pp.429-435 and in *Hall's Chronicle* pp.796-797

posthumously, despite him never having been charged with heresy during his lifetime or given a chance to recant. This fact, together with the desecration of Tracy's remains by order of the same convocation, created much ill feeling even amongst those who believed in purgatory and the role of the saints. Two years later, Henry would punish those involved severely while Anne would make her feelings known on the matter by becoming a patron of Tracy's son.[290]

It is probable that the camels and their keepers were sent to the Tower of London where a menagerie was kept. It is unknown how long they survived.

The variety of Imperialist attitudes to Katherine's case coming to court is fascinating. The Emperor's demand that not a day's delay occurs is totally unreasonable given that it took a month to get a letter from Rome to England. Even if Henry and his Privy Council were to meet the same day to reply – and it must be presumed they would wish to take legal advice and discuss the situation carefully rather than rush – it would take another month to get the response to Rome. Delays might have been frustrating to Doctors Mai and Ortiz who lived there but justice demanded that time was taken. Ortiz' theory that there should be no trial because Katherine was obviously right is plain ridiculous. Chapuys' argument that the case should be decided against Henry because he was in contempt shows a desire to apply different standards. Katherine had refused to accept the authority of the legatine court at Blackfriars in exactly the same way that Henry had refused to recognise that of Rome, yet the case went on without Wolsey and Campeggio issuing a verdict against her. The only common thread between their attitudes is a lack of respect for process or any interest in an open search for the truth.

Cardinal Trani's intervention is significant. He was recognised as the most godly of all the cardinals, a man who took the Holy Bible and his faith seriously. The decision to send him for "re-education" conjures up images of totalitarian regimes and certainly does not support the pope's claim to neutrality.

It is unclear why Anne should be ecstatic at the clergy recognising Henry's position and agreeing to pay a fine. If this really was news which brought her joy, she must have been a most unusual young woman. Most females of her age would have been more excited by gifts, entertainments or the prospect of getting married, not a vote in convocation.

The recognition of Henry's earthly supremacy was in line with the commandment of St Peter who had written: "Be subject for the Lord's sake to every human institution whether it be the Emperor as supreme or to governors as sent by him." (1 Peter 2:13-14)

Chapuys' comment about England being nothing but a "tributary" of Rome relates to the shameful events of three centuries before. Following King John's refusal to accept Langton as Archbishop of Canterbury, Innocent III had excommunicated the King and placed the country under an interdict. After five years, King John surrendered "to our lord Pope Innocent and to his Catholic

---

290 See January 1533 below. LP 12.2.1304

successors, the whole kingdom of England and the whole kingdom of Ireland, with all their rights and appurtenances, for the remission of our own sins and of those of our whole race as well for the living as for the dead." In return for a tribute of one thousand marks per annum, John and his successors would be entitled to reign. The document remains one of the darkest in England's history but is even more shameful for the papacy. The idea that any king should be forced to yield their entire country to a foreign power was bad enough but to claim such an act was necessary "for the remission" of sins was to fly in the face of the entire Christian faith. Just why did Innocent III imagine Jesus had died on the cross? (Matt 26:28) It remained a document which the Imperialists and popes valued highly and they would use it to justify their efforts to deprive Henry of his throne and later his daughter Elizabeth.

March 1531

Events

- Chapuys ridicules the opinions of Marc Raphael, the ex-chief rabbi brought from Venice by Henry VIII (LP 5.120).
- James V of Scotland tells the Emperor that he distrusts England and France and asks if he has a sister, niece or daughter he can marry in order to create an alliance (CSPS 4.2.605, 653).
- Mai removes references to Katherine sleeping with Arthur for fear it will harm her case. He urges the Archbishop of Santiago to prepare witnesses in Spain according to the questions devised earlier (LP 5.130).
- Henry sits in judgment at a heresy trial and releases a preacher who has denied papal supremacy saying: "This proposition cannot be counted as heretical for it is both true and certain." Chapuys blames Anne's malign influence saying that she and her father are "more Lutheran than Luther." (CSPS 4.2.664)
- Francis sends another protest on Henry's behalf to the pope, this time drafted by Jean du Bellay. He advises Henry to have the issue sorted in England by clergy there (LP 5.151).
- Cardinal Cesi urges the Imperialists to agree to a two year delay in Katherine's case (CSPS 4.2.667).
- the Emperor thanks the pope for making two Spaniards cardinals but says he wants three more (CSPS 4.2.661).
- the Duke of Mantua is told by the Emperor that he must remain with Julia of Naples, despite Julia vowing not to defend the case (CSPS 4.2.643, 661).
- the Turk threatens Hungary (LP 5.137).
- in an audience with Henry, Chapuys tells him that the Emperor's efforts to have the case heard swiftly at Rome are a mark of his great love for his uncle and his deep concern that Henry should not have to endure any

more sleepless nights agonising over whether his marriage is incestuous (CSPS 4.2.664).
- Henry tells the nuncio that he does not care if the pope excommunicates him for Jesus said that people should only obey God (LP 5.148).
- Sir Thomas More, together with Bishops Stokesley and Longland, reads the verdicts of the universities regarding Henry's "marriage" to the members of the House of Lords and then the House of Commons with instructions that they should share them with their constituents. Chapuys – who was not there – reports that the Commons were unimpressed and upset. Edward Hall – an MP who was there – said: "When these determinations were published, all wise men in the realm much abhorred the marriage: but women and such as were more wilful than wise or learned, spake against the determinations and said that the universities were corrupt and enticed so to do, which is not to be thought."[291]
- the convocation of Canterbury order that the body of William Tracy be dug up and burnt in public to demonstrate the wickedness of his heresies (LP 5.928).
- Cardinal Loaysa says that "everyone knows" the Emperor is "an angel."[292]

Comments

Chapuys' desire to blame Anne for everything which he regarded as bad is frankly comical. Henry was a very able theologian who spent considerable hours studying his Bible as well as the works of the church fathers. His exchanges with ambassadors frequently contain quotations from the Scriptures. Henry did not need Anne to instruct him in the subject. He was a capable judge, indeed finding some faults in the unnamed preacher's teaching which he was required to retract. As for the idea of her being more Lutheran than Luther, there is no evidence that Chapuys had the slightest understanding of Luther's theology so he could not have defined Anne's beliefs in this manner even if he had known them.

It is difficult to regard Chapuys' comments about Raphael as anything but antisemitic. His presumption that he himself understood the Hebrew scriptures better than a chief rabbi is extraordinary and his criticism betrays the fact that he had not even read Deuteronomy 25. The text is quite clear and exactly how Raphael explained it. A man might marry his widowed sonless sister-in-law but only for the purposes of raising up heirs for his dead brother not himself. If he wanted children for himself, he needed his own wife. As to the claim that Henry was angry with Raphael, he remained in his employment for at least the next three years even accompanying the court to France in 1532. As Raphael was in his seventies by this stage, it is likely that his employment was ended by his death rather than anything else.

---

291 *Hall's Chronicle*, p.780.
292 Parker, *Emperor*, p.211.

The idea of digging up a dead man for the purpose of punishing him is likely to seem repugnant to most people today but it was not not a unique case. In 897, Pope Stephen ordered that his predecessor's body be exhumed, dressed in full papal regalia, and tried for behaviour inconsistent with his office. Pope Formosus was found guilty – being dead he clearly could not enter a plea – and his body desecrated before being thrown in the Tiber. It was washed up and a monk declared that as miracles had been reported by those who touched it, Formosus must be a saint. Pope Stephen was in consequence arrested, jailed and murdered, probably to avoid the scandal of another trial.

The university opinions read included six from France and two from Italy. Three of them (all French) said that marriage to a brother's wife was invalid if the first union had been consummated but they were not asked to debate if it was legal if the first had not been consummated so it would be unwise to draw the conclusion – as some modern writers have – that they were not truly supportive of Henry. The King had undoubtedly approved the questions which were sent out. The university of Bologna, said of any marriage to a brother's wife that: "we witness and without any doubt do steadfastly hold that this marriage should be horrible, accursed, to be cried out upon and utterly abominable not only for a Christian man but also for any infidel, unfaithful or heathen." The University of Padua wrote: "such marriage is no marriage, yea it is to be abhorred and cursed of every Christian man and to be abominate as a grievous sin and that it is as clearly as can be forbidden under most cruel penalties by the law of nature, of God and of man. And that the pope, unto whom the keys of the Kingdom of heaven be committed by Christ, the Son of God, hath no power to dispense by right and law for any cause or suggestion or excuse that any such matrimony should be contract. For things which be forbidden by the law of God be not underneath his power but above it. He is vicar of God only in such things as God hath not determined Himself in His law but hath left them to the determination and ordinance of man."

Henry's comment to the nuncio was pointed. He was quoting Matt. 4:10 which described how the devil offered Jesus rulership of the world if only he would follow him, an offer Jesus rejected by quoting Deut. 6:13-14 that people should only obey God. Chapuys' Biblical knowledge does not seem to have been sufficient for him to pick this up but Henry was effectively telling the nuncio that obeying the pope in order to gain authority was like obeying the devil. Whether the nuncio recognised the reference is not known.

April 1531

Events

- Francis sends Henry an ornate clock with moving planets on the dial (LP 5.187).

- in Rome, Doctors Mai and Ortiz argue about how Katherine's case should be handled. Mai, as a canon lawyer, says that if they can prove Katherine was left a virgin by Arthur, there will have been no affinity and hence no impediment. Ortiz, as a theologian, favours arguing that the prohibition in Leviticus is human rather than divine law and hence the pope can dispense. Ortiz adds that he feels so strongly about Katherine's case that he would willingly suffer martyrdom to defend her cause (CSPS 4.2.686).
- from Antwerp, Vaughan sends Henry a copy of Tyndale's *Answer to More* which he has painstakingly copied out because of the poor print quality of the original (LP 5.201).
- Henry Percy is elected a Knight of the Most Noble Order of the Garter (LP 5.204). Financial problems force him to alienate considerable lands (LP 5.220.17).
- Henry seeks a further six month delay in proceedings at Rome or the hearing being moved to a neutral country. He tells Bennet to warn the pope that: "here lieth a great number in wait to hear of open dissension between the pope and Us; and as soon as that trumpet bloweth, they will think it a most propitious occasion to strike at his power, which is in all points abhorred, as he and other his predecessors hath used it." The Privy Council are agreed that should Henry be summoned to Rome then this will be the issue upon which "We shall expunge finally his high power." Henry orders Bennet to "abuse them as they have abused us for they have been to us always like a willow tree, showing fair buds and leaves without any fruit." (LP 5.206; SP vol. 7 pp.297-299) Acknowledging the pope may retaliate, he adds: "I know his excommunications are not to be feared when right is on the other side" (CSPS 4.2.699). Chapuys thinks that Henry's policy is to delay proceedings until the pope dies in the hope that his successor will be more amenable to Henry's demands (LP 5.171).
- Katherine tells the Emperor that she needs the verdict before parliament resumes in October. She is, however, prepared to go to parliament herself to defend "my truth and my rights." (LP 5.176). She writes: "I shall not desist from my prayer until I see full justice done unto me for, as Your Highness well knows, I have truth and right on my side. To uphold and defend these is a meritorious work in the eyes of God and the greatest service man can do." (CSPS 4.2.681)
- the Archbishop of Toledo reports finding a letter by Katherine's father saying she was a virgin when Arthur died but he agreed to say she was not to please the English (CSPS 4.2.710).
- Edmund Howard (Anne's uncle and the father of Kathryn) becomes the Comptroller of Calais (LP 5.220.14)
- Mary has indigestion and Henry refuses to visit her. Chapuys, who admits the condition is not life threatening, claims Anne will not let Henry go because she is jealous of his love for his daughter. Chapuys says Anne hates Mary even more than she does Katherine for this reason. He also reports Norfolk's fear that Anne will be the ruin of the family saying that

- Henry is already complaining that Katherine never nagged him like she does (LP 5.216).
- the Duke of Mantua asks the pope for Catherine de Medici's hand in marriage despite still being wed to Julia of Naples (CSPS 4.2.698). He also asks Ferdinand, the Emperor's brother, to see if he can get him the heiress of Montferrat as a wife. The heiress happens to be the younger sister of his first wife. Ferdinand writes to the Emperor saying that he needs money and acting as a marriage broker for the Duke would be a good way of earning some (CSPS 4.2.701).
- the pope's twenty year old 'nephew', Hippolito Medici, rows with the pope saying he cannot live on less than 700 crowns a month and he wants to give up being a cardinal. Announcing his wish to contest the rulership of Florence with his cousin Alessandro, he departs Rome (CSPS 4.2.703, 704).
- the pope expresses a preference for the Dauphin to marry the daughter of his stepmother, Eleanor, rather than any daughter of the Emperor (CSPS 4.2.700).
- Anne's desk is garnished with laten and gold at a cost of £2 4s 7d. Henry also pays the bill for her embroiderer, William Lylgrave, at £18 14s 9 ½d. (PP pp.123, 128)[293]
- the rent for George Boleyn's house at Greenwich is paid by the King - £20 for two years (PP p.128).
- a reward of £5 is paid to "young Mr Weston", Henry Knyvet and Thomas the jester (PP p.126).

Comments

George was a Gentleman of the Privy Chamber, one of around half a dozen men who attended the King. None of the others had their rent paid. Since his duties required him being frequently at court, where his wife also served, it is unclear how much time he spent at the house in Greenwich. Only a few weeks before, a farm had been purchased for Anne at Greenwich.[294] Assuming she was not planning to do a Marie Antoinette and amuse herself with a model dairy, let alone take up ploughing, the gifts suggest a conscious desire of Henry's to keep them both close but also capable of separation should the need arise.

Henry was a keen collector of clocks. His privy purse expenses show numerous purchases of them as well as the employment of two clock-makers at £4 per annum in 1521 and a keeper for the clock at Hampton Court at £2 per annum.

---

293 Laten is the material used for church brasses.
294 See February 1531

It is unknown what service Weston, Knyvet and the jester had performed to earn the £5 reward. It may have been related to an entertainment over Easter.

Hippolito's income was in Tudor terms worth about £2000 a year, the equivalent of a senior member of the nobility.

It is unsurprising that Ferdinand thought that helping the Duke of Mantua with his matrimonial arrangements would be lucrative. On past history, he could expect a long career in such a role! Even Henry never proposed to two women at the same time. Mantua's request for the sister of his first wife was no doubt inspired by the fact that her brother had died in March leaving her an attractive fortune.

Despite living in England for thirty years, Katherine seems to have had no understanding of the role of parliament. Her statement that she is willing to go there to defend her case is interesting in light of her refusal to attend the legatine court at Blackfriars.

Mai's proposal to argue Katherine's case on the basis of her virginity was rather dangerous. Canon lawyers were not united on the definition of affinity, disagreeing on whether it stemmed from vows or intercourse. Even if they were to settle that point, it was not clear that it had any relevance to the case. Gratian's *Decretum* which was the recognised handbook of canon law and which the pope and cardinals were meant to use when coming to judgment declared: "If someone is betrothed to a woman and, because of his death, he does not know her, his brother cannot take her as a wife."[295] If in a fit of gallantry, or in response to financial rewards, the papal court did accept Mai's claim, it would then arguably play into Henry's hands because the application for dispensation made in 1502 was for affinity and if there was none, it would follow that those seeking the dispensation had lied. Canon law stated that any bull granted on false information was obreptious and hence automatically invalid. For Mai to propose such a case was a clear sign of the desperation felt by Katherine's supporters at Rome.

The first half of 1531 sees Henry showering Anne with expensive gifts every month. Was this just a token of his love or was he trying to appease her as efforts to delay things in Rome continued. The process had already been running for four years. Did she think it would never end? Was she starting to doubt Henry's commitment to her? Does the fact that she apparently received no gifts during the second half of the year indicate that she had been appeased or that she had gone off to sulk at Hever again?

It is interesting that Vaughan thought Henry might like Tyndale's book and his copying it all out was an act of true dedication. The 15,000 word volume denies purgatory and the need for clerical celibacy. It says that scripture is the sole ground for faith and that tradition has no role. It argues for the need to have the scriptures available in English so that people can read them for themselves and not be reliant on interpreters. It criticises the concept of a

---

295 C27, q2, c11

treasury of merit accumulated by the saints and says that people are saved by faith in Jesus alone, not by works or the advocacy of saints. It talks of Jesus' death being a once for all time sacrifice and the mass being a memorial of that and not a further sacrifice. It discusses the infamous Hunne case.[296] Finally, Tyndale condemns the pope for taking the Bible and "putteth it under his feet and treadeth on it in token that he is lord over it that it should serve him and he not it." What Henry might have liked was Tyndale's remark that papal lawyers had "no more skill of the scripture than they that never saw it: yea, and have professed a contrary doctrine."

May 1531

Events

- Henry reads Tyndale's *Answer to More* and describes it as seditious, unlearned and slanderous. He decides he does not want Tyndale to ever return to England (LP 5.248).
- the convocation of York grants Henry £18,840 0s 10d to obtain pardon for Praemunire (LP 5.225).
- Nicholas Raince, Francis' permanent ambassador in Rome, tells Montmorency that the pope's love for Francis could be a benefit to Henry's case (LP 5.231). Gregory Casale tells Henry the case is going so badly that his only hope lies with French influence. Great hopes are placed on the impending visit of the Cardinal Bishop of Tarbes (LP 5.229).
- Katherine suggests that she and Henry go to visit Mary, He tells her that she can go if she wishes and stay there too permanently. Katherine replies that she will never leave her husband's side, even for her daughter (LP 5.238).
- Henry commences a major building project at Westminster (LP 5.238, 260, 261). He starts converting Wolsey's old home of York Place into Whitehall Palace.
- the Cardinal Bishop of Tarbes arrives in Rome and urges the creation of four more cardinals – two for France and two for England and requests that Henry's case be heard at Cambrai or Avignon (LP 5.255). Henry says he would be pleased to welcome the pope to these locations (LP 5.274).
- the cardinals refuse to create the four cardinals but also reject the Emperor's nominee on grounds he is a murderer (CSPS 4.2.733).
- Henry asks his ambassador at Rome to protest at the excommunication of King John of Hungary without so much as a hearing. He believes this was done at the request of the Emperor whose brother also claims to be King of Hungary (LP 5.274).

---

296 See January 1530 comments.

- from Venice, Niño reports rumours that Francis is negotiating with the Turk with a view to creating war in the east for the Emperor (CSPS 4.2.714).
- an Imperial court finds that the Duke of Ferrara is entitled to keep Modena and Reggio. The pope, who claims them as part of the Papal States, complains to the Emperor and says he expects him to overturn the verdict (CSPS 4.2.725). The English celebrate a rupture between pope and Emperor and hope it will benefit their cause (CSPS 4.2.720).
- talking of the annulment, the Duke of Norfolk tells Chapuys: "The Devil and no other must have been the originator and promoter of this wretched scheme." (CSPS 4.2.720)
- the pope tells the Imperial ambassador that his plan is to take Henry's case as slowly as possible in the hope that Henry will give up and go and marry Anne thereby settling the matter. Dr Mai replies that such a course of action will be to the ruin of Christendom (CSPS 4.2.732).
- James V of Scotland withdraws his bid for the hand of Catherine de Medici in the hope that he'll obtain a Danish princess instead (LP 5.257).

Comments

Anne was an active participant in Henry's building plans not only poring over the plans with him but visiting the site and offering suggestions based on her experience of French palaces.[297]

One wonders who Norfolk thought was responsible for the annulment process beginning. Most people today, and many then, believed it was Henry although others blamed Wolsey or the Bishop of Tarbes. Suggesting the King was the Devil would be distinctly unwise. Norfolk had ordered a play showing Wolsey going to hell though not as Satan. Norfolk was generally pro-Imperial so it must be assumed that his comment meant he was pointing a finger at the French, though this may have just been a front put on for the benefit of Chapuys.

Henry did eventually take the pope's advice and simply marry Anne. Christendom was not ruined.

June 1531

Events

- Wolsey's ex-physician, Dr Agostini, has an audience with the Emperor at Ghent. The Emperor is astonished to hear of how Henry spent ten hours examining a heretic. Agostini reports that Campeggio is upset that he has been stripped of his role as Cardinal Protector of England. Keen to

---

297 Simon Thurley, *The Royal Palaces of Tudor England* (Yale 1993 p.50; Simon Thurley, *Houses of Power* (2017) p.217

continue his European travels, Agostini asks Norfolk to secure him an official role so that he can serve Henry more fully (LP 5.283).
- the Cardinal Bishop of Tarbes tells the pope that he carries a book containing Henry's arguments. The pope tells Dr Ortiz that he will seek to get hold of this so that the Imperial lawyers can prepare a refutation to it. Suspicious of the pope's enthusiasm to read the book, Tarbes passes the book instead into the safe hands of the English ambassadors (LP 5.284, 309).
- Nicholas Shaxton is held in custody by the Bishop of Norwich for denying purgatory and clerical celibacy (LP 5.297).
- in Antwerp, English translations are published of the books of Isaiah and Jonah (LP 5.303).
- the law faculties of Orleans and Paris declare that Henry's summons to Rome is unlawful and that if the papal court refuse to admit his excusator, the entire legal process at Rome is null and void (LP 5.306).
- Henry tells the papal nuncio that he does not care what the pope does: "I will do here as I think best." (CSPS 4.2.739).
- a deputation of some thirty lords and bishops is sent to Katherine to seek her agreement to have the case heard outside Rome. She refuses claiming that the pope represents God on earth and therefore eternal truth, and hence no other judge is possible. She denies Henry's supremacy of the church in England saying that all spiritual matters, including anything related to the sacrament of matrimony, belong to the pope alone. She also takes the opportunity of again denying that her marriage to Prince Arthur was consummated (LP 5.287).
- suspecting he favours Katherine following a remark made about wishing all lawyers involved in the annulment case could just be packed off to Rome to debate it there, Anne tells Sir Henry Guildford that she will have him dismissed as Comptroller of the Household when she is Queen. Guildford retorts that she will not be able to do so as he is resigning now. Henry tells him to ignore the talk of a woman and refuses to accept his resignation but Guildford departs anyway (LP 5.287).
- an English dialogue is published setting out Henry's case. Chapuys dismisses it as "feeble" saying that Katherine's virginity means there is no issue and the violent language therein will encourage people to support her (CSPS 4.2.753).
- the pope says he would rather Catherine de Medici marry the Duke of Mantua (CSPS 4.2.743). Dr Mai suspects that she will, however, marry the Duke of Orleans because the pope wants her to become Duchess of Milan. If the aged, sick and childless Duke of Milan dies without issue – as seems probable – the duchy reverts to France and would go to the Duke of Orleans. The pope also thinks that the pro-French Florentines would like the match and a union with the French royal family would boost his standing in the world, even though it would annoy the Emperor (CSPS 4.2.746).

- relations between Doctors Ortiz and Mai further deteriorate with continued rows about Katherine's case and squabbles over precedence which see Dr Ortiz riding his horse up level with Dr Mai's instead of staying behind thus provoking Dr Mai to speed up as they race to the papal palace. Mai says the Spaniards despise Ortiz and the Romans laugh at this ultra touchy and vain little man (CSPS 4.2.748).
- in Ulm, the mass is abolished and altars are broken. They are replaced with services of Holy Communion or the Lord's Supper celebrated at plain tables (CSPS 4.2.755).
- Mendoza, the Imperial ambassador to England before Chapuys, is given his cardinal's hat (CSPS 4.2.741).[298]
- Chapuys advises Katherine to bribe some people to go to the Low Countries and swear her marriage to Arthur was not consummated and that they heard Henry say so. To his disappointment, he fails to find anyone willing to go, a decision he attributes to fear (CSPS 4.2.753).
- William Brereton protests when a sturgeon he is due to take to Henry is stolen. (LP 5.316).
- Henry Norris obtains the manor of Langton in Rutland following the death of the Dowager Duchess of Buckingham (LP 5.318.10).

Comments

It is unknown why Agostini was in Ghent and how the trip was funded if he was not there on official business for either Norfolk or Henry,

The translation of Isaiah into English is particularly significant as it is regarded by Christians as the most important prophetic book. It is the basis for much of the teaching regarding the messiah and has long had a major role in evangelism. The familiar Christmas readings such as "the people that walked in darkness have seen a great light" and "unto us a son is given" as well as the Good Friday readings about the suffering servant, all come from Isaiah. It is a volume of great poetry and this fact, together with its message, meant that once heard in English, people would be unlikely to want to go back to having it in Latin. Given that translations of the Scriptures were still banned, only those willing to risk purchasing an illegal import and subsequent charge of heresy could enjoy it.

Henry's decision to spend from 9am to 7pm debating theology with a heretic shows how seriously he took his role as Defender of the Faith. He was not some libidinous fool who devoted his days to pleasure while being pushed around by clever ministers, as some modern portrayals like to suggest. He was the most intellectual prince in Europe and his knowledge of the Bible surpassed most of the clergy – and certainly critics like Chapuys. Henry may not have been an original or systematic thinker like Calvin but he had a passion for the truth and the salvation of souls, his own and other people's.

---

[298] The election had taken place on March 9th 1530.

Katherine's view of papal supremacy is predictable and never changed. What is more interesting is Norfolk briefing Chapuys about an encounter which he admits Katherine won. If Chapuys is to be believed, Norfolk's support for Anne was not entirely robust though he also comments "I had no doubt that his thoughts on the subject differed from his words." Since we do not possess Norfolk's correspondence which might have revealed his true feelings on the subject, we are unable to judge the point. As Anne's uncle, he would have expected to gain if she became queen and this prospect would have over-ridden any personal dislike he may have felt for her. He may have simply been hedging his bets by trying to keep on good terms with Chapuys because, if the annulment failed and Katherine remained Queen of England, his support would stand him in good stead for further reward from the Emperor. Norfolk saw Henry and Anne together regularly which Chapuys did not and he may have felt that her hold on the King was not as secure as everybody thought.

Dr Mai may have been right about the Romans laughing at Dr Ortiz but one suspects they were laughing at him too. What the Emperor and his ministers thought as they read the complaints being made by each party against the other is not known. Possibly, they just turned the page…

Anne's behaviour with Guildford is petulant at best, threatening at worst. It clearly demonstrated a lack of maturity, grace and political discretion - no doubt why Chapuys repeats the story. However, his account may not be entirely accurate. Guildford's wish that all the lawyers go off to Rome to debate the annulment is not necessarily a vote of support for Katherine. It is likely that Churchill had times that he wished that the war was over so his government could deal with other things, but that does not mean he supported Germany, and certainly many people in the United Kingdom became heartily tired of hearing about Brexit in the second decade of the twenty-first century whether they were supporters or opponents of the proposal. Guildford may have just been tired of the arguments. He was by this time forty-two and probably a sick man: he died just under a year later. Guildford was not only Comptroller but one of the MPs for Kent and he had been in Henry's service for over twenty years. He had been Master of Horse from 1515 to 1522 and was frequently to be found enjoying masques, jousts, and games of cards with the King. In 1525 he worked with Anne's father on the Amicable Grant and in December 1529 on the articles against Wolsey.[299] Living at Leeds Castle in Kent from 1512 onwards, just twenty-two miles from Anne's home of Hever, Henry Guildford had probably known her since childhood given he had been married to her cousin.[300] He was an experienced courtier and his response to Henry's young lady friend presuming to lecture him on loyalty is understandable. Guildford was also a friend of Sir Charles Brandon and brother in law of Nicholas Carew. Yet

---

299 Guildford had accompanied Wolsey on his 1527 mission to France.
300 Guildford's first wife, Margaret Bryan, was niece to Thomas Boleyn. See Appendix 6: Key Relationships. They married in 1512 and had no children. She died before the annulment crisis began.

Chapuys was wrong when he said that Guildford left over the incident. He may have gone home for a few days but he was still Comptroller when he died.

The dialogue which Chapuys describes but does not name must have been the *Glass of Truth*. Some writers have suggested it was issued later but evidently Chapuys had seen it or a draft copy.[301]

The pope's desire to see his "niece" Catherine de Medici marry the second son of the King of France, despite being aware that this would upset the Emperor, shows Clement was not a coward but simply selfish. The Duke of Orleans was Henry's godson so the match could have helped his case.

The destruction of altars and abolition of the mass would happen in England in Edward's reign. It was not until the late nineteenth century following the influence of the Oxford Movement that the word altar started to be used again by Anglicans and non-churchgoers though it is incorrect. Altars are places of sacrifice and the Church of England continues to teach that Holy Communion is a memorial of the once for all time sacrifice of Jesus. As Article XXX1 states:

> The offering of Christ once made is that perfect redemption, propitiation and satisfaction for all the sins of the whole world, both original and actual; and there is none other satisfaction for sin but that alone. Wherefore, the sacrifice of masses in the which it was commonly said that the priest did offer Christ for the quick and the dead to have remission of pain or guilt, were blasphemous fables and dangerous deceits.[302]

July 1531

Events

- Alessandro de Medici is welcomed as Duke of Florence and the city pledges loyalty to the Emperor (CSPS 4.2.757).
- Henry tells his ambassadors in Rome that he has not given up hope that the pope will act reasonably "though we trust him not perfectly" because of his ability to "fashion his communications as may make for his purpose." He stresses the verdicts against the case being advoked and says they are to tell the pope that scholars agree "that our marriage is null, invalid, wicked, an obscene pollution, abominable, incestuous, detestable to God

---

[301] The dating of this tract has produced considerable debate, see especially Richard Rex, 'Redating Henry VIII's a Glasse of the Truthe', *The Library*, March 2003 4(1):16-27; Steven Haas, 'Henry VIII's Glasse Of Truthe', *History*, (October 1979) pp.353-362. It could not have been the university determinations because they were not issued as a dialogue.

[302] Heb. 9:28, 10:10

and odious to men" and that no pope has the authority to issue a dispensation against divine law. Henry is willing to attribute the pope's behaviour to poor advice and to forgive him if he will issue a fresh decretal commission for the annulment to be heard in England by the Archbishop of Canterbury with a promise not to interfere or over-rule this. Henry offers suggestions for other judges such as a panel with one nominee each for himself, Katherine, the pope and Francis or else the abbots of Westminster, Hyde and Winchcombe.[303] Regarding Katherine's "invented" claim of non-consummation with Arthur, they should rehearse the evidence presented to Wolsey and Campeggio "being so evident and manifest in law, as no proof may or ought to be admitted to the contrary" and because it is "most certainly true." They are to tell the pope "the matter must have an end." They are also to offer Henry's help to the pope to secure the marriage of his "niece" Catherine de Medici with Francis' second son, Henry's godson (LP 5.326, 327).[304]

- Francis tells Henry that the pope has promised the Cardinal Bishop of Tarbes that he will not issue a verdict against him even if the case lasts twenty years (LP 5.328). Henry seeks to obtain this promise in writing from the pope (LP 5.327).
- Chapuys admits that the law will presume Katherine consummated her marriage to Arthur given she slept in his bed and that testimonies of what Arthur said on the subject will make it impossible to prove she did not. Her only hope, in his view, is character witnesses to her virtue. If, however, more universities support the illegality of the advocation, he thinks her case almost hopeless (LP 5.340).
- the pope manages to secure a loan of the book the Cardinal Bishop of Tarbes gave to the English and he promptly lends it to Dr Ortiz who proclaims it the work of the devil and says that all the opinions pro Henry have been bought and are worthless (LP 5.342). Meanwhile, Katherine's negative response to Henry's suggestion that the case be heard outside Rome is hailed as a speech inspired by the Holy Spirit and worthy of St Catherine herself and deserving of publication (CSPS 4.2.766).
- the Emperor refuses to return Tyndale to Henry saying there is no evidence that he has done wrong and he believes Tyndale is being persecuted for his support of Katherine (LP 5.354).
- Katherine condemns the pope for denying her justice but expresses confidence that testimonies of her old Spanish servants regarding her marriage to Arthur will win her the case (LP 5.355). Unknown to her,

---

303 Respectively, John Islip, John Salcot and Richard Munslow. Salcot became Bishop of Bangor around Christmas 1533 and had helped secure the vote for Henry at Cambridge. Islip was a member of the Privy Council and became an advocate of Henry's Supreme Headship. All three attended over eighty per cent of days in Parliament. Lehmberg, *Reformation Parliament*, p.41-43. 257

304 SP vol.7 pp.305-316.

these have not even been sought yet with the Emperor issuing a reminder on July 31st (LP 5.362).
- Henry departs Windsor leaving Katherine behind. An exchange of letters follows. Chapuys contrasts Katherine's submissive replies with Henry's rudeness which he attributes to Anne dictating the letter! (LP 5.361)
- the Imperial lawyers in Rome tell Chapuys that if proof could be found of Henry committing adultery with Anne, the pope would be willing to issue a censure. Chapuys admits that there is no hope of that but says the papal nuncio is willing to send a notarised letter regarding Henry's angry language to him if that would help (LP 5.361).
- George Throckmorton receives nine offices worth £39 10s 10d a year (LP 5.364.4). William Carey's brother, John, gets two manors in Wales (LP 5.364.25). George Boleyn is appointed keeper of Hatfield Regis at £3 0s 6d a year and together with his father, offices in Essex worth £16 1s a year (LP 5.364.9,28).
- Dr Ortiz complains that a benefice he was granted in Spain a decade before remains closed to him. The pope excommunicated the patron and put the whole village under interdict as well as advoking the case to Rome and issuing an inhibition against proceedings in Spain. Following pressure from Ortiz and the Empress, the pope has agreed to revoke the advocation but the case has yet to be heard in Spain (CSPS 4.2.766).
- the pope says he is prepared to offer the following concessions to the German Lutherans – communion in both kinds, an end to clerical celibacy and the redefinition of mortal sin as only those acts which are committed against divine law (CSPS 4.2.769).
- an abbot arrives in England to commence a visitation of the Cistercian monasteries. Henry refuses to permit this to happen. Chapuys claims this is because Henry has claimed to be king, emperor and pope in England (LP 5.361).
- the papal auditors thank the Emperor for their rewards. Capisucio wants his paid to his cousin, Cardinal Cesarino, but Simonetta wants his direct (CSPS 4.2.758).
- the Emperor proclaims that his primary and principal object in defending Katherine is "that the authority, power and dignity of the pope and of the apostolic see should be preserved from the calumnious attempts of those who wish to impeach and restrain the same." (CSPS 4.2.768)
- Henry has talks with Joachim, the French ambassador, about the possibility of himself and Francis supporting the Duke of Saxony and other German princes in their dispute with the Emperor (LP 5.337).
- Anne has a row with Henry's brother-in-law, Charles Brandon, allegedly accusing him of having incestuous sexual relations with his daughter (CSPS 4.2.765).
- building work continues apace at Westminster Palace. A painting of Henry's coronation is created for the Low Gallery near the gardens and recently extended orchard. Lodgings are built for Anne below the library. Rooms

are set aside for Thomas Boleyn and Henry Norris. A new gallery is built with four cases for Henry's clock collection. Henry is so keen for the project to be completed that he orders candles so work can continue through the night (LP 5.952).
- Katherine's chaplain, Thomas Abell, publishes his book I*nvicta Veritas*. Edward Wootton seeks to obtain a copy for Reginald Pole but reports they are not sold openly and hence very difficult to find (CSPV 4.673).

Comments

It is evident that the records for the summer of 1531 are incomplete for Henry on several occasions refers to letters from ambassadors which are no longer extant.

The Emperor's belief that Tyndale was a keen supporter of Katherine can only have stemmed from Chapuys' recommendation of Tyndale's *Practice of Prelates*. Had he read the tract himself, he would not have defended him.[305]

Three words spring to mind regarding Dr Ortiz – pot, kettle, black. At the same time that he was condemning the English for use of financial rewards, he was arranging them for Imperial supporters. Bribery existed on both sides and if opinions in favour of Henry's case were to be discounted on those grounds, so should the decisions for Katherine. As regards his benefice in Spain, Ortiz' arguments that the case should be heard in Spain where it began and all the witnesses live, rather in Rome where nothing has happened for years, is a repeat of the points Henry has been making about his annulment case – grounds Ortiz has condemned as unreasonable.

The pope's offered concessions to the Lutherans are significant. They were to be used only as needed in negotiations but they are in advance of papal policy in the twenty-first century. People were burnt at the stake by Bloody Mary for such demands and yet here the pope is agreeing to them.

The Emperor's stated objectives in defending Katherine show the impossibility of an amicable end to Henry's case. The Emperor and pope were interested in the authority of Rome: Henry in the word of God. Indeed, the omission of any desire to find the truth amongst the Emperor's goals is indicative of his attitude.

Henry's request for another decretal commission and pollicitation may seem curious. This had been Wolsey's policy and it had ended in failure, not because the documents had not been issued but because the pope had failed to honour them. It followed the pope verbally promising the Cardinal Bishop of Tarbes that he would never issue a verdict against Henry. Given the situation could not just rest, Henry's interpretation of this was that the pope must want somebody else to give the verdict and who more suitable than the Archbishop of Canterbury? The second prong in Henry's strategy at this point was to separate the pope from the Emperor through reminders of the Imperial decision regarding the Duke of Ferrara, by creating a marriage alliance between the pope

---

305 See December 1530 Comments

and Francis and possibly rewarding Cardinal de Medici with an abbey in either France or England. Henry thought that if such an alienation could be achieved, the pope would issue the desired annulment. Had he known that the pope had given his legal team's arguments to the opposition, he would have realised that the pope's claim to impartiality was a blatant lie.

Chapuys is the only source for Anne's accusation of the Duke of Suffolk. At this point, Brandon had two married daughters and two still at home – Frances aged fourteen who was betrothed and Eleanor who was eleven or twelve. Is it credible that Brandon was sexually abusing his own daughters, the King's nieces? If Henry had believed this, Brandon would have lost his head. Nothing further was said about the matter so it seems safe to clear Brandon of this serious charge of child abuse. How then did Chapuys get it wrong? Brandon did have a twelve or thirteen year old ward who was promised to his son so could have been referenced as a daughter. The age of consent was twelve in Tudor England but sexual activity at this age was very rare, primarily because the purpose of intercourse was seen as procreation and the age of menarche was normally at least fifteen in this period. Following the death of his wife, Brandon would eventually marry the said ward but it would be unwise to infer from this that they were involved years earlier. Many people meet their future spouse in childhood without there being any inappropriate contact.[306] Could Anne have made some comment about Brandon securing the wardship of the wealthy heiress with a view to having her himself should his wife die young and the barb have been misreported to suggest that this was a present and not future relationship? Brandon's wife, Mary, did not enjoy good health. Or did Anne make a reference to Brandon marrying a woman and her niece and the word was changed to daughter either by Chapuys or by whoever told the story to him?[307] If Anne really did make such an accusation, it would be proof of her having a foul mind and evil nature, and if that is the case, it is hard to imagine that Henry would have married her. Brandon was not just his brother-in-law but his closest and most loyal friend. Henry could accept Brandon and Anne not liking each other much but not his future queen spreading scurrilous lies about someone so close to him and who was father of the second in line to the throne.[308] The likelihood must be that Chapuys got it wrong.

---

306 For example, Queen Elizabeth II met Prince Philip of Greece when she was thirteen but did not marry him until she was twenty-one.

307 Prior to marrying Mary Tudor, Brandon had married Anne Browne and Margaret Mortimer who were aunt and niece.

308 Brandon's son, the Earl of Lincoln, died in March 1534 but prior to that, he was second in the succession behind Henry's daughter. Although the Brandons were friends of Katherine, their first loyalty was to Henry so if Henry wanted an annulment, so did they. It is likely, however, that they wished Henry had picked a different future bride.

The archives show at least three rebuttals of Abell's book were produced, the first ran to over three hundred pages and was entitled *A confutation of Abel's babbling*.[309]

When Henry rode off from Windsor, was it his intention never to see Katherine again or was he hoping to pressurise her into submission? If she had accepted her status as Dowager Princess of Wales she would no doubt have been welcomed at court as Anne of Cleves would be in years to come when she became the King's honorary sister – though whether Anne would have been there with a friendly smile or developed a sudden headache and taken to her room is less certain. Why did Henry do it otherwise? He liked to take his lead from the Old Testament which spoke of the need to cast aside foreign women that might lead a person into idolatry and false belief.[310] Katherine's adherence to the pope and belief in his right to dispense against God's word certainly bordered on idolatry.

August 1531

Events

- Thomas Wharton seeks support from Thomas Cromwell for a court case having already sought support from Henry and Anne (LP 5.367).
- Katherine tells the pope she would rather die than have her case heard outside Rome (LP 5.366).
- a new Venetian ambassador arrives in England, Carlo Capello (CSPV 4.683).
- the pope asks Henry for financial support to fight the Turk (LP 5.374). He denies promising the Cardinal Bishop of Tarbes that he would avoid giving a verdict for twenty years but admits that with the right paperwork he could devise delays of at least ten years (LP 5.359).
- the Venetian, Mario Savorgnano, Count of Belgrade visits England and goes to see both Henry and Katherine (CSPV 4.682).
- Campeggio fulminates against the wickedness of the universities who have said that popes cannot dispense from divine law in any circumstance. He opines that opposing the authority of Rome and questioning it should not be allowed (LP 5.366).
- representatives arrive from Savoy to ask Thomas Boleyn if he has persuaded Henry to finance the Duke's planned war to obtain restitution of Cyprus, something Boleyn had promised to do when he was in Italy, Boleyn tells them that the court is on progress and they should come back in the spring (CSPS 4.2.778).
- Francis arrests a bishop for treason (LP 5.384).

---

309 LP 5.1. The handwriting is that of the Earl of Derby, Anne's cousin and uncle by marriage. He had married Norfolk's daughter and half sister successively. At the time of writing, Derby was twenty-two.
310 Ezra 10:3,10-11; Deut. 7:3-4; 1 Kings 11:2; Mal. 2:11

- eighteen priests are charged with the attempted murder of Stokesley, Bishop of London, and of assaulting his staff in an attack which lasted almost two hours. They were protesting against increased taxes (LP 5.387).
- Henry Norris secures a manor in Buckinghamshire (LP 5.392.4).
- George Boleyn wins £58 shooting against the King at Hampton Court (PP p.56).
- Thomas Bilney is tied to a stake and burned alive for giving the anchoress at Norwich a copy of Tyndale's *Obedience of a Christian Man* and his translation of the New Testament into English.[311]

Comments

When working under the direction of Wolsey, Boleyn was an effective diplomat but the prospect of becoming the King's father-in-law seems to have gone to his head and turned him into a veritable loose cannon. If historians living centuries later regard it as obvious that Henry was not going to fund a war in Cyprus, why did Boleyn – who knew Henry well – suggest otherwise? For once, Chapuys' comment is appropriate: Boleyn was "insane."

Claiming she would rather die than have the case held outside Rome demonstrates Katherine's love of histrionics. It was neither a measured or reasonable response.

The details of Wharton's case are unknown since he comments that the bearer of the letter will update Cromwell verbally, but it is an early example of someone making suit to Anne as the "coming" queen rather than to Katherine.

Savorgnano's report is fascinating. It is an informal account with descriptions of places he visited, such as Dover Castle and Canterbury Cathedral. He describes London as a "very notable city… very rich, populous and mercantile, but not beautiful." He stayed with the Venetian ambassador and was escorted to the palaces by Marc Raphael, the ex-rabbi whom Henry had brought to England and who had taught Savorgnano Hebrew. The palaces impressed him with their wealth, craftsmanship and fine galleries. He was clearly bowled over by Henry saying: "he is very tall of stature, very well formed and of very handsome presence, beyond measure affable and I never saw a prince better disposed than this one. He is also learned and accomplished and most generous and kind." That Henry embraced him enthusiastically, although a stranger, demonstrated to him Henry's impetuous, warm and emotional nature. He did not meet Anne and merely records that she was held to be a "young woman of noble birth though many say of bad character" because she was inciting Henry away from Katherine. He visited Katherine at The More where he found her dining with thirty maids of honour standing as an escort and fifty staff waiting upon her. He numbered her household at two hundred and said she was "rather small. If not handsome, she is not ugly. She is somewhat stout and has always a smile on her countenance." He went on to

---

[311] Bilney's story is told in John Foxe, *Acts and Monuments,* vol.4 pp.623-639 and in John Strype, *Ecclesiastical Memorials* (1822) vol. 1 part 1 pp.311-314.

visit the fifteen year old Princess Mary whom he described as short, beautiful and musically gifted.

The arrest of Poncher, Bishop of Paris, for treason is worth noting in relation to what happened later with Bishop John Fisher. The allegations against Poncher had been made as far back as 1529 and related to his behaviour when Francis was in captivity. Having jailed him, Francis contacted the pope seeking permission to hold a trial and execute him, should he be found guilty (LP 5.958). Negotiations regarding this were ongoing when the bishop died in captivity. A few years earlier, the Emperor had arrested the Bishop of Zamora for treason in Spain. He sought permission from the pope to torture him to elicit a confession (CSPS 3.1.364). As this was not forthcoming, the Emperor had him executed without trial and was consequently excommunicated by the pope. With Fisher, Henry had him tried without asking the pope and when he was found guilty, executed. The pope expressed absolute horror and threatened him with excommunication. Unlike the Emperor, Henry chose not to buy a pardon but rather to reiterate his right to punish clergy who were guilty of treason. He may have had the same idea in 1530 with Wolsey though he died before any formal charges were even laid. The cases of Poncher and Zamora are a reminder that Henry was not acting in any unusually evil manner but just as other rulers did when faced with treason.[312] Bilney represents a classic example of how a man's opinions could change. In his early life, he was an orthodox Roman Catholic but he suffered fear of death because, no matter how many pardons he bought or pilgrimages he went upon, he did not believe his sins were truly forgiven. His life was changed by reading Erasmus's translation of the New Testament from the original Greek, and in particular 1 Tim. 1:15 which said that Jesus saved. Like Martin Luther, his new awakening led him to want to share the good news with others. In December 1527 he was prosecuted for heresy and he recanted only to feel such guilt afterwards, that he returned to his former opinions and shared them with greater zeal. His key beliefs were that prayers should be directed through Jesus alone and not the saints, and that worship and the New Testament should be available in English to facilitate universal understanding. Amongst those who admired him were Hugh Latimer, whom he converted, and Matthew Parker, the former of whom was claimed by Anne Boleyn to be one of her bishops while the latter became her chaplain in 1535 and subsequently Archbishop of Canterbury under Elizabeth I.[313] Parker was present at Bilney's death. Anne's own religious opinions are discussed

---

312 Whether Fisher's denial of Henry's supremacy deserved the death penalty is a separate debate. He claimed he did not do so maliciously but the volume of his works in favour of the papacy make it hard to see how anyone could not interpret them in this light. However, what was absolutely certain was that he persistently urged the Emperor to invade England in support of Katherine – and inciting a foreign ruler to invade your own country has been a crime classified as treason everywhere and at all times.

313 LP 10.797. Latimer became Bishop of Worcester in 1535 after Ghinucci was removed.

elsewhere but Bilney's execution is a stark reminder of the danger which Anne ran by possessing Tyndale's works herself and by her support for English language Bibles. Those cynics who tend to decry Henry's changes of opinion during his life and attribute them to political convenience should also take heed. Bilney was not the first or the last to experience mid life conversion and to feel so strongly that God had intervened to awaken him to truth, he was prepared to face a hideous, public death. This was not a secular age and Henry's pursuit of the annulment stemmed from his belief that the sin of his 'marriage' to Katherine had not been forgiven. Readers may find such faith hard to understand but it is essential to accept the reality of its existence across all levels of society if one is ever to understand Tudor England.

September 1531

Events

- it is revealed that Henry Percy owes the King £10,169. 16s. 2d (LP 5.395).
- following a poor harvest, the export of corn and other food is banned (LP 5.413).
- Katherine claims The More is one of the worst houses in England and says she would rather be a prisoner in the Tower (LP 5.416).
- Henry appoints Edward Lee, his almoner and ex-ambassador to Spain as Archbishop of York and Stephen Gardiner, his secretary, as Bishop of Winchester (LP 5.418,419). Foxe is appointed almoner in Lee's place, Chapuys claims by Anne Boleyn (CSPS 4.2.796).
- the law faculty of Paris declares Henry's citation to Rome invalid and says that the papal court's refusal to accept the excusator is illegal (LP 5.424). Francis tells the pope he cannot proceed in this unjust and illegal way (LP 5.433).
- Chapuys reports that Paris is now voting on whether the pope could dispense even if Katherine's first marriage was unconsummated. He attributes this to English fears because they know the Imperialists can prove she was a virgin when she married Henry (LP 5.416).
- Princess Mary gets a new wardrobe including a black velvet nightgown, three French hoods, sixteen pairs of velvet shoes, two dozen pairs of gloves, several gowns and other items made from a vast collection of velvet, silk, satin and fur (LP 5.439).
- Francis' mother, Louise of Savoy, dies (LP 5.454). Henry orders the English court into mourning blue (LP 5.512).
- accounts of St Martin's monastery at Dover reveal that it made £113 18s 9d profit in the last year and distributed 16s 4d in alms – less than a five hundredth part of its income (LP 5.446).
- Dr Mai continues to send urgent requests from Rome for documentation. He has still not seen the "Spanish brief" nor does he have a copy of the 1529

legatine court proceedings at Blackfriars. As he reminds the Emperor, what is being heard is Katherine's appeal against that court: it is not an advocation of the whole case. He is also still awaiting statements from Katherine's staff regarding her time with Arthur. Despite this, the Emperor orders no delay (CSPS 4.2.792, 798).
- also in Rome, the English seek a new commission to have the annulment case heard in England. Amongst their arguments they note that all the auditors in the Rota are Imperial employees, a fact which Dr Mai admits will require some effort to defend (CSPS 4.2.789).
- the Emperor continues to press for three more cardinals, including a hat for the bishop rejected on grounds he was a murderer. Eventually one is agreed, but not that one (CSPS 4.2.782, 792).
- Cardinal San Quatuor dies. To Imperial horror, the pope proposes replacing him with Ghinucci. This would result in Ghinucci, who remains Henry's man, having free access to all the pope's correspondence including that with the Emperor (CSPS 4.2.792). Meanwhile, as Mai reminds the Emperor, the cardinal's death means that the 2000 ducat pension he received is now available and he asks which other cardinal the Emperor wishes to reward (CSPS 4.2.832).
- the Cardinal Bishop of Tarbes returns to Rome and has a lot of meetings with the pope, worrying the Imperialists who are unable to discover the reason (CSPS 4.2.783).
- the pope sets out his conditions for a General Council. It must be held in Italy. The Emperor must attend from start to finish. The agenda must be limited to the war against the Turk and problems of Lutheranism (CSPS 4.2.800).
- a plot to assassinate Renée's husband, Ercole of Ferrara, is uncovered (CSPS 4.2.792).
- the pope is upset that letters said to be by him promising Henry his annulment and Francis the hand of Catherine de Medici for his son in return for stopping a General Council being held, have been sent to the Emperor. He claims they are forgeries and blames the Duke of Ferrara. Mai says he does not believe the pope would write such letters but he fears they represent his sentiments. He describes the pope's public neutrality as a character "flaw" they simply have to endure (LP 5.406).
- Henry purchases 185 acres around St James in London (LP 5.406).
- a story is told of how a house on the River Thames in which Anne Boleyn is dining is surrounded by an angry mob of seven to eight thousand women who seek to drag her out and kill her. Anne is forced to escape by boat across the river. It is noted that a number of the protesters are actually men in disguise. (CSPV 4.701).

Comments

Percy's debt in modern money is over seventy million pounds.

Katherine's claim about The More is absurd. It was a property held by Wolsey as Abbot of St Albans and considered sufficiently palatial for him to stay there as well as the King and various diplomats.[314] Campeggio described it in 1529 as "a very fine palace" (LP 4.5995), this in the same month, Henry formally secured the palace from the new abbot (LP 5.405). When the Venetians visited Katherine at The More a few weeks earlier, she had over two hundred staff in attendance. If Katherine – or Chapuys who reported the remark – seriously believed this was the worst house in England, they should have gone and seen how the poor lived in their dark and draughty homes with no chimneys, sanitation or glazed windows and only mud floors.

The probability of the Duke of Ferrara forging the pope's letters is minute but it shows the level of suspicion felt against him in Rome. The year closed with the Duke's ambassador still boycotting the papal court in protest at the slanderous accusation (CSPS 4.2.576).

It is difficult not to feel sorry for Dr Mai who was charged to prosecute a case without delay but not given copies of the necessary papers. Chapuys had sent a copy of the legatine court proceedings but evidently the Emperor had not sent it on. After all the arguments about the legitimacy of the infamous "Spanish brief", it must be wondered why the Emperor had not only refused to give it to the envoy whom the pope sent for it but also not given it to Katherine's defence counsel in Rome. What was he hiding?

The expenditure on Mary's wardrobe represents a significant charge and shows Henry's love for her and that he had no wish to reduce her status. Mary was fifteen at the time.

Chapuys' allegation about the debate in Paris is rather odd. Previously he had said that Katherine's virginity was impossible to prove after twenty-two years but now he claims the Imperialists have the proof – even though Dr Mai in Rome is obviously unaware of this. His sneering at the idea of affinity commencing with vows rather than sexual intercourse shows his ignorance of canon law and the Bible. Also worth noting is his claim that Anne appointed Foxe the royal almoner. Quite why Chapuys should believe Henry was suddenly unable to appoint his own almoner and need to depute the task to Anne is unclear – no doubt because the idea was so silly. The only person who appointed Henry's almoner was Henry. Anne may or may not have suggested Foxe but she certainly did not have the authority to appoint him.[315]

---

314 The King had stayed there twice in 1530 following the completion of recent building work which he had authorised (PP p.37, 40, 49, 74). He would stay there again with Kathryn Howard, Gareth Russell, *Young, Damned and Fair* (2017) p.163

315 Foxe had been active in promoting the annulment and the year before had completed the *Collectanea satis copiosa*, the basis for the *Glass of Truth,* and he was working on a volume introducing the 1531 Determinations.

The story of Anne's flight from the mob is very strange. Thomas Boleyn had been given Durham Place which was in the Strand with an entrance direct from the River Thames so it is entirely possible that she was dining there.[316] It is also conceivable that she could have been a target of hatred for her perceived role in the fall of Queen Katherine. However, the only reference to the event comes from a letter sent to the French ambassador in Venice. The name of the letter writer is not known but as the remainder of the letter concerns meetings held at the French court, outfits worn and arrangements for the servants of Louise of Savoy, it is likely that the author was a courtier. The letter was in Italian so he could have been a clergyman serving there or a visiting dignitary. If the sender had been the Venetian ambassador to France or some official, the name would have been recorded while a merchant would have been unlikely to have the access required to obtain the other information given. The author says that he has heard the story from an unnamed source so clearly it is a case of reporting an incident at least third hand. Somebody would need to have witnessed the event in England and taken the news to France and then told the unnamed writer who in turn told the French ambassador in Venice who then told the Venetian authorities. From a historian's point of view, the provenance of the evidence is not overwhelming and there is the key point that nobody else mentioned it. The author says it was hushed up because women were involved, the inference being that women were silly creatures so what they did was of no importance, but he also says that many of the "women" were actually men and a mob of that size would represent a threat to public order regardless of gender. Could there really have been such an attack on Anne which Chapuys did not discover? If there had been, would Henry not have given orders to increase patrols in London or put additional guards around the palaces? The anonymous correspondent mentions that Jean du Bellay, Bishop of Bayonne had just returned to France from England so could he have told the tale? It would seem uncharacteristic but if he was the source, it would lend considerable credence to the story. Whatever the truth of the matter, it shows the way gossip spread from one country to another, especially if the story was something which the teller hoped was true. If it did happen, Anne must have been terrified by the incident.

October 1531

Events

- the new Venetian ambassador in England reports Henry has asked Ferdinand, the Emperor's brother, to obtain the hand of Mary of Hungary, regent of the Low Countries, as his new wife (CSPV 4.686).

---

316 It was a prestigious address being next door to Wolsey's York Place and owned by him as Bishop of Durham. Wolsey's successor, Cuthbert Tunstall, gave it to Henry two months after Anne's execution noting that Thomas Boleyn had been resident there until this time. The surrender coincided with Boleyn's removal as Lord Privy Seal (LP 11.203.3), *Statutes of the Realm* vol.3 pp.687-688.

- the annulment case opens at Rome. Henry is cited for contempt due to his non appearance (LP 5.467). His excusator, Edward Carne, appears with a letter sent by Henry which bears his seal but not his signature. This renders the document inadmissible and results in further delays (LP 5.473).
- Katherine's lawyers, in an opening statement, claim Prince Arthur publicly announced he was impotent and alleges the dispute between her father and his over her dowry was liable to lead to war and this justified the dispensation for her to marry Henry. They say that as any dissolution of the union would provoke war between England and the united forces of the Emperor, Hungary and Portugal, the "marriage" must be maintained. They express the belief that there is no limit to papal authority and say he can even dispense brothers to marry their own sisters (LP 5.468). Dr Ortiz says the consummation of Katherine's marriage to Arthur is irrelevant as affinity is only a concept of canon law (LP 5.492).
- Jean du Bellay, Bishop of Bayonne makes a flying visit to England and dines with Henry, Anne and her parents (LP 5.488).
- Henry tells his ambassadors to withdraw from the papal court if the case continues: "We do not think it proper to adorn the court with our representatives, and to honour him at our great expense, who is most hostile to us and who is plotting against us." (LP 5.464; SP vol. 7 p.324). Dr Mai admits that Henry's threat has worried the cardinals and asks the Emperor to send a letter to encourage them (CSPS 4.2.812). Henry adds that he did not seek a break with Rome but rather desired friendship, however, given "the Emperor's authority is greater with the pope than the truth's" the situation is impossible. "Words or letters are no longer believed. Always, one thing is said or done while another is pretended." But "we know these tricks by experience." (SP vol. 7 pp.325-327).
- the food situation in England deteriorates and there is fear of famine (LP 5.472).
- another deputation of lords is sent to ask Katherine to agree to the case being heard in England. She refuses saying it is necessary for the pope to judge because his job is to define the law and set an example to the world. She expresses confidence in the integrity of the papal court and denies the possibility of any intrigue or unfair influence there (CSPS 4.2.808). Throwing herself on her knees, she loudly begs the lords to persuade Henry to abandon his scandalous example and return to her, but if he will not, she declares that she will go wherever he sends her, even willingly surrendering herself to be burnt at the stake. Chapuys – who was not there but told about it – reports all her attendants gathered round her and promptly burst in tears (LP 5.478; CSPS 4.2.808).
- Anne allegedly sends a message to the Bishop of Rochester suggesting he should abstain from attending the next session of Parliament lest he become ill again (LP 5.472).

- Thomas Boleyn obtains two parks in Kent (LP 5.506.16) and Henry Norris is made Chamberlain of North Wales (LP 5.506.25).
- Chapuys complains that living miles away from court and having few visitors means he is unable to obtain credible information about events to pass on. He asks the Emperor for more money so he can try to remedy the problem with suitable bribes to key individuals (CSPS 4.2.814).
- Dr Ortiz reports the sorrow felt in Rome by news that Katherine has been evicted from Henry's palace and is living in penury without any household staff. The pope tells him that Henry has denied the story (CSPS 4.2.812).
- on the 21st, Dr Mai sends yet another appeal for a copy of the proceedings of the legatine court held in England in 1529 (CSPS 4.2.817). Chapuys sends a further copy to the Emperor – his fourth (LP 5.488).
- a French envoy is sent to the German princes in accordance with Henry's suggestion made in July (LP 5.337, 472).
- the Roman Catholic cantons of Switzerland secure a major victory over the Protestants at Kappel. Zwingli is killed. The event causes great rejoicing at Rome (CSPS 4.2.822).[317]

Comments

The lack of a signature was a cunning and successful ploy to delay proceedings in Rome. Whoever thought of it deserved a pay rise.

To allege that England and Spain were about to go to war in 1509 because Katherine's dowry had not been paid indicates utter desperation on the part of the Imperial lawyers. No such threat existed. Their testimony to the court was an absolute and blatant lie. If Henry's team had not refused to recognise the court, they could have launched a counter suit for perjury. As for the idea that Prince Arthur emerged from his bedroom following his wedding night and announced to all the court that he was impotent… It is too laughable to merit further comment.

Katherine's loud proclamations on her knees that she was willing to be sent to the stake represent another example of her love of public histrionics. Nobody had ever suggested such a fate. She was simply playing to the gallery – the Tudor equivalent of getting herself interviewed on prime time television or establishing an active social media presence. Chapuys makes a point of saying that those sent to her spoke softly and asked to address her privately but she chose to gather her court and raise her voice so all could hear. If she seriously believed that Rome was a haven of integrity, she was delusional, and if she was able to make the allegation with a straight face simply for effect, she was an astounding actress. Not even those who lived and worked at the papal court would have made such a claim.

---

317 Martin Luther also said "How well God knows his business." Philip Hughes, *A Popular History of the Reformation* (New York, 1957) p.139

The story of Anne's message to the Bishop of Rochester is told by Chapuys. It does not feature in Fisher's first biography which was compiled by Richard Hall who handled his papers and interviewed his staff and friends. No trace of such a letter has been found since in diocesan records. Where Chapuys got the story from is a mystery but evidently he did not check it before he sent the report.

The rumours at Rome about Katherine's living conditions can be traced to Chapuys and the deliberately misleading information he sent the Emperor.

It is unknown where the Venetian ambassador got his story that Henry was planning to discard Anne and marry the Emperor's sister. It is easy to mock the story but it might have been a solution to the impasse and Mary of Hungary was twenty-six and therefore of childbearing age. Did a courtier suggest it or Henry throw the idea out to create more confusion? Might Henry and Anne have been having a row and he turned round and threatened to replace her with someone else? Or was it just a case of someone pulling the leg of the new ambassador and not expecting him to take it seriously? Mary, a childless widow, had already decided she would never marry again though nobody outside the Imperial family knew of this private vow (CSPS 4.2.586).

The civil war in Switzerland – then a collection of cantons rather than a unified state – was important not just for the battle against heresy but because foreign princes were accustomed to using it as a recruiting ground for mercenaries. If the inhabitants were engaged in internal warfare, neither the Emperor nor Francis nor the pope nor anyone else could hire them to fight their own wars.

The prospect of famine was not only bad for the people affected and for the economy but it weakened the defences of the country against its enemies because emaciated and exhausted men could not fight. At the time, it would also have been interpreted as a sign of divine displeasure, though Henry's enemies were unable to claim that God was angry at him seeking an annulment because the food shortage was European wide.[318]

November 1531

Events

- it is revealed that following Henry's request for reduced fees for the bulls for Winchester and York, the pope has cut them to 20,000 ducats (LP 5.512).
- Dr Mai finally receives the witness statements from Spain but finds only two appear relevant. He continues to await the transcript of the legatine court and the original of the controversial "Spanish brief" (LP 5.516).

---

318 In December 1527, Wolsey had told Gregory Casale that if the annulment was not granted, God would visit the country with famines, war and discord (LP 4.3644; SP vol.7 p.19).

- Chapuys reports that he has been unable to find anyone willing to say that war with Spain was raging or imminent at the time of Henry's accession. Katherine's response to the question was that she knew nothing of politics (CSPS 4.2.818).
- Henry's daughter Mary leaves for Richmond. Chapuys tells the Emperor that Anne procured her eviction as she saw her as a threat and Anne's rule is law (CSPS 4.2.818; LP 5.546).
- Stephen Vaughan sends Tyndale's exposition of 1 John to Henry together with Barnes' *Supplication* (LP 5.533)
- in Rome, the excusator, Carne, is rejected by the Rota and the question returns to Consistory (CSPS 4.2.835).
- an envoy arrives from the Duke of Cleves to discuss a potential marriage between the Duke's son and Henry's daughter (LP 5.548).
- skirmishes and arguments erupt along the border with Scotland. Henry tells his sister that since her son, James V, has a "possibility of succession" to the crown of England, she should advise him to act more reasonably or the English people will reject him as unworthy of the throne (LP 5.537,3).
- Katherine and Chapuys disagree over tactics to put pressure on Henry. Katherine believes the Emperor should use rigorous words to show his support for her. Chapuys proposes interrupting trade since causing people to lose their livelihoods and go hungry will make them liable to rebel. He asks the Emperor for permission to go to Rome to support her case there (LP 5.546).
- anxious to protect public health as plague rages, Henry issues an order exempting the eight physicians who cover the whole of London, from keeping watch at night (LP 5.549; CSPV 4.702).
- Joachim, the French ambassador, tells Anne she will soon be queen and claims the Emperor will not object to this. Anne replies that she would rather wait for the honour and her happiness than be beholden to the Emperor (CSPS 4.2.838).
- the university opinions regarding the annulment are published in English (LP 5.546).
- the pope continues to express hopes that his "niece" Catherine de Medici, will marry the Duke of Milan but admits that negotiations are not going well (CSPS 4.2.841). Meanwhile the French, who still want her to marry the Duke of Orleans, propose that the Duke of Milan marries instead Jeanne of Navarre, the potential bride discarded by the Marquis of Mantua two years before (CSPS 4.2.832).[319]
- reports are received of French attacks on Spanish ships in defiance of the peace. The pope predicts that there will soon be war as Francis still wants Milan and he believes Francis and Henry are fomenting division in Germany. To cheer him up, Mai obtains an astrological forecast predicting that Francis and his sons will all meet grisly ends (CSPS 4.2.841).

---

319 Jeanne was the niece of Francis I of France, her mother being his sister.

- Katherine writes to the Emperor claiming that her suffering would be enough to kill ten others and that no Christian has ever suffered so intense an agony. She reiterates that she has done nothing to deserve it, offending neither God nor the King. She says the saints in heaven are on her side and will force Henry and those who intentionally drove him into "this error" to admit this. Meanwhile, she complains her enemies are pampered and feasted and blames the pope (CSPS 4.2.819).
- the ex-Venetian ambassador to London, Lodovico Falier, returns home after three years and gives a report to the Signory which covers England's wealth, military capabilities, judicial system and political outlook. He describes the Duke of Norfolk as xenophobic but waxes lyrical over Henry:

> In this eighth Henry, God combined such corporal and mental beauty as not merely to surprise but to astound all men. Who could fail to be struck with admiration on perceiving the lofty position of so glorious a prince to be in such accordance with his stature, giving manifest proof of that intrinsic mental superiority which is inherent to him. His face is angelic rather than handsome, his head imperial and bald, and he wears a beard contrary to the English custom. Who would not be amazed when contemplating such singular corporal beauty coupled with such bold address, adapting itself with the greatest ease to every manly exercise. He sits his horse well and manages him yet better; he jousts and wields his spear, throws the quoit and draws the bow admirably; plays at tennis most dexterously; and nature having endowed him in youth with such gifts, he was not slow to enhance, preserve and augment them with all industry and labour. It seeming to him monstrous for a prince not to cultivate moral and intellectual excellence, so from childhood he applied himself to grammatical studies and then to philosophy and holy writ, thus obtaining the reputation of a lettered and excellent prince. Besides the Latin and his native tongue, he learned Spanish, French and Italian. He is kind and affable, full of graciousness and courtesy and liberal, particularly to men of science whom he is never weary of obliging… He appears to be religious; he usually hears two low masses and on holy days high mass likewise.

Falier adds that since the fall of Wolsey, Henry has taken over the government and is now much less liberal though "He gives many alms, relieving paupers, orphans, widows and cripples." Nonetheless, he says he is wealthy with a million in gold as ready money which will be augmented if he obtains the money he is owed which amounts to almost a quarter of a million pounds, more than twice his annual income. His breakdown of Henry's situation is as follows:[320]

Income	£	%
Revenue from Crown lands	38,000	36.2
Customs	30,000	28.6
Confiscations from convicted felons	10,000	9.5
Wardships	10,000	9.5
Receipts from vacant benefices[321]	8,000	7.6
Fines	5,000	4.8
Charges for the seal	2,000	1.9
Revenue from lands in Calais and Guisnes	2,000	1.9
	105,000	

Expenditure		
Gifts	24,000	22.9
Court including wages of over 500 staff, an armed guard of 300 men, 8 chaplains, heating, food, entertainments, administration	20,000	19.0
Parks and game preserves	10,000	9.5
Ambassadors, envoys and couriers	8,000	7.6
Soldiers in fortresses and on the borders	6,000	5.7
Privy Chamber	6,000	5.7
Cavalry	4,000	3.8
Buildings	2,000	1.9
Alms	2,000	1.9
Total	88,000	
leaving a surplus of	17,000	16.1

He adds that the church in England is very wealthy with an income of £1.2 million, the monasteries having an income of £30,000. He believes exports to be worth two million in gold. He reveals that Henry has some three hundred horses in his stables ranging from the finest Barbaries for racing to basic ponies for messengers with other breeds for hunting, jousting and other uses. He estimates Henry's military capabilities to be 150 sail, 4000 cavalry and 60,000 infantry (CSPV 4.694).

---

320 Falier's report gives all figures in ducats but they have been converted here to sterling using the exchange rate of five ducats to the pound which he supplied.
321 Traditionally, the monarch left bishoprics empty for a year in order to enjoy the income before an appointment was made.

Comments

Chapuys' failure to find anyone to say war existed in 1509 is unsurprising since there was none. Katherine's protest that she knew nothing about politics is ludicrous given her father had appointed her his ambassador, a role she actively fulfilled, such as seeking to negotiate a match between her widowed sister, Juana, and her father in law, Henry VII.[322] In December 1508, she had been principal attendant on Mary Tudor when she wed the future Emperor, Katherine's nephew, Charles, a union which proved the close alliance between the countries.[323] Katherine knew the truth and chose to withhold it because it did not help her case.

Twenty thousand ducats – between £4000 and £4500 – is worth around £3 million today. It is not known what original figure was demanded but judging by the wonder expressed at the significant reduction allowed, it was probably at least double this. It is not surprising that people criticised the greed of the papacy and felt that the money could do more good in England. By contrast, the patents for Henry Fitzroy when he joined the nobility cost £13. 6s. 8d.[324] Not all charges for documentation to confirm position were exploitative, just those from Rome.

Mary had never lived with her parents: royal children did not. They had their own nurseries and then households which were separate, partly for reasons of health and security, but also to give them some experience of governing first a house and then a property and later larger estates as they grew up. From 1525 to 1528, Mary had been based in Ludlow on the Welsh border. Richmond Palace was not far from London and Mary's removal after a visit was perfectly normal and a responsible act given plague had broken out in the city. It also kept her close enough should Henry decide the Duke of Cleves' envoy should be introduced. Chapuys' claim that it was the result of Anne's plotting is at best a sign of him being misinformed, at worst another example of his love of mischief making.

It was expected that all able bodied adult London men would take their turn in the night watches over the city. Henry's exemption shows the extent of his involvement in government. Tired physicians were no use to patients and if they were on watch, they were unavailable to treat the sick. The population of London at this time is not known exactly but the Venetian ambassador estimated it at 70,000 that autumn (CSPV 4.694) though some later historians have thought it was rather less.[325] It is likely that there was around one physician to every nine thousand or so people. As their services would have

---

322 CSPS 1. 551
323 James Gairdner, ed., *The Spousells of the Princess Mary* (Camden Society, 1893) p.26
324 Murphy, *Bastard Prince,* p.59. This was a standard rate, not specially discounted.
325 For example, Peter Clark and Paul Slack, *English Towns in Transition 1500-1700* (Oxford, 1976) p.63.

been expensive, for many people, the only medical care they could expect would have come from an apothecary.

Henry's comments about the possibility of James' succession are interesting. Was he considering Mary's status now suspect or expressing a fear that the annulment case would not be settled before his own death and this would prevent him having children by Anne or anyone else? Did the Earl of Lincoln, then aged nine and son of his sister Mary by her husband Charles Brandon, Duke of Suffolk, appear sickly? Alternatively, there was his bastard son Henry Fitzroy, the Duke of Richmond, who was twelve; or his cousin the Marquess of Exeter who was thirty-three.[326] Or was Henry simply holding out a carrot to avoid the expense of a stick?

Katherine's letter is remarkable. To describe her claim to have suffered more than any other Christian who had lived in the previous one and a half thousand years as being an exaggeration is an understatement: it was literally untrue. Her statement that she had never offended God is equally so. Katherine's reputation for piety, buoyed up by Imperialists, does not sit well with such a notion. As it says in 1 John 1:8: "if we say we have not sinned, we deceive ourselves and the truth is not in us." Christianity teaches that the only person not to have offended God through sin was Jesus, and this is a fundamental which Katherine should have known. The assertion that the saints are lined up ready to punish Henry's advisors when they get to heaven is also bizarre. The Bible teaches that God will judge, that hell is the place for punishment rather than heaven, and it commands "love thy enemies." Four years into the crisis and she was still talking about not deserving what has happened, completely ignoring the fact that the issue is the legality of the "marriage" and not her. Perhaps it was inevitable that someone brought up in a palace would think the entire world revolved around herself but it is difficult to avoid the suspicion that Katherine was showing signs of madness. Her sister Juana had been incarcerated for years on these grounds, though some historians have queried if her son, the Emperor, did that simply so he could enjoy the Spanish throne himself.

Falier's report is interesting not just for what it says but what it does not say. There is no mention of Thomas Cromwell as a significant figure at court nor of Anne's father, though both are listed amongst the members of the Privy Council together with Norfolk, Suffolk, Fitzwilliam, Shrewsbury and Gardiner.[327] He describes the King, Queen, Mary and the Duke of Richmond but not Anne. Given she was the most talked about woman in Europe, this omission suggests he had not met or seen her during his three years' sojourn at the English court and it casts further doubt on Chapuys' claim that she was much in evidence and politically active. Either that or he thought the likelihood

---

326 Son of Henry's mother's younger sister and consequently a grandson of Edward IV. He was executed for treason in 1538.
327 He also lists a Lord Darcy whom he says was Comptroller but that role was held by Sir Henry Guildford. It is possible that owing to Guildford's ill health, somebody else was doing the work temporarily at the time Falier made his list.

of her becoming queen was too remote even to mention. The analysis of Henry's expenditure may not be exact but it is a potent reminder of how in the days of personal rule by monarchs, they also had to pay the bills. Too often, the impression is given that Henry pocketed all the income from the later Dissolution of the Monasteries for himself and squandered it on pleasure and gifts to courtiers. In fact, the majority went on defending the country against expected invasion in 1540 and in the war which followed. This was long before the time when there was a separate department for national defence or diplomatic service funded by parliament. If Falier's figures are even approximately right and Hall's claim that the Praemunire fine of 1531[328] represented the costs of the annulment after almost four years (with three more to go) is true, it can be seen what a huge investment Henry was placing in his campaign.[329] Falier's figures for Church wealth also help to explain the resentment felt by the laity and the growth of anticlericalism. Henry's investment in horses is a reminder of why the post of Master of Horse – at this point held by Sir Nicholas Carew – was so important.

For those brought up on the Holbein portrait and the various portrayals and caricatures of Henry in books and movies, Falier's account may raise a disdainful smile but it is important to remember that Falier was not employed by Henry, had no expectation of ever seeing him again or being rewarded by him. He was endeavouring to present an objective report to help the Venetian authorities understand better the man with whom they were often called to deal in matters of war or international trade. It should not therefore be rejected as simple sycophancy but rather as something which helps us to understand what Anne saw in Henry – action man, charmer, and dazzlingly intelligent. They were not attributes anyone would ever apply to Francis or the Emperor or, most likely, any of the other men at court.

Chapuys' promotion of trade disputes which would result in the impoverization and possibly death of innocent English sailors, weavers, dyers and farmers, simply to support Katherine's claim to Julius II's bull being valid, is another reminder that he was a nasty and obsessed little man.

The arguments attached to the university opinions are discussed more fully in Was Henry married when he met Anne? Having shown how marriage to a brother's wife was against the law of God and of nature, the book said "none authority of man can extend or stretch so far that it may release by any dispensation the forbidding of God." It described the pope's dispensation to Henry and Katherine as nothing but a perversion and abuse of power and a worthless attempt to give "lewd liberty to sin." It followed that "they may, yea and are bound, for the love and religion that they owe to God not only to break straight away such marriages but also with a stable and steadfast stomach and such as a Christian man ought to have be bound to withstand and resist valiantly the pope although he would threaten them by a thousand cursings and

---

328 See February 1531
329 The £105,000 would be worth around £80,000,000 today.

excommunications... Christian men if their private conscience, enlightened with the Holy Ghost and knowledge of holy scripture, as it ought to be, hath moved them unto it they may without any jeopardy yea and are bound to make a divorce with her, whom both nature and the law of God doth forbid them to have to their wife: and to deliver themselves from that untrue and only presumed and pretended marriage." It ended by saying the evidence was clear and "it seemeth to us best here, to conclude and make an end of our work, and not to tarry the any longer." [330]

The French proposal that the Duke of Milan marry Jeanne of Navarre was a ploy to ensure he could not beget an heir: Jeanne was still a toddler.

Feminist historians sometimes like to quote Chapuys' comment about Anne ruling Henry and similar remarks made by him and others as evidence of Anne being a strong woman with a modern habit of speaking her mind. She may or may not have been so but this comment should not be interpreted in this manner. Ambassadors – particularly those for Spain – had a long tradition of claiming that English kings were ruled by the women around them. They said this of Cecily Neville and Edward IV as well as of Henry VII and his mother. It was a way of denigrating English kings and Englishwomen in general,[331] Englishmen too were hostile to the idea of a strong woman. The Earl of Warwick had condemned Henry VI in the previous century as a man who "does not rule but is ruled" by his wife. [332] Fisher's eulogy of Margaret Beaufort by contrast, said she was "full obedient and tractable."[333] The ideal woman and role model for every female at the time was the Blessed Virgin Mary whose abiding characteristic was unquestioning obedience.[334] Rather than flinging up our hands in horror at such misogynistic remarks or giving them a positive gloss which is diametrically opposed to the intentions of the original writers, we need to simply accept them as shining a light on the world in which Henry and Anne lived, the better understanding of which should always be our goal, and remember that until the late twentieth century, the figures of the female battleaxe and henpecked husband were regular and totally acceptable comic characters.

December 1531

Events

- the Bishop of Cordova sends the pope 16,000 ducats worth of gifts in order to get permission to bequeath his estate as he chooses (CSPV 4.707).

---

330 *Determinations* p.38, 136, 151-154.
331 Queen Isabella of Castile was hardly a model of their idealised docility.
332 Elizabeth Norton, *Margaret Beaufort, Mother of the Tudor Dynasty* (2010) p.54
333 John Fisher, *The Funeral Sermon of Margaret Countess of Richmond* ed. J. Hymers (1840) p.109
334 Luke 1:38.

- the envoy from Cleves departs without Chapuys discovering his mission (CSPS 4.2.853).
- Norfolk's brother-in-law, Rhys ap Gruffydd, is executed for treason. Chapuys claims Anne demanded this because he spoke disparagingly of her (LP 5.563).
- negotiations for a new trade treaty with the Low Countries begin (LP 5.564).
- George Constantine is arrested on suspicion of heresy and imprisoned in Thomas More's house in Chelsea (LP 5.574).
- in Rome, the English demand the issue of the excusator be debated in a public session of Consistory. They also enter protests against the auditors of the Rota on grounds of political bias. A further delay is granted to allow them to summon new lawyers. The pope promises this will be the last but Dr Mai does not believe him. Mai says the cardinals ("devils") are all in favour of the case never ending, some because they are pro-France, some because they have received bribes or hope for one, and others because they hope the situation will resolve itself and go away (CSPS 4.2.857). Cardinal Ancona urges delay lest a verdict provoke war which would consume resources needed to fight the Turk (CSPS 4.2.872).
- from Antwerp, Vaughan advises Cromwell that the swell of opinion in favour of a return to Biblical truth will continue: "Let the King be assured that no policy or threats can take away the opinions of his people until he fatherly and lovingly reforms the clergy, whence spring both the opinions and the grudges of the people." (LP 5.574).
- Katherine continues to petition the Emperor to press the pope to issue a verdict in her favour. She maintains Henry is a good and virtuous man who has been led astray with empty hopes and false opinions but expresses confidence that God will hear her prayers and enlighten him to the truth (CSPS 4.2.860, 877).
- Paul Casale, younger brother of Gregory, is murdered on his way to Naples to obtain opinions on behalf of Henry (LP 7.86).[335] The Duke of Mantua's brother describes him as "young, virtuous and lovable and not a little esteemed by His Holiness."[336]
- Tewkesbury is burnt at the stake for denying purgatory, saying that faith alone saved and for reading with approval Tyndale's *Obedience of a Christian Man* and *Parable of the Wicked Mammon* (LP 5.589).
- a new French ambassador arrives, Pomeray, and is welcomed by Anne Boleyn with a banquet. He is granted apartments at Bridewell Palace (LP 5.614).
- Henry Percy meets the Earl of Bothwell who says he wants to leave Scotland and join Henry's service. Bothwell reports that James V wants to be Duke of York and believes the pope and Emperor can obtain him this honour (LP 5.595, 597).

---

335 Pocock, *Records*, vol. 2 p.511
336 Fletcher, *Our Man in Rome*, p.168

- Bennet, Henry's ambassador in Rome, returns home to discuss the situation. Henry tells him to use all means available to delay the annulment case until the Emperor returns to Spain, something he estimates will not happen for at least six months. Henry authorises a reward for Cardinal Ancona including a French bishopric, if Bennet believes it will encourage him to "prevent wrong." Henry further proposes Avignon as a neutral place suitable for the case to be heard (LP 5.610).
- John Brereton, a royal chaplain, is awarded a prebend at St Stephen's, Westminster (LP 5.627.20).
- still upset at Katherine's removal from court, Dr Ortiz tells the pope that Anne Boleyn has had a miscarriage in an attempt to pressurise him into ordering Henry to restore Katherine and expel her. Mai tells Ortiz that it will not happen and Ortiz retorts that if it does not, he will go and denounce the pope as a sinner to his face and tell him that his negligence is causing God to pour out his wrath on Europe (CSPS 4.2.872).
- as rumours of impending Turkish attack flood Rome, Dr Mai tells the pope that if Francis and Henry refuse to give financial aid, he should excommunicate them both and deprive them of their kingdoms (CSPS 4.2.864).
- the Emperor assures the pope he will use all means in his power to enforce his sentence in the annulment case when it comes (CSPS 4.2.867).
- Francis brokers a peace between the Lutheran and Roman Catholic cantons of Switzerland (CSPS 4.2.871).
- the pope endeavours to secure a reliable spy in Francis' court (LP 5.565).
- Henry tells the papal nuncio that the pope is unreasonable: "Whenever I happen to ask for a thing that I consider just and right, the answer is that 'law forbids' or that the rules of the Chancery and the style of the Roman court are against it. Whereas if the Emperor asks for anything, His Holiness immediately derogates all laws, rules and styles to please him." He adds, "I care not if sentence be pronounced against me. I know what to do." (CSPS 4.2.853)
- Gregory Casale tells the pope that the Emperor's denial of Henry's authority as monarch and efforts to humiliate him in Europe have created a rupture which will never heal (CSPS 4.2.878).

Comments

Paul Casale died on 27th November and the news reached England on 17th December (LP 5.586). He had served as papal nuncio to England in December 1529. Whether he was killed by highway robbers or Imperial agents is unknown. Paul was in his mid-twenties at the time.

It is interesting to speculate how the Emperor proposed to enforce the pope's verdict. Would he lead his army into England, collect Katherine from wherever she was living at the time, then take her to Henry and lock the pair of them in a bedroom until Henry had fulfilled his conjugal responsibilities?

Would Anne be removed kicking and screaming and sent to Hever with a lifelong guard placed round the castle to prevent her escape or sending letters or messengers to Henry? If the pope gave his verdict for Henry, would the Emperor instead lead his army to escort Katherine back to Wales as Dowager Princess then return to London to sit down for a meal with Anne? Did he imagine the people of England, and Henry's own armed guard and courtiers, would all sit back while he did this? The Emperor was not such a fool. It was a meaningless promise.

Katherine's prayers that Henry would be enlightened to the truth were answered – but not as she anticipated.

It is unknown if the John Brereton rewarded was the brother of William but William certainly did have a brother John who was in holy orders (LP 9.504.13).[337]

The usual interpretation of James' wish to be Duke of York was that he wanted to be recognised as second in line to the English throne. If this is the case, it is interesting because there was little related tradition. The first second son of a monarch to bear the title was Richard, best known as the younger of the Princes in the Tower. The second was the future Henry VIII. In both cases the expectation would have been that the elder brother would become king and have their own heirs. In the fifteenth century, Edward, Duke of York had become Edward IV but the crown was achieved by battle and the title came from his father who was great-grandson of Edward III.[338] James' own grandson would eventually become King of England in 1603 but this was mainly because Elizabeth had no children and he was the nearest relative – as well as being Protestant, male and English speaking, all considered benefits at the time.

Using a false allegation that Anne had suffered a miscarriage to try to force the pope into issuing a letter of condemnation indicates the type of dirty tricks employed by Henry's enemies. To use an anachronism, it was not cricket.

The authorisation to Bennet to make an offer to Ancona is worth noting for two reasons. Firstly, the fact that Henry could offer a French bishopric shows how closely Francis was involved in the annulment campaign. Secondly, his explanation of it as an encouragement is a reminder that people of the time thought differently to us today. We view gifts as inherently suspicious and expect transparency but then it was the custom to reward someone financially in return for a favour either granted or anticipated. Indeed, the Bible commended the practice of giving gifts in order to secure access to "great men."[339] Bribery, by contrast, was the offering of a reward for a favour which

---

337 E.W. Ives, *Letters and Accounts of William Brereton of Malpas* (Lancashire and Cheshire Record Society vol. CXVI. 1976) p.32, 62. William's brother John had grants in LP 9.504.13 and LP 10.392.50.

338 Edmund, first Duke of York, was the fourth son of the monarch, the second to fifth were Edmund's son, grandson, great-grandson and great-great-grandson respectively.

339 Prov. 18:16

was not otherwise expected and was condemned in the Bible.[340] The practice of gift giving was universal internationally right down to local level. The pope would have been horrified if anyone accused him of accepting a bribe from the Bishop of Cortona, although most people today would interpret the event as such. The 16,000 ducats in modern money would be worth over £22 million, which puts most recent scandals involving people accepting money into context. It is easy for people who have guaranteed incomes paid safely into the bank, plus pensions and health insurance, to adopt a holier-than-thou attitude toward those in the sixteenth century but it is not a fair response. Sixteenth century officials did not have modern remuneration packages. There were no pension schemes and salaries were paid intermittently with people often having to wait years to receive anything: they were frequently left out of pocket. Revenues from land were variable with war, plague or poor harvests capable of decimating expectations and couriers bearing cash could be ambushed and killed. That individuals sought security in a very insecure world is not surprising. It may not have been ethical but was almost unavoidable. Both sides paid rewards but whilst the English filed letters about payments away and published them, the Imperial archives rarely seem to have considered such records worthy of being kept and certainly have not wished to see them published!

The Gruffydd case is interesting. As a young lord in 1529, Rhys had entered into armed conflict with Lord Ferrars at Carmarthen Castle as part of a power dispute. Ferrars and Gruffydd both claimed the other reached for their knife first and Wolsey chose to release Gruffydd on a bond for good behaviour. This was one of Wolsey's last acts and his actions may have been influenced by a desire to find favour with Norfolk at a time when he himself was falling from power following the failure of the legatine court. In September 1531, Gruffydd was arrested and sent to the Tower for treason. He was accused of discussing a prophecy that James V of Scotland would, with the aid of the Welsh, Irish and Manxmen, topple Henry VIII: "James the King of Scots with the red hand and the raven shall conquer all England." Gruffydd's symbol was the raven and it was said that having raised men to bring this prophecy to fulfilment, he would be rewarded by James by being created Prince of Wales. No evidence was presented to show that James V knew anything about the plot and there was no actual rebellion. Gruffydd was convicted of having "imagined and compassed traitorously and unnaturally the death and destruction of the most royal person of our sovereign lord and the subversion of this his realm" based on evidence from a servant who alleged he had been present at the discussion about the prophecy and from Gruffydd's uncle who claimed the said servant visited him and asked him to arrange mortgages to raise funds for the insurrection.[341] Gruffydd protested his innocence and was supported by his wife. Interestingly,

---

340 Prov. 17:23
341 *Statutes of the Realm*, vol. 3 p.415.

neither Norfolk nor Anne stepped in.[342] Did they believe he was guilty or did they regard a family member being accused of treason as being noxious to their own position, rather like many today would shun someone accused of being a paedophile or drug dealer? The case has attracted some attention in modern times with complaints that there was no written evidence presented, only hearsay.[343] However, it must be remembered that legal practices were very different in the sixteenth century. Few traitors were stupid enough to commit their crimes to paper so oral testimony was not unusual. Anne Boleyn, herself, would be convicted of treason based on hearsay and Wolsey too faced treason charges over the contents of a letter which was never written but simply reported to have been discussed by a servant. Gruffydd was not given details of the charges against him until the day, nor the opportunity to call witnesses or to cross-examine his accusers but this was normal practice at the time: Anne Boleyn's trial was exactly the same. Prophecies were taken seriously in this era and they could lead to death as the Duke of Buckingham (Norfolk's father in law) and Nun of Kent found.[344]

However, the suggestion that Gruffydd and his servant were executed because Gruffydd spoke ill of Anne Boleyn is just Chapuys repeating a vicious rumour. Chapuys himself reports it as such, though a number of later writers unfamiliar with his habits have quoted it as a fact.[345] Rather it is evidence that Chapuys' lack of reliable information, combined with his belief that everyone opposed Anne with the same fervour as he did, was causing him to credit idiotic rumours. A report received at Venice the same month told how Anne and Henry had got married and returned to the palace where a nobleman abused them and

---

342 Gruyffdd had married Catherine Howard, half sister of the Duke of Norfolk, she being the daughter of Thomas Howard's second wife and he the son of the first wife. This also made him Anne's half uncle.

343 W. Llewelyn Williams, 'A Welsh Insurrection', *Y Cymmrodor* 16 (1903), 1-95; Victoria Flood, 'Political Prophecy and the Trial of Rhys ap Gruffydd, 1530–31', *Studia Celtica*, vol. 50, no. 1 (2016), pp.133-150. For a more balanced view by a legal historian, see John Bellamy, *The Tudor law of Treason: an introduction* (1979) pp.240-241. Gruffydd's descendant said that Rhys was twenty-three when he died but Williams believes he could have been slightly older. Chapuys uses the adjective "young." An account of the case appears in *The Reports of Sit John Spelman* vol 1 (1977) pp.47-48 which says the jury took two hours to determine that treason had taken place. The accusers may have been acting from malicious motives but that is a separate issue. The legal process was followed correctly..

344 In 1529, the Earl of Desmond told the Emperor that an ancient prophecy said that an Earl of Desmond would conquer all England and he suggested this was a reason for the Emperor to send him arms and men so he could commence war in pursuit of his destiny. (LP 4.5501). In 1530, William Harlock was held in the Tower for disseminating prophecies relating to the Earl of Desmond and the King of Scots in Somerset and elsewhere (LP 4.6652).

345 Llewelyn Williams suggests that Gruffydd was a loyal Catholic who opposed Anne who was a Protestant but, quite aside from the lack of any evidence about Gruffydd's thoughts on the annulment, Anne was also a loyal Catholic.

was promptly beheaded in the midst of the palace for their entertainment (CSPV 4.724). The Venetians had more sense than to give this tale credence but perhaps Chapuys heard it and put two and two together to make a whole lot more than four. There is no evidence for Gruffydd speaking either for or against her and as part of the Howard family, he had more to gain from her becoming queen than her fall. Treason was punishable by the death penalty and always had been: Anne did not set the punishment. Nor did she compose the indictment (which made no mention of her) or serve on the jury. His death was a product of the fear of the perceived threat from Scotland which was concentrating government minds at this period and concern about the raising of men in Cornwall by magnates that summer for unspecified reasons.[346] not due to Anne throwing some hissy fit and demanding her boyfriend have him executed. Contrary to Chapuys' comments, Rhys' widow described Anne as her only hope and one "to whom I am much bound" indicating that she certainly did not see her as an enemy but rather as a friend.[347]

History should be based on evidence but it is hard not to wonder how Anne felt as she prepared to spent another Christmas with Henry simply as his favourite. The lack of correspondence by her which would reveal this is a major problem for academics, though perhaps a gift to fiction writers and dramatists who are thereby enabled to create their own responses.

1532

January 1532

Events

- the pope sends a demand for money to wage war against the Turk to Francis and Henry (LP 5.693, 695).
- Francis, the Cardinal Bishop of Tarbes and Cardinal Du Prat all protest to the pope regarding the illegality of Henry's citation to Rome and the impossibility of justice being done when it is impractical to transport the necessary witnesses there (LP 5.697, 704, 706).
- whilst the French ambassador, Pomeray, continues to dine regularly with Henry, Chapuys is forced to rely for news on merchants, Katherine's physician, the papal nuncio and informers since he is not welcome at court and the French ambassador refuses to tell him anything. He tells the Emperor that the Cleves envoy came to buy horses, that Reginald Pole has been sent abroad to prevent him speaking in the parliament which has been summoned to deal with Katherine, that a new ambassador is on his

---

346 LP 13.2.804.
347 LP 9.577.

way from England to him, that Henry has demanded an Act giving him the property of every nobleman on death even if they have adult sons and that Thomas Boleyn is about to be made a duke (LP 5.737, 762). All are untrue.
- the Reverend Hugh Latimer is summoned by Stokesley, Bishop of London, for speaking against prayers to saints and advocating that the laity be allowed to read the Bible (LP 5.703).
- in Rome, the English protest that the Emperor and Mai have sent letters forbidding their lawyers in Bologna and Padua from coming to Rome. Cardinals Farnese, Monte, Cesi and Trani support them and delay is granted till February (LP 5.731).
- the French ambassador at Rome blames the Emperor's influence across Italy for the poor treatment of the English cause (LP 5.729).
- news is received in England of the death of the reformer Oecolampadius at Basle (LP 5.739).
- Dr Ortiz persuades the pope to send a letter to Henry telling him to dismiss Anne and take Katherine back. Ortiz' draft which includes automatic excommunication for Henry if he does not comply within fifteen days is rejected (LP 5.738) and the result is a friendly hope on the pope's part that Henry might follow his suggestion and send Anne away until a verdict is pronounced. The pope warns Henry that his bad example is likely to encourage heresy, which he is sure that Henry as Defender of the Faith would not want and expresses his hope that the rumours of him and Katherine living apart are untrue (LP 5.750).[348] Unimpressed, Ortiz tells the Emperor that as God's minister on earth, it is his duty to use his sword to punish the enormous sin Henry has committed by sending Katherine away (CSPS 4.2.893). He tells the pope that Henry is deliberately hindering the Gospel (LP 5.738).
- Henry rewards many people with new year gifts including his daughter, Anne's parents, her brother and sister, Francis Weston and Henry Norris. Katherine gets nothing and her gift to him of a gold cup is returned. Gifts Henry accepts include a chess set, a mirror, marmalade, embroidered collars, parmesan cheese, treacle, gloves, books, a greyhound, a falcon, horses, cushions, a pair of virginals, sturgeon and a box with an image of the French princes (LP 5.686). Anne sends him some hunting darts and he gives her "a tapestried room with a bed of cloth of gold and silver, and crimson satin with rich embroidery more highly prized that the rest." (CSPS 4.2.880).
- Mai says he believes the cardinals will continue to agree delays as long as the threat of a General Council exists (CSPS 4.2.884). The pope, however, tells him "I do promise most solemnly and upon my faith, that after this delay I myself will be your advocate and proctor." (CSPS 4.2.892)

---

348 Pocock, *Records,* vol. 2 pp.166-168

- Henry has a heated exchange with the papal nuncio over Katherine. Henry points out that he gave her four houses to choose from and her income, household and state remain the same as before the separation adding it is no business of the Imperialists if he choose to locate her elsewhere, continuing "since they insist upon her being my wife it follows that I am head of the family; she must therefore obey me" (CSPS 4.2.887). Henry adds an accusation that the Rota is corrupt and like the pope unfit to judge. The nuncio admits that the pope is not a learned man but says he has good advisors and claims the pre-eminence of Rome and of the pope is indisputable. Henry scoffs and says he will never accept the judgment of the pope and does not care if he is excommunicated before walking out (CSPS 4.2.887, 892).
- an English translation of the Acts of Praemunire is published in parliament ((LP 5.721.3).
- the ex-rabbi Marc Raphael assists in the resolution of a trade dispute between Venice and England (CSPV 4.726).
- bad weather sends the court indoors for entertainment. A dancing dog brings laughter while many games of tennis provide exercise and an opportunity for gambling on the result. Francis Weston wins £4 playing tennis. Henry spends evenings playing shovelboard (a form of shove ha'penny) but his lack of success means George Boleyn wins £45 from him (PP pp.186, 188, 189).
- Henry asks Gardiner to persuade Francis to agree to a new treaty. The Emperor, he admits, never fails to take offence so "he may trouble and unquiet the state of us and of our realm, not ceasing to stir, provide and encourage other princes and people against us." Pointing out that the disaffection of the Lutheran princes from the Emperor represents an opportunity, he says they should not "lose this goodly occasion the like whereof shall not perchance in many years be given unto us." He proposes Francis send a further envoy to Germany to promise the princes aid if they will continue in their defiance. They should then move toward a mutual defence agreement with each party promising military and financial aid if one of the others is attacked. Henry says no money should be given to the princes unless they make this commitment. He adds they should not provoke the Emperor to open war until he returns to Spain but notes there is no indication he will go there for a "long season." Gardiner is to make sure that he does not give Francis the impression that Henry feels any need of such a treaty, merely that the idea is "for the mutual interest and commodity of us both." (LP 5.711)[349]

---

349 Pocock, *Records*, vol. 2, pp.157-65. Discussions regarding France and England aiding the Germans had been ongoing since July 1531, see LP 5.337, 472.

Comments

The pope's letter is interesting as much for what it does not say as for what it does. The verbs used are *prosequmur* and *hortamur*, i.e. urge and exhort, not words of command. There is no mention of excommunication and Katherine is referenced as his queen and accepted wife of more than twenty years rather than as his true and undoubted wife. Anne is not described as Henry's mistress, just as a woman who shares his house. It is easy to see why the Imperialists were dissatisfied with it. Most importantly, although addressed to Henry, it was not sent to him but to the Emperor for him to do with it what he wished.

Even if Katherine was Henry's lawful wife – which she was not – she was not the only woman to be sent away by her husband. The Duke of Norfolk, Henry Percy and Thomas Wyatt all lived apart from their wives and across Europe, many men at all levels of society did the same. Did Dr Ortiz imagine that the Emperor should – or could – use armed force to compel every man to live permanently with his own wife? Arguing that separation was a sin against the sacrament of holy matrimony was one thing but claiming that Henry alone should be punished was simply unfair.

The pope's promise to be Mai's advocate and proctor hardly implies neutrality. Henry's suspicions were well founded, though given the pope was renowned for not keeping his promises, perhaps Henry did not need to be quite so worried.

The proposed defence treaty indicates that behind his bluster, Henry did have some concerns about the Emperor taking action against him, either directly through invading via Ireland, Scotland or the Low Countries, or indirectly through trade. Francis was keen on avenging his defeat at Pavia but after the disastrous and expensive war in Italy and his capitulation at Cambrai, his desire to wage war on the Emperor was tempered by a recognition that this was not the time.

Henry's comment about being head of the family seems misogynistic to modern ears but was in line with Biblical teaching and contemporary belief.[350] Women promised to obey their husbands as part of their marriage vows and the attribute which Chapuys most frequently praises in Katherine is her obedience.

Anne's gift to Henry of darts for boar hunting was obviously appreciated because he still had them when he died in 1547. The inventory records them as "staves trimmed with crimson velvet and fringed with red silk."[351] The information that Henry gave Anne a bedroom for New Year – the custom of giving gifts at Christmas only began in the nineteenth century – comes from Chapuys. The official records of what he sent people contains a diplomatic blank against her name!

---

350 1 Peter 3:1-6, Eph. 5:22-4
351 Suzannah Lipscomb, *The King is Dead*, (2015) p.207

John Oecolampadius was one of the most important Biblical scholars of his generation. An expert in Greek, Latin, Hebrew and Aramaic[352], he had advised Erasmus on manuscript sources for his 1516 New Testament. He supported Henry's case because Leviticus was binding on all people for all time whereas Deuteronomy was a dispensation merely for the Jews at a particular time, commenting to Zwingli that Henry's struggle might be long but it was a "labour not to be repented of."[353] He believed that the Bible, rather than tradition, was the source of faith and enlightenment and that the text should be interpreted using the linguistic tools and historical understanding of the scholar rather than allegorically but he remained firm in his conviction that no correct interpretation could be gained without the assistance of the Holy Spirit. He advocated the use of the Hebrew over the Greek in Old Testament studies and taught that the Gospel did not simply involve salvation but right living due to the Law being written on men's hearts.[354] Oecolampadius was also a theologian of great renown and his teaching on the Eucharist would greatly influence Thomas Cranmer and the development of Anglican liturgy in the reign of Edward VI.

February 1532

Events

- Cardinal Ancona and his nephew demand church offices in France worth a minimum of 6000 ducats per annum each plus bishoprics in England and valuable jewels on deposit in return for their help (LP 5.777, 778).
- Anne's uncle Edmund Howard (father of Kathryn) admits to debts of over £400 in Calais and asks Cromwell to secure him an annuity since his family refuse to help (LP 5.786).
- a proclamation in Amsterdam bans the sale of cloth made outside the Empire (LP 5.804).
- Dr Ortiz, still unhappy that the pope has not threatened to excommunicate Henry, writes to the Emperor suggesting he instruct the pope to do so (LP 5.809).
- the French ambassador at Rome says Henry is "quite badly handled" at the papal court and that this goes "against God and reason".[355] He advises the only way to influence the pope is to hit him financially (LP 5.781, 810). Chapuys reports that parliament is debating just such a measure (LP 5.832).

---

352 Aramaic was the language spoken by Jesus and the disciples.
353 Hastings Robinson (ed.) *Original Letters relative to the English Reformation* (Parker Society, 1847) p.551
354 Jer. 31:33
355 Nicolas Camusat, *Meslanges Historiques* (Troyes, 1619) p.174. Summarised at LP 5.781, 783.

- Warham, Archbishop of Canterbury, protests formally about legislation which threatens papal authority and Church prerogatives (LP 5.818). Henry replies that since a Christian's primary duty is to God, it would not be schismatic to adhere to the Word of God when Rome not only misinterprets the Holy Scriptures but sets an example to the world totally opposed to the life and teaching of Jesus. He points out that there is nothing in the Bible to show Rome has any superiority so its power is usurped. Henry says that following the pope means forsaking Christ and he will never do that. He assures the Archbishop that "we shall never separate from the universal body of Christian men" i.e. the true Church (LP 5.820).
- Chapuys reports that Henry is seeking the right to appoint to English benefices which he regards as the pope's own prerogative (CSPS 4.2.907).
- Gregory Casale, England's Italian ambassador in Rome, is granted an annuity of £ 46 13s 4d (LP 5.5.838.7).
- the pope tells Dr Mai that Bennet, England's English ambassador in Rome, has said the French are untrustworthy allies and that Katherine is the most suitable woman in the world to be Queen. Mai tells the Emperor that he "knows for a fact" that Henry is not so much in love with Anne as before and hence seeks an honourable escape from the mess he is in and he claims Norfolk and Gardiner share Bennet's opinions (CSPS 4.2.909).
- in Rome, arguments about the excusator continue. Tempers flare so much that the English are able to hear the row in another room (LP 5.796, 797). Henry tells his team to continue to oppose the citation on grounds it was not served correctly and that kings cannot be summoned. What, he asks, is there to stop the pope summoning all monarchs and then taking their territories? He reiterates that it would be dangerous for him to leave England, that Rome is unsafe with the Emperor's army there and the Turk threatening, and his safety on the journey could not be guaranteed. He expresses wonder at the pope admitting he has done wrong but refusing to correct it and enquires why the pope's ability to do right is less than his ability to do wrong (LP 5.836).
- Gardiner suggests that Francis' talk of marrying one of his daughters to James V was just a delaying tactic to annoy the Emperor. Henry accepts the explanation doubtfully attributing it to Grand Master Montmorency's pro-Scottish leanings and warning that if such a marriage did take place, it would end the Anglo-French alliance (LP 5.807). Nonetheless, he requests Gardiner obtain a portrait of Francis and his sons for his palace wall (LP 5.791).
- plans are drawn up to defend the border with Scotland amid fears of invasion (LP 5.807, 832).
- Henry receives a lion from Germany (PP p.193)
- George Boleyn wins a further £41 from the King at shovelboard (PP p.195)

Comments

Chapuys' condemnation of Henry for wanting to appoint to English benefices is unfair. Both Francis and the Emperor were allowed to do this in their own domains (CSPS 4.2.913).

It is interesting to see Edmund Howard seeking help from Thomas Cromwell rather than his niece Anne. Did he think Cromwell had more influence with Henry or did he suspect that Anne would be guided by his elder brother, the Duke of Norfolk, whom he believed did not trust him?

The argument about the excusator went on for months. Should he be admitted or not? If so, should his argument be upheld? His presence in Rome was a master stroke on Henry's part for he claimed to represent England rather than the King. There being no precedent for such a role in the papal court, there were no procedures to follow so the lawyers could argue *ad infinitem*. Henry could thus tie the Imperial lawyers up in knots and frustrate Katherine's desire for a sentence. Did Henry hope that if this went on long enough Katherine would either give up or agree to have the case held in England or in neutral France? He was preventing a sentence against him but not getting any nearer marrying Anne or having the male heir he craved, and all the time the clock was ticking on his and her fertility levels.

With hindsight it is easy to dismiss Henry's fears of war but the Emperor had made overtures to Ireland and Scotland and he ruled the Low Countries and had family links to Denmark, all convenient places from which to launch an attack on England. Keeping the Emperor busy in Germany and Hungary and maintaining the Anglo-French alliance were important policy initiatives.

Writers sometimes make the mistake of claiming Henry opposed the church: he never did so. The church is defined as the body of Christ – part being on earth (the church militant) and part being in heaven (the church triumphant). Henry came to oppose Rome but never Jesus. In all his writings and statements he backs up his arguments with quotations from the Bible. He was a deeply pious prince on a crusade, not a wilful megalomaniac seeking to supplant the pope for his own emotional and financial gain. Ortiz' suggestion that the Emperor give the pope orders indicates his own belief that the papacy owed obedience to secular rulers rather than vice versa – an opinion he regarded as heretical when voiced by Protestants or Henry VIII.

The account of Bennet's meeting with the pope is bizarre. He wrote no report of any such meeting and nor had Henry sent orders for him to say such a thing. If he did speak to the pope as described, Bennet was acting traitorously. If he did not, what sort of political game was the pope playing in saying that he did? Dr Mai said he hoped it was true but admitted his doubts.

A modern historian has described Cardinal Ancona and his nephew as the two most corrupt cardinals in Rome.[356] It is an apt judgment.

---

356 Fletcher, *Our Man in Rome,* p.169. Ancona's nephew, Cardinal Ravenna, would go on trial for corruption in 1535.

March 1532

Events

- Thomas Boleyn denies the right of the pope and clergy to pass laws effective in England. Chapuys describes him and Anne as "true apostles of the new sect" (LP 5.850).
- the Duke of Norfolk visits Dover to discuss plans for a new harbour and fortifications (LP 5.850).
- James V of Scotland requests the hand of Francis' daughter in marriage. The ambassador suspects Francis will refuse and offer him the daughter of the Duke of Guise or Vendôme instead (LP 5.855, 898).
- the mother of one of the Emperor's chaplains agrees to testify that Katherine was a virgin when she married Henry (CSPS 4.2.917).
- Cranmer and Elyot send a report of Reformed worship at Nuremberg. Elyot remains tasked with arresting William Tyndale (LP 5.869).
- a pro-annulment preacher in Salisbury is hissed at by women (LP 5.879).
- Pomeray, the French ambassador, notes he is treated like a prince by Henry being allowed an apartment in the palace and sharing meals with the King (LP 5.883).
- Parliament passes an Act restricting the payment of annates to Rome. Chapuys reports resistance in the Commons necessitating a division but Henry reports that the initiative for the Act came from there. Henry tells his ambassador in Rome that if the pope should complain that parliament discussed the matter at all, they are to tell him that Henry permits free speech (LP 5.879, 882, 898).
- Cardinal Trani, the third highest ranked cardinal in Rome, offers to become Cardinal Protector for England (LP 5.880). Henry is happy with the idea and suggests either Monte or Farnese as alternatives (LP 5.886).
- negotiations with cardinals Ancona and Ravenna continue. Henry warns that rewards will only be paid after they have proved their loyalty and ability (LP 5.887).
- George Boleyn is sent to France. Jean du Bellay believes he has been sent by Henry directly and without the approval of Norfolk or the Council (LP 5.882).
- legal wrangles continue in Rome including two weeks spent arguing over the definition and use of the word peremptory. The English describe the Imperialists as "chiding and scolding and alleging laws and decisions that never were" (LP 5.892). The Imperialists accuse the English of wasting time. The argument continues to be over whether the excusator should be admitted, a matter which needs to be settled before he can submit his case that Henry should not appear in Rome.[357] Only after that has been decided

---

[357] An English summary of Carne's twenty-five conclusions which he submitted for debate appear in CSPV 4.743.

can the case regarding the validity of the "marriage" begin. The Rota have already voted against the excusator unless he has a mandate from Henry for the main case. The Rota's verdict is not binding on Consistory and the English say it should not be revealed because it would be likely to prejudice the debate in the latter. As Cardinal Ancona, leading canon lawyer, supports the English on this point and adds that a case can only be heard where it is safe for the petitioner (i.e. Henry) as well as the defendant, Dr Mai despairs. If Katherine's case is decided by the Rota, he feels sure of a verdict in her favour but he acknowledges that if it goes to Consistory, it could easily be lost as the cardinals include many men whom he says are more interested in faction and enhancing their chances of becoming the next pope than in her (CSPS 4.2.921, 925).
- Cardinal Loaysa, an Imperialist, cheerfully tells the Emperor that his work of fighting Lutheranism is so important that he must have no thought of returning home to his wife or children in Castile until victory is won, even if he is away for a dozen years or more (CSPS 4.2.916).
- the Empress, herself daughter of the previous king of Portugal, tries to secure a verdict for Katherine from the University of Lisbon (CSPS 4.2.924).
- a nurse and midwife is provided for Bridget, wife of Sir Nicholas Harvey, at the King's expense (PP p.197)
- the Duke of Ferrara sends Henry some falcons (PP p.198).
- Venice votes (194 for: 4 against) to allow all but two of their subjects to support Henry by writing or at Rome if they so wish. The two they say must remain at Padua are lecturers whom they claim cannot be spared without risking the studies of the students there (CSPV 4.747).

Comments

Henry did not usually pay medical bills when court ladies had babies as this would have been the responsibility of their husbands and Bridget is one of only two ladies to be so honoured. The other was the Countess of Worcester in February 1530 (PP p.22). Both ladies were noted as close friends of Anne Boleyn. It is likely that the payment was made following Henry agreeing to be godfather to the child in question.[358]

James V would go on to marry Guise's daughter. The resultant child would be Mary, Queen of Scots.

The Emperor had already been away from home for over two years. Given he was quite fond of his wife, he probably did not share Loaysa's sentiments.

Annates were effectively a tax equivalent to the first year's income of a bishop or archbishop and which had to be paid before the said bishop was allowed to receive any of the income which went with the job. They had been introduced around two hundred years before. The sums required were huge and

---

358 Both of Bridget's husbands served Henry as ambassadors overseas so his gift to her was an expression of regard for their service.

generally involved the bishop-elect having to take out a loan. Given the life expectancy of the period, it was not unusual for a bishop to die before this loan was paid. Meanwhile, money had to be raised and that would have come from church lands via farm or property rentals, and from churches. Although there is no proof, because the opinion poll had yet to be invented, it is fairly safe to assume that the husbandmen, tailors and farm labourers who worked so hard to put food on their own tables were less than inspired by the thought of working harder and longer to raise money so that the pope in Rome could enjoy a luxurious existence.

Hall records that it was revealed during the debate that between 1489 and 1531, £160,000 had been paid in annates to Rome – worth around £1.1 billion today or £24 million a year, a sum he describes as "incredible."[359] Hall also observed that MPs were concerned to learn that Spanish bishops did not have to pay annates, something Chapuys admitted. It should be remembered that the money passing out of the realm was not paper or like some modern electronic transfer, it was actual gold coins. Tudor monetary theory was limited but it was deeply concerned about this one way passage of wealth. After all, the pope was not going to come to London with a ship full of coins and spend them all purchasing English goods for the benefit of English merchants, farmers and craftsmen. Once the money was sent to Rome, it was gone.

That the call to abolish annates came from the Commons is supported by a petition referring to them as unjust and "against the law of God," this based on St Peter's condemnation of Simon Magus who sought to buy a position in the church and from which event the word simony derives (LP 5.721.5, Acts 8:18-23). The petition is undated but probably dates from the start of the year when plans for parliamentary business during the coming session were drawn up. In 1404, Parliament had described annates as a "horrible mischief and damnable custom" so the antipathy was not new.[360]

Traditionally, it is Thomas Cromwell who is credited with the idea of using annates as a lever against the pope but it is more probable that it came from the French. In 1438, the Pragmatic Sanction of Bourges had stopped the payment of annates to Rome and successive French kings used the prospect of revoking this agreement as a carrot to obtain favours from the pope for over seventy years. It was Francis who eventually did so in 1516 with the Concordat of Bologna which reinstated annates in return for papal support for French claims in Italy. Francis' move was deeply unpopular in France because the policy had worked well.[361] In 1522, Adrian VI had declined to act against

---

359 *Hall's Chronicle*, p.785 The Act gives the same figure but says the period was from 1487. It says that this is just the figure for annates and excludes all other monies paid to Rome. At the time the bill was passed, there were five ducats to the pound. During the period in question, eighty-two bishoprics had changed hands so the average fee per time was £1,951 in Tudor money, or about £13.6 million today.
360 Geoffrey Parmiter, *The King's Great Matter* (1967) p.185
361 Robert Knecht, 'The Concordat of 1516: a reassessment', *Historical Journal* vol 9 (1963) pp.24-27.

France on grounds "such a step would be immediately followed by a stoppage of all supplies of money from that kingdom" and because he knew the "French King would become a protector of the Lutheran heresy and make a resettlement of ecclesiastical order in his dominions."[362] Given the amount of time that Henry and his ministers spent with their French counterparts, it is not surprising that the English Reformation should demonstrate so many similarities with French policies of the fifteenth century. The only surprise is the lack of attention given to this fact by English historians.

It might be wondered why the bishops opposed the restraint of annates when they had most to gain from the practice ending. The reason was simple: the pope was their boss and they did not wish to upset him. It was this demonstration of disloyalty which led to Henry's famous comment a few weeks later that the clergy were only half his subjects.

The Act was also highly unusual because it was conditional. It gave Henry until Easter next year to negotiate with the pope to see if he would "reasonably, to compound, either to extinct and make frustrate the payments of the said annates, or first-fruits, or else, by some friendly, loving, and tolerable composition, to moderate the same, in such wise as may be by this his realm easily borne and sustained." Only if the pope refused was the payment to be reduced to a flat five per cent of the profits on any benefice. Parliament was clearly not optimistic that the pope would generously abolish annates because the Act continued that if the pope should "unjustly, uncharitably, and unreasonably, vex, inquiet, molest, trouble, or grieve our said sovereign lord, interdict his heirs or successors, kings of England, or any of his or their spiritual or lay subjects, or this his realm, by excommunication, excommengement, interdiction, or by any other process, censures, compulsories, ways or means" then such punishments should not be "published, executed, nor divulged, nor suffered to be published, executed, or divulged in any manner of wise" and clergy must continue to celebrate "all manner of sacraments, sacramentals, ceremonies, or other divine service of Holy Church, or any other thing or things necessary for the health of the soul of mankind."[363] Not only does this Act demonstrate the low opinion of the papacy with its belief that the pope would, far from turning the other cheek as Jesus commended, resort to revenge which punished wholly innocent people at a profound level, but it was passed months before Henry married Anne. Hence, when in the months that followed Henry said he would ignore papal condemnations, he was acting in accordance with parliament's wishes rather than acting the part of an autocrat. The Act was confirmed in 1534.

Chapuys describes the use of a division in the Commons as a new thing. It is the first mention of such an event so he may have been right in this, but it is equally possible that it had happened before and he reported it because it was new to him. Chapuys does not appear to have had much idea about

---
362 Pastor, History, vol. 9, pp.2010202.
363 Gee and Hardy, *Documents Illustrative* pp.180-186.

parliamentary procedure. Edward Hall, an MP who was there, makes no mention of it suggesting the practice did not seem novel to him.

Cardinal Trani was a highly respected figure in Rome with a keen interest in the Bible. His support for Henry is worthy of note. Unfortunately, he did not have the opportunity to become Cardinal Protector of England because Francis intervened to secure his support for himself (LP 5.1110).

It is unknown exactly when and why George Boleyn went to France. Perhaps Henry thought it was cheaper after losing so much to him at shovelboard! Most likely it was to repeat Henry's request for a meeting with Francis. The fact that other members of the Privy Council were not involved indicates it was a private mission.

April 1532

Events

- Henry re-organises his Privy Chamber into two shifts each of which attend him for six weeks before having six weeks off. They are: (LP 5.727)

Job Title	Shift A	Shift B
Principal Lord	The Marquess of Exeter	George Boleyn, Viscount
Groom of the Stool[364]	Sir Henry Norris	Sir Thomas Heneage
Gentlemen	Sir Nicholas Carew	Sir Francis Bryan
	Sir John Russell	Sir Edward Neville
	Sir Anthony Browne	Sir Thomas Cheyney
	Sir Richard Page	John Wellysbourne
	Francis Weston	Sir Henry Knyvet

- the pope explains to the Emperor that given Katherine has suffered no real harm in England, he sees no reason to excommunicate Henry (LP 5.934).
- Katherine receives a copy of the pope's January letter urging Henry to restore her and send Anne away until sentence is given. She brands it useless and decrees that it should not be served on Henry (CSPS 4.2.931, 943).
- the French ambassador expresses his belief that Henry should cease spending time and money on trying to obtain a solution from the pope and follow the example of Louis XII of France by simply marrying the woman of his choice (LP 5.941).

---

364 The senior gentleman who acted as manager for the other team members.

- trade talks with the Low Countries continue but little progress is made as each side accuses the other of seeking unreasonable terms to favour their own subjects (LP 5.946).
- in Rome, Carne, the excusator, delivers a new protestation alleging that Italy is unsafe for Henry, particularly with the threat of Turkish invasion. He argues his points with the cardinals for three weeks. The Imperial lawyers and Katherine's proctor decline to participate so the English file a complaint against them for contempt (LP 5.972).
- Norfolk's eldest son is betrothed to Frances Vere, daughter of the Earl of Oxford. He is nineteen, she fifteen. Chapuys remarks that the bride is no catch and claims Anne forced Norfolk to arrange the match for fear his son would marry Henry's daughter, Mary, and this would raise Norfolk's stature in the King's eyes enabling him to use his influence to have Katherine restored and Anne dismissed (CSPS 4.2.934).
- it is reported in Venice that Henry, Francis, the German princes and the disputed King of Hungary have formed a league with the support of the Turk. Princess Mary will wed John of Hungary and as soon as the Turk attacks Italy, the various league members will immediately launch attacks of their own against whichever part of the Emperor's domains are nearest. The informer adds that the Duke of Albany is to command the league's army (CSPS 4.2.928).
- a German envoy arrives in Rome claiming to represent a team of Lutheran preachers. If the pope will donate five hundred crowns, he promises that this highly effective group will re-convert Luther himself and the Duke of Saxony back to papal allegiance. The pope, who has been studying the Augsburg confession with his advisors, agrees (CSPS 4.2.932, 937).
- William Peto, provincial of the friars at Greenwich, preaches a sermon before Henry saying that princes should beware evil advisors who lead them from the truth. After the service, Henry speaks to Peto who brings up the subject of the annulment whereupon an altercation follows. When Peto seeks permission to visit Toulouse for a chapter meeting, Henry agrees and takes the opportunity of his absence to send one of his own chaplains to Greenwich to speak in favour of the annulment. The warden objects and Peto returns home to deal with the furore. Henry demands the warden is deprived but Peto refuses saying he has done nothing wrong. Henry has both men imprisoned. Chapuys gleefully reports that Peto's motive for going to Toulouse was not a chapter meeting but to get a book printed in support of Katherine which he did (LP 5.941).
- a group of Norfolk's retainers led by Richard Southwell invade the sanctuary at Westminster where Sir William Pennington, kinsman of the Duke of Suffolk, is hiding. They murder him there. Learning of the atrocity, Suffolk gathers his men to pursue the killers but Henry steps in to stop the situation escalating and has the perpetrators arrested. The Venetian ambassador says that he has heard the murder resulted from a private

quarrel but also that it stemmed from the Duchess (Henry's sister) using "opprobrious language" about Anne Boleyn (CSPV 4.761).
- the bishops tell Henry that they cannot support the annulment unless the pope does so because they have taken oaths of allegiance to him (CSPV 4.761). A furious Henry gives the Speaker and a group of M.P.s copies of the said oaths saying that: "We thought that the clergy of our realm had been our subjects wholly but now we have well perceived that they be but half our subjects, and scarce our subjects." The oath taken by the bishops went:

> I, (name) from this hour forward, shall be faithful and obedient to the pope, St Peter, and to the holy church of Rome. …
>
> I shall not consent that they shall lose either life or member or shall be taken or suffer any violence or any wrong by any means. …
>
> The rights, honours, privileges, authorities of the church of Rome and of the pope and his successors. I shall cause to be conserved, defended, augmented and promoted.
>
> I shall not be in counsel, treaty or any act in the which anything shall be imagined against him or the church of Rome, their rights, states, honours or powers, and if I know of any such to be moved or compassed, I shall resist it to my power and as soon as I can, advertise him or such as may give him knowledge.

Hall says concern over this oath was one of the reasons why the pope was deprived of his jurisdiction in England.[365]
- George Boleyn returns from France and together with his father, wins several games of bowls against the King earning £54 15s. They relax afterwards with fresh oranges (PP p.203, 209-211).

Comments

Norfolk's son married Frances the following year but they did not live together until she was eighteen, a reminder that although the legal age of consent for girls was twelve, few contemporaries believed that sexual activity was advisable at that age. Chapuys may have dismissed her charms and fortune but she was an acceptable match. His theory of a paranoid Anne forcing the union reflects more on Chapuys' mentality and wishful thinking than on reality.

The fact that Katherine refused to have the pope's letter served on Henry is worth noting. Many historians mention the letter but neglect to point out that the named recipient did not get it.

---

365 *Hall's Chronicle*, p.789

WHY IT TOOK SO LONG   423

The informer in Venice evidently had great communication skills if he was able to convince people of such an outlandish tale as the new anti-Imperial alliance. It is a reminder that people faced with the threat of war are prone to set reason aside and also that in the absence of an independent news service against which stories could be verified, rumours took on a disproportionate importance.

The story of William Peto is often misrepresented. He did not preach against the annulment before Henry, he challenged him after the service. Given he was seeking a favour from the King in the form of a permit to travel overseas and he was not despatched forthwith to the Tower, it may be supposed the debate was rather more civilised than Chapuys portrays it.

The Privy Chamber re-organisation is interesting because it casts light on Anne Boleyn's fall. Norris, Page and Weston from the first shift were all arrested with Browne being involved in the accusations and Carew in the plot to replace Anne with Jane Seymour. None of those in the second shift were involved at all. It is also worth noting that Russell and Cheyney were in separate teams. Presumably the bad blood engendered by the wardship battle had not entirely died away. George Boleyn's position as a Viscount was far below that of Exeter who was a Marquess and cousin to the King, but George was expecting to become the King's brother-in-law. In 1526, Francis Weston had been a page so he had clearly risen through the ranks.[366]

Obviously all those involved were born at least three hundred years before birth registration, but so far as can be known, the approximate ages of the attendants were: Shift A – Exeter (34), Norris (50), Carew (36), Russell (47), Browne (32), Page (40), Weston (21). Shift B – Boleyn (28), Heneage (52), Bryan (42), Neville (61), Cheyney (47), Wellysbourne (32), Knyvet (28).[367] Henry was 40. With the exception of Weston, they were largely men who might be expected to be of some maturity, though that does not always go hand in hand with age.[368]

The chief duty of the Principal Lord was to act as Henry's companion. The Groom of the Stool cared for Henry's intimate physical functions as well as handling his petty cash and valuables including jewels. The Gentlemen helped dress the King, attended him in public, carried out confidential work for him and provided entertainment for him in terms of music or sporting activity.

The clergy oath clearly shocked M.P.s and Henry and it is easy to see why. A person's first loyalty should be to their country not an overseas power, and at this date, the pope was very much the ruler of the papal states and a secular prince.

No murder should be taken lightly, but such a deed carried out in the sanctuary of a church is an horrific act of desecration. Pennington was married to Suffolk's first cousin once removed. Suffolk's biographer expresses his

---
366 LP 4.1939. It is unknown when Weston started in the role.
367 Henry Knyvet and Francis Bryan were both first cousins of George Boleyn as were Henry Norris and Nicholas Carew by marriage. See Appendix: Key Relationships
368 Proof of the shift system in operation can be found in Husee's report of April 1534 when he notes that Bryan was not working at the same time as Norris, LP 7.428.

belief that it was indeed a private quarrel because Pennington had been involved in previous property disputes with Howard supporters whose lands bordered his own.[369] It also makes more sense than the idea that it had anything to do with Suffolk's wife. Mary was too astute, having been an English princess from birth and also Queen of France, to comment upon Anne openly regardless of what she might have felt. Mary was also indisputably loyal to her brother. Moreover, why kill Pennington over something she said? The allegation tells us nothing about the opinions of the Duchess of Suffolk but a great deal about the mood of the time and the willingness to believe in the existence of opposition to Anne in high places. It is also interesting that Chapuys failed to hear about the event. With regard the Southwells and their associates, they were briefly imprisoned before being tried and released upon payment of a fine and pardoned (LP 5.1139.11, 1336). The fact that they were friends of Thomas Cromwell probably helped.

May 1532

Events

- the home of Cuthbert Tunstall, Bishop of Durham, is raided in search of treasonous or anti-annulment works. Nothing is found. It is suspected he was warned (LP 5.986, 987).
- parliament vote a tax to raise money for fortifications along the border with Scotland. It is less than Henry requested. During the debate, an MP had said Scotland could not afford to invade without Imperial aid and the best way of preventing that was for Katherine to be restored. An angry Henry summons the Speaker and a group of M.P.s to rebuke them for interfering in a private matter. He tells them that "conscience, caused me to abstain from her [Katherine's] company, and no foolish or wanton appetite: for I am forty one years old, at which age the lust of man is not so quick, as in lusty youth." (LP 5.989)[370]
- Henry reports Peto and Elston to the pope and asks that a senior member of their order be sent to try them. At Chapuys' prompting, the papal nuncio writes to the pope advising him not to do so and Katherine asks the Emperor to do likewise (LP 5.989).
- James V expresses disappointment that he cannot marry the Emperor's sister but promises to accept a Danish princess as he has proposed (LP 5.1004).
- Henry Percy is appointed Sheriff of Northumberland for life. As the role offers the chance to make a considerable sum, he agrees to pay the Exchequer £40 per annum for the privilege (LP 5.1008).

---

369 Gunn, *Charles Brandon*, p.125
370 *Hall's Chronicle*, p.788

- Pomeray, the French ambassador, returns to France on business. Chapuys wonders why and suspects that it is to discuss the situation in Scotland (LP 5.1013).
- after two months the excusator Edward Carne finishes presenting his case to the cardinals. The pope decrees the Rota must now provide them with legal advice on all Carne has said together with advice on Mai's arguments for the Imperialists before they can debate their decision (LP 5.1014).
- the papal nuncio complains to Norfolk that a preacher called the pope a heretic. Norfolk says that he would have had the man burnt alive if he could but Thomas Boleyn and someone whom he would not name disagreed. Chapuys assumes he means Anne Boleyn (CSPS 4.2.951).
- the Commons present a supplication to the King complaining about the church making laws inconsistent with civil and common law, about heresy trials where people are condemned without evidence against them being presented, about excessive fees in church courts and delays to probate and about the lack of able clergy at parish level (LP 5.1016). Henry asks convocation to reply. Their response is that their judicial power is scriptural and they cannot give away power given to them by God (LP 5.1018, 1019). Henry passes their response to the Commons saying: "we think their answer will smally please you for it seemeth to us very slender."[371] The bishops also submit a counter petition seeking stronger laws against heretics (LP 5.1017). Chapuys says that if parliament has its way, the church will have less authority than shoemakers who are able to pass laws for their own profession and he prays that God will send down such remedy as the intensity of the evil requires (CSPS 4.2.951).
- on 16th May, the clergy submit. They agree to make no new laws without Henry's consent and to a review being held of all existing laws. The submission is received by the King, Thomas Cromwell and three of the lords (LP 5.1023).
- Sir Thomas More resigns as Lord Chancellor and is replaced by Audley. More claims that the pay is too low but Chapuys thinks it is because he fears being drawn into conflict with Henry (LP 5.1046).
- the Emperor hurts his leg while hunting (LP 5.1027; CSPS 4.2.953).
- the Scottish parliament promises not to pass any legislation prejudicial to the pope (LP 5.1030).
- Henry seeks the support of cardinals again for the election of Ghinucci (LP 5.1036).
- Edmund Howard (father of Kathryn) declares that though he has many kin, including those in high places, he has fewer friends than anyone (LP 5.1042).

---

371 *Hall's Chronicle* p.789

- on the 13th, the papal nuncio delivers the pope's letter of January 25th to Henry. He responds: "I am very much surprised that the pope still persists in his folly and wants me to recall the Queen to my house, for since His Holiness chooses to consider her my legitimate wife, it is evident that the right of punishing her for the rudeness with which she has treated – and is daily treating – me, belongs exclusively to me, not to His Holiness or to anyone else." Chapuys fears it will be ignored as the letter is so ineffective and reports that Henry is sending Katherine to another house further away (CSPS 4.2.952).
- Henry Norris is made steward of Lewisham and East Greenwich, both then part of Kent, at £3 6s 8d per annum. The grant is made at the King's palace of Placentia at Greenwich as part of the ceremony in which Audley replaces More (LP 5.1065.22, 1075).
- Baron Montfalconet, the Emperor's envoy, reports Henry will give nothing toward the war against the Turk. He observes Katherine still loves Henry and that she believes he will obey the eventual verdict from the pope and take her back treating her better than ever. Katherine is also sure that the verdict will mark the revival of the Anglo-Imperial alliance in place of the Anglo-French (LP 5.1059).
- Dr Ortiz continues to press the Emperor to demand the pope threaten Henry with excommunication if he does not take Katherine back. He says that given the pope is clearly unwilling to issue a verdict, it is the Emperor's job to stand up for the sacraments. If Henry refuses – as Ortiz expects – God will rain down terror on him as a mark of divine wrath (CSPS 4.2.947).
- the pope says that if the French disturb Italy, the Imperial army should cause trouble for them elsewhere. A bemused Dr Mai comments that the pope is like the Bible, his every word contains a mystery! (CSPS 4.2.950)
- two giant fish, each more than thirty feet long, are caught in the Thames. Gloomy Londoners predict it is an ill omen (CSPV 4.773).
- Cardinal Salviati complains about the atrocities being committed by Imperial forces under Marquis del Vasto. He observes that the pope made a league with the French for less (CSPS 4.2.950).
- Chapuys is confused by the visit to Henry of a Neapolitan noble from France. He hears he has brought two ships laden with artillery to take to Danzig but much searching by Chapuys' agents fails to locate the vessels. He starts to wonder if the interpreter misunderstood or if he has been deliberately misled. Although he sets agents to watch the ports, the gentleman departs with Chapuys none the wiser (LP 5.1013, 1046, 1059).

Comments

As usual, Chapuys immediately sprang to accuse Anne of supporting the preacher who called the pope a heretic. She may have done so but the preacher could not have done this without the support of the King and it is entirely possible that Henry was the person whom Norfolk was trying to avoid naming for fear any criticism of him would be regarded as treason. Henry had suggested the pope was a heretic himself in November 1529.

The decision of the nuncio to serve the pope's letter urging Henry to restore Katherine and send Anne away is significant. The letter had been sent to the Emperor rather than Henry and he had sent it on to Katherine who said that she did not want it served. Chapuys knew this because he had reported her wishes to the Emperor on 29th April. The nuncio worked very closely with Chapuys so would have acted after talking to him. Had Katherine changed her mind or was Chapuys so keen for the letter to be served that he decided he knew better than her and so told the nuncio to go ahead?

It is interesting that the lords who accepted the submission of the clergy did not include Thomas Boleyn or his son. According to Chapuys, they were the ringleaders of the campaign against the church so it is surprising that they did not wish to be there to mark their triumph – unless they were not as anticlerical as he claimed. The submission of the clergy has attracted a huge amount of academic coverage but not everybody at the time saw it as significant. West's account of events written just a few days later does not even mention it (LP 5.1059). Henry was not doing something new but following the example of his predecessor William the Conqueror who refused to allow convocation to "ordain or forbid anything save what had first been ordained by himself as agreeable to his own will."[372]

The right claimed by the church to pass its own laws may seem an archaic issue but it was a topic much to the fore in 1928 when parliament rejected the revised prayer book drawn up by convocation. The church decided to use it anyway and went on to introduce Series 2, Series 3, the Alternative Service Book and Common Worship, even though the legality of these remains open to debate amongst some evangelicals.

More's biographer, Nicholas Harpsfield in 1557, claimed that he resigned due to ill health and following doctor's orders that he should take a complete rest.[373] He may have been ill but it is generally supposed that his resignation was a protest at the Submission of the Clergy. At his trial, he accused Henry of violating Magna Carta and his coronation oath to protect the

---

[372] Gee and Hardy, *Documents Illustrative*, p.59 quoting Eadmer. In the same document, it was reported: "He would not then allow anyone settled in all his dominions to acknowledge as apostolic the pontiff of the City of Rome, save at his own bidding, or by any means to receive any letter from him if it had not first been shown to himself." William also wrote to the pope to explain why he had rejected a suggestion that he pay homage to him: "I refused to do fealty, nor will I, because neither have I promised it, nor do I find that my predecessors did it to your predecessors." ibid. p.57 The Conqueror was clearly a monarch after Henry's own heart.

[373] Harpsfield, *Thomas More*, p.20.

church.[374] In this, he was wrong on both counts. Notwithstanding the millions of Orthodox Christians, More believed that the only true church was that headed by the pope and the English church could not separate from it any more than a leg could declare itself independent of a body. However, on 24th August 1216 the pope had declared Magna Carta 'null, and void of all validity for ever' and it made no sense for a man who supported papal authority over England to cite a document which a pope had declared invalid. As regards the coronation oath, Henry was upholding that absolutely in seeking to prevent the English church passing their own laws. Convocation consisted only of clergy, generally bishops and archdeacons. The church was the body of Christ and consisted of all those who had been baptised, both clergy and laity.[375] By involving the laity in the review of legislation, Henry was making an important point about the nature of the church. Many of his contemporaries, including More and Chapuys, defined the church as the clergy but this was untrue as is demonstrated throughout the New Testament.[376]

Chapuys' comment about shoemakers was irrelevant. Their regulations only affected themselves while church laws affected everyone. People could be imprisoned or fined or lose their livelihoods at the church's pleasure without redress. Even their corpses were not safe.

It is often held that Henry had given up on Rome by this stage but his efforts to have Ghinucci made a cardinal suggest that this was not quite the case. Despite some discussions, no new Cardinal Protector had been appointed for England and Henry may have wanted to wait until Ghinucci was elected so that the role could go to him.

This month shows the importance of reading a variety of texts. Montfalconet's report states that sermons are being preached daily in Katherine's favour. That may have been the case somewhere but evidently not everywhere for Hall – a native Londoner rather than a visitor who probably spoke no English – said of this same time: "The King was openly rebuked by preachers for keeping company with his brother's wife."[377] The Venetian ambassador also reported that many sermons were being preached about the annulment, some strongly backing Henry, others Katherine (CSPV 4.767).

Placentia, also known as Greenwich, was where Henry had been born, although the palace had been rebuilt during his childhood by his father. Similar in size to Hampton Court, it boasted tennis courts, a tiltyard, a cockpit and a fine banqueting house plus extensive stables and an armoury where it is likely that some of Henry's suits of armour (visible today in the Tower of London) were made. Henry and Anne spent considerable time there. It was also used for

---

374 Ibid. p.57
375 Pope Francis commented that clergy comprised only one per cent of the Church which is why lay involvement at all levels was vital, *Hope* p.206
376 Preventing the church passing laws without royal approval also ensured that the church could not legislate against the King.
377 *Hall's Chronicle*, p789

important visits and spectacular events, so for Norris to be made the Keeper of the manor was a sign of great favour.[378]

Katherine's efforts to protect Peto and Elston were an act of direct disobedience to Henry, the man whom she claimed was her husband. Modern readers might admire her spirit but it was a breach of the vows she had made at her wedding and coronation.

Historians should restrict themselves to the evidence and not indulge in speculation, but it is hard to resist wondering how much laughter was heard around the court as they heard of Chapuys' fruitless ship-hunting exploits.

June 1532

Events

- the Emperor tells Dr Ortiz not to seek a second letter from the pope to excommunicate Henry but rather to devote his time to supporting Dr Mai in obtaining a verdict (CSPS 4.2.956). Dr Ortiz replies that Katherine appears to have changed her mind and now wants such a letter sent. He claims Henry is living in mortal sin and will be damned unless he leaves Anne who is the conduit of Satan. Regarding the place of the trial, he says it must be in Rome because only the pope can determine the extent of his own authority (CSPS 4.2.960).
- the Turkish fleet leaves Constantinople heading toward Sicily (LP 5.1092; CSPS 4.2.959).
- the pope selects Cardinals Monte and Ancona to advise him on the annulment (LP 5.1095). Monte writes to Henry promising his service (LP 5.1074). Ancona accepts 2,000 ducats from the Emperor to support Katherine but Mai thinks he is making promises to Henry too (CSPS 4.2.965).
- Chapuys continues to spend time trying to discover the motives of the recent Neapolitan visitor to court. He sends a man to follow him to France and arranges for the Regent of the Low Countries to send a party of gunmen to assist in the planned ambush: the Neapolitan evades them (CSPV 4.778). Chapuys also bribes the landlord of the house where the Neapolitan's captain is living (still minus ships) to spy on him. He learns the captain is very fond of backgammon (CSPS 4.2.962).
- Pomeray, the French ambassador returns from a visit home with two greyhounds sent as a gift from Francis to Henry and agreement to a new treaty of mutual defence (LP 5.1109, 1117).

---

378 For more on Greenwich in this period, see Clive Aslet, *The Story of Greenwich* (London, 1999) pp.40-62 and Simon Thurley, *The Royal Palaces of Tudor England* (Yale, 1993).

- Norfolk says that Mary remains the heir and will do so unless Henry has a son by another marriage. He believes Mary will retain her precedence over any future daughters Henry might have and claims that anyone who suggests that Mary is illegitimate will be beheaded (LP 5.1131).
- Anne Boleyn is granted two manors in Middlesex (LP 5.1139.32).
- from Rome, the Bishop of Auxerre reports that the pope pays the Emperor 50,000 crowns per month and becomes daily more of a slave to him (LP 5.1128)
- Chapuys reports on the questionable loyalty of two of Henry's ambassadors. Sir Thomas Elyot returns from the Imperial court and promptly sends a coded report on his briefing with Henry to the son of Dr Puebla in Spain (CSPS 4.2.957). Meanwhile, Sir John Wallop departs for France saying that he wants to be the one to execute the pope's eventual verdict and bring Katherine back to Henry. A confident Chapuys predicts that the pope's verdict will give the Emperor more power in England than he has ever had (LP 5.1109).
- Henry visits the Tower of London to inspect its ability to withstand attack and to view the artillery and ammunition levels therein (CSPV 4.778).
- Dean John Barlow dines with an Imperial councillor named Heylwigen at an inn in Brabant. He says that Henry was told by his confessor around 1523-4 that his "marriage" to Katherine was forbidden by divine law. Admitting that he knows both Bessie Blount and Anne Boleyn, he says Anne is pretty but less beautiful than Bessie, also more eloquent, graceful and comes from a better family. He denies that Anne is Henry's mistress and confirms that Henry ended the relationship with Bessie before she married (LP 5.1114; CSPS 4.2.967).
- Christian of Denmark, the Emperor's brother-in-law who was deposed in 1523, is ship wrecked and falls into the hands of his enemies (LP 5.1110, CSPV 4.778).
- plans are made for Henry's bastard son, the Duke of Richmond aged twelve, to spend some time in France (CSPV 4.782).
- Francis is frustrated by the pope. Having been asked by the pope for galleys to defend Italy against the Turk, he prepares them – only to discover that the pope has decided to use Imperial ones instead without telling him (LP 5.1103, 1125). Increasingly suspicious of the pope's promised neutrality, he suggests the pope's "nephew" Cardinal Medici come to France as a hostage. Dr Mai advises the pope to send the young cardinal to Hungary instead (CSPS 4.2.965).
- the cardinals refuse to consider the Imperial candidate, Muxetula, for election on ground he is of Jewish descent (CSPS 4.2.965)

Comments

One suspects that nobody ever accused Dr Ortiz of being indecisive or lacking in conviction. A famous satire existed entitled *Julius Exclusus,* in which the author imagined Julius II excommunicating St Peter for failing to agree with him.[379] It is easy to imagine Dr Ortiz being caricatured in the same way. He would have been apoplectic with rage had he discovered Jesus letting Henry into heaven and no doubt hurried to tell him that loving thy enemies was a divine joke not a command. Indeed, Dr Ortiz may even have tried to excommunicate Jesus!

Two thousand ducats in modern currency would be worth almost £3 million. It was not a little reward which the Emperor gave Ancona.

It is unknown what use the Emperor found for the information that the Neapolitan's captain enjoyed backgammon or whether he found this level of detail in Chapuys' reports impressive or irritating. Chapuys neglected to report on the failed ambush: the Venetian ambassador did that.

Heylwigen's account of his conversation with Barlow has attracted interest because it provides a rare eye-witness description of Anne Boleyn.[380] The document is not without difficulties. The two summaries in the English *Letters and Papers* and the *Calendar of State Papers: Spain*, differ in key respects, a fact which led Professor Ives to do his own translation[381] Heylwigen admits that Barlow did not speak Flemish which presented another opportunity for confusion.[382] At this date, Bessie Blount remained an unmarried widow so it was perhaps not too surprising that Heylwigen would suppose Henry would seek to marry her in the hope of legitimating his son by her, the Duke of Richmond. Belated legitimisation of a child conceived in adultery was illegal but if Henry was confirmed not to have been married to Katherine, no adultery was involved. Richmond was a healthy thirteen year old son and ideal candidate for heir to the throne. The interesting thing is that somebody in Heylwigen's position did not know Henry intended to marry Anne. Perusal of correspondence by Imperialists such as Chapuys and Loaysa give the impression that the whole of Europe knew and was scandalised, but here we have one of the Emperor's own councillors from the nearby Low Countries who is unaware.[383]

---

379 Opinion is divided over whether Erasmus or Richard Pace wrote the work. For further discussion see Diarmaid MacCulloch, *The Reformation*, p. 99. Given the political nature of the work, it was published anonymously,

380 Barlow was involved in the annulment as early as 1523 and took Henry's secret message to Knight in 1527. It was said of his relationship with Anne that he "always belonged to her, had his promotion by her and had been ambassador for her in divers places beyond the sea" (quoted in Starkey, *Six Wives*, p.305). He was also her chaplain for a time. In short, he knew her extremely well and would have been very familiar with Bessie Blount too.

381 Eric Ives, *Anne Boleyn* p.51. Ives adds that when Barlow heard of Anne's arrest in 1536, he presumed it was a vicious rumour promulgated by her enemies and set out to arrest the informer who had the effrontery to suggest that given Barlow's closeness to Anne, he must have been party to her adultery so should be in the Tower himself. *Ibid.* p305.

382 For discussion of this document, see When was Anne Boleyn born?

Ex-King Christian spent the remainder of his life as a prisoner of his uncle Fredrik I of Norway.

Why was Richmond being sent to France? To improve his fluency in French which was the language of most European courts; to enable him to spend time with leading political figures in France and develop relationships with those of the coming generation; to broaden his education and to demonstrate that Henry intended his son to have a public role when he grew up. There is no reason to suppose he considered making Richmond his heir but he probably saw him as fulfilling the sort of role which Brandon or Norfolk did in his own reign. For Francis, being entrusted with Henry's precious and entirely beloved son, was a very great honour and sign of the closeness of the alliance and Henry's trust in him. After all, should things go wrong, Richmond's presence would give Francis a key bargaining tool as a hostage.

July 1532

Events

- a young priest takes some angels (coins worth 8s 6d) and files them down. He tries to sell the filings to a goldsmith but has no joy. He tries three or four more but is unable to secure what he deems an acceptable offer. He is reported to the authorities, arrested, tried and sentenced to death. Chapuys, claims the unnamed priest was one of the two most loved men in England and that he acted in the simple belief that his actions were legal. He decries the fact that the priest was condemned by a civil court and executed without being defrocked first and says this shows the extremities to which the English clergy are reduced. To further enhance his story, he claims Henry pardoned a Frenchman for the same offence and that Thomas Boleyn asked Anne to intercede for the man with Henry but she refused saying there were too many priests in England anyway (CSPS 4.2.972).
- Henry formally founds a new college at Oxford – a re-foundation of that Wolsey was building (LP 5.1179).
- the Duchess of Norfolk tells Cromwell that some of Suffolk's servants have vowed revenge against the Southwells for the murder of William Pennington (see April 1532) and Cromwell promptly tells the King. The Duke of Norfolk apologises to the next messenger Suffolk sends to court saying he knows it is untrue. Suffolk fires off a furious letter to Cromwell complaining about him passing on gossip without investigating its

---

383 In October 1533, a month after the birth of Elizabeth, Henry received an offer from Sigismund of Hungary that he should marry his eighteen year old daughter described as "very beautiful..full of juice" and likely to be fertile, LP 6.1292. The news of Henry's marriage to Anne had evidently not reached Hungary by early summer when it may be presumed the messenger set out for England.

WHY IT TOOK SO LONG 433

veracity and saying that if he had thought any of his servants had behaved in that manner, he would have punished them himself before personally handing them over to Henry for judgment (LP 5.1183).
- the Emperor remains ill at Ratisbon. The condition is serious but not life threatening (LP 5.1186; CSPS 4.2.973).
- Henry sends thanks to Montmorency for accepting his request and negotiating a meeting between himself and Francis at Calais and Boulogne in the autumn. The French ambassador plays a key role in the arrangements and reveals Henry wants to bring Anne and leave Katherine at home (LP 5.1187).
- Henry cancels his summer progress and returns to London to prepare for the trip. Chapuys comments that he has heard rumours the King had to come back because crowds of women kept abusing Anne (LP 5.1202).
- the pope continues to refuse to give any money toward the Emperor's defence of Europe against the Turk (CSPS 4.2.971).
- Dr Agostini, travelling with his patient Cardinal Campeggio, asks Cromwell to discover why the Duke of Norfolk is upset with him and to secure a reconciliation (LP 5.1188).
- Edward Seymour, brother of Jane and employee of the Duke of Richmond[384] receives a loan of £1000 from Henry (LP 5.1205).
- Anne Boleyn gives the French ambassador a greyhound and a hunting outfit.[385] He reveals he is often paired with Anne when they go hunting with Henry and says the gift is a way of Henry honouring Francis indirectly "because that which the Lady does is all at the commandment of the said King." (LP 5.1187)
- Francis Weston and his wife are allowed to receive her inheritance now she is of age (LP 5.1207.4).
- James Butler, Anne Boleyn's original intended husband, is appointed Treasurer of Ireland (LP 5.1207.15).
- Henry jokes that Spanish dress makes a woman look like a devil (LP 5.1187).
- having received legal advice from the Rota, the cardinals are left to discuss whether the excusator should be admitted. After three sessions, they are unable to agree. It is decided to give Henry until October to send a proctor for the case and if he does not, to condemn him for contempt and continue without his input (LP 5.1157). The Imperialists claim this is a victory for Katherine (LP 5.1151) but the pope and Cardinals Monte and Ancona tell

---

384 Murphy, *Bastard Prince*, p.161
385 Ives, A*nne Boleyn*, p.196 has stated that the letter was written by Pomeray who was the French ambassador at the time and who accompanied Henry and Anne on their truncated progress that summer citing as evidence correspondence of du Bellay showing he was in France at this date. The original letter was transcribed by Le Grand from the royal archive at Bethune where it was attributed it to Jean du Bellay, a statement copied by the editors of *Letters and Papers.* The ending of the letter is not consistent with du Bellay's usual style in either the blessing or the signature. Le Grand, *Histoire*, vol. 3 p.557.

the English it is a victory for them (LP 5.1171-1173). The French say that if a vote had been taken, the old and wise cardinals would have backed Henry but they are in a minority. They add that the foolish majority support Katherine not from conviction but due to fear of the Emperor (LP 5.1170).[386]

- although the pope vows to excommunicate anyone who reveals details of what happened at any of the meetings of the cardinals, some details emerge. Ancona argued in favour of the excusator but when that motion seemed destined to fail, he decided to recommend that Henry send a proctor arguing that such would not be at risk in the same way that Henry might be. A decision to this effect was made. Ancona was supported by Cardinal Monte with Bennet noting that the pope had taken both men to be his advisers in the case. The idea of having the trial at a place indifferent was not wholly ruled out although it was agreed that finding any location acceptable to both sides was almost impossible and "Ancona said the style here is that the cause, if it be advoked hither should not be committed to any" which meant even if the taking of evidence was carried out away from Rome, the verdict would have to come from the pope alone since it was his responsibility to define the limits of his own authority and what the Bible meant. The cardinals accept Ancona's recommendation and agree delay is essential as things might change (LP 5.1172-1173).
- the English go to the pope to protest about the decision. They say that it makes no sense to admit a proctor but not an excusator and that the failure to reach a judgment on the excusator or the articles presented is a tacit rejection of them. On this basis, they tell Henry: "it is to be supposed they will be more difficult in the principal cause to serve Your Highness' cause according to justice." (LP 5.1172) On being told that the question of the admission of the excusator was doubtful, Carne retorts: "in every learned man's opinion besides them and the part adverse, the matters be most clear and relevant." He ends his report saying sadly "if our lives had lain upon it, we could do no more than we did." [387]
- Casale tells Henry that the cardinals in Rome "for fear dare not, or else for affection will not, minister justice" and he expresses frustration at the failure of the French to come through with the promised rewards. He says he knows at least nine abbacies are vacant in France and Cardinal Ancona knows it too. Casale says this makes it increasingly difficult to keep Ancona devoted to Henry and he warns the King that if he is unable to obtain help from the French, he should step in to ensure they do not

---

386 Nicolas Camusat, *Meslanges Historiques (Troyes, 1644)* p. 176b
387 The reports summarised in LP 5.1172 and 1173 are available in Pocock, *Records,* vol. 2. Carne and Bonner's (1172) is pp.292-298, Casale and Bennet's (1173) pp.288-292. Some damage to the originals means there are some gaps in the text. The authors also recommend Cardinals Trani, San Severino, Cesarini, Monte and Grimani as deserving letters of thanks from Henry for being "sincere friends".

hinder his cause by publicising the vacancies. Since no legal decision is made without Ancona's involvement and he is an old man who may not be around much longer to help, the situation is difficult (LP 5.1173, 1174).
- Dr Ortiz, in receipt of a letter from Chapuys saying that the pope should excommunicate Henry if he is unwilling to give a verdict before the summer vacation, goes to see the pope to demand this. The pope refuses and says they must wait until October to see what Henry will do before any further action is taken. Ortiz says it is essential that Henry is excommunicated for the mortal sin of casting off Katherine and that if the pope fails in his duty, he will stand up on the Day of Judgment and accuse him before God of apostasy. Ortiz claims that at this point, the pope changed colour and began to tremble with emotion. Protesting: "I am not a lawyer" the pope said he should go and see Cardinal Ancona, though not until the following day. Next morning, Dr Ortiz duly hastens off to see Ancona who tells him exactly the same thing, wait. Once again Dr Ortiz gets angry before departing. He makes further attempts to see the pope and cardinal only to discover both have developed sudden illnesses and are now far too sick to see him! (CSPS 4.2.979)
- at Ratisbon, agreement is reached between the Emperor and the Lutheran princes. In return for toleration of their faith – provided that no innovations are made – until matters can be settled by Imperial Diet or General Council, they will support him with money and arms for the war against the Turk (CSPS 4.2.982).
- the wife of Henry Percy claims that he has admitted a pre-contract with Anne Boleyn. Her letter to her father, the Earl of Shrewsbury, is passed by him to the Duke of Norfolk who takes it to Anne. She denies it and takes the letter to the King demanding a full investigation to clear her name of this libel. This is granted and Percy is summoned to London to be interrogated by Norfolk and other members of the Privy Council. He denies the allegation and repeats this statement under oath on the sacrament before the archbishops of Canterbury and York (Warham and Lee).[388]

Comments

Aside from his parishioners, probably nobody knew the unnamed priest. Justice Spelman did not even believe the man's name worthy of recording in his report of the case.[389] Coin clipping was against the law and had been a capital offence since 1275. The priest was not unaware of what he was doing. Chapuys was not such a fool as to believe that coin clipping was a minor offence and his suggestion that the priest may have thought it was comparable to reducing the

---

388 Paul Friedmann, *Anne Boleyn* vol. 1 pp.159-161. His source was a letter by Chapuys to the Emperor dated 22nd July 1532 which is not in the *Calendar of State Papers: Spain* but which he found in the Imperial archives at Vienna.
389 Spelman, *Reports*, p.49

size of large wafers at Holy Communion is laughable. As for the fact that the priest was executed as such and not defrocked first so he could be punished as a layman, Spelman noted that the judges in the case universally agreed that given the charge was high treason, no such step was required: nobody was above the law. Chapuys told the story simply as a means of blackening Anne's reputation in the eyes of the Emperor. It might also be wondered where he got the tale from. Thomas Boleyn was hardly likely to have related the conversation to Chapuys: they were not on friendly terms. At best it could have come from a servant eavesdropping, but possibly it was third or even fourth hand. Earlier in the same despatch, Chapuys related how he discussed with the papal nuncio the pros and cons of exaggerating the truth about the Turk to the Duke of Norfolk so by his own admission, he was not afraid of repackaging the facts to suit his audience. There is, however, another aspect to this story which enhances its comedic appeal. Chapuys evidently regarded Anne's supposed comment that there were too many priests in England as horrifying and evidence of her dangerously heretical opinions but Thomas More, a man whom he admired and viewed as the embodiment of Roman orthodoxy, had not only said exactly the same thing but committed it to print in his 1528 reply to Tyndale: "ye should not of priests have the plenty that ye have...there be too many."[390] Strange that for More to say it was fine but when Anne agreed with him, Chapuys saw that as heresy.[391]

The ability of the clergy to claim exemption from punishment in civil courts was a long standing grievance and one to which Henry was particularly sensitive. In 1512, Parliament had passed a law limiting benefit of clergy to a small degree. In response, in 1514, Pope Leo X had ruled that no layman could ever exercise authority over a priest, even a king.[392] An almighty row broke out with the church upholding the papal decree saying the exemption was a divine right and basing their argument on two texts, "honour thy father and thy mother" (Ex. 20:12) and "touch not my anointed" (Ps. 105:15) - a curious claim since both refer to the laity in the actual Bible. They even threatened to excommunicate anyone who tried to judge a cleric. In a debate at Baynard's Castle, Henry declared: "By the ordinance and sufferance of God we are King of England and kings of England in time past have never had any superior but

---

390 More's views on the inadequacies of the clergy and their excessive numbers are discussed in Hughes, *The Reformation in England*, vol. 1 pp.86-88.

391 In Thomas Starkey's *Dialogue between Reginald Pole and Thomas Lupset* ed. Kathleen Burton (1948) pp.78, 83-84, Reginald Pole also opines "priests are too many, and yet good clerks too few; monks, friars and canons are too many, and yet good religious men too few" adding that there be "no small number idle and unprofitable, which be nothing but burdens to the earth." The work was not authorised by Pole but Starkey had lived with him and knew him well so there is no reason to suppose that such was not his opinion.

392 He added that not only were "ecclesiastical persons" exempt from tithes and other taxes, any who paid them or accepted them, would be excommunicated. Decree 8 of the fifth Lateran Council, 5th May 1514.

God only." He refused the Archbishop's demand for the pope to adjudicate on the legitimacy of the statute and threatened the clergy with the Act of Praemunire whereupon they backed down. Yet the issue had not gone away and it was one of the grievances aired in Fish's *Supplication of the Beggars* who wrote in despair "what law can be made against them? "[393] The case of the coin clipping priest was, therefore, a reiteration of Henry's position from eighteen years before and the decision to execute him as a priest would have been very popular with the majority of the population. Chapuys was out of touch in his criticism.

Cromwell's hurry to report an unsubstantiated rumour to Henry may have been fuelled by fear that, if it was found to be true and he shown not to have said anything, he would be in trouble or it could have been an attempt on his part to show himself loyal in the hope of making Henry think he was indispensable and so gain favour. The incident casts light on Cromwell's character which is worth remembering when it comes to his role in Anne Boleyn's 1536 fall.

Henry's return to London was to prepare for the trip to France. The rumour which Chapuys so mischievously repeated about it being a response to popular protests arose because the planned visit was kept secret from almost everyone, including himself as Imperial ambassador, until the arrangements were more advanced. With no official announcement of the trip, people simply speculated. The French ambassador who was there made no mention of any protests along the route. Chapuys himself later admitted that the return was due to the French trip so it is sad to see the false rumour repeated as fact in so many books today.

Excommunication should be a last resort punishment, a verdict that the offence the person has committed is so heinous that they are no longer fit to be in the presence of their fellow Christians nor to receive the Body and Blood of Christ at Holy Communion. Dr Ortiz believed that Henry was guilty of adultery which would have breached the Ten Commandments and if Henry had been guilty, such a verdict might have been applicable after other means had failed. However, revealing what is said in Consistory did not breach any commandments of God. Archbishop Warham issued a similar threat to the convocation in England.[394] It is hard to imagine that when Jesus gave his followers the keys to heaven and hell that he meant them to be used in this way.

Were it not so important a case with so serious repercussions, it would be tempting to laugh at the idea that the only person who could define the limits of the pope's power was the pope. It is the sort of philosophy beloved of dictators. Clement is often seen as weak but he had been taught by Machiavelli who was so close a friend that he dedicated a book to him and visited him in

---

393 For a fuller account of the problems in 1512-1514, see Gwyn, *The King's Cardinal*, pp.47-50. Simon Fish, S*upplication of the Beggars* (1529) p.8. Parliament would pass further laws to limit benefit of clergy in 1534 and 1536, see Lehmberg, *Reformation Parliament*, pp.185, 230.
394 Lehmberg, *The Reformation Parliament* p.99

1525 after he became pope.[395] Pomeray's comments about Anne are extremely important. He saw her almost daily. He chatted to her, dined with her, went shooting with her and he was selected to accompany Henry and Anne when they went on progress. This is in marked contrast to Chapuys who was ostracised from court and who never spoke to Anne. Chapuys describes Anne as manipulative, cunning and extremely temperamental. Pomeray saw her as a non-political, gentle and obedient, loyal lady friend of Henry's. It is remarkable that so many writers seem to cite the Chapuys view over the French and it seems likely that this largely stems from a preference in the twentieth and twenty-first century to see women as powerful and independent figures with humility and obedience being seen as highly undesirable traits. Nonetheless, historians should seek the truth not try to shape the facts to fit their own beliefs.[396]

The allegation of a pre-contract between Anne and Percy was malicious. Percy's wife wanted a separation and this was the only way by which she could think to get one. It may also have been a political attempt to scupper the wedding of Henry and Anne which was expected to take place very soon. That the inquiry took place is confirmed by Percy himself (LP 10.864) but Chapuys is the only source for how it came about and it is unknown, therefore, when exactly the letter was written. Such a serious allegation would have been treated with due urgency but if Percy was at home in Northumberland, it would have taken a few days for him to get to London.

August 1532

Events

- the Turkish army arrives at the Danube. They bring twelve elephants who are so terrified by the cascading, fast running and overflowing river that they refuse to cross until propelled forward by hot irons. Meanwhile, a Venetian vessel is taken by the Turks and its crew killed. The Imperial navy masses at Naples to try to stop the Turks entering the Adriatic (LP 5.1223).
- preparations begin for Henry's trip including the manufacture of new jewellery and robes (LP 5.1237, 1239). Chapuys says that Anne has written to her closest friend and companion, the lady who is to her like a sister, telling her that she anticipates that this journey will see her achieve the objective for which she has most longed. Assuming she means her wedding to Henry, Chapuys immediately advises the Emperor to have

---

395 Pastor, *History*, vol. 10 p.340
396 In 1540, the Duke of Norfolk, expressed astonishment at the idea that a monarch would take political advice from a woman, a reaction which suggests that he did not think Henry had done so from Anne, LP 15.223

armed Flemish ships sent out into the English Channel to prevent the trip taking place (CSPS 4.2.986).
- two Florentine sculptors, Maiano and Rovezano, continue work on Henry's tomb (LP 5.1244)
- Henry Percy reports a number of violent clashes along the border with Scotland and advises the King that James V has sent four thousand Scots to Ireland and five hundred archers (LP 5.1246).
- Francis tells his ambassador in Rome that should the pope ask why he is meeting Henry, he should say that they intend to discuss the dangers posed by the Turk (LP 5.1253).
- Henry agrees to pay his ex-brother-in-law, the Earl of Angus, £1000 per annum until he is restored to his estates in Scotland provided that he maintains his loyalty to him and not James (LP 5.1254).
- Katherine's chaplain, Thomas Abell, is sent to the Tower for his book *Invicta Veritas* while government officials try to secure all copies and remove them from sale (LP 5.1256).
- Archbishop Warham dies on the 23rd creating a vacancy for the role of Chancellor of the University of Oxford. Henry proposes Bishop John Longland of Lincoln and asks that the first debate be on the subject of the power and primacy of Rome (LP 5.1273).
- in the days before his death, Warham drafts a defence against the charge of Praemunire. He states that bishops are made by election in Rome and not at consecration and that their first loyalty is to the pope on grounds he is "head of all Christian men" while Henry is just head of Englishmen. Claiming Thomas Becket was a martyr, he warns of the dire fate which befell other kings who attacked the church, such as Richard II who was dethroned and says any area which holds a bishop prisoner will be placed under interdict and the two dioceses nearest to it. He justifies his stance on the Donation of Constantine which he says shows the primacy of the spirituality over the temporal (LP 5.1247).[397]
- Henry receives the gift of a melon from an Italian admirer as well as pears from the gardens of Hampton Court, cucumbers from Greenwich and three gifts of bowls of filberts (PP pp. 242-243, 248-249). Anne is given a stag and a greyhound by Lady Russell, both of which she gives to the King at Woodstock (PP p.245)
- in Rome, Dr Ortiz continues his campaign for Henry to be excommunicated despite being told to calm down by Cardinal Mendoza and ordered to stop by Dr Mai. After a month of refusing to see him, the pope relents only to be treated to further accusations of how he is failing Christ and the church and faces destruction on the Day of Judgment for his sins. The pope points out that there is no evidence that Henry is committing adultery with Anne and that his keeping Katherine from him is a perfectly

---

[397] For the draft of his address, see James Moyes, 'Warham: an English primate on the eve of the Reformation', *Dublin Review*, vol 114, (April 1894) pp.390-419

reasonable response while the case is being heard since it involves his conscience. Dr Ortiz refuses to listen and demands another brief to excommunicate anyone in England who preaches against the validity of Katherine's "marriage" and says the pope must appoint Abell an apostolic preacher to signify to Henry that Abell is right. The pope sends Ortiz away and refuses to see him again. Dr Mai says Ortiz is harming the cause but Ortiz says if the pope is well enough to see the English and French daily, he can see him and he would rather upset the pope than risk the wrath of God by failing in his duty. Dr Ortiz then goes home and writes a letter to the Emperor's Chancellor demanding that Mai be censured for lack of commitment (CSPS 4.2.984, 988).

Comments

Many readers may be able to think of people whom they would term the "colleague from hell" but Dr Ortiz would be hard to beat for the title. Condolences must go out to the pope and Dr Mai and the elderly Cardinal Ancona having to endure his rants.

If Warham had lived to deliver his draft speech, it is certain he would have found himself in the Tower. Referencing rebellions which toppled anointed kings would have been unsafe whoever was on the throne, as the Earl of Essex would discover in 1601. Richard II was not removed by Henry Bolingbroke for attacks on the church or because he allowed Parliament to pass the Statute of Praemunire and it is questionable – to be polite – that Edward III's fatal stroke was an act of God for this reason. As for his appeal to the Donation of Constantine, this was known to be a forgery so Warham's citation of it is most peculiar. Warham was a very old man at this point so perhaps his draft demonstrated confusion. His references to Becket and the Constitutions of Clarendon were inflammatory. The Constitutions had been the subject of Becket's row with Henry II. In simple terms, Henry II wanted clergy who committed serious crimes such as rape or murder to be punished in the civil courts like anyone else: Becket argued they should only be defrocked and face no censure unless they repeated the crime. Regarding the creation of bishops being by the pope and not consecration, this was simply historically untrue. The Greek word which was translated as bishop appears in the Old Testament, a period when there was certainly no pope and in the New Testament, appointment was by laying on of hands.[398] If Warham had lived, one can only hope he would have had the sense to revise it drastically before opening his mouth.

---

398 In the Old Testament, the word appears at Num 4:16,31:14; Judges 9:28; 2 Kings 11:15,18,12:11; 2 Chron. 34:12,17; Neh. 11:9,14,22; Job 20:29; Isa. 60:17. In the New Testament, see 2 Timothy 1:6-7, also Acts 6:6; 14:23. Once again, no pope was involved in these appointments.

A large body of Scots being sent to Ireland just as Henry was planning to leave England taking most of his nobility and army with him was not the sort of act which would have been viewed with anything but deep suspicion.

Chapuys does not name the close female friend of Anne Boleyn. It is unlikely to have been Bridget, the wife of Sir Nicholas Harvey. She had left Anne's service to have a child in the spring and her husband had died on the 5th August. To have urged her to drop everything to come to France for a wedding would have been insensitive.[399] It may have been the Countess of Worcester or Anne Wingfield.

Living in an era where every supermarket has melons on the shelves almost every day of the year and seeing the wonder expressed at a gift of one here is a reminder of how times change. Henry may have had more palaces, horses, jewels and precious objects than most of us but we have the better diet. It is also interesting to note how, whenever Henry was on progress, poor people would resort to him bearing gifts of fresh produce from their gardens. A cynic might say that they only did this in order to earn a reward but it might also be argued that they took gifts because they loved their monarch.

September 1532

Events

- worried by a lack of communication from Henry and no news on promised rewards to Cardinal Ancona, Gregory Casale leaves Rome to see the King in person (LP 5.1321).
- the papal nuncio in England warns the pope that Parliament is set to pass legislation against him in the autumn. At his request, the pope draws up two briefs, one telling Henry not to allow Parliament to do so and the second instructing the clergy not to agree to any such bills (CSPS 4.2.991).
- Dr Ortiz is upset when he discovers that the cardinals did not actually vote and give a verdict against Henry and the excusator as he had thought and indeed told other people. He persuades the pope to have Cardinal Cesi write the decision to delay up as a minute (CSPS 4.2.996). He is also upset when he learns that not only is there to be no brief excommunicating Henry until at least October but nor will there be one in favour of Thomas Abell either. Having promised these to Katherine and Chapuys, he feels distinctly embarrassed (CSPS 4.2.990, 1000). He fears the pope will grant neither brief until after Henry's meeting with Francis and the Emperor has defeated the Turk. Given this could take some time,

---

399 Chapuys' letter was written on 26th August and he says Anne's letter was written less than a week earlier by which time she would have known of Sir Nicholas' death.

he urges the Emperor to demand the excommunication first expressing the belief that as soon as it is issued, the people of England will rise up and topple Henry from his throne (CSPS 4.2.997).
- the Bishop of Bayonne, Jean du Bellay, becomes Bishop of Paris.
- at Rome, an alleged conspiracy involving Cardinal Colonna and the French ambassador is discussed. Suspicions that the rumours might be true are strengthened when the French ambassador is spotted digging a large hole in his garden and burying what is thought to be a box of papers (CSPS 4.2.992).
- Katherine continues to complain about the pope not giving a verdict in her favour. She says that the way the English treat the pope is as disrespectful as the Turk and as dangerous for the future of the Christian faith. She adds that because she still loves Henry, she will not criticise him directly but leave Chapuys to do so (CSPS 4.2.994).
- the pope hears that Stokesley, Bishop of London, has changed sides and is now supporting Katherine. He also suspects that the Duke of Norfolk is not as committed to the annulment as Henry thinks and so he advises the Emperor to make every effort to be a good friend to the Duke (CSPS 4.2.991).[400]
- Henry reacts angrily when he is handed the letter from the pope telling him to send a mandate or the case will go ahead without him. He declares: "I will never put up with it." (CSPS 4.2.993) He says the pope has usurped authority and permits a book to be published explaining why which Chapuys promptly sends on to the pope (LP 5.1316).
- at Windsor Castle, Anne Boleyn is created Marquess of Pembroke with lands in Wales to give her an income of £710. 7s. 10d and in England to give her £ 313. 5s. 3d, total £1023. 13s. 2d. Her robe for the ceremony costs £8 with a further £82. 9s. 8d spent on silks for hangings. All the nobility are present and the Duke of Norfolk's daughter carries her train. Pomeray, the French ambassador, plays his part and after the ceremony, a mass is celebrated at which a new Anglo-French treaty is signed (LP 5.1274, 1285, 1370.1). The Imperial ambassadors in France and England spend the rest of the month trying (and failing) to discover the terms of the treaty (LP 5.1292, 1337).
- Cardinal Loaysa hopes Anne's new title means that Henry is about to marry her off to one of his nobles or a Frenchman (CSPS 4.2.1012).
- the Emperor, duly recovered, sets off for Vienna ready to take on the Turk (LP 5.1277).
- one of Cromwell's friends sends him a hawk noting that as he is inclined to be fat, he should take more exercise (LP 5.1281).

---

400 Thomas Winter in Padua heard it was Gardiner who had left court but Gardiner accompanied Henry to France as did Stokesley (LP 5.1453). Mai had also heard it was Gardiner (LP 5.1291). Most likely whoever left was absent simply to prepare for the trip.

- an account book shows the complexity of Cromwell's financial dealings, some being of his own accord and others undertaken on behalf of Henry. Amongst those owing money are Thomas Wyatt and William Brereton (LP 5.1285).
- further violent skirmishes take place on the border with Scotland. Henry makes discreet overtures to some of James' discontented nobles while encouraging the Earl of Angus to go and "annoy" Scotland. When James complains, Henry replies that if he was acting justly, there would be no problems (LP 5.1286, 1367).
- Thomas Cranmer remains at Ratisbon seeking a response from the Emperor and his council regarding the trade treaties with the Low Countries (LP 5.1290).
- an outbreak of plague at Dover causes Henry to delay his trip to France by ten days and to change his sailing arrangements (LP 5.1292, 1316).
- work continues at the Tower of London including a new bridge to the Queen's apartments, an improved garden for the Queen and a new roof and floor in the Queen's great chamber. Margaret Beaufort's rooms are converted into a wardrobe for Henry and the White Tower is refaced and given four new turrets (LP 5.1307).
- William de Langais, brother of Jean du Bellay, arrives from France with a personal invitation for Anne from Francis. Chapuys waspishly suggests Francis wants to thank her for being a better and cheaper ambassador for France than Wolsey, adding she has better access to the King and is more cunning and malicious (CSPS 4.2.995).
- preparations for the trip to France continue. Henry orders new jewellery and plate, sharing his pleasure in the designs with Anne (LP 5.1237, 1299). Henry Norris is kept busy moving diamonds, pearls and gold from one palace to another (LP 5.1335).
- Francis' wife has a miscarriage (LP 5.1337).
- an official announcement says that the purpose of the trip is so that Henry and Francis can make plans for the defence of Italy should the Emperor be defeated by the Turk and turn south (LP 5.1308).
- examinations of Peto, Elston and the other friars at Greenwich begin. Cromwell believes eight support Katherine, ten Henry. Each man is interviewed separately (LP 5.1312, 1313).
- Chapuys rebukes Pomeray for repeating a rumour he knew to be untrue and sanctimoniously talks of how only the wicked circulate such things and this for their own dark purposes. He claims Pomeray was unable to find words to reply (CSPS 4.2.995).
- Croke congratulates Henry for his book, the *Glass of Truth*, and says it has convinced many. He also thanks him for the offer of a teaching post at his new college in Oxford but comments that he would rather teach divinity than Greek (LP 5.1338, 1372).
- Canon John Brereton is granted a pardon for seeking a bull from the pope to hold multiple benefices (LP 5.1379.13)

- Chapuys fails to discover what the meeting in France is to be about. He concludes that only Henry, Anne and Pomeray know and is upset none of them are telling him (CSPS 4.2.993).

Comments

Anne was created a peer in her own right, hence she was a Lady Marquess rather than a Marchioness, i.e. wife of a Marquess. As this was a novel idea, even contemporaries tended to refer to her as a Marchioness. The income from the lands was less than stated because she was committed to paying varying pensions and grants from them, thus the Welsh income dropped from £710. 7s. 10d to £510. 1s. 11d. Although Anne had received many gifts of things like clothes and jewellery over the years, she remained financially dependent on Henry, or in event of them separating, on her father. This grant changed that but also made her the most senior female member of the nobility after the royal family. As she was to be presented to Francis and his courtiers, Henry needed to take this step to avoid uncomfortable issues regarding precedence and protocol. The grant was, however, of an annuity from the lands rather than the lands themselves which remained the property of the Crown.[401] Something not noted at the time was that the majority of the lands Anne received in South Wales had been part of the dowry given to Margaret of Anjou. With the agreement of Parliament in 1453, Margaret had surrendered them for alternative properties so they could be given to Henry VI's uncle, Jasper Tudor, but the fact that they were part of a queen's dowry was significant and should have been recognised as indicating Henry's intentions toward Anne.

The repairs at the Tower, particularly the improvements to the Queen's apartments were not for the benefit of Katherine but part of Henry's preparations for Anne's coronation. Although Chapuys reported rumours of Henry being about to marry Anne, he never seems to have wondered why the work was being done on this part of the Tower.

The pope's comments about Norfolk and Stokesley indicate that he was still being fed Chapuys' poisonous, and often untrue, reports.

Pomeray was probably struck dumb, not by Chapuys' brilliance as an orator but by his effrontery in criticising him for repeating a rumour given Chapuys' reports show he did it all the time.

October 1532

Events

- Henry orders the Duke of Norfolk to get Katherine's jewels so that Anne can wear them to France. An outraged Katherine tells the hapless messenger: "I would consider it a sin and a load upon my conscience if I were

---

[401] They would form part of her jointure, see Appendix 5: Anne's Property Holdings.

persuaded to give up my jewels for such a wicked purpose as that of ornamenting a person who is the scandal of Christendom and who is bringing vituperation and infamy upon the King through his taking her with him to such a meeting across the Channel." Henry then sends a gentleman of his own Privy Chamber to get them, reminding her that his sister, Mary, Duchess of Suffolk, had been happy to hand over the jewels she had as Queen of France.[402] This time, Katherine obeys (CSPS 4.2.1003).
- Cardinal Loaysa prays that Henry's meeting with Francis will go badly and the two princes will be divided (CSPS 4.2.1005).
- Chapuys reports that Henry spent some time with his daughter and would have spent longer except that Anne sent two of her servants to listen in (LP 5.1377).
- the pope's "nephew", Cardinal Medici, is arrested by Imperial troops on a warrant from the Emperor himself. The pope summons the Imperial ambassador and Cardinal Loaysa to complain at this affront to the dignity of a member of his family and representative of the Apostolic See. The arresting officers are persuaded to take the blame saying that they misread the warrant which was for Medici's travelling companion, but Cardinal Medici's staff say that this is untrue and the warrant was for him. The fact that the French ambassador told the pope the Emperor had ordered the arrest before it happened strengthens Clement's doubts. Nonetheless, the pope accepts the Emperor's apology reluctantly and arranges to meet him in Bologna next month (CSPS 4.2.1007, 1012, 1014).
- Dr Ortiz, fearful that the pope will delay any activity on the annulment until after his meeting with the Emperor urges that Henry be excommunicated now (CSPS 4.2.1010).
- Dr Mai gets the annulment case referred back to the Rota but admits that there is no desire on the part of anyone at Rome to see the case concluded. He suspects that Sir Gregory Casale has been despatched with a secret message from the pope to Henry because Casale is such a "great favourite" of his. His newly returned colleague, Pedro de la Cueva, admits the pope is afraid of France and England not only renouncing allegiance to him as nuncios there have advised but sending armies to Italy, though he notes the pope is skilled at making promises to both sides whilst doing nothing (CSPS 4.2.1004, 1014, 1016).
- after frustration at Guintz, the Turk retreats from Hungary. The Emperor departs Vienna planning to return to Spain from Genoa but travelling via Mantua and Bologna where he intends to meet with the pope (CSPV 4.818). Thomas Cranmer, travelling with him as English ambassador,

---

402 Mary Brandon did not travel to France. Some have suggested this was a snub to Anne but she was a very sick woman at this point and died only a few months later. Professor Richardson observed that a letter written by Mary in March 1533 was "in the wavering hand of a very sick woman." Walter Richardson, *Mary Tudor: the White Queen* (1970) p.253.

reports on the havoc wreaked by unpaid Imperial troops which has much angered the German princes. Apologising for being unable to discover what progress Duke Frederick of Saxony might have made with the Emperor on Henry's behalf, Cranmer asks for instructions regarding the annulment case at Rome (LP 5.1449).
- Wolsey's son, a student in Padua, asks Thomas Cromwell for funds. He complains that Bonner, whom Wolsey told to treat him as a son, is instead persecuting him (LP 5.1453).
- plague is rife in London and Kent. The law courts are closed and the scheduled meeting of Parliament in November is postponed to February 1533. A national search for vagrants believed to be spreading it is organised and a curfew imposed (LP 5.1450, 1466, 1515).
- Anne Boleyn tells a friend that she will not be marrying in France because she wants to be married at Westminster (LP 5.1377).
- Henry Norris considers employing the Duke of Richmond's early tutor, John Palsgrave, for his son (LP 5.1478).
- Henry Percy advises the King that James V is vulnerable given his usual ally, France, is now his friend and the Emperor is busy with the Turk. He notes that many nobles are disaffected and says this represents an opportunity for Henry who "taking your time, shall with a small power, having a greater ready if need shall require, which they think shall not, obtain what purpose as shall stand to your most gracious pleasure concerning the realm of Scotland."[403] Later in the month, bands of Scots take the opportunity of Henry's absence to invade England and burn down villages on the border, in one case abducting and murdering a heavily pregnant woman. Counter-raids in reprisal follow (LP 5.1460). The Venetian ambassador reports that a herald arrived from Scotland to declare war and Henry told him that he had no wish for a war with his nephew but that if James chose to invade, he would meet the same fate as his father (CSPV 4.811).[404] In Rome, the pope announces that a war between the two countries is imminent (CSPV 4.815). As a result of tensions on the border, no northern lords are permitted to accompany Henry to France.
- a tract advises Henry to return the church to the state in which it existed at the time of the Ascension urging him to employ his supremacy to "pluck down the pope and his ministers of his law from the high altar in the quire and spurn them out of Christ's holy church to make that place holy." (LP 5.1501).
- Henry and Anne finally depart for France, staying with Sir Thomas Cheyney at his home of Shurland on the Isle of Sheppey en route.[405] They spend the

---

403 SP vol. 4 p.619
404 James IV, husband of Henry VIII's elder sister Margaret, was killed in battle by the English in 1513 at Flodden.
405 It is likely that being an island, Sheppey was free from plague. Evidence from the other island off Kent shows that it suffered very few outbreaks compared to the mainland, see Margaret Bolton, 'The Experience of Plague in East Kent, 1636–38',

first five days together in Calais where Henry takes the opportunity of viewing the fortifications and ordering work (LP 5.1495) and also going shopping.[406] An anonymous observer reports that Anne accompanies Henry everywhere and is treated as if she is queen (CSPV 4.824). During the evenings, they play cards and dice, Anne winning 15s at the former and Francis Weston £46 13s 4d at the latter. Henry then departs to spend three days with Francis at Boulogne. His party is met by Francis' three sons. Francis says that he is more bound to Henry than anyone in the world and tells his sons: "My children, I am your father, but to this Prince here you are as much bound, as to me your natural father, for he redeemed me and you from captivity: wherefore on my blessing I charge you to be to him loving always."[407] There are lavish entertainments, hawking expeditions, church services and summit meetings between Henry, Norfolk, Suffolk and Gardiner on one side and Francis, Montmorency, Chabot and Cardinal Du Prat on the other.[408] Other meetings are held separately involving theologians with Marc Raphael on hand to explain the Hebrew Torah (LP 5.1429, CSPV 4.822) and with Casale. The party then travel to Calais for three days of feasting and further meetings. Henry's bastard son, the Duke of Richmond aged twelve, rides out to meet them. Following a banquet, Anne spends time dancing and chatting with Francis. Henry jousts and plays tennis with Cardinal Lorraine and the Duke of Guise and enjoys performances from French singers.[409] An exchange of honours takes place with the Dukes of Suffolk and Norfolk being elected to the French Order of St Michael and Montmorency and Chabot being elected to the English Order of the Garter. Treaties are signed with regard the raising of armies in event of the Emperor being defeated by the Turk and the negotiation of a European wide peace with Casale, Ghinucci and Cranmer to handle talks for the English. It is also agreed to send Cardinals Tournon and Grammont (Bishop of Tarbes) to Rome and that Francis will offer one of his daughters as a bride to James V on condition that he cease hostilities with Henry. After an exchange of gifts, the Kings part and Henry prepares to return home having impressed his hosts that "he is a handsome and gracious prince." (LP 5.1481, 1482, 1484, 1485; CSPV 820, 822, 823, 824).[410]

Local Population Studies, Vol. 96, Number 1, Spring 2016, pp. 9-27

406 He spends over £740 on jewels – Richard Turpin, T*he Chronicles of Calais,* ed. J. G Nichols (Camden Soc.1846) p120
407 *Hall's Chronicle* p.791
408 The French representatives were respectively Grand Master, Lord Admiral and Chancellor of France.
409 *Chronicles of Calais* pp.119-120.The Duke of Guise would become grandfather to Mary, Queen of Scots. Cardinal Lorraine was then aged thirty-four. Henry must have greatly enjoyed the performance of Francis' jester for he gave him £40, almost ten times that which he gave to each of the singing groups.
410 Camusat, *Meslanges Historiques,* p.108

- Casale leaves with a reward for Cardinal Ancona to be granted if the excusator is admitted. Henry warns this is "a matter so evident and manifestly just in the opinion of all learned men here" that failure to grant it would "cause us little to trust any other matter to be further obtained by their (Ancona and Ravenna) means." Casale's instructions meanwhile are to "use and make as much instance and sticking as you possibly may" until after the Emperor leaves Italy (LP 5.1493). Henry doubts the pope will issue a verdict against him and dismisses the recent ban on English appeals as nothing "but decrees of popes given in their own favour to the hurt and prejudice of all them that shall be grieved by them, taking away refuge and remedy of wrongs which is defence granted by law of nature and not to be in anywise taken away." He cites in his support the ruling of the Council of Nicea (LP 5.1493).
- the reformer John Frith is thrown in the Tower where he is chained. Frith is twenty-nine[411]

Comments

There are a number of accounts of the visit to France: an official English report, a French report, a lengthy account with considerable extra detail in Hall's Chronicle plus other information in the Chronicle of Calais (believed to have been composed by Richard Turpin, a constable there at the time) and in French and Venetian sources[412] The accounts have different slants, some concerned with the expenses, others with the clothes, others with politics, but they all tell the same story and none of them list Anne's father as being part of the English party. The only reference to him is found in a manuscript owned by the Marquis of Bath which lists those due to attend and how many attendants they were allowed to take.[413] It seems inconceivable that Anne's father did not go to France but the fact that no eyewitness or official account mentions him suggests he was absent. As Anne's father, an erstwhile envoy to the French court and one of Henry's senior courtiers, he would have been expected to play a prominent role in proceedings yet he attended no meetings, took part in no

---

411 For a full biography of John Frith see Foxe, *Acts and Monuments*, vol. 5 pp.2-17. In 1573, Foxe edited Frith's works.

412 See *Hall's Chronicle* pp.790-794, Alfred Hamy, *Entrevue de François Ier avec Henry VIII à Boulogne-sur-Mer, en 1532* (Paris, 1898)

413 HMRC *Manuscripts in the Library of the Marquess of Bath* (1904) p180. The list shows Thomas Boleyn entitled to 24 men as other earls and bishops, George Boleyn 12, Thomas Cromwell 10 like most of the Privy Chamber excepting Henry Norris and Nicholas Carew who both had 15. William Brereton had 6 and Mark Smeaton 2, Thomas Wyatt 4, James Boleyn 10. In total, the list indicates 2773 people accompanying Henry but it is unlikely that all went due to the plague. John Stow, *Annals of England*, (1603) p.944 refers to James, Edward and William Boleyn as well as Viscount Rochford (George) but not Thomas. The five earls present were Arundel, Oxford, Surrey, Rutland and Derby.

entertainments, rode with no welcoming parties, received no gifts.[414] He was not present at the Garter meeting held at Calais.[415] He was not listed as being in London with the Privy Council so where was he? Did he go to France and become ill and spend the entire time shut up in his hotel room so nobody saw him? Was he taken ill before the party sailed and compelled to remain at Hever or Dover? George Boleyn is listed as being amongst the lords. Anne was said to have had ten or twelve ladies but these are not named. Her mother could have been amongst them, but as Countess of Wiltshire and sister of the Duke of Norfolk, it would be surprising if nobody mentioned her. Nor is it certain that her sister was there. At the Calais banquet on the 27th, Anne entered masked with six other similarly attired dancers. They were revealed to be Lady Mary (her cousin), Lady Derby (her step-aunt), Lady Fitzwalter (sister of Lady Derby), Lady Rochford (Anne's sister-in-law), Lady Lisle (a friend of Anne and wife of Henry's bastard uncle) and Lady Wallop (wife of the ambassador). Authors often assume that the Lady Mary was Anne's sister but this is unlikely because this was not her usual title and her name appears first in the list, indicating a precedence which the widowed Mary Carey simply did not possess. Lady Mary was the Duke of Norfolk's daughter who had held Anne's train when she became Marquess of Pembroke and who was known by that title and who would have outranked the other women. So, at this moment of triumph, it seems Anne was rather lacking in family about her.

Another aspect on which all the accounts agree was the luxury involved. Both kings wore doublets encrusted with rubies and diamonds worth £100,000 apiece. Henry wore a collar containing fourteen rubies as large as eggs with other precious stones worth over £90,000. Anne's jewellery included twenty rubies and two diamonds and Francis gave her another diamond worth 16,000 crowns then or about £26 million today (LP 5.1376). The food served included swan, venison, quail, pheasant, salmon, tench, roast eel, oyster, cod, custard, fruit and tarts. Hall says that there were forty dishes in each of the first two courses and seventy in the third adding "to tell the riches of the cloths of estates, the basins and other vessels which was there occupied, I assure you my wit is insufficient, for there was nothing occupied that night, but all of gold." The rooms were lined with valuable tapestries, pearl encrusted velvet hangings, gold plate. Henry's accounts show the trip cost him £4033. 10s. 11d in entertainments alone with a quarter of this being spent on food for four days at Calais.

If the object of the trip was to convince French clergy of Henry's case – and it is not clear that they needed any further convincing – it might have been thought Henry would have chosen different bishops to accompany him. Longland was his confessor, Gardiner his secretary, Stokesley had been active

---

414 It would have been expected for him to accompany Suffolk and Norfolk at the summit rather than Gardiner. The exclusion of Cromwell should be noted by those historians who seek to credit him with a major role at this point.
415 J. Anstis (ed.) *The register of the most noble Order of the Garter,* vol. 2 (1724) p.389

in Henry's case since December 1529 but Clerk had been one of Katherine's supporters. Henry's reference to the French supporting his argument about the excusator could indicate the verdicts previously passed in Paris or discussions during this trip. On the last day of the month, Francis would write to his own ambassador at Rome saying that the pope was wrong to summon Henry.

The French trip marked Anne's acceptance on the public stage as Henry's intended queen. The title of the official English account, *The Manner of the Triumph*, is revealing.[416] Henry was not prepared to wait any longer to settle his affairs.

The account of Katherine's reaction to the request for her jewels is well known and it must be assumed that she was angry, though whether the words quoted were genuine or Chapuys' is another story. At the 1529 legatine court, Katherine was described as speaking in broken English so the use of a word like vituperation would seem surprising, unless she was exaggerating her familiarity with the language for effect in court. Once again, Katherine blamed Anne for allowing herself to be taken to France rather than Henry for taking her. Although the member of the Privy Chamber sent to collect the jewels is not named, the likelihood is that it was Henry Norris who as Groom of the Stool was entrusted by the King with tasks involving valuable jewels, large sums of money and where tact was required. There is nothing to suggest that Anne demanded the jewels herself: it appears to have been Henry's idea.

Chapuys' willingness to believe ill of Anne is further demonstrated in his description of her sending spies to hear what Henry said to Mary. Presumably he heard this from one of Mary's servants but what were Anne's servants doing out riding with Henry? Is it likely that any of the riders would have left their position in the procession to eavesdrop? If anyone had come so close to the King without authorisation, would not his guard have told them to move? The idea that Henry was terrified by the presence of these spies and immediately ceased the conversation like a small child caught with his fingers in the sweet jar, is just laughable. It is difficult to credit this story at all and one must suspect that Chapuys' informer either made it up or else applied a substantial amount of re-interpretation to it.

Cranmer's letter of 20th October indicates that he had no idea that he was about to be recalled to England let alone appointed Archbishop of Canterbury. He expected to travel with the Emperor through Italy and on to Spain. His comment that the French ambassador would speak to Duke Frederick and advise Henry shows the closeness with which the ambassadors were working.

Whilst the sentiments of the author who sought to return the church to its early purity were no doubt sincere, the ascension marked a rather too early date. Christianity was still a sect of Judaism at this point.

---

416 *The Maner of the Tryumphe of Cales and Bulleyn* is reproduced in Hamy *Entrevue* pp. xxxviii-xlv. It was so popular that a second enlarged edition was printed, Hamy's book highlighting the additions.

The Imperial army did not achieve victory in battle over the Turk, though reading the Imperial rhetoric of the time, it is easy to think this was the case. The town of Guintz – or Kőszeg in modern Hungary – put up a stellar defence and thereby delayed the Turkish army for so long that it not only gave the Emperor time to assemble a large army but it meant that the weather made further campaigning in the area impossible until the spring, hence the Turkish decision to withdraw.

The fact that the reward was only to be paid to Ancona if the service was performed is a sign that it was not a bribe – which is a payment in advance for someone to do something which would they would not normally do – but what it says, a reward for a job well done, in modern terms, a bonus or tip. The ethics of those type of payments is also open to debate but people who wish to condemn the Tudor world should remember that the twenty-first century is not blameless.

One of the texts central to Christianity is the sermon on the mount which begins with the beatitudes which include "Blessed are the peacemakers" (Matt 5:9). It must be concluded that this was not a text which Cardinal Loaysa took very seriously.

By contrast, John Frith, who was one of the greatest figures in the English Reformation, was a man of "friendly and prudent moderation in uttering of the truth, joined with a learned godliness. ...Where necessity did not move him to contend, he was ready to grant all things for quietness' sake. ... Dexterity of wit was in him, and excellency of doctrine." Frith's works reveal him to have been far and away the greatest theologian of his era. His Biblical knowledge was second to none and he espoused those practices so close to Henry's heart of studying the text in the original Hebrew and Greek and seeking the meaning of it, rather than following the medieval tradition of starting with a doctrine and then using the Bible as a source book to justify it. This latter approach was the one adopted by Bishop John Fisher whose works Frith courteously and expertly destroyed.[417]

November 1532

Events

Reader, she married him![418]

---

417 See Was Henry married when he met Anne?
418 *Hall's Chronicle*, p.794.

Other Events

- severe weather and storms force Henry and Anne to remain in Calais. Some of those who depart are driven back to port while others are forced into Flanders. Great anxiety is felt for those who have not returned for fear that they have drowned. Severe flooding occurs at Antwerp and gales cause much damage. Norris and Norfolk are taken ill (Hall p.794, LP 5.1509, 1579). Henry returns to England on the 14th and stays at Dover until the 18th when he moves on to Canterbury. The next day, he continues on to Sittingbourne and on the 20th he reaches Stone near Dartford. On the 23rd, he reaches Eltham.(PP pp.273-275).
- Henry tries again to have Ghinucci elected a cardinal (LP 5.1522).
- divisions continue between the Observant Friars at Greenwich. Richard Lyst, a lay brother who admits that Anne's charity has saved him and his mother, seeks her assistance as Katherine's supporters – particularly Forrest and Peto – endeavour to convert others to their opinion while Friar Laurence is in Calais (LP 5.1525, 1591).
- Henry's son, the Duke of Richmond, together with Norfolk's son, the Earl of Surrey, depart Calais to join the French court where they will reside alongside Francis' own sons (LP 5.1529).
- Montpesat replaces Pomeray as French ambassador at the English court. Katherine tells Chapuys that she hears he supports her which is why he has not been given lodgings in a royal palace like his predecessors. A hopeful Chapuys vows to investigate (LP 5.1579).
- the Marchioness of Exeter forwards an unsigned letter to Chapuys telling him that the pope is to be told to issue the annulment as he promised in 1527 or return the case to England or else Francis and Henry will renounce their allegiance. It adds that Casale believes the pope will issue such a verdict as soon as the Emperor returns to Spain which prompts Chapuys to tell the Emperor to get a verdict fast (LP 5.1531).
- Dr Mai refuses to take Dr Ortiz with him ever again when he meets with the pope. Dr Ortiz complains to the Empress. He denies his behaviour upsets the pope and claims it is simply because his superb arguments are so true and unanswerable that the pope is left feeling embarrassed and inadequate (CSPS 4.2.1025).
- the Imperial ambassadors complain to the pope that Henry has taken Anne to France and the pope agrees to generate a brief telling Henry to restore Katherine and separate from Anne until a verdict is given. He says the brief will be dated in November but will not be issued until after he has met with the Emperor in Bologna and it will only take effect a month after it is actually presented to Henry. Dr Ortiz complains that it should have been sent while Francis and Henry were together, a time "when Satan has shamelessly planted his banner by the pernicious example of this woman." (LP 5.1567)

- the brief composed says that if Henry arranges his own annulment outside Rome and marries anyone else, the union will be void and both he and his bride will be excommunicated. Nonetheless, the pope says he hopes that once this "cloud of error" has passed, Henry will return to be a loyal son of Rome (LP 5.1545).
- the instructions to the two French cardinals say they are to complain about exactions made on the expedition of bulls and to warn the pope that any delay in granting the annulment will be seen as a refusal and result in France and England stopping all money going to Rome and summoning a General Council. Francis proposes to meet the pope at Avignon after his meeting with the Emperor and to bring Henry with him so that the affair can be finally settled (LP 5.1541).
- Chapuys tells the Emperor that the cardinals have been sent to urge the pope to support the Vayvod John in Hungary and that parliament has been delayed until their return (LP 5.1531, 1579)
- Katherine tells the Emperor that he must instruct the pope to ignore every word the cardinals sent by Henry and Francis say. She describes the annulment debate as being a "second Turk" and admits she does not know which is more damaging. She expresses the opinion that all the thunderbolts in England fall on her (LP 5.1520; CSPS 4.2.1027).
- a Flemish captain reports on a conversation which he says a friend of his had with Gregory Casale. He alleges that Anne blamed Casale for her not being married prior to the trip and he told her that the pope was afraid of the Emperor which is why Henry and Francis decided to despatch the cardinals. The Fleming says he hopes the Emperor will get a verdict before the cardinals reach Rome and warns that Francis and Henry are planning mischief in Italy and a strict watch is needed against this (CSPS 4.2.1028).
- the Venetian ambassador to France meets Casale who tells him that all will be made clear in six weeks or so: "obedience will be withdrawn from the pope. Something will be done." Casale says that the pope will only have himself to blame for not allowing the annulment case to be decided in England (CSPV 4.829).
- Casale complains that the 40,000 crowns promised by Francis for distribution as rewards is not forthcoming. His application for the 3,000 promised by Francis to Cardinal Monte is declined on grounds it is not yet time. Nonetheless, he sends his brother to ask the Cardinal to stop the pope giving any verdict until he returns from Rome in the spring (LP 5.1547).
- following on from her visit to the Tower of London prior to her journey to France, Anne selects a cupboard from there to be delivered to her apartments (LP 5.1548).
- Thomas Cranmer leaves the Emperor at Mantua. The Emperor commends his diligence and Cranmer's replacement, Hawkins, says that he has made many friends by his gentle courtesy and done much good for Anglo-Imperial relations. He returns carrying a book about papal power noting

that Anne told him "that it was Your Highness' commandment that we should seek out such books." (LP 5.1551, 1564; SP vol. 7 p.389)
- trouble continues on the border. James V blames the English and issues a proclamation that any Scotsman who speaks to an Englishman will be put to death (LP 5.1558, 1559).
- Henry expresses his doubts that the Emperor will reach Spain before the end of the year although Chapuys notes he seems very happy that he is going there (CSPS 4.2.1030).
- it is reported that the Italians blame the Emperor for the coming of the Turk into Europe and they "say he doth many things for money which be very ungodly." (LP 5.1564; SP vol. 7 p.390)
- at Rome, the English launch another appeal against the pope's refusal to admit the excusator (CSPS 4.2.1029).
- the Imperialists decide that Francis' offer of his daughter to James V is a sign of fear (CSPS 4.2.1031).
- the pope claims that Henry planned to marry Anne in France but news of the Imperial victory over the Turk forced a change of plan (CSPS 4.2.1031).
- Dr Mai tells the pope that information from England says the English are likely to rebel in support of Katherine so it is his duty to issue his verdict to prevent civil strife. He hopes the prospect of rebellion will assuage the pope's fear that a verdict will encourage scandal and division (CSPS 4.2.1031).
- the Duke of Cleves dies[419]

Comments

Dr Mai's belief that the English were about to revolt can only have come from Chapuys. Like many of Chapuys' reports, it was totally untrue. One can only speculate on what difference it would have made to Henry's cause had the truth been known at Rome.

The unsigned letter which the Marchioness forwarded was supposed by Chapuys to have been written by her husband or Carew. It might have been thought she would have known her own husband's writing and Chapuys had so many dealings with Carew, he ought to have recognised his.

The report of what Anne said to Casale is passed on at best third hand. Casale was a highly experienced and trusted diplomat. He was unlikely to have let slip anything he should not have done, though he may have expressed opinions with a view of deliberately misleading England's enemies. Telling one of the Emperor's subjects that Henry was not planning to do anything and that he believed the pope was afraid of the Emperor was a good way to send a reassuring and false message across. Giustinian's account of his conversation with Casale is more credible but also intriguing. What did he mean by six weeks and something being done? Six weeks would represent roughly the end

---
419 Father of the future Queen of England, Anne.

of the year when the Emperor was due to reach Spain, though problems with obtaining galleys at Genoa and poor weather meant Henry saw this as doubtful. He could have meant that at that point, the pope was expected to issue his verdict, either for or against Henry. Or he could have known that Henry was about to marry Anne and assumed that this would become public knowledge in about six weeks time resulting in a final breach with Rome.

Why did Henry marry Anne at this point after waiting so long? He admitted that Francis advised him to do so and it is likely that Casale said the same on grounds he saw no prospect of the pope actually making a decision. After parading Anne in France, she may have pressurised Henry into doing so before they returned to London, although given the marriage was not made public, any hopes she might have had of it clarifying her status, would be disappointed. Were the severe storms a factor in Henry's timing? A threat of loss of life may have convinced him of the need to father a son as soon as possible. It is impossible to say. At this stage, the couple took their preliminary vows which created a binding marital union: solemnisation followed in the new year.[420]

Henry's journey back to London from Dover was quite leisurely and involved a trip to Sandwich. It is unknown if Anne accompanied him on this. Stone was the childhood home of the recently widowed, Bridget Harvey, but she may not have been present being still at her late husband's house. Stone was a regular stopping place on journeys from London to the coast.

December 1532

Events

- Thomas Cranmer begins his journey home but severe weather delays him (LP 5.1620).
- Francis thanks Henry for allowing his son to reside at his court and says he now feels as if he has four sons (LP 5.1627).
- William Brereton travels to Kent to inspect property for Henry (LP 5.1631).
- Henry is disappointed to learn that the pope is going ahead with his meeting with the Emperor. It will delay the Emperor's return to Spain (LP 5.1633).
- the new French ambassador Montpesat tries to convince Chapuys that the two French cardinals are travelling to Bologna of their own free will without any instructions or funding from either Francis or Henry. Katherine tells him that Henry has paid out £6000 though her spies have not been able to find out whether this is to cover expenses or rewards when they arrive. (LP 5.1633).

---

420 For a full account of their marriage, see When did Henry and Anne marry?

- Henry takes Anne and the French ambassador to see progress on the new works at the Tower and shows them the Treasure House giving the latter a fine gilt cup worth £173. 2s. 1d (LP 5.1633, LP 6.228; CSPV 4.836).[421]
- Henry Percy updates the King on his raids into Scotland as tension mounts (LP 5.1633, 1635, 1638, 1670, 1671).
- despite being told by Dr Mai to stay in Rome, Dr Ortiz decides to follow the pope to Bologna. He tells the empress that she should keep any letters which Katherine sends her because he is convinced she will soon be canonised and that many miracles will occur thanks to her intercessions and this will make the letters valuable relics (CSPS 4.2.1034).
- the King of Portugal tells the Emperor that he is happy to send an ambassador to England if he thinks it will help. He does not understand the matter so is reluctant to meddle but his lawyers have assured him that Katherine is right (LP 5.1643).
- Gregory Casale asks for guidance. Does Henry wish him to continue opposing the pope or simply to ignore him? If he is to do the former, should he be doing it in Henry's name or unofficially? (LP 5.1648).
- Agostini arrives at Bologna with Campeggio. He reports that the cardinals are very nervous about what the French cardinals will do and because they know they are bringing substantial learned opinions to support the argument that Henry should not be required to appear in Rome (LP 5.1657). Cardinal Loaysa offers to go incognito to the house occupied by the French cardinals to find out their plans so the pope can prepare his response (CSPS 4.2.1032).
- the Emperor, who arrives at Bologna on the 10th, rewards Campeggio with a bishopric. In order to ensure the pope's obedience to his wishes, he installs two hundred of his soldiers inside the palace they share, five hundred outside and stations an army of six thousand Germans around the town (LP 5.1660).
- Bonner reports gleefully on the rigours of the journey experienced by the pope and cardinals in reaching Bologna. Hearing that they have had to endure straw mattresses instead of feather beds, he writes that he "would have caused them to lie on the boards with sorrow or else have set fire in the straw" (LP 5.1638).
- Cardinals Egidius and Ancona die. The death of the latter is seen as a major blow because both the pope and the Emperor regarded him as an expert and were awaiting his opinion. The Duke of Mantua's brother, a friend of the Casale family, tells Sir Gregory that Ancona's nephew, Cardinal Ravenna, claims to have a copy of Ancona's writings. Casale goes to see him and reports Ravenna's claim that "not only one time but many", Ancona told him "his vote and opinion, when he should come to give

---

[421] The Venetian ambassador reported that Henry took his daughter Mary to the Tower but Chapuys would have known if that had happened and he specifically says Henry took Anne to show her progress on the Queen's apartments there.

sentence: the which vote was in the favour of Your Majesty." Casale's letter continues: "the pope will believe what Ravenna doth say, being of such great reputation with His Holiness as he is; and because also he being accounted rather Imperial than otherwise, it cannot be thought otherwise, that he declaring the vote of his uncle in the favour of Your Highness and against the Emperor, he doth it for none other [reason] but to tell the truth, without respect to any person." He adds that a vote in Henry's favour by Ancona is likely to make the Emperor change his mind "which at this time is most hard to do, he having a contrary opinion therein." Dr Mai visits Ravenna on the Emperor's behalf and tells him that the Emperor "would more believe the said vote, then all the books and men in the world." However, suspicion arises when Ravenna refuses to simply hand over the papers and only promises to reveal it when the time is right. The English say he will only receive the promised reward if he produces it promptly and it is in Henry's favour (LP 5.1659, 1662, SP vol. 7 pp.398-400).
- Henry gives Anne £ 1,188. 11s. 10d worth of gilt plate, mostly from his stores including some with the royal arms, but a few pieces from that left by Sir Henry Guildford. The collection includes 29 bowls, 9 cups, 4 flagons, 6 goblets, 6 salts, 19 pots, 20 trenchers, 7 basins and 9 chandeliers (LP 5.1685). He also pays his goldsmith to emboss the new plate with her new coat of arms (LP 6.32).
- the pope tells Bennet that though his canon lawyers said that popes could dispense from Levitical prohibitions, they also agreed that for a dispensation to be valid, the cause cited must be true and he admitted to having known for the past two years that this requirement "in this case doth not appear." He says that if Henry will only be patient he will do all "that may be pleasant and profitable to Your Highness; adding yet, that this is not to be done with a fury, but with leisure, and as occasion shall serve." (LP 5.1659, SP7 p.402)
- the Turkish ambassador in Venice admits that the Sultan was encouraged by the German princes and Francis who all hate the Emperor. (CSPS 4.2.1036)
- Hawkins, translating a tract in support of Henry, advises the King that he may need to make some changes as the Italians are most adverse to studying the Bible (LP 5.1660).
- Thomas Boleyn orders a cuirass from Venice (CSPV 4.838)
- the Duke of Norfolk seeks to have the body of his ancestor, Thomas Mowbray, the first Duke who died in 1399, returned to England from Italy (CSPV 4.837).

Comments

The gift of plate was substantial and the fact that so many pieces bore the royal arms was a clear signal of Anne's new status even though her marriage to Henry was not yet public knowledge.

Bonner became famous for burning Protestants under Mary. His fondness for such a mode of killing evidently stretched back to this date.

Bennet's letter telling Henry that the pope has admitted that he has known for two years that Henry's argument that the bull is invalid because the cause given was untrue must have provoked a roar that was audible across the entire palace complex. If the pope knew this, he should have given his verdict accordingly. To go on to say that things should be handled leisurely after keeping Henry waiting for five years was extraordinary. No wonder Henry had despaired. The pope's admission is also a sign that he doubted the authenticity of the "Spanish brief" with its reference to Julius making the grant for "other causes" also. Given the Emperor had refused to allow the pope to see the document and the failure of his own staff to locate any reference to the original, his suspicions are understandable.

It is amusing to wonder how Cardinal Loaysa thought he might disguise himself and infiltrate the lodgings of the French cardinals. The Cardinal Bishop of Tarbes knew him well so would have been likely to recognise him. It is not the sort of activity in which you would expect a senior dignitary of the Roman church to be engaging.

The fact that Katherine is supplying Chapuys with information about Henry's activities is interesting. Not only would making such reports to a representative of a foreign power be construed as treason – she was after all Queen of England though she tended to forget this when it suited her – but it shows she was employing a network of spies and informers. It might be argued that this was fair and Henry did the same, but it is not behaviour which receives the attention it deserves.

Considering that the pope employed Ancona as his advisor and spent hours with him, it is curious that he claims not to know his opinion. If Ravenna really had Ancona's writings, he should have taken them immediately to the pope: that he did not suggests he was lying. On 4th November, Ravenna had written to his sick uncle to say that money had been received from Henry but they should wait to see what the Emperor offered before making any decisions. In late 1535 when Ravenna was charged with corruption, it was revealed that he had hired someone to forge papers in his uncle's name to be sold to the highest bidder.[422]

Given Casale had been able to speak to Henry at length only a few weeks earlier, it is a sign of the rapidly changing situation that he felt the need for new instructions.

---

422 Fletcher, *Our Man in Rome*, pp.179-180

1533

January 1533

Events

- preparations are made for the continuing war with Scotland (LP 6.37,51,71).
- Chapuys apologises to the Emperor for not having been able to find out what was agreed when Francis and Henry met (LP 6.19).
- the pope invites Francis and Henry to attend a General Council (LP 6.11,12,13).
- Thomas Abell, Katherine's chaplain and author of *Invicta Veritas*, is released from the Tower on condition that he neither writes nor preaches until at least two weeks after Easter (LP 6.19).[423]
- the Emperor tells Chapuys that the pope is willing to have the annulment case heard outside Rome and says he will agree if Katherine accepts the proposal and provided that Anne is sent away from court until the verdict is given and also that Francis and Henry both promise not to do anything derogatory to the interests of the pope in the meantime (LP 6.23).
- Henry sends a number of New Year gifts. Recipients include Henry Norris, Francis Weston, Thomas and George Boleyn, Anne's uncle James Boleyn, Richard Page, and Ladies Shelton and Wingfield (LP 6.32).
- at Bologna, Dr Ortiz wonders why the pope will not give sentence against Henry given he has sent no proctor. He cheers himself up with the thought that if Henry refuses to obey the brief and take Katherine back, the pope will deprive him of his kingdom and the Emperor will then be responsible for instituting a new ruler who will be friendly to Imperial interests (LP 6.53).
- on the 10th, Henry solemnises his marriage to Anne Boleyn (CSPV 4.893).
- on the 26th, Thomas Audley is created Lord Chancellor (LP 6.73).
- Henry loans Cranmer £1000 to pay for the bulls from Rome to make him Archbishop of Canterbury (CSPS 4.2.1043). Bonner praises Cranmer as a man "of singular good learning, virtue, experience, and all good parts" noting that the entire nobility support him (LP 6.101, SP vol. 7 p.411).
- an apprentice petitions Cromwell for permission to go abroad to work. He had written a tract on justification by faith which so angered the Bishop of London that he lost his job with the result that nobody was now willing to employ him (LP 6.99, 100).
- the French cardinals have an audience with the pope and agree that he will travel to meet Francis in May after the Emperor leaves Italy. The pope promises to resolve Henry's case then in a way which he hopes will give him "much profit" and tells him to expect "a good resolution to be had"

---

[423] Easter was celebrated on 13th April.

(LP 6.38, 92, SP vol. 7 pp.408-9). Francis sends a special envoy to update Henry stressing the need for secrecy because if the Emperor finds out, he will stay in Italy to stop the pope leaving (LP 6.91).
- the papal nuncio meanwhile tells Henry that the pope is willing to have the case heard in a neutral country before a legate or refer it to the General Council, whichever Henry prefers. The nuncio implies that Gregory Casale had secured this concession from the pope which surprises Henry who says he never authorised him to make any such request. Henry tells Casale that his coronation oath prevents him submitting to a foreign jurisdiction unless Parliament agrees, which he says they will not. Admitting, however, that the offer has given him more hope than he has had before, he tells Casale and Bennet to get the case transferred back to England. After all, if the pope is willing now for it to be heard outside Rome, it should be no problem to convince him that it should be in England where the witnesses reside. Meanwhile, he sends them copies of the treaties made between his father and Katherine's parents highlighting the paragraphs which confirm that her union with Arthur was consummated and that great amity existed between the countries which renders the motive of preventing war untrue (LP 6.102).
- Henry appoints Cromwell to investigate the William Tracy will fiasco and to punish the perpetrators (LP 6.40). The Chancellor of Worcester is fined £300 for exhuming and burning the body.[424]
- the Duke of Mantua sends Henry some breeding mares and Henry responds by sending him horses in return (CSPV 4.840).
- Norfolk admits that he does not understand the rights and wrongs of Henry's case and he has no interest in trying. He accepts that people more learned than himself say the King is right and says that England needs the situation settled. He claims the pope supports the Emperor not just from fear but because he hopes to secure good marriages and positions for his many relatives (CSPS 4.2.1043).
- Bonner arrives in England and spends the morning of the 25th with Henry at Westminster where he is shown for the first time the treaties made by Henry VII with Ferdinand and Isabella. He tells Bennet, still in Italy, that a return of the case to England is imperative because anything less will cost the pope Henry's loyalty and warns that things are being done "beyond your expectation and mine and contrary to the same." Bonner also comments that the argument that the pope cannot change a decree of his predecessor is disproved by the case of Alphonso IX whose marriage to a cousin as permitted by Pope Celestine was annulled by Pope Innocent just a few years later on grounds no pope had the authority to permit such unions (LP 6.101, SP vol 7 pp.410-416).[425]

---

[424] *Hall's Chronicle* p.796. For details of the Tracy case see February 1531 above.
[425] Marriage to a cousin was not forbidden in the Bible but had been banned by Pope Gregory the Great.

Comments

The list of New Year gifts includes nothing to Anne's mother or sister, but the original document appears incomplete which could account for this. Lady Shelton was Anne's aunt and would later head the nursery of the young Princess Elizabeth. James Boleyn was the Hebrew scholar who had also attended Henry and Anne in France. The Lady Wingfield mentioned is Elizabeth, wife of Sir Anthony, not Bridget who had been Lady Harvey since 1525 and was referenced as such in the Privy Purse expenses (see March 1532). Interestingly, Henry Norris is the first name on the list, which strongly suggests it was not drawn up by officials working in order of precedence but by the King himself who began with those closest to him and whom he most wished to reward. Jane Seymour's brother, Edward, appears on the list as he did in 1532, a reminder that he did not owe his career advancement to his sister but she to his.

The likes of Chapuys and Ortiz, and indeed remarkable numbers of later historians, have regarded Henry's case as totally doomed from beginning to end, but it appears that things were starting to move Henry's way. The only problem for the King was that it was rather late because he had already married Anne and she was pregnant, though he would not have known this at this point. The pope's continued delaying tactics and refusal to give a sentence or even to see the brief served – its creation was more a sop to the Imperialists than a real threat against the King – were all signs that he had no intention of supporting Katherine. Chapuys claimed that Henry was refusing to give the nuncio audience because he was so afraid of being served a verdict or excommunicated but Henry's own letter indicates that he had met with him. They had just not told Chapuys!

Chapuys also failed to find out about Cranmer being chosen as Archbishop of Canterbury until after Cranmer returned in early January. He was astonished but the Venetian ambassador had predicted this in August 1532.[426] Too often it is said that Cranmer only got the job because he supported the annulment but he was eminently well qualified. As a churchman, he was a doctor of theology with more than ten years of lecturing behind him. As a politician, he had served as ambassador to the Emperor and as an envoy in Italy and Spain. In these roles he had proved effective and made friends and cultivated excellent international contacts, quite unlike the irascible Gardiner. Moreover, the pope would have known Cranmer so there was no need for Henry to justify his recommendation for the role. The cost of the bulls at £1000 is virtually the same as the income just granted to Anne Boleyn as Marquess of Pembroke and equates to around seven million pounds today. With such fees, no wonder the pope had no wish to upset Henry and lose the money.

---

426 CSPV 4.799

Henry's appointment of Cromwell to investigate the affair of William Tracy's will is significant as another example of him using his supreme headship to curtail the excesses of convocation. The fine handed out to Worcester was enormous, equivalent to just over two million pounds today. Sadly, those responsible would have simply passed the cost on to others through increased fees.

A full discussion of the dates of Henry's marriage to Anne exists in the chapter When did Henry and Anne marry? It is significant that the source for the date being the 10th was George Boleyn who was surely in the best place to know.

Bonner's meeting with Henry on the morning of the 25th is worth noting because that is the same morning that some others say Henry married Anne. Also interesting is the fact that he was shown the treaties made just after Prince Arthur died, all of which agreed that the union with Katherine had been consummated and had been signed by her parents. These treaties had been known by Wolsey so where had they been for the last five years? Some unknown person was working hard on Henry's behalf. The discovery of the Alphonso IX case was also significant since it answered one of the pope's chief excuses to Henry namely that he was bound by the judgment of his predecessors. Moreover, the annulment had been issued despite three children having been born to the union.[427]

Why was Abell told to keep quiet until after Easter? We know that at Easter, Anne would be proclaimed queen but very few people at the time would have known this, maybe not even Anne herself. Chapuys, who ordinarily looked for hidden meanings in every event, does not seem to have queried this term at all. It demonstrates that Henry was working to a plan, not simply responding to events as they came along.

Gregory Casale was probably astonished to be criticised by Henry for his efforts to secure a hearing on the annulment in a neutral country. In April 1531, Henry had told Bennet to achieve this and in December 1531 he had suggested to the pope that this might be acceptable to him. Casale would have seen both letters.[428] Whatever conversation Henry had had with Casale in France, he had evidently not said that he was closed to the possibility of a solution from Rome, even though he was prepared to take matters into his own hands if none could be achieved.

It is good to read Bonner's tribute to Cranmer. A pity he did not have this in mind when he supported Bloody Mary in having him burnt at the stake.

---

427 Alphonso IX of Castile lived at the end of the twelfth century and was an ancestor of the Emperor and his wife. The dispensation for his marriage to his cousin Beatrice was of third degree affinity.
428 LP 5.206, 610.

February 1533

Events

- the war with Scotland intensifies with Henry Percy leading raiding parties over the border. Lawson suggests the northern abbeys be required to pay more toward their defence given the prodigal spending habits of their abbots (LP 6.107, 124, 125, 143-146, 163, 185-186). Francis seeks to arrange a meeting between Henry and James V but although Henry is keen, the Scottish king retorts that he expected France to support him against their common enemy, England, not make peace (LP 6.184, 190).
- Montpesat, the French ambassador, is shown the offer from the pope delivered to Henry via the nuncio. He tells Francis that Henry is willing to respond to the pope with good words until he sees whether his deeds match his promises but warns that Henry "has too little trust" in the pope.[429] (LP 6.110). Langais is sent by Francis to update Henry with the news of what the Cardinal Bishop of Tarbes and Tournon have negotiated and reports that Henry is very pleased and plans to send Norfolk or Thomas Boleyn to the meeting in May between Francis and the pope (LP 6.184).
- Richard Lyst asks Anne to pray for him as he does for her daily. Not only is he unpopular with his brethren at Greenwich because he supports her – he says they tease him by calling him her chaplain – but he has now been ostracised for questioning the death of Brother Raynscroft in prison, following what he sees as false accusations. He believes Raynscroft was murdered. He assures Anne that although he has often suffered rebukes and trouble in her defence of her cause, he is glad to do so as should be anyone "in the cause of his friend" (LP 6.115, 116, 168).[430]
- Parliament opens. Amongst the bills to be considered is one which requires anyone accused of heresy to receive details of the charges and to be told who has made them. If the accusers or any of the judges are found to have a private grudge against the person, the case shall be dropped. Another seeks to alter the taxation system since currently farmers pay 1s 8d per acre for land under the plough but only 1½d per acre for land used for grazing. This discrepancy is resulting in land being turned from food production to sheep which represents a risk to national welfare (LP 6.120).
- George Throckmorton becomes involved in a dispute over rights to land in Essex and Warwickshire. His opponent in the case is the King (LP 6.128).
- Dr Ortiz discovers that Henry had slept with Anne's sister and had sought a dispensation to marry Anne though he remains unaware that the pope actually issued the said dispensation back in 1528. He is also informed

---

429 Camusat, *Meslanges Historique,* p.122
430 H. Ellis, *Original Letters Illustrative of English History,* vol 2 (1846) p248

that Francis and his sister both oppose the annulment and that Francis told Henry this when they met in Calais (CSPS 4.2.1044). In a letter later in the month he expresses the hope that the war in Scotland will prove beneficial to Katherine's cause (CSPS 4.2.1048).
- the pope refuses the idea of the Archbishop of Canterbury judging the annulment case (LP 6.139) though he is happy to confirm Cranmer's appointment to the role. The fees will be 10,000 ducats for the annates, 1500 ducats to Campeggio for proposing him in Consistory, 4000 ducats in rewards to the pope's staff and a further 1000 ducats for the pallium (LP 6.177). Katherine asks the Emperor to tell the pope not to allow the appointment until after a verdict has been given (LP 6.142).
- Bennet says he does not believe Cardinal Ravenna will hand over Ancona's opinion or his own until he is paid and points out that the Emperor has offered Ravenna 6,000 ducats to support Katherine (LP 6.139).
- the pope issues an indulgence promising seven years remission of purgatory and seven years without need to fast during Lent to anyone who provides a Scot going to the Holy Land with food or clothes (LP 6.140).
- the Marquis of Montferrat, uncle of the Duke of Mantua's first and third wives, is excommunicated for retaining a pension which Cardinal Trivulcio claims. The Emperor offers him the hand of Julia of Naples, the Duke's second wife but he thinks she is too old (LP 6.156). Another obstacle to the match is that the Marquis is Bishop of Casale and vowed to celibacy (LP 6.261).
- Henry proposes to prosecute the Bishop of St Asaph, Henry Standish, for Praemunire (LP 6.157).
- the Count of Cifuentes is sent to replace Dr Mai as Imperial ambassador to the pope (LP 6.178). D'Inteville replaces Montpesat in England (LP 6.160).
- Chapuys is confused by Henry inviting the papal nuncio to attend Parliament and to dine. The nuncio refuses to reveal what is going on. Chapuys suspects that Henry has made some deal with the pope and that this show of unity is to reassure the M.P.s that he has this support. He expresses the belief that the nuncio proposed a place indifferent for the case to be heard simply to help the pope who is totally unwilling to try it himself and wants someone else to take responsibility. However, the condition set by the pope for the place indifferent is that Henry send Anne away and take Katherine back which Henry utterly refuses, telling the nuncio: "I will do nothing of the sort and for this reason: her obstinacy, disobedience and extreme rigour towards me have been such that a reconciliation is quite impossible." Chapuys describes Henry's refusal to go to Rome as the most outrageous thing ever (CSPS 4.2.1047).
- Katherine says that even if Henry does agree to take her back, she will not agree to the case being heard anywhere but Rome. She claims that she does not want the verdict so much for herself but because it will be to the honour and benefit of the Emperor (CSPS 4.2.1047).

- another mystery which Chapuys seeks to solve is where Melanchthon is hiding. He has been told that the great German reformer, the colleague of Luther, is living in one of Henry's palaces ready to advise the King on how to seize church property and generally annoy the pope, this because Henry's own efforts to annoy Clement have not worked! Chapuys is also told – whether by the same person or not is unclear – that Henry is planning a conquest of Flanders, news he sends to the Emperor immediately (LP 6.180).
- Chapuys says that Henry cannot survive an hour without Anne. He tells the Emperor that this weakness in Henry should be exploited. If the pope will excommunicate Anne, nobody will complain because everyone hates her and it will encourage open protests. If he can get the pope to issue the verdict while the war with Scotland is ongoing, this will cause mayhem as the realm will then be under interdict and people will have no overseas trade to support themselves whilst also being at war. The expected result from this, Chapuys claims, will be a rising and the murder of Anne Boleyn. If the pope will not issue a verdict, the interdict will suffice (LP6. 142). He reiterates this advice in a later letter and complains that Cranmer has two preachers living in his home who have spoken against Katherine and should therefore – in Chapuys' view – have been burnt at the stake (CSPS 4.2.1048).
- Henry shows his Privy Councillors as well as selected lawyers and bishops, the treaties made by his father and Katherine's parents with the passages confirming that Katherine and Arthur had consummated their union highlighted. Katherine complains that people will think she is a liar for saying otherwise (LP 6.142, 160).
- after twice reporting that Anne has said she and Henry will be married soon, Chapuys discovers that they have already tied the knot. He claims Cranmer performed the ceremony and that her parents and brother were in attendance together with two of her favourites whom he does not name. He adds that previously Thomas Boleyn had opposed the match (LP 6.142, 160, 180).
- the pope signs a treaty with the Emperor which includes a clause that Henry's annulment case shall only be heard at Rome and that the brief excommunicating Henry shall be executed (LP 6.182). He also asks the Emperor to attack Constantinople but the Emperor refuses saying he lacks the resources, though he tells his wife that given the scant support he gets from the pope, he would not wish to take the risk (CSPS 4.2.1046).
- the pope tells Hawkins that the canon lawyers agree that the Levitical prohibitions are moral laws. Some say he can dispense from them for a good cause, others that he cannot, but that when the request was made for Henry to marry Katherine back in 1503, there was no good cause. This is the same as he told Bennet in December 1532. Hawkins asks why if the pope knows this, he does not do something about it. The pope replies that he cannot do anything unless Henry sends a mandate. Hawkins, in

frustration, enquires why he needs a mandate from the King given he claims a higher mandate from God which requires him to do justice promptly and not to act "for certain worldly respects." The pope does not reply (LP 7.177).[431]

- Henry tells his ambassadors they should only pay Ravenna if they see Ancona's report in full, are able to have the handwriting verified and obtain a notarised copy, warning them of the ease with which someone else could fabricate a verdict against him or alter the original. He repeats his refusal to have the case heard in Rome and says that as he is not bound to appear there – citing the legal opinion of the University of Orleans – he is not bound to send a mandate. He comments "We know what the pope should do, what he ought, and what he may do… He hath done us extreme and intolerable wrong." He tells them to remind the pope that St Peter was a fisherman who made great catches[432]: "Princes be great fishes, and must be with polity handled, and with evident and manifest right entertained, and neither can they, nor will, abide wrong, nor the shadow or visage of wrong." Referring to papal authority and the fact that for the first fifteen centuries of the church's existence no pope had claimed the power to dispense from Leviticus, he writes: "by the amplification of their authority giving dispensation in our case, we be wounded, so now by the modifying thereof that we may be healed." Henry also asks them to tell the pope that they have heard rumours of a brief against him but they are sure they must be untrue because neither they, not the excusator, have been informed about it. Henry knows the brief does exist but is upset that it was produced at the Emperor's request without even the courtesy of a notification to his own ambassadors (LP 6.194, SP vol 7 pp.416-421).

- the Emperor tells the pope that he should set as a condition for the marriage of Catherine de Medici with Francis' second son the suspension of any further action regarding Henry's annulment. The pope refuses saying this is not relevant to a marriage treaty (LP 6.201)

- in Flanders, plans are made for publishing the pope's letter to Henry of March 1530. The notice accompanying this is to say that all who have aided Henry in his case in any way, including all his councillors, are excommunicated and that the whole realm is under interdict – something completely untrue (CSPS 4.2.1050).

- Audley, the Lord Chancellor, is awarded a £225 pension from the revenues of Westminster Abbey. Chapuys claims this is evidence of Henry plucking the feathers of the clergy's nest (CSPS 4.2.1053).

- on the 4th, Humphrey Wingfield becomes Speaker of the House of Commons and is knighted four days later (LP 6.142)

---

431 SP vol. 7 pp.424-425
432 Luke 5:6, John 21:11

Comments

Richard Lyst was an apothecary whose customers had included Thomas Wolsey. He mentions in his letter that following the recent death of his wife, he wishes to be ordained and he went on to achieve this ambition. In 1535 he was appointed vicar of St Dunstan in the West in London, a position he held until 1556.[433] This was the church in which Tyndale had once preached and where Simon Fish had been buried. Lyst's messenger to Anne was Dr Goodrich who became Bishop of Ely in 1534.

The Throckmorton case is unimportant in itself but worth noting as background given the acrimonious discussion which would take place a month later when Throckmorton would accuse Henry of sleeping with Anne's mother and sister.[434] He said that he was told this by his cousin Friar Peto whom he claimed accused Henry to his face of the same in the garden at Greenwich after his controversial sermon of April 1532. Throckmorton does not record what Henry said to Peto. His account was written in 1537 and was confused as he has Thomas More serving as Chancellor when the Act of Appeals was being debated, something which did not happen as More resigned ten months previously. Throckmorton had been a Squire of the Body to Henry from 1511 so the fact that he was not aware of these two alleged affairs is significant given he was a close body servant of the King at the time he said they took place. He had also worked for Wolsey who surely would have been in a position to know. It is also deeply disturbing that Throckmorton heard the story from a man who was Henry's confessor. Presumably Peto heard about Mary Boleyn when Henry confessed his adultery with her but such a revelation should have been kept private and not exploited, and augmented, for political gain.

It is often difficult to get an impression of people laughing in the past but the person who convinced Chapuys that Melanchthon was hiding in a palace somewhere and that Henry was about to wage war on Flanders must have been doubled over in hysterics when he realised that Chapuys had taken him seriously and reported this news to the Emperor. What Charles V made of such outlandish tales is unknown. Chapuys' comment that Melanchthon favoured the annulment demonstrates how little he understood Lutheranism, something also shown by the frequency with which he labelled people as Lutherans who were nothing of the sort.

Chapuys' account of Cranmer conducting a wedding is obviously yet another of his false reports but it is interesting that he does not claim that Anne's sister was there. His belief that anyone who spoke against Katherine should die at the stake is alarming to say the least. As for his sanctimonious criticism of the pension for Audley, he must have forgotten his own application for a benefice to fund himself.[435]

---

433 Henry Ellis, *Original Letters*, vol 2 p.246, 269
434 LP 11.952
435 See November 1530

The affairs of the Duke of Mantua and his family must have provided employment for a whole team of canon lawyers in Rome. Despite his vows of celibacy, John George, Marquis of Montferrat was granted a dispensation to marry the Emperor's cousin, Julia, but he died nine days later. Spanish troops promptly moved in and occupied Montferrat for three years. The speed at which annulments and dispensations could be granted to Mantua's family was in sharp contrast to Henry VIII.

How did Ortiz find out about Mary Boleyn and the dispensation? He does not say though he records it as a new fact.

The plan to send either Norfolk (who admitted he did not understand the case) or Anne's father (whom the pope had refused to see before) is rather strange. A better choice would have been Thomas Cranmer. However, Henry might have changed his mind had the meeting ever happened.

That people were afraid of papal censures of interdict and excommunication is not just a sign of their economic concerns but their spiritual. Their fear was the greater because they were not allowed to read the Bible in English so did not know that, as John says, "God is love." (I John 4:8,16)

The papal fees for Cranmer's creation as Archbishop totalled 16,500 ducats which was around £3750 then or about £26 million today. It is not known what interest – if any – Henry might have charged on his loan to Cranmer to help pay for them but his loan covered less than a third of the cost. The new Archbishop would have been left in dire financial straits for years.

It is difficult to find polite words to describe the pope's behaviour in February 1533. On the one hand, he was reaching out to Henry with the offer of a place indifferent and sending olive branches via the French whilst at the same time signing a treaty with the Emperor denying the very things he had promised. The treaty was signed on the 24th, the day after Chapuys wrote to the Emperor to report Henry had married Anne, so it is clear that the pope was not responding to the news. Chapuys' courier had probably not even left England at this point and it is inconceivable that the nuncio would have discovered the marriage a month earlier and got the news to Rome without telling Chapuys. In fact, the pope reneged on the treaty by not executing the brief of excommunication so he showed himself as untrustworthy to the Emperor as he did to Henry. It is no wonder that faith in the pope was woefully low on all sides. Henry was totally right to doubt the pope's word.

Katherine most evidently did want the verdict for herself but her belief that vindication of her "marriage" to Henry would be a boon for the Emperor is a reminder that she continued to look at the question from the perspective of Spain. She had been Queen of England for over twenty years but had no desire to identify with that country. It is a stark contrast to the utter loyalty of other consorts to their new country, men such as Prince Albert and Prince Philip and women such as Margaret of Anjou. It is very sad that a woman who was so loved by the English people should have been so totally dismissive of their land and it is hard to imagine how she regarded her "Spain first" principle as being in any way a mark of loyalty to the man she claimed to be her husband and to whom she had made vows of obedience.

Christians are meant, by definition, to base their lives on that of Jesus. Could anyone imagine Jesus rejoicing in the thought of innocent men, women and children losing their lives and homes in war on grounds this might benefit in some way a particular person in a totally unconnected lawsuit? Katherine herself never expressed such noxious opinions. Being nasty seems to have been a key characteristic for those wishing to enter the Emperor's employment. Ortiz, Loaysa, Chapuys and Garay are four of the most repellent characters in the entire sixteenth century.

March 1533

Events

- Henry announces his intention of reversing the surrender of England to Rome made by King John three centuries before (LP 6.235).
- a visitation begins of Anne's properties in South Wales (LP 6.200).
- the Emperor seeks to have three people elected cardinal and succeeds in obtaining one. Francis seeks to have two elected and also gets one. Francis' second candidate – the one who fails – is Ghinucci, Bishop of Worcester. The French cardinals – Tournon and Tarbes – say the Emperor and his agents menaced the cardinals in consistory for eight hours to obtain this result. Loaysa is particularly vociferous in saying the Emperor will not accept Ghinucci (LP 6.201, 206).
- Hawkins comments to Henry from Rome that the pope is motivated only by worldly concerns and the claim that Katherine believes England is unsafe for her is being used simply as an excuse (LP 6.206).
- the French continue to try to broker a peace – or even a truce – between England and Scotland (LP 6.212, 242, 259). Chapuys, however, suggests that the pope might like to sponsor James V to continue the war (CSPS 4.2.1056).
- D'Inteville, the Bailly of Troyes, arrives as new French ambassador. Jean du Bellay's brother, Langais, makes a four day visit to the English court and has an altercation with Chapuys when the latter claims that the Emperor has always shown obedience and respect for the pope. Langais reminds him that it was the Emperor who held the pope captive in 1527. Chapuys denies that was the Emperor's doing and claims that the pope was released as soon as the Emperor found out. Langais remarks that it was not before a substantial ransom had been paid (LP 6.212).
- the English ambassadors in Rome rally to the support of Sir Gregory Casale saying that he did his best to get the pope to agree to transferring the case back to England but when it was clear that the pope would not agree to this saying "stand not upon that for if ye do, ye shall destroy all", he

proposed the place indifferent as the best solution. They warn Henry that this is the only alternative to Rome which can be agreed (LP 6.222, 225, 226).
- having failed to locate Melanchthon in any of the royal palaces, Chapuys concludes that he is not in England but he saves face by telling the Emperor his belief that an envoy from the reformer has arrived. He bases this claim on the fact that a German is being dealt with by Cromwell rather than Norfolk which must mean he is of low rank and not from a prince (LP 6.212). Later in the month he is able to ask the King about it who tells him the man has been sent by the Landgrave of Hesse (LP 6.235).
- Anne gives a banquet on the 24th and takes the opportunity of exhibiting all her new gold plate. She sits in the Queen's chair next to a proud Henry who comments to the Duchess of Norfolk that this shows Anne to be a worthy bride as this is a rich marriage portion. A disgruntled Chapuys, who is not invited, complains that Anne and Henry did not speak loudly enough for his spies to hear their conversation! (CSPS 4.2.1055, LP 6.212)
- Cardinal Ravenna recommends keeping his late uncle's vote for Henry a secret so that he does not suffer a loss of reputation at Rome. He tries to negotiate a new benefice in England (LP 6.227).
- George Boleyn is sent to France to tell Francis that Henry has married Anne in order "to have male succession and posterity, by which we will establish (God willing) the quiet rest and tranquillity of our kingdom and dominion." He is to say that Henry has done this following Francis' advice to delay no longer but instead to consummate his union with Anne. He is to thank Francis for being a "true brother and friend" to Henry and to advise that God's pleasure is apparent in that the succession appears "already in good appearance of advancement" i.e. Anne is pregnant. He is to say the news of the marriage has not yet been made public but will be obvious soon, by Easter at the latest. He is to pass on Henry's hopes that Francis will tell the pope not to interfere and will delay signing the marriage agreement for his son with Catherine de Medici until the pope agrees to admit the excusator. Henry helpfully sends George with a draft letter for Francis to have copied out and sent to the pope (LP 6.230).[436] Francis reads this and tells Henry it is too inflammatory. Reminding him that the idea of a meeting with the pope to settle the annulment was Henry's own and that Francis has managed to arrange this through his own cardinals, he amends it to offer his protest to the pope about the excusator not being admitted which is something no previous pope has ever refused and to urge that the case be delayed until the meeting in May. He further recommends to Henry that Norfolk, rather than Thomas

---

436 SP vol. 7 pp.427-437. It is indicative of George's fluency in the language that the instructions are in French not English.

Boleyn, be sent to the meeting if Henry is unable to attend in person on grounds sending Anne's own father might aggravate the situation. George returns Francis' draft which Henry accepts (LP 6.254, 255, 282). Meanwhile, Francis sends a handwritten letter of congratulation to Anne Boleyn (LP 6.242).
- Henry arranges for a sermon to be preached before himself, Anne and the Privy Council saying that subjects should pray that God forgive the King for living in adultery so long with his brother's wife and that they should urge him to marry as soon as possible to secure the succession. The preacher adds that the King might even take a woman of non-royal birth for such a noble cause, citing the example of David who fathered the mighty and wise Solomon on Bathsheba who was a commoner, rather than on his first wife, the princess Michal, daughter of King Saul (LP 6.235).
- Chapuys finally has an audience with Henry which involves the usual disagreements about the power of the pope and the role of the Emperor. Chapuys suggests that if the pope rules against Katherine, she could go to Spain and rule there, a move which would enable the Emperor to travel more with his wife. Henry suggests that having been absent from Spain for over thirty years, the people there do not give a fig about her, but Chapuys reassures him that they adore their "holy princess", a comment which leaves Henry speechless (CSPS 4.2.1056).
- Henry expresses the belief that "the pope will never consent to a General Council whatever briefs he might have issued on the subject for the pope, fearing the great injury that he may receive on that score, will take good care not to convene the council." (CSPS 4.2.1056)
- the Cardinal Bishop of Tarbes is taken ill and remains behind in Bologna when everyone else moves back to Rome. He is visited by Dr Mai (LP 6.208, 259).
- Henry appoints his uncle, Arthur Plantagenet, Lord Lisle, as Deputy of Calais. Keen to make sure of his rights, Henry sends agents to take all the pheasants which the last Deputy had and return them to England, leaving Lisle with just a young cock and hen and the hope of more birds to be born in future (LP 6.277, 300.21).
- Cranmer is consecrated Archbishop of Canterbury. Before he takes his oath of loyalty to the pope, he makes a formal protestation that this is only in so far as it does not run counter to his loyalty to the King which comes first (LP 6.291).
- Norfolk tells the papal nuncio that since the pope refuses to act, the decision will be made in England (CSPV 4.867).
- a bill banning appeals to Rome in the future and the continuance of any already in process is introduced to Parliament. The Commons support the theory but are nervous that upsetting the pope might result in an interdict which would stop trade and lead to widespread poverty, even starvation (LP 6.296).

- Charles Brandon is granted the wardship of Henry Grey, Marquis of Dorset (LP 6.300.21).
- Thomas More tells Erasmus that he has composed his epitaph which includes a boast "I molested the heretics, for I so hate that folk that, unless they repent, I would rather incur their animosity, so mischievous are they to the world."(LP 6.303)
- Henry's leading councillors publicly predict that the pope will betray the Emperor and say that if he does not, other princes will follow Henry's example in removing their obedience from Rome (CSPS 4.2.1057).
- Anne's household is appointed (CSPS 4.2.1057, CSPV 4.872).
- Henry gives Anne the manor of Much Waltham in Essex and an annual rent of £102 15s 6d from the town of Bristol for life. This is part of her jointure with the citation saying it is "for the great zeal, love and hearty affection that His Majesty beareth unto his most dear and entirely beloved wife, Queen Anne, and in consideration of the marriage had and solemnised between His Grace and the said Queen Anne." Confirming previous grants to her also, the Act declares that from 21st March 1533, Anne be "enabled, legitimated and able to sue in her own name by the name of Anne, Queen of England and of France and Lady of Ireland" and to receive all profits, issues, commodities and advantages of those lands to her own benefit for "the great costs expenses and charges which his said most dear and well beloved wife Anne Queen of England must of necessity sustain and bear in her chamber and otherwise" and may "dispose the same at her own will and pleasure by her discretion as if she were a woman sole."[437]

Comments

It is striking that Ghinucci, Hawkins, Bennet and Bonner all write in support of Gregory Casale to Henry and that they even speak to the pope about it. Henry's criticism of Casale (see January 1533) had stung and was felt to be unfair. Their concerted support shows the respect in which Casale was held, something even the Imperialists admitted when they noted he was a favourite of the pope's (see October 1532).

Foreign affairs were ordinarily the domain of the Duke of Norfolk. Chapuys' assumption that if Cromwell was involved it must mean the visitor was of little importance and not a good Roman Catholic is interesting, even if not correct. He notes the visitor spoke Italian, a language with which Cromwell was familiar but Norfolk not (LP 6.212).

D'Inteville is the figure on the left in the famous painting by Holbein, *The Ambassadors*. The man on the right was Georges de Selve.

---

[437] *Statutes of the Realm*, vol. 3 pp.479-481. The jointure was made by Letters Patent and confirmed when Parliament sat.

Easter in 1533 fell on 13th April, a month after George was sent to France.[438] The timing must have been as soon as Anne felt sure she was pregnant. Medical books of the period suggested that "quickening" occurred at three months though Anne's hopes would have been raised at the first period she missed. It would have taken a few days to prepare George's eleven pages of instructions and arrange his journey so, if she was three months gone, the supposition must be that she conceived in early December, some two to three weeks after making her preliminary vows to Henry.[439] It is a matter of speculation how long Henry would have waited to announce his marriage had Anne not become pregnant. If he had found her barren, would he have denied the union and simply married again?

Was Henry dumbfounded by the force of Chapuys' argument that Katherine was holy and likely to be given the job of ruling Spain should the case go against her (Chapuys' theory) or amazed by the thought that Chapuys actually seemed to believe what he was saying? There is no evidence that the Emperor wanted anyone to rule Spain for him and if he had, there was always his mother who was the rightful queen and whom he kept incarcerated on grounds of madness.

Francis' advice to Henry was very sound. Since the demise of Wolsey, Henry had lacked any statesman of international calibre to counsel or represent him which meant his reliance on the French alliance was not just based on their support for the annulment or potential military aid, but their political advice. The Cardinal Bishop of Tarbes was able to achieve far more at Rome than Bennet, Bonner and Hawkins ever could. Henry conversed frequently with the French ambassadors and took them to meetings of the Privy Council. He was particularly close to Jean de Bellay and Giles de Pomeray. Norfolk was the highest ranking councillor in England but rather a plodder. He was like the tourist who studies the phrase book before going abroad and as a result is able to ask directions and make purchases but only so long as the person to whom he speaks uses words which were in the phrase book: if the person to whom the tourist speaks uses different ones, he is lost. Norfolk could carry out orders faithfully but he lacked political initiative.

Regrettably, Francis' letter to Anne has not survived. The fact that it was handwritten by the King was seen as a huge honour. Normally, letters were written by secretaries and only signed by royalty.

The Cardinal Bishop of Tarbes died in March 1534 just three days after the verdict given at Rome against Henry but the lack of reference to him after this time indicates that he was ill for months.

---

438 He was appointed on the 11th March, LP 6.229.
439 Normally, a queen would take to her chamber to prepare for the birth a month in advance but Anne retired on 26th August and gave birth twelve days later. Either Elizabeth was early or Anne was hoping to suggest that Elizabeth was not conceived until after final vows had been taken. Preliminary vows did create a legal marriage but the church taught that consummation should not occur until after solemnisation.

Lord Lisle's wife, Honour, was a friend of Anne Boleyn's. She danced with her before Francis and corresponded with her and sent her gifts. Henry's concern about the pheasants throws light on his character and capacity for detail. He was very much like his father in many ways and certainly believed that if you took care of the pennies, the pounds would take care of themselves.

The wardship grant was to prove highly significant because the young Marquis would marry Brandon's daughter and produce Lady Jane Grey who became queen of England in 1553.

The documents do not list the appointments to Anne's household though the identity of a number of the individuals become obvious as time goes by. Her uncle James Boleyn became her chancellor, Lord Thomas Burgh her chamberlain, Sir Edward Baynton vice-chamberlain, George Taylor her receiver-general and William Coffin her Master of Horse. What was noted was that Henry made the appointments, not Anne. He had so little belief that she would need a full time secretary that he left her to use Uvedale, the man who served his son Richmond, in this capacity.[440] It was taken for granted that a husband would appoint his wife's staff so nobody quibbled about this, even one assumes Anne.

March saw Henry and his Council in more confident mood than they had been for some time. The meeting with the pope was in process of arrangement and indicators of the pope being willing to compromise gave grounds for optimism. The Imperialists, meanwhile, were despondent. After six years, they had not been able to persuade the pope to give a verdict in Katherine's favour. Writers with the great benefit of hindsight tend to downplay Imperial concerns but very few people would have risked money on Henry not winning his case at this point.

It is sometimes said that England ceased to be a papal fief in 1365 which was when Parliament determined that no monarch "could bring the realm and kingdom into such thraldom and subjection but by common consent of Parliament, the which was not done; therefore that which he [John] did was against the oath at his coronation."[441] However, a debt cannot be cancelled unilaterally and this conception of Parliamentary power did not exist in the early thirteenth century. In 1365, Parliament was angry because Urban V had sent a bill for over thirty years of unpaid tribute and the King was upset because the said pope had refused to issue a dispensation for his son Edward to marry the heiress of Flanders, not because the match offended canon or divine law but simply because the pope was French and he thought such an alliance would be dangerous for France. The declaration of 1365 was made not as a statement of political principle but in response to Urban's behaviour. The Statutes of Praemunire and Provisors were re-issued at the same time.

---

440 Ives, *Anne Boleyn* p.265. Her chaplains included William Latimer and Matthew Parker.
441 Richard Hart, *Ecclesiastical Records* (Cambridge, 1846) p.15

Henry's comments about reversing King John's surrender show that he believed England had remained a papal fief beyond 1365. Indeed, he told Sir Thomas More around 1520 that he was "bounden unto the see of Rome... for we received from that our crown imperial."[442] Too often, writers suggest that Henry broke with Rome in some petulant fit having failed to get his annulment. This is untrue. The church existed in England prior to the arrival of Roman Christianity in 597 and England was recognised as a sovereign state from that time until 1213. Henry's restoration of national and church independence was an immense and extraordinary achievement and his comments demonstrate that this was not the result of some accident of fate but a clear policy on his part.

April 1533

Events

- convocation votes that no pope could lawfully issue a dispensation for a man to marry his brother's wife if the first marriage was consummated. They also determine that Katherine's marriage to Arthur was consummated on the basis of the witnesses at Blackfriars and the confirmation of this in the treaty signed by her parents and the pope's own brief (LP 6.311)[443]
- Henry grants Cranmer permission to hear the annulment case at Dunstable and arranges for him to receive copies of all the learned opinions from across Europe, the treaties relating to Katherine and Arthur's marriage and the transcripts of the legatine court hearings from 1529. Cranmer decides to have the witnesses re-examined for himself and summons Rowland Lee, one of Henry's chaplains, to Lambeth (LP 6.332, 333, 386).
- the Act in Restraint of Appeals is passed (LP 6.324).
- Henry complains that Irish merchants are unloading their goods in the "creek of Liverpool" to avoid paying customs at Chester (LP 6.319).
- Henry commissions Thomas Boleyn to go to France to secure a tighter alliance with France (LP 6.407). This follows fears that Francis might not send an army if the Emperor invades.
- Tyndale warns John Frith, still in prison, to avoid debates on the mass (LP 6.403).
- George Boleyn is granted a wardship (LP 6.419.8).
- Fredrik, King of Norway and Denmark, dies.
- Mary, regent of the Low Countries, asks the English ambassador if rumours that Henry has married Anne are true. He admits that he does not know and complains to Cromwell that he has received no news from England for six months (LP 6.371, 372).

---

442 William Roper, *Lyfe of Sir Thomas More*, ed. E. V. Hitchcock (EETS, 1935) p.68
443 Pocock, *Records*, vol. 2 pp.449-459 includes the names of the signatories.

- an anonymous tract is published which claims the pope offered Henry a dispensation to marry a French princess but that God sent Anne instead (LP 6.416).
- Bishop John Fisher is arrested on the 6th for alleging that George Boleyn went to France to offer money to Cardinal Du Prat (Chancellor of France) and Cardinal Lorraine which they could then use to bribe the pope to accept Henry's marriage to Anne. Unsurprisingly, Chapuys believes the story (CSPS 4.2.1058).
- on Wednesday 9th, Henry sends Norfolk, Suffolk and Exeter to tell Katherine that he married Anne more than two months ago and that henceforth she herself is to be known as the Princess Dowager. Katherine will have all the estates she inherited at Arthur's death and if she needs additional funds to maintain her in appropriate state, Henry will be happy to grant her whatever is necessary. Katherine retorts that she would sooner go door to door begging than ask him for help (LP 6.324, 351).
- on Thursday 10th, Chapuys reports that Cranmer has performed the betrothal of Henry and Anne and told people he will solemnise the union after Easter. Chapuys also claims Cranmer will judge the annulment in a secret place so Katherine will know nothing about it. He tells the Emperor that aside from a dozen or so people close to Anne, the entire country is desperate for the Emperor to invade and "eradicate the poison of the lady" adding that Henry will be the first to flee. He recommends that the Emperor launch attacks on English ships and fund James V to invade from Scotland (CSPS 4.2.1058).
- despite Imperial protests, on Good Friday (11th) the pope decides to recall the brief ordering Henry to expel Anne and restore Katherine. Dr Ortiz tells the Emperor that he thinks the pope has sent Henry a private absolution (LP 6.341). The Venetian ambassador in Rome says that the pope claimed he only wrote the brief because the late Cardinal Ancona advised him to do so (CSPV 4.877).
- on Easter Saturday (April 12th) Anne attends Mass with all the state of a queen and is prayed for by name as Queen Anne. Two days later, Chapuys protests to Henry. In an angry exchange, he tells the King that he should have more respect for God: Henry replies that his conscience and God are on excellent terms. Chapuys casts doubts on Henry having more children which elicits a response: "Am I not a man like others? I need not give proofs to the contrary or let you into my secrets." Chapuys concludes from this that Anne is pregnant. Chapuys reiterates that the idea of having the annulment case heard in England is fundamentally unfair because all the clergy will be bribed or terrified into supporting the King and says that Henry's behaviour is scandalous. Henry comments that: "if the world finds this new marriage of mine strange, I find it still more so that the pope should have granted a dispensation for the former" without having the power to do so. He reminds Chapuys that the pope promised to have the case settled in England and then broke his word so he is the one at

fault. When Chapuys says Henry deserves excommunication, Henry answers that the Emperor deserves it more "because he has long opposed me, not allowing me to get out of the sin in which I was and has put off my marriage." As tempers become more ragged, Henry asks Chapuys if the Emperor told him to speak to him in this manner and Chapuys admits he has not. Henry reminds him that the role of an ambassador is to promote amity not dissension and ends the audience (LP 6.351; CSPS 4.2.1061).
- on Tuesday 15th, the Venetian ambassador, Carlo Capello, dines with Henry and Anne, her father and brother, the Duke of Norfolk and the Marquis of Exeter. He salutes her as Queen and congratulates her on her marriage and new status (CSPV 4.873).
- the Count of Cifuentes arrives in Rome to replace Dr Mai as Imperial ambassador. He tells the pope on the 19th that unless a verdict is given soon, Henry will marry Anne. The pope asks what the Emperor's response would be if that happened and Cifuentes replies that the pope should just give a verdict in Katherine's favour and find out. He also reassures the pope that in his opinion, there is no chance of Henry doing this (CSPS 4.2.1059).
- Katherine tells Chapuys that she does not want the Emperor to wage war on her account (LP 6.391).
- the Emperor finally returns to Spain. His privy council debate what action should be taken regarding England. They note that there is no grounds for military action since Henry has not harmed Katherine or Mary and nor has he threatened the Emperor or broken the terms of the treaty of Cambrai or any of the other agreements which exist between England and Spain. They believe that the pope is unlikely to give judgment against Henry for he is "very cold and indifferent in this matter and most tolerant with regard to the English king." Even if the pope did pronounce, Henry would ignore it. They agree that the case is no longer about Katherine for whom nothing can be done but that the focus needs to switch to protecting Mary's right of succession. They deliberate on whether Katherine should be recalled to Spain but offer the Emperor no advice on that point. They recommend that the King of Portugal and Ferdinand send letters to the pope and that a special envoy be sent to England to instruct Chapuys on how to behave so that he does not exasperate Henry and make the situation worse for Katherine and Mary. The Emperor reads the report and writes the word "no" against this last suggestion (CSPS 4.2.1064).
- preparations for Anne's coronation begin (LP 6.391, 395, 396, 420, 421).
- George Joye welcomes the marriage of Henry and Anne by sending them both two leaves of Genesis in English and asking for a licence to print an entire Bible (LP 6.458).
- Chapuys sends an urgent appeal to the Emperor for money saying that tradesmen are so convinced that he will now have to leave the country,

they are demanding payment of their bills and refusing him further credit (CSPS 4.2.1058).
- Henry orders twenty thousand bows from Germany (LP 6.593).[444]
- at the very end of the month, news reaches Rome that Henry and Anne are married (CSPV 4.881).

Comments

Sadly, Frith did not take Tyndale's advice[445] and he fell into the trap of responding to an attack by Thomas More. In July 1533, Frith would be martyred by being burnt at the stake, but his ideas lived on. The failure of Henry to recruit him for his annulment cause due to differences over purgatory and the mass was understandable in context of the times but had Henry been better informed, he would have found a champion whose eloquence and logical ability would likely have been of immense benefit to him.

Chapuys and other Imperialists persistently claimed that people were bribed or bullied into supporting Henry but this is far from the case. In the lower house of convocation, fourteen of twenty-three declared marriage to a known brother's wife to be against divine law, seven disagreed, one could not make up his mind and one said it was against divine law but the pope had the power to dispense anyway. Thus forty per cent failed to fully support Henry – hardly indicative of them being the bought or cowed assembly which Chapuys claimed. In the upper house, the vote was 253 in Henry's favour and 19 opposed – an overwhelming ninety-three per cent vote of support. The opponents included Bishop John Fisher of Rochester and Katherine's Spanish confessor, George Athequa, who was Bishop of Llandaff. On the issue of the consummation of Arthur and Katherine's marriage, the vote was almost unanimous in the lower house and forty-one to six in the upper.[446] Chapuys' attitude was based on his utter refusal to believe that anyone would support Henry by choice or conviction. Along with other Imperialists, he firmly believed that any books or arguments against the validity of Katherine's marriage must have been secured by nefarious means. Many later writers have blindly accepted this viewpoint because they too have failed to spend time studying Henry's case and so assumed he was wrong. Different opinions will always exist but it should be accepted that a great many people studied the case carefully and concluded Henry was right on the basis of the evidence presented. They did not need to be bribed or bullied into submission.

---

444 A letter is sent saying that the wood is to be cut on 4th June. Allowing for the time taken to get letters across the continent, the order must have been placed in April.

445 Tyndale's letter is undated so may have been written earlier in the year.

446 The full report is given in David Wilkins, *Consilia Magnae Britanniae et Hiberniae*, Vol. 3 (1737) p.765. No figure appears for the vote on consummation in the lower house. The convocation at York would debate the same questions in May and voted 49 to 2 that the marriage was against divine law (a 96 per cent vote for Henry) and 48 to 2 on the question of consummation.

Further evidence of Chapuys occupying some different plane of reality exists in his claim that the entire country is desperate for the Emperor to invade and that Henry would be the first to flee in terror. To paraphrase a famous Churchill aphorism, Henry would have been on the beach to see the Emperor off in person and he would have had the nation behind him. They may not have approved of his union with Anne but they had no wish to see their country overrun by foreign soldiers or become an outpost of the Empire. The people remembered the Emperor's armies had been responsible for the Sack of Rome even if Chapuys chose to forget this. As Francis was to observe in 1535, the English would never accept a foreigner ruling them (CSPV 5.84).

Henry's offer to Katherine of additional income if she required it was perfectly fair. Cranmer's court was set up at Dunstable in order to be near to Katherine at Ampthill so that it would be easy for her to attend, not in any effort to deny her justice. She was invited to attend but declined to either appear herself or send any lawyers to represent her.

The story of George Boleyn and the bribe is utter nonsense. Henry openly had no faith in the pope and no respect for his authority so why would he have wanted to risk a huge sum of money in this way? Why would Cardinal Du Prat be involved given he had played virtually no part in the matter to date? If Henry had ever thought of such a plan, it would have been activated through the Cardinal Bishop of Tarbes or Gregory Casale in Rome. Of course, neither Fisher nor Chapuys were privy to the instructions Boleyn received. The story was simply the product of febrile imaginations.

The thoughts of the Spanish privy council are fascinating. They seem ready to abandon Katherine and it is probable that if the pope had proposed an agreement whereby Mary would remain heir unless Henry had a son – on grounds the union with Katherine was entered into in good faith albeit without a valid bull - this could have formed the basis of a settlement, notwithstanding the objections Anne would have made. Unlike Chapuys, they see no grounds for war but they also have no confidence in the pope passing a verdict in Katherine's favour. Most interesting of all is the council's belief that Chapuys is making a difficult situation much worse – a view it would be impossible to contradict given the evidence – and the Emperor's refusal to do anything about it.

The decision to go ahead with Anne's coronation on June 1st is interesting in light of her pregnancy and the recent revelation of the marriage. People would not have had time to digest the change let alone accept it. That Henry wanted to show off his new wife because he loved her and was proud of her is understandable, but coronations take time to prepare. Planning for the pageants to be performed when Arthur married Katherine began seventeen months before the wedding.[447] Henry's mother had not been crowned until November 1487, more than a year after she had given birth to the son and heir

---

447 Michael K. Jones, Malcolm G Underwood, *The King's Mother* (Cambridge, 1992) p.77.

and almost two years after her wedding to his father.[448] The fact that people were able to get everything ready in such a short time is testimony to their industry and enthusiasm. Henry was clearly in a position to control the work of his own staff but he had no such authority over all the guilds and organisations who took part.

The Act in Restraint of Appeals is one of the most significant pieces of legislation passed in this period. Chapuys was persistently to claim that it was aimed solely at Katherine which was, like many of his allegations, false. Appeals to Rome existed in all sorts of cases including wills, marriages and divorces, tithes and offerings. If, for example, a farmer leased land from a monastery and there was a dispute about the value of his property and produce which was not resolved in the English church courts, the farmer's only hope was to appeal to Rome. Since the expense of such a course of action was prohibitive, to say nothing of impractical given the distance involved, it meant the farmer had no option but to pay what his landlord demanded. In the case of Tracy's will, the church court had posthumously decreed him a heretic leaving his widow homeless and his son disinherited with their only hope being an appeal to Rome. As the Act observed, the existing appeals process resulted in "great inquietation, vexation, trouble, cost and charges" and meant justice was not done. The decision to have all cases settled in England or Wales was, therefore, a huge benefit to thousands of people. Moreover, the Act confirmed that this change was not a novelty but a restoration of what "hath always been thought and is also at this hour" and in line with laws passed by previous English monarchs to safeguard people "from the annoyance of the See of Rome" and the "intermeddling" of all "foreign princes or potentates of the world."[449]

The Act was unusual in that it included a retrospective element applying it said to cases "already commenced, moved, depending, being, happening, or hereafter coming in contention, debate, or question" which did affect Katherine but it also applied to many others who were no doubt overjoyed at the prospect of saving a lot of time and money. As with the Act restricting annates of March 1532 – which remained conditional and not fully ratified – it said that "any foreign inhibitions, appeals, sentences, summons, foreign citations, suspensions, interdictions, excommunications, restraints, judgments, or any other process or impediments... from the see of Rome, or any other foreign courts or potentates of the world, or from and out of this realm" should be ignored and the clergy continue to celebrate the sacraments. It made it an offence for anybody resident within the country – not just citizens so it applied to Katherine and Chapuys – to seek judgments from overseas, to act in any way which might impede justice being done at home, to speak or do anything in derogation of any verdicts issued by English courts, and said that anyone found

---

448 Henry had been crowned just after Bosworth and before he married. Henry VIII had "married" Katherine before his coronation so theirs had been a joint ceremony.
449 *Statutes* vol. 3 pp.427-430. Also available in Gee and Hardy, *Documents Illustrative*, pp.187-194.

guilty, together with their "comforters, abettors, procurers, executors, and counsellors" would be subject to the penalties listed in the Statutes of Provisors and Praemunire, i.e. loss of all property and imprisonment at the King's pleasure.[450]

The Act is most famous for its preamble which declared "this realm of England is an empire and so hath been accepted in the world, governed by one supreme head and king, having the dignity and royal estate of the imperial crown of England" and that everyone in it, be they clergy or laity "be bounden and ought to bear, next to God, a natural and humble obedience: he Henry being also institute and furnished by the goodness and sufferance of Almighty God with plenary, whole and entire power, pre-eminence, authority, prerogative and jurisdiction, to render and yield justice and final determination to all manner of folk, residents or subjects within this his realm." At this period, the word empire simply meant an area which was totally under the rule of one person: it did not have the overtones of colonialism which it had later.[451] Thus by this Act of Parliament, the shameful surrender of the country to the pope by King John three centuries before was undone.[452] Henry restored the independence and sovereignty of England.

May 1533

Events

- Cranmer begins hearing the annulment case on May 10th. Katherine refuses to appear and is pronounced contumacious as at Blackfriars in 1529. He pronounces his verdict on May 23rd saying the marriage of a man to his widowed sister-in-law was forbidden by divine law (Lev 18:16) and as such "it was impossible for the pope to licence any such marriage."[453]

---

450 Lehmberg suggests that the Act had been drafted in September 1532, before Henry and Anne went to France and before their marriage, *Reformation Parliament* p.104. The similarity of the wording of the Act with that of Praemunire indicates that the composers had a copy of the earlier statute in front of them.
451 The word empire is still used in the original sense sometimes as a jest, for example when minor officials are described as empire building or gardeners are said to have their own little empire in their garden shed.
452 See February 1531 Comments. For a detailed analysis of the antecedents for this use of the imperial title by English Kings over the previous century and a half, see S. J. Gunn, *Early Tudor Government* (1995) pp.164-167, 198-199
453 *Works of Thomas Cranmer* vol. 2 p.245

> The said pretended marriage always was, and still is null and invalid, that it was contracted and consummated contrary to the will and law of God, that it is of no force or obligation, but that it always wanted, and still wants the strength and sanction of law ; and therefore we sentence, decree and declare, that it is not lawful for the said most illustrious and powerful prince Henry VIII. and the said most serene Lady Katherine, to remain in the said pretended marriage.[454]

Five days later at Lambeth Palace he declares that Henry and Anne's marriage had been validly contracted.[455] (LP 6.461, 469, 496, 497).
- Chapuys is summoned before the Privy Council and warned that ambassadors are not above the law and if he should seek to present, circulate, or in any way promote papal publications, he will be judged guilty of Praemunire. (LP 6.465). Chapuys tells them that the Act of Appeals is illegal because the Anglo-Imperial treaty forbids the passing of laws which are prejudicial to Spanish subjects. He is reminded that Katherine is an English subject due to her marriage. Chapuys pounces that they have denied she is married to Henry but they retort she became English through her marriage to Arthur (LP 6.508). Foxe tells him not to "create disturbances" in England and states that the pope "has no authority whatever among us; he has nothing to do with either temporal or spiritual matters in this kingdom." Thomas Boleyn accuses Chapuys of being two-faced and Cromwell proclaims "my countrymen are not people to allow themselves to be conquered without resistance." (CSPS 4.2.1072, 1073) Undaunted, Chapuys tells the Emperor that everyone else in England is desperate for him to invade and they tell him this because he is a "friend of peace" (CSPS 4.2.1076, 1077).
- the Duke of Norfolk and George Boleyn leave for France to meet the pope at Nice alongside Francis to finally settle the annulment crisis (LP 6.476, 541).
- Katherine is told that she can live on her income as Dowager Princess of Wales which is 24,000 ducats a year. (LP 6.530, 556).
- Chapuys reports a conversation with Norfolk in which the latter said that Thomas Boleyn had pretended to be mad in a bid to deter Henry from marrying Anne and commented that Henry was "continually inclined to amours"(CSPS 4.2.1077). Chapuys then packs his bags confident that the Emperor will withdraw him from England (CSPV 4.889, 923).
- Jean D'inteville, French ambassador at Henry's court, notes that his brother, the French ambassador at Rome since 1530, had on several times "heard the pope say that where this king's great matter is concerned, it would be

---

454 Herbert, *History*, p499
455 Rymer, *Foedera,* vol. 14 pp.470-1

better for everyone if he just wentahead and married her," something he says Henry could use in his defence.[456]

Comments

The 24,000 ducats would be worth just over thirty million pounds today. Clearly the sum was not for Katherine's use alone and she had to pay her staff from this and maintain her properties but it does show that Chapuys' claim that Katherine was reduced to penury was a blatant lie. In June, he went further and suggested to the Emperor that the Spanish grandees write to Henry offering money to help her manage in the hope this would shame Henry into providing more than what he regarded as a meagre amount (CSPS 4.2.1091).

If Thomas Boleyn had feigned insanity, surely someone would have noticed and mentioned it, most especially Chapuys himself? Boleyn had worked hard to see his daughter as queen and even though the strain of the campaign had involved rows with Anne, as is evident by her comment that her father had not wished to see her pregnant (LP 6.556), he certainly did not oppose her marriage. Regarding the comment about "amours", the word can be used for any sort of passion or enthusiasm, not necessarily love affairs which is how people today tend to interpret it. Henry had been fired to write a book against Luther and to study New Testament Greek and to build new palaces, all projects into which he threw himself whole heartedly – until something new came along to interest him. However, we only have Chapuys' word for it that Norfolk said "amours." If we had Norfolk's account of the conversation, it may have been rather different.[457]

It is a wonder that Chapuys' nose did not scrape the paper as he described himself as a "friend of peace." The man was utterly delusional. His hopes of leaving were also dashed. The Emperor took events much less to heart than he did.

June 1533

Events

- Anne is crowned at Westminster Abbey. Francis Weston is one of those knighted as part of the celebrations. Her uncle, the Duke of Norfolk, and her brother George, miss the event being in France but her parents are there. No mention is made of her sister Mary. Representatives of France and Venice feature prominently and report it to have been a great success:

---

456 Guy and Fox, *Hunting the Falcon*, p.264
457 Henry had not been deterred from a union with Katherine by her sister, Juana, being declared insane.

Chapuys is not invited and claims it was the opposite. It is believed that Henry spent over £20,000 on the event (CSPV 4.912, CSPM 911).
- Francis sends Anne a celebratory litter with rich hangings and three fine beasts to pull it. The delighted Anne immediately takes it for a three mile drive (LP 6.720).
- Marguerite de Navarre, Francis' sister, says that she loves Henry and Anne as if they were her own brother and sister. She also reveals that Francis' marriage to the Emperor's sister has broken down (LP 6.692).
- Anne tells the Venetian ambassador that she believes God has inspired Henry to marry her, noting he could have found a greater lady but not one more anxious to do her duty as queen (CSPV 4.924).
- after a long period of ill health, Henry's younger sister, Mary, the Dowager Queen of France and Duchess of Suffolk, dies aged thirty-eight.
- Henry formally appeals to a General Council[458]
- Katherine orders new liveries for her staff, emblazoned with the initials "H and K" (CSPV 4.923).

Comments

It is sometimes suggested that Marguerite's absence at Calais indicated her disapproval of Henry and Anne's relationship: her own comments indicate otherwise. In July 1534, Anne was to say of Marguerite "that she hath ever entirely loved [her], and never doubted of correspondence on her behalf" (LP 7.958) while in August 1535, Marguerite and her husband summoned representatives of the universities of Orleans, Poitiers, Toulouse and Montpelier as well as the head of the Charterhouse in France to debate Henry's case against the pope.[459] They had not been asked to do this but did it freely to show their support.

Analysis

Most people will be familiar with the game where a prize is hidden and people are required to search for it with the person who hid it advising them if they are close (warm), far away (freezing), almost there (hot) etc. It is possible to compare Henry's quest for an annulment to this game. At the outset, the prize seemed in direct sight and he simply had to take it so he was warm. Imperial success in the war placed an obstacle in his path which cooled him off but the pope's promises of a hearing in England left him in a warm place again. The loss of the war in Italy followed by the pope abandoning his allies for the

---

458 Rymer, *Foedera* vol. 14 p.478
459 LP 9.238. All found in Henry's favour.

Emperor and reneging on his promise to Henry plunged the King into the freezer. Without Wolsey's guidance he had to find a new route to the prize and at first his progress was slow like an athlete without a coach. Nonetheless, Henry pursued his quest and through 1532, he was getting warmer by the day. He had French support and the agreement of the pope to come and settle the matter in person at Nice with signs that the Emperor too was open to discussing a solution. Henry was hot and he reached out to grab the prize by marrying Anne – and overbalanced in the process which tumbled him back into the cold, giving a lifeline to Katherine's supporters who, up until that point, had been very pessimistic about their chances. As the long history of the six years given above has shown, Henry's quest was far from being a lost cause and he came very close to winning his case.

So why is it that so many historians seem to suppose Henry was doomed to failure and his request for an annulment was unreasonable? Partly it is because of the general lack of understanding of Henry's case which has led them to conclude it was weak, something which was clearly not the case as the chapter "Was Henry VIII married when he met Anne?" has shown. Also, it is a judgment largely based on the benefit of hindsight. At the outset, there was no reason to suppose that he would not have been able to obtain an annulment quite easily. In the first place, there was considerable precedent in his favour. As Henry pointed out, popes had granted annulments for less reason before, for example:

Louis XII of France[460]

At the age of twelve, he married his second cousin once removed, Jeanne de Valois, the sister of Charles VIII, also twelve. After twenty-two years, more than half being spent living together as man and wife, Louis XII decided to seek an annulment on grounds the union was unconsummated due to witchcraft. Although the couple had not had children, Jeanne claimed that the union had been consummated and there were witnesses of Louis leaving his wife's bed and telling courtiers on occasions that he had "mounted my wife three or four times during the night." When reminded of these boasts, Louis replied that he did: "not believe it to be the case that he had intercourse with her, neither with mindset of a married man nor in reality at all", indeed it was impossible because he "did not ever sleep with her when they were both nude." The suit caused immense scandal but Louis was determined as he wished to marry Anne of Brittany, who was not only the widow of his predecessor Charles VIII but also Jeanne's sister-in-law and a wealthy heiress. In September 1498, the pope accepted a generous pension from Louis to his son, Cesare Borgia, and issued the dispensation for the new marriage to go ahead. Three months later, the annulment of the previous union with Jeanne was issued, supposedly on grounds Louis had been forced into the marriage against his

---

460 See D. L. D'Avray, *Papacy*, pp. 87, 145-53.

will.⁴⁶¹ Jeanne departed to a nunnery. Louis' new marriage produced two daughters both of whom were well known by Anne Boleyn: Claude – who married Francis I and whom Anne Boleyn served – and Renée. After the death of his second wife, Louis married Henry's younger sister, Mary, once again celebrating his wedding night with boasts of his multiple mountings to his courtiers. After Louis died, Mary married Charles Brandon, Duke of Suffolk and returned to England.

Margaret of Scotland ⁴⁶²

The elder sister of Henry VIII, she had married James IV of Scotland. Following his death, she chose to marry the Earl of Angus in August 1514 but within two years, the marriage was in trouble and in 1518 she discovered he had another woman. The situation was resolved when Angus conveniently remembered that he had been betrothed to his lady friend when he married Margaret and hence not free. Pope Clement VII claimed to believe this and granted an annulment specifying that the daughter of his marriage to Queen Margaret be declared legitimate on grounds it was genuine amnesia and not a case of Angus lying either when he made his wedding vows or now. Henry's response to this decision was condemnation of it as frivolous and false.⁴⁶³

Charles Brandon, Duke of Suffolk

Aged around nineteen, Brandon fell in love with Anne Browne who was the daughter of Sir Anthony, lieutenant of Calais.⁴⁶⁴ They married but whilst she was pregnant, Brandon left her to marry her aunt who was some twenty years older than him but very wealthy. Having obtained her assets, he applied to have this second union annulled on grounds that at the time he had married her, he had forgotten she was a member of his family and consequently the dispensation granted to allow the marriage was invalid. Conveniently for him, the aunt was mother-in-law to his father's first cousin which was hardly close affinity but he thought it sounded better than mentioning the existence of his wife because bigamy was a crime. This union being annulled, Brandon then married his first wife Anne again who died of complications from childbirth only a few years later. He next married his eight year old ward, Elizabeth which gave him access to her income and meant he obtained the title of Viscount Lisle. In February 1515, he married Henry's sister Mary, the widowed Queen of France, but it was unclear whether he had actually obtained an annulment of his union with Elizabeth beforehand. As the bride had been a child and the union

---

461 Pastor, *History*, vol. 6 , p.57. The fact that Louis was about to invade Italy in pursuit of his claim to Naples may have helped the pope's decision.
462 See D. L. D'Avray, P*apacy,* pp.171-73
463 LP 4.4131. See a fuller account of Margaret's case in March 1528 Comments
464 Her brother Anthony Browne (d. 1548) was a member of Henry's Privy Chamber and her sister Elizabeth became Countess of Worcester and friend of Anne Boleyn, though she was believed to have betrayed her.

was unconsummated, there was evidently no problem with it being annulled but questions about Brandon's status at the time he wed Mary, not only in relation to his previous union with Elizabeth but also with Anne and her aunt Margaret, led to Brandon asking the pope for a clear annulment of all his previous unions and a statement confirming the legitimacy of his marriage to Mary and his children by her and by Anne. This was duly granted thanks to the efforts of Gregory Casale thirteen years after the marriage to Mary in a document which was a masterpiece of vagueness.[465]

Ladislaus II of Hungary[466]

Married Barbara of Brandenburg when he was twenty and she was twelve. Owing to war keeping the couple apart the union could not be consummated and after two years Ladislaus decided to seek an annulment. Barbara's father offered him her ten year old sister instead but Ladislaus refused, though he did pay the angry father compensation. He agreed not to pursue the separation but nonetheless on 4th October 1490, Ladislaus married Beatrice of Naples. Following suit, in 1493, Barbara was betrothed to someone else, this also illegally though the groom renounced the union when she was jailed. In 1500, Alexander VI (the Borgia who had recently annulled Louis XII's marriage) finally annulled Ladislaus and Barbara's marriage on grounds of non-consummation despite admitting that the reason for this was simply Ladislaus' disinclination and not his capability. He justified the grant because "no small dangers to Christendom" could easily result if the King lacked offspring. At the same time, the pope also annulled Ladislaus's union with Beatrice which had failed to produce any children in ten years on grounds that Ladislaus had forgotten he was married at the time and hence the union was bigamous. Beatrice, who protested as the innocent party that she had no wish to have her marriage annulled, was ordered by the pope to pay a 25,000 ducat fine and take an oath of perpetual silence regarding the case.[467] Ladislaus remarried and had a daughter who married the Emperor's brother and nephew of Katherine of Aragon, Ferdinand.

Alphonso IX of Leon [468]

In 1191, Alfonso married his cousin Teresa of Portugal using a papal dispensation for first degree consanguinity. Notwithstanding Alphonso and Teresa having three children, Celestine III annulled this union in 1196 on grounds of them being blood relatives. Given the couple knew this and so did he, this collective amnesia must have stemmed from bribery. A year later, Alphonso married another cousin, Berengaria, using once again a papal dispensation for first degree consanguinity issued by the said Celestine. In

---

465 See May 1528
466 The case is discussed in D. L. D'Avray, P*apacy, Monarchy and Marriage, 800-1600* (Cambridge, 2015) pp.163-168
467 John Skinner, *An Ecclesiastical History of Scotland* vol. 1 (1788) p.446
468 He was g-g-g-g-g-g-g-g-g-grandfather of Charles V.

1198, a new pope was elected, Innocent III, and he said that Alphonso's second marriage should not have been allowed on grounds that marriages to a cousin were against the law of God and his predecessor had no authority to issue a dispensation in the first place. Marriages to cousins were not forbidden in the Bible, only by the church, but this was an extremely relevant case since it showed one pope overturning a dispensation issued by another and saying the first pope had no authority to issue it – exactly what Henry was arguing in his own case. Innocent III threatened Alphonso with excommunication if he did not leave Berengaria but the couple – who had not requested any annulment – stayed together until 1204 by which time they had five children. The irony of a man-made law being declared the law of God whilst one stated clearly in the Bible was branded human, cannot have been lost on Henry. As part of the terms of the annulment, the pope declared the children legitimate.[469]

Henry IV of Castile[470]

Katherine of Aragon's half-uncle, he married Blanche of Navarre in 1440 and sought an annulment thirteen years later on grounds of non-consummation. Since it was not deemed politic to brand the King as generally impotent, the pope agreed to place the blame on malign influences, i.e. witchcraft, which meant that Henry was only impotent with Blanche. Henry remarried and had a daughter but this led to a civil war over the succession which was won by Katherine's mother who went on to rule as Isabella of Castile. Her claim that Henry IV could not possibly have fathered the heiress was made in opposition to the papal ruling, indicative of how respect for papal authority depended on the pope agreeing with her. In reality, the annulment was granted due to changing political alliances, Castile believing they would benefit more from one with Portugal than with Navarre.

Federico Gonzaga, Marquis of Mantua

He had married Maria of Montferrat in 1517 when he was seventeen, but relations became strained when he had a child by his mistress the same year. Another child followed whereupon Maria – according to the Marquis, most unreasonably – tried to poison the mistress. He decided to seek another wife and in 1528 he was granted an annulment from Maria by Clement VII who was able to find grounds in return for the Marquis returning two prisoners to him. The Marquis had previously been commander of the papal armies which may have assisted his suit. In March 1530, Maria's brother died but the news did not reach the Marquis in time to stop him marrying Julia of Naples, in return for which he was made a Duke. The discovery that his ex-wife was now heir of Montferrat meant the Marquis decided to seek an annulment from Julia on grounds that the first annulment had not been given for due cause and was

---

469 A more proper ground for the second annulment would have been that the first annulment was granted on farcical grounds and not legal in the eyes of God.
470 See D. L. D'Avray, P*apacy, Monarchy and Marriage* pp.123-127

therefore invalid meaning he was really still married to heiress Maria and his union with Julia was bigamous! This inventive claim failed because Maria died just six months later leaving the Marquis in need of new grounds, his next effort being Julia was older than he had supposed. Whether the fact that he had not bothered to ask in advance of the wedding was due to him being a gentleman or the fact that the Emperor offered him such rewards to marry her was not clarified. He then suggested that he had been forced into the match despite him being a grown man of thirty-one and a renowned soldier at the time. The Emperor ordered the pope not to allow any annulment, Julia being his kinswoman[471]. The Marquis offered to marry the pope's "niece" Catherine de Medici to try to get out of his union with Julia but in the end, he had to resort to bribery, the Emperor accepting 50,000 ducats in return for which he told the pope to generate an annulment on whatever grounds he wished. The Marquis then obtained a dispensation to marry the sister of his dead first wife. His relationship with his mistress was not affected by these shenanigans.

Had he known about it, Henry might also have given the example of his predecessor King John who married Isabella of Gloucester who was his second cousin in 1189 when he was still a prince. The Archbishop of Canterbury promptly annulled the match saying they were too closely related and excommunicated them. John appealed to a papal legate and obtained a dispensation which allowed the marriage to continue so that John could continue to derive income from her lands but on condition that the union was not consummated, the legate – and clearly the pope who supported the decision – evidently regarding the match as an infringement of Lev 18:6.[472] Twelve years later, and by now king, John petitioned successfully for his marriage to be annulled on grounds it should not have been authorised it in the first place on grounds of consanguinity and he promptly wed a French heiress instead.

And there are writers who claim that Henry had a poor case!

There are those who have made the point that in all the above cases, the pope acted in line with canon law and this meant he was in the right. The obvious response to this might be to quote Mr Bumble in *Oliver Twist* who commented that if that was what the law said, "the law is an ass – an idiot."[473] Others might think of the old adage about the international quality standard ISO 9001 that it does not ensure a good product, just a good administration system: a company might churn out square wheels but yet pass with flying colours provided that the paperwork was correct. As Henry noted, canon law was meant

---

471 See Appendix 6: Key Relationships
472 The verse merely refers to those "near of kin" which the Roman Church interpreted as including cousins.
473 Charles Dickens, *Oliver Twist,* (1838) chapter 37.

to be about applying God's justice, not quibbling over technicalities. Not every law which exists is ethical. The transportation of slaves across the world and of Jews to concentration camps was carried out in accordance with laws of the time and usually with correctly completed paperwork, but nobody would suggest those activities were right just because the law said so. The Council of Trent said that annulments might be granted if an impediment was discovered afterwards "if it was not unlikely that he (or she) should be ignorant."[474] To imagine that people were likely to be unaware of the existence of a current wife or family member is stretching credulity to breaking point.

Moreover, the personnel involved in Henry's case were friendly to him which meant it was a reasonable expectation that they would assist him. Although the pope had never visited England, he had corresponded closely with both Henry and Wolsey for some years prior to the annulment crisis. In February 1514, when he was still Cardinal Medici, Henry had appointed him Cardinal Protector of England and Medici was instrumental in obtaining the title Defender of the Faith for him.[475] In October 1523 Wolsey said that he and Medici were of one mind in all matters.[476] When Medici became pope, Wolsey went into raptures describing him as a "gift of God", a man of "virtue, wisdom, experience" and the person whom:

> I, above all spiritual persons living, have in mine heart most loved and been affectionate unto; assuring you that I cannot with my tongue or pen express the inward joy, which I have taken and do take to see him, whom I have so long and so much loved, honoured and been so entirely dedicated unto, thus called by God to the supreme place and governance of Christ's religion, being, as I take God to record, far more joyful thereof, than if it had happened upon mine own person. For surely, besides the manifold particular causes moving the King's Highness and me most specially to desire the exaltation weal and comfort of so great, so faithful, constant, and perfect a friend, as His Holiness hath hitherto been unto us, having firm and undoubted hope that the sincere love and steadfast affection, heretofore surely established, rooted and knit, is and shall be forever most assuredly permanent and indissoluble on either party.[477]

---

474 J. Waterworth (trans), *The Canons and Decrees Sacred and Ecumenical of the Council of Trent* (New York, 1848) p.201. Chapter 5

475 LP 1.2639; LP 3.1335, 1895.

476 LP 3.3389. See also LP 3.1325 where Medici reiterates his close friendship with Wolsey. For Medici's early service for England and Wolsey see LP1.2642, 3301.

477 LP 3.3659; SP vol. 6 pp.222-223

Nor was this just idle flattery. Other people recognised the close relationship between the trio. When Medici became pope, Henry received letters of congratulations on his candidate's victory.[478] In 1525, the Imperialists thought the pope was simply the puppet of Henry and Wolsey, an opinion shared by the Venetians.[479]

In return, the pope acknowledged that his election was due to a large degree to Henry and Wolsey and he promised that he would always be grateful and do anything he could to please them.[480] He expressed his love and admiration for Wolsey and those who knew him believed he was totally sincere in this.[481] Indeed, one of his first acts when he became pope was to appoint Wolsey, legate for life, an honour previously unknown.[482] Moreover, since 1213, England had been a fief of the papacy meaning that he was required to do his best for it and his vassal, Henry.[483] Ghinucci was to play a key role in the annulment, particularly with regard the scholarly research efforts in Italy, but also within the Vatican. He had first come to England in 1520 when Cardinal Medici wrote that, although he wished to come and see his friend Wolsey, he could not leave Italy but had instead arranged for his closest friend Ghinucci to come as papal nuncio. He said Ghinucci was very high in the affection of Pope Leo X and would act as a totally trustworthy conduit so that he, Wolsey and Henry could exchange secrets and plan policy.[484] At Medici's request, Henry granted Ghinucci the bishopric of Worcester in 1522.[485] In 1527 when the annulment crisis began, Ghinucci was recognised as being one of the pope's two most influential advisers, the other being the Datary Giberti: both were anti-Imperial.[486] Moreover, he had been secretary to Julius II and although he had not personally been involved in the raising of the dispensation for Henry and Katherine in 1504, this meant that he had crucial inside knowledge of the way the system worked, something especially valuable when the matter of the 'Spanish brief' arose. Over the coming six years, Henry would persistently seek to obtain a cardinal's hat for Ghinucci, something opposed by the Imperialists because they feared his influence and debating ability. They only relented in 1535 when the crisis was over. Ghinucci was extremely loyal to Henry and a staunch believer in his case and it was unsurprising that when Henry removed

---

478 LP 3.3579, 3587.
479 LP 4.1767, 2111.
480 LP 3.1981, 3549.
481 LP 3.1325; LP 4.1777, 1866. Across Europe, Wolsey was greatly respected, especially since his triumph with the Treaty of London. At home, his industry and attention to detail were second to none, though his wealth and power aroused jealousy.
482 LP 1.2201; 3.651, 2771; 4.15
483 See comments April 1533
484 LP 3.784, 853, 897.
485 Medici had been offered the bishopric in 1521. LP 3.1298, 1335, 1348, 1349.
486 CSPS 3.2.3; LP4.2685

him as Bishop of Worcester following the break from Rome, he awarded him a handsome pension of 1500 ducats or £375 per annum.[487]

Cardinal Campeggio was also well known to Henry and Wolsey having spent eight months in England in 1518-19. Another regular correspondent of Wolsey, he became Cardinal Protector of England when Medici became pope which meant he was England's spokesman in the Vatican giving Henry grounds to have confidence that he would put the welfare of the country first. It was Campeggio who introduced Gregory Casale to Henry's service by bringing him to England as one of his servants. Casale was then a teenager but so impressed Henry that he knighted him and recruited him. Casale was close to the pope and sheltered with him during the Sack of Rome.

Thus, although Henry had no resident English cardinal in Rome, he had good friends there, people whom he would have assumed he could trust to help him or give him good advice. In fact, only Casale and Ghinucci did this.

Another point, generally neglected by English historians, is that Henry was a highly respected figure in Rome. No other monarch had written a book against Luther. The pope and cardinals were in awe of his learning and it is significant that they did not choose to debate with him on a theological level but preferred to focus the debate on the shifting sands of canon law which they could define as they wished.

Significant too is the fact that Henry had been led by the pope to believe he had his support. If the idea of annulling the "marriage" had been as heinous as some modern writers have suggested, the pope should have dismissed it when it was first mentioned. He did not and for some time, actually did his best to help Henry. In July 1528 he issued the pollicitation meaning Henry had a document, signed by the pope, which said that marriage to a brother's wife was "contrary to the laws both of God and man" and in which the pope promised never to advoke the case to Rome, to ensure speedy justice and declared that any acts against the pollicitation were null and void. Is it any wonder that Henry was angry when the pope broke his word and that he viewed the proceedings at Rome as invalid? He was right.

(ii)

With so much in Henry's favour, why did it all go wrong? The timing of key events in the war in Italy was particularly unhelpful. The pope was taken prisoner just after the annulment case began. Naples fell while Campeggio was en route to England resulting in the pope's command that he protract the case as long as possible. The war was finally lost at Landriano, just after the legatine court had opened. Indeed, Henry was unlucky throughout the case. Staffileo died too soon. The pope's illness at the start of 1529 created a real possibility of a successor who supported Henry – but the pope recovered. It is possible that Wolsey's death too came as an unwelcome surprise to the King who may have

---

487 LP 6.1281

had an ulterior motive in summoning him to London to face supposed treason charges.

The emergence of the 'Spanish brief' was also bad timing because it delayed the opening of the legatine court and meant that time was spent discussing questions which were not part of the original decretal commission. Although it supported Henry by confirming the consummation of Katherine's marriage to Arthur, the reference to "other causes" was a major setback. Initially, Henry had argued that the dispensation had been granted under false pretences: he was under age and there was no prospect of war between England and Spain. This meant that the pope could annul without any loss of reputation because Julius had erred in granting the document through no mistake of his own. The brief ended that plan which forced Henry to pursue his point that Julius was acting *ultra vires,* not an option the pope would consider because it threatened his own authority. Although nineteenth century investigation proved the authenticity of the brief – whether the actual document presented to Ghinucci was a copy or original cannot be proved – at the time, neither side felt convinced it was genuine. The fact that it had not been registered properly worried the pope and the Emperor. The truth was that Julius II had sanctioned a deliberately false date on the document which explained why nobody could find it in the registers for the time it was supposedly issued. Henry was totally right to question the legality of the document and even if it had genuinely come from the Vatican rather than being the creation of a forger, it was an extremely shoddy piece of work and the falsified date made its acceptance as evidence debatable to say the least.

The war in Europe was a major obstacle to Henry's case. The refusal of Venice to return Ravenna and Cervia despite the many requests of Francis and Henry, hardened the pope's heart. If Henry had managed to secure them, the pope might have granted the annulment as he rewarded others for good service, but Henry was in no position to return Florence to the pope which he wanted even more.

Henry was of the view for a long time that the pope was afraid of the Emperor and many modern writers refer to the pope as the Emperor's captive while glossing over the fact that this episode was only for a brief period. If the pope had been that scared, surely he would have issued a verdict in Katherine's favour in 1529 or afterwards. He did not choose to do so and the correspondence of the Imperialists shows that at the time when Henry's marriage to Anne became public, they still had little confidence that the pope ever would support Katherine. In fact, the pope pursued the same policy throughout the six year crisis – promising everything to everyone before burying his head in the sand and hoping the problem would go away by itself.

Finally, Katherine was far better at public relations. By making a big feature of her claim to be a virgin when she married Henry, she portrayed herself as an innocent victim, a female in need of protection, a successor to all those revered virgin saints in history, not least of which was the Blessed Virgin herself. It attracted the chivalrous at the time and has continued to do so ever since. Not only did it win hearts, the claim had the great benefit of being totally impossible for anyone to prove or disprove.[488]

(iii)

It is necessary to look at the personalities of those involved. The Emperor had no interest in the rights and wrongs of the case and was only concerned about the scandal and repercussions.[489] He wanted to see Henry and Katherine's daughter, Mary, inherit the throne because she was his cousin and he had every chance of ensuring she married one of his relations and thus added England to the Imperial dominions.[490] His concern was not with his aunt's welfare but the political map of Europe and the potential for Habsburg dominance. He had learnt Katherine was sterile as early as 1525 and had no desire to see Henry marry a fertile woman, unless she was his own kin.[491] If Henry had offered to marry another of the Emperor's relations instead of Anne, he would have accepted with alacrity and sent Katherine into a nunnery so fast that her head would have spun. For all his claim to be keen to see the case settled, he did not even bother to ensure that the lawyers representing Katherine at Rome were paid which meant they drifted off to do work which did pay and with-held work they had done.[492] It was hardly a sign of commitment. When news was brought to him in 1536 of Katherine's death, the appalled papal nuncio observed "he danced and celebrated until dawn."[493]

The Emperor's treatment of women in his family was atrocious. He deliberately stole from his mother and lied to her so that he could rule in her place. He employed people to dress up as clergy and carry fake bodies past her window repeatedly so that she would believe she was being confined for her own safety due to a severe outbreak of plague. He told his sister to marry Francis knowing he had venereal disease because the alliance was more important than her health. He over-ruled the advice of others to demand his eleven year old niece engage in sexual intercourse to cement another political alliance. In 1530 he had his own seven year old bastard daughter branded when she disobeyed him. Henry's treatment of Katherine and Mary pales in comparison.[494]

---

488 It was also irrelevant. The Bible prohibited a union with a brother's woman. It did not add in brackets, unless she is a virgin.
489 The word scandal appears in relation to the annulment in the CSPS six times in 1527, nine in 1528, ten in 1529, twenty-four in 1530, twelve in 1531, six in 1532 and seventeen in 1533.
490 Mary did marry the Emperor's son when she became queen but Philip left her at the first opportunity and she died childless so England escaped this fate. He then proposed to Elizabeth I who refused him. He also tried to take the country by force but the Armada was defeated.
491 LP 4.1484
492 LP 6.656, 725; CSPS 4.2.1066
493 Parker, *Emperor*, p.246.
494 Parker, *Emperor*, pp.xvi, 80, 157, 212, 215, 628.

His attitude to the church was little better. In September 1526, the Emperor reminded Clement VII that "you cannot be unaware that you became pope through my intercession and with my help" and said that if he did not start showing some gratitude, he would take his revenge either by calling a General Council or on the battlefield. He repeatedly claimed that it was his Imperial duty to uphold papal authority despite being the man whose troops had twice caused the pope to flee for his life, had held him prisoner for six months and who had attacked and murdered numerous clergy and religious and desecrated churches. Is it any wonder that Wolsey treated this jaw droppingly audacious claim with well deserved contempt. [495]

His employees, followed by a number of modern writers, liked to contrast the one they termed "Charles the divine" with Henry but the Emperor acted in a very similar way which made his stance against Henry's actions two-faced to say the least. In 1526, the Emperor summoned a council of bishops to ask them if for a "just cause" he could wage war against the pope. They confirmed that he could, so he did. In the same year, the Emperor was excommunicated for the torture and garrotting of Bishop Acuña of Zamora. Far from expressing any concern about this punishment, the Emperor merely did his penance, paid the fine and was re-admitted to the church a few weeks later. He made deals with Lutherans when it suited him, following the advice of his confessor, Loaysa, that "you should not scruple to make use of them, even though they are heretics because since your own heart is without sin, their errors will not prevent your success." Indeed, the Emperor went further and wrote: "perhaps at some point it will turn out that Martin Luther is the one doing the right thing." He defended the rights of his subjects, be they in Spain or Germany, to have their court cases held at home rather than in Rome. [496] Towards the end of his life, the Emperor advised his son and heir to always be submissive to the pope but only so far as the policy fitted in with the needs of Spain and the rights of the Crown: "but do this without any prejudice to the pre-eminences, prosperity and peace of the said kingdoms." [497] The Emperor was a fine exponent of the maxim, "do as I say but not as I do."

In short, the Emperor's motivation throughout the annulment crisis and beyond was political and owed nothing to love for an aunt he barely knew. Opposing Henry's plans was simply a lever to crack the alliance which England had made with his enemy, France. When the situation changed, he ordered his ambassador to pay his respects to Anne Boleyn, an instruction which must have left Chapuys incandescent with fury. Later on, the Emperor's son would seek to marry Anne's daughter, despite Imperial policy officially being that she was a bastard and notwithstanding Philip's prior consummated marriage to her sister.[498]

---

495 Parker, *Emperor*, p.169
496 On July 3rd 1519 he signed the Wahlkapitulation which prohibited any German ruler or subject being summoned before a foreign jurisdiction.
497 Parker, *Emperor*, pp.103, 151, 166, 209, 418

The character and behaviour of the pope has been much debated over the years with even many Roman Catholics finding it hard to defend. Many have called him weak but this was not the view in 1527 when the crisis began. In December 1521, he was branded a tyrant and a liar by his fellow cardinals while Francis described him as a warmonger and threatened to withdraw French allegiance from Rome should he be elected pope.[499] He was not afraid of battle being involved in the capture of Milan in November 1521 and the saving of Bologna in April 1522.[500] He was recognised as being pope in all but name during the reign of his cousin Leo X and was the effective governor of Florence. The fact that Florence revolted at the first opportunity and declared itself a republic suggests he was not viewed as some benign, godly leader: indeed, he worked with Machiavelli. Throughout his career, he was very much a political animal. During Leo's papacy, he attended meetings with diplomats and campaigned against the French.[501] In 1519, he opposed the election of Charles as Emperor.[502] As pope, he made alliances with other Italian princes and encouraged war against the Emperor despite accepting rewards from him.[503] Immediately after Francis' capture at Pavia, he started making proposals for the division of France.[504] He granted a dispensation to the Emperor to marry Eleanor of Portugal because he knew the Emperor was promised to Henry's daughter and he believed that the breach of this arrangement would provoke Henry into joining his own league and sending money to aid the war.[505]

He was ambitious and had no compunction about lying to achieve his goals. He promised the French that he would abandon the Emperor and ally with them if they would only cast their votes for him at the papal election.[506] In October 1525 he admitted that he had no scruples about dissembling and breaking his promises if it suited his political goals.[507] The Venetians entered an alliance with him but admitted they did not trust him.[508]

Those who saw him regularly such as Gregory Casale and John Clerk, shared this opinion. Casale predicted that the pope would change sides if it suited him and he did.[509] When Clement was elected, Clerk advised Wolsey to delay making the customary vow of obedience because the new pope was having talks with the French who were Henry's enemies at the time. Clerk's

---

498 Evidently the moral outrage they alleged at Henry having relations with the two Boleyn girls, did not apply to the Habsburgs.
499 LP3.1895, 1947. When Medici was elected, it was without the French votes. LP 3.3464
500 LP 3.1795, 1809, 2211
501 LP 3.1101, 1209, 1325
502 LP 3.137, 149.
503 LP 3.36; LP4.1197,1624, 2227, 2267.
504 LP 4.1197
505 LP 4.1523, 1771
506 LP 3.1895
507 LP 4.1719
508 LP4.1824
509 LP 4.1885,1966,2317,2399

term of opprobrium for the man was the strongest any bishop was ever likely to use and certainly showed a lack of respect for his character. Clerk wrote: "Judas is not sleeping."[510] Even the pope's close friend Ghinucci noted he was a man prone to waver and change his mind if he saw some personal advantage in doing so, commenting that he lacked "a manly spirit."[511]

From the Imperial side, the Emperor called him a "villain" in 1525 while his ambassador Soria observed the pope had "scarce interest" in serving God.[512] Mai observed he was "rather too prone to change his opinion" and angrily told him to his face that "it is a wonder to me how lightly Your Holiness holds promises made."[513] He later condemned his "vacillating conduct" and lies while the Emperor's aunt Margaret, Regent of the Low Countries, described the pope as a man of "inconstant humour and fickle disposition."[514]

Given the unanimity of negative opinions about the man from both sides, it may be wondered that Henry took so long to realise that he was not going to get what he wanted. It is easy to be clever with hindsight but Henry was very much a "cup half full" man rather than a "cup half empty." He was aware of political realities and knew that dissembling was sometimes necessary but he expected that the many positives in the relationship over the previous thirteen years would stand him and his case in good stead. Henry had always been loyal to the pope and unlike the Emperor, had never attacked Rome let alone done so twice. As a man of honour himself, Henry thought that deep down, the pope must be so too. In fact, the only time when the pope behaved in the manner of St Peter, was when Wolsey fell. When Jesus was arrested and faced death, Peter denied any association with him three times. When Wolsey, one of the most senior figures in the Roman church, was stripped of his authority and subsequently arrested with the prospect of death before him, the pope distanced himself from him so fast that no cock would have had time to crow.[515] Of course, Peter repented of his failings and went on to play a key role in the early church with tradition saying he gave his life as a martyr for Jesus. Pope Clement by contrast showed no remorse.

The pope should have overturned Julius' bull as *ultra vires*. As pope, he claimed to be the heir of St Peter who had stated clearly that in any situation of

---

510 LP 3.3651.
511 LP 4.2155, 2317. Ghinucci was not referring to the pope's physical bravery as much as his lack of integrity.
512 Parker, *Emperor*, p.151, 166
513 CSPS 4.1.41, 97. Bishop Firmilian of Caesarea had concluded Stephen was not a valid pope because his mind was so slippery and the heir of St Peter was meant to be a rock, Wilhelm Hartel (ed.) *Cyprian Epistulae* vol. 3 (1871) p.418
514 CSPS 4.1.173, 647
515 Luke 22:54-62. It might be objected that historians should be objective and not seek to bring religion into things and asking what Jesus would have done is not appropriate. However, the pope was the Vicar of Christ. It was his job to act as Jesus' mouthpiece. It is therefore entirely relevant to compare the behaviour of the pope against the teaching of scripture.

conflict, a person should obey God rather than man (Acts 5:29). Indeed, the pope should have annulled the "marriage" upon his election and not waited for Henry to raise the matter, being proactive in the matter of morality like some of his predecessors. The allegation he made that he was unable to overturn a decision of his predecessors was a blatant lie as history showed. Indeed Julius had issued the fateful dispensation despite a ruling to the contrary of Innocent. If Clement felt doing that would be damaging to papal authority[516] or politically difficult, the very least he should have done was order Katherine to submit to the legatine court held at Blackfriars in 1529 and rejected her appeal outright. The legates had been appointed by him as his representatives so Katherine's rejection of them was a rejection of papal authority. Moreover, appealing before a verdict was issued was prohibited by canon 35 of the Fourth Lateran Council and the terms of the legatine commission prohibited appeals, so he was utterly in the wrong when he advoked the case. This is quite aside from the injustice of the claim that the case had to be sent to Rome because it was unfair to hear it in England when Henry was a party. The pope was also a party so how could it be heard in Rome and by himself?

Thus, Henry faced a man who was not so much weak but of no integrity. In the television series *Yes Minister,* Sir Humphrey lists the six key skills which a government minister should possess: the ability to blur issues, conceal errors, delay decisions, dodge questions, juggle figures and bend facts.[517] Clement VII was an expert in all areas. Inadequate in theology and canon law by his own admission, he was simply a disgrace to his office.[518] When Clement died in 1534, Rome rejoiced and his tomb was defaced, with the text amended from Clemens Pontifex Maximus to Inclemens Pontifex Minimus.[519] Henry was not alone in his dim view of the man but it was unfortunate for his case that he was forced to deal with such a person.

The other key player in the crisis was Francis I. His role is often overlooked but if he had not supported Henry, it is difficult to see what Henry could have done, particularly after the fall of Wolsey which cost Henry his most experienced adviser. Francis invested considerable time and money into sending ambassadors to Rome to plead Henry's case. He offered him the services of legal advisers and theologians across France as well as considerable face to face advice, both directly and through ambassadors such as Joachim, Jean du Bellay and Pomeray. A cynic might suggest that Francis' motivation was simply to secure Henry's alliance against the Emperor but this is too simplistic. France had a long tradition of opposing the encroaching demands of the papacy and was a great upholder of conciliarism. Experts such as du Bellay

---

516 The saying "pride comes before a fall" may apply.
517 Series 2, episode 7, *A question of loyalty*.
518 He did have some good qualities. He was a patron of Michaelangelo, intervened to help the Jews in Portugal and set up the Confraternita della Carita to provide Christian burial for the destitute. Unlike some of his predecessors, he was never accused of being a drunkard, glutton or sexually incontinent.
519 Herbert Vaughan, *The Medici Popes* (1908) p.342; LP 7.1263

had no doubt that Leviticus was divine law and beyond the pope's power to dispense and there was consistency in their position: France had opposed the granting of the dispensation back in 1503. The arguments produced to uphold Henry's arguments that no prince ever had, or should be, summoned to Rome like some lackey, were perfectly valid. Across Europe, French representatives worked alongside the English to support Henry's case. The fact that they did not generate long gossipy reports like Chapuys means their role has been rather neglected but it was very real and highly significant. Henry had no resident cardinal of his own in Rome and was deeply reliant on Tarbes who not only worked tirelessly for him there but conferred gravitas on his campaign and enjoyed almost unequalled access to the pope, as well as being able to draw on years of diplomatic experience at the highest level. Indeed, it was because so much French effort had gone into obtaining papal consent to the annulment that Francis would lose his temper with Henry when the carefully arranged meeting with Clement in 1533 was sabotaged by Bonner.[520]

And what of the women involved? It is impossible not to feel sorry for Katherine despite her histrionics. Her stubborn insistence that her father would never have told her to do anything wrong is quite touching, even if she was probably the only person on the planet ever to trust Ferdinand of Aragon. At no point during the entire crisis did she express any willingness to see what the Bible said. Instead, she based her entire case on what the pope said, though only as long as he agreed with her. As Edward Hall commented of Katherine's reaction to Henry and Anne's marriage and her return to the status of Princess Dowager: "she (as women love to lose no dignity) ever continued her old song trusting more to the pope's partiality than to the determination of Christ's verity."[521] She continually bleated that she had not deserved what was happening, completely failing to recognise that the case was against the "marriage" and not her personally. Of course, any middle aged woman would feel resentment if the man they considered their husband preferred a younger and probably prettier woman, particularly when the romance was being conducted publicly. Katherine may have been pious in conventional terms but she was still human and subject to jealousy. Nonetheless, what did she expect to gain from her intransigence? Was it likely to make Henry fall in love with her? If he had been forced to restore her to the same palace as queen, it would not have been a marriage in any real sense. They would have lived in separate apartments and the most she might have hoped for was the chance to glimpse him walking across a garden. What is particularly sad is that the English people seem to have loved her as their queen but yet she had no respect for them or their laws. In July 1533 she told Mountjoy that she did not consider herself in any way English and that she took more pride in being the daughter of Ferdinand and Isabella of Spain than being Queen of England.[522] After more

---

520 LP 6.1426
521 *Hall's Chronicle* p796.
522 CSPS 4.2.1100

than thirty years in the country, it was a remarkably frank rejection. Small wonder Henry despaired.

The biggest mystery remains why Katherine never experienced any scruple of her own about her "marriage." She was universally agreed to be a devout Christian woman and she was also educated. Did she think God's commandment not to marry a brother's wife did not apply to royalty? Did she mentally add the words "unless the pope says so"? Or could it be that she was not actually reading the Bible at all or being very selective in her choices or passages? Her decision not to allow her daughter to be taught the Old Testament suggests she thought there was something to hide.[523]

Yet, notwithstanding the sympathy one might have for her position, it remains true that Katherine was a liar. She lied about the brief. She lied about the quality of homes she had and her standard of life. She lied about the political situation of the first decade of the century and her knowledge of it. She lied about the risk to her safety and the amount of legal support she had in England.[524] Furthermore, her allegations about things Henry said proved impossible to verify as well. Such behaviour was not entirely novel. She had lied about her first pregnancy in 1510 and if she told her confessor that her marriage to Arthur was consummated and her duenna that it was not, then she must have lied to one of them too.[525] People like their history to be clear cut with obvious saints and sinners and Katherine has widely been portrayed as a saint for centuries but she was far from this. Reminding people of her lies and treasonous activities is likely to result in the same response as historians have faced when listing out the terrorist activities of the suffragettes – horrified denial – but the facts are clear and sympathy for her position should not be allowed to obscure the truth.

As for Anne's feelings, we know very little. She left no letters that revealed them and we only have the occasional reference to some comment she made in the reports of Chapuys who was never there to actually hear her say those things and whose reliability is highly suspect. In the early days of the crisis, we know that Henry kept her informed of progress even allowing her to eavesdrop on a briefing with Chapuys,[526] but there is no way of knowing what transpired between them in the later years. Their conversation behind closed doors was known only to them. Did Anne seek to advise Henry or simply calm him down or cheer him up as circumstances required? The image of her actively leading him astray stems from Katherine who refused to blame Henry for anything and the tradition of attributing unpopular policies to advisers about the King rather than the monarch himself, not from any concrete evidence.

---

523 Mattingly, *Catherine*, p.141
524 Henry provided her with Flemish lawyers. It was the Emperor who refused to permit them to assist her.
525 See How did Katherine become Queen of England.
526 CSPS 4.1.492

(iv)
   What mistakes did Henry make? He did not trust Gregory Casale's judgment sufficiently which led to him underestimating the Imperial leanings of the pope. Long before the Sack of Rome, the pope had written of his hatred of the French (LP 3.1325) and he had accepted Imperial rewards (LP 3.36). Instead, Henry assumed for a long time that the pope's behaviour toward him was the product of his fear of the Emperor but whilst the pope's experiences in 1526 and 1527 at the hands of Imperial armies must have made a deep impression on him, the precise nature of that could only be identified by a psychologist. The pope would also have had a fear of Francis whose armies had also entered Italy. The evidence suggests that the pope's desire to remain neutral and avoid making any decision was a clear policy on his part and Henry was slow to recognise this. Casale told him in February 1529 that the pope would never annul for this reason.
   He failed to appreciate the enormity of the problem facing him despite his servants doing the sums. The college of cardinals contained normally between thirty and forty members of which only around half a dozen were French or Venetian and therefore likely to be favourable to Henry. The majority of these men did not reside at Rome so were unlikely to be in college to vote for him, unlike the Imperial cardinals most of whom did live in or near Rome.
   Henry should have carried out his threat to remove his ambassadors from the Imperial court in order to prompt the Emperor to withdraw Chapuys in a tit-for-tat. Chapuys had no interest in fostering better Anglo-Imperial relations, just upholding the Emperor's interests. In his mind, England was an insignificant backwater which should have been keen to become an Imperial fief, not an independent kingdom with rights to make its own laws and decisions. Chapuys encouraged treason at Henry's court and his obsessive devotion to Katherine made a difficult situation considerably worse and removed any chance of there being a negotiated settlement. As the Spanish council admitted in 1533, a less feisty individual might have been able to handle things much better for all concerned. Even worse was the impact which Chapuys had on proceedings at Rome. His continual claims that England would revolt if Anne became queen, together with his comments about Anne plotting to kill Katherine and Mary, were believed by the pope and this created a fear of issuing a judgment in Henry's favour. His lies about Henry's treatment of Katherine and Mary also strengthened the Emperor's resolve to resist as did his persistent claims that the entire country, bar the Boleyn family, supported Katherine. This was simply untrue as would be shown in 1534 and 1535 when oaths were administered to the adult population requiring them to accept the legitimacy of Henry's marriage to Anne. Some people may not have liked it but from a population of around three million, the objectors were barely two hundred. The government had no means of coercing such a number so the lack of dissent shows the match cannot have been that unpopular.
   Henry could have made an effort to recruit the reformer John Frith who was one of the most gifted theologians of his day, not only putting John Fisher

in his place but converting Thomas More's son-in-law from his opinions about purgatory. Frith was more polite than Tyndale, intellectually extremely able and had a tremendous talent for establishing a case and proving his point. He made a very good impression on everyone who met him, including his opponents, and he would have added polish and gravitas to Henry's campaign.

With regard to winning support at home amongst his councillors and the population at large, Henry should have made it abundantly clear that it was not his intention to bastardise Mary. She was the innocent victim of Julius II's bull and popes were not averse to legitimising children in such circumstances. Leaving Mary as heir until a son came along would have reduced resistance to the annulment.[527] It would also have been a potentially effective bargaining point with the Emperor. If the pope had agreed to annul the "marriage" leaving Mary as legitimate, the Emperor's posturing would probably have ended.[528]

He could have asked the Emperor for a bride from amongst his many relations and given up Anne and the French alliance. The Emperor would have abandoned Katherine for the chance to separate Henry from Francis and he would have seen the family honour as upheld if Henry had married another of his own. Until the peace of 1529, he could have sought the hand of Eleanor, the Emperor's sister. She had been contracted to Francis as part of the Treaty of Madrid but he did not want her and a deal could have been made, although being twenty-eight, Henry may have felt she was too old.[529] Similarly, he could have sought a Medici bride with the same result.

Henry also had the opportunity to marry Bessie Blount who had already shown herself capable of bearing him a healthy son as well as two sons to her husband, She was widowed in April 1530 and did not marry until the summer of 1532. She may have been more acceptable to his courtiers.

On a more cynical level, he could have offered Mary as a bride to one of the pope's family. The Medici were an ambitious clan and the pope would have been only too happy to have one of his own as potential king of England. He would undoubtedly have annulled Henry's marriage and declared Mary legitimate, just as Henry requested in 1527, if such a prize had been offered.[530]

Perhaps too Henry should have sought to marry Bridget Wingfield instead of Anne. Bridget was a veritable son machine having eighteen children in just over twenty years of marriage, seven of them sons and most of whom who grew to maturity. The Boleyn women were not so fertile.

---

527 If Mary had supported her father and the laws of England instead of maintaining the supremacy of Rome, she would not have been bastardised. The unfortunate situation in which she found herself was entirely of her own making.

528 In 1536, the idea of legitimising Mary was proposed as part of a peace agreement with the Emperor but by then Elizabeth had been born and Mary's disobedience had meant Henry was unwilling to consider the idea, LP 10.351.

529 Eleanor had a daughter from her first marriage but had no further children in twenty years of marriage to Francis. She was born in 1498.

530 Mary was suggested as a bride for Alessandro de Medici in February 1534 by the French but Henry rejected the idea, Friedmann, *Anne Boleyn*, vol 1 p.274, 296.

(v)

    Should Henry have been able to foresee what would happen? He had been warned. Erasmus had condemned canon lawyers for "weaving together six hundred laws in the same breath no matter how little to the purpose...quite losing track of the truth in question while they go on disputing." He described how theologians would "ordinarily accommodate to their own purpose four or five little words plucked out from here and there even depraving the sense of them if need be; although the words which precede and follow these are nothing at all to the point or even go against it....You can imagine how much pleasure it gives them to shape and reshape the holy scriptures as if they were made of wax."[531] The twisting of Deuteronomy was a case in point.

    Tyndale likewise had spoken of the Bible having "but one simple literal sense" which certain theologians with "arguments of philosophy, and with worldly similitudes, and apparent reasons of natural wisdom" used to wrest "the Scripture unto their own purpose clean contrary unto the process, order and meaning of the text."[532] The argument over whether Leviticus 18 was natural, divine or man made law demonstrated this. He spoke of canon lawyers as having "no more skill of the Scripture then they that never saw it: yea and have professed a contrary doctrine. They be right hangmen to such as desire the knowledge of the scripture."[533] This was undoubtedly true as the claim that marriage to a wife's sister was equivalent to a brother's wife showed, the former never being condemned in the Bible only by canon law. In the *Obedience of a Christian Man*, a volume Henry is said to have observed was a book all kings should read, Tyndale condemned how the pope, cardinals and canon lawyers mocked the laws of God and the "many years they will prolong the sentence with cavillations and subtlety, if they be well moneyed on both parties" before deciding "he that hath most money, hath best right...in defiance of God's ordinances." It is easy to imagine Henry nodding his head vigorously as he read that bit.

    And John Frith too spoke of canon lawyers as being "clean ignorant of Scripture" and "the malicious ministers of their masters the devil" who "condemn all things that they read not in their law." He wrote: "The pope and bishops keep their own traditions and laws, but the law of God is clean out of their minds. The pope sayeth, 'ye shall in all things follow the church of Rome (by that meaneth he himself and his cardinals) and as for the Scripture, it standeth in my power and authority, for I may make of it whatsoever I will. I am Lord of the Scripture to allow and disallow it, for of me doth it take its full authority.'" Frith warned: "reason not with him. You may show him the scripture, but it availeth not, for he will wrest it and wring it into a thousand

---

531 *Desiderius Erasmus, Praise of Folly* trans. Betty Radice, (2004) pp.56,61, 81
532 Henry Walter (ed.), *Doctrinal Treatises of William Tyndale: Preface to the Five Books of Moses* (Cambridge, 1848), p.393. The Preface was written in 1530.
533 William Tyndale, *Answer to More's Third Book chapter XVI* in *Whole Works of Tyndale, Frith and Barnes* p.319

fashions." If someone decides to stand by the Bible and "will not forsake the truth, they will condemn him without audience, for fear of losing of their temporal winning." He added: "The pope hath Judas' mind, for you get nothing of him without money."[534] Rome never did admit Henry's excusator.

Henry might also have taken note of Campeggio's suggestion that his daughter Mary should marry her half-brother, Richmond and interpreted this as a sign of how little the pope respected Levitical law.[535] If this was his attitude in 1528, there was no reason to suppose he would uphold Henry's case.

Given the number of times Henry was told to marry Anne without waiting for a verdict, it might be wondered why he did not heed this advice. The main reason was that he wanted his marriage to Anne to be legally watertight and he lived in a world which defined morality by the law. There was no independent sense of ethics which might say a law was bad: something was moral if it was legal and immoral if it was not. This changed with the Reformation and the spread of printing and education which led to people generally having access to the Bible and so enabling them to redefine their sense of right and wrong. Henry's determination to secure his case on the Bible shows he was ahead of his time but his dedication to the legal campaign is a salutary reminder that his motivation was succession not Anne. He loved and wanted her but not so much that he would jeopardise his dynasty for her.

Question: Why did it take so long for Henry and Anne to marry?

Answer:

Firstly, Henry had to cast off the belief of his youth, long encouraged by men like Wolsey, that the pope had authority in England, was knowledgeable about the Bible and seriously committed to pastoral care when he was instead a political figure concerned with his own authority. As a man of honour himself, Henry assumed that others were the same. He was naive.

Secondly, Henry was a victim of discrimination and political skulduggery. A blacksmith, for example, who brought Henry's case would have had no problem in obtaining an annulment quickly and cheaply. The technicalities invalidating the 1504 dispensation were genuine and as Henry Ansgar Kelly – a canon law expert and no supporter of the King – admitted, "canonical precedent" at this period was to annul marriages made with defective permits: "the juridical practice on which Henry based his appeal was considered quite respectable and it has persisted to this day."[536] Unfortunately for Henry, his "wife" had influential friends at Rome who were keen to obstruct justice, chiefly in the hope that Mary would succeed her father and marry a Habsburg, thereby adding England to the Empire.

---

534 Works of John Frith in *Whole Works of Tyndale, Frith and Barnes*, pp. 116, 81, 101,104, 106, 100. 99.
535 LP 4.5072; Lev. 18:9
536 Kelly, *Matrimonial Trials*, p.140.

Aftermath

Imagine a comprehension exercise. A text is presented which reads: "And the Lord spake...Thou shalt not uncover the nakedness of thy brother's wife...Ye shall keep my ordinance..I am the Lord your God."[537] It is followed by the first question, Who says 'Thou shalt not uncover the nakedness of thy brother's wife'? The answer is obviously the Lord.[538] Yet, on 8th July 1533, the pope and his cardinals voted that this was not the correct answer: rather, it was man and thus the pope had absolute authority to disregard it (LP 6.808). The denial that Leviticus was the word of God remains, arguably, the most self serving ever to come from the Vatican but since the cardinals agreed that popes could not overturn the law of God, their only option when faced with the reality of them doing so, was to deny that the said law was divine. Besides, denying their ability to dispense would result in a substantial loss of income given the amount they charged for issuing dispensations. It is hardly surprising that Henry treated the decision with the contempt it deserved.

It had taken over six years for Rome to issue an opinion on this point but it was not the verdict which Katherine or her supporters craved. It was just a statement of principle with no mention of her case at all. Indeed, six days later, the pope advised the Emperor that problems with the paperwork for her case prohibited any final decision. Moreover, the decision passed was not unanimous. When Capisucio, Dean of the Rota, claimed that it was proven that England and Spain were at war in 1509 and suggested that Jesus' "Blessed are the peacemakers" abrogated Leviticus, Cardinal Tournon rightly walked out in disgust. The same Dean also announced that he had found witnesses to confirm that Henry as a child had raised the application for a dispensation in 1502 – another blatant lie (CSPV 4.925). He also stated that Prince Arthur had been impotent though the cardinals declined to rule on whether this was true or not Capisucio had persuaded them to issue the verdict that Leviticus could not be divine law on grounds that Manuel of Portugal had married two sisters in succession, something which he wrongly stated was forbidden in the Torah. Arguing that the pope would not have been able to issue a dispensation if it had been divine law, he pronounced the case proven. If the cardinals had been given copies of the Bible or known the text, they would have realised the falsity of the claim. They might also have wondered whether the failure of the Almighty to drop a thunderbolt on the pope as he signed the dispensation was really a winning argument for its legality. What is clear is that Capisucio was a disgrace to his office.

---

537 Lev. 18:1,16,30
538 Modern Biblical scholarship might dispute such but that emerged centuries on from this period so is irrelevant to this study.

Two days later, the pope wrote to Henry warning him that if he did not separate from Anne by the end of September, he would face excommunication. In his letter, he explained why he had suddenly decided to proceed in the matter. He was angry that Archbishop Cranmer had presumed to give a decision in a case which he had advoked to Rome. Cranmer's verdict that Henry's marriage to Anne was valid was thereby declared null and void and the offspring of the union illegitimate (LP 6.807, 953, 1448). In short, the pope had reacted not to Henry's marriage which he had known about for some time but to Cranmer's verdict which he only learned about in mid June (LP 6.643). The French cardinals immediately protested about the pope's action (CSPV 4.939).

Given that Anne was expecting their first child, Henry refrained from telling her the news in case it caused a miscarriage (LP 6.918). He continued to fulminate against the pope, something Chapuys repeatedly claimed upset the entire country but the French reported that, whilst Anne remained unpopular, the denial of papal authority was extremely well received (LP 6.1435). Henry withdrew his ambassadors from Rome and the papal nuncio left England.

The pope was due to go to France in the autumn for the marriage of Catherine de Medici with Francis' second son and he had promised to sort Henry's case then so there was considerable anger on the part of the English and French that he had acted precipitately. Henry argued that Francis should cancel the meeting and he sent George Boleyn to try to persuade him but Francis argued he could do more good by talking to the pope face to face about the situation, though he did send a strongly worded complaint to the pope about his actions. Meanwhile, John Fisher, Bishop of Rochester, told Chapuys that the Emperor should now send his army to England because waging war on the sinful Henry would be as pleasing a work to God as waging war on the infidel Turk (LP 6.1164). Two weeks later, Fisher repeated this request for an invasion (LP 6.1249).

In September, Anne gave birth to Elizabeth. Although there was disappointment that the child was a girl, she was very healthy and Henry and Anne anticipated further offspring.

In October, the pope and Francis met. The King and his Chancellor worked hard on Henry's behalf and continually challenged unsubstantiated claims made by papal lawyers. Cardinal DuPrat said that it was wrong for the pope to order Henry to return to Katherine when that union was against divine law. Simonetta did not dispute that, merely said the pope required Henry to live with Katherine, not sleep with her! (LP 6.1331). The Cardinal also pointed out to Simonetta that it was illegal under canon law for the pope to have annulled the marriage of Henry and Anne on grounds it had been celebrated in defiance of his prohibition because the said order had only been served on Henry and Anne had not been even cited or warned of the prospect of excommunication if she went ahead. Simonetta did not reply because the procedure was indeed iicit and indefensible.

Exactly how much progress had been made at the meeting is unclear but in November, the insolent behaviour of Bonner and Gardiner who had been sent to represent English interests and deliver Henry's appeal to a General Council, resulted in a major row. Francis thundered: "as fast as I study to win the pope, ye study to lose him" and told Henry that Bonner had undone in minutes what he had spent hours trying to achieve.[539] A furious pope told Francis to abandon Henry but he refused (LP 6.1426, 1427). This was less because Francis approved of Henry having Cranmer issue verdict than because he wanted Henry's support for his own future wars.

The row caused a serious rift in the Anglo-French alliance. Francis was angry that Henry had not told him in advance about Cranmer's verdict: Henry thought Francis should have refused to give his son to Catherine de Medici in protest at the pope's behaviour. Jean du Bellay was sent to soothe the troubled waters and engage in some earnest negotiations at Rome where the pope resurrected the idea of a hearing at Cambrai with the verdict coming from Rome. This proved to be a non-starter since Katherine refused to have the case heard anywhere but Rome and Henry refused to have any verdict from there (CSPM 927, 928).

It might be thought that the Imperialists were triumphant at this point but they were deeply concerned about the Medici-Orleans marriage. Not only was the groom the son of Francis, their long time enemy, but he was Henry's godson. The prospects for the pope favouring Henry's case when the present furore died down seemed high, especially given the pope had just created four French cardinals and was talking about giving hats to three more anti-Imperialists, one of which was Ghinucci (CSPS 4.2.1155). Nor were they happy when the pope gave the newly weds the duchy of Urbino which he said was part of Catherine's inheritance. The Imperial ambassador complained that this gave the French territory in Italy again which was a threat to their own lands. The pope's response was to smile and explain it was a meaningless gesture because women could not inherit Church land, something he had neglected to tell Francis (CSPS 4.2.1403). When the announcement was made of Anne's second pregnancy in January 1534, Katherine's supporters were left convinced that there was no chance of her restoration or Henry returning to Rome (LP 7.96, 114).

Yet on 23rd March 1534, the case was suddenly decided. The impetus came as a result of letters sent by Katherine and Chapuys which stated that the lives of Katherine and Mary were at risk unless a verdict was given. The circulation of some of Henry's statements against Rome also hardened the hearts of some cardinals who had previously opposed action (CSPM 943). Only twenty-two cardinals were involved, less than half the number eligible to attend, and the debate itself was extremely acrimonious and lasted almost twelve hours. None of the eight French cardinals were present.

The verdict was that Henry's union with Katherine was "canonical" i.e. it complied with canon law. It did not state that it was moral or that it complied

---

539 Bonner upset Francis again in 1540 to such a degree that the French king demanded his removal, LP 15.121.

with the teaching of the Bible. The decree further declared his marriage to Anne "null, unjust and attempted" and their daughter, Elizabeth, "illegitimate." It also, rather optimistically, said that Henry was required to pay the costs of the case. The judgment was not to be sent until after Easter and there was no way of enforcing it.[540] Two cardinals immediately applied to the Imperial ambassador at Rome for pensions as payment for their votes and he recommended rewards for several others (CSPS 5.27, 29).

Given that in 1528 the pope had offered a revised dispensation on grounds that the original issued by Julius II was inadequate, something even most Imperialists agreed, this was perhaps a curious judgement, albeit predictable given the cardinals were effectively ruling on themselves. Jean du Bellay had said only eight days earlier that he did not see how any such verdict could be given because there was no doubt whatsoever that the problems raised by Henry such as the fact that his parents and Katherine's mother had died between the dispensation being issued and used (LP 7. Appx.12) were absolutely genuine.[541]

In fact, the Imperial party, led by Cardinal Campeggio, employed a highly irregular argument in order to obtain this decision. He claimed that the case must be judged only on the basis of material presented up to the time Katherine made her appeal. Given that the only things to have happened at Blackfriars up to that point was that the judges had been sworn in and the King welcomed, this meant that no evidence was presented at all. Proof of the deaths of Henry VII and Isabella, proof of Henry being under age when the marriage was first suggested, proof of his protestation, witness statements relating to whether or not Katherine and Arthur consummated their marriage, the expert opinions of universities across Europe, were all ruled inadmissible.[542] It was a brilliant, if utterly unethical, way of ensuring nothing which might harm the Imperial cause could be raised or discussed. Campeggio said that whether the marriage was against divine law or not and whether the dispensation was flawed or not were immaterial: Henry's use of the dispensation when he made vows to Katherine validated it and their union had confirmed peace between England and Spain, even if it had not been necessary to do so (CSPS 5.1.76).

Jean du Bellay reported that six cardinals did their best to protest against this reasoning. They included Cesi, one of the three canon law experts authorised by the pope to advise him on the case, and De Cupis who was said to be the holiest man in Rome.

The real reason for the verdict was not because Henry's case was weak either in canon law or theology. By the pope's own admission, Henry was right on both counts. He agreed Julius should not have issued the dispensation because there was insufficient cause and it was against divine law but he maintained that Julius had the power to issue a dispensation in theory. As he

---

540 CSPS 5.1.29, Kelly, *Matrimonial Trials*, p.169.
541 For a full explanation of Henry's arguments see Was Henry married when he met Anne?
542 The witness statements were read to the cardinals in June 1533.

said in September 1530, he would never issue a verdict "which will destroy that authority." (LP 4.6638) The argument of canonicity was not based on the format of the 1504 dispensation but on the wider principals of canon law which related to papal power. In 1075 *Dictatus Papae* was issued by Gregory VII which made a number of claims in this regard. In an open attack on the Orthodox churches, it stated that the Roman Church was the only true church, those who were not members were not catholic and that the pope's title was unique. It said the pope had authority to absolve Christians of their obedience to their earthly rulers and claimed the pope himself was a saint due to the merits of St Peter and that the church could never err. It said that any judgments made by him could not be retracted and that he could be judged by nobody, including a General Council. It added that nobody could condemn anyone who made an appeal to the pope and that important cases should be referred to Rome, though it did not say that they had to be judged there. It also said that only the pope's own verdict could make any book or chapter of the Bible, canonical or deny it.[543] The status of this pronouncement was open to debate but it was unsurprisingly much beloved by successive popes. At his consecration, Innocent III claimed to be: "constituted mediator between God and mankind; on this side of God, but beyond man; less than God, but greater than man; who judges all cases but is judged by no one."[544] On the basis of this, Julius' dispensation had to be valid because his position as pope meant nothing he did could be judged by anyone but God – and certainly not Archbishop Cranmer. Inerrancy meant that the dispensation created a precedent proving that popes could rule on the matter, from which it followed that Leviticus could not be divine law.

Of course, Henry disagreed. Gregory VII's pronouncement had been issued a thousand years after the death of Jesus and was not supported by the Bible. It had also not been universally accepted for the previous four hundred and fifty years. The 1393 Statute of Praemunire had been passed against papal transfers of bishops without royal authorisation. Papal judgments had been overturned by their successors and by councils. When in 1302 Boniface VIII issued *Unam Sanctam* declaring that there was no salvation without obedience to Rome, the French declared it heretical and set up their own pope at Avignon, just one of many schisms of varying durations in the church's history.[545] The response from England in 1534 was therefore swift – acts of Parliament formally severing links with Rome. There were to be no appeals, no monies paid, no prayers for the pope's well being and the earthly head of the church in England was confirmed to be Henry. In early 1531, Cardinal Ancona had expressed the position of Rome: "canon law must take precedence over all other laws whatsoever, even those of the Kingdom itself."[546] Henry now

---

543 Clauses 2, 6, 11, 17-22, 27.
544 Corinne J. Vause and Frank Gardiner (trans.) *Between God and Man* (Washington, 2004) p.24.
545 The Orthodox churches had already rejected such a claim and continue to do so.
546 Hughes, *The Reformation in England*, vol. 1 p. 378

changed that. Canon law ceased to be taught at university and civil law became supreme.

Nonetheless, the story does not end there. Rome had finally given a decision but it had no impact and nor could it. The pope and cardinals could hardly board a ship to England and invade the country, marching to Kimbolton to collect Katherine and then take her to Henry and force the two of them into the joys of matrimony. It was again said that if Henry ignored it, he would be excommunicated which he did but nothing happened. The sentence was suspended, initially thanks largely to the efforts of the French and later due to the Emperor.

On 25th September 1534, pope Clement VII died. He was replaced by Cardinal Farnese who took the name of Paul III. His first policy was to try to heal the breach with Henry but that changed following the execution of Bishop Fisher on 22nd June 1535, just one month after he had been elected a cardinal. The pope was outraged that anyone should sit in judgment on a clergyman let alone execute him without papal consent. He claimed not to know that Fisher had been tried and found guilty of high treason but he did not let this fact alter his opinion. His predecessor had ignored the fall of Wolsey but Paul III insisted that an attack on a cardinal was an act of contempt against the Holy See. He wrote to Francis and the Emperor urging them to deprive Henry of the crown of England and expressing his wish to excommunicate Henry immediately and have all trade with England cease.[547]

These proposals were rejected by both sides. Francis argued that the punishment was far too severe which was true. Nobody had suggested deposing the Emperor when he was excommunicated in 1526 or cutting off trade with all his dominions. Francis said that while he would not join Henry in breaking with Rome, he would continue to support him in his marriage to Anne and in his right to pass laws in England as he saw fit.[548] Francis knew that if the Emperor deprived Henry and installed a puppet ruler in his place, that would make France entirely encircled and this was not in the interests of its national security. Besides he, wanted Henry's support for his Italian ambitions. From the Emperor's point of view, he feared excommunication would make Henry take an even harder line against the pope and thus ruin any chance of a reconciliation, plus the prospect of France waging war on Henry's behalf against him was not one he relished.

Despite all the arguments about Henry's alleged "marriage" to Katherine over the years, it is worth noting that the excommunication was issued not because of Henry's treatment of her or because of his marriage to Anne. It was because of his treatment of a convicted traitor who happened to be a cardinal. The irony of an excommunication following a breach of the civil law rather than a breach of the sacrament is obvious. Evidently, the pope was less concerned about the sacraments than the status of his staff.

---

547 LP 8.1095, 1117
548 LP 9.148, 941, 947

After Katherine's death in January 1536, the Emperor was content to seek a new alliance with Henry – political reality taking precedence over his promises to the pope. The death of Anne Boleyn five months later led to the pope himself again making overtures to Henry, bow to me and I will increase your power but Henry was not to be fooled. He no doubt thought of how Jesus had been tempted in the wilderness by the devil who offered him all sovereignty, to which Jesus responded: "Get thee behind me, satan, for it is written 'Thou shalt worship the Lord thy God and him only shalt thou serve."[549] For Henry, the break with Rome had not been about Anne, though the annulment crisis was the catalyst, rather it was the product of considered thought and genuine conviction. Henry had correctly realised that followers of Jesus were called Christians for a reason, namely that they believed Jesus and his law to be supreme. They were not called Churchians because the church was not the goal of obedience. The pope and the Imperialists failed to appreciate this, effectively making an idol of the institution. Almost five hundred years on, England continues to have a monarch who is Supreme Governor of the Church of England and to take pride in being an independent sovereign nation which believes in civil law.

Although apologies have been issued to descendants of slaves and abused native peoples, the Vatican has yet to express sorrow for the gross way in which Henry VIII was treated and it continues to view England as an errant papal fiefdom instead of a sovereign state.[550] However, at the Council of Trent which began just after his death, it did go some way toward trying to save its blushes. In 1563 it said that dispensations should never be given below the second degree – Henry and Katherine's had been issued in the first – and could not be given at all even by the pope, in every case prohibited in Leviticus. It also confirmed that Leviticus was the Word of God, describing God as "the author" and the text having been dictated by the Holy Ghost, a view confirmed in 1965 in *Dei verbum* which proclaimed: "Since everything asserted by the inspired authors or sacred writers must be held to be asserted by the Holy Spirit, it follows that the books of Scripture must be acknowledged as teaching solidly, faithfully and without error that truth which God wanted put into sacred writing."[551] Indeed, current Roman Catholic teaching that homosexuality is sinful is based on Leviticus 18:22 being divine law.

Yet whilst the story of Anne and Henry's long battle to get married will continue to generate different theories, the greatest mystery is surely the willingness of so many people to claim Katherine was Henry's wife despite the fact that the verdict in her favour was illogical, political and made by a man who was not a valid pope at all according to the Roman church's definition of *Cum tam divino*, any more than was Julius II who issued the notorious dispensation. The majority of those who refer to her as "wife" are not even

---

549 Luke 4:8
550 In 1935 it canonised the convicted traitor, Bishop John Fisher.
551 Waterworth, *Canons and Decrees,* pp.194, 201, 18; *Dei Verbum* chapter three.

committed Roman Catholics and it is hard to imagine they all believe in the rights of the college of cardinals to overrule Parliament. The pope today must dearly wish that all his pronouncements were greeted with such willing obedience.

When did Henry and Anne marry?

The question of when Henry and Anne married may seem a strange one to ask for people today who are accustomed to royal weddings being big, public events accompanied by much festivity and merchandising, but it was only in the twentieth century that members of the royal family began to marry in public.[1] The marriages of Henry's parents and grandparents had all been private as had his own two weddings to Katherine, the second taking place in his privy closet with only a couple of witnesses and the former being held in such seclusion that nobody at the time, or since, has ever located the date for the event. Thus, it is not surprising that mystery surrounds the marriage of Henry and Anne. They would have regarded it as something private, a deeply serious religious occasion which was not something to trumpet to all and sundry. Yet news of the wedding did spread quite fast:

> The King, after his return, married privily the lady Anne Boleyn on St Erconwald's Day [14th November][2]

> The King now impatient of further delay determined to marry Anne Boleyn secretly on the 14th day of the following November [1532][3]

These two quite categorical statements, the first from a strong supporter of Henry and the latter from a notorious opponent of Anne Boleyn might be taken as the definitive answer to the question set except that not everybody reported the same thing. In a letter to his friend and fellow ambassador, Nicholas Hawkins, Thomas Cranmer said that he was told it took place "about St Paul's day."[4] The Imperial ambassador in England, Eustace Chapuys, said it took place on the feast of the Conversion of St Paul which is January 25th.[5] Which is right and why is there this discrepancy?

The first point to note is that there was more than one date which could be described as St Paul's day. Since the time of Richard II, the biggest festival in London had been held to honour St Erconwald and this was held at St

---

1 The wedding of Katherine and Arthur was the exception in centuries of history.
2 Edward Hall, *The Union of the Two Noble and Illustre Famelies of York and Lancaster* ed. H. Ellis (1809) p.794
3 Nicolas Sander, *Rise and Growth of the Anglican Schism* ed. David Lewis (1877) pp.92-93
4 J. E. Cox ed., *Miscellaneous Writings and Letters of Thomas Cranmer* (1846) p.246. The letter was dated 17th June 1533 so written after Cranmer's enquiry into the marriage.
5 CSPS 4.2.1072

Paul's.[6] Arthur and Katherine's wedding had been celebrated on this day to take account of the crowds being in London and the fact that it was a holiday. To London residents like Edward Hall and Archbishop Cranmer, St Paul's day could mean the day when everybody went there for feasts and celebrations, i.e. 14th November. For a foreigner such as Chapuys, if he heard a reference to St Paul's day, he would assume it meant the feast of the conversion in January because he was unfamiliar with local customs and did not speak English. This explains why two traditions existed but since Cranmer did not explain what he meant by St Paul's day, it is necessary to look at the reliability of the other sources.

Edward Hall's reference to the wedding comes at the end of his account of the trip to Calais. In his version, Henry and Anne married at Dover as soon as they arrived back in England. Hall's description of the journey to and from France and the meeting of Henry and Francis is extremely full and contains a large number of details not to be found in other accounts. It was evidently the work of an eyewitness, be that Hall himself or his source. Thus, Hall clearly had access to information from those close to Henry and Anne on the trip and there is no reason to doubt his information. Hall was writing at the time so cannot be accused of inventing a date to save Queen Elizabeth from allegations she was conceived before her parents were married, something which might have happened had he been writing decades later.[7] Moreover, his date of 14th November was accepted by Nicholas Sander who was an outspoken enemy of Henry and Anne and who would have been only too pleased to be able to employ a later date so he could accuse them of having sexual intercourse prior to marriage. The chronicler Holinshed also quoted this date.

By contrast, Chapuys' reliability is extremely poor. On 23rd February 1533, he stated that Thomas Cranmer had performed the wedding ceremony with Anne's parents, brother, two of her female friends and one of the royal chaplains there.[8] On 31st March, he said that he expected the marriage to be solemnised at Easter.[9] On 10th April, he said that Cranmer had only seen Henry and Anne betrothed and the wedding would take place in April or May.[10] On 15th April he reported that none of the Privy Council attended the wedding (including presumably Anne's father and brother who were members) while on 18th May he said several had.[11] On 10th May, he said that it took place after Bonner's return from Rome – and Bonner's letter of 31st January reveals that he did not see Henry until the 25th January. Two years later, he announced that the

---

6 Richard Grafton, *Grafton's Chronicle* (1809) vol 1 p.460
7 The chronicle is not a diary. Immediately after naming the wedding day, Hall adds that "very few" knew until Easter. It is probable that he wrote up the events of each year at the end of the same from notes he had written throughout.
8 LP 6.180. Cranmer specifically stated that he did not do this and was not there.
9 LP 6.296
10 LP 6.324
11 LP 6.351, 508.

celebrant was an Augustinian friar named George Brown.[12] A reasonable conclusion would be that Chapuys did not know.

Furthermore, the November date makes sense because Henry himself said that he had taken Francis' advice of October 1532 to marry rather than wait on the pope.[13] Also attending that meeting of the two kings had been Sir Gregory Casale who would have passed on the latest news from Rome and his own perspective of the state of Henry's annulment campaign.

There is another account of the wedding by Harpsfield. Writing some twenty years after the event, he said it was solemnised by Henry's chaplain Rowland Lee with just Henry Norris and Thomas Heneage of the Privy Chamber present and Lady Berkely attending Anne.[14] He does not give the date saying only that it took place at Whitehall before dawn. In his account, Lee asked Henry for the papal dispensation for the wedding to take place saying "it is expedient that the licence be read before us all or else we run – and I more deep than any other – into excommunication in marrying Your Grace without any banns asking and in a place unhallowed and no divorce as yet promulgated of the first matrimony." Henry assured Lee that a dispensation existed but said that he did not have it with him and since going to fetch it would attract attention, Lee should continue without which Lee did.

Harpsfield's story is often quoted but is it credible? Henry Norris was head of the Privy Chamber so it is entirely probable that Henry would have been accompanied by him, but the staff of the Privy Chamber worked in shifts and Heneage was employed to cover Norris when he was away, so it would be extremely odd to have both men present at the same time.[15] Anne would have been accompanied by someone and it could have been Lady Berkely. It is impossible to say to whom she was closest at the time or who was working that day. It is perhaps a bit strange that she did not choose her mother instead. Even if Harpsfield was right about those present, how did he come by the information? None of them were likely to have ever spoken to him: he was an infant at the time of the event. Anne and Norris were both dead and Henry was hardly going to grant an interview on his deathbed giving details of the event to a teenage Harpsfield. Moreover, Harpsfield's aim in writing was to uphold papal authority and expose what he regarded as the wickedness of Henry and Anne; his intended audience was Katherine's daughter, by then Queen Mary. It is beyond credibility that Lee would have demanded a papal dispensation at this

---

12 LP 8.121
13 LP 6.230, SP vol 7 p427
14 *Nicholas Harpsfield, Pretended Divorce of Henry VIII ed. Nicholas Pocock (Camden 1878) pp.234-5.* Lady Berkley was Anne Savage whose brother John had been the first husband of William Brereton's wife. Ives suggests that William Brereton might have been in attendance also, *Anne Boleyn* p.211. Since Anne Savage did not marry Lord Berkley until February 1533, if Harpsfield was right about her attending the wedding as Lady Berkley, it would mean that he thought Henry and Anne married nearer Easter.
15 LP 5.927

point and listed all the objections which might be made. Harpsfield has invented the exchange for the single purpose of showing Henry acting in defiance of the pope. The touches about dawn, banns and unconsecrated ground were added just to cast further doubt about the legality of the ceremony. Weddings had to be celebrated between eight in the morning and noon before witnesses to be valid and canon law desired them to take place in church after banns, though this was not actually a fixed legal requirement.[16] It is clear that Harpsfield composed his account not as an independent, factually based narrative for the benefit of later historians but as a piece of political propaganda for the use of contemporaries. He was a canon lawyer and his goal was to describe an event which breached canon law in as many regards as he could imagine in order to discredit Henry's marriage and Elizabeth's status.

Finally, there is the report of Sir John Wallop who was English ambassador in France. He said that he was told by King Francis that Henry and Anne married on January 10th. This was the date given to him by George Boleyn who had been sent by Henry to inform Francis about the event.[17] This report is seldom referenced by historians but is surely the most accurate of all given the source. Henry knew when he got married whereas the likes of Chapuys relied on rumour mongers and guesswork. Moreover, George Boleyn was probably in attendance at the wedding.

So does this mean that Hall and Sanders got it wrong? No. The question of the date of Henry and Anne's marriage has been much discussed over the years but generally from a modern standpoint which does not take into account the different situation which existed in Tudor times. We think of a marriage taking place in a single ceremony but traditionally, marriage involved two separate services. At the first stage, known as betrothal or spousals, the *de futuro* or vows of intention "I will" would be taken with the agreement between the families following.[18] In the case of wealthy families, the negotiation of a property settlement could take some months while with a poor couple, it could be agreed in minutes. Only after these arrangements had been made would the second ceremony, with the *de praesenti* "I do" vows, take place.[19] It was to cater for a delay between the services that the second service involved a

---

16   A marriage without banns was officially classed as clandestine but remained valid provided that the consent of both parties had been freely given. The time regulation was binding and this meant that the Emperor's own marriage was invalid because it took place at two in the morning (LP 4.2022), a fact of which Harpsfield was probably unaware.
17   CSPV 4.893
18   This stage could take place before a priest or privately. If the latter, it was classified as clandestine regardless of the number of witnesses present.
19   Couples in a hurry could omit the betrothal stage but this was frowned upon unless there was a good reason, such as one party being close to death.

repetition of the *futuro* vows before the *praesenti* ones in order to confirm that the couple were still willing to take on the commitments of matrimony.[20]

In some cases, there might be a third stage which involved a nuptial mass. Ordinarily, this was part of the second ceremony but in cases where the marriage had taken place by proxy or where it had been impossible to celebrate mass for some reason, there would be a separate solemnisation. The union of Henry and Katherine demonstrates this with *praesenti* vows being taken in the autumn of 1504 and solemnisation only in June 1509 by which point Henry had come of age.

However, in canon law, a couple was legally married after the first ceremony. As it said in Gratian's *Decretum*: "They are truly called married after the first pledge of betrothal, although conjugal intercourse is as yet unknown to them."[21] In most cases, the second service was confirmation, a public proclamation of the fact that the couple were now about to put their promises into action and commence living together as man and wife. The analogy is not exact but it is rather like the situation with a coronation. That event publicly confirms accession and enables the monarch to make vows to the country and receive the blessing of the church, but it does not change his or her status. The monarch accedes upon the death of the previous sovereign and attends his or her coronation as monarch just as the betrothed bride and groom enter the church for the wedding as husband and wife.

The key difference in law between a couple who had taken *futuro* vows only from one which had taken *praesenti* as well rested in the indissolubility of the union. Prior to the couple having consensual intercourse, the union could be annulled. Depending on the situation, this could happen by mutual consent or it might require a formal licence from the church.[22] However, once intercourse had taken place, no prospect of annulment or divorce existed.

A clear example of this changing understanding of how marriages are dated rests in the case of Henry and Jane Seymour. Every textbook today states that Henry married Jane on 30th May 1536 having been betrothed on the 20th May, the day after Anne's execution. Yet contemporary sources do not say this. They state that Jane and Henry married on the 20th.[23]

---

20 The failure of the Book of Common Prayer to include a separate order for the first ceremony led to its gradual disappearance by the time of the Civil War. The modern wedding service continues to have this double set of vows.

21 Case 27 q2 c6.

22 For more on this subject see Henry Swinburne, A *Treatise of Spousals* (1686). There were additional regulations in cases where one or both parties were under age when they took their vows.

23 Richard Hall, *Life of Fisher* ed. Ronald Bayne (1926) p140; Sander op.cit p134; Henry Clifford, *The Life of Jane Dormer, Duchess of Feria* ed. Joseph Stevenson (1887) p42; Charles Wriothesley *A Chronicle of England* ed. William Douglas Hamilton (1875) p.43; Edward Herbert, *The History of England under Henry VIII* ed. White Kennett (1870) p.335; John Foxe, *Acts and Monuments* vol. 5 ed. S. R. Cattley (1837) p.137

Thus, when Hall said that Henry and Anne married on November 14th, he was referring to first vows which were legally binding. The second ceremony confirming the marriage presumably took place on January 10th. Cranmer says that he heard about it a fortnight or so later which fits in with his arrival in the country around January 20th and him being at court on the 26th.[24]

To those committed to the belief that Henry was actually married to Katherine at the time, the wedding – on either date – was illegal because the pope had not issued any ruling and also bigamous. To all those who recognised that Henry's "marriage" to Katherine was invalid, Henry was a free man so there was no problem.

Also worthy of note is that Elizabeth was born on September 7th 1533. Given Anne only took to her chamber eleven days before the birth indicating the baby was due in the last week of September, it must be presumed that Elizabeth was premature and she was conceived on or after January 10th.[25] It is therefore evident that Henry did not marry Anne because she was pregnant, a lie frequently repeated. After all the years of waiting, and given both Henry and Anne were devout Christians, they were not likely to "jump the gun" as it were. When Anne married Henry, she would have been a virgin. The fact that so many people today seem to find that hard to believe says more about them than it does about her.

Although no document provides us with details about the wedding such as what the bride wore, we can recreate the two scenes to a large degree without indulging in reckless flights of fancy.

The first service at Dover would have been of only a few minutes duration with Henry and Anne in their ordinary clothes – if a king can ever be said to wear such – standing before a priest with, probably, just her brother and uncle in attendance. Her father had not travelled to France so was unlikely to have been at Dover unless he had recovered from his sickness while Henry and Anne were in France and gone to meet them.[26] They would have been asked if there was any impediment to their union and they would have said no. They would then have promised to marry one another and Henry would have given Anne a ring. Very simple and could have been held in any room.

---

24 LP 6.73.
25 She was due to reach Greenwich to take to her chamber on Tuesday 26th August 1533, LP 6.1004. It is likely that she rested the first day after the journey and that the traditional mass with prayers for a safe delivery which preceded the queen entering her room took place the following morning. A queen was expected to take to her chamber a month to six weeks before her child was born. As Anne was described as being fit and well just days before, they may have opted for the shorter period.
26 See Why did it take so long for Henry and Anne to marry? October 1532 comments.

The second service would have been held in one of the chapels which existed in all the royal palaces, though Henry could have asked a chaplain to consecrate a different room for temporary use as a chapel. The only necessary furniture would have been an altar plus two prayer desks or prie-dieus. It is likely that Henry and Anne would have met in a room nearby and entered the chapel together, their guests and attendants following.[27] Anne would have stood on Henry's right in accordance with Ps. 45:9. Both Henry and Anne would have been dressed in their finest clothes which meant they would have literally sparkled with precious stones. It was not traditional for brides to wear all white until the reign of Queen Victoria[28] so it is unlikely that Anne did so, though given it was January, her robes were probably trimmed with ermine. She might have worn blue, a colour associated with virginity through the Blessed Virgin Mary, or silver to represent the white worn by the saints in heaven (Rev 7:9-14), or crimson or purple which were symbolic of royalty, or even green and white which were the colours of the Tudor dynasty. Her hair would have been loose but her head would have been covered, perhaps with a coronet in line with her status as a Lady Marquess or with a small hat. This was to meet the requirements of 1 Cor 11:3-13 which requires women to cover their heads in church or at prayer as a reminder that they are subject to men and God. Given the time of year, Anne may not have been able to carry flowers so might have carried instead a small book of prayers or psalms, perhaps with some dried rosemary inside, the symbol of remembrance, or – if she was really romantic – possibly some dried petals from a rose which Henry had given her months before.

The couple would have taken their positions in front of the priest who would have led the service in accordance with one of the recognised orders. There was no uniform text across the country but the most common versions were Sarum or York and given Henry and Anne were in the south, it is probable that they used Sarum. The text of the service is given in full in the Appendix but the outline of the service would have been as follows.

The priest would have welcomed everyone with the words, "Lo, brethren" rather than "Dearly beloved." He would have reminded them of the serious nature of marriage and asked, firstly the congregation and then the couple, if there was any lawful reason why they should not be married. He would next have asked first Henry and then Anne if they were willing to enter into marriage. Having received confirmation from each of them separately (I will)[29], he would have asked who was giving Anne away. It is probable that her father stepped up at this point. The handover was symbolic. The father recognised that he had been entrusted with Anne's care by God when she was born and he now returned her to God, who was represented by the priest, who in turn gave her to her husband just as God gave Eve to Adam (Gen 2:18,21-

---

27 The idea of the bride entering in a separate procession is later.
28 Katherine of Aragon wore white when she married Arthur. It was noted because it was unusual.
29 This repeated the betrothal to ensure that consent still existed.

22). The vows were then exchanged in words which remain familiar today, for richer, for poorer etc. There were a couple of differences. Both sets of vows included the words "if holy church it will ordain" as a reminder of church authority. Anne would also have promised "to be bonny and buxom in bed and at the board." Bonny meant good and the definition of a good wife was to be found in Prov 31:10-31. Buxom meant obedient and this was enjoined both physically in terms of sexual intimacy (1 Cor 7:3-4) but also generally in the home (at board). As marriage signified the union between Christ and the Church – a relationship in which the Church evidently owed obedience to God and not vice versa and nor were they equals – so the bride of a man owed him obedience. Her subjection to her husband was a mark of her reverence for Christ.[30] The concept appals many people today but is scriptural and neither Anne nor Henry would have queried it in the slightest.[31] The ring would then have been produced and blessed before Henry placed it on the third finger of Anne's right hand with the words beginning: "With this ring I thee wed."[32] The ring represented eternity since it had no end and the touching of Anne's fingers as the persons of the Trinity – Father, Son and Holy Ghost – were named, was a reminder of how God was making the marriage and how they would be employed to work with God in the act of creation. The priest would have pronounced them man and wife, no doubt eliciting a relieved smile from everyone present, before Psalm 128 was read. Ordinarily, the priest or an assistant read this alone but given that both Henry and Anne could read, they may have joined in. A series of prayers followed before everyone stood to recite the Nicene Creed, the statement of belief which unites all Christians.

At this point, the focus of the service would have moved toward Holy Communion. The format of the mass followed the usual custom. The priest would have given the customary warning that receiving the sacrament was not something to be taken lightly and that only those who were in love and charity with their neighbours and who had confessed and received absolution should partake. Although people like Henry attended mass several times a day, he would only have received on special occasions such as festivals and at his own wedding. Duly warned, everybody would have knelt down. Aside from the bride and groom, nobody would have had or expected pews or kneelers: the hard floor was customary. Confession and absolution followed.[33] Traditionally, a canopy was held over the couple at this point whilst a separate blessing was given and they were invited to kiss the pax. The Sarum order allowed the groom to kiss the bride at this point, theoretically with a holy kiss of peace.

---

30 See discussion in Gregory of Nazianzen's thirty-seventh oration 'On the Words of the Gospel', question 7.
31 Gen 3:16; 1 Cor 14:34; Eph 5:22-24; Col 3:18, Tit 2:4-5; 1 Pet 3:1-6
32 The left hand was later specified in the *Book of Common Prayer* and remains the usual hand.
33 Private confession and absolution would have been expected as well as public confession as part of a group. In Protestant churches, public confession is the norm rather than private.

Cranmer would later cut this option out as it was often the occasion for behaviour not consistent with the occasion.[34] If a canopy was used when Henry married Anne, there must have been people there to hold it which would have meant more witnesses and more chance of the news being spread.[35] The couple would then have received the sacrament, it being regarded as important that a couple's first meal together was Holy Communion to symbolise the centrality of Christ in their lives.[36]

At the end of the service we may assume Henry would have kissed his bride, shaken hands with everyone and there would have been a lot of smiles and laughter as they worked out how they could leave the room without being seen and the secret coming out. Anne would have had to remove her new ring and conceal it somewhere. In short, it would have been a very conventional affair with a radiant bride and a doting groom who were very much in love and not a little relieved to have finally tied the knot.

Question: When did Henry marry Anne?

Answer
The "I will" vows were taken on November 14th 1532 and the final "I do" vows on January 10th 1533.

---

34 The idea of kissing the pax was removed too, though revived in the form of passing the peace in the 1970s by Anglo-Catholics.
35 A canopy was usual but not essential. In the circumstances, it is likely that it was omitted.
36 One of the reasons for weddings being held in the morning was that people were meant to fast before receiving Holy Communion and it was not held reasonable to expect them to go without food for most of the day.

What was Anne's life like as Queen?

For many people, the horror of regular performance review by their employer is a part of life. Assessment is made on the basis of a job description, which may or may not have any bearing on what the day to day job entails, and that is followed by the uncomfortable silence while the boss tries to compose some targets to be met while the employee crosses everything they can in the hope that the objectives will be better than last year's. Anne Boleyn did not have to endure such events. In her early days as a maid of honour, there might have been a probationary review but certainly there was nothing further. After all, the role of queen does not come with a formal list of duties to be undertaken or an outline of personal characteristics or skills required to do the job, broken down into essential or desirable with asterisks to indicate where training might be supplied. The absence of these modern day human resource niceties meant that Anne was left on the one hand, subject to everyone's varied expectations which meant she was likely to disappoint many, but on the other hand, gifted with considerable freedom on how to interpret her role. So where did she start?

Although not of royal birth herself, Anne had been at court since childhood. She had witnessed the behaviour of Margaret, Regent of the Low Countries and Queens Mary and Claude of France as well as seeing how other senior French ladies such as Marguerite d'Angoulême and Louise of Savoy acted. When she returned to England, she served Queen Katherine and possibly worked in other households too. These experiences would have taught her a great deal about dignity, patronage, managing staff and how to put on a public show. Her observations of kings Henry and Francis would have shown her what different monarchs expected of their spouses. She also had the opportunity to observe the Emperor briefly in the days before he was married. Beyond all that, she must have received advice from her parents, both of whom were seasoned courtiers. All this, combined with the six years of waiting before she married Henry, meant that Anne should have been very well prepared for her new life as Queen of England.[1] The only question would be, how she was going to define it.

Just over a century before Anne became Queen, Christine de Pizan wrote *The Treasury of Ladies* which was a guide to how royal ladies should behave. It is unknown if Anne ever saw it but Francis' great-grandmother had a copy so it is possible.[2] The volume will be used here to set a contemporary standard against which Anne might be assessed.

The first duty of any queen, wrote Christine, was to serve God. She should be "always striving to do good, never idle." She should have her

---

1 Officially, she was also Queen of France because the English monarchs maintained their claim to the country as well as Lady of Ireland.
2 Christine de Pizan, *The Treasure of the City of Ladies*, translated Sarah Lawson (2003) p.xix

almoner make enquiries in every town where the poor live, where those who have fallen on hard times are, poor widows, women in childbed, students, poverty stricken priests and then "secretly send gifts to these good people by her almoner without even the poor knowing who is sending them." She should spend her afternoons in good works and ensure that her ladies do the same. Christine wrote: "Know truly that the goods of which you have such an over abundance belong to the poor and not to you. You are a thief and you steal from God if you are able to go to the aid of your neighbour and yet you do not help him."[3]

Her next duty was to her husband. She should obey him without complaint in all things and always support him, refusing to hear any ill reports of him. If he did something wrong, she should admonish him gently or if he committed a graver sin, send her confessor to advise him. She should converse regularly with his doctors, cooks and senior personal attendants to ensure that he was receiving the best service to ensure his well being. If he should be unfaithful to her, "she must put up with all this and dissimulate wisely, pretending that she does not notice it."[4]

As a mother, she should visit her children often and be vigilant about their education, ensuring they not only pursue learning but attain discipline and develop a desire to serve God. "Children are the greatest haven, security and ornament that she can have."[5]

As an employer, she should set a good example. In addition to attending worship daily, listening to sermons and reading devotional works herself, she should make certain her ladies had access to the same. She should correct their faults and not scold them or act ungraciously, and dismissal should be a last resort for those who fail to improve. She should forbid indecent words and literature and ensure that their games and laughter are kept in moderation. She should control access to her apartments so that men whose intentions are dishonourable are prevented from entering.[6]

She should use her position to do good, accepting petitions, employing wise personnel and seeking always to bring peace to any situation of conflict. Never should she seek to avenge herself on anyone who has wronged her.[7]

With regard her personal behaviour, Christine wrote: "Chastity she will have so abundantly and with such purity that in neither word nor deed, appearance, ornaments, nor bearing, conduct, social pomp nor expression, will there be anything for which she could be reproached or criticised... Sobriety will prevent her from saying any word, especially in a place where it could be passed on and reported, that she has not well examined." However, she warned that this will not necessarily be enough for "the better and more virtuous a lady

---

3   Ibid. p. 15, 25, 35.
4   Ibid. pp.36-38
5   Ibid. p.19
6   Ibid. pp.31-32, 51-53, 133
7   Ibid. pp.23, 33-34, 45

is, the greater the war envy very often makes against her." When someone makes false reports seeking to alienate her from her husband "as often happens to many ladies without cause, she will not seek, nor wish, nor try to obtain their punishment...[but] pray to God for them that He may have mercy on them. Nor will she ever...bear a grudge against anyone who has done her a great injury, being mindful of the great injuries Our Lord suffered for us." Since "it is difficult to be among the flames without getting burned...she will take all adversity willingly for the love of Our Lord and will give thanks to Him for it with a good heart."[8]

This then was what Anne was expected to do and it is safe to assume that Henry would have agreed with every word of the above advice. In addition to providing her with an income and apartments in his various palaces, he established a household to support her in her new role. It is unknown how much say Anne had in the appointments but the senior personnel were chosen, or at least approved, by the King himself. She commented on her accession that she had thanked him for supplying her with "faithful and expert officers" - before turning round and telling her new employees that it was up to them to prove by their "virtuous conversation and government" that they were worthy of Henry's recommendation.[9]

The head of her household was her Chamberlain, Thomas, Lord Burgh, but most of the day to day work was deputed to her Vice-Chamberlain, Sir Edward Baynton. Her chancellor was her uncle, James Boleyn.

For guidance, she had a group known as the Queen's Council. This consisted of her receiver-general, surveyor, attorneys, solicitors, auditors and clerk of council. Her receiver-general was George Taylor whose wife was half-sister to Nan Gainsford, one of her maids; her surveyor was John Smith whose brother worked for Lord Lisle. The minutes of her council have not survived so it is impossible to see who attended regularly and to assess their contribution.

Other people she employed included chaplains to celebrate mass and preach and an almoner whose role was to distribute charity on her behalf. This latter was an ordained priest so also able to celebrate mass and preach. Anne's chaplains included Matthew Parker (later Archbishop of Canterbury), Hugh Latimer (later Bishop of Worcester), William Betts, William Latymer and Nicholas Shaxton (later Bishop of Salisbury). Her almoner was John Skip.

The two male employees whose roles required them to spend most time alone with Anne were her secretary John Uvedale, who also served the Duke of Richmond in the same capacity and William Coffin, her Master of Horse.[10]

Her female staff would have included a group of Ladies of the Household who attended her at major events such as the visit by Chabot. These

---

8   Ibid. pp.8,19-20,30,32,44
9   Maria Dowling (ed.), *William Latymer's* Cronickille *of Anne Bulleyne* (Camden, 1990) p.48
10 Despite this contact, neither man was named as a suspected lover when she fell.

were high ranking individuals and included her cousin Mary Howard who married Henry's bastard son, the Duke of Richmond, in 1533, also Lady Margaret Douglas who was Henry's niece, being the daughter of his elder sister by her second husband.[11]

Her regular attendants were the Ladies of her Privy Chamber and the Gentlewomen of the same. The former were from noble families, the latter from the gentry. The theory of drawing attendants from both sectors was to symbolise how the lords and commons supported the Queen as they did the King in Parliament. Their role was to act as her companions, to run confidential messages and to shield her from unwelcome petitioners. They also dressed her and cared for her jewels and petty cash and took care of her personal needs such as bathing, use of the chamber pot, issues related to menstruation and pregnancy. Members of this group included the Countess of Worcester, Lady Anne Cobham, Ladies Anne and Elizabeth Wingfield, Margery Horsman and Anne's sister-in-law, Viscountess Jane Rochford.[12] Lady Bridget Harvey also served briefly.

Below this group came the Ladies Attendant who fulfilled a similar role to the grooms in the King's Privy Chamber and were all married. They tidied rooms, laid fires, replaced rushes and old candles and summoned food. Mrs Jankyn was probably one of these.

Next came the Maids of Honour who were generally young and invariably single. Few of them stayed long because having secured a husband, they usually went to live with him and start a family, though some later returned as a Lady Attendant or Lady of the Privy Chamber. They were the ones who took the food or clothes at the doors of the Privy Chamber and handed them to the Ladies Attendant who would serve or dress the Queen accordingly. The maids also ran minor errands and provided entertainment through dancing, singing or playing instruments. They accompanied the Queen when she processed down the corridors to mass or to the great hall to dine and created a decorative backdrop when she was greeting visitors. Supervising the maids would have been one of the Ladies or Gentlewomen of the Privy Chamber who took the title of Mother of the Maids. In 1534, this was a Mistress Marshall.[13] Anne's Maids of Honour included her cousin Mary Shelton, Jane Seymour, Joan Guildford, Jane Ashley, Anne Parr and also Nan Gainsford.[14]

---

11 She was resident at court and regarded as close to Anne, LP 7.Appx.13
12 A Thomas Horsman was a server to Henry VIII and had a son in 1536 who became an M.P. Margery married in 1537 so was probably of similar age and most likely a sister. There was also a John Horsman to whom Francis Weston owed money when he died (LP 10.869). It was common for household staff to be related to one another.
13 LP 7.8
14 Other staff mentioned as receiving gifts at New Year 1534 included Mistress Gamage, Nurse, Holland, Morris, Tops, Hills and Ashley (LP 7.9.2). At New Year 1532, before Anne became Queen, the only ladies listed were Anne Savage, Anne

In addition, Anne's household included a large number of other servants such as cooks, laundresses, cleaners, needlewomen, gardeners, falconers, brewers, chandlers, waiters and personnel in her stables and kennels. She would also have had medical staff including a doctor and apothecary. There were security guards, ushers and food tasters too. Amongst the specialist staff was Joan Wilkinson, her silkwoman.[15]

Anne evidently took her queenship seriously. After her coronation, she called her senior staff together and told them that she gave "most hearty thanks to Almighty God for that it hath pleased Him of His bountiful clemency and only goodness to call me to this high and royal estate. It stands to reason that I should most humbly acknowledge my obedient duty to my sovereign who, amongst all the rest of his ladies, hath vouchsafed to accept me as most worthy to enjoy his most gracious personage." She said that as a queen it was her duty to keep herself "pure and undefiled" and to maintain her "house and court so well ruled, that all that see it may desire to follow and do thereafter and all who hear may desire to see it." She explained that this was because "the royal estate of princes doth far pass and excel all other estates and degrees of life and doth represent and outwardly shadow unto us the glorious and celestial monarchy which God the governor of all things doth exercise in the firmament." To this end, her intention was that her household be a place where there was "no pampered pleasures, no licentious liberty or trifling idleness, but virtuous demeanour, godly conversation, sober communication and integrity of life."[16] It was an ambitious target, so how did she do?

With regard to Christine's first requirement of a queen that she be charitable, Anne excelled. A memoir written by one of her chaplains noted how she ordered her staff to buy great quantities of canvas and flannel to be cut into smocks, shifts, shirts and sheets for the poor which her ladies and maids of honour then made up. On progress, Anne would send messengers ahead to each parish church where they would ask the wardens for the names of those most in need of them, ensuring that full details were given of the size of each family and the ages of its members so that the correct items could be sent. To most of those in need, she gave a shilling which was equivalent to three days wages but where the need was great, she gave much more. Pregnant women were given a pair of sheets and two shillings each. In all cases, the gifts were dependent on those in need being of good character and having fallen on bad times through no fault of their own. The most usual grounds for such poverty were old age, widowhood and long or short term sickness but natural disaster and cattle plague could be factors too. In 1535, she gave a man and his wife who had lost their entire livelihood due to the last, twenty pounds to rebuild, urging them to

---

Jocelyn, Margery Horsman, Jane Ashley and Mistress Wriothesley (LP 5.686). Jane Ashley's sister-in-law Kate would become nurse and subsequent governess to Princess Elizabeth.

15 An excellent study of Kathryn Howard's staff and their work can be found in Gareth Russell, *Young, Damned and Fair* (2017) pp.140-149.
16 Latymer, *Cronickille*, pp.48,50.

return for more if that sum was insufficient. Other families got three or four pounds to purchase one or more cows, something valuable for providing them with milk and cheese as well as, eventually, meat.[17] Her silkwoman recalled that Anne thought "no day well spent wherein some man had not fared the better by some benefit at her hands."[18] Anne was, however, aware that simply giving alms was not enough. She took a keen interest in schemes to benefit the poor long term by providing work to keep them away from begging and to generate an income. William Marshall dedicated a work to her outlining how the poor were maintained in Ypres and she was so impressed that at the time of her death, she was in process of implementing a scheme by which regional officials would be sent money to buy "stock there to be employed to the behoof of poor artificers and occupiers."[19]

Latymer especially noted Anne's generosity to those who would today be termed asylum-seekers. She helped a number of people who fled religious persecution in France to not just make a new home but find employment. Amongst those was Nicholas Bourbon whom she brought to England in 1534 having learned he had been imprisoned in France for speaking out against papal authority.[20] After her fall, Bourbon paid tribute to her bravery in doing this, writing "No one would be able to, or would dare to, bring help, only you oh Queen: you, oh noble nymph both can and will dare, as one whom the King and God Himself loves. How can I express my thanks, still less, oh Queen repay you? I confess I lack the resources but the spirit of Jesus which inflames you utterly, He has the wherewithal to give you your due." She then employed Bourbon as a tutor to four boys, all of whom were around ten years old. They included the sons of Henry Norris, of Nicholas Harvey, of her sister Mary Carey and of John Dudley.[21]

As Queen, she was required to wash the feet of the poor toward the end of Lent, a service designed to remind the most powerful of how Jesus had washed the feet of his disciples at the Last Supper. Given that Anne does not seem to have been naturally inclined to humility, this must have been difficult for her, but she did it, kneeling on the floor, washing and drying the feet and then kissing them. After this, she would distribute the Maundy money, a set

---

17 Latymer, *Cronickille*. pp. 44-45, 51. The making of shirts and smocks is confirmed by George Wyatt, Samuel Singer (ed.) *Life of Cardinal Wolsey*, vol. 1 (1887) p.445 and by John Foxe, *Acts and Monuments*, ed. Stephen Cattley, vol.5 (1846) pp.60-61.
18 Foxe, *Acts and Monuments* vol. 5 p.60
19 Foxe, *Acts and Monument* vol. 5 p.135. Marshall's work was entitled the *Form and Manner of Subvention of Helping for Poor People.* In the Parliament after her death, an Act was passed for the relief of the poor nation wide.
20 Latymer, *Cronickille* p.56
21 E. Ives, 'A Frenchman at the court of Anne Boleyn', *History Today*, August 1998, pp.22, 25. To write so positively within two years of her execution for adultery, incest and treason, indicates that Bourbon had no doubts that she was innocent of all charges.

sum for each person, there being one there for each year of her life. Latymer notes how Anne decided to augment the usual sum by a further 6s 8d, an increase of some twenty per cent.[22]

Christine's next set of requirements related to the queen as a wife. It is impossible to know exactly what is going on in anybody's marriage but Anne did make a few comments which give a hint as to her relationship with Henry. Around five months before she died, she told her aunt "I have daily experience that the King's wisdom is such as not to esteem" repentance when somebody has no choice.[23] In the Tower, she queried whether her husband was putting her through such a traumatic experience "to prove me."[24] At her trial, following the verdict against her being pronounced, Lancelot de Carles claims she said, "I have always been faithful to the King. I do not say that I am perfect. I have not shown him the humility as I ought to have done seeing his generosity and the great sweetness which he bore me and the great honours he laid upon me. I have often entertained fantasies against him in my jealousy."[25] Henry may have given her reason to be suspicious of him but as Christine would have said, and he allegedly advised Anne himself less than a year after they wed, she should simply have closed her eyes and made no comment.[26]

Infuriating though such an attitude might be to us today, it is Anne's comments about Henry's attitude to apologies and her idea that he would even consider throwing her into the Tower on false charges just to test her love for him, which are truly disturbing. Chapuys may have continually carped on about how Anne was the dominant partner but this would not have been a scenario which she would have recognised. In February 1535, the French envoy reported that she was ill at ease in her husband's company, her eyes forever darting across to him and his councillors demonstrating she believed she was being watched. Moreover, having stressed how suspicious Henry was of the behaviour of the French, she admitted that this was putting her into a worse position than she had held before she married and she told Gontier she dare not speak or write to him because she was afraid.[27] Gontier attributed her state of mind to her concern for Henry's pleasure and desire to see him pleased by the ongoing negotiations, but that her love should generate such distress seemed as worrisome to him as it should us today. Living with a grumpy Henry was evidently not a pleasant experience.

---

22 Latymer, *Cronickille*, p.53. 6S 8d would have been just over three weeks wages for a labourer.
23 LP 10.307.ii
24 LP 10.797
25 Lancelot de Carles, *Trial and Death of Queen Anne Boleyn* (1545) f.36 lines 1001-1009.
26 CSPS 4.2.1123
27 Jean le Laboureur (ed.), *Les memoires de Messire Michel de Castelnau*, vol. 1 (Brussels, 1731) p.412. A summary is in LP 9.174. Gontier quotes her as using the verbs *craindre* meaning afraid, *perdre* meaning lost and *désoler* meaning grieved.

Christine did say that it was part of a wife's duty to send staff to gently admonish her husband if she became aware of him committing a sin or being led astray. There is clear evidence of Anne doing this. She was evidently unhappy about the proposal to close all the smaller monasteries and she sent Hugh Latimer to "induce the King's grace to the mind to convert them to some better uses... to places of study and good letters and to the continual relief of the poor."[28] She arranged a number of sermons on this subject including one by her almoner, John Skip, which was delivered less than a month before she fell.[29]

Anne was also diligent in seeking to find ways to amuse and please Henry. When he was concerned about papal authority, she encouraged people to go in search of books to help his studies.[30] When he was downhearted, she arranged banquets and entertainments for him.[31] At dinner, she would arrange for theological debates to take place. Henry enjoyed these very much and sometimes continued the debate afterwards with people by letter.[32]

Anne's primary duty as queen was to produce a son and heir, as well as preferably a spare. This was made clear at her coronation when various characters stepped forth to sing or recite verses to her. They included:

> O every one that sees these shows, that sees Anna in her passing beauty riding through the city, do you bring incense; and pray first that the crown may sit well on her forehead; then that in a short while she may bless her country and her Prince with a son; finally that, seeing her aged lord surrounded by brave grandchildren, she may with him pass to the starry realms of bliss.
>
> Citizens, make merry, and dance, and pray! 'Tis Heaven gives her to thee, happy Britain. Anon she will bear a brave son to rule by his parents' side as they grow old; nay, already does her child's life beat. Therefore at the behest of Heaven go, Queen, where your lot calls you; take your sceptre, take to you your crown! Hie you to your palace and your Prince's arms, while the streets ring again with songs!
>
> Anna comes, bright image of chastity, she whom Henry has chosen to his partner. Worthy husband, worthy wife! May heaven bless these nuptials, and make her a fruitful mother of men-children.[33]

---

28 Latymer, *Cronickille*, p.57. The author was no relation of the future bishop.
29 LP 10.615
30 LP 5.1564
31 For example, LP 8.876
32 Latymer, *Cronickille*, p.62
33 Frederick Furnivall (ed.), *Ballads on the Condition of England in Henry VIII's and Edward VI's reigns* (1868-1872), pp.382-383, 386

Obviously, Anne failed in this key role and there can be no doubt that this was the chief cause of her fall. Even if Henry had grown to dislike or possibly hate her, if she had given him a couple of healthy sons her position would have been secured, though she might have been sent to live in a separate palace and only joined him in public for special occasions. Anne had three pregnancies during her three year marriage. The first resulted in the birth of Elizabeth, the future virgin queen who reigned from 1558 to 1603. A French poem describes Anne as having an easy labour (the author was male) but being saddened by the child's gender.[34] Neither the second or third pregnancy resulted in a live child.

The second conception took place in November 1533, just two months after Elizabeth's birth. Since Anne would have remained apart from Henry until she was churched in mid October, this indicates a healthy fertility.[35] The pregnancy was revealed in January and by April, Anne was said to be displaying "a goodly belly."[36] A silver cradle was commissioned from the royal goldsmith and she and Henry were described as enjoying life to the full.[37] The royal couple had been planning a second trip to France but at the start of June, Henry decided that he would go alone and leave Anne as regent. The date given for his departure varied from late August to early September, the change of date undoubtedly reflecting some adjustment in when the baby was due.[38] Henry would not have wished to miss the birth and hoped to be able to announce the arrival of a son to Francis in person. The last reference to the pregnancy is on 24th June when Kingston observes that Anne has "a fair belly as I have seen."[39] Something evidently went wrong either on the evening of 8th July or the morning of the 9th because on the former date, Henry was actively planning his journey whilst on the 9th, George Boleyn was suddenly despatched to France with urgent instructions to have the trip rescheduled to the following spring. In order not to cause offence to the French king, George was to say the request

---

34 Lancelot de Carles, *Trial and Death of Queen Anne Boleyn* (1545) f.8 lines 150-157, 169

35 Churching retains its place in the *Book of Common Prayer* to this day, though it has become a less used rite since the 1960s. It is frequently misunderstood as relating to cleansing but the Church's teaching is quite clear that women go to give thanks for their survival of childbirth and hopefully the gift of a new life. The rite looks back to the example of Mary but is not intended as a bloodless recreation of the Temple ceremony as laid down in Lev. 12:2,4-8; Luke 2:24.

36 LP 7.96, 114, 556

37 LP 7.1668, 823

38 LP 7.784, 785, 877

39 LP 8.919. This entry has been mistakenly calendared under 1535. Anne was not pregnant that summer and the letter was written from Greenwich which is where Anne and Henry were staying in June 1534. On that date in June 1535, they were at Windsor.

came from Anne who was close to her time and wanted Henry with her.[40] News of the child's loss was kept secret for some time, though those who saw Anne arriving alone at Guildford at the end of the month would surely have been able to see for themselves.[41] Chapuys had remained in London so he knew nothing about it and he told the Emperor on 27th July the pregnancy was going to plan.[42] It was not until the end of September that he reported Anne had not had a child, and he then claimed this was because she had never been pregnant, going on to say that Henry was so angry at the deception that he had started romancing an unnamed woman.[43] Such a tale shows the way in which Henry's government worked. The King was never wrong and if it was learned that his wife had either miscarried or delivered a premature stillborn son, the Imperialists would have taken it as a sign of God's anger at his repudiation of Katherine, and hence the blame must be laid on Anne. Thus, the excuse was born that the pregnancy had been a phantom of her imagination. It is easy to imagine how Anne must have felt being placed in this role. She had been forced to face the physical and emotional pain of losing a child, one that was probably male judging by Henry's comments when she miscarried in January 1536, and also to endure public humiliation in the face of the court.[44]

What happened at the start of July is necessarily unknown. No official report was made and even if one had been written, medical knowledge of the time was such that it would probably not have revealed much to us today. She may have suffered some internal damage because it was almost fifteen months before she conceived again and during this period came the first signs of stress in the royal marriage. Henry was said to be flirting with other women and Anne was described as showing visible signs of strain and hysteria.[45] Henry's desire to see Elizabeth married to Francis' son, Angoulême may indicate that he lacked confidence that Anne would conceive again. In May 1535, he commented that the idea of sending the young prince to England had been discussed by the two kings at Calais late in 1532 and that then "there was no such just urgent nor honourable cause (saving only amity) to require the same, as there now is." Henry wanted Angoulême sent immediately and only if the French "will by no mean, reason nor persuasions be allured nor induced to condescend thereto" should they suggest he come in 1540 when Elizabeth would be seven and the betrothal take place. He acknowledged that the French might refuse on grounds that Henry might have sons of his own by then and

---

40 LP 7.958, 965
41 LP 7.989. When Henry's bastard son Richmond died in July 1536, he tried to keep that secret too.
42 CSPS 5.1.75
43 CSPS 5.1.90
44 In February 1535, a drunken woman in Suffolk was arrested for saying that Anne had given birth to a stillborn child the summer before, LP 8.196. There is nothing to suggest that the woman had any actual knowledge of the event but it shows the existence of gossip around the country.
45 LP 7.1257, 1369; LP 8.48, 174

said if that was the case, Elizabeth could go to France instead. Yet his desire to have Angoulême educated in England was because he might "succeed the King's Highness in the Imperial Crown of this Realm in the right and title of the said Lady Princess."[46] Had he genuinely expected Anne to bring forth sons, it is hard to see why he would have placed such urgency on Angoulême's arrival.[47]

In the event, the talks for Elizabeth's marriage to Angoulême failed at the end of June 1535 and Anne became pregnant again in mid October of the same. This third pregnancy lasted seventeen weeks and ended with the miscarriage of a male foetus.[48]

Anne shows every sign of having been a devoted mother. She visited Elizabeth regularly.[49] In her last month, she not only made arrangements for her daughter to be cared for – significantly not by her family but by her chaplain, Parker – but purchased a number of garments and caps for her.[50] Prior to her marriage she had expressed a desire for a large family describing children as "the greatest consolation in this world."[51] Sadly for her, that was not to be.

Her marriage to Henry made Anne stepmother to two teenage children. Mary was then sixteen and Richmond thirteen. The stereotypical image of young people portrays them as moody, obstreperous and self absorbed. Mary was all these things: indeed, the truculent teen was very much the step-daughter from hell. Her first encounter with Anne would have been in June 1522 when both were involved in the celebrations of the Emperor's visit but it is improbable that the six year old Mary would have noticed her. Like other royal children, Mary had her own household so was not regularly at court except at Easter and Christmas. In September 1525, she visited her parents at Ampthill but there is no reason to suppose Anne was there.[52] Thereafter, until May 1527, Mary was in Ludlow so she was not a witness to Henry's growing interest in Anne.[53] After that brief visit to court, Mary departed again and it is unknown

---

46 SP vol.7 pp.610, 612. A summary is in LP 8.793
47 On 1st March 1534, while Anne was pregnant, the only legitimate male heir to the throne, Henry Brandon who was the eleven year old Earl of Lincoln and the King's nephew, died, LP 7.281. This would have made the situation particularly dangerous. The only heirs were a legitimate six month old baby girl and Henry's two bastards, Mary and Richmond.
48 LP 10.282.
49 For example, P 7.171, 530, 1297
50 LP 10.913; J. Bruce and T. Berowne (eds.) *Correspondence of Matthew Parker* (Parker Society, 1853) p.59
51 CSPS 4.1.224
52 Frederick Madden, *Privy Purse Expenses of the Princess Mary from December 1536 to December 1544* (1831) pp.xxx, xlii
53 Mary did visit her father again in September 1526 at Ampthill and it is just possible that Anne was present though far from certain, SP vol.1 p.177. Even if Anne had been at court, it is unlikely that her duties would have seen her path cross with the ten year old Mary.

when she first got to hear of the proposed annulment. In the summer of 1528, she was with her parents at Ampthill while Anne was at Hever suffering from the sweat. Until the end of 1533 when she was stripped of her royal status and moved into the household of Henry and Anne's daughter Elizabeth, Mary continued her peripatetic movement from one royal household to another. She barely saw either of her parents and certainly had no opportunity to get to know Anne Boleyn. The fact that the two barely met, combined with all the tales being poured into Mary's ears that Anne was the wicked woman seeking to break up her family, meant that the relationship of step-mother to child was almost doomed from the outset. Anne tried to extend a hand of welcome but her overtures were rudely rebuffed.[54]

Although Chapuys preferred to claim that Anne was the instigator of Mary's separation from her father and the source of the harsh treatment he alleged she received at the hands of Anne's aunt who was put in charge of the household, it is clear that Henry was the driving force behind it all. His intention had been to leave Mary as legitimate but her stubborn refusal to accept instruction on the case meant his attitude changed. Mary owed him obedience as his daughter and as his subject she was required to abide by the law: her complete denial of Anne's title of queen was treason. Her chaplains and mother were quick to tell her that she should not exercise her mind in thinking about the Bible in case she draw a conclusion which was not in line with the views of Rome but they encouraged her to exert her personal, untrained judgment in terms of the law.[55] Mary's stance was criminal and unreasonable. It was like the Prince of Wales today announcing that he was not prepared to have any contact with the governments of India or Pakistan because he had unilaterally decided that he was not willing to recognise the statutes passed by Parliament which recognised the independence of those two countries. How was Anne supposed to act toward such a child? If she did lose her temper and comment that Mary deserved execution – and the alleged comment was passed on at least third hand by Anne's enemies – she was doing no more than telling the truth.[56] If Henry had been aware of how Mary was plotting with Chapuys to secure her own removal into the hands of his enemy, the Emperor, her fate would have been sealed. It must have been extremely difficult for Anne to cope with this wilfulness and the only saving grace must have been that she did not have to share her home with the girl.

Yet, Anne continued to try to build a relationship with Mary. At the start of 1536, she wrote to her aunt observing "considering the Word to God to do good to one's enemy, I wished to warn her" of the consequences of disobeying

---

54 CSPS 5.1.22
55 Frederick Madden, *Privy Purse Expenses,* p.lvii. Her mother told her to "go no further with learning and disputation in this matter" and "meddle nothing." LP 6.1126
56 LP 8.1105; CSPS 5.1.141

her father.[57] When Katherine died, she sent a message to her vowing that if Mary would only relent, she would do her best to be a second mother to her.[58] Mary's response was to ignore the gesture and proclaim that she would rather die.

In Mary's defence, it could be argued that she was just the victim of the vicious public separation of her parents and certainly the trauma of such an event would have generated scars. In more recent times, Prince Harry has spoken of his mental problems following the equally public and acrimonious breakdown of his parents' marriage. Whether Henry's annulment was transformative or whether Mary was naturally prone to obstinacy, histrionics and a refusal to accept advice like her mother, can never be known. She may have had psychiatric problems like her maternal aunt, Juana. In 1535, it was reported that Mary believed herself to be the wife of the Dauphin and publicly expressed her confidence that he would soon come to take her away.[59] She had been betrothed to him when she was two but that had lasted only a couple of years.[60] In 1521 she was betrothed to the Emperor to whom she sent an emerald ring in March 1525 saying she hoped he was being faithful to her.[61] Following the Emperor discarding her, she was promised to Duke of Orleans in May 1527, this at an age when she was fully aware of what was happening. Why then in 1535 she should have thought she was the legal wife of the Dauphin is impossible to imagine.

It is important not to impute Mary's later bloody character to the years she spent as Anne's step-daughter even though indicators of intolerance might be seen. The best indicator of Mary's nature at this time is to be found in an incident which occurred a month after Anne was executed. It was then that Mary finally agreed to obey her father and she took an oath on the Bible promising to abide by the laws of England. This meant recognising that her parents' "marriage" had been invalid from the outset and that the pope had no authority outside his own diocese of Rome. No sooner had she signed the papers but she appealed to the said pope for an absolution.[62] It was wilful treason. She smiled dutifully at the King whilst behind his back she made contact with England's greatest enemy. Faced with a step-daughter of such mentality, there was no hope for Anne ever making progress with her.

Much less is known about Anne's relationship with Henry Fitzroy, the Duke of Richmond. She saw a lot of him because he was often at court and the premier peer in the kingdom as well as being married to her cousin, Mary Howard. She sent him gifts each New Year including a bay horse with saddle, a

---

57 LP 10.307.ii.
58 LP 10.141.
59 LP 9.566
60 LP 3.4504
61 LP 3.1150, 1802; 4.1240
62 LP 11.7.

silver salt and a ring, a cruse and a bonnet.[63] No records survive of what he sent her. When Anne fell, Henry told his son that she had planned to kill him but no evidence to support such a claim has survived and there is no way of knowing if Richmond believed it. It is likely that the relationship between Anne and Richmond was cordial but not especially warm. Neither probably felt that they had much in common with the other and Richmond's presence was a constant reminder of Anne's own failure to bear a son.

Being Queen meant managing a household of at least two hundred people and Anne's goal was to run a tight ship. She permitted no arguments, fights or immorality amongst her staff and insisted that they attend divine worship on a daily basis. If people disobeyed, she would allow two or three private admonitions before resorting to a public dressing down. She told her managers that if the person continue to disobey and be "found void of grace and without hope of recovery, you shall banish and expel them from my court, never to be admitted again within the precincts of the same." Her chaplain said that "many times" she summoned her Maids of Honour to her chamber to "give them long charge of their behaviours and telling off for spending time in vain toys and poetical fantasies."[64] Her silkwoman, who served other queens, said she "never saw better order" than amongst Anne's ladies who were kept so busy they had no leisure for vain pastimes.[65] Anne was not, however, one of those who demand "do as I say but not as I do." She urged her chaplains to correct her if she behaved in an inappropriate manner because she wanted to yield "good example to others." She also made a point of reading from the English Bible which she had set up on a lectern in her apartments for them to read.[66]

Anne was not an uncaring employer. When Mrs Jankyn heard that her husband, who ordinarily worked in the Queen's pantry but was away sick, was in need of her attendance at his bedside, Anne not only told her to leave immediately but provided her with horses and a year's wages to cover the costs of the journey and extraordinary medical expenses.[67] When the uncle of her receiver-general's wife faced poverty due to old age and infirmity, she sent to Lord Lisle in Calais urging him to send a man to him to discover his needs and to meet them. Just over a month later, it was reported that this had happened.[68] She also believed in being generous to her staff considering them first for any vacancies which came her way. She explained: "since I enjoy their service they may have some portion of my living."[69]

---

63 Beverley Murphy, *Bastard Prince* (2001) pp. 127, 149, 153.
64 Latymer, *Cronickille*, p.62
65 Foxe, *Acts and Monuments*, vol. 5, p.61
66 Latymer, *Cronickille*, pp.49, 50, 60, 62-63. Anne preferred reading the Bible in French but wanted to set a good example.
67 Latymer, *Cronickille*, p.52
68 LP 8.110, 123, 371. George Gainsford was uncle to Anne's maid Nan Gainsford and to the wife of her receiver-general..
69 Latymer, *Cronickille*, p.67

Given the revelations which allegedly came out when Anne fell, it might be wondered whether she really did maintain such a strict household. An often quoted letter is that of her Vice-Chamberlain, Edward Baynton, who spoke of her ladies dancing and having a very merry time.[70] What is less often pointed out is that the letter was written about the coronation festivities, a period which would be expected to involve unusual levels of partying. That there was music and dance in her apartments does not mean that the atmosphere was ungodly. Many Tudor dances were slow and stately with a bare minimum of human contact. Men from the King's Privy Chamber did visit but the number of ladies in attendance meant they were not unchaperoned. Anne's comments in the Tower about how she had taken Norris and Weston to task for their visits show she did try to maintain order. In this, she was not always supported by the King. When she asked her sister-in-law, Jane Rochford, to dismiss one of her junior staff for flirting with him, Henry promptly countermanded the order and expelled Jane instead![71] A more serious instance of supervisory failure was that of Lady Margaret Douglas, one of her principal ladies, who was courted by Anne's half-uncle, Thomas Howard, and entered into a clandestine marriage with him probably in April 1536. It is doubtful that Anne knew anything about this and likely that the couple took advantage of the confusion about the court as a result of rumours regarding Anne's position in order to go ahead. The union was never consummated and when Henry found out a couple of months after Anne died, he sent both parties to the Tower.[72]

Being queen, gave Anne access to a considerable sum of money which she could use as she wished as well as many opportunities for patronage although she seemed to use these sparingly. She sought the grant of a farm in Caernavon for one of the footmen who served her infant daughter and an advowson in Bristol for her vice-chamberlain and chaplain.[73] A set of accounts for 1534-5 reveals that her income from land was just over five thousand pounds. Of this, a fifth was spent in wages and annuities, five per cent in New Year gifts, almost an eighth on her stables and thirty per cent on charity.[74]

She received requests for help, though usually she was seen as a secondary source of assistance. In 1534, the earl of Oxford asked her to follow up on a request which he had made to the King two years before.[75] Lady Lisle was advised to seek her help in a dispute about a weir.[76] Elizabeth Staynings,

---

70 LP 6.613.
71 LP 7.1257.
72 An Act of Attainder was passed against Howard for treason. *Statutes of the Realm* vol.3 pp.680-681. For more on the case see David Head, 'Beying ledde and seduced by the Dyvll', *Sixteenth Century Journal*, vol. 13 (1982) pp.3-16
73 LP 7.89; LP 8.900
74 LP 9.477. In modern money, she had an income of around thirty-five million pounds.
75 LP 7.594
76 LP 8.892

asked Lady Lisle if she could obtain an audience for her with Anne so she could seek her help in obtaining the release of her husband, Walter, from debtor's prison: Henry Norris had already been recruited to petition the King directly.[77] Lady Anne Skeffington sought her assistance after her husband died on royal service in Ireland and she encountered problems getting her goods back to England.[78] Anne also received a petition for assistance in a chancery case, for which an identical request had been sent to Archbishop Cranmer.[79] At one point, she became involved in the very long running saga of Whetyll who had been granted a spear's place at Calais by Henry in 1531, only to be denied this by the Lieutenant Lord Lisle who said he would rather go to jail than employ such a person.[80] Perhaps prudently, she declined to intervene further and the arguments continued after her death. Two people who did win her favour were Thomas Winter, Wolsey's son and Richard Tracy, son of William whose will had proved so controversial.[81]

Anne was a clear believer in education which she thought would enable a new generation to "order and correct all unlawful and ungodly laws and consequently establish all godly and good in God's commonwealth." She maintained John Bekynsaw who was studying in France as well as various men at Oxford and Cambridge, amongst them the monk John Eldmer, and she encouraged others to do the same.[82] It was noted that any poor student who could obtain a recommendation to her through one of her chaplains was likely to be assisted.[83] Early in 1536, she intervened with Henry to have the tax burden of the University of Cambridge reduced.[84] She founded a grammar school in Stoke by Clare which boasted a number of free places alongside those for fee payers as well as at least eight choral scholarships which were designed to enable bright students from poor backgrounds to receive a bursary to study at Cambridge for six years. The school also offered lectures on the Bible in English and Latin for adults.[85] She expressed the intention that her daughter be taught Latin, Hebrew, Greek, Italian and Spanish so she could judge things for herself.[86] Sadly, Anne's death meant that Elizabeth never received instruction in Hebrew though she did become one of the best linguists of her age.

---

77 LP 7.735, 845. He was freed in January 1535, LP 8.89. There is no evidence that Anne granted an audience and the release of Staynings was credited to Norris.
78 L 10,185, 317. She also asked Cromwell to intervene.
79 LP 7.569, 570
80 LP 7.386. For other correspondence on the case, see LP 5.318.5; LP 6.983; LP 7.533, 1220, 1532, 1535 1540, 1543, 1581; LP 8.14,632; LP 10.406, 635, 669, 672, 707, 708, 789, 1101.
81 LP 7.964; LP 12.2.1304
82 LP 4.6788; 8:710; Latymer, *Cronickille*, pp. 56-57, 59
83 J T Bruce and T T Perowne (eds.), *The Correspondence of Matthew Parker* (Parker Society, 1853) pp.2-3
84 LP 8.1067; LP 10.243, 345
85 John Strype, *Life and Acts of Matthew Parker* vol. 1 (Oxford, 1821) pp.16-18.
86 Latymer, *Cronickille*, p.53

Of course, not all of Anne's time was spent in good works, attending church or distributing patronage. She lived in her own suite of rooms and would have attended mass each day before taking breakfast. Her time thereafter involved business but also reading, sewing, playing her lute, going to watch Henry play bowls or tennis, and when the weather was fine, hunting and archery. She also shopped, spending time with jewellers, merchants and dressmakers as well as commissioning gifts and sending staff on book buying expeditions. In the evening, she would normally dine with Henry and participate in whatever entertainment was planned. This might involve cards, music, dancing or watching some performance, perhaps a short play or a demonstration by acrobats or a wrestling match. Some nights, Henry would go to her room but on others he would return to his own suite where he might drink and gamble with the Gentlemen of his Privy Chamber.

When Christine wrote that good women were sometimes the victims of lies concocted by the envious, she cannot have imagined that a queen would face execution as a result. The idea of enduring misfortune for the sake of Jesus went back to the Bible and Anne accepted this. She told the Ives family who had lost everything that God had chosen them as a vehicle for the demonstration of his power and that he commonly "tries his elect as gold in the furnace by loss of goods, sickness or other adversities that they, in these transitory vanities, should profess their humble acknowledging of greater benefits. Be you nothing dismayed herewith but proceed in your godly purposes and let not the railing reproaches of the enemies of God's glory daunt your undefiled conscience. God will preserve you and raise you."[87] In the Tower, it was her faith which kept her strong. Her first words upon hearing the verdict of death were to thank God and say: "Thou art the way, the truth and the life. Thou knowest if I have deserved this death." Back in her room, she told her weeping attendants that she had no need of solace because she had absolute confidence that she was going to heaven "the happy place of true fulfilment leaving here all unhappiness." She said it was necessary to accept God's will even when one did not understand it.[88]

Overall, it can be seen that Anne tried her best to be a good queen and to make a positive difference to the world. Having supplanted the popular Katherine, she faced an uphill battle for acceptance but it is likely that if she had been granted time, she would have succeeded in winning love and admiration from her subjects.

Question: What was Anne's life like as queen?
Answer
      Some part pleasure, some part privilege, but for the great part, duty.

---

87 Ibid. p.55
88 Lancelot de Carles, *Trial and Death of Queen Anne Boleyn* (1545) f.36 lines 989-90; f.42 lines 1170-1176; f.44 lines 1187-88

Was Anne a Protestant?

In the eyes of John Foxe, the great martyrologist who did so much to expose the horrors of Bloody Mary's reign of terror, Anne Boleyn is portrayed as a champion of the reformed faith. In the memoir written by her chaplain, William Latymer, Anne is seen as a devout and godly woman who based her life on the Bible.[1] Their lead has been followed by a number of later historians who have been inclined to see Anne as some sort of protestant, but was she?

Any discussion of the issue needs to begin by accepting that Anne Boleyn was a deeply committed Christian. Her faith sustained her through the long years of waiting for Henry to marry her and through the dark days in the Tower. Her final words on earth were a quotation from the Bible. In our more secular age, such a way of life can be misunderstood. What do words like church and faith mean? The philosopher Roger Scruton wrote: "Church is not just a place where people get together to announce their adherence to a set of laws or to bone up on the principles of Biblical theology. It is a place where people come to encounter God...The religious life is one lived in the full consciousness of judgment and it requires a constant search for absolution – for the cleansing of the soul that comes when the fault is atoned for and forgiven. We can most easily accomplish this if we recognise that the world is a gift and our life a part of that gift. We are called upon to give thanks and the being whom we thank is the one who grants absolution, since our faults are forms of ingratitude, failures of love. That is the meaning of the two commandments that Christ put above all others and on which 'hang all the law and the prophets.'"[2]

Scruton's answer highlights what faith really meant to Anne. She sought to encounter God and believed that she had an active relationship with him through prayer and sacrament and studying the Bible. She believed in judgment and sought forgiveness through regular confession and absolution. She believed that God guided her actions and was the source of all her blessings, for which she gave thanks, and also of her trials which she attributed to him testing or punishing her. God was not an abstract being but a living person, as real as Wolsey, and moreover, he was a constant presence with her, as inescapable as the darkness that always accompanies the blind. God was not something reserved for Sunday mornings or a useful argument with which to taunt her enemies. It was because she knew God as friend and saviour – and royalty had few trusted friends – that she was always seeking to please him. Naturally, she let him down at times, but that desire to please was the motivating factor in both her life and Henry's. She believed she had been called to be Queen and this awesome responsibility meant she gave considerable

---

1   Maria Dowling (ed.), *William Latymer's Cronickille of Anne Bulleyne (Camden, 1990)*
2   Roger Scruton, *Our Church* (2012) pp.209, 215-216.

thought to her behaviour. Her influential position is why it is so important today to seek to ascertain what she did believe and where she sat in the spectrum of opinions which existed at that time.

Many writers use the simplistic distinction of protestant and catholic to define what they perceive to be the two great parties though some have preferred to use the word evangelical in place of protestant on grounds that supporters of reform in this period rarely adopted all the tenets of protestant faith. Whilst it is true that neither Anne nor her friends expressed the beliefs later associated with Calvin, the word evangelical is not helpful because it remains in use for a particular grouping in the current Church of England, a group many of whose beliefs would be equally foreign to Anne Boleyn, and is also widely used in America for still different views. A better choice of word would be reformed because that sums up what Anne and those around her wished to achieve, the reform of abuses in the Church.

If reformed is to be used of one party, what of the other? The most commonly used word is catholic which is totally wrong and impossible to justify. The Nicene Creed is accepted by Anglicans, Orthodox, Baptists, Methodists, Pentecostals and every other body which acknowledges Jesus as the son of God and saviour and it refers to them all being part of the "one, holy, catholic and apostolic church." It is not peculiar to Rome. The word catholic means universal and refusing to use it for protestants today is discriminatory and insulting.[3] Other writers use the phrase "old faith" which is also deeply offensive to protestants who believe that they are following the teaching of the New Testament and that it is the Church of Rome which represents the new teaching due to its espousal of traditions developed since that time.[4] Given the distinguishing feature of the two groups at the time was acceptance or denial of the authority of the pope as Gardiner observed in his *Of True Obedience*: "this I utterly deny that God ordained the bishop of Rome to be the chief as touching any absolute wordly power: of this is the question: in this point the whole cause consisteth," the two terms used here are reformers and papists.[5]

Notwithstanding the fact that many writers have defined the difference between the two in very basic terms such as a belief in or denial of justification by faith alone, the actual points of disagreement in Tudor times were considerably broader and might be summed up as follows. It might be noted that the questions over which people fought and increasingly died, were not part of the Nicene or Apostles' Creeds which did not mention sacraments or define the method of atonement.

---

3   Clause 26 of the 1087 *Dictatus Papae* defines catholic as obedient to Rome.
4   See, for example, Bullinger's *The Old Faith* (1537) translated by Coverdale (Parker Society, 1844). For more discussion on this work, see Peter Stephens, 'Bullinger's Defence of the Old Faith,' *Reformation and Renaissance Review*, vol 6 (2004) pp.36-55.
5   Quoted in James Muller, *Stephen Gardiner and the Tudor Reaction* (New York, 1926) p.64. Cranmer used the word papistical in the same way, LP 9.592,

Bible

1) Papists believe that access to the Bible should be restricted: reformers believe in the Bible being easily accessible, both in physical terms and through the use of everyday language. In June 1533, Cochleus wrote to James V warning that if it was translated into English, people would read it and use it to decide between papists and reformers with the result that the "majority being carnal" would conclude that Luther and his associates had a truer understanding of St Paul than the pope.[6] The Council of Trent in 1546 upheld the authenticity of the Latin Vulgate on grounds "the lengthened usage of so many ages, has been approved of in the Church, and be, in public lectures, disputations, sermons, and expositions" and advised that other editions offered no "utility."[7] Pope Gregory VII ruled: "it was pleasing to God Almighty, and not undeservedly, that the Sacred Scripture should be obscure in certain places, lest, if it were freely open to all, it would perhaps become worthless and would be subject to scorn, or it would perversely lead the mind into error." For this reason he prohibited translation from the Latin and ordered rulers "to resist, for the honour of God Almighty, this vain temerity in all men" which made them seek the Word of God in their own language.[8] Even when an English translation approved by Rome did appear in 1610, the editors described as an "erroneous opinion" the ideas that a vernacular edition was necessary or that the Holy Scriptures "ought or were ordained by God to be read indifferently by all."[9]

2) Papists believe that Christians need instruction to interpret the Bible correctly: reformers believe this is unnecessary and that people should use their God given minds to do so and trust in the guidance of the Holy Spirit.[10] The second decree of the Council of Trent in 1546 condemned any who "presume to interpret the said sacred Scripture contrary to that sense which holy mother Church, whose it is to judge of the true sense

---

6   LP 6.608

7   Second decree of the fourth session, April 1546. J. Waterworth (trans.), *Canons and Decrees Sacred and Ecumenical of the Council of Trent* (1848) p.19. In the discussions, the delegates went further claiming the Vulgate represented "more correctly" the Greek and Hebrew texts, not only as they existed but those lost to history, p.lxxxix. A group under Cardinal Pacheco wanted all vernacular translations banned but this proposal was not carried. Vega noted that the Vulgate was not held to be free of all textual errors but was perfect in all matters of faith and morals, p.xc -xc1.

8   Jacques Migne, (ed.) *Patrologia Latina* (Paris 1854) vol. 147 col. 555, translation by Adam Bishop. In 1713, the bull *Unigenitus* described the Jansenists demand for a vernacular Bible as "scandalous, pernicious, rash, injurious to the Church and her practice."

9   Introduction to the Rheims-Douai Bible.

10   See Rom. 14:5; 1 Cor. 10:15; 1 Thes. 5:21

and interpretation of the Holy Scriptures, hath held and doth hold; or even contrary to the unanimous consent of the Fathers."[11]

3) Papists use the Septuagint (Greek translation) as the basis for the Old Testament: reformers use the Hebrew original text. The Septuagint includes additional books such as Ecclesiasticus, Tobit, Baruch and is generally more messianic. For example, the Septuagint refers to a virgin giving birth, the Hebrew to a young girl. Crucially, the Septuagint includes 2 Maccabees 12:40-45 which is the basis for the belief in the efficacy of prayers for the dead.[12]

4) Papists believe in the equal authority of "written books, and the unwritten traditions... as having been dictated, either by Christ's own word of mouth, or by the Holy Ghost"[13]: reformers only accept the authority of the Bible. Thus, for example, papists believe that those referenced in the Gospels as Jesus' brothers and sisters were Joseph's children by a previous marriage and that Mary's parents were Joachim and Anna, while reformers deny both statements because they stem from tradition only and not the Bible. Papists, such as More, say that the nature of the relationship was revealed by the Holy Spirit which, being part of the Trinity, makes it true.[14]

5) Papists believe that scripture should be interpreted using scholastic and allegorical methods: reformers support only the common sense meaning of the text. Examples of the former include the dimensions of Noah's ark representing the proportions of Jesus' physical body, and the parable of the Good Samaritan indicating how the inn (representing the Church) offers shelter from the bandits (representing Satan).

6) Papists use the Bible to support their beliefs: reformers base their beliefs on the Bible. For example, Fisher used Psalm 66:12 which refers to passing through fire and water as justification of his belief in purgatory whilst the reformer Frith pointed out that the psalm was written about the exodus.

Law and ceremonies

1) Papists tend to view all things as permissible unless forbidden by God: reformers prefer to restrict themselves only to things permitted by God. Thus papists pour oil at baptism and light candles while reformers dismiss these as empty ceremonies.

---

11 Waterworth, *Canons*, p.19
12 Pole in particular argued for this book to be declared canonical at the Council of Trent, Waterworth, *Canons*, p.lxxxiv
13 First decree of the fourth session of the Council of Trent. Waterworth, *Canons*, p.18. Pius IV placed tradition first with the Bible following in the Trentine Creed of 1564.
14 Thomas More, *The Workes of Sir Thomas More* (1557) p. 143 from *The Dialogue concerning Heresies*.

2) Papists believe in the existence of seven sacraments: reformers accept only two or three.[15]
3) Papists believe that during Holy Communion, the bread and wine become truly the Body and Blood of Christ but only the bread should be distributed: reformers say that the body and blood are symbols of Christ's spiritual presence and both bread and wine should be shared as at the Last Supper.[16] Since papists regard the Mass as a sacrifice, they celebrate using an altar. Reformers argue that the only acceptable sacrifice was made once and for all by Jesus and so they use an ordinary table.
4) Papists believe that worship should be in Latin: reformers that it should be in a language which people understand.[17]
5) Papists believe that the canon law has authority: reformers only accept the authority of the Bible.[18] An example of this is Cardinal Pole condemning Henry for marrying Anne whom he says was in the same first degree of affinity to him as Katherine, something only true in canon law.[19] The Council of Trent declared anathema anyone who believed that only those impediments laid down in Leviticus existed or who denied the Church's right to create their own impediments.[20]

The Church

1) Papists believe that the keys to heaven and hell refer to church discipline: reformers to the preaching of the gospel. In his *Obedience*, Tyndale wrote that they were "nothing else save knowledge of the law and of the promises or Gospel" citing Luke 11:52 in support.[21]

---

15 Baptism and Holy Communion were agreed by all but only Luther accepted penance.
16 Reformers differed widely in their opinions regarding how Jesus was present in the sacrament but all rejected transubstantiation. The issue became much more of a dividing line in the years after Anne's death.
17 In 1563, the Council of Trent admitted that the sacraments could be administered "even in the vernacular tongue, if need be" according to a format which would be issued, Waterworth, *Canons*, p.214. It was to take some four centuries before the Mass was celebrated in English. In a brief of 12th January 1661, Alexander VII condemned all translations of the mass and declared that any attempts to do so would result in an interdict, John McManners, 'Church and Society in Eighteenth-Century France' in ed. Henry and Owen Chadwick (eds.) *Oxford History of the Christian Church* vol.2 (Oxford,1998) p.45
18 Luther famously burnt the canon law.
19 Joseph G Dwyer (trans), *Pole's Defence of the Unity of the Church* (Maryland, 1965) p.188
20 Waterworth, *Canons*, p.194. Canon III
21 William Tyndale, *The Obedience of a Christen Man* (1528) p. liiii. This view echoes Deut. 30:15 where Moses says that God has given the Law which gives life to those who choose to keep it and death to those who disobey.

2) Papists believe in a sacerdotal priesthood: reformers in the ministry of all believers. This caused papists to define the Church as the organisation rather than the entirety of its members. When More claimed Henry VIII had broken the first clause of Magna Carta "that the English Church shall be free, and shall have its rights undiminished, and its liberties unimpaired" he was thinking thus. By contrast, Henry recognised that the Church included the laity which meant they had rights over the clergy in some areas and over property.
3) Papists believe that the pope has authority over the entire Christian Church: reformers believe that he is simply the Bishop of Rome and his pastoral responsibilities and authorities do not extend beyond his own diocese.
4) Papists believe that the Church is of necessity a single entity because it is the body of Christ on earth and Jesus had one body with one head: reformers believe that the body is made up of many members all of whom have a role to play. Those members include national and regional churches as well as the eastern Orthodox tradition. Reformers see the Church on earth as having many members and regional leaders united under one divine head.
5) Papists stress that salvation is through Jesus as set forth through his earthly body, the Church: reformers see salvation as being through Jesus' physical body when on earth and mystical body in heaven.[22]

Salvation

1) Papists believe in the necessity of faith and works for salvation: reformers in justification by faith alone. To reformers, good works are simply the result of faith and evidence of the Holy Spirit within, a thanksgiving for salvation and not a contribution toward it.[23]
2) Papists believe that Christians can merit God's favour either through their own good works or through the intercession of the saints: reformers believe that everything comes only from Christ and people can earn no merit whatsoever.[24]
3) Papists define the righteousness of God as his just punishment of people for their sins: reformers define it as the imputation of God's own inherent righteousness to humanity as an act of love. Righteousness is not therefore something to be earned but a passive acceptance through faith which itself comes from grace.[25]

---

22 It is significant that followers of Jesus are called Christians and not Churchians.
23 Canon IX of the Council of Trent declares that anyone who says that nothing but faith is required is anathema, Waterworth, *Canons*, p.45
24 See the papal bull of 1343 *Unigenitus Dei Filius*
25 The tension between the two aspects of God as judge and loving father is something which has occupied theologians for centuries. Anselm, some four centuries before Anne was born, expressed the dilemma – to be just, God must punish sin to show it

4) Papists believe that remission of punishment can be bought through indulgences and gifts made to the Church: reformers oppose any such thought of mercenary transaction and see all punishment due as being removed by forgiveness which is freely given through grace by a loving God. The reformers Roy and Barlow wrote: "Of Christ our merciful Saviour, they make a judge full of terror only threatening our damnation, whose favour as they falsely fain we cannot be able to obtain without saint's mediation. They say that holy men's suffrages, pardons, masses and pilgrimages for sins make satisfaction. They bid us in our works to trust whereby they say that we must deserve our salvation. Faith little or nothing they repute."[26]

What then can be said about Anne's position on any of these points? She left no written testimony so we are forced to try and piece together her views based on her actions in life and things she is supposed to have said. This last category is particularly difficult because it is impossible to know if her words were accurately recorded and attention is needed to the context. Considerable focus has been laid on words spoken by her in the Tower but words spoken at times of severe stress may not truly represent regular opinions. Many people today on learning they are terminally ill might complain that it is not fair and they do not deserve what is happening – though if asked at any other point in their life whether they thought that all the good things they enjoyed in life were signs of God rewarding them for their faith and the bad things indicators of punishment for sin, they would almost certainly have said no, and quite possibly added they did not believe in God anyway. Similarly, it has been said that when men go over the top into battle, there are no atheists, even though they might have been quite numerous six months before in the comfort of the mess room. Moreover, opinions change as people develop. What Anne thought in 1526 may not have been the same as she thought in 1536. Faith is not a "tick box" exercise, a case of believe that, believe that etc. It is about a personal relationship with the Almighty and nobody at the time, and certainly nobody since, can know what Anne or Henry or anyone else said in their private prayers. Nonetheless, aware of the problems involved, it is important to make the effort because Anne's faith was a vital part of her life and if we want to understand her as a person, we need to try to discover her feelings on these matters.

---

is serious, but to be loving, God must forgive. It is important to recognise that imputation does not make someone righteous just as electing someone to a golf club does not instantly make them an expert player: rather it confers upon them the rights of membership and the opportunity to improve their game.

26 *Rede me and be not wroth* (1528) lines 1409-1421.

Anne and the Bible

Anne was a passionate advocate of Bible translation. She used a French version herself but she set up an English one in her chambers for her maids to read, and used it herself occasionally to encourage them.[27] Long before she became Queen, she read the epistles of St Paul in French.[28] She later owned a copy of the epistle and gospel readings for each of the Sundays of the year with the text in French and the commentary in English plus a French psalter and a French translation of the book of Ecclesiastes.[29]

To us, this may not seem too remarkable but Anne did this at a time when vernacular translations were prohibited by Article VII of the 1408 Constitutions of Oxford unless they had been sanctioned by the bishops, which they had not been. Anyone who read such a work, be it publicly or privately was to be excommunicated and if the translation was deemed heretical, the law of 1401 specified the punishment to be burning alive at a stake. She owned a copy of Tyndale's New Testament (1534 edition) which survives and the English Bible referenced by Latymer must have been that produced by Coverdale in 1535. Henry, advised by Skip, Shaxton and Latimer who would all go on to serve Anne, had pronounced Tyndale's work to be heretical in May 1530. The chief reason for this was that Tyndale had chosen to use words which accurately reflected the Greek original but which were not in line with the teaching of Rome, e.g. congregation for church, repentance for penance, elder for priest, love for charity.[30] Thomas More had devoted thousands of words to condemning Tyndale over this, not because he thought Tyndale had misunderstood the Greek but because he said the changes were misleading and liable to result in disobedience to Rome and schism. Congregation, for example, could be used of any gathering including infidels and was not exclusive to Christians while repentance meant a change of heart and was distinct from the sacrament of penance which Rome taught was necessary for salvation.[31] Moreover, Tyndale's New Testament included marginal notes and introductions to each book. Many of these notes were uncontroversial and

---

27 Latymer, *Cronickille*, pp.62-63. Anne's lack of Latin meant she could not have read the Vulgate.
28 Witnessed by Louis de Brun during Lent, 1529, Eric Ives, *Anne Boleyn* (1986) pp.316-317.
29 James P Carley, *The Books of King Henry VIII and his wives* (2004) pp.125, 128. The presence of Anne's coat of arms as Marquess of Pembroke dates the *Pistellis and Gospelles* book to late 1532.
30 For example, congregation in 1 Tim. 3:15, repentance in Luke 15:7, elders in Titus 1:5 and love in 1 Cor. 13:13. Tyndale's work did not include verse numbers but they have been used here for ease of reference.
31 Gregory Martin, *Discoverie of the Manifold Corruptions of the Holy Scriptures* (1582) took the same line. What mattered was not the accuracy of the translation from the original sources but its consistency with the doctrine as defined by Rome and its contribution to religious experience.

merely explanatory of unusual words but some, particularly those in Romans, staunchly opposed the concept of salvation by works, for example "deeds are an outward righteousness before the world and testify what a man is within, but justify not" (Rom 2:130), "in works may no faith be put for by them no man is justified before God, but by Christ's blood only" (Luke 17:10). Against a passage in which Jesus condemned the pharisees for creating regulations which prevented people approaching God, the note read "the false and wicked doctrine of the papists" (Luke 11:52).

Coverdale's Bible had been dedicated to Henry but was equally offensive to the papists. Not only did it use the same contested words such as congregation and love, but it had a title page which showed all the disciples being sent off with keys, an image captioned with the text of Mark 16:15 "Go ye into all the world and preach the Gospel." For the papists, who interpreted Matt. 16:19 as a gift of the keys to Peter and his descendants alone this was clearly heresy, though the reformers could justify it by Matt 18:18 and John 20:23 when the keys were given to the disciples as a group.

Thus, Anne's possession of these two works, and her public display of the latter and encouragement of people to read it without seeking the interpretation of a priest, showed her not only flouting the law but firmly identifying herself with the reformers.[32] The idea of reading the Bible itself would have seemed unusual to her contemporaries. In a survey of 869 clergy in the diocese of Norwich covering 1500 to 1550 just ten possessed Bibles.[33] During training, they would have chiefly read the *Glossa Ordinaria* and *Sentences* of Peter Lombard rather than the Bible and in parish ministry, they would have used the Breviary and Missal. Anne's uncle, the Duke of Norfolk, Henry's leading noble adviser, famously boasted that he had "never read Scripture in English nor ever would."[34] As a humanist prince and keen student of Erasmus, Henry was not opposed to the idea of vernacular scriptures and had queried whether an authorised English translation should be produced in 1530.[35] Matthew Parker said that Anne strongly encouraged him in this idea and it is possible that his researchers for the *Collectanea Satis Copiosa* uncovered

---

32 Tyndale included what is known as the Johannine comma, a phrase added to the Vulgate in the sixth century which mentioned "the Father, the Word, and the Holy Ghost: and these three are one." The words were first quoted in Greek in 1215 and added to a Greek manuscript of the New Testament held in the Vatican by a copyist in the late fifteenth century. Erasmus had excluded them in the first edition of his Greek New Testament but pressure from Rome had forced him to restore them in the later edition which Tyndale used. In Coverdale's edition and the Great Bible authorised by Henry in 1539 to be set up in parish churches, the words appeared in brackets to show they were not original. For more detail on this subject see Bruce M. Metzger, *A Textual Commentary on the Greek New Testament* (Stuttgart, 1993).
33 Derek Wilson, *The People's Bible* (2010) pp.15-16
34 LP 16.101
35 *Hall's Chronicle* p.772

evidence of Anglo-Saxon translations which might have reassured Henry of the provenance of such a plan.[36]

Not only did Anne publicly use a vernacular Bible, she did her best to support those involved in the publication and illegal importation of such works. In May 1534, she had Richard Herman, an English merchant in Antwerp who had lost his livelihood because he had "with his goods and policy help the setting forth of the New Testament in English" restored.[37] In 1528, she had urged Wolsey to forgive Thomas Garrett, the parson of Honey Lane, who had been suspended for owning heretical books which were unspecified but probably included Tyndale's work.[38] She received a petition from Thomas Alwaye which cited her support for others who had suffered for possession of the same.[39]

Her beliefs about scriptural interpretation are also made clear in a letter from Cranmer to Latimer where he advises him that when preaching before her, he should stick to the plain and literal meaning of the text and avoid allegorical or anagogical approaches.[40] This was a view she shared with Henry whose fondness for quoting Nicholas of Lyra, a keen proponent of this approach, is evident. She firmly believed that clergy should preach, something very few did. To this end she encouraged the appointment of reforming bishops such as Latimer, Shaxton and Goodrich whilst also vowing that as long as she had breath in her body, she would not allow "poor gospellers" to perish.[41] When Edward Crome, whom she had appointed as vicar of Aldermanbury, failed to take up his new role in what she considered a reasonable period, she wrote to berate him saying that his duty was to go and further virtue, truth and godly doctrine, things which were lacking and which made his immediate resort to the parish imperative.[42]

---

36 In the Anglo-Saxon era, the Venerable Bede had translated the Gospel of John and at Lindisfarne, a monk wrote a word for word translation below the Latin text of the Gospels to help students. King Alfred had the first fifty psalms, the four Gospels and Exodus chapters 20 to 23 translated into English.
37 LP 7.664; LP 9.746
38 LP 4. Appx.197
39 Ives, *Anne Boleyn*, p.315
40 LP 7.29
41 Latymer, *Cronickille*, pp.55, 59
42 LP 7.693. Crome had been investigated three years earlier for suspected heresy and forced to confirm he accepted the use of images, prayers for the dead, intercession of the saints and that a vernacular Bible was unnecessary where truth necessary to salvation might be known to the people by other means, such as through the sacraments, LP 5.129.

Anne and law and ceremonies

That Anne believed that the Bible was the supreme judge in cases of marriage impediments and not the canon law can be safely presumed from the fact of her own marriage to Henry.

There is no reason to suppose that she questioned the validity of any of the sacraments. When someone sought to dedicate a book to her which questioned the mass, she refused permission.[43] In the Tower, Anne asked for the sacramental bread to be left in her closet, a clear indicator that she believed that it had been transformed into the body of Christ.[44] Protestants would not feel any requirement for this believing that Christ was everywhere and could be prayed to from anywhere.

On the scaffold, she asked for the prayers of onlookers "as I depart to Jesus, in order that the record of my sins does not stain my soul after I am gone."[45] She did not ask for prayers after her death. This may indicate that she had doubts about the doctrine of purgatory.

Although Anne was allegedly sufficiently traditional to consider going on a pilgrimage, there is no evidence that she ever did.[46] On progress in 1535, she sent her staff to investigate the supposedly miraculous blood of Hailes. They reported it was nothing but duck's blood or else melted red wax, which prompted her to complain to the King. The offending object was removed, though the monks put it back after the royal couple had gone.[47] Her objections were based on the falsity of the claims made by the monks which meant that people were being taught incorrect things about the love of God. She did not oppose the veneration of images in itself but did feel that the practice was open to abuse and this is probably why a petition was made to her on behalf of Thomas Patmore who spoke out on the subject.[48]

Shortly before her death, her almoner preached a sermon before the King defending such practices as holy water. It is likely, though not absolutely certain, that he represented her opinion in this, arguing that focus should be kept on the main issues and not on the destruction of things indifferent.[49]

A long standing tradition records that Anne gave her ladies prayer books and there have been various claims over the centuries that particular volumes held in libraries or stately homes are one of such gifts. Although there is no

---

43 LP 10.371
44 LP 10.793
45 Lancelot de Carles, *Trial and Death of Queen Anne Boleyn* (1545) f.44 lines 1229-32
46 The allegation that she had such an idea came from Chapuys who did not hear her say the words himself. Even if she did say them, it is unknown if she was being serious or jesting. Paul Friedmann, *Anne Boleyn* (1884) vol. 1 p189
47 Latymer, *Cronickille*, p.61
48 Thomas Freeman, 'Research, Rumour and Propaganda – Anne Boleyn in Foxe's book of Martyrs', *Historical Journal* vol. 38 no 4 (1995) pp.813-814.
49 LP 10.615

conclusive evidence to connect any of these with Anne, it is entirely likely that she did give them such books. At the time, there were primers which contained the Lord's Prayer, Ten Commandments, Hail Mary, Apostles' Creed and a selection of devotional material such as the Penitential Psalms or graces to be used before and after meals.[50] Some of these were small enough to be worn as girdle books. The key point, regardless of the exact contents, was that the material was in English. Anne was so convinced of the need for people to worship in their native tongue that she went to Syon Abbey to distribute copies of such books telling them the repetition of Latin words which they did not understand was without value and a means of pretending holiness which was inconsistent with humility. Instead she wanted them to use prayers in English "that they might understand what they did pray for and be stirred to greater devotion."[51]

Anne and the Church

Anne was a proud member of the Church of England. It is often said that Henry created this but that is untrue.[52] The church of England began the moment the first convert to Christianity was made in the country, an event which probably occurred a few decades after the death of Jesus. Centuries before Augustine arrived on English shores as an emissary of Gregory the Great, English bishops had attended church councils on the continent, for example at Arles in 314 and the Celtic church was flourishing in many parts of the country. Henry's break with Rome restored the national independence of the church in line with history and the Bible. In Revelation, Jesus sends a message to seven independent regional churches and Paul sent epistles to churches in Thessalonica, Ephesus, Galatia, Philippi, Corinth and Rome. Neither Jesus nor Paul sent a letter to the bishop of Rome and asked him to distribute it, nor did they suggest that the teaching they were sending had to pass through such a person in order for it to be valid. The papacy in the sense that Henry and his contemporaries would have understood it, i.e. as a superior overall authority, did not exist until the fifth century, a time as distant from Jesus' own as the Tudor one is from us. Henry had no concept of creating something new and there is no reason to imagine that Anne ever thought differently. To this day, the Church of England identifies itself as part of the "one, holy, catholic and apostolic church." It baptises people and ordains ministers into the worldwide

---

50 The penitential psalms are numbers 6, 32, 38, 51, 102, 130 and 143. The Ten Commandments existed in two versions, one Roman, the other Reformed which followed the Hebrew division. Without knowing the books Anne gave, it is impossible to say which version she espoused.
51 Latymer, *Cronickille*, p.61
52 The allegation often made that he broke with Rome to marry Anne is also false: he married her first.

church of God, not into itself alone.⁵³ In its Prayer Book, begun under Henry but issued fully by his son, it states that its form of worship shows it to be one with the universal Church though formulated in accordance with English practice. The 1534 Act prohibiting Peter's Pence says that the Church of England will never "decline or vary from the congregation of Christ's Church in any things concerning the very articles of the catholic faith of Christendom or in any other things catholic declared by holy scripture and the Word of God necessary for salvation."⁵⁴

The concept of restoration to an earlier golden age was a crucial part of the reformers philosophy. Generally today, we think of things new as representing improvement but they had little faith in humanity. Original sin meant all were corrupt so the only way of alleviating God's displeasure was to look to the past and seek to recreate what God had intended in Eden and then Galilee.

Anne completely supported the view that the pope was nothing but the Bishop of Rome and had no authority outside his diocese. She told a delegation of abbots that she lamented "to see how obstinately you have departed from God's true religion and forsaken due obedience to your sovereign and most cowardly yielded the same to the usurped power of the bishop of Rome whose detestable sleights and frivolous ceremonies you have taken to be the pillar of your fantastical religion and, like dissembling hypocrites, have ascribed your erroneous superstitions to the censure of the blind pastor."⁵⁵

Anne's books bear testimony to her belief about the nature of the keys and authority in the church. She had copies of Simon Fish's *Supplication of the Beggars* (1529) and William Tyndale's *Obedience of a Christian Man* (1530), both of which were banned.⁵⁶ Mere ownership alone would not be proof of her approval of the contents: many people today have a shelf of glossy cookery books next to the microwave used to heat their ready meals. However, Anne passed both on to Henry with passages highlighted showing she had read them and accepted their arguments. Tyndale's book named the pope as Antichrist and defined the keys as preaching. It provided considerable evidence that the papal claims to universal sovereignty were not biblical and therefore not to be accepted.⁵⁷

Fish described the pope as a warmonger, "a cruel devilish bloodsucker drunken in the blood of the saints and martyrs of Christ." He wrote: "there is no purgatory but it is a thing invented by the covetousness of the spirituality only to translate all kingdoms from other princes unto them. There is not one word spoken of it in al holy scripture." He went on: "if that the pope with his pardons for money may deliver one soul thence, he may deliver him as well without money: if he may deliver one, he may deliver a thousand: if he may deliver a

---

53 As per 1 Cor. 1:2
54 *Statutes of the Realm* vol. 3 p.469
55 Latymer, *Cronickille*, p.58
56 David Wilkins, *Concilia* vol. 3 (1737) p.727; LP 5. Appx.18
57 For more on this work, see December 1530 in Why did it take so long?

thousand he may deliver them all, and so destroy purgatory. And then is he a cruel tyrant without all charity if he keep them there in prison and in pain till men will give him money."[58] Fish condemned the clergy in England as parasites and "strong puissant and counterfeit holy, and idle beggars and vagabonds" who took money and kept it for themselves rather than giving to the poor. He complained that they were above the law, citing the case of Richard Hunne as an example of how if a man criticised them, he would face false heresy charges and even murder with his killers escaping scot free. After comparing their lack of obedience to civil power to Jesus' own obedience, Fish told Henry: "they will not let the New Testament go abroad in your mother tongue lest men should espy that they, by their cloaked hypocrisy, do translate thus fast your kingdom into their hands, that they are not obedient unto your high power, that they are cruel, unclean, unmerciful, and hypocrites, that they seek not the honour of Christ but their own, that remission of sins are not given by the pope's pardon, but by Christ, for the sure faith and trust that we have in him."[59]

Neither book could be construed in any way as supportive of the papists cause.

Anne and Salvation

Anne's good works were legion. She and her ladies engaged in sewing shirts for the poor, following the example of Tabitha (Acts 9:39) and she was prodigious in her almsgiving. In the Tower, she spoke of going to heaven because she had done "many good deeds in my days."[60] This could reflect a papist belief in merit or it could show that she considered the good works she had been enabled to do were signs of God having chosen her and endued her with grace. A marginal note to 2 Pet. 2:3 in Tyndale's New Testament which she owned read "he that hath such works may be sure that he is elect and that he hath the true faith." Jesus had said "by their fruits ye shall know them," a sentiment repeated by John who added: "whoso keepeth his word, in him verily is the love of God perfected: hereby know we that we are in him."[61] Amongst the books which Anne possessed, she had a commentary on Ecclesiastes which said that "Faith, having reconciled us unto the Father doth get us also the Holy Ghost which yieldeth witness in our hearts that we be the sons of God." This faith was then the "means whereof we be well prepared for to keep the law of God which is but love: and without the which it is as well possible for us to keep the said commandments as unto the ice to abide warming and burning in the fire." It was faith which "maketh us good workmen to make good fruits and maketh us good trees for to bear good fruit."[62] Ecclesiastes is an ancient

---

58 Simon Fish, *A Supplicacyon for the beggers* (1529) pp. 6,10
59 Ibid. pp. 3,9,11-12
60 LP 10.797
61 Matt. 7:20; 1 John 2:3,5
62 Ives, *Anne Boleyn*, pp.322-323

work of Jewish wisdom literature so it clearly did not discuss medieval Roman doctrines such as the treasury of the saints, but Anne's possession of the work suggests that she inclined to the view that faith saved and works were a consequence of it.

It is, however, impossible to say conclusively what she meant by her words at the Tower. She was speaking at a time of severe pressure, not reading from a weighty theological treatise which she had prepared earlier. Justification by faith alone might have been a key issue for professional theologians but Anne was not one. She was an ordinary woman, elevated to a rare position, doing her best to make sense of the mystery of grace.[63] Although many modern writers have tried to suggest the distinction between faith and works is a black and white issue and therefore her words represent a clear sign of her religious preferences, this is not the case. Faith today is often seen as a conscious decision to accept a set of propositions such as might be embodied in a creed or confession, an intellectual or emotional act unlike the performance of good works which generally requires physical effort. Throughout the centuries, Christianity has often presented such a view developing a bewildering array of different creeds and articles with members of different churches often being told that failure to adhere to these propositions is liable to cost them salvation. Such a process does not exist in Judaism and it is significant that the word faith does not exist in the Old Testament and where the concept appears, it simply indicates trust. It is clear that when Jesus spoke of the need to believe in himself, he was employing this Jewish understanding of faith as trust.[64] His understanding of religion was covenantal and obedience based. When asked by the rich young man how to get to heaven, Jesus spoke of works and in the parable of the two sons he similarly praised the one who did, not the one who said. He stressed that doing good was the duty of the faithful, not meritorious in itself with grace being pre-eminent.[65] James, brother of Jesus and first head of the Church, writing to Jews, stressed works and denied that faith alone could save.[66] Paul's comment that salvation came from grace alone and not works was addressed to a Gentile community which defined faith as belief and was not a denial of the importance of good deeds which he said followed.[67] The key issue is not the distinction of faith and works but the word 'alone.' Thus Anne's comment regarding good deeds was wholly in line with the Biblical tradition

---

63 In 1602, some seventy years after the Reformation began in England, Josias Nicholls observed it was common amongst those attending church to believe that people could earn salvation by being good. Quoted in Patrick Collinson, *The Religion of Protestants* (1982) p.202
64 John 10:9, 14:6, 17:20-21.
65 Mark 10:17-21; Matt. 21:28-32; 7:16-20; Luke 17:10; Matt. 20:1-16.
66 James 1:22-24, 2:14-18. Modern textual critics would question whether the epistle was by James or one of his followers but his actual authorship was not doubted in the Tudor period.
67 Eph. 2:8-9. At the Council of Trent, Canon 1 denies the possibility of salvation by works alone, Waterworth, *Canons*, p.44.

that faith and works were inextricably intertwined since both were the product of the Holy Spirit. It reflected Cranmer's teaching that faith without works was "only a painted visor."[68] It was not definitively either papist or reformed.

Although negative evidence is always hard to assess, it is worth observing that there are no records of Anne purchasing any indulgences. This is not to say that she never did so, merely to observe that her surviving expenses do not show her spending her money in this way.

Conclusion

Considering the evidence in the four areas, it is clear that Anne was a reformer in many ways. It is worth querying where Anne obtained her interest in the subject. Often, it is suggested that it was Marguerite of Navarre but Anne left France at the end of 1521, before Marguerite is known to have had any enthusiasm for the subject. She may have been influenced by her brother, George, who was known to be a keen supporter of reform. Or she could have developed her opinions based on her own observance of things about her or from conversations with the clergy with whom she came into contact. Anticlericalism in England was widespread at this time and the abolition of papal authority was not accompanied by any mass rallies in its defence, but Christian faith was thriving. A comparison today might be that many express cynicism about politicians but they still believe passionately in democracy. The views which Anne was perceived to hold would have made her appear a threat to the majority of the population who, as Eamonn Duffy's various works have shown, enjoyed a religion which was based on the idea that forgiveness could be bought, that holy water could cure ague and carrying a saint's statue round a field would prevent weeds. Responsible Roman clerics would have branded such things as superstitious or abuses and agreed that reform was needed, but they were a minority. A largely illiterate population valued ceremonies above the printed word and feared change. To be called a reformer, was not generally a compliment.

To try to step beyond what is certain to argue she was either a proto-protestant or conservative humanist is a pointless exercise. Even if we were to know her opinions on every point, the likelihood is that she would not fit into any specific category any more than anyone else. Today, there are Labour voters who agree with some elements in the Tory manifesto and vice versa. There are large numbers of Roman Catholics who do not accept the prohibition on contraception or the doctrine of transubstantiation, just as there are Anglicans who express doubts about elements of the Nicene Creed or actually pray for the dead. There have been Christians of all denominations who have

---

68   J. E. Cox (ed) *The Works of Archbishop Cranmer,* vol. 2 (Parker Society, 1846) p.86

ignored Biblical teaching on providence and spoken of luck. Inconsistency is part of being human and using one's own mind.

Yet, it is important not to discard the use of the word protestant completely. It arose in 1529 when the princes who favoured Luther's reforms protested against the Emperor who sought to prevent them. Those who protested did so on the basis of the following key points:

a) that only a General Council freely summoned – as distinct from one summoned by the pope – could rule on doctrine
b) that the Holy Bible was "holy, divine, invincible, constant" also "pure, clear, clean and right" and contained "all things needful for Christian men to know." That "only the word of God and the holy Gospel of the Old and New Testaments, as contained in the biblical books, shall be preached clearly and purely, and nothing that is against it. For with that, as the one truth and the correct rule of all Christian doctrine and life, no one can err or fail, and whoso builds on it and endures shall prevail against all the gates of hell. Nevertheless, on the other hand, all human additions and trifles shall fail, and cannot stand before God."
c) that rulers have a duty to "give a true, sound answer for our doctrines, lives, governments, conduct and actions regarding such matters, before Almighty God." This involves banning all "things would bring about contention, tumult, revolt and every misfortune among people in general." Instead, each prince must legislate, using the Bible as their standard "for the maintenance of God's Word, and for the souls, bodies, lives and property of himself and his subjects, for freedom, defence and protection" and the promotion of "peace and unity." Failure to do this would mean denying "that He has redeemed us from sin, death, the devil and hell; it will give the Lord Christ ground also to deny us before his Heavenly Father."
d) that "in matters concerning the honour of God, the welfare and salvation of our souls, each stand for himself and must give account before God."
e) that God "will give his Holy Spirit to lead us into all truth; through which we may come with unanimity to a just, true, life-attaining, saving Christian faith, through Christ, our only Mercy-seat, Mediator, Advocate and Saviour."

Taking this declaration of Spiers as the definition of the word protestant, it can be seen that Henry was most assuredly one of them. He believed in the supremacy of general Councils over popes. He considered it his sacred duty to protect the souls of his subjects by leading them into what he believed was the truth as defined by the Word of God even if this meant disobeying international authority. He legislated in line with Biblical teaching and within a couple of years of Anne's death, ensured that a copy of the Holy Scriptures in English was set up in every parish church in the country. Anne lacked the same authority except in her own household and there she too set up a Bible and encouraged her staff to conduct themselves according to God's law. The fact of her marriage to Henry indicates her belief that the Bible contained all that was necessary for salvation and she had no requirement for papal blessing.

Question: Was Anne a Protestant?

Answer
According to the original definition as laid down in 1529, yes. According to later definitions of faith, no.

Why did Anne fall?

This hotly debated topic has produced four main theories. The first is that Henry was a wicked man who deliberately ordered the execution of his wife on trumped up charges in order that he could marry his new love, Jane Seymour. The second is that Henry was duped into executing her by false evidence generated by the machiavellian Cromwell who plotted her downfall in order to save his own neck. Whether he did this because he felt threatened by her criticism of the dissolution process or because he was determined to replace the French alliance with an Imperial one or in order to gain control of the Privy Chamber is something about which the proponents of the plot theory disagree. The third view argues that Anne was somehow to blame, either because she was an actual adulteress or she flirted irresponsibly. A fourth view claims that Anne was a victim of medical ignorance which saw her failure to bear a healthy son in 1536 as the result of sin.

In order to answer the question here, some background will be given to the situation in April 1536 before a detailed analysis of the events from the second half of that month up to the death of Anne on 19th May.

England's relations with the Emperor had been largely acrimonious for over a decade and worsened when Henry formally discarded the Emperor's aunt, Katherine of Aragon, and removed her daughter Mary from the succession; but the Emperor was a realist. As early as February 1534, he had accepted that Anne was there to stay and recognised his need to conciliate Henry to prevent him supporting Imperial enemies in France, Italy, Denmark and Germany. Provided that Henry did not mistreat Katherine or Mary, the Emperor was prepared to posture his opposition to Anne while in reality opposing any further action against Henry by the pope.[1] In fact, Henry continued to stir up trouble in Denmark and Germany and in September 1535 sent Gardiner to France to encourage Francis to start waging war against the Emperor with an offer to fund a third of the costs.[2] The death of the Duke of Milan at the end of October 1535 meant the necessity of making a new alliance with England became the Emperor's new and absolute priority. Everyone knew that Francis would seek to regain the duchy by force and the Emperor wanted to make sure that Henry did not assist him. He faced the problem that Henry knew that the Duke's death had increased England's bargaining power so a new treaty would not be easy to obtain.

By contrast, since 1526, England and France had been in close alliance. Henry had supported Francis in his efforts to obtain the release of his sons from Imperial captivity while Francis had supported Henry in his annulment from

---

1 CSPS 5.1.9.
2 LP 9.443.

Katherine. The relationship had been strained by Henry's break from Rome in 1534 and the execution of Bishop John Fisher which aroused outrage in France.[3]. Henry wanted Francis to withdraw his allegiance from Rome to increase pressure on the pope to withdraw the verdict against himself but Francis was not willing to do this at this particular time. He knew he would need papal support to get Milan back from the Emperor and the affairs of the placards in the autumn of 1534 had created fears of growing Lutheranism in France.[4] Francis told Henry that he would continue to defend his annulment and the legitimacy of his marriage to Anne but he would not join him in any war against the pope, a position he was maintaining to the end of 1535.[5] Francis' stand meant negotiations for the marriage of the young Princess Elizabeth to Francis' son, Angoulême, eleven years her senior, broke down in the summer of 1535. Nonetheless, despite the difficulties, the alliance remained.

Meanwhile, in a personal sphere, Henry and Anne's marriage had begun well with the birth of Elizabeth in September 1533. A boy would have been preferred but the baby was healthy and Anne soon pregnant again. The loss of what was almost certainly a son at the start of July 1534 created a rift between them. As had happened with Katherine, Henry chose to seek solace with other women, though whether any of the relationships went beyond flirting is uncertain. This time, Anne did not become pregnant again swiftly and as the months passed, Henry must have started to doubt. In May 1535, he drew up plans for Elizabeth's marriage which was due to take place in 1540. He said that if he had two living sons by then, she would go to France and be brought up there for her life as a French princess. If, however, he had none and Elizabeth continued to be the heir, Angoulême would need to move to England so that he could be educated in English language, customs and laws ready for when he became king.[6] Nonetheless, it was reported in June 1535 that Henry doted on Anne more than ever and in the middle of October 1535, she conceived.[7] She wrote to her aunt in January 1536 that she hoped for a son and Chapuys confirmed that Henry was also confident this would happen.[8] Although Chapuys was to claim on 25th February 1536 that Henry had not spoken ten times to Anne since the start of December, this does seem unlikely.[9] Henry and Anne had enjoyed their progress in the autumn of 1535 and shown every sign of being extremely happy together. She was carrying what both hoped would be a prince, the birth of which would effectively stop the clamour

---

3   LP 8.909, 985.
4   The placards were an attack on the mass. For more details see R J Knecht, 'Francis I: Defender of the Faith?' in E. W. Ives, R J Knecht, J. J. Scarisbrick (eds) *Wealth and Power in Tudor England* (1978) pp.119-125
5   LP 9.826, 941, 947, 1000.
6   LP 8.760, 792, 793
7   LP 8.876
8   LP 10.282, 307.ii.
9   LP 10.351.

for Mary's return to the succession. Christmas 1535 was probably a very merry affair and Anne had every reason to look forward to 1536.

Two events radically changed the situation both personally and politically in January 1536. On the 7th, Katherine died and on the 29th, Anne miscarried.

Henry's reaction to Katherine's demise was relief: "God be praised that we are free from all suspicion of war." He dressed in yellow and proudly paraded the two year old Elizabeth around the court.[10] He then looked to both France and the Emperor to see which would make him the better offer in return for his favour and an alliance. Anne's reaction was to send a message to her aunt who had care of Katherine's daughter, Mary, asking her to tell Mary that if she would only obey the King, she would try to be a second mother to her. This kind offer to the bereaved teenager was reported to the Emperor by the ever suspicious Chapuys as a feint, Anne simply seeking to gain Mary's trust so she could poison her more easily.[11]

Anne's miscarriage of a son of seventeen weeks gestation was a cruel blow to both parents. Chapuys reported that Henry had been heard to say on the morning of the 29th that he had been bewitched into marrying Anne and he considered the union null and void as a consequence. Proof that it was thus, said Henry, was his lack of sons so he wanted to take another wife.[12] Chapuys thought this speech improbable but what he did not know, and presumably neither did his informer, was that Henry had spoken just after being told the news that he had lost another son: he was distraught and not speaking rationally. It was twelve days before Chapuys learned what had happened and he then claimed that Henry told Anne "I see that God will not give me male children" adding, "When you are up, I will come and speak with you."[13] He also reported that a traumatised Anne had made the situation worse by seeking to pass the blame on to Norfolk for scaring her when he broke the news of Henry's serious fall at a joust a few days before.[14] Chapuys dismissed this argument on grounds Norfolk had told her gently, conveniently neglecting to mention he was not present to know anything about it. Given the universal belief that a fright would cause a miscarriage, it must be wondered why Norfolk chose to tell Anne at all. It was said in France that Henry had been unconscious for two hours, a story that almost certainly was spread from

---

10 LP 10.54, 141.
11 LP 10.141. The Emperor's reaction to Katherine's death was recorded by the papal nuncio at his court: "he danced and celebrated until dawn." Geoffrey Parker, *Emperor* (Yale, 2019) p.246. Chapuys would no doubt have been as horrified by this display from her nephew as the nuncio.
12 LP 10.199.
13 CSPS 5.2.29.
14 Modern medical research has confirmed that stress is a factor in miscarriage and that sons are more likely to be lost than daughters. Alice Klein 'Rethinking Miscarriage", *New Scientist*, 8th August 2020 pp.41-4

Chapuys to Hannaert, his opposite number at that court.[15] If Henry had died, Anne would have become Governor for Elizabeth under the terms of the Act of Succession. Since he recovered, this did not happen but the prospect of Anne in this position may have influenced what was to happen that spring. It would not have been a scenario likely to put joy in the hearts of many on the Privy Council. Most importantly, even if Chapuys was right about the words said after the loss, there is no way of knowing how they were spoken. Was Henry angry or sad? What else was said during the exchange and what happened later? Did Henry and Anne cry together over their shared loss or turn their backs on one another? We can speculate, but that is all we can do because we do not know. A couple who lose a child are likely to experience many emotions and also to want some privacy. It is easy with some imagination and hindsight to develop theories where there is an absence of evidence, but great caution is needed least the theory morph into "fact".

It was on February 17th that Chapuys first mentioned Jane Seymour.[16] He noted that several people had told him that the King had sent her great gifts in the last few days.[17] The story told decades later of Anne miscarrying following the discovery of Jane sitting on Henry's knee was clearly a fabrication.[18] If Jane really had been in such a position, it might be supposed that the couple were alone with the door shut. Anne would not have been walking about unattended which means that Henry and Jane would have had to be so engrossed, that they failed to hear the footsteps and the guard saluting and the door opening in time for Jane to move. Moreover, given that none of the three were likely to talk about the incident, the only way there could have been a witness was if he or she also managed to get through the door remarkably fast. The story's chief value is what it shows about people's perceptions of Henry: they clearly thought he was a man without honour who cheated on his wife. They also had no difficulty believing Jane was a strumpet with no respect for holy matrimony either.

Jane at this time was around twenty-eight. She had joined Anne's staff three years earlier and was granted a New Year's gift in 1534 alongside other maids of honour, though she may not have been at court for the whole period since.[19] She was a second cousin of Anne Boleyn and came from a family with a

---

15 LP 10.294. Chapuys had not thought the fall sufficiently serious to tell the Emperor when he wrote to him on the 29th January though he did mention it to Granvelle the same day, LP 10.200.
16 LP 10.282
17 CSPS 5.2.21. The same letter is calendared as the 10th in LP 10.282 where it says "many say he has lately made great presents" though the original uses *plusieurs* (several) and *ces jours* (these days).
18 Henry Clifford, *Life of Jane Dormer* (1887) p.79
19 LP 7.9. She had not been in Anne's service in 1532 because Lady Lisle's staff were required to explain her identity when she married Henry, something which would have been unnecessary had she been part of Anne's household when she visited Calais in October that year, LP 10.1069. There is a possibility that Jane left court

long history of service to the Crown. One of the many stops on Henry and Anne's summer progress had been at the home of Jane's parents.

On 18th March 1536, Chapuys reported that Henry was still enamoured of Jane and toward the end of that month, he recounted a story which he had heard from both Sir Thomas Elyot and the Marchioness of Exeter, that Henry had sent Jane a purse of gold coins. According to them, she promptly flung herself on her knees protesting that as a virtuous maiden, she could not possibly accept such a present from a married man – before adding the comment that if she was about to marry, she would be happy if Henry would send it back again! Even Chapuys thought this sounded a staged performance and commented that she was being well tutored by Carew and friends. Henry's response, was similarly staged for public circulation. He vowed that he would not see her again except when her family were available to chaperone her.[20] It may be pondered whether this charade was performed because there was gossip that Jane was already the King's mistress. The Exeters were friends of Chapuys so it is also possible that the story was fed to him deliberately in order to encourage him to support Jane's case, it having been revealed to him already that she supported the restoration of Mary.

Yet, the fact that Henry was being unfaithful to Anne – at least in mind – did not mean he had any intention of leaving her. Henry demonstrated his commitment to Anne by arranging for her to be recognised by Chapuys on Easter Tuesday 18th April. This was a hugely significant step. Chapuys' hatred of Anne was infamous and he must have loathed bowing to her but the Emperor had written to him on 28th March specifically saying that she was not to be considered a barrier to a new alliance.[21] Doubtless, Henry wanted to see if the Emperor's alleged desire for amity was real by engineering the confrontation of Anne and Chapuys, but he would not have permitted this public encounter had he thought any disrespect would be shown to his queen.[22]

Following the exchange of courtesies at the chapel door, Henry met with Chapuys to discuss the Emperor's proposals for a new alliance. It was immediately obvious that Henry did not support them. He told Chapuys that Milan and Burgundy belonged to Francis not the Emperor. He said that England's relations with the papacy were none of the Emperor's business and

---

early in 1534 to marry William Dormer but returned when the match fell through toward the end of that year. Such was the tale told by Dormer's daughter: Clifford, *Jane Dormer* pp.41-43.

20 LP 10.601. The despatch is dated 1st April but refers to an incident several days before.
21 CSPS 5.2.40. The summary at LP 10.575 is not entirely reliable.
22 The sight of Chapuys bowing to Anne would have had the added benefits to Henry's mind of reminding the French that his undiluted favour towards them was not guaranteed and of sending a message to Mary's supporters that her position was untenable. Chapuys admitted that this was exactly the reaction which followed, LP 10.699. He commented that the only reason he had not kissed Anne's hand was because he had heard that she was not entirely in Henry's favour, LP 10.720

that if he wanted a rapprochement with Rome, he would use his own ambassadors and did not need any Imperial help. He said his relationship with Mary was similarly nothing to do with the Emperor and vowed to treat his daughter according to her obedience. He then launched into a tirade over the Emperor's ingratitude over the years and his machinations at Rome to prevent Henry's annulment. Finally, he told a stunned Chapuys that unless the Emperor was prepared to write to himself admitting his fault and begging forgiveness, he was not willing to proceed with talks of a new treaty.[23] To add to the injury, Henry summoned the French ambassador and reported the whole day's affairs to him.

Given that Chapuys had been working with Cromwell to try to bring about a new alliance, this left the Imperial ambassador with the proverbial egg on face. He tried to save his reputation by assuring the Emperor that the entire Privy Council supported him and that Cromwell had taken to his bed in sorrow, but it was clear that any hopes which the Imperialists might have had that Henry was about to renounce France in their favour, return to Rome and reinstate Mary, were just pipe dreams.[24] Chapuys was so desperate to argue that he had not misread the political situation totally that he told the Emperor on 29th April that Nicholas Carew's election to the Garter on the 23rd was a sign of Anne's lack of influence, deliberately implying George Boleyn was the only other candidate when in fact there were twenty. That Carew was chosen at the request of the King of France was something which Chapuys knew well and he admitted his in his letter to Granvelle of the same day.[25] He clearly did not think that the Emperor would be pleased to know Henry was doing a favour for France. He also failed to mention that Carew was married to Anne's cousin.

Even if Anne was angry at Henry's behaviour with Jane, she still felt perfectly assured of her position. She continued to intercede successfully on behalf of those who sought her help, such as the University of Cambridge and she was not afraid to use her role to warn her husband when she felt his ministers were exploiting him.[26] Whether she saw John Skip's controversial sermon of April 1st before he preached it is unknown but it is reasonable to assume that it reflected her views. The French, whose ambassadors spent much

---

23 LP 10.699.
24 LP 10.699, 700.
25 LP 10.752, 753. The promise to appoint Carew had been made in June 1533 and confirmed in February 1535 but was first discussed in May 1533, LP 6.555, 707 and LP 8.174. Records of the Garter show that Carew received ten votes and George Boleyn five with George being the sixth most popular choice of twenty nominees. There were ten electors each of whom had three votes. J. Anstis (ed.) *The register of the most noble Order of the Garter*, vol. 2 (1724) pp.398-401. George had also been nominated in 1532 and 1535 and Chapuys had not claimed any political significance for George's failure to secure election on either occasion.
26 LP 10.345, 615.

more time at court than Chapuys, still believed she wielded considerable influence and worried that she might be an obstacle to their plans.[27]

This then was the situation in the third week of April, 1536.

That Anne's fall was sudden and unexpected was universally agreed by contemporaries. There are two key accounts of how it came about. Alexander Ales was in London at the time and he reported that enemies of the Gospel "entered into a conspiracy" which was led by Stephen Gardiner, Bishop of Winchester, who "wrote to those friends whom he had in the Court of the King of England, conspirators like himself, to the effect that certain reports were being circulated in the Court of the King of France, and certain letters had been discovered, according to which the Queen was accused of adultery."[28] His view was supported by the martyrologist John Foxe.[29]

An alternative view is presented by Lancelot de Carles who was also in London at the time and employed by the French ambassador. He recorded that a noblewoman was criticised by her brother for her lax morals and she responded by saying it was unfair to criticise her when the Queen behaved in a much worse manner. She said that Anne frequently slept with her brother, George Boleyn, and told her own brother to ask Mark Smeaton if he wanted to know more.[30]

At this point the two stories merge. The allegations were reported to the King who ordered an investigation. In Lancelot de Carles' version, he warned those who spoke out that if it was found that they had lied, they could expect to face execution themselves.[31] That Henry would have acted in this way is entirely credible and he would have been irresponsible not to take the allegations seriously. It was what he did in 1541 when allegations regarding the behaviour of Queen Kathryn Howard were made.[32] It is likely that he also remembered the practice of his father when faced with such a circumstance, namely that he should "keep it to himself and always grope further" whilst setting spies on the party accused.[33]

Both accounts have something to commend them. Ales was not a courtier but he knew Thomas Cranmer well and his landlord knew Cromwell.

---

27 LP 10.443.
28 *Calendar of State Papers; Domestic 1558-9*, 1.1303, Alexander Ales to Queen Elizabeth, 1st September 1559
29 S, Cattley (ed.), *Foxe,'s Acts and Monuments* (1837) vol. 5 pp.136-7. Foxe noted how Gardiner continually told Henry that Anne would never be accepted by the rest of Europe.
30 Lancelot de Carles, *Trial and Death of Queen Anne Boleyn* (1545) ff.14-15, lines 338 to 372.
31 Ibid. f.19 lines 484 to 486.
32 H. Nicolas (ed.) *Proceedings and Ordinances of the Privy Council* vol.7 (1837) pp.352-355. For fuller accounts see Gareth Russell, *Young and Damned and Fair* (2017) and Lacey Baldwin Smith, *A Tudor Tragedy* (1961)
33 LP 3.1282. Ales confirmed that Anne was being watched.

Foxe's sources included Mary, Duchess of Richmond, one of Anne's chief ladies and Henry's daughter-in-law; Anne's chaplain, Matthew Parker; her silk woman, Joan Wilkinson; and George Constantine who worked for Henry Norris. Ales and Foxe were, therefore, in a better position to know the truth than the likes of Chapuys, but the possibility of interpreting events according to a certain agenda cannot be ruled out either by the authors or their sources. The English have long enjoyed trying to cast blame on to the French and by the time Ales and Foxe wrote, they had witnessed Gardiner's murderous activities during Mary's reign.

Nonetheless, Gardiner was at the French court where rumours were circulating. In July 1535, Francis I had commented that Anne had never lived virtuously when in France and still did not do so, though it should be stressed that his comments were made just after the negotiations for his son to marry the Princess Elizabeth had broken down, something which had no doubt left him angry and keen on recrimination.[34] Even before Katherine died, Francis was said to have expressed the hope that as soon as she did so, Henry would discard Anne and marry his eldest daughter, Madeleine, and when the news broke a month later that Katherine was dead, there was open speculation that this would happen.[35] The pope was told and Chapuys admitted to hearing the reports in March.[36] On May 15th, having just been told of Anne's arrest, the Emperor sent Chapuys urgent instructions to prevent such a match and instead try to persuade Henry to take the Portuguese princess who was young and apt to bear sons.[37] Further credence to the story is given by the French actually offering Henry the hand of Princess Madeleine within a week of Anne's execution.[38] This would not have happened unless they had reason to suppose Henry would favour the proposal which suggests that Francis or Montmorency had raised the subject informally with Gardiner or Wallop and also with Castlenau, their resident ambassador at the English court – who clearly had no idea that Henry's relationship with Jane Seymour was serious.

It may also be that the papal nuncio's famous report that Francis in March 1536 had spoken of one of the Boleyn sisters as "a great ribald, the most infamous of all" referred to Anne not Mary: after all, Mary had only spent some six months at the French court when she was about twelve while Anne had been there for six years.[39] This phrase has been subject to immense scrutiny and a vast amount of hyperactive speculation over the centuries but it should be noted

---

34 LP 8.985
35 LP 9.970; LP 10.170
36 LP 10.601. The story was still being circulated in France in May: LP 10.838. The pope backed the idea seeing it as a possible means of restoring Anglo-Papal relations and was disappointed when Henry married Jane instead.
37 LP 10.888.
38 LP 10.1069, 1070.
39 LP 10.450. Faenza clearly believed Francis was talking about Mary but it does seem likely he was confused. There is no reason to suppose that when Francis admitted to have known Mary years before, he meant in a sexual way.

that the word ribald had other definitions than whore.⁴⁰ It could mean blasphemous. Anne was associated with reformers who might be considered heretics by some but neither she nor Mary could be considered to have held strikingly shocking beliefs in their youth which is the period of which Francis was speaking. Another meaning was disobedient, wilful, lacking in respect for men, preferring to pursue their own ideas and pleasures without regard for others. This was almost certainly the sense meant when Wolsey called Margaret, Regent of the Low Countries, a ribald in 1525.⁴¹ However, the most common meaning in France of ribald at this time was simply low born and it is probable that Francis was making the point that Anne was not of royal blood and hence she was unsuitable – unlike his own daughter – for the role of Queen of England.

Whatever meaning was intended and whichever sister was meant, the key point was that Francis was speaking disparagingly of Henry's Queen and her family to a foreign envoy just weeks before her fall. Ales was almost certainly wrong in believing there was an organised conspiracy but the idea that an Englishman would have conveyed such news had he heard it is certain. If Francis was allowing such rumours to be spread, it suggested that he was not serious in his protestations of friendship for Henry and this presented a risk. If France allied with the Emperor, England would not only be isolated but it could become an object for shared invasion. Certainly, as will be seen, the French were actively involved in Anne's fall, though not necessarily instrumental in it. The fact that no letter of this nature survives does not mean one was not written: the evidence presented against Anne was all destroyed and it would have been amongst it.

Lancelot de Carles' version that the investigation began as a result of an accidental remark by one of Anne's ladies also contains a ring of truth.⁴² Husee said that the principal source was the Countess of Worcester who was one of Anne's leading ladies while her brother, Sir Anthony Browne, was employed by the King.⁴³ An anonymous French chronicler repeats this claim.⁴⁴ Cromwell on 14ᵗʰ May would also say Anne's ladies brought matters to light.⁴⁵

---

40 See the *Oxford English Dictionary*, also Lucas Harrison, *A dictionarie French and English* (1570); John Florio, *A worlde of wordes* (1598). Francis spoke in French and Faenza translated his words into Italian.
41 LP 4.1379.
42 As the English writers blamed the French, so the French blamed the English. Kathryn Howard would later be brought down following an enquiry which was prompted by revelations about her private life from an ex-member of staff, LP 16.1334
43 LP 10.953. William Brereton was receiver for Browne's lands.
44 Nicholas Pocock (ed.), *Records of the Reformation*, vol. 2 (1870) p.675.
45 LP 10.873. The letter clears Gardiner and Wallop of being the instigators of Anne's fall but notes they may have beard rumours of Anne's misbehaviour in France. Cromwell does not name the ladies involved.

Can the two versions be reconciled? It is possible. A letter may have come from France which raised questions about Anne's conduct there before she met Henry while the Countess' comments came after an investigation had started. Accusations that Anne had been unfaithful while Queen were of a much more serious nature. Such a pattern of events would also explain why Anne's fall took place over more than a week. Alternatively, as will be shown below, these two accounts may simply reflect what the government wanted people to think because they were afraid people might otherwise blame the King for instigating it all.

The first event in Anne's fall is usually said to be April 24th when two commissions of oyer and terminer were established, one for Middlesex and the other for Kent.[46] However, something had to have occurred for that to happen and it may be significant that Cromwell was said to have left court on the 21st for some undisclosed reason, though the only source for this is Chapuys and it could be that Cromwell simply used that as an excuse to avoid a further meeting with him.[47] Many staff have been told to announce their master is out when he is in the next room. On Sunday 23rd, the French ambassador spent a long time at court and Henry made the very unusual request that he travel in person to speak to Francis and that he make the journey post, which meant travelling at the greatest speed possible. The French king at the time was at Lyons, some five hundred miles away. Given it was an offence for an ambassador to leave his post without the direct permission of his own sovereign, Castelnau would not have agreed to do this unless something extremely significant had happened. Chapuys assumed that the English were about to make the French some great offer because they were afraid of the Emperor making peace, but he was simply speculating.[48] It is possible that a letter from France had been received and Henry wanted to know if his ally was allowing disrespectful talk about Queen Anne at court. If so, this was likely to led to a serious breach in amity. Or it could be that news had been received of Anne's behaviour in France which suggested she might have entered into a pre-contract there which could be used as an excuse for a second annulment. Henry had disclosed full details of his meeting on the 18th with Chapuys to Castelnau the day after and Castelnau had despatched a letter to Francis on the 19th so there was no reason for him to make the journey concerning that.[49]

If the investigation was triggered by a revelation from the Countess of Worcester, it is difficult to explain why over a week passed before those named were arrested, unless the lady's initial comment to her brother was significantly less detailed than what she subsequently told Cromwell. Yet, there is another candidate for the role of whistleblower from amongst Anne's staff – Jane

---

46 LP 10.8
47 LP 10.700.
48 LP 10.720; CSPS 5.2.47
49 LP 10.688, 759. Henry met with Castelnau on the 25th and 30th April to discuss terms of a new alliance, LP 10.760.

Seymour. On the same day that the commissions were set up, April 24ᵗʰ, Henry bestowed an annuity on Jane Seymour of one hundred marks.[50] This was an enormous sum – more than seven times her annual income and some eight times that of most parish clergy.[51] It is impossible to say why Henry did this but it is incontrovertible evidence of his close relationship with her and the fact that he intended it to continue. Had she provided damning evidence against Anne – it is inconceivable that Henry would not have asked her – and this annuity was her reward? Was it really a coincidence that the annuity and the commission were raised at the same time? There were other possibilities which could have prompted Henry's generosity. Jane may have just agreed to become his wife: it is known that they discussed marriage before Anne was arrested.[52] Had Jane suggested to Henry that she was pregnant with his child? Such a sum would have been sufficient to establish a household of her own. Despite her public performance of being the virtuous maiden when she returned Henry's gold a month earlier and his pronouncement that he would henceforth only see her when she was chaperoned, there is nothing to say that she had not already slept with him. If he thought she was pregnant, it would explain the rushed removal of Anne and his joyful conduct all the time she was in the Tower. There is no evidence that she was pregnant but she could have been mistaken or simply lied. Her behaviour in encouraging the attentions of her employer's husband scarcely demonstrates a sense of ethics. It might also explain why the coronation which Henry planned for her in July was postponed and then cancelled.[53] At the time, it was said there would be no coronation until Jane was pregnant.[54] Whatever Henry's motive for the annuity, it is a very significant event in the story and one which historians have generally overlooked or deliberately suppressed.

Commissions of oyer and terminer were set up on an occasional basis throughout the period to deal with serious cases of treason, murder and revolt in the counties involved. Examples include Thomas More, Bishop John Fisher, the Carthusians, Hale, the Prior of Worcester and for the Kent insurrection of 1528.[55] The precise nature of the suspicions giving rise to the two commissions were not included so it is possible that their establishment at this point was coincidental – though the fact that they only produced evidence against Anne, George Boleyn, Henry Norris, William Brereton, Francis Weston and Mark

---

50 LP 13.1.1520.ii. It may have been agreed a day or two before. The instruction would have been given to Cromwell who would have had to find a clerk to prepare the paperwork for Henry to sign.
51 Michael Zell, 'The Personnel of the clergy of Kent in the Reformation Period', *English Historical Review* vol. 89 no CCCLII (1974) p.529; J. Caley and J. Hunter (ed.) *Valor Ecclesiasticu*s, six volumes (1810-1834)
52 LP 10.908.
53 LP 10.908, 909; LP 11.47.
54 Charles Wriothesley, *A Chronicle of England*, ed. William Hamilton, vol. 1 (Camden Society, 1875) pp.55-56; LP 11, 8, 528.
55 LP 4.4301; LP 8.609, 886, 974; LP 9.90.

Smeaton, would suggest that they had been set up to investigate the Queen. The writs for the commissions were signed by Audley rather than Henry but it would be unwise to infer from this that he did not know about them. The Lord Chancellor was within his rights to establish commissions and if Henry had asked for an enquiry to be made, this was the way to do it.

Although twenty men or more might be named to such commissions, only four were required to act at any time and it appears that in practice, those involved in 1536 were Norfolk who originally questioned then arrested Anne; Cromwell; Audley; the treasurer Fitzwilliam; and Paulet who was comptroller of the household. It is unlikely that the presence of Thomas Boleyn who was named as a member was required except at the final meeting when the results of the investigation were officially handed over by the commission to the grand jury.[56] The job of the commissioners was to investigate. Questions to be asked of witnesses would have been devised by Cromwell and he would also have generated any supplementary questions having read the depositions collected. Based on the commission's findings, Cromwell would have drawn up the charges if he felt there was a case to answer, possibly with the assistance of lawyers. His own legal background might have rendered this unnecessary but in such a high profile case, discussion with the Lord Chancellor almost certainly occurred. The King would definitely have been involved.

The next day, Tuesday 25th, saw the Privy Council meeting from morning to nearly ten at night. Castelnau arrived at court with his bags packed ready to receive his final instructions prior to starting his journey and was told they were not ready for him and he should come back on the 27th.[57]

On the same day, Nicholas Carew sent a message to Mary telling her that she should be of good cheer and that her enemies – by which he meant Anne's family – would soon be putting water in their wine. This last is a rather obscure comment but it could be a case of Chapuys again missing a biblical reference. Jesus' first miracle was the miracle at Cana where he turned the water in containers into fine wine and this was done at a wedding feast. By implying the process would be reversed, Carew was offering a broad hint that the Boleyns would be suffering because Henry was about to make a new marriage.[58]

Also on this day, letters were sent to Pate, the English ambassador with the Imperial court, and to Gardiner and Wallop, the English ambassadors in France.[59] Much attention has been paid to the letter to Pate because it refers to Anne as our "most dear and most entirely beloved wife" and says "there is great likelihood and appearance that God will send unto us heirs males to succeed us."[60] This has been interpreted by some to show that Henry was still

---

56 Judge John Spelman was listed on both commissions but his memoir gives no indication that he was involved until the days of the actual trials.
57 LP 10.752
58 LP 10.752; John 2:7-11.
59 LP 10.725, 726.
60 SP vol.7 pp.683-688.

committed to Anne at this point and anticipated having children by her. Three things need to be remembered. Firstly, this was the conventional description of Anne: it was used, for example, in the Act of Succession.[61] Secondly, the reference to the likelihood of sons was made by Chapuys whose argument to Henry was that whilst sons might be expected, in case they did not come, Mary should be returned to the succession. Henry was just quoting him and not expressing any opinion of his own.[62] Thirdly, although the letter was signed on that date, it had been in production for some days. Cromwell admitted to Chapuys on the 21st that he had been supposed to draft it on the 19th but had been delayed owing to issues arising from letters received from France.[63] Furthermore, although the letter defended Henry's annulment from Katherine, it did not explicitly mention his marriage to Anne. The two issues were separate. Some historians have failed to appreciate this but consider the following analogy. Before an election to a council seat can take place today, the previous incumbent needs to resign or die but it does not automatically follow that the election of a successor is carried out legitimately: fraud may be employed, expenses may be corrupt, the candidate may be ineligible. Similarly, whilst the legitimacy of his marriage to Anne depended on Henry being single at the time, his status did not guarantee that the marriage was legal in every way because more than one condition was required by canon law. Thus, Henry's defence of the annulment cannot be interpreted as commitment to Anne.

By Wednesday 26th with the Privy Council again meeting all day, Anne was aware that something was afoot. She spoke to her chaplain, Matthew Parker and asked him to take care of Elizabeth if anything should happen to her.[64] What she thought might happen, Parker did not reveal but it is significant that she thought the crisis related to herself and not international relations.

Meanwhile, Cromwell sat down with the Dean of the Chapel Royal, Richard Sampson, for extensive talks. Chapuys was told by Sampson's servant

---

61 *Statutes of the Realm*, vol. 3 p.473. Edward IV used this wording on 13th April 1465, Gemma Holman, *Royal Witches* (2019) p.214.

62 "On Tuesday last past repaired unto Us, then being at our manor of Greenwich, the Emperor's Ambassador here resident; and on his master's behalf,... made unto Us certain overtures.... The second overture and request was that, forasmuch as there is great likelihood and appearance that God will send unto Us heirs male to succeed Us in the Crown of this our Realm We would vouchsafe, at his contemplation, to legitimate our daughter Mary, in such degree, as in default of issue by our most dear and most entirely beloved wife the Queen, she might not be reputed unable to some place in our succession."

63 CSPS 5.2.43a. On the same day, Chapuys wrote to Granvelle saying Cromwell had taken to his bed in sorrow that plans for the new Anglo-Imperial alliance were going so badly. Given his letter to the Emperor of the same day refers to numerous communications between himself and Cromwell, it must be assumed that at most it was for a brief nap.

64 LP 10.748; J. Bruce and T. T. Perowne (eds.) *Correspondence of Matthew Parker* (Parker Society, 1853). p.59. It cannot be known if she made similar requests of her family or if she thought they might fall with her.

that it was to discuss plans for him to replace Pate, something he found hard to believe.[65] Sampson had been involved in Henry's annulment from Katherine from the outset and was a respected canon lawyer. He had served as an overseas diplomat in 1529 but he was not a regular traveller on behalf of Henry.[66]

On the 27th April, writs were issued for a new Parliament, even though the previous one had been dissolved less than a fortnight earlier. It has been suggested that this was to deal with extinguishing papal authority but it is not obvious why at this point, such an objective would have been thought so urgent that members needed to be summoned back so soon.[67] Most members were landowners and June was a particularly busy time of year with the harvest soon to start. The proposed act was important but surely could have waited until the autumn or have been handled in the session which lasted from February 5th to April 14th. It seems more probable that the writs were sent out because it was expected that Parliament would be involved in some way in the current crisis, either in redefining the succession or by proceeding against Anne by Act of Attainder.[68] Quite possibly, Henry and Cromwell were uncertain at this point. Presumably early investigations had shown there was a serious issue and they wanted to preserve their options while they awaited further findings. There was ordinarily a six week interval between sending out writs and Parliament actually assembling so the subsequent decision to go for trial rather than wait for an Act of Attainder indicates Henry's desire to have the matter handled swiftly.

The Privy Council met again on the 27th and Castelnau returned as directed to collect his instructions and go to France. He expressed surprise that the message he was to take was nothing like that which he had expected to take and decided to send a messenger instead. Chapuys said that the ambassador was not pleased.[69]

It may be supposed that the Council meeting did not last all day because there is evidence of other business being contracted. Lord Lisle's staff were at court regarding the planned royal visit to Dover where a new harbour was being built. Henry wished to inspect the works and Lisle wanted to take the opportunity to travel from Calais to see him. Henry Norris obtained permission from the King for him to do this on the 27th whilst Margery Horsman assured Warley, one of Lisle's men, that Anne was very much looking forward to seeing Lady Lisle on Friday 5th May. It was said that the royal couple would leave

---

65 LP 10.753.
66 LP 4.3302, Appx.240. Sampson would represent the King at Cranmer's court which annulled Anne's marriage. Less than a month after this, he became Bishop of Chichester, LP 10.1256.19.
67 LP 10.736. E. W. Ives, *Anne Boleyn* (1986) p.363.
68 Anne and George were tried in the court of the High Steward by their peers because Parliament was not sitting. In 1542, Kathryn Howard was given the option of facing trial there but declined hence she was condemned by Act of Attainder, *Journal of the House of Lords* vol. 1 p166
69 CSPS 5.2.47. Castelnau's visit to court is confirmed by Warley, LP 10.748.

London after the May Day jousts and be at Rochester on the 2nd before journeying south via Canterbury. Cromwell advised that he would like to return to Calais with Lisle so he could review work there.[70]

Also on the 27th, Bishop John Stokesley of London was asked about whether it would be possible to annul Henry's marriage to Anne. Lord Montagu, who told Chapuys the next day about this, did not reveal who had asked the bishop, only reported the bishop's sage response that he would only answer that question if it was put to him by the King in person, and even then he would like to know what response Henry wanted in advance.[71] It is impossible to interpret this event without knowing the identity of the querent. If the question was being asked by Cromwell or one of the commissioners, it would suggest that Henry was still considering a solution which left Anne alive and was unaware of it being a case of treason which was punishable by death. Or the person asking could have been one of Jane Seymour's supporters who was aware that Henry wished to marry her but did not know anything about the investigation into Anne. Given that Cromwell was consulting Sampson, it seems more likely that the enquiry to Stokesley was unofficial.

On Friday 28th April, Anne went shopping. The day before, she had bought some fringe for a saddle for Henry's niece, Margaret Douglas. Now, she purchased some silver and gold fringe plus some black silk edging and a set of gold and silver buttons as a present for Henry to decorate his saddle.[72] This may have been intended for the Dover trip or just as a gift. The fact that she was buying him presents just four days before her arrest is particularly poignant. She evidently knew that he was unhappy with her and that he was involved with another woman but the purchase suggests she had no idea that she would be kneeling before an executioner just three weeks later.

While she shopped, the Privy Council met.

Saturday 29th saw Chapuys write to Granvelle to tell him that nothing important was happening in England.[73] The success of Cromwell in keeping the investigation into Anne away from Chapuys who had spies everywhere is worthy of note, especially by those who like to regard Chapuys as a reliable witness of events.

Meanwhile, Anne had an exchange with Mark Smeaton, one of the court's musicians. She saw him beside a window looking miserable and asked him why. He said it was no matter and she told him that he should not expect her to speak to him because he was not a gentleman – a slightly odd comment given she had initiated the conversation. Mark replied that: "A look suffices."[74] It was a completely inconsequential exchange which Anne revealed while in the Tower. She said it was the first time she had spoken to Mark since she and Henry had returned from their progress in October 1535. She mentioned it

---

70   LP 10.738, 747, 748.
71   LP 10.752
72   LP 10.913.
73   LP 10.753
74   LP 10.798.

when expressing her mystification why anyone should accuse her of committing adultery with Mark: he had only entered her privy chamber once in all the time she had been queen.[75] In 1541, Thomas Wyatt would similarly speak of the effect of sudden imprisonment and the impact it had on the mind, commenting on his hours of torment as he racked his mind "perusing all my deeds to my remembrance whereby a malicious enemy might take advantage by evil interpretation."[76]

On Sunday 30th, Henry wrote to Gardiner and Wallop in France. The letter spoke only of Henry's desire for a new treaty of mutual defence, his opposition to Mantua as a venue for any General Council and his refusal to contribute toward the cost of Francis' invasion of Savoy, though he did not rule out the possibility if the war was to be waged against the Emperor in Flanders.[77]

The Privy Council continued to meet. Either before or after that, Henry was seen arguing with Anne in a window at Greenwich Palace. Anne had Elizabeth, then aged two and a half, in her arms. Alexander Ales, who was waiting for the meeting to finish so he could present his papers, said he could not hear what was being said "but the faces and gestures of the speakers plainly showed that the King was angry."[78]

On the same day, whether before or after is again unknown, Anne had a row with Henry Norris. She asked him why he did not marry her cousin and he said he preferred to wait. Anne accused him of looking "for dead men's shoes, for if aught came to the King but good, you would like to have me." A horrified Norris denied that any such thought had ever crossed his mind. Later on the Sunday, Anne sent him to tell her almoner, John Skip, that she was a "good" woman.[79] It was a curious course of events and some historians have seen it as deeply significant, suggesting that Henry was angry because he had heard what was said and interpreted it as treason. This is highly speculative. Baynton referenced the conversation in a letter to Fitzwilliam written on the 3rd of May but this does not prove it had become the subject of court gossip: he may have been told by Fitzwilliam who was one of the principal leaders of the investigation and seeking Baynton's assistance in obtaining testimony about Anne from her ladies.[80] Anne revealed the argument when in the Tower. At that

---

75 The charge later made against Anne was that she had slept with him in 1534.
76 G. F. Nott (ed.) *The works of Henry Howard earl of Surrey and of Sir Thomas Wyatt the elder* (1816) vol 2 p.279
77 LP 10.760.
78 *Calendar of State Papers; Domestic* 1.1303, Alexander Ales to Queen Elizabeth, 1st September 1559
79 LP 10.793. Good in this context would have been perceived to mean faithful and obedient to her husband, It was not expressive of general behaviour such as generosity to the poor, kindness to animals, possession of the seven Christian virtues.
80 LP 10.798. Baynton was Vice-Chamberlain of Anne's Privy Chamber. His letter shows he knew that Mark had confessed but Norris and George Boleyn had not so he was clearly being informed about events. Baynton was not one of the commissioners and he would not have been at the Tower at the interrogations.

point she knew she had been accused of adultery with Smeaton and Norris and it appears that someone had said Norris had confessed. Knowing that she had not committed adultery with him, Anne sought in her mind to find what cause Norris might have had to accuse her and she thought it must be this event, where, in speculating on what would happen after Henry died, she was arguably guilty of treason. There is no evidence that what was said was deemed significant by the investigators. It did not feature in any of the indictments against her and there is nothing to suggest it was ever mentioned at any of the trials.[81]

Secrecy continued to prevail over what the Privy Council were deliberating upon but one announcement was made at eleven that night: Henry and Anne's trip to Dover, scheduled to commence the following day, was postponed for a week.[82] It is unknown who told Anne, or when, or what excuse was given.

Finally on the 30th, Mark Smeaton was arrested.

Monday 1st May saw the annual May Day celebrations. Henry attended with Anne but left early. It is assumed that news had been passed to him that a confession to adultery had been obtained from Smeaton. He rode off with Norris and took the opportunity to quiz him about the allegations about Anne, reportedly offering him his life if he would only confess to having known her intimately himself.[83] This intervention could be indicative of the feeling Henry had for his closest servant or a sign that he had so much confidence in Norris' loyalty that he assumed he would be willing to lie to the investigators in order to help Henry win his case. Norris refused to confess anything so the King, either being unconvinced of his innocence or just angry at his refusal to lie, ordered Norris' detention as soon as they reached Westminster. He was placed into the safekeeping of the Treasurer, Fitzwilliam, and sent to the Tower the next day.

Also on the 1st May, Cromwell returned Hackney to the King, a house which he had been given only seven months earlier and spent considerable funds on updating. MacCulloch is right to query why in the midst of everything which was happening, Cromwell wanted to spend time on something which was surely not urgent. His suspicion is that the intention was that the King then offer it to Henry Percy – from whom it had been taken a year earlier – to encourage Percy to "recall" a pre-contract with Anne.[84] If this is true, the plan failed for Percy repeated the statement he had made in July 1532 under oath and on the sacrament before the Privy Council and both Archbishops, that no such pre-contract existed.[85]

---

81 The dates on which Anne was supposed to have discussed marrying one of her lovers were all months earlier.
82 LP 10.787.
83 T. Amyot (ed.) 'A Memorial of George Constantine', *Archaeologia* vol. 23 (1831) p.64
84 Diarmaid MacCulloch, *Thomas Cromwell* (2018) pp.340-341, 611.
85 LP 10.864.

On Tuesday 2nd May, Anne was arrested. She was questioned first at Greenwich by her uncle, the Duke of Norfolk who was accompanied by Fitzwilliam, Paulet and unnamed other members of the Privy Council. She later complained that she had been "cruelly handled."[86] Norfolk then took her by barge to the Tower of London. Upon arrival, she asked if she would be placed in a dungeon but was told she would stay in the same apartments which she had used before her coronation three years earlier. She had been told that Norris and Smeaton were already there but had no idea about the whereabouts of her brother. She was also unaware of the identity of the third person with whom she was supposed to have committed adultery. Interestingly, she expressed concern for her parents and brother but not her sister.[87]

That George Boleyn was arrested on the 2nd too is certain though some confusion exists about whether it was before or after Anne. He was supposedly taken at Whitehall which indicates – if true – that aware of some danger to his sister, he had left Greenwich to try and speak to the King on her behalf.

News of Norris' arrest had spread and on the 2nd, Roland Bulkely of Gray's Inn wrote to his brother in North Wales urging him to hurry to London to plead with the King on his behalf.[88] Sadly for him, the servant was stopped by Rowland Lee who reported the letter, which appeared to slander the Queen, to Cromwell saying he hoped the contents were not true.[89] Chapuys also learned of the arrests that day which provoked a triumphant letter to the Emperor, though he remained unclear about the details. He thought Smeaton was one of Anne's staff and that Norris had been arrested for failing to reveal the affair.[90] Keen to claim some credit for his own role in encouraging Jane, he then expressed the hope that the Emperor would now "augment his kindness" to himself.[91]

That night, according to Chapuys – who was not present – Henry told his son, the Duke of Richmond, that he had escaped the terrible fate of being poisoned by Anne together with his half-sister, Mary.[92] Whether this ever happened is open to doubt. Chapuys was obsessed with the idea that Anne wanted to poison Mary and repeatedly expressed this suspicion to the Emperor so it may be that the scene was largely a development of his own mind and that all Henry had said to his son was that he should thank God that no harm had come to him because Anne had been arrested for plotting.[93] Cromwell would later tell Gardiner that there was "a certain conspiracy of the King's death

---

86 LP 10.797.
87 LP 10.793.
88 A more cynical interpretation was that he wanted his brother to hurry to plead for some of Norris' assets.
89 LP 10.785, 820.
90 LP 10.782.
91 LP 10.783.
92 LP 10.908. Chapuys gives no hint on the identity of his supposed informer to this exchange, a conversation which if it did happen, one might have supposed would have taken place in private rather than before witnesses and Imperial spies.

which extended so far that, all we who had the examination of it, quaked at the danger His Grace was in."[94] However, on the 23rd April, the day before the commissions of oyer and terminer were set up, Henry had met with Katherine's physician, the man whom Chapuys claimed would be able to provide proof that Katherine was poisoned. The supposed evidence for this was the candle maker's discovery whilst embalming her that her heart was black.[95] That a candle maker was not a skilled surgeon with a deep understanding of human anatomy and the principles of forensic autopsies is obvious and Henry was no fool, but it is possible that in the fervid atmosphere of the time, a seed of doubt was sown which he then passed on to his son.

Clearly considerable activity was going on behind the scenes but by May 3rd, all the government had was Mark's confession. Norris may have been tricked by Fitzwilliam into revealing some gifts or words which could be twisted into treason, but he had not confessed to adultery.[96] Baynton said that he thought it would be unwise to proceed if Mark's confession was all that could be produced.[97] It may be that he feared it had been obtained under duress or it could be because Smeaton was a commoner. Lord Dacre had been cleared of treason by his peers on grounds the witnesses against him were not gentlemen so their word could not be trusted.[98] People might also regard the idea of the Queen consorting with a humble musician as literally beyond belief. For Henry to charge Anne with adultery only for her to be cleared, would definitely damage his reputation – as George IV would later find when he tried to extricate himself from Queen Caroline.

Anne's women were certainly being questioned though not all were being as co-operative as the government wanted. Baynton expressed his disappointment that Margery Horsman was refusing to reveal anything against Anne.[99] One lady who clearly did subsequently co-operate was Anne's sister-in-law, Jane Rochford. The fact that the prosecution were able to quote words she allegedly told her husband, indicate her involvement because George clearly did not tell then and nobody else would have been in a position to supply this information. Given Jane's apparent distress at George's incarceration, it may be that she spoke out simply with a view to destroying Anne and her words were simply twisted by Cromwell so they could be used

---

93 For example, CSPS 5.1.10, 57, 86; LP 7.171, 10.141. In April 1533 he had warned that "when this cursed Anne has her foot in the stirrup, you may be sure she will do the Queen all the injury she can, and the Princess likewise" LP 6.324.
94 LP 10.873.
95 LP 10.141
96 Amyot, *Constantine*, p.64
97 LP 10.799.
98 Edward Herbert, *The History of England under Henry VIII* (1719) p.530. Eleven of the jurors involved would also sit in judgment on Anne and George so it was not an idle fear, LP 7.962.
99 LP 10.799.

against her husband.[100] According to the French ambassador, Jane Rochford had taken part in a demonstration in support of Henry's daughter, Mary in October 1535 and this must have soured both the marriage and her relationship with Anne. Indeed, it is hard to believe she would have kept her job after such behaviour.[101]

This may have been the point at which Jane Seymour was removed to Carew's house at Beddington, seven miles away.[102]

It was on Wednesday 3rd May that Archbishop Thomas Cranmer reached Lambeth having been summoned by Cromwell. As the latter's letter has not survived, it is not known when it was written but probably on the 1st. Cranmer had evidently been told of the reports of adultery but he had also been warned not to approach the King. Given his position and usual easy access to Henry, this might have seemed strange but Cranmer presumed it was because Henry was upset and he wrote a letter to him urging him to endure misfortune like Job and join him in praying that Anne be found innocent. He said he was "clean amazed, for I had never better opinion of woman" but expressed confidence that Henry would not have taken the drastic step of having her arrested without due cause. He added: "If it be true that is openly reported of the Queen's Grace, if men had a right estimation of things, they should not esteem any part of Your Grace's honour to be touched, but her honour only to be cleanly disparaged." He paid tribute to Anne's dedication to the Gospel and reminded the King that all – including Henry – had offended God and were in need of mercy. Having written thus far in his letter, he was summoned to Whitehall where he was shown what were said to be proofs of Anne's guilt. He returned to Lambeth and completed his letter by expressing his sorrow.[103]

Despite convincing Cranmer, concerns remained about the strength of the government case. Four more arrests were made – William Brereton, Francis Weston, Richard Page and Thomas Wyatt.[104] Why they were chosen is unclear. There is nothing to suggest that they were arrested as a result of anything Anne said, although it is possible that Kingston wrote further letters disclosing her comments from the Tower which have not survived.[105] It may be that they were

---

100 LP 10.798. There is no evidence that she accused her husband of incest with Anne.
101 LP 9.566. The note is in D'Inteville's handwriting, Paul Friedmann, *Anne Boleyn*, vol. 2 (1884) p.128.
102 CSPS 5.2.55. The actual date of the move is not recorded. Anne had also been ensconced at Beddington in 1529 to keep away from Cardinal Campeggio, David Starkey, *Six Wives* (2004) p.340.
103 Gilbert Burnet, *History of the Reformation*, ed. Nicholas Pocock vol.1 (1865) pp. 320-322, summarised in LP 10.792
104 Constantine says that he spoke with Brereton at 9a.m. on the "Thursday afore May Day" i.e. 27th April and that Brereton observed that "there was no way but one" with the matter. He adds that Brereton was arrested the same afternoon. This appears to be a transcription error in the printed text as the arrest most likely took place on 4th May, the Thursday aft May Day. Amyot, *Constantine*, p.65
105 Kingston said that Anne referred to an exchange with Weston but this seems to have been in response to being told of his arrest since the words were not treasonous and

named during the interrogation of Anne's staff. However, it is interesting to note that those whose positions came under threat at this time were linked. Henry's Privy Chamber was organised into two shifts and it is significant that Norris, Page and Weston were all members of the first.[106] Moreover, Browne, whose sister allegedly started the crisis, was also part of the same group, as were Carew and the Marquess of Exeter who were actively promoting Jane Seymour. The last member of the team was John Russell whose glowing comments about Jane made just after Anne's fall suggest that he was similarly involved. Brereton was also linked to this first shift.[107] By contrast, with the exception of George Boleyn, no member of the second shift was involved. Whether this concentration of arrests related to one small team, none of whom were politically important, constitutes evidence of faction is open to debate. It could simply indicate that this team was poorly supervised and so gave rise to rumour or that there were catastrophic personality clashes between the members.

Meanwhile, Henry's reaction to all that was happening was to withdraw himself from all business by day and to go out partying by night. He allegedly commented on one occasion that he thought Anne had been with over a hundred men and offered to show the Bishop of Carlisle some verses he had written about it some time before.[108] It could be that his behaviour was an act of bravado but the sight of the King celebrating the fall of the woman whom he had loved so greatly did not impress people and ironically did more to raise support for Anne than any number of sermons or statutes in her favour. It also made it hard to credit that he was suffering bodily harm as a result of her behaviour, which was one of the charges which would be laid against her.

A piece of evidence which would be produced at the trial was the deathbed statement of Lady Wingfield, a document which has not survived. She was said to have been an employee of Queen Anne but who was she? There

---

not used in either the indictment against him or the Queen, LP 10.793. The letter is undated though the editors have chosen to calendar it on the 3rd which would make it before the arrest.

106 LP 5.727

107 It is not clear if Grooms were divided into shifts as well although it would seem probable. Brereton was further employed by Browne, the two men both having the Earl of Worcester as their brother-in-law. Browne's sister was the Earl's wife while Brereton's wife was the Earl's sister. It is also possible that Brereton was related in some way to Anne. Her father's first cousin, Francis Cheyney, married Werburga, daughter of John Brereton. After Cheyney's death, she married Sir William Compton who was a close friend of Anne's father.

108 LP 10.908, 909. The source for the story is Chapuys who said he was told by Carlisle – the party organiser – himself. He does not give the date of the incident but it had clearly taken place since his previous letter to the Emperor written on the 2nd May so may have been after the conviction of the men and possibly after Anne's as well. The story does, however, seem totally improbable unless one is to credit that Henry had known of Anne's adultery for a long time ("*longtemps*") and chosen to ignore it.

were four Lady Wingfields during Anne's life, though never more than three at a time.

The usual identification is Bridget (née Wiltshire) who had married Sir Richard Wingfield but she had been widowed in July 1525. Although the exact date of her re-marriage is unknown, it was probably early in 1526 judging by the number of children she went on to have. When she joined Anne's household in 1530 and when she left to have a child early in 1532, it was as Lady Nicholas Harvey.[109] She did not return to her employment at court and never served Anne after she became queen. In August 1532, Bridget was widowed again but she remarried and became Lady Robert Tyrwhitt. The date of this marriage is unknown but was probably in the late summer of 1534 since a grant was made then to Sir Robert of lands she had inherited from her second husband.[110] She went on to have at least two children by him, something which indicates that the marriage must have lasted at least two years due to the human gestation period, and probably longer given that women's fertility decreases with age so it is very unlikely that Bridget, by then in her early forties, would have conceived immediately after the first birth. Thus, although her date of death is unknown, there is no reason to suppose that she was not alive in the spring of 1536. Her husband did not remarry until 1538 at the earliest and widowers at this time generally remarried within six months of their wife's death. Most significantly, the person who said that the deathbed statement came from Lady Wingfield was Justice John Spelman, a man accustomed to accurately recording the names of witnesses.[111] It is inconceivable that he would have referred to Bridget by a name which she had not borne for more than ten years, especially given he knew personally the other Lady Wingfields and also Bridget's husband who was an Esquire of the Body. For these reasons, Bridget can be eliminated as a candidate.

There were three other Lady Wingfields. Sir Richard's brother, Robert, was married to Joan (née Poynings) and Anne spent time with her in 1532 at Calais where Joan had lived since 1523. Joan never worked for Anne and was still alive in 1539 when Robert died so can be discounted as the source of the deathbed statement. Sir Anthony Wingfield was married to Elizabeth (née de Vere) but she outlived her husband who died in 1552 so again can be discounted. Elizabeth may have worked for Anne because she received a New Year's Gift from the King in 1532 and 1533, though there were usually some forty female recipients of such and they certainly did not all serve her.[112]

The last Lady Wingfield was Anne (née Wiseman), wife of Richard and Robert's brother, Humphrey. A lawyer by profession, he had begun his career as an employee of the Duke and Duchess of Suffolk, the Duke being his first

---

109 CSPS 4.1.345; PP p.197.
110 LP 7.1217.12. In June 1529, a grant was made to William Brereton of the lands his wife had inherited from her first husband when the couple married, E. W. Ives, *Letters and Accounts of William Brereton of Malpas* (1976) p.14.
111 J H Baker (ed.), *The Reports of Sir John Spelman*, vol. 1 (1977) p.70.
112 LP 5.686; LP 6.32

cousin. In February 1533, Humphrey became Speaker of the House of Commons which prompted Henry to knight him which naturally raised his wife from Mistress Wingfield to Lady Wingfield. The lack of any staff lists for Anne during her time as Queen makes it uncertain if this Lady Wingfield worked for her but it is very possible. Employees were generally selected from the families of existing staff and Sir Humphrey's wife had the added advantage of being a kinswoman of Anne's mother, Elizabeth Boleyn.[113] Sir Humphrey was also an employee of Anne's uncle, the Duke of Norfolk. Certainly, a Lady Wingfield received a New Year's gift in 1534 which may have been her since the wife of Sir Anthony could have been having a child at this time.[114] The exact date of Lady Anne Wingfield's death is unknown but is likely to have been in 1536 because in a letter to Cromwell of 1537, Sir Humphrey referred to it as having cost him a lot of money.[115]

Support for Cromwell procuring a deathbed statement from Lady Wingfield can be found in the fact that he preserved a letter definitely written by Anne who tells the recipient "next mine own mother, I know no woman alive that I love better." The letter is undated but Anne signs herself as Anne Rochford indicating that it must have been written between December 1529 and the end of August 1532.[116] At this date, Bridget was Lady Harvey and she was known in Anne's household by this name. The only Lady Wingfields alive in the 1529 to 1532 window were Joan and Elizabeth, the two ladies who indubitably survived her.[117] Neither of them are known to have been emotionally close to Anne but her personal correspondence has not survived and her whereabouts between 1522 and 1527 are uncertain so it is impossible to know whom she considered her friends. The letter in question is not addressed. The assumption of the recipient rests in a note written on it by another hand "to my Lady Wingfield this be delivered." Mary Anne Wood guessed it was for Robert's wife, Joan which is possible.[118] Anne was planning a visit to Calais in 1532 which may have prompted correspondence, though why Lady Joan would have sent Cromwell a copy of one such letter is hard to imagine. It could also have been addressed to Elizabeth who was attached to the court at this time. However, if the note was added in 1536 when the document was given to Cromwell, the recipient could be the wife of Sir Humphrey who had become Lady Wingfield when Anne was Marquess of Pembroke.

---

113 Anne Wingfield's aunt was the sister of Thomas Howard, the second Duke of Norfolk and hence aunt of Anne Boleyn's mother
114 LP 7.9
115 LP 12.2.1342. The biography on the History of Parliament website states that death occurred before January 1537. The wealth of his wife is affirmed by the loan she made to the tenant of Bromley hall, LP 7.1672
116 Prior to December 1529 she was Anne Boleyn and after August 1532 she was the Marquess of Pembroke.
117 Humphrey had yet to be knighted so his wife was Mistress not Lady Wingfield.
118 Mary Anne Everett Wood, *Letters of Royal and Illustrious Ladies,* vol.2 (1816) pp. 74-75.

The letter bears no relation to the case against Anne in 1536 so the question arises of how Cromwell came into possession of it and why he bothered to keep it. There is no reason to suppose that either of the living Lady Wingfields sent him the document but Sir Humphrey was a close friend of Cromwell's and would have spent time sorting through his wife's possessions after her death. The letter reveals that Anne was concerned that there had been a disagreement between herself and the recipient but gives no clue as to the nature of this and urges her to "leave your indiscreet trouble" which was upsetting God and herself. Indiscreet at this time meant unwise or frivolous so the trouble may have been financial.[119] According to the inscription on the tomb of Sir Humphrey's wife, she was "graced with modesty, manners, affability, and good parentage, and acceptable to all; and so liberal to the poor as is incredible."[120] Inscriptions are designed to flatter but this does not mean that they are untrue and Anne Boleyn was also renowned for her charitable work which may have been grounds for a friendship between them.[121] Humphrey Wingfield also shared Anne's passion for education, employing resources from a monastery dissolved by Wolsey to establish a school, a project in which it is reasonable to suppose he was supported by his wife.[122] Given the likelihood that the recipient was the deceased Lady Wingfield, it increases the probability of her employment by Anne when she was Queen. The letter may have been given to Cromwell to show that the recipient was close to Anne and therefore in a good position to know her secrets which were about to be revealed in the deathbed statement. Whether what Sir Humphrey told Cromwell or the two men produced as a statement bore any relation to what the dying Lady Wingfield said, is another question. Sir Humphrey was a cousin of the Duke of Suffolk and supporter of Henry's daughter, Mary, so may have been hostile toward Anne's position even if they shared some views on reform. Although the date of the deathbed statement's production and Cromwell receiving the letter are unknown, it seems likely that the two events took place during the first week of May and the suspicion must be that the former was manufactured to bolster the case, it being impossible for anyone to refute the evidence of a dead witness.

On Sunday 7th May, letters were sent out to every county sheriff explaining that the reason for the summons to a new Parliament was to deal with important matters which had only just arisen and which related to the surety of the King's person and the succession of the realm.[123] Some recipients might have hoped that this meant Mary was to be restored but most would have

---

119 *Huloets dictionarie* (1572)
120 J. H. Lawrence-Archer, *An Account of the Sirname Edgar* (1873) p.41
121 Maria Dowling (ed.), *William Latymer's Cronickille of Anne Bulleyne* (Camden, 1990) pp.44-45
122 Diarmaid MacCulloch, Thomas Cromwell (2018) p.112; E. W. Ives, 'Anne Boleyn and the Early Reformation in England', *Historical Journal*, Vol. 37, No. 2 (1994) p.399
123 LP 10.815.

been confused, especially having spent much of the previous year administering the oath required of all people to swear "to bear faith, truth, and obedience only to the King's majesty, and to his heirs of his body of his most dear and entirely beloved lawful wife Queen Anne, begotten and to be begotten." The letters provided a hint that some act of treason had been discovered.

Henry would have been receiving daily updates on the investigation and around a week after Anne was arrested, he made the decision that sufficient evidence had been amassed to support a successful prosecution. On Tuesday 9th May, writs were sent out summoning jurors for the trial of Norris, Smeaton, Brereton and Weston. The story of their conviction together with that of George and Anne is in the next chapter. Page and Wyatt would later be released without charge. Some writers have considered that Wyatt secured his release by providing evidence against Anne basing their claim on a poem he wrote which includes the words "I was made a filing instrument to frame other" excusing his behaviour because "youth did me lead and falsehood guiled."[124] Such an interpretation presupposes that the poem was autobiographical and that it relates to 1536 and not another event. Wyatt was thirty-three when Anne fell so hardly a youth. It is more likely that Wyatt survived because he was a close friend of Cromwell's and Page because his wife was the mother-in-law of Edward Seymour, Jane's brother.

Given that an accusation of adultery with just one person would have sufficed to destroy Anne, why did the government charge five men? Lacey Baldwin Smith noted that those involved had been brought up on the theory of needing copious evidence.[125] It was not for nothing that Henry's case against his "marriage" to Katherine became known as the *Collectanea Satis Copiosa.* Only having one man might also be considered a risk: Baynton had told Fitzwilliam and Cromwell that he felt more paramours were needed if the charges were to stick. Other motives for accusing so many may have been to show Anne was an insatiable monster to destroy any support she might have claimed. If this is the case, it suggests that Chapuys' frequent claims that the entire country hated her were untrue. Two eye witnesses to reactions to the news of her arrest showed stark differences. De Carles described rejoicing and little children dancing in the street while Ales noted "the tears and lamentations of the faithful who were lamenting over the snare laid for the Queen, and the boastful triumphing of the foes of the true doctrine." A further reason may have been to try and show that Anne was seeking to avoid her primary duty which was to produce an heir. It was believed that frequent intercourse left the womb too slippery with semen to hold a child.[126] Another possibility is that it was to preserve Henry's reputation. To be cuckolded by one man might generate suspicions that he was unable to satisfy his young wife but if she could be shown to be sharing her favours with many, it would imply there was something wrong with her and the image of the

---

124 Kenneth Muir and Patricia Thomson (ed.), *The Collected Poems of Sir Thomas Wyatt* (Liverpool, 1969) p.14
125 Lacey Baldwin Smith, *Anne Boleyn: The Queen of Controversy* (2013) p.180.
126 Tracy Borman, *Private Lives of the Tudors* (2018) p.89.

virile Henry would remain intact. Alternatively, the government may have simply charged all those whom the investigation had suggested were culpable.

Why did Henry believe such horrific stories about his own wife? In part, it may have been because he had put her on such a pedestal during their courtship that it was inevitable she sink in his estimation later on because it was simply impossible for anyone to live up to such expectations. It might also be remembered that jealousy is not the most rational of emotions and is apt to accept the most sinister interpretations of innocuous events. It is possible that, with her husband's eyes wandering, Anne had been trying to make herself more attractive recently. Women in such circumstances often try changing their hair or scent or clothes. Henry might have thought nothing of this until somebody brought to him the allegations of adultery whereupon they would have taken on a whole new and ominous significance.

Yet, from Henry's perspective, the evidence was compelling. Smeaton had confessed that he had slept with Anne on three occasions. Other statements had been provided by those closest to her and who were taken to be people of integrity. The Countess of Worcester was a peeress and wife of one of his Privy Councillors. Nan Cobham was kinswoman of another courtier.[127] Lady Wingfield was wife of the Speaker and a relation of his brother-in-law, Charles Brandon. Moreover, Henry was enjoying a relationship with one of Anne's maids-of-honour. He must have discussed what went on in her mistress' rooms with Jane, even though she was unsurprisingly not called to testify. Who knows what tales Jane might have dreamt up? Given her own plans to marry Henry as soon as he was free, Jane was not going to say Anne was a model of godly propriety. She would have stuck the knife in with relish as hard as she could.

A further factor in Henry's reaction would have been the death of his last two children by Anne. Just as he believed that the loss of his children by Katherine had been due to divine displeasure, so it followed that God was punishing him now. This must have been very confusing for Henry. He had no doubts that he had been right to leave Katherine and he was equally convinced that God had chosen to open his eyes to the fallacy of papal authority. Henry believed he was God's chosen. The only conclusion he could draw was that Anne was not similarly chosen. She must be evil and how did a wicked woman behave? Well, adultery, incest and plotting murder seemed pretty good grounds for defining her as such.

As historians, we can only assess situations based on written evidence but Henry knew the people involved very well and he found the claims plausible. No doubt, given his feelings for Jane, he wanted to believe the allegations but he was not a fool. In 1543, Cranmer's enemies sought his destruction and the Archbishop told the King that he had no objection to being sent for trial because he trusted in justice. Henry replied: "What fond simplicity

---

127 She went on to serve Katherine Parr but her identity is unknown. Guy suggests she was a niece or cousin of Lord Cobham, John Guy, Julia Fox, *Hunting the Falcon* (2023) p.280

have you! ... If they have you once in prison three or four knaves will be soon procured to witness against you and condemn you."[128] In Cranmer's case, Henry intervened because he deeply admired his Archbishop and knew he was innocent. Similarly, in 1546, Henry prevented Katherine Parr's fall which was being plotted by his ministers.[129] By contrast, in 1536 with regard to Anne and those accused with her, he allowed the prosecution to go ahead and take its course because he genuinely thought they were guilty. This is proven by the fact that Henry was willing to sign death warrants for five men whom he had known very well over a long period of time. Norris was at least forty and had been in close attendance on the King for over twenty years. He was trusted not only to care for Henry's body but his jewels and cash. Nobody knew Henry better and it is evident that the King regarded him as not just a servant but a friend. Honours were heaped on Norris from 1515 right through to March 1536.[130] Weston was twenty-five and had served the King for at least ten years and was a regular companion of his at sports and play. He was also evidently friends with the French ambassador who intervened unsuccessfully for his pardon.[131] Brereton was around fifty and had been at court for many years, though he was in addition a major landowner and administrator for the crown so frequently away from court. George Boleyn was just over thirty and had been in royal service since childhood. He had undertaken some diplomatic work in France but was primarily a boon companion of the King. Smeaton had joined Henry's service after the fall of Wolsey in 1529 but the King would have known him before that. As a musician, he was not on the same social level as the others but given Henry's love of music and long employment of him, he was clearly someone whom the King admired and probably worked with on compositions or performed alongside. It is certain that in mid April 1536, Henry had no desire to be rid of any of them, and if such a thought had entered his head, all he had to do was dismiss them.

    Contrary to the portrayal of the King in some of the more lurid popular histories, Henry was not a bloodthirsty psychopath who chopped heads off without reason or just for fun. If Anne's fall had been precipitated simply by Henry wanting to be rid of her, a perjurer could have been found to swear to a pre-contract with her. The marriage could then have been annulled and Anne despatched to a nunnery or into exile. That Henry did not do this is a sign of his his new belief that these long standing servants and friends were depraved monsters who had been systematically cuckolding him over the years. His anger at being betrayed by those he trusted was greater than if they had been

---

128 J. G. Nichols, *Narratives of the Reformation* (Camden, 1859) p.255.
129 J. J. Scarisbrick, *Henry VIII* (1968) pp.478-81.
130 LP 10.597.27.
131 LP 10.908. Chapuys' account is supported by Lancelot de Carles' poem which devotes nineteen lines to describing Weston's talents and the campaign to save him, a contrast to the other accused who are not mentioned, f.29-30, lines 788-807.

complete strangers.[132] He was merciless towards all those involved, though he remained supportive of those they left behind.[133]

Around this time, Henry wrote his only letter to Jane Seymour. Undated, it refers to "a ballad lately made in great derision against us."[134] Evidently, gossip was already being spread that Henry's motives in discarding Anne might not be entirely honourable and it would continue to grow. By the end of June, Dr Ortiz at Rome was reporting that Jane was already five months gone with the King's child and this was why Anne had been executed.[135]

Meanwhile, Anne may have written to Henry. The document which survives is in an Elizabethan hand and there are a number of reasons for doubting it is even an authentic copy.[136] However, Anne had expressed the desire to write to her husband so what remains may have been based on an original and then just enhanced by an unknown person.[137] The fact that it was stored among Cromwell's papers would suggest that there had been a letter of some sort though Henry probably never saw it. That she would have declared her innocence and asked that he destroy only herself and save the life of her brother is entirely conceivable. There is little sign of humility in the letter which could also be in keeping with her character and her status, though she would have been advised to act otherwise, as Wolsey famously told Henry's sister Mary in 1515.[138] The letter is extremely articulate which is one of the grounds some have used for doubting Anne wrote it, but she would have had

---

132 A comparison might be drawn with Henry's anger when Brandon married his sister without permission, LP 2.224.
133 At the end of June, the brothers of William Brereton and Henry Norris both received grants of lands and positions which had been held by the newly executed. The King also granted the estates which Brereton's widow had inherited from her first husband back to her and intervened with Thomas Boleyn to obtain money for George's widow. Such generosity was not normally expected by the families of traitors. LP 10.1256.8, 29, 30, 52.
134 Jasper Ridley, *The Love Letters of Henry VIII* (1988) p.75. The letter was written between Jane's removal to Beddington which probably took place around the 3rd May and her return from there on the 14th, LP 10.908.
135 LP 10.1213. Similar thoughts were reported from people in England, e.g. LP 10.1205. Such rumours represented a real danger to Henry's reputation at home and abroad.
136 LP 10.808. The full text is in Burnet, *History,* vol 4 pp.291-292. Burnet notes that the document he saw had been badly burned. He also says that Anne sent a second message to Henry on the night before she died in which she thanked him for advancing her from a gentlewoman to a Marquess and then to a Queen and now to the ranks of the saints – vol. 1 p.327. He does not say if this was a verbal or written message but the assumption would have to be that it was written and he saw it prior to the Cottonian fire. Since it has not survived, the handwriting cannot be examined for authenticity but even if it was genuine, it seems certain that nobody would have been brave enough to deliver such a missive to the King.
137 LP 10.798. Kathryn Howard would write to Henry during her imprisonment, HMRC, *Calendar of the Manuscripts of the Marquis of Bath* (1904) vol. 2 pp.8-9.
138 LP 2.227.

plenty of time in the Tower to polish her drafts and there may have been input from her almoner who visited her. Besides, we have too little of Anne's correspondence to be able to reliably assess her literary skills. It is a letter which many would like to be genuine though it is clearly not. Whether it contains a partial truth will be forever unknown.

On Friday 12th May, Norris, Weston, Brereton and Smeaton were convicted of high treason. Amongst those affirming their guilt was Anne's father, Thomas Boleyn. Immediately, the Duke of Norfolk was appointed Lord High Steward and commanded to convene a trial for George and Anne. The necessary writs went out the following day. Six trials had taken place before the Lord High Steward since 1415 and on three occasions, the accused had been cleared but that was evidently not considered a possibility this time.[139] Proof that the result was a foregone conclusion can be found in Anne's household being broken up.

It was probably on the 12th, that Henry wrote to Queen Mary, Governor of the Low Countries, summoning a swordsman from St Omer to behead her. The letter, no copy of which exists in the archives, was no doubt sent by special courier, quite possibly carried by one of the Privy Chamber. St Omer was in the Low Countries which was governed by the Emperor's sister and normally contact with her would have been through, or at least notified to, Chapuys as the Imperial ambassador at court, yet he clearly knew nothing about it and those involved in the case were not told either. Spelman, for example, refers to the swordsman coming from Calais, which would no doubt have been his port of embarkation but was not his home: it seems likely the swordsman was ordered to say nothing and leave people to make their own assumptions.[140] That the request for the swordsman was sent before Anne's trial is based on the fact that even if someone travelled post and the swordsman was able to depart at a moment's notice, it would have taken a minimum of three days to get the man to London, more depending on the tides and weather in the English Channel. The Spanish chronicler claims nine days passed from the despatch of the letter to the man's arrival.[141] It seems likely that the executioner did not arrive until the 18th because Anne's execution, which had been expected that day was put off until the 19th.[142] Furthermore, it was only on Tuesday 18th that Henry wrote to Kingston, the Constable of the Tower, telling him that "moved by pity," he had decided that he did "not wish the same Anne to be committed to be burned

---

139 Barbara Harris, 'The Trial of the third Duke of Buckingham: a revisionist view', AJLH, vol. XX (1976) p.19.
140 Spelman also noted that the judges on the 15th complained when the Duke of Norfolk sentenced Anne to be burnt or beheaded at the King's pleasure. The treason acts specified that the punishment for a female traitor was burning so to give the King a choice meant the verdict was technically disjunctive. Evidently, Norfolk knew what the King had done even though it was not revealed to the court. J H Baker (ed.), *The Reports of Sir John Spelman,* vol. 1 (1977) p.70.
141 Martin Hume (ed.) *Chronicle of King Henry VIII. of England* (1889) p.70.
142 LP 10.902; Carles f.41-43, lines 1149 to 1195.

by fire" but rather "the head of the same Anne shall be caused to be cut off."[143] If the Spanish Chronicle is correct – and it is not a document famed for its accuracy – that would mean Henry wrote even before the first trial was held.

His choice of an Imperial executioner is interesting. Queen Mary, said that Henry wanted the Imperialists to have the honour of exacting "vengeance" on Anne and she is likely to have drawn this conclusion from whatever Henry wrote to her.[144] But what did he mean?

Although everyone knew that the Imperialists blamed Anne for Katherine's removal, Henry never wavered in his conviction that his "marriage" to Katherine was invalid. If it had not been Anne who benefited from his understanding of the situation, it would have been someone else. Thus, there was no reason for Henry to hire an Imperialist as an act of repentance. Nor, was he motivated by some idea that the move would please the Emperor and make him more likely to come to terms. Henry's position with regard to the Emperor's requirements did not change and it would be the Emperor who would be forced to back down. So why was he inviting the Imperialists to wreak their revenge on the woman they called the Concubine? Could Henry have become so convinced of Anne's evil nature by the adultery allegations that he was now prepared to believe she had tried to poison Katherine? Given Henry's letter to Mary has not survived – itself interesting – it cannot be known what he was thinking.

On 14th May, two days after the conviction of the commoners, Cromwell wrote to Gardiner advising him that he would be getting £200 because "his Majesty doth not forget your service." This could be assumed to represent a saving on the annuity of this value which had been paid to George Boleyn out of the diocese of Worcester of which Gardiner was bishop but the wording suggests it was meant as a personal reward and the promise of something to follow for Wallop, who was certainly not paying an annuity to anyone, supports this.[145] Gardiner evidently wrote back complaining he was not getting £300 which prompted stiff responses from Henry and Cromwell.[146]

On Monday 15th May, Anne and George were tried and found guilty of treason. The next day, Archbishop Thomas Cranmer visited Anne. What was said remained secret but Kingston reported that Anne afterwards expressed some hope that she would be allowed to retire to a nunnery, the exit plan offered to Katherine in 1529.[147]

On 17th May, the men were executed. George Constantine attended and reported that Norris said almost nothing and that Brereton, Weston and Boleyn only confessed the fact that they deserved to die in language typical of the

---

143 TNA C 193/3, fol. 80.
144 M. Gachard, *Analectes Historiques* (Brussells, 1856) pp.17-18.
145 LP 10.873, 878. If a reward was involved, it suggests that Ales' allegation about Anne's fall being precipitated by a calumny from France may deserve more serious attention than it is usually given.
146 LP 11.28, 29.
147 LP 10.890.

period. To modern eyes, their words sound like an admission of guilt but they were just a reflection of the Christian belief in the total depravity of humanity unless relieved by grace. Weston's words bear a striking resemblance to the words of St Augustine's *Confessions*.[148] Smeaton, a man who shared their faith but had not been educated to the same eloquence, simply said "I have deserved the death" which is more likely to mean that he repented his false confession than he was maintaining his admission of adultery.[149]

Also on the 17th May, Archbishop Cranmer pronounced the annulment of Henry and Anne's marriage. Reasons for that are discussed in a later chapter but it was something which Anne knew was going to happen. Many since then have mocked at the apparent anomaly of someone being convicted of adultery when not legally married. This was not a mistake or part of some devilish plan. The treason acts related to the behaviour of and due to the king's companion.[150] It was reasonable to assume that a queen was married to a king but Anne had been crowned and consecrated and did not owe her title simply to being Henry's wife. Her position was recognised by Church and Parliament and the annulment did not alter this.[151]

On Friday 19th May, Queen Anne Boleyn had her head cut from her body. As soon as Henry heard the news of her head bouncing across the scaffold with eyes still flickering, he galloped off to see Jane Seymour.[152] Almost five hundred years later, his image has not recovered. As John Foxe commented, "to such as can wisely judge upon cases occurring" it was "a great clearance" unto Anne of the charges brought against her.[153]

---

[148] The *Book of Common Prayer* confession used daily includes "there is no health in us" whilst that at Holy Communion has "we acknowledge and bewail our manifold sins and wickedness...provoking most justly thy wrath and indignation against us." Such words were, and are, used alike by people from Jack the Ripper to the most saintly maiden aunt. Article nine of the Church of England confirms that everyone is "by nature inclined to evil" and "deserveth God's wrath and indignation."

[149] Amyot, *Constantine*, p.65.

[150] *Statutes of the Realm* vol. 2 p.319. Companion was the usual Norman-French word for consort so implied wife but was not legally restricted to it.

[151] Kathryn Howard was stripped of her title before execution, LP 16.1366

[152] LP 10.926. Spelman said her head was removed with one blow and "fell to the ground with her lips moving and her eyes moving." Spelman, *Reports*, vol. 1, p.59

[153] Thomas Freeman, Research, Rumour and Propaganda – Anne Boleyn in Foxe's book of Martyrs, *Historical Journal* vol. 38 no 4 (1995) p.810. Burnet commented similarly: "nothing did more evidently discover the secret cause of this queen's ruin, than the King's marrying Jane Seymour the day after her execution." Burnet, *History* vol.1 p.332

Conclusion

In 1527, Henry took advantage of a chance comment by the Bishop of Tarbes to start the annulment from Katherine. He had wanted to leave her for some time but not known how. In 1536, a very similar situation arose. Henry was disappointed with Anne: she had promised so much but failed to produce a son. He knew it was not his fault for he had proved that by siring the Duke of Richmond. He may have sought to prove it again with Jane, but whether he did or not, his worry about the future remained. He was not averse to the idea of discarding Anne but it was not clear how he could do it. The only grounds for a divorce would be her adultery and even if proof of that was to be found, he could not remarry during her lifetime since the church taught that marriage was till death. An honest annulment seemed improbable given the huge efforts which had gone into ensuring his marriage to her was legally watertight and could take a long time, something the middle aged Henry did not have. Although Anne lacked foreign relations with powerful armies lined up to defend her, Henry would have suspected that she would not meekly accept the bastardisation of their child and go quietly. The accusation of treason opened a new possibility: her execution. As a widower he would be free to start again. It would meet Henry's sense of justice which required the guilty to be punished. Moreover, a verdict of treason did not require proof of adultery.

The events of late April and early May are not demonstrative of any orchestrated plan or dastardly plot by some individual or group against the Queen, but rather of the government responding to Henry's wishes. Although there are those who would like to see Henry as a cold blooded wife murderer, it seems he was genuinely convinced that Anne was guilty. The idea that a vengeful Cromwell concocted the whole scheme to dupe Henry makes no sense. The men accused were not politically important and nor did they form any sort of united faction. None of them represented a threat to him or to the progress of the reformation and nor were they obstacles to Anglo-Imperial or Anglo-French alliances. The claim made by Cromwell in June that he had masterminded Anne's fall because he was so distraught at the idea of not having an Anglo-Imperial alliance was part of his campaign to convince Chapuys that he was the only man able to persuade Henry to go down this route. The higher his value in the eyes of Chapuys, he would have realised, the greater his chance of a generous reward from the Emperor. In the same conversation, Cromwell claimed Henry was keen to make Mary his heir, which was untrue. Although many later historians have quoted Chapuys' letter as if it were evidence of a fact rather than a comment, it is clear that Chapuys himself did not believe that Cromwell had this sort of power. He noted that if Cromwell ever originated any measure, Henry would automatically suspect and oppose it "even if he should otherwise deem it acceptable and in conformity with his own views."[154]

---

154 CSPS 5.2.76

Something else which Cromwell told Chapuys was that the investigation into Anne began after he read a Flemish astrological forecast which suggested the King's life was in danger from those closest to him. No such document has been found but people at this period did generally believe in signs from the stars. Recorde later noted that the fall of princes was always indicated in advance through an act of "God by the signs of heaven." Paulet, a key player in the investigation into Anne, was a sponsor of astrologers as was Henry himself.[155] Nonetheless, Chapuys' claim that Cromwell attributed the discovery of Anne's evil machinations to a forecast could simply be Chapuys trying to suggest to the Emperor that he was partly responsible himself for her fall; after all, Chapuys had told the Emperor in March 1535 that he owned a forecast showing Henry being endangered.[156]

Yet, even though the idea of Cromwell masterminding some plot entirely on his own to destroy Anne should be discarded, it does not follow that her fall was entirely the result of what was perceived to be her errant behaviour. A month after her death, on 14th June, Anthony Browne, brother of the Countess of Worcester and the man who had allegedly first spoken out against Anne, found himself facing interrogation over his devotion to Mary and a possible conspiracy to return her to the succession.[157] Francis Bryan was also questioned for the same together with the Marquess of Exeter and Fitzwilliam, both of whom had been active in building the case against Anne, as well as Jane's supporter, Carew. The possibility that a rumour had been heard about Anne and was exploited by supporters of Mary, not necessarily with the aim of destroying her but of overturning the Act of Succession, should not be overlooked. It is easy to assume that any plot which existed had the goal of Anne's death but she may have fallen simply as collateral damage in one which had the sole objective of restoring Mary. Henry's daughter evidently thought Anne was an obstacle to her prospects commenting a week after Anne's execution that "nobody durst speak for me as long as *that* woman lived, which is now gone."[158]

Sometimes cited to support the plot theory, in December 1536, the papal nuncio in France, Faenza, claimed that Henry had told Jane that Anne "had died

---

155 Keith Thomas, *Religion and the Decline of Magic* (1971) pp.342-343, 354. It is not obvious what signs an astrologer might have used to justify any prediction. There were no malefic planetary aspects or transits at the time and none which would have shown up as derogatory to Henry's nativity. The existence of a forecast may have been used to support the case made but it is unlikely to have been the starting point of it.
156 LP 10.1069; LP 8.327. The original is fully quoted in Friedmann, *Anne Boleyn* vol. 2 p.58. The exact meaning of the word Chapuys used is uncertain and it may have been a verbal prediction rather than a written one.
157 LP 10.1134. Francis Bryan was also questioned.
158 LP 10.968. Her comments were another sign of her delusional state. Mary was not in disgrace due to anything Anne had said or done but purely because she had defied the law. As she would learn, Anne's death did not help her cause. The only solution for her was to obey.

in consequence of meddling too much with State affairs."[159] Faenza had never been to England and is not known to have had any contacts in England or to have been in receipt of letters from Chapuys, though he was a close friend of the English ambassador at the French court, Wallop. This would justify little credence being given to his claim except for the fact that six weeks earlier, an unnamed French diplomat who was certainly at Henry's court, noted that the King had "often" told Jane not to meddle with his affairs.[160] The diplomat concluded that Henry was referring to Anne by this warning, though even if that were true, Faenza's interpretation of the comment is open to doubt. It could mean that Henry believed Anne had been a victim of plotters but it could equally mean that he did not want Jane becoming politically active in the way that Anne had done: the French were very aware of Anne's pro-French support and may have seen her fall as an attack on them, even though her relationship with them had cooled by that point. Even if Henry had said what Faenza claimed, rather than what the eyewitness said, it would not follow that Henry therefore thought she was innocent, just that her crimes were exposed by people for their own ends rather than from loyalty to him.

However the process which led to Anne's spectacular fall began, Henry seized the opportunity and ensured it was followed through to the conclusion he required. His lack of favour toward her meant that comments, which would either not have been made previously or would have seen those responsible facing death, were now deemed acceptable, even dutiful. The allegations may or may not have been invented deliberately to free the King to marry Jane but there was a conscious decision to magnify and twist innocent events into something sinister. A tiny puff of smoke was fanned into a mighty conflagration and it consumed the lives of six innocent people in the process.

Could Anne have prevented what happened? If she had given birth to a thriving son in July 1536 as expected, there is no reason to suppose she would not have enjoyed a long life. Even a healthy daughter would have saved her by giving Henry confidence that a son would follow, Her failure to do that, combined with the way she had upset those who were closest to Henry and so best placed to help her should she get into trouble, meant she was in a dangerous position. Anne understood this, though it is probable that she only feared an annulment attempt. She cannot have imagined in her wildest dreams that anyone would contemplate putting her on trial for incest with her own brother.

Jane's role in Anne's fall is not entirely clear. There is no doubt that she was actively seeking to incite her employer's husband into adultery, a mortal sin which might cost him his soul. It is possible that Jane's lack of education meant she actually thought that Henry and Katherine had been legally married and so saw her own behaviour as a bit of tit-for-tat, but she was evidently seeking the crown for herself. Publicly she was playing the role of demure

---

159 LP 11.1250
160 LP 11.860

damsel in the calculated manner of any modern media manipulator or spin doctor, whilst privately she was acting as the Lady Macbeth of character assassination. Henry may have been seduced by Jane's presentation but it is improbable that he was in love with her for within a month of Anne's demise, he was expressing regret that he had married her.[161]

The fact that Henry had already promised himself to Jane even before Anne was arrested, let alone been tried and condemned, is why later generations have not seen him as Henry the Great. Yet the rumours about Anne which emerged in April would have seemed heaven sent to him and indeed contemporaries across Europe lost no time in saying that it was a sign of God's special favour to Henry that these things had come to light.[162] Indeed, the 1536 Act of Succession said that "God of His infinite goodness, from whom no secret things can be hid, hath caused to be brought to light, evident and open knowledge" of the problem.[163] Henry would undoubtedly have shared this belief and this, combined with what he would have seen as God's evident non-acceptance of his marriage to her as demonstrated by the lack of sons, meant he had no hesitation in believing the evidence presented to him. He thought that she and those accused with her were traitors and death was the penalty prescribed for the crime. He would have signed the death warrants with a clear conscience. The story that on his deathbed almost eleven years later, Henry repented having realised that Anne had never been unfaithful to him, is something many would like to be true but impossible to prove or disprove.[164]

Question: Why did Anne fall?

Answer
Henry believed she was a traitor and he considered he had the right to punish her both as his wife and his subject.[165]

---

161 LP 11.8. Henry was not expressing sorrow that Anne was dead, just that he had not taken more time to choose another bride.
162 For example, see LP 10.888, 947, 970, 974, 977.
163 *Statutes of the Realm*, vol. 3 p.656
164 Burnet, *History* vol.3 (1866) p.207. The story was told by Thevet in his *Cosmography* (1563) p.xvi. As Burnet comments, a friar was unlikely to willingly express support for Anne so Thevet probably wrote what he thought was true.
165 LP 10.1069.

Was Anne's conviction fair?

A belief in the need for justice to be fair is deep seated and the supposition by many, both then and since, that Anne was not guilty of adultery has led to questions being raised about the trial process. This section seeks to examine this question by looking at the charges laid against her, the jurors involved, and also by comparing her experience to that of other high profile people to face trial such as the Duke of Buckingham (1521), Lord Dacre (1534), Thomas More (1535), Thomas Cromwell (1540) and Queen Kathryn Howard (1541).

The first point which needs to be made is that Anne was convicted of high treason, the same as her brother, Henry Norris, William Brereton, Francis Weston and Mark Smeaton. Notwithstanding the popular misconception, she was not convicted of adultery which was not an actual crime. But what was treason? Three Acts defined it which are listed below. The numbering of clauses has been added to ease reference in what follows.

The Treason Act of 1352 listed:

1. When a man doth compass or imagine the death of our lord the King or of our lady his Queen or of their eldest son or heir;
2. if a man do violate the King's companion or the King's eldest daughter unmarried or the wife of the King's eldest son and heir;
3. if a man do levy war against our lord the King in his realm or be adherent to his enemies in his realm, giving to them aid and comfort in the realm or elsewhere and thereof be attainted by open deed;
4. if a man counterfeit the King's Great or Privy Seal or his money;
5. if a man bring false money into his realm counterfeit to the money of England knowing the money to be false;
6. if a man slay the Chancellor, Treasurer or one of the King's justices.[1]

A final clause commented: "because that many other like cases of treason may happen in time to come which a man cannot think or declare at this present time; it is accorded that if any other case supposed treason which is not above specified, doth happen before any justices, the justices shall tarry without going to judgment of the treason, till the cause be showed and declared before the King and his parliament whether it ought to be judged treason or felony." In 1416, coin clipping was added by this means to the list and attempting to poison a bishop likewise in 1531.

---

[1] *Statutes of the Realm* vol. 2 pp.319-320. The Act was passed in the spring which owing to the year then commencing on 25th March, meant contemporaries cited it as 1351. Here, because the year has been assumed to begin on January 1st, the year of 1352 is given.

In the 1533 Act of Succession, treason was defined as when anybody after 1st May 1534:

1. by writing, or printing or by any exterior act or deed, maliciously procure, or do, or cause to be procured or done, anything or things to the peril of your most royal person;
2. or maliciously give occasion by writing, print, deed or act whereby your Highness might be disturbed or interrupted of the Crown of this realm;
3. or by writing, print, deed, or act, procure or do or cause to be procured or done any thing or things to the prejudice, slander, disturbance, or derogation of the said lawful matrimony solemnized between your majesty and the said Queen Anne;
4. or to the peril, slander, or disherison of any the issues and heirs of your highness, being limited by this Act to inherit and to be inheritable to the crown of this realm;
5. [in event of a regency] by writing or exterior deed or act, procure or do or cause to be procured or done any thing or things, to the let or disturbance of the same. [2]

The Treason Act of 1534 covered anyone who did:

1. maliciously will, wish or desire by words, writing or by craft, imagine, invent, practice or attempt, any bodily harm to be done or committed to the King's most royal persons, the Queen's, or their heirs apparent;
2. or to deprive them or any of them of the dignity, title or name of their royal estates;
3. or slanderously and maliciously publish and pronounce by express writing or words that the King our sovereign lord should be heretic, schismatic, tyrant, infidel or usurper of the crown;
4. or rebelliously do detain, keep or withhold from our said Sovereign Lord, his heirs or successors, any of his or their ships, ordnance or artillery or other munitions or fortifications of war [3]

In each case, the punishment for treason was death: burning for a woman and being hanged, drawn and quartered for a man. Conviction meant that the property of the traitor reverted to the Crown. Anyone who abetted a traitor was considered guilty of the same offence and failing to reveal treason was judged misprision.

Thus for Anne and her fellow accused, a charge of high treason was extremely serious. Some of the treason definitions above were clearly

---

[2] *Statutes of the Realm* vol. 3 pp.473-474
[3] Ibid. pp.508-9

inapplicable. Nobody suggested they had taken royal ships or counterfeited coins or murdered the chancellor. Yet the indictments against them were framed in order to obtain a verdict of high treason. The charges against Anne were as below.

1) "That the Lady Anne, Queen of England, having been wife of the King for the space of three years and more in contempt of the marriage so solemnised between her and the King and bearing malice in her heart against the King following her frail and carnal lust did falsely and traitorously procure, by means of indecent language, gifts and other acts therein stated, divers of the King's daily and familiar servants to become her adulterers and concubines so that several of the King's servants, by the said Queen's most vile provocation and invitation, became given and inclined to the said Queen."

A series of charges then followed all of which were in the same format. They gave a date and place on which the Queen "procured, by sweet words, kisses, touches, and otherwise" a named man "to violate her" then listed the date and place of the actual adultery adding "they had illicit intercourse at various other times, both before and after, sometimes by his procurement, and sometimes by that of the Queen." With regard to George Boleyn it accused her of "alluring him with her tongue in the said George's mouth, and the said George's tongue in hers, and also with kisses, presents, and jewels; whereby he, despising the commands of Almighty God, and all human laws" on a specific date "violated and carnally knew the said Queen, his own sister." The dates given were:

Name	Procured	Adultery	In Middlesex
Norris	6th Oct 1533	12th Oct 1533	Westminster
George	2nd Nov 1535	5th Nov 1535	Westminster
Brereton	3rd Dec 1533	8th Dec 1533	Hampton Court
Weston	8th May 1534	20th May 1534	Whitehall
Smeaton	12th Apr 1534	26th Apr 1534	Westminster

Name	Procured	Adultery	In Kent
Norris	12th Nov 1533	19th Nov 1533	Greenwich
George	22nd Dec 1535	29th Dec 1535	Eltham
Brereton	16th Nov 1533	27th Nov 1533	Greenwich
Weston	6th Jun 1534	20th Jun 1534	Greenwich
Smeaton	13th May 1534	19th May 1534	Greenwich

The charge continued:
"Furthermore that the said George Lord Rochford, Henry Norris, William Brereton, Francis Weston and Mark Smeaton, being thus inflamed by carnal love of the Queen, and having become very jealous of each other, did in order to secure her affections, satisfy her inordinate desires and that

the Queen was equally jealous of the Lord Rochford and the other before mentioned traitors, and she would not allow them to show any familiarity with any other woman without her exceeding displeasure and indignation and that on the 27th November 1535 and other days at Westminster, she gave them gifts and great rewards to inveigle them to her will.

2) Furthermore that the Queen and the other said traitors, jointly and severally on 31st October 1535 and on 8th January 1536 and at various times before and after, compassed and imagined the King's death and that the Queen had frequently promised to marry someone of the traitors whenever the King should depart this life, affirming she never would love the King in her heart.

3) Furthermore that the King having within a short time before become acquainted with the before mentioned crimes, vices and treasons, had been so grieved that certain harms and dangers had happened to his royal body.

4) And thus the Queen and the before mentioned traitors had committed the before mentioned treasons in contempt of the King and to the danger of the King's person and body, and to the scandal, danger, detriment and danger of the issue and heirs of the said King and Queen."[4]

The key word in the first charge was "malice." The Acts of 1533 and 1534 had both specified that malicious words or deeds against the King were treasonous.[5] Adultery was an act in contempt or derogation of the royal marriage which was treason according to the third clause of the Act of Succession.[6] The reference to Anne's lovers being "given and inclined to the said Queen" implied that the loyalty which they owed Henry was being taken away and switched to her. If any was guilty of treason, it followed that this meant they were adherent to one of the King's enemies and guilty of giving comfort to them, an offence under the third clause of the 1352 Treason Act. The allegations relating to gift giving and tongues in mouths and jealousy were irrelevant and added to give substance and prurient colour to the rest: none were criminal offences. Willing adultery on the part of the Queen was not an offence envisaged by Edward III's government but was construed as her abetting the said traitorous violation which made her equally culpable. As the 1352 Act had said, in cases where they was a query, the King could define

---

[4] LP 10.876. See also *Third Report of the Deputy Keeper of the Public Records* (1842) pp.242-245.

[5] More and Fisher argued that they were not guilty of treason because they did not speak maliciously but the judges disallowed their plea on grounds the adverb was not key.

[6] Only the adultery with George Boleyn, Mark Smeaton and Francis Weston were said to have taken place after 1st May 1534, the date from which the Act of Succession applied.

treason with the aid of Parliament if it was sitting. In 1542, faced with Kathryn Howard, Parliament would clarify that adultery of a Queen was high treason.

The second charge of imagining the King's death was explicitly a reference to the first clause of the same Act. The inclusion of the allegation that she had promised to marry one of the men was important because it meant that those involved had not just imagined the King's death but planned to act upon it. Common law had treated words without deeds as treason since the late fifteenth century but this confirmed an act had taken place, not just a thought. In 1530, Wolsey was accused of asking for a treasonous letter to be written and he was arrested, even though no such letter was ever written.[7] In 1521, Buckingham was condemned on the basis of treasonous words and thoughts only.[8]

The third charge related to the first clause of the 1534 Treason Act in that by their activities, Anne and her paramours had caused the King distress and bodily harm. Upsetting the King had been regarded as treason ever since a ruling of 1477.[9]

The fourth charge referenced the fourth clause of the Act of Succession because the scandal imperilled the future of the Princess Elizabeth.

It is clear that the charges brought were carefully worded to cover offences under all three Acts, the first three clauses of 1352, the first, third and fourth of 1533 and the first of 1534. To employ such a range demonstrates the government's determination to secure a conviction – or perhaps the weakness of its case.

All of the accused pleaded not guilty to each of the charges except for Smeaton who pleaded guilty to adultery alone in breach of the 1352 Act.

The trials of Anne and George took place at the Tower in a hastily convened court of the Lord High Steward. Having been introduced to the judges, a clerk read the indictments and this would have been the first time that George and Anne heard the actual charges against them. They would then have been asked to enter a plea of guilty or not guilty. They were not allowed to challenge any of the judges, all of whom were peers, and nor were they allowed legal counsel or to call witnesses on their own behalf. This was entirely in line with normal practice as it had existed for centuries.

The jury did not hesitate to find all six guilty, but were they? At one level, it is clear that they were not for investigation of the dates and places given shows that the individuals were not normally at the location on the date

---

[7] L. R. Gardiner, 'Further News of Cardinal Wolsey's End,' *BIHR*, vol. lvii (1984) p.103. Wolsey died before he could be tried.

[8] Barbara Harris, 'the Trial of the third Duke of Buckingham: a revisionist view', AJLH, vol. XX (1976) p.21

[9] John Bellamy, *The Tudor Law of Treason: an introduction* (1979) p.11. Thomas Burdett was condemned for casting the King's horoscope to discover when he would die and then sharing this information. It was held that by so doing, Burdett weakened the love which subjects had for their monarch which caused the King such sadness that it reduced his lifespan.

concerned. The phrase "and in other places and on other days before and after" was common in all treason indictments and was not specific to this case. It enabled a conviction to be gained even if the date shown could be disproved on grounds the crime happened on a different date.[10] Adultery was not something which was likely to have actual eye witnesses but the law required that dates be given. In the case of Anne Boleyn, her offences with Weston, Smeaton and her brother were shown to have occurred while she was pregnant. This was almost certainly deliberate. It was believed that if a woman had intercourse while pregnant, she risked the life of the unborn child. Given both pregnancies ended with the death of the foetus, an implication might be drawn that Anne and her lovers had sought to imperil the issue of the King which was treason. The interval between procuring and the act of adultery was important here because it showed pre-meditation to do evil. To lawyers of the period, whether an act had actually taken place was less important than showing the intention. If a person planned to commit a crime, they argued, they were already guilty. It was a line of argument used by Jesus in the Sermon on the Mount when he said that any man who looked on a woman with lust was already guilty of adultery (Matt. 5:28). In 1542, Kathryn Howard was found guilty of treason on grounds she intended to commit adultery, not that she actually did.[11] However, it is important not to focus too much on the issue of whether Anne did or did not commit adultery. There is no evidence that she did. It would not have been in character for her to do so and she denied it under oath and on the sacrament. The charges against her covered many elements of the treason laws to ensure conviction was inevitable. A charge that her behaviour had caused the King stress was vague enough to mean anything and it could be argued that any argument which she had ever had with him was evidence of her treating him and their marriage with contempt. If her reaction to hearing of Henry's accident in January had been to wonder what would happen next, a lawyer could twist that into her imagining the King's death. Anne did not have to commit adultery to be found guilty of treason.

Given this was the case, why was adultery included on the indictment? Throughout history, the way to attack a woman has been to challenge her sexual behaviour. The allegation does not have to be true or even credible to do damage, as claims of paedophile tendencies made against some politicians and celebrities today have shown. Yet the specifics of adultery and incest may have been chosen intentionally. Prior to her marriage, Anne was widely recognised to be a virgin. Even her worst enemies accepted this, and it is certain that a lot of money would have been available from Imperial coffers, if someone had been able to prove otherwise. As Queen, Anne had continued to espouse godly behaviour through her charitable works and her support of certain preachers. She may have been hated for supplanting Katherine and encouraging reform,

---

[10] Ibid. p.129
[11] Gareth Russell, *Young and Damned and Fair* (2017) pp.342-3, 367. The intention alone constituted misprision. *Statutes of the Realm* vol. 3 pp.857-69

but there had not been the slightest hint of any personal lack of integrity in her lifestyle. To proclaim such a person guilty of adultery and incest was therefore shocking but it was also revenge. When Henry argued that his "marriage" to Katherine was invalid, the Imperialists had been offended because they thought the idea that Katherine had willingly entered into an incestuous marriage with her husband's brother was libellous. Since they did not recognise the annulment, they viewed Anne as an adulteress. The first charge against her was liable to win support from those who thought that way because if Anne had been willing to commit adultery, as they saw it, with Henry, why would she hesitate to commit adultery with others? Even if she had not, in their eyes she was already guilty.[12] Similarly, as Katherine had been accused indirectly of incest, what better retaliation could there be than to charge Anne with the same crime? Thus the sexual element of the charges against her not only created sympathy for Henry who had found himself yoked to such a wicked nymphomaniac, but they destroyed Anne's credibility and satisfied the desire on the part of Katherine's supporters to punish her, eye for eye, tooth for tooth, incest charge for incest charge.

The records of the trial itself have long disappeared so it is impossible to know what evidence was brought forward. Although some have hinted that the absence is suspicious and wondered if Elizabeth had material defamatory to her mother destroyed when she came to the throne, there is no reason to think this happened. Accounts of interviews, signed depositions and confessions are missing from other treason trials. Once the person had been convicted, those involved would have seen no reason to keep the papers, any more than anyone today would keep last month's shopping list.

Chapuys reported that no witnesses were called which he described as unusual though he was no expert on English law or history. At the trial of the Duke of Buckingham which was similarly held before the Lord High Steward, four witness statements were read and at the Duke's request, the four men were brought in to confirm them. Two witnesses were used at Dacre's trial and one at More's.[13] Smeaton's confession was inadmissible at Anne's because as a convicted traitor, his word was considered untrustworthy. However, the jurors would have known of it from talk of his conviction.

Judge John Spelman, who was actually present, said that the chief evidence presented came from Lady Wingfield whom he said "had been a servant to the said Queen and of the said qualities; and suddenly the said Wingfield became sick and a short time before her death showed this matters to one of hers."[14] How this evidence was introduced is necessarily unknown. Did somebody testify to having heard her revelations and then sign a deposition about it? If so, when? Unless she had died very recently, the person who heard

---

[12] Queen Mary in the Low Countries typified this response. She did not believe Anne was guilty of the charges laid against her but she thought she was responsible for destroying Katherine's "marriage" so had no sympathy for her, LP 10.965
[13] William Cobbett, *Collection of State Trials*, vol 1 (1809) pp.291, 408.
[14] J H Baker (ed.), *The Reports of Sir John Spelman*, vol. 1 (1977) p.70

the claims would have been guilty of misprision of treason for not speaking sooner. This use of hearsay evidence was entirely in line with court practices of the day and would continue to be so until the late seventeenth century though it would not be allowed today.[15] The significance of the chief evidence coming from somebody who was dead and unable to confirm or deny it, is obvious. At the time, though, a deathbed statement was considered to be especially valuable because it was thought nobody would want to meet their maker with a lie on their lips.[16] Spelman does not specify what Lady Wingfield was supposed to have alleged but it is possible that it related to the incest story. Her husband, Sir Humphrey, was a close friend of Cromwell's and his son would later become the biographer for Katherine's daughter, Mary, suggesting they were pro Imperial.

The French ambassador, Castelnau, was also at the trials and a gentleman in his household, Lancelot de Carles, wrote an account which quoted George Boleyn as saying he was condemned "only on the word of one woman" but does not name her.[17] John Husee, told the Lisles that the Countess of Worcester gave the principal evidence but that there was also some from Nan Cobham and another maid of Anne's whose name he did not record.[18] How this evidence was presented is unknown. There may have been signed depositions or, more likely, a clerk may have given a verbal summary of what they said. None of the trio were in court to confirm their reported evidence. Cromwell gave an interesting reason for the lack of detail: it was too abominable to reveal![19]

There were at least two pieces of written evidence. One was a letter which Anne had written in 1533 to tell her brother that she was pregnant. The prosecution alleged that she told him because he was the father, an

---

[15] Margery and Frederick Schauer, 'Law as the Engine of State: The Trial of Anne Boleyn', *William and Mary Quarterly* vol. 22 (1980) p.75

[16] A dead witness was employed in the annulment of Henry's marriage to Anne of Cleves, LP 15.850 (7).

[17] Lancelot de Carles, *Trial and death of Queen Anne Boleyn* (1545) f.32. The ambassador would not have attended alone but it is impossible to say which of his staff accompanied him. The amount of detail given in Lancelot's account about expressions, seating arrangements, judges kissing a crucifix, the significance of the direction in which the axe faced, all suggest he was present. The inaccuracies in his account such as George being tried before Anne can be explained by the fact that he was writing a literary work not a journalistic report, and Anne's trial was the highpoint with the drama of George's case told before to add tension.

[18] Since he knew Margery Horsman well, it may be assumed it was not her. If it had been George's wife, he probably would have named her and she was a Gentlewoman of the chamber not a maid of honour. A possibility is Bess Harvey who lost her job around this time, though it is unclear whether Anne dismissed her or Jane simply refused to take her on with the other maids-of-honour LP 11.1134.

[19] LP 10.873.

interpretation that did not convince people at the time who thought it entirely normal that a mother-to-be would inform her family of such news.[20]

Chapuys told the Emperor that George had read out – despite being ordered not to do so – a piece of paper which claimed that Anne had told her sister-in-law, his wife Jane, that Henry "was not skilful in copulating with a woman and had neither expertise nor power."[21] Chapuys had this information from his spy but it must have been such a sensational moment that the spy was able to remember it clearly. Given that, aside from the judges present and the court officials, there was an audience of over two thousand people to the trial, it is surprising that the incident was not recalled elsewhere.[22] The reason for this revelation being introduced into proceedings was to show that Anne had sufficient knowledge of men in order to compare Henry's performance. If she had been a virgin when she married him and faithful ever since, she would not be able to do this. It also suggested that Anne was unsatisfied with Henry which, not only supported the view of her being unnaturally sexually ravenous, but meant she was not having orgasms. Medical theory of the time taught that unless a woman did so, she would not conceive.[23] Given the primary duty of a queen was to produce an heir and at least one spare, this showed she was unfit for the role. Although it can be seen why the prosecution regarded Anne's alleged statement as supporting their case, the introduction of it was risky and one can only wonder how Henry reacted when he was told what had happened – if anyone was that brave. To be cuckolded by a monster might earn him sympathy but a public revelation that he was less than a model of virility, was quite damaging to his image. It may be no accident that the famous Holbein portrait of him with outsized codpiece was painted and circulated a year later.

Very little is known about the charge of compassing the King's death. The latter of the two dates given was 8th January 1536, the day on which news of Katherine's death reached the court. Was it thought that Anne's first reaction had been that this event would somehow enable her to rid herself of Henry and marry one of her lovers? At Buckingham's trial, Chief Justice Fyneaux had advised the jurors that "if one intends the death of our lord the King, it is high

---

[20] *Calendar of State Papers; Domestic* 1.1303, Alexander Ales to Queen Elizabeth, 1st September 1559
[21] LP 10.908
[22] Indeed, the omission from other accounts raises doubts about the veracity of the story. Chapuys' report is curious in many ways. He suggested to the Emperor that Anne was charged with poisoning Katherine which she was not and that George failed to answer the charge that he had questioned Elizabeth's paternity, something also not part of the indictment. These were additions to the story made by Chapuys to bolster his belief that Anne killed Katherine and that Elizabeth was a bastard and to justify his campaign to have Mary reinstated in the succession. Along with the other accused, George had been charged with bringing the issue of Henry and Anne into disrepute but not only is that not the same as questioning Elizabeth's paternity, but the court record shows George clearly pleaded not guilty and was not silent.
[23] Betsy Rowland, *Medieval Woman's Guide to Health* (Ohio, 1981) p.167. The theory was Galen's.

treason."[24] It must be presumed that the argument would have been that Anne, and whomsoever she married, were effectively seeking the throne for themselves because under the 1533 Act of Succession, Anne was to be regent if Elizabeth succeeded. As Elizabeth was only two years old, that would have meant that Anne could have expected to be effective ruler for at least a dozen years.

Assuming some evidence was presented, the question would remain of how it was obtained. There were rumours that Smeaton had been tortured, something which should not have happened without a signed writ from the King.[25] Perhaps one did exist and was destroyed with the rest of the papers. Perhaps, those involved took a chance and racked him anyway as happened later with Anne Askew. Perhaps he spoke of his own volition: Lancelot de Carles specifically states that he did this, though he may have simply been repeating the official assurance given to the French.[26] Even without violence, there were means to persuade witnesses to speak, a promise of a favour or money, the threat of repercussions if they did not 'remember' what Cromwell wanted. Ales confirmed that bribes were offered and promises made to Anne's staff and this would not have happened had those involved not been sure of Henry's support. Today, how information is obtained is key to its validity but then things were very different. Treason was a very serious charge and it was deemed essential to the realm's safety that a conviction was obtained. The use of false witnesses was not only accepted but recommended. Sir Thomas More, who had been Lord Chancellor and therefore the senior legal figure in England, had justified the use of people known to be liars in heresy and treason trials "because the crime is so great and so odious, that therefore it is worthy to be handled with the more rigour and the less favour." He said "reason moveth and necessity compelleth" the acceptance of witnesses who would not be accepted in any other sort of court least otherwise "all such crimes should pass forth unpunished, and thereby should the world swarm full of such mischievous people for lack of proof and trial in the matter."[27] He had also recommended the summary execution of traitors without indictments or trial.[28]

Cynics also recognised the use of perjury in cases involving landowners. In 1537 it was admitted that if "a knight or a lord that had lands or goods to

---

[24] Harris, *Trial*, p.21. At least four of the judges for Anne and George had also served on the jury for Buckingham.

[25] T. Amyot (ed.) 'A Memorial of George Constantine', *Archaeologia* vol. 23 (1831) p.64 "The saying was that he was first grievously racked, which I could never know of a truth." Constantine was employed by Norris and attended school with Brereton.

[26] De Carles f.19 line 477. The fact that he mentioned the subject is indicative of it being a topic of debate.

[27] Thomas More, *Dialogue,* book 3 chapter 3. More's own conviction on the basis of the perjured evidence of Richard Rich might be held to be a case of sad but poetic justice.

[28] Bellamy, *Treason*, p.231

lose then he should lose his life" because a "false wretch" would be paid to testify against him by those who anticipated benefiting from the accused's conviction.[29]

Whatever was said, the prosecution's case was circumstantial. George Boleyn had spent a long time alone with Anne in her room: surely they could not be talking, they must have been having sex. She danced with gentlemen of the King's Privy Chamber, but did not her enjoyment of this pastime signify a more intimate relationship with them? It was pretty pathetic and even Chapuys said the conviction was "by presumption and not evidence, without proof or valid confession." He suggested her real fault was laughing at the King's dress and poems which the prosecution had alleged was a crime.[30] Lancelot de Carles said that Anne turned to the judges at the end and told them: "the reason why you have condemned me is other than you could have deduced from what has been presented."[31] He adds that her sober, constant and unflustered defence together with her expression which "made more effect than her words" meant "those who saw did not believe her guilty."[32]

So why was she condemned? It is easy to criticise the judges for their servility in supporting Henry in murder but that would be unfair. At the time, there was no concept of innocent until proven guilty but rather the reverse.[33] It was assumed that the commission and grand juries had done their job and that the defendant was guilty, unless they could prove otherwise. In Anne's case, a court had already found four men guilty of having slept with her and sought the King's demise so how could they realistically find her innocent without overturning the verdict of the previous court?

A final word should be said about the juries involved. A fair trial to us requires that those sitting in judgment are not related to the accused or involved in the case in any way. Was this what happened with Anne and those charged with her?

Hardly. As Paul Friedmann demonstrated back in 1884, the jury for Norris, Brereton, Weston and Smeaton included William Musgrave who owed Cromwell £1340, Giles Alington who was son-in-law to Thomas More's widow and Walter Hungerford who was the son-in-law of Lord Hussey, ex-chamberlain of Mary's household and a close friend of Chapuys.[34] The grand juries for Anne and George included Giles Heron who was married to More's daughter.[35] Yet this was totally normal practice at the time because in treason trials, the prosecution had the right to select the jury.[36]

---

[29] LP 12.2.655
[30] CSPS 5.2.55. This was not part of the indictment.
[31] De Carles f.36 lines 996-998.
[32] Ibid. f.35 lines 950-952
[33] Schaurer, *Law as the Engine of State*, p.73
[34] Paul Friedmann, *Anne Boleyn*, vol. 2 (1884) pp.270-271.
[35] LP 10.876.7
[36] Schauer, *Law as the Engine of State*, p.62

With regard the twenty-five judges who tried Anne and George, they were selected from the peerage which was so intermarried that it was inevitable that many of them were related to one or both of them or to the four men already condemned.[37] The full list is given in an appendix and it shows that the judges included the chamberlain of Anne's household, the husband of the Countess of Worcester and kinsman of Nan Cobham and who testified against her and George's father-in-law. It could be argued that they were in a particularly good situation to know the truth so not necessarily hostile jurors. They were also dependent on Henry for their well-being and a failure to convict could have brought them into suspicion of abetting traitors. Thomas Boleyn was not part of the jury though Chapuys says that he requested to be present at the trials of both of his children, possibly to give them moral support or perhaps to distance himself from their crimes.[38]

Question: Was Anne's conviction fair?

Answer
Not by modern standards but the trial process was absolutely fair by Tudor ones and conducted in full public view. With regard to the verdict, the most eloquent comment on proceedings came from Anne herself. On being arrested, she asked if she would be denied justice. She was told that even the poorest subject of Henry VIII could be sure of that. Her response? A bitter laugh.[39]

---

[37] The Duke of Norfolk as Lord High Steward was in charge of proceedings and not a judge. The Earl of Northumberland sat in judgment on Anne but was taken ill so did not sit for George's trial. LP 10.876.8

[38] CSPS 5.2.55. Boleyn had attended the trials of Norris, Weston, Brereton and Smeaton.

[39] LP 10.793

Why was Anne's marriage annulled?

Imagine the scene. You have spent years of your life making the King's marriage watertight. You've seen it confirmed by parliament, lawyers, even the Archbishop of Canterbury and you have overseen thousands of people across the country taking an oath of loyalty to the couple. After considerable struggle, the marriage has been recognised by the Emperor. There is no longer any doubt about its legitimacy. You believe you deserve a reward so when a summons comes from the King, you approach cheerfully wondering what might be in store. Will it be a title, a house, maybe a pay increase? The King greets you with a smile and tells you that he has a new project for you – dissolving the said marriage. As your jaw drops at the thought of starting over, he adds with a beam that you have just less than a month to complete the task as he has already made plans to marry Jane Seymour.

It is sometimes said that Henry could easily have obtained an annulment of his marriage to Anne and that the fact that he had her executed instead indicates he was a vicious murderer. This is totally wrong. The people who have made such a claim are united by one assumption: they accept the validity of Henry's "marriage" to Katherine and in consequence consider that his marriage to Anne was obviously invalid because Katherine was still alive when it took place. The fallacy of this opinion has already been shown but even the most dedicated supporter of Katherine needs to accept the fact that Henry had absolutely no doubts about the illegality of his "marriage" to her. He believed he was single when he married Anne and his opinion never changed. If asked on his deathbed to name his first wife, he would not have named Katherine. Thus, any quest for an annulment from Anne could not be sought on that basis or any other which might suggest that the unfortunate union with Katherine had ever been valid. Moreover, the fact that the task set was difficult is evident by Cromwell spending four days in discussions with Sampson on the subject. If Anne's biographer, Friedmann, had been correct about it being so simple, the meeting would surely have only taken a few minutes.[1] The court convened by Cranmer to investigate the matter also lasted several days.[2]

Henry's annulment from Anne was shrouded in secrecy which gave rise to different theories about the grounds used. Spelman reported that many said it was a pre-contract on Anne's part.[3] Chapuys was disappointed that it was not

---

1 Paul Friedmann, *Anne Boleyn*, vol. 2 (1884) p.240.
2 Henry Ansgar Kelly, *The Matrimonial Trials of Henry VIII* (1976) pp.244-245.
3 J H Baker (ed.), *The Reports of Sir John Spelman*, vol. 1 (1977) p.59. If this had been the case and Percy had been the excuse, his marriage would have been automatically dissolved by the same pre-contract. This did not happen proving that this was not the grounds used. Wriothesley made the same mistake, Charles Wriothesley, *A Chronicle of England*, ed. William Hamilton, vol. 1 (Camden

because that would have suited his low opinion of her. Instead, he thought it had been granted because of Henry's relationship with Mary Boleyn which seemed to him a dishonourable excuse and meant the King was guilty of incest, coincidentally one of the acts for which Anne had just been executed.[4] Given the lack of documentation on the trial process, speculation is, and was then, inevitable but it is possible to work out what happened.

Under canon law, in order to obtain an annulment, Henry would need to prove one of the following:

1. he or Anne had been forced into the match
2. he or Anne was under age, fourteen for him and twelve for her
3. they were related in some forbidden degree and they had no valid dispensation
4. he or Anne was married or contracted to someone else at the time
5. he or Anne was insane and therefore not capable of making promises
6. he or Anne was in holy orders or had taken vows of celibacy
7. he or Anne was an unbaptised pagan
8. he or Anne was impotent and unable to consummate the marriage

In addition, for a marriage to be fully canonical, the wedding needed to be celebrated:

1. either after banns had been publicly read or a licence obtained
2. during the hours of daylight
3. by an authorised clergyman
4. on consecrated ground[5]
5. before witnesses.

Failure to meet one of this second group of conditions was not considered sufficient to annul a marriage though it could cause legal problems for any children seeking their inheritance and result in it being classified as clandestine. More commonly, clandestine marriages occurred when a couple took vows to one another without banns or a licence or the presence of a priest. Common law recognised the full legality of such unions as did the Church, though the Church held they could be dissolved in certain circumstances.

For Henry, the options were very limited. He and Anne were clearly adults at the time they married and both were baptised and practising Christians. Neither of them had taken holy orders and nor were they insane. The fact that they had a daughter was proof that the marriage had been

---

Society, 1875) p.41.
4   LP 11.41.
5   Property could be consecrated for the purpose. This might happen if someone was very ill or a monarch wished to use a particular room.

consummated. Despite Henry's comment about being bewitched, there is nothing to suggest anyone ever considered claiming that he had been forced into the marriage. There was a precedent for using witchcraft as grounds for an annulment but Henry's words had been spoken in the heat of his distress at losing his son and were not a statement of proposed policy.[6] In 1534, he had used the same language with regard to Wolsey having urged him to write a book against Luther.[7] This left just two options, one being the existence of a previous spouse and the other an impediment for which there was no valid dispensation.

Henry's marital history was clear. Although his enemies might have argued his "marriage" to Katherine was legal and it was true that he had wed Anne before Thomas Cranmer pronounced the annulment of that union, there was no possibility of Henry re-opening that issue which would have meant acknowledging papal supremacy. Besides, a marriage contracted during annulment proceedings was retrospectively validated by the annulment decree of the first. Cranmer had been acting entirely in accordance with canon law when he pronounced Henry and Anne's marriage legal in May 1533.

Anne's marital history had been investigated thoroughly when she first became involved with the King. Questions had been asked about her relationship with Henry Percy and that matter would be raised again in 1532 and once more in 1536 while she was in the Tower.[8] Faced with an absolute denial of the existence of any pre-contract, taken certainly in his case under oath and quite probably Anne also, that was also a non starter.

If Percy could not be presented as a valid previous spouse, an alternative would be needed. In 1527, a dispensation had been received from the pope for Henry to marry someone who had been promised in marriage before she was seven years old and it has been speculated here that the prospect of such a match could have explained why Anne was sent abroad at such a young age.[9] However, even if the man was still alive and could be found, the fact that there had been a dispensation meant he was equally unsuitable for Henry's purposes.

Another option might have been to find a French beau, either real or fantasy. It would not have been beyond the realms of possibility for someone to be found who would claim to having made vows to Anne and had sex with her in return for a generous reward. That solution would genuinely have met the requirement for information which only came to light after the marriage and it would have had the added benefit of enabling the English to do something which they have loved for centuries, blame the French.

---

6   Archbishop Henry Chichele had annulled the marriage of the Duke and Duchess of Gloucester in 1441 for witchcraft, Kelly, *Matrimonial Trials*, p.242. Canon law permitted annulment on grounds of impotence due to witchcraft but this was no help to Henry, D. L. D'Avray, *Papacy, Monarchy and Marriage 800-1600* (Cambridge, 2015) p.123.
7   LP 7.152.
8   LP 10.864
9   See *Was Anne the cause of the breakdown of Henry's "marriage" to Katherine?*

Yet, it was not a straightforward process to use a pre-contract to break a marriage. Canon law stated that if a couple made promises to one another in the future tense, they were lawfully wed but they could dissolve that union by mutual consent or by one party taking vows in the present tense to someone else.[10] If the promises had been made in the present tense but the relationship not consummated, this constituted public honesty which meant that a dispensation was required but Henry had one of these.[11] The only time when a pre-contract was absolutely binding and destructive of future relationships was if it was consummated.[12] Anne was recognised by Henry as well as by her enemies, to have been a virgin when she married him so the only way in which the government could win the case would be to hire a perjurer, French or otherwise.

Most likely, the idea of using the excuse of a pre-contract was rejected deliberately both for the improbability that it would work and because it risked Anne's conviction. In 1540, the Lord Chancellor would warn Henry that he should not annul his marriage to Kathryn Howard on such grounds because it "might serve for her defence."[13] Henry believed an unfaithful Queen should be punished. He wanted the annulment but not if it could call into question Anne's guilt.

That left the question of an impediment which had not been lawfully dispensed. At the time Henry married Anne, he had a dispensation from the pope dated April 1528 which allowed him to marry almost any woman in England.[14] It covered anyone who had made an unconsummated marriage, had been betrothed as a young child, was related to him spiritually (a god child or god sister), was a blood relation up to second cousin, was related to any woman with whom he had ever slept, had entered into a clandestine betrothal, plus anyone who had incurred any degree of affinity to him as a result of illicit coitus. Such a complex list of possible impediments were not meant to reflect all the obstacles which he might face with Anne but to allow Henry some flexibility should he choose after all to marry someone other than her while he was awaiting his annulment from Katherine. The papal dispensation did state that it was only operative if that union had been validly dissolved but it could not be attacked on those grounds due to the principle of retroactive validation which existed in canon law.

With such a comprehensive dispensation, it is understandable why those involved in trying to find a way of breaking Henry's marriage to Anne had such

---

10 There were some exceptions to this. For a good guide to canon law on this point see Henry Swinburne, A *Treatise of Spousals* (1686) and John T. Noonan's translation, *Marriage Canons from the Decretum Of Gratian and the Decretals, Sext, Clementines and Extravagantes* (1993).
11 The lies of Spelman and Wriothesley would not have known of this document.
12 As Cranmer told Henry with relation to Kathryn Howard, words be "sufficient to prove a contract, with carnal copulation following." SP vol. 1 part 2 p.690
13 SP vol. 1 pt. 2 p.692
14 LP 4.3913

a hard time. Cranmer found the case so challenging that he declined to ever reveal the grounds employed, though he did issue the necessary decree which was ratified a month later by convocation and then by Parliament. It is evident he did so reluctantly and that he continued to have doubts about Anne's guilt. In the early hours of May 19th, the day of her execution, he was pacing his garden at Lambeth unable to sleep when he told Ales: "She who has been the Queen of England upon earth will today become a Queen in heaven."[15] If he had thought her guilty, he would have presumed she would be on her way to hell.

The second Act of Succession passed in June 1536 said that Anne had revealed a hitherto unknown impediment to Cranmer when in the Tower, but failed to disclose it on grounds it was covered by the seal of the confessional – a very handy excuse. Had there been a simple pre-contract or breach of affinity or consanguinity regulations, there would have been no reason for such secrecy. Since the government was happy to brand Anne an incestuous and traitorous nymphomaniac, it seems improbable they would have hesitated about publishing details they could proclaim further indicated her duplicitous and evil nature. A number of historians have taken this reference to a revelation by Anne literally but it was just a cover and a means of passing the blame on to her.[16] No fault could ever be suggested on the part of the King.

Thus, the only possible grounds left was to claim that the dispensation itself was illegal, the route taken when annulling the match with Katherine. The 1534 Act against Exactions Paid to the See of Rome had declared future dispensations from Rome illegal but accepted those issued prior to 12th March 1533 provided that they were in accordance with the laws of God and of the realm.[17] This naturally excluded the one issued by Julius II permitting Henry to marry Katherine, his brother's widow. The dispensation of 1528 included a clause dispensing the impediment created in canon law by Henry's relationship with Mary Boleyn. The 1533 Act of Succession stated that marriage to a wife's sister was against God's law but defined marriage as any union which was solemnised in church and consummated.[18] As Henry had not been married to Mary Boleyn which meant there was no impediment to him marrying Anne. The Act, therefore, effectively deemed the 1528 dispensation unnecessary – unless Anne was forbidden to him by one of the other clauses such as being his god sister – which solved the embarrassment of Henry using a document issued by Rome.

---

15 *Calendar of State Papers; Domestic* 1.1303, Alexander Ales to Queen Elizabeth, 1st September 1559
16 Ives' theory that in 1528 Henry had not known the pope lacked the authority to dispense, and this was a new revelation pointed out by Anne in 1536 is improbable. Eric Ives, *Anne Boleyn* (1986) p.406
17 *Statutes of the Realm* vol. 3 pp.465, 470.
18 Ibid. pp. 472, 475. For more on this doubtful, though traditional, interpretation of the Hebrew text regarding sisters, see *Was Henry married when he met Anne?* The text forbade a man having a contemporaneous relationship with his wife's sister but not one after his wife had died.

In the summer of 1536, less than two months after Anne's death, two new Acts were passed relating to the Succession and Dispensations. The latter declared all papal bulls and dispensations issued prior to 3rd November 1534 void except for those relating to marriage which would remain valid unless the union breached the regulations of the 1536 Act of Succession.[19] This Act rehearsed the list of prohibited matches as laid down in Leviticus, including that of wife's sister, but it crucially redefined the qualifying relationship. Now, instead of needing to have solemnised and consummated a marriage, it said where "any man know carnally any woman, that then all and singular persons being in any degree of consanguinity or affinity to any of the parties so carnally offending shall be deemed and adjudged to be within the cases and limits of the said prohibitions of marriage." Since Henry admitted having slept with Mary Boleyn at least once and Anne was her sister, this meant that she was now forbidden to him. The Act said that if anyone's marriage was now found to breach the 1536 Act, regardless of when it had been contracted, it was to be dissolved. It went on to legitimate existing annulments of such couples, regardless of the grounds employed for the separation:

> Any person or persons of what estate, dignity, degree or condition so ever they be, who hath been heretofore married within this Realm, or in any other the King's Dominions, within any the degrees above rehearsed, and by any the Archbishops or Ministers of the Church of England be separate from the bonds of such unlawful marriages, that then every such separation shall be good lawful firm and permanent for ever, and not by any power authority or means to be revoked or undone hereafter. And that the children proceeding or procreate under such unlawful marriage shall not be lawful nor legitimate, any foreign laws licences dispensations or other thing or things to the contrary thereof notwithstanding.[20]

To describe this as legally questionable would be something of an understatement: Acts are not meant to be retrospective.[21] A reason had been found to annul Henry's marriage to Anne but the law did not exist at the time Cranmer issued the document. It is small wonder that Cranmer never published his reasons for annulling Henry and Anne's marriage. Presumably he had been advised of the forthcoming legislation and was not simply psychic but the document as issued on May 17th 1536 would not have stood up to any sort of scrutiny. Anne was truly Henry's wife.

---

19 Ibid. p.672.
20 Ibid. p.658.
21 The 1531 Determinations had quoted St Ivo as saying that man who married the sister of a woman with whom he had previously must be forcibly divorced, Edward Fox, *The determinations of the moste famous and mooste excellent vniuersities* (1531) pp.73-74.

It can be argued that it was the 1533 Act which was the problem because it defined affinity in terms of marriage only and not from any act of sexual intercourse which was the definition in Rome's canon law until 1917.[22] This touches on the issue of whether English law is supreme in England, something Henry and most of the population would have averred but staunch supporters of papal supremacy such as Fisher and Chapuys, denied. English common law had never regarded acts of sexual intercourse outside the bonds of matrimony to have created ties of affinity. Besides, as Cranmer himself had ruled in 1533 illicit coitus was not an impediment of divine law but canon law so Henry's relationship with Mary Boleyn was not covered by either the 1533 or 1534 Acts.[23]

That the annulment came after the conviction for adultery makes obvious sense, although the treason acts did not specify that the Queen had to be the king's wife. The question remains of why bother to annul the marriage after sentence of death had already been pronounced? Henry would be a widower in a few days and so indisputably free to marry whomsoever he liked, provided that they were of age, single and not related to him in a forbidden degree.[24]

One possible contributory reason was to declare that Henry had been a single man his entire life. If Jane had suggested to Henry that she was pregnant, the legitimacy of that child might be disputed if it was evident that it had been conceived as part of an adulterous union and that would have meant continued problems over the succession. By annulling Henry's marriage to Anne, no such issues would arise. There is no evidence that Jane had voiced such a thought but it would explain the frantic events of April and May 1536. Annulling his marriage to Anne may have reflected Henry's desire to both distance himself from the monstrous image of her which his prosecution had created and to cover his guilty conscience.

However, the main reason for annulling the match was because it was the easiest way to bastardise Elizabeth and since English law did not allow a marriage to be annulled unless both parties were alive, it followed that the annulment had to be issued before Anne's execution.[25] Legally a child of an

---

22 For more on the changing concept of affinity see *Was Henry married when he met Anne?*
23 Kelly, *Matrimonial Trials*, 232. Illicit coitus was only added to canon law in the eleventh century.
24 Jane was Anne's second cousin which meant she was related to Henry in the third degree of affinity as a result of Henry's relationship with Anne and Mary regardless of whether affinity was defined as stemming from marriage or illicit intercourse.
25 William Blackstone, *Commentaries on the Laws of England* (1825)p. 434. When Richard III seized the throne, he justified his move in *Titulus Regius* by saying that the Princes in the Tower were illegitimate, M. Pronay and J. Cox (ed.), *The Crowland Chronicle Continuations* (1986) p.161. Regardless of whether that claim was or was not true, the marriage of Edward IV not been annulled in his lifetime and Richard had previously recognised the offspring as rightful heirs. The justification was therefore utterly illegal as well as immoral.

annulled union was not illegitimate if the parents had entered into the match in good faith which is why it was necessary to claim that Anne had withheld crucial information and thus not taken her vows in good faith. As an adult, Elizabeth would dispute this suggestion saying her mother "had wanted nothing but marriage with the King, with the authority of the Church and of its Archbishop, therefore if she was deceived, she acted in good faith."[26] This is true but it is probable that Anne agreed to take the blame voluntarily. Cranmer had visited her in the Tower in part to help her prepare for death and they must have discussed the situation. Cranmer was Elizabeth's godfather and would have shared Anne's concern for her future. They may have thought that by supporting her removal from the succession they were giving her the best chance of survival and future happiness.

From Henry's perspective, by bastardising both his children and then ensuring that the subsequent Act of Succession allowed him to name his own successor in event of a lack of legitimate issue, he opened the door to making Richmond his heir. This was something which the Privy Council had suggested.[27] At the time, Richmond was an apparently healthy seventeen year old, handsome, intelligent, sporting, a model prince whom many would have welcomed as king. [28]

Question: Why was Anne's marriage annulled?

Answer
Not withstanding the comment in the 1536 Act of Succession that "Your Majesty, not knowing of any lawful impediment entered into the bonds of the said unlawful marriage," the annulment was predicated on his prior relationship with Mary Boleyn.

---

26   Lisa Hilton, *Elizabeth I: Renaissance Prince* (2014) p.84. Her comments were recorded by the Venetian ambassador, Giovanni Michiel in 1557.
27   LP 10.1069.
28   Chapuys advised the Emperor not to object to the clause allowing Henry to name his successor on grounds he felt it was obvious the King would select Mary, LP 11.40. If Richmond had shown any signs of being ill in the spring, it might have increased the pressure on Anne's position with Henry regarding the need to try and father another son as especially urgent, though he could have tried for this with Anne. Richmond died a few weeks after Anne.

Conclusion

We began with the popular view of Henry and Anne's relationship:

> Dastardly Villain Henry falls for Feisty Temptress Anne and decides to divorce his wife Saintly Victim Katherine. Given he has No Case and the pope is a prisoner, this represents an Impossible Task for Wolsey. When Wolsey suffers inevitable failure, Dastardly Villain Henry destroys him before spending almost three years sitting around waiting for Clever Clogs Cromwell to come along and sort the mess out for him. Dastardly Villain Henry sets up his own church to get His Own Way and marries Feisty Temptress Anne. She has a daughter which leaves him Not Pleased so he finds Another Woman. Clever Clogs Cromwell then dupes Dastardly Villain Henry into murdering Anne on trumped up charges leaving the king free to marry Innocent Little Jane.

Investigation of the facts, presents a very different case.

Following the death of Prince Arthur, Katherine's parents being desperate to maintain the alliance with England because they want assistance in their war with France, bribe the pope to do something which had never happened in the entire history of the Church, and allow a man to marry his brother's widow. Henry queries the legitimacy of this document on his accession but is reassured by Katherine's father. He "marries" Katherine but a succession of losses means his doubts remain. In 1524 he separates from her. Three years later, a comment by a French bishop convinces him that he was right all along and he seeks an annulment. Given the pope is an ally and at war with Katherine's nephew, he expects a rapid resolution of the issue giving him the chance to make a new alliance, possibly with France. Advice that Princess Renée appears unable to have children causes him to look closer to home and his attention falls on Anne Boleyn. Meanwhile, the war in Europe turns against England and her allies and what should have been a simple process becomes complicated. Anne remains sceptical that it will work out but he encourages her and shortly after her twenty-first birthday, she agrees to marry him.

The pope says that Henry is right on both the canon law and theological fronts and promises to give a verdict in his favour. However, he reneges on his promise in order to secure Florence for his family.

Henry secures learned support from across Europe and marshals a formidable case but it is to no avail. In the end, and in accordance with New Testament teaching, he returns the English church to the independence which it had before the arrival of Augustine from Rome. His union with Katherine is pronounced null and void on grounds no pope can overturn the Word of God.

Henry marries Anne and has a healthy daughter but two miscarriages follow. These two events create some strain on the marriage but Henry continues to fight for her acceptance by people in England and overseas.

In 1536, Henry instigates an investigation into Anne, probably following a rumour of her infidelity. Cromwell is cobbles together a case against Anne based on innuendo and an alleged statement from a deceased courtier. Henry genuinely believes in her guilt and orders her removal and death. He then marries Jane Seymour, a lady with whom he had dallied in the aftermath of the loss of his son by Anne.

In 1547, Henry dies. A few years later, the Council of Trent rules on marriage and declares that no dispensations should be given for first degree affinity or consanguinity. They also rule on the status of the Bible and confirm that Leviticus is the Word of God.

Appendix 1 The Bull and the Brief

The controversy over Henry's annulment centred around the two documents known as the bull and the Spanish brief. The bull was the official permit issued by Julius II with one copy sent to Henry VII so that his son could marry Katherine and the second copy sent to her parents. The brief was a letter sent by the same pope to Katherine's mother.[1]

The differences between the bull and the brief were as follows:

1. Bull refers to the peace and friendship between "Ferdinand and Isabella, Catholic king and queen of Spain and Sicily, and the aforesaid King and Queen of England"
Brief says between "the aforesaid King of England and our beloved son in Christ King Ferdinand and our beloved daughter in Christ, Isabella, Catholic Queen of Spain and Sicily."[2]

2. Bull says that Katherine's marriage to Arthur had been "perhaps" consummated.
Brief says it had been consummated "through carnal union".

3. Bull says the "said Arthur" had died
Brief says "nevertheless and because lord Arthur" had died

4. Bull says "And whereas you desire to contract a lawful matrimony between you by present words"
Brief refers to this desire later in the paragraph

5. Bull refers to a bond of peace and amity
Brief refers to ties of peace

6. Bull says the motive of the applicants is that the bond should be more durable
Brief says motive is because the bonds might not last without some bond of affinity

7. Bull says the grant is for the "advancement of blessed peace and concord"
Brief refers to this and certain other causes (unspecified)

---

1 An English translation of the two documents can be found in D'Avray's *Dissolving Royal Marriages* pp.232-234. For the story of the two documents, see How did Katherine become Queen of England?
2 Note that Queen Elizabeth of England is omitted from the brief but not the bull. She died on 11th February 1503, before either document was issued. She was alive when Katherine married Arthur and the reference in both documents is to this union.

8. Bull says pope has granted the dispensation in order to make the bond of peace and amity more durable
Brief says the pope has been moved and inclined to grant it because the peace might not last and for other reasons

9. Bull says that supplication has been made
Brief adds that it has been made in due humility

10. Bull says the dispensation has been made "by a gift of special grace"
Brief makes no such reference

11. Bull says it removes the impediment of affinity as well as any obstacles arising from "papal and other contrary constitutions and ordinances"
Brief does not specify the impediment being dispensed.

12. Bull says Henry and Katherine may marry either publicly or privately and lawfully remain so
Brief says they may lawfully contract and remain in a marriage in public or privately

13. Bull says that if Henry and Katherine have already married either publicly or privately and had a child, the child shall be legitimate
Brief says the children shall be legitimate even if they have already married

14. Bull includes a provision that it is null if Katherine has been raped.
Brief has no such provision.

15. Bull refers to being enjoined to carry out penance
Brief reverses the clauses so that penance is enjoined

16. Bull includes a final clause saying that all who question the decision shall be cursed
Brief has no such section

Both documents were dated 26th December 1503 in the first year of the papacy of Julius II. Although this makes it appear that the date is the same, in fact the date on the brief is impossible. On papal bulls, the year ran from 25th March to 24th March whilst on briefs, the year ran from 25th December to 24th December.

1503 was the year of three popes. Alexander VI died on 18th August. Pius III was elected on 22nd September but died on 18th October. Julius II was elected on 1st November. Thus, in documents, the following regnal years applied:

Bull
25th March 1503 to 24th March 1504 was
  Alexander VI year twelve,
  Pius III year one,
  Julius II year one

Brief
25th December 1502 to 24th December 1503 was
  Alexander VI year twelve,
  Pius III year one,
  Julius II year one

25th December 1503 to 24th December 1504 was
  Julius II year two

Hence the date of 26th December 1503 was within Julius' first year for bulls but the second year for a brief. If the brief was written in Julius' first year as the document stated, it would mean the date was really December 1502 which was eleven months prior to his election.

Both dates were false because in July 1504, the pope wrote to say that he had yet to grant the dispensation.[3] They were actually issued later that year.

---

3   CSPS 1.396

Appendix 2   The Love Letters

Seventeen letters written by Henry to Anne Boleyn exist at the Vatican. None of them are dated and over the years, many writers have developed their own theories about when they were written. A few can be dated with a fair degree of accuracy because of the content, for example, Henry's letter telling Anne that Cardinal Campeggio has arrived at Paris must relate to mid September 1528 because Campeggio arrived there on the 14th and it would have taken only a few days for the news to reach London. Other letters contain few or no clues but, unless we are to believe that Henry wrote a letter to Anne when she was in the next room, they must all belong to one of the periods during which Anne and Henry were separated. Those periods were:

1) mid June to mid August 1528 when Anne was sent to Hever due to the sweat[1]
2) late August to early December 1528 when Anne was sent from court pending the arrival of Campeggio[2]
3) December 1529 to mid January 1530 when Anne went home for Christmas following an altercation with Henry[3]

There is the possibility of a further separation during the summer or autumn of 1531. The Privy Purse accounts, which had previously contained regular references to her contain none from June to November of that year inclusive. Perhaps she took the opportunity to visit friends or family while Henry was busy. A separation at this point would make sense of the letter in which Henry refers to working on his book. The exact date of the *Glass of Truth* has been disputed by historians but the publication window is generally agreed to be between late 1531 and 1532 although Chapuys seems to have seen a copy, possibly a draft, in June 1531.[4]

The letters are listed below in what would appear to be their chronological order. Each one is referenced by its calendar number in *Letters and Papers of Henry VIII* and its Harleian number. As the text of each letter is easily accessible from multiple books and websites, they are only summarised here. None of Anne's letters to Henry survive.

---

1   LP 4.4391, 4649
2   CSPS 3.2.541; LP 4.5016.
3   CSPS 4.1.241, 252
4   Richard Rex, 'Redating Henry VIII's A Glasse of the Truthe', *The Library*, March 2003, 4(1):16-27; Steven Haas, 'Henry VIII's Glasse Of Truthe, *History*, (October 1979) pp.353-362; CSPS 4.2.753. An alternative theory is that Henry was referencing the *Collectanea Satis Copiosa* which Heneage says Henry was working on in June 1528 (LP 4.4409). This, however, was a collection of documents which the King reviewed rather than a prose creation.

Separation 1

LP 4.4410　　　　　　　Harleian 9
Language　　　　　　　English
Form of address　　　　Darling, sweetheart
Approximate date　　　Around 15th June 1528
Content
Henry tells Anne that he has told her father to take care of her newly widowed sister.

LP 4.4403　　　　　　　Harleian 3
Language　　　　　　　French
Form of address　　　　Beloved
Approximate date　　　Around 20th June 1528
Content
Henry reassures Anne that her brother has recovered from the sweat and that he himself has not caught it. He tells her that women seem less liable to catch it and those who do, suffer less.

LP 4.4383　　　　　　　Harleian 12
Language　　　　　　　French
Form of address　　　　Mistress
Approximate date　　　Around 23rd June 1528
Content
Henry tells of his dismay that Anne has the sweat. He sends her his physician.

LP 4.4477　　　　　　　Harleian 13
Language　　　　　　　English
Form of address　　　　Darling
Approximate date　　　Early July 1528
Content
Henry updates Anne on which courtiers have had the sweat and tells her that Carey's sister is unsuitable for the role of Abbess of Wilton.

LP 4.3218　　　　　　　Harleian 4
Language　　　　　　　French
Form of address　　　　-
Approximate date　　　July 1528
Content
Henry admits to confusion about Anne's feelings for him. Some passages in her letters appear positive, others less so. He asks her to confirm her intentions and

promises that if she wants a "special relationship" with him, he will abandon all other women and take her as his only love. He admits to having loved her "for more than a year."[5]

LP 4.3221   Harleian 1
Language   French
Form of address   Mistress and friend
Approximate date   July 1528
Content
Henry hopes Anne is missing him as he misses her and sends her a bracelet containing a portrait of himself. He expresses his confidence in her unchangeable affection.

LP 4.4537   Harleian 11
Language   French
Form of address   Mistress, friend
Approximate date   July 1528
Content
Henry asks her to tell her father to come to London two days earlier than planned so that preparations for Campeggio's arrival can be made.

LP 4.4648   Harleian 7
Language   English
Form of address   Darling
Approximate date   Early August 1528
Content
Henry tells Anne that Wolsey has secured her accommodation in London

Separation 2

LP 4.4742   Harleian 6
Language   English
Form of address   Darling
Approximate date   Mid September 1528
Content
Henry advises Anne that Cardinal Campeggio has arrived at Paris.

---

5   The dating of this letter is crucial. Writers who have assumed with the benefit of hindsight that Henry began the annulment in order to marry Anne have presumed that it was written much earlier before the process began but the evidence does not support this.

LP 4.3220	Harleian 10
Language	French
Form of address	Mistress
Approximate date	October 1528
Content	

Henry complains that Anne has not written to him lately so asks if she is well. He sends her a hart and comments that he would rather have her with him than her brother.

LP 4.4894	Harleian 17
Language	English
Form of address	Sweetheart
Approximate date	October 1528
Content	

Henry says he rejoices that she has given up what he terms her "vain thoughts and fantasies" and is now being reasonable. He assures her that Campeggio genuinely is ill and has promised not to be imperial in the matter of the annulment.

LP 4.4539	Harleian 15
Language	English
Form of address	Darling
Approximate date	Late Autumn 1528
Content	

Henry expresses his surprise that people in London know about their meetings and urges her to be more discreet

LP 4.3990	Harleian 14
Language	English
Form of address	Darling, sweetheart
Approximate date	November 1528
Content	

Henry asks her not to detain two men en route to Rome too long long as they are going to the pope and "the sooner we shall have word from him, the sooner shall our matter come to pass.[6]

---

[6] Vannes and Bryan. Some writers have thought the reference was to Gardiner and Foxe who travelled in February 1528 but Anne was with Henry at this point and Gardiner and Foxe were travelling with the pope's representative, Gambara, so it is inconceivable that they would either have taken him to meet her or left him standing outside while they went in. By contrast, in November 1528, Anne was at Hever with her mother (LP 4. Appx.206).

Separation 3

LP 4.3219 Harleian 8
Language French
Form of address -
Approximate date December 1529
Content
Henry reveals his pleasure that Anne remembers him despite having chosen a place other than that which he gave her.

LP 4.3326 Harleian 2
Language French
Form of address Mistress
Approximate date December 1529
Content
Henry expresses his disappointment that Anne has apparently declared she will not return to court and he wonders why. He hopes she will tell him the report is untrue.

LP 4.3325 Harleian 5
Language French
Form of address -
Approximate date January 1530
Content
Henry thanks her for the New Year gift she sent him of a damsel in a ship. He forgives her and hopes she will do the same for him and that she will remain firm in her purpose.

Separation 4

LP 4.4597 Harleian 16
Language English
Form of address Sweetheart
Approximate date Summer 1531
Content
Henry says he has spent four hours writing his book. He is now looking forward to seeing her soon and hopes he will be able to kiss her "pretty" breasts.[7]

---

7   It is particularly disappointing that Anne's response to this letter is unknown. Henry may have been talking about a pleasure he was confident of enjoying or he could have simply been expressing a wish the fulfilment of which Anne had no intention of permitting until she had a wedding ring.

Appendix 3   Henry and Anne's Wedding[1]

The Betrothal – November 1532

(Henry and Anne stand before the priest who faces the congregation.)

Priest

Henry, do you swear by God and his holy saints herein and by all the saints in paradise, that you will take this woman whose name is Anne to wife if the church permit and love, honour, hold and keep her, hale and sick as a husband oweth to keep his wife, and all other for her to leave and hold thee only to her as long as your either life lasteth?

Henry

I will

Priest

Anne, do you swear by God and his holy saints herein and by all the saints in paradise, that you will take this man whose name is Henry to husband if the church permit and obey him and serve him, love and honour and keep [him when] hale and sick as a wife oweth to do the husband, and to leave all other men for him and hold thee only to him whilst your either life lasteth?

Anne

I will

(Henry and Anne join hands)

Priest

Thus ye affiance yourselves.

(A sermon on the serious responsibilities of marriage follows. Henry and Anne bow their heads for a blessing and leave amid congratulations from the witnesses.)

---

[1] Taken from John Blunt, *The Annotated Book of Common Prayer* (1866) pp.261-274. The text here is given in English but the service may have been in Latin.

The Wedding – January 1533

(Henry and Anne stand before the priest who faces the congregation.)

> *Priest*
> Lo brethren we are come here before God and his angels, and all his hallows[2], in the face and presence of our mother holy Church, for to couple and to knit these two bodies together: that is to say, of this man and of this woman. That they be from this time forth, but one body and two souls in the faith and law of God and holy Church. For to deserve everlasting life, whatsoever that they have done here before, I charge you on God's behalf and holy Church, that if there be any of you that can say anything why these two may not be lawfully wedded together at this time, say it now, either privily or appertly[3], in helping of your souls and theirs both.
>
> *(turning to bride and groom)*
> Also I charge you both and either, by yourself, as ye will answer before God at the day of doom, that if there be anything done privily or openly, between yourself: or that ye know any lawful letting why that ye may not be wedded together at this time: say it now, ere we do any more to this matter.
>
> Henry, wilt thou have this woman to thy wedded wife and her love, honour, hold and keep, hale and sick as a husband oweth to keep his wife, and all other for her to leave and hold thee only to her as long as your either life lasteth?[4]
>
> *Henry*
> I will
>
> *Priest*
> Anne, wilt thou have this man unto thy husband and obey him and serve him, to love and honour and keep [him when] hale and sick as a wife oweth to do the husband, and to leave all other men for him and hold thee only to him whilst your either life lasteth?[5]

---

2   saints
3   openly
4   If York vows were used, the words would have been: Wilt thou have this woman to thy wife: and love her and keep her in sickness and in health, and in all other degrees be to her as a husband should he to his wife, and all other forsake for her; and hold thee only to her, to thy life's end? Sarum vows were more common.
5   If York vows were used, Anne would have been asked: Wilt thou have this man to thy husband, and to be buxom to him, serve him and keep him in sickness and in health: And in all other degrees be unto him as a wife should be to her husband, and all other to forsake for him: and hold thee only to him to thy life's end?

Anne

I will

Priest

Who shall give this woman?

(At this point, somebody, possibly Anne's father would have taken her right hand and given it to the priest. He would then have given her hand into Henry's right hand. Henry would then speak, either repeating the words after the priest or saying them from memory.)

Henry

I, Henry, take thee Anne to my wedded wife to have and to hold fro this day forward for better: for worse: for richer: for poorer, for fairer for fouler: in sickness and in health: till death us do part, if holy church it will ordain, and thereto I plight thee my troth.

(Henry would then have let Anne's hand go and the process would be repeated in reverse with her taking his hand and saying, either after the priest or from memory.)

Anne

I, Anne, take thee Henry to my wedded husband to have and to hold fro this day forward for better: for worse: for richer: for poorer: in sickness and in health: to be bonny[6] and buxom[7] in bed and at the board till death us depart if holy church it so ordain and thereto I plight thee my troth.

(Henry and Anne would then loose their hands and Henry would place on the priest's service book a ring and some money. In the past, this was likely to represent the dower but increasingly the money became associated with the priest's fee for performing the ceremony. A blessing would have been said over the ring and it would probably have been doused with holy water. The priest would then return the ring using three fingers of his right hand – symbolising the Trinity – to Henry who would have taken Anne's right hand[8] in his and said as follows.)

Henry

With this ring I thee wed, and this gold and silver I thee give, and with my body I thee worship[9], and with all my worldly cathel[10] I thee endow.

---

6 Good
7 Obedient
8 The Sarum rite states clearly "et manu sua sinistra tenens dexteram sponsae." i.e. take in his left her right
9 Honour
10 Goods

THE WEDDING SERVICE

In the name of the Father (touching the ring to her thumb)
In the name of the Son (touching the ring to her forefinger)
In the name of the Holy Ghost (touching the ring to her middle finger)
Amen (placing it upon her fourth finger)

(At this point Henry and Anne would have knelt down on cushions or at prayer desks)

Priest

They that God hath joined, let no man dissever.

Forasmuch as this Henry desireth this Anne to be his wife in the Lord, and this Anne desireth this Henry to be her husband in the Lord, and one hath made the other a promise of holy and Christian matrimony, and have now both professed the same openly, and have confirmed it with giving of rings each to other,[11] and joining of hands: I the minister of Christ and the congregation pronounce that they be joined together with lawful and Christian matrimony, and I confirm this their marriage in the Name of the Father, the Son, and the Holy Ghost. Amen.

God the Father bless you, God the Son keep you, God the Holy Ghost lighten your understanding: the Lord mercifully with his favour look upon you, and so fill you with all benediction and grace, that you may have remission of your sins in this life, and in the world to come, life everlasting.

All

Amen

Reading by one of the clergy, Psalm 128

Blessed are all they that fear the Lord and walk in his ways.
For thou shalt eat the labours of thine hands: O well is thee, and happy shalt thou be.
Thy wife shall be as the fruitful vine upon the walls of thine house.
Thy sons like the olive branches round about thy table.
Lo, thus shall the man be blessed that feareth the Lord.
The Lord from out of Zion shall so bless thee that thou shalt see Jerusalem in prosperity all thy life long.
Yea, that thou shalt see thy children's children and peace upon Israel.

(All kneel.)

---

11 Women did not give men rings. The plural refers to the betrothal ring given in a previous ceremony and the wedding one at this point. The "each to other" references the vows taken.

Priest

Lord, have mercy upon us.

All

Christ, have mercy upon us.

Priest

Lord, have mercy upon us.

All

Our Father, which art in heaven, hallowed be thy Name.
Thy kingdom come.
Thy will be done in earth, as it is in heaven.
Give us this day our daily bread, and forgive us our trespasses,
as we forgive them that trespass against us.
And lead us not into temptation; But deliver us from evil.
Amen.

Priest

O Lord, save thy servant, and thy handmaid

All

Who put their trust in thee.

Priest

O Lord, send them help from thy holy place

All

And evermore defend them.

Priest

Be unto them a tower of strength,

All

From the face of their enemy.

Priest

O Lord, hear our prayer.

All

And let our cry come unto thee.

Priest

THE WEDDING SERVICE

O God of Abraham, God of Isaac, God of Jacob, bless these thy servants, and sow the seed of eternal life in their hearts; that whatsoever in thy holy Word they shall profitably learn, they may in deed fulfil the same. Look, O Lord, mercifully upon them from heaven, and bless them. And as thou didst send thy blessing upon Abraham and Sarah, to their great comfort, so vouchsafe to send thy blessing upon these thy servants; that they obeying thy will, and always being in safety under thy protection, may abide in thy love unto their lives' end; through Jesus Christ our Lord.
Amen

Merciful Lord, and heavenly Father, by whose gracious gift mankind is increased; We beseech thee, assist with thy blessing these two persons, that they may both be fruitful in procreation of children, and also live together so long in godly love and honesty, that they may see their children Christianly and virtuously brought up, to thy praise and honour; through Jesus Christ our Lord. Amen.

God, who by thy mighty power hast made all things of nothing; who also (after other things set in order) didst appoint that out of man (created after thine own image and similitude) woman should take her beginning; and knitting them together, didst teach that it should never be lawful to put asunder those whom thou by matrimony hadst made one: O God, who hast consecrated the state of matrimony to such an excellent mystery, that in it is signified and represented the spiritual marriage and unity betwixt Christ and his Church; Look mercifully upon these thy servants, that both this man may love his wife, according to thy Word, (as Christ did love his spouse the Church, who gave himself for it, loving and cherishing it even as his own flesh) and also that this woman may be loving and amiable, faithful and obedient to her husband; and in all quietness, sobriety, and peace, be a follower of holy and godly matrons. O Lord, bless them both, and grant them to inherit thy everlasting kingdom; through Jesus Christ our Lord. Amen.

Almighty God, who at the beginning did create our first parents, Adam and Eve, and did sanctify and join them together in marriage; Pour upon you the riches of his grace, sanctify and bless you, that ye may please him both in body and soul, and live together in holy love unto your lives end. Amen.

(All stand to recite the Nicene Creed.)

Priest
Good men and women, I charge you by the authority of holy church,

that no man nother[12] woman that this day proposeth here to be communicated that he go not to God's board, less[13] than he believe steadfastly, that the sacrament that he is about here to receive, that it is God's body flesh and blood, in the form of bread; and that which he receiveth afterward, is nothing else but wine and water, for to cleanse your mouths of the holy sacrament. Furthermore, I charge you that no man neither woman go to God's board less than he be of his sins clean confessed, and for them contrite; that is to say having sorrow in your hearts, for your sins. Furthermore, I charge you if there be any man or woman, that beareth in his heart any wroth or rancour to any of his fellow Christian that he be not there houselled[14], there to the time that he be with him in perfect love and charity, for he who so beareth wroth or evil will in heart, to any of his fellow Christians, he is not worthy his God to receive; and if he do, he receiveth his damnation, where he should receive his salvation. Furthermore, I charge you that none of you go to God's board today, less than he be in full will and purpose for to cease and to withstand the deeds of sin. For who proposeth now to continue in sin again after this holy time he is not worthy to receive his God; and if he do, it is to him great peril. Furthermore, I charge you both men and women that haveth servants, that ye taketh heed that they be well governed in taking of meats and drinks, for the peril that may befall, through forfeiting of meats and drinks.[15] Also ye shall kneel down upon your knees, saying after me, I cry God mercy, and our lady saint Mary, and all the holy company of heaven, and my ghostly father, of all the trespass of sin that I have done, in thought, word, or in deed, from the time that I was born, to this time; that is to say in Pride, Envy, Wroth, Sloth, Covetousness, Gluttony, and Lechery.[16] The Commandments, diverse times I broke. The works of mercy not fulfilled.

All (kneeling)

Almighty, everlasting God, the Father of our Lord Jesus Christ, the Maker of all things, the Judge of all men, we acknowledge, and we lament that we were conceived and born in sins, and that therefore we be prone to all evils and we are sorry for it with all our hearts. Have mercy upon us, most gentle Father, through thy Son our Lord Jesus Christ

(The priest pronounces absolution and commences the consecration of the

---

12 Nor other
13 Usage of the time preferred less where we would use unless.
14 Receive the host, i.e. the bread representing the body of Christ.
15 This is a reference to receiving Holy Communion not a comment on the importance of good diet.
16 The seven deadly sins as defined by the pope, interestingly listed before the Ten Commandments.

elements)

All
O Lamb of God, have mercy upon us.
O Lamb of God, have mercy upon us.
O Lamb of God, grant us thy peace

(The bread is broken and distributed and a prayer of thanksgiving said by the priest ends the service.)

Appendix 4   The coronation of Anne Boleyn

Although an account of the coronation of Anne Boleyn was published in 1533, it primarily dealt with the pageantry of the procession through the streets and the banquet which followed.[1] What follows here is a re-creation of the service based on the accounts given by Legg of the coronations of Queens Eleanor and Henrietta, wives of Henry III and Charles I respectively.[2] Coronations are very traditional events and many of the elements which occurred in Anne's coronation also featured in that of His Majesty King Charles III in 2023, although Anne, being the wife of a king rather than a ruler in her own right, was not required to take vows or don sacerdotal robes and there was no recognition.

The coronation festivities began on Thursday 29th May with Anne being taken by barge from Greenwich to the Tower of London wharf amid a flotilla of boats, her journey accompanied by music and gun salutes. Henry met her there and stayed with her. On Friday, at the Tower, the King created nineteen Knights of the Bath, amongst them Francis Weston and the brother of George Boleyn's wife. It is unknown if Anne attended this ceremony. Saturday was occupied by a lengthy procession through the city with various stops at which pageants were performed, one of which involved the prophecy: "Queen Anne when thou shalt bear a new son of the King's blood, there shall be a golden world unto thy people." Her route took her from the Tower to Westminster Hall via Fenchurch Street, Gracechurch Street, Leadenhall Street, Cornhill, St Paul's, Ludgate Hill, Fleet Street, Temple Bar and Charing Cross. After refreshment, Anne retired to spend the night at the palace of Whitehall.

Coronation day itself began early. The Lord Mayor of London, together with the Aldermen, went to Westminster Hall to join the Abbot and his monks, the clergy and singers of the Chapel Royal, the judges of the King's Bench and the members of the House of Lords, all of whom were in full ceremonial dress. Anne arrived just after 8 a.m. walking under a golden canopy carried by the barons of the Cinque Ports with her ladies following and took her place under a cloth of state. Anne wore a white dress decorated with pearl studded tongues. An Imperial source suggested that this represented "tongues pierced with nails

---

1   *The noble tryumphant coronacyon of quene Anne, wyfe unto the most noble kynge Henry the VIII* (1533). See also the account in LP 6.601 item 3 and Hall pp.799-805. Edward Hall was an eye-witness to the event as was John Spelman whose account appears in LP 6.583. Further accounts can be found in LP 6.583 to 585

2   L. G. Wickham Legg, *English Coronation Records* (1901). Anne's coronation would have been in Latin but it is given here in English based on Legg's translation. As Henrietta was a Roman Catholic, the service was not carried out as planned. It is reasonable to assume, however, that those who drew up the initial order used that composed for James I and Anne which in turn would have been based on Henry VIII's, the last monarch to have a queen consort.

to show the treatment which those who spoke against her might expect"[3] but the significance of the touch related to the date. Anne's coronation took place upon Whitsunday, one of the three major festivals in the Church year. It commemorated the gift of the Holy Spirit which appeared as "cloven tongues like as of fire" on all those filled with a love of the Gospel.[4] On top, she wore an ermine edged cloak or surcoat of purple velvet lined with crimson taffeta. Her hair was loose as was traditional and topped by a gold bejewelled circlet. From there, the procession moved into Westminster Abbey.

Anne's entrance was heralded by a fanfare followed by the singing of Psalm 122 which begins: "I was glad when they said unto me, let us go into the house of the Lord." This psalm had been used for centuries at this point and would continue to be used.[5] Anne made her way to a square platform which had been set up in the middle of the Abbey between the stairs up to the quire and the steps down to the altar. The platform had been carpeted and railed and contained a chair of state upon it, i.e. a padded chair beneath a canopy of gold which was almost certainly trimmed with the Tudor colours of green and white. As part of the procession, the Marquis of Dorset bore the sceptre; the Earl of Arundel, the rod; and the Earl of Oxford, the crown which would be used in the ceremony.

The choir sang again and then Anne went down to the altar and prostrated herself before Thomas Cranmer, Archbishop of Canterbury, who said:

> Almighty and everlasting God, the fountain and wellspring of all goodness, who dost not reject the frailty of the woman, but rather vouchsafest to allow and choose it, and by choosing the weak things of the world, doest confound those that are strong, who didst sometimes cause thy people to triumph over a most cruel enemy, by the hand of Judith a woman; give ear we beseech Thee to our humble prayers, and multiply thy blessings upon this thy servant Anne, whom in all humble devotion we do consecrate our Queen. Defend her with thy mighty hand, and with thy favour protect her on every side, that she may be able to overcome and triumph over all her enemies, both bodily and ghostly; and that with Sarah, Rebecca and Rachel, and other blessed and honourable women, she may multiply and rejoice in the fruits of her womb, to the honour of this Kingdom, and the good government of God's holy Church, through Jesus Christ,

---

3   LP 6.585. The editor of the volume suggests that it may have been written by Chapuys.
4   Acts 2:1-13.
5   It was used in 1953 and 2023 and also for the entrance of Catherine Middleton at her wedding to Prince William.

> who vouchsafed to be born of a most pure Virgin, that He might visit and redeem the world; who liveth and reigneth, with Thee Father, in the unity of the Holy Spirit, throughout all ages, world without end. Amen.[6]

The eagle shaped ampulla of holy oil together with the golden spoon[7] was then handed to the Archbishop who continued:

> God who only hast immortality, and dwellest in light, who cannot be approached, whose providence is never deceived, who hast made all things that are, and that are to come, and callest the things that are not, as the things that are; who callest down the proud from their seat, and doest exalt the humble and meek: we humbly beseech Thee for thy unspeakable mercy, that as for the good of thy people the Jews, thou didst deliver Queen Esther from captivity, and didst bring her to the bed of Ahasuerus, and to the society of his kingdom: so for the good of thy Christian Flock, Thou wilt of thy Mercy, by our ministry, advance thy servant Anne to the most high and royal company of our King, that she continuing always in the chastity of princely wedlock, may obtain the crown that is next unto virginity, and may in all things and above all things, study always to please Thee the living God, and by this holy inspiration to perform those things that are acceptable unto Thee, through Jesus Christ our Lord. Amen.

Anne then rose and her attendant removed her coronet so that the Archbishop could anoint her. She then knelt on the altar steps and bowed her head while he made the sign of the cross upon her saying:

---

6 Ghostly enemies are spiritual rather than supernatural. The story of Judith appears in the Apocrypha. Sarah, Rebecca and Rachel were respectively the wives of the patriarchs, Abraham, Isaac and Jacob and their stories are all to be found in the book of Genesis.

7 The golden spoon is believed to be the oldest item in the coronation regalia dating back almost a thousand years. It is on display at the Tower of London and the only item used at Anne's coronation which still exists. The eagle shaped ampulla made in 1661 was based on the medieval one used for her which was in the same shape, this due to a medieval legend of the Blessed Virgin presenting such an item to archbishop Thomas Becket. The St Edward's crown used for Anne was destroyed in the civil war and a replacement made in 1661

ANNE'S CORONATION

> In the name of the Father, the Son and of the Holy Ghost, let the anointing of this oil, increase and establish thee for ever and ever. Amen

Anne then rose so that her attendant could open her purple robe whereupon the Archbishop anointed her on the breast saying:

> In the name of the Father, and of the Son, and of the Holy Ghost, let the anointing of this oil, increase thy honour, and establish thee for ever and ever. Amen.

Having thus been anointed in two places to represent the consecration of her heart and mind to God, Anne knelt again while the Archbishop said:

> O almighty and everlasting God, we beseech Thee of thy goodness, to pour out the spirit of thine abundant grace and blessing, upon this thy servant Anne, that as by the imposition of hands, she is this day crowned Queen; so she may by thy sanctification, continue always thy chosen and worthy servant, that she may never hereafter fall from this grace, through Christ our Lord. Amen.

Anne's robes were then restored and the choir sang another anthem while she was led up to her chair of state. The archbishop followed and she held out her right hand to him so that he could put the ring of the Queens of England upon her fourth finger saying:

> Receive this ring the seal of a sincere faith, that thou mayst avoid all infection of heresy, and by the power of God compel barbarous nations, and bring them to the knowledge of the truth. Amen.

> God to whom belongeth all power and dignity, grant we beseech Thee to thy servant Anne, by the sign of Christian faith, prosperous success in this her honour, and that she may continue firm in the same, and endeavour always to please Thee through Christ our Lord. Amen.

The Archbishop then went back down the steps and picked up St Edward's crown from the cushion on which it rested and laid it upon the altar. He said:

> O God the crown of the faithful, who dost crown their heads with a crown of precious stones, bless and sanctify this Crown, that as the same is adorned with many precious stones; so thy servant that weareth the same may of thy grace be replenished with thy manifold gifts of all precious virtues through Christ our Lord. Amen.

Cranmer then processed back up the steps and stood in front of Anne. He lifted the crown then set it down upon her head saying:

> Receive the Crown of glory and honour of joy, that you may shine in brightness, and be crowned with everlasting gladness. Amen.

> Seeing you are by our ministry solemnly consecrated for our Queen receive the crown of royal excellency which is placed upon your head by the episcopal hands of us (though unworthy) and as you are crowned with gold and pearls so labour to be beautified with the gold of wisdom and the pearls of virtue, that after this life ended you may with the just virgins decently meet the everlasting Bridegroom our Lord and Saviour Jesus Christ and enter into the kingly gate of the heavenly court by His help, who with the Father and the Holy Ghost liveth and reigneth, one God world without end.[8] Amen.

Anne was the only Queen Consort ever to have been crowned with the St Edward's crown which was ordinarily reserved for the sovereign alone. It had been used for Henry but not Katherine. The significance of Henry allowing it to be used was not lost on people of the time. Anne was being proclaimed queen in the richest sense and all the blessings which were believed to stem from contact with what was deemed a holy relic due to its association with Edward the Confessor, king and saint, were being called down upon her and the child in her womb. She was literally consecrated with oil and majesty.

Next, the sceptre and the ivory rod with a dove were presented to the Archbishop. The sceptre represented justice and the rod, equity and mercy with the dove symbolising the Holy Spirit. Anne turned over her hands and into her right hand, Cranmer placed the sceptre and into the left the rod before saying:

---

8 A reference to the parable at Matt. 25:1-12.

> O Lord, the fountain of all good things, and the giver of all perfection, grant unto thy servant Anne that she may order aright the high dignity that she hath obtained, and with good works establish the glory that Thou hast given her, through Jesus Christ our Lord. Amen.

As she sat there thus bearing the symbols of majesty, the choir sang the *Te Deum*, the ancient hymn of praise which begins "We praise Thee, O God: we acknowledge Thee to be the Lord."

After the singing, Anne moved to the throne set up for her where the St Edward's crown was replaced with a lighter one made for the occasion.[9] This was made of gold and formed of six crosses each set with a large sapphire, these being interspersed with thirty-two pearls. A further gold cross surmounted these studded with a large diamond. A purple velvet cap inside was designed for comfort.[10] Sapphires were said to signify wisdom and pearls purity while the thirty-two stones represented the number of years which Jesus was believed to have lived. Given the original crown was said to weigh five pounds, it may be assumed she was duly thankful for the exchange.[11] Two bishops then took centre stage to read from the Bible. The first reading was from 1 Pet. 2:13-17 which concerned obedience to the monarch; the second from Matt. 22:15-22 wherein Jesus commended people to "Render unto Caesar the things which are Caesar's and unto God the things which are God's."[12] The choir then sang the Nicene Creed followed by the words:

> Let my prayer come into thy presence as the incense, and
> let the lifting up of my hands be as the evening sacrifice.

During the creed, the Bible was taken to Anne for her to kiss.

Music was played as Anne descended to the altar to make her offering. In accordance with tradition, this was a gold mark plus the bread and wine in St Edward's paten and chalice. These items would have been handed to her. This done and a prayer being said, she returned to her platform and knelt while Psalm 5:1-3 was sung. The mass was then begun which would have included prayers for the King but, in a break with tradition, not for the pope. When the *Agnus Dei* or "O Lamb of God, have mercy upon me" was reached, Anne's crown and purple robe were removed as a sign of humility before God and she went down to kneel at the altar and kiss the pax. There she said to the Archbishop:

---

9   The St Edward's crown was returned to the altar.
10 Gareth Russell, *Young and Damned and Fair* (2017) p.159
11 Edward Twining, *A History of the Crown Jewels of Europe* (1960) p.132.
12 Lev. 26:6-9 with its promises of a time of peace and plenty to come may have been read in addition. It is unclear when this passage was removed from the service.

> I confess to God, to the Blessed Mary, to all Saints, and to you, father, that I have sinned grievously, in thought, word, and deed, by my own fault; I beseech Holy Mary, all the Saints of God, and you, father, to pray for me.

Cranmer responded:

> Almighty God, have mercy upon thee, and pardon thee all thy sins, deliver thee from all evil, preserve and confirm thee in good, and bring thee to everlasting life.

Anne responded "Amen" and he continued:

> The Almighty and merciful Lord grant you absolution and remission of all your sins, time for true penance and amendment of life, the grace and consolation of the Holy Ghost.

Anne then repeated her "Amen" and received the bread. She returned to her chair while the choir sang. The Archbishop completed the mass and all stood as the Gloria in Excelsis was sung. Anne, once again crowned and in her purple robe, processed to the shrine of St Edward to make an offering and then withdrew briefly into a chamber set aside for her use on the side while the congregation all donned their coronets and the trumpets were prepared. A fanfare sounded and Anne emerged to begin her majestic procession back through the Abbey and out via the west doors to the waiting crowds outside as Psalm 61, believed to have been used at the coronation of King Solomon, was sung. She carried the sceptre and rod and her father walked at her right hand side.[13] From there, they all returned to Westminster Hall where the King was waiting with a magnificent banquet. Given Anne was five months pregnant at the time, it must be supposed that she was heartily glad of a chance to relax slightly and sit down.

---

13 The orb was not in use for coronations at this date.

Appendix 5   Properties of Anne Boleyn

Ordinarily in Tudor times, a woman would be maintained by her father before marriage and her husband afterwards but Anne had to wait a long time before she married. In the case of wealthy and noble men, income would be given to the wife to provide her with an independent income for herself and her household and this was known as a jointure. Since married women did not have the right to own property in their own right before the 1882 Married Women's Property Act, Parliament passed an Act when Anne married Henry which allowed her to have the legal status of a femme sole which meant that she could own property and make contracts in her own name. The Act said that she was "enabled, legitimated and able to sue in her own name by the name of Anne, Queen of England and of France and Lady of Ireland" to receive all the profits of the lands for her own benefit to be used toward "the great costs expenses and charges which his said most dear and well beloved wife Anne Queen of England must of necessity sustain and bear in her chamber and otherwise." Her property portfolio included some estates which she was granted outright for the term of her natural life and others which remained owned by the Crown but from which the income was given wholly to her. The income would have included rents, fees for leases, grazing and fishing rights, sale of timber, resources and marriage rights of wards, fairs and markets, advowsons and goods seized from felons and outlaws. All of the estates would have been managed for her and it is unlikely that she would have visited many of them. These lands were:[1]

Essex

Bourehouse – Leased from Waltham Abbey by Thomas More's brother-in-law in 1522 and subsequently by More himself in 1526 at £6 per annum. It had previously been leased by the grandparents of More's first wife, Jane Colt. It was part of the grant when Anne became Marquess of Pembroke and within Nether Hall manor in Roydon.

Coggeshall – part of the grant when Anne became Marquess of Pembroke and valued at £100 per annum. There may have been a family link to this area because in 1442, Richard Boleyn served on a jury there.[2]

---
[1] *Statutes of the Realm* vol. 3 (1817) pp 479-481
[2] M. L. Holford (ed.), *Calendar of Inquisitions Post Mortem, Vol. 26, 21-25 Henry VI, 1442-1447* (2009) p.35

Filols or Felix Hall – part of the grant when Anne became Marquess of Pembroke and family home to Jane Seymour's sister-in-law, Catherine, the wife of Edward.

Much (or Great) Waltham – granted on 21st March 1533.

Roydon – rented by the Morris or Morice family originally from Christ's College, Cambridge (founded by Henry VIII's grandmother Margaret Beaufort) but then directly from the Crown at £53 per annum. It was part of the grant when Anne became Marquess of Pembroke and after Anne's death, the income was given to Henry's daughter, Mary.

Hertfordshire

Hunsdon – originally owned by the younger of the Princes in the Tower, Henry VII had granted it to his mother, Margaret Beaufort.[3] After her death, it was let to Anne Boleyn's grandfather and following his demise, Henry Norris was appointed bailiff, doubtless because Henry wished to stay there on occasion.[4] In 1528, William Carey died of the sweat there while the King was in residence. In 1531 it was returned to Anne's uncle, the Duke of Norfolk, but income from the land was given to Anne upon her creation as Marquess of Pembroke in October 1532.[5] Henry spent considerable sums enhancing the estate during Anne's lifetime. Between 1526 and 1534 he spent £2,900 (worth some twenty million today) on new chimneys, tiles, wainscot, locks and glass for various rooms.[6] His daughters Mary and Elizabeth both lived there at various times. In 1559, Elizabeth I granted the estate to her cousin Henry Carey, son of Anne's sister Mary Boleyn, a man whom she had created Lord Hunsdon.

Pishiobury – purchased from Lord Scrope to be added to the Hunsdon estate. Although it was part of the grant when Anne became Marquess of Pembroke, the actual sale had not been completed at the time.[7] The estate included a deer park and two water mills which were leased out, one for grinding corn and the other for fulling wool.

Stanstead Abbots – part of the grant when Anne became Marquess of Pembroke, it had been obtained from the Abbot of Waltham a year earlier.

---

[3] Richard, Duke of York, who married Anne Mowbray the daughter of the Duke of Norfolk. Anne Mowbray was the third cousin of Anne Boleyn's mother. She inherited it from her father and predeceased her husband hence it fell into royal hands.
[4] LP 4.3622.27 in November 1527. Confirmed LP 4.5336.10 February 1529
[5] LP 5.1370.3
[6] LP 7.250
[7] The grant was confirmed after the sale in November 1534, LP 7.1498.1

Weston – another manor which had come into the Crown's possession upon the death of the younger of the Princes in the Tower, it contained a deer park. After Anne's death, the income from it was granted to Jane Seymour and later to Katherine Parr. The grant was made a month after Anne became Marquess.[8]

Middlesex

Cold Kennington – also known as Kempton, it was a manor of Sunbury and granted to Anne on 30th June 1532. Income came to her from arable land and pasture as well as woods, a mine and a stone quarry.

Hanworth – granted to Anne when she was Lady Anne Rochford by letters patent on 2nd July 1532, the property included a royal residence but the house had been held for some years previous by Francis Weston's father, Richard, who was its keeper and then by Stephen Gardiner. It was said to include extensive gardens and an orchard as well as a deer park. As with Cold Kennington, she was to hold the property for her lifetime rent free but to pay from the income the "cost and charges for keeping of the said park."

Somerset

Curry Mallet – part of the Duchy of Cornwall and primarily farmland.

South Wales

Camrose, Cilgerran, Diffryn (next Bryn), Emlyn, Cefn-drum, Llangynog, Llanstephan, Roch, Manorowen, Trayn Clinton and Ystlwyf had all formed part of the dowry granted by Henry VI to his wife Margaret of Anjou and had been subsequently granted to Jasper Tudor, Henry VIII's great-uncle.[9] The lands included forest but also a slate quarry at Trayn Clinton and mills at Llanstephan and Haverfordwest also a weir at the former. They were granted to Anne when she became Marquess of Pembroke together with St Ishmail's, Haverfordwest and Lewston. Several of the properties had been held by Rhys ap Gruffydd who had been executed for treason in December 1531 but was married to Anne's aunt, Katherine Howard.[10]

---

[8] LP 5.1499.23
[9] Chris Given-Wilson et.al (ed.), *Parliament Rolls of Medieval England*, (2005) March 1453 and October 1495. For more on Jasper's estates see Roger Thomas, *Political career, estates and connection of Jasper Tudor, Earl of Pembroke and Duke of Bedford*, PhD thesis, Swansea 1971
[10] Emlyn, Llanstephan, Cilgerran, Manorowen, Havefordwest

Caerleon – two corn mills and a fulling mill plus a fishery were added a month after Anne became Marquess.

Coedrath Saundersfoot – income from at least two coal mines was were added a month after Anne became Marquess.

The following properties were granted to her when she became Queen.[11] Unless otherwise stated, they were all manors from which she obtained rental income.

Berkshire

Benham Lovell
Bray
Cookham
Hampstead Marshall
Newbury
Stratfield Mortimer
Swallowfield
Wokefield

Buckinghamshire

Bierton
Claydon
Langley Marish
Waddesdon
Wendover
Wraysbury

Cambridgeshire

Wratting

Dorset

Alderholt
Cranborne
Creech
Gillingham
Gussage
Knowle
Marshwood
Pimperne
Portland
Steeple
Tarrant Gunville
Wareham
Weymouth
Wilksworth
Wyke

Essex

Bardfield End
Bradwell
Claret Hall
Dedham
Hadleigh Castle
Havering atte Bower
Langham
Latchley
Thaxted
Tilbury (mussel farm)

Gloucestershire

Barnsley
Bisley
Brimpsfield

---

[11] LP 7.419.25. They had previously been granted to Katherine in June 1509, LP 1.94.35

Charlton
Doughton
Miserden
Somerford Keynes

Hampshire

Andover
Headbourne Worthy
Hook Mortimer
Odiham

Herefordshire

Kingsland
Marden

Hertfordshire

Anstey
Berkhamsted
Hitchin
Kings Langley
Standon

Kent

Deptford
Erith
Kingsdown
Shillingheld (Chilham)
Southfleet
Swanscombe
Tonge

Lincolnshire

Deeping
Grantham
Kelby
Stamford

Middlesex

Baynards Castle
West Ham

Norfolk

Barney
Bircham Tofts
Fulmodeston
Great Snoring
Grimston
Thursford
Walsingham (including mill)
Wighton

Northamptonshire

Fotheringhay Castle
Nassington
Upton
Yarwell

Oxfordshire

Finmere

Somerset

Bridgwater Castle
Exmoor Forest
Haygrove
Helwell
Mendip Forest
Milverton
Odcombe

Suffolk

Clare
Erbury (Clare)
Hundon

Langham
Layham
Stratford St Mary
Sudbury
Woodhall

Surrey

Banstead
Charlwood Park
Pirbright
Shere
Walton-on-the-Hill

Sussex

Duncton

Wiltshire

Chelworth
Chippenham
Compton
Corsham
Cricklade
Devizes Castle
Ditchampton
Highworth
Marlborough (town)
Marston Meysey
Melksham Forest
Pewsham
Rowde
Sevenhampton
Tockenham
Vastern Park
Winterbourne
Wootton Bassett (town)

Wotton-under-Edge

Worcestershire

Bromsgrove
Clifton upon Teme
Feckenham Forest
Norton
Oddingley
Wyche

Appendix 6   Key Relationships

In most books, large complicated family trees are provided. Here, I have deliberately opted for multiple simplified trees to show the links between two or more people or families, e.g. the Boleyns to the Wingfields. The names of those who sat in judgment on Anne in 1536 are underlined. Italic print denotes illegitimacy.

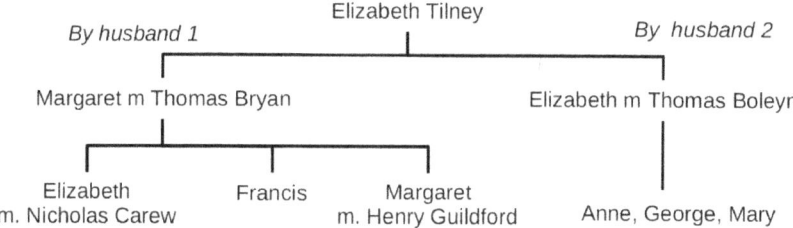

Boleyn – Bryan - Carew

Elizabeth Tilney

By husband 1 — *By husband 2*

- Margaret m Thomas Bryan
  - Elizabeth m. Nicholas Carew
  - Francis
  - Margaret m. Henry Guildford
- Elizabeth m Thomas Boleyn
  - Anne, George, Mary

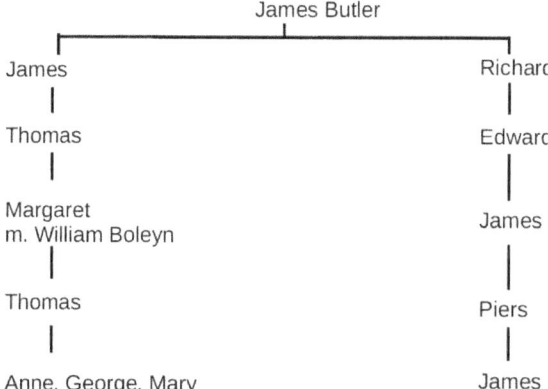

Boleyn - Butler

James Butler

- James
  - Thomas
    - Margaret m. William Boleyn
      - Thomas
        - Anne, George, Mary
- Richard
  - Edward
    - James
      - Piers
        - James

Boleyn - Cheyney

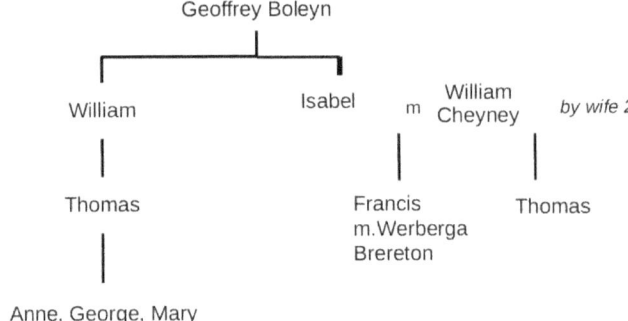

Boleyn - Cobham - Wyatt

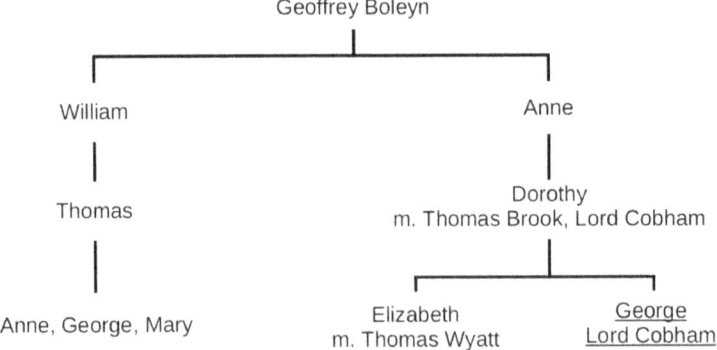

Boleyn - Derby

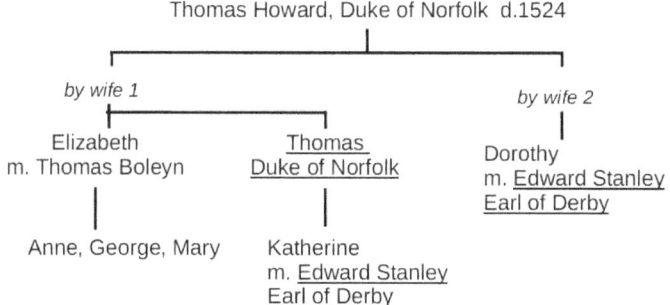

Boleyn - Gryfydd

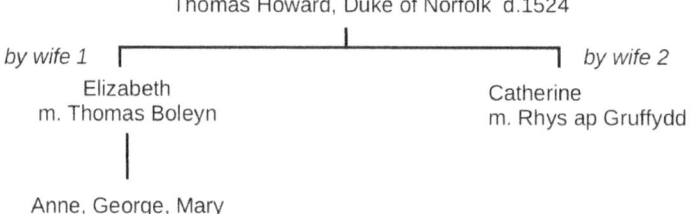

Boleyn - Knyvet

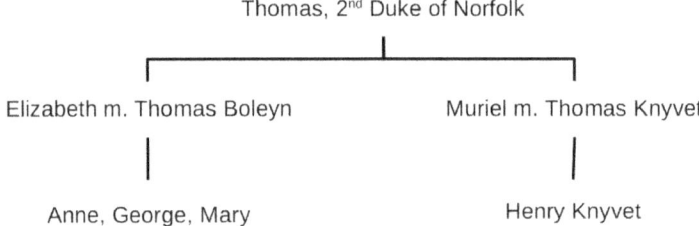

Boleyn – Norris 1

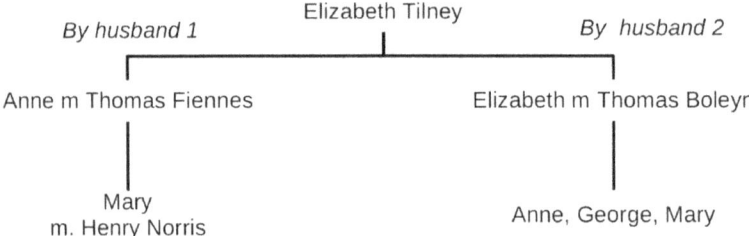

Boleyn – Norris 2

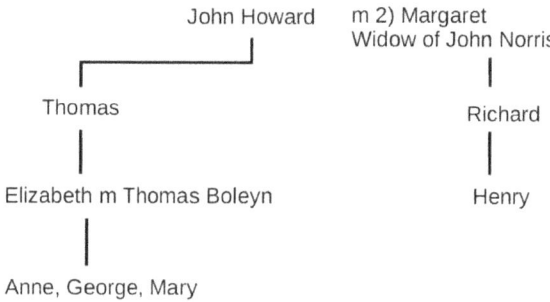

Boleyn - Seymour

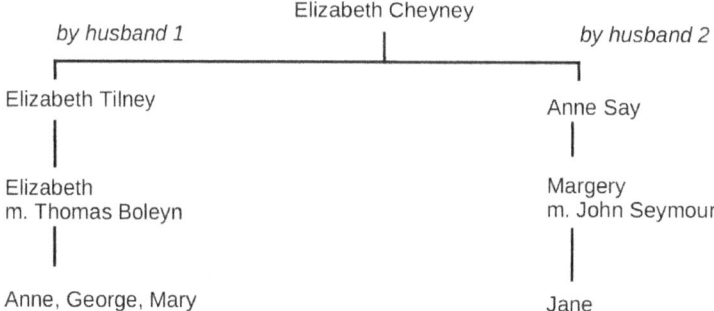

Boleyn - Wingfield

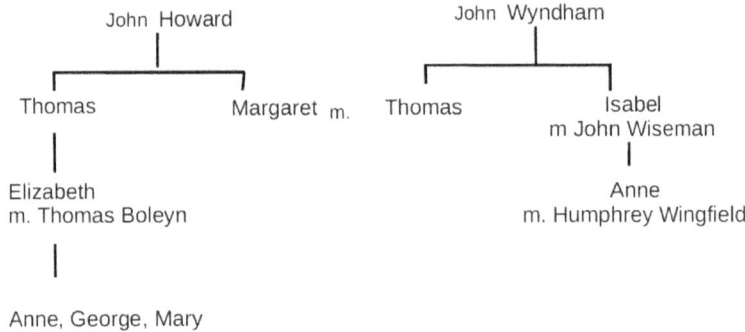

Henry - Boleyn

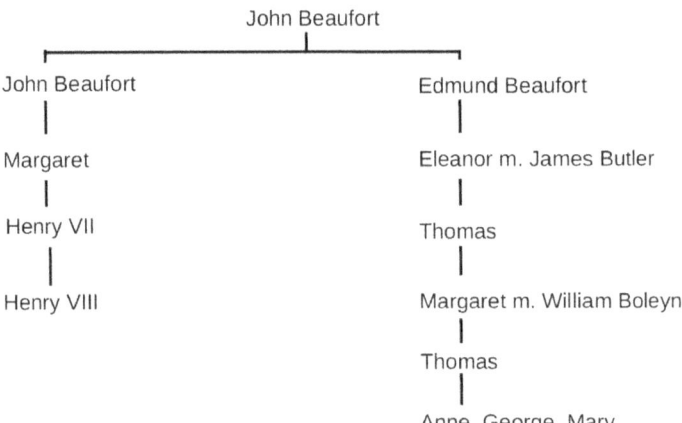

KEY RELATIONSHIPS

Henry - Brandon

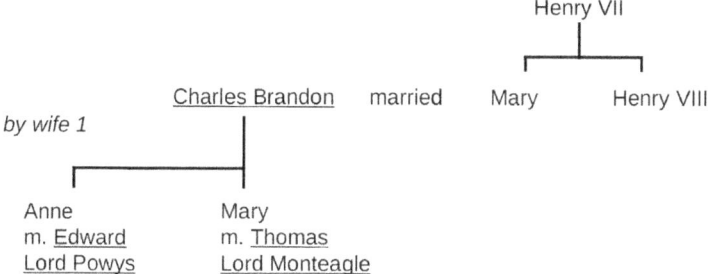

Henry – Buckingham

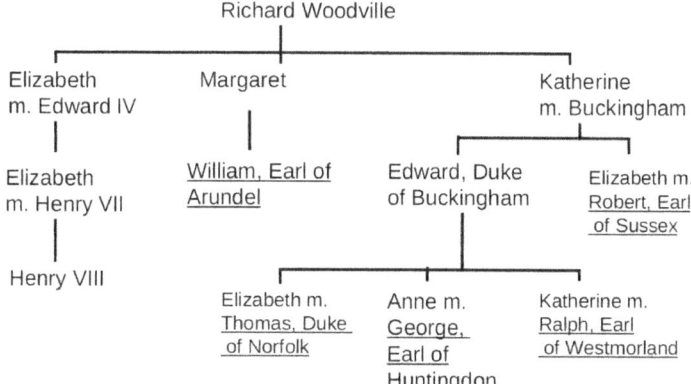

Henry – Carey - Percy

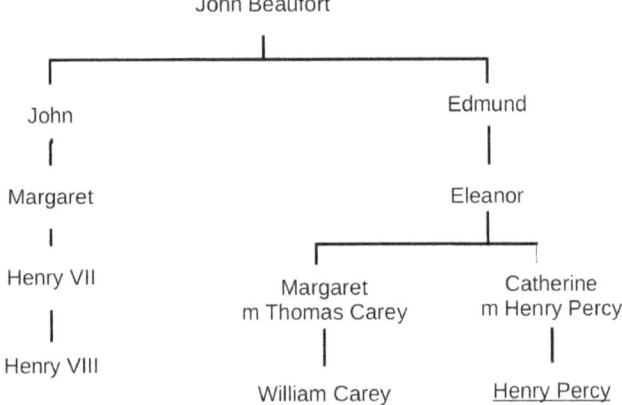

Henry - Exeter

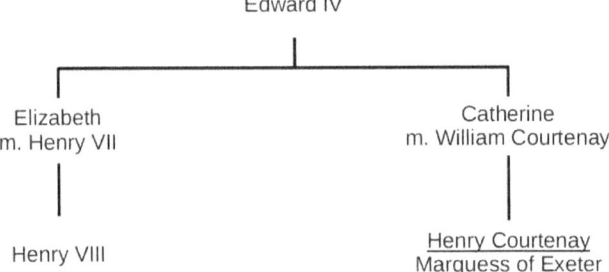

KEY RELATIONSHIPS

Henry - Katherine

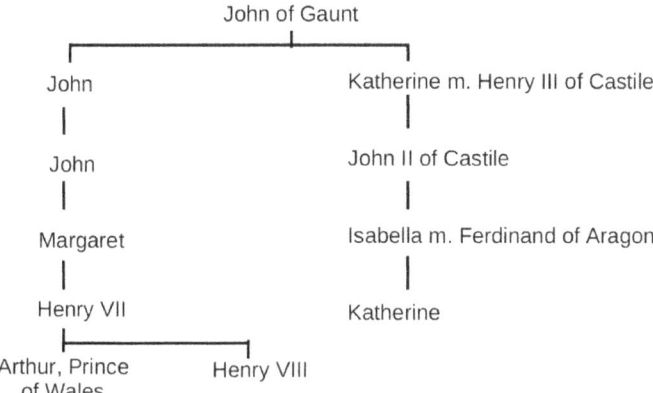

Henry - Kildare

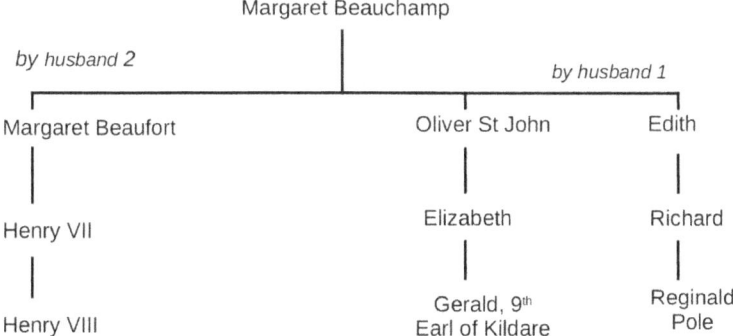

Henry – Lisle - Dorset

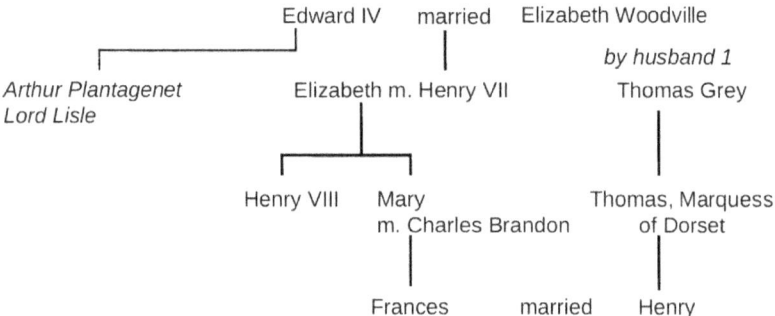

Henry - Norfolk

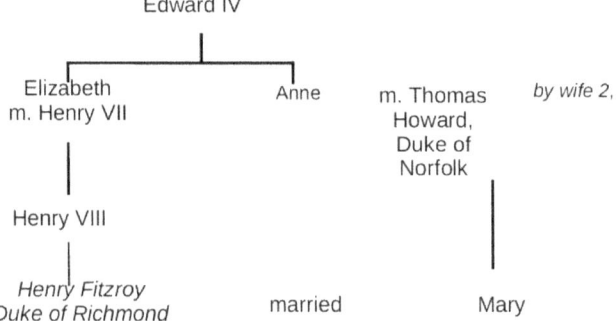

KEY RELATIONSHIPS

Henry - Parker

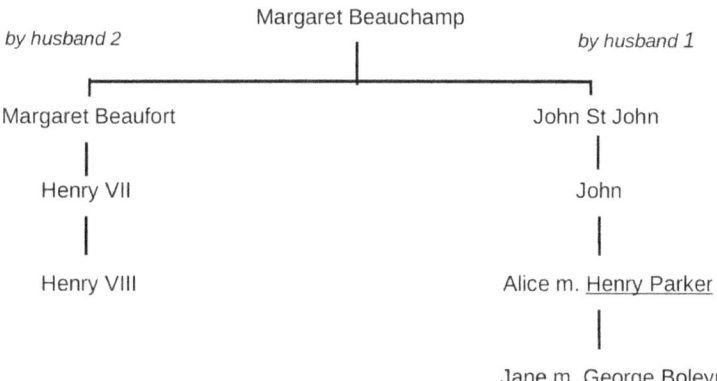

Henry - Pole

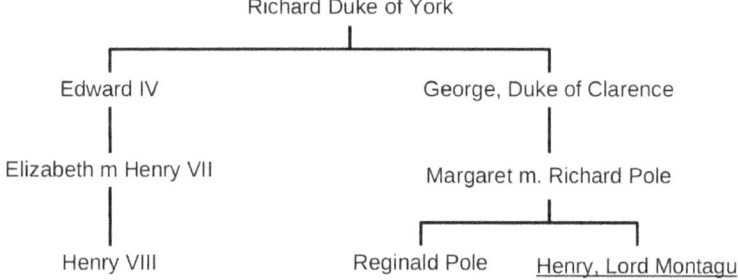

Henry - Renée

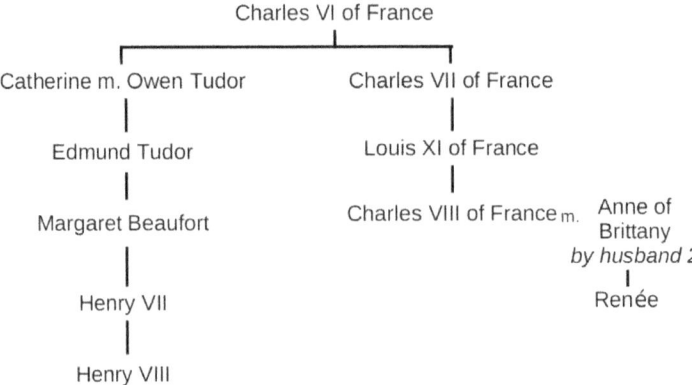

Henry – Worcester - Brereton

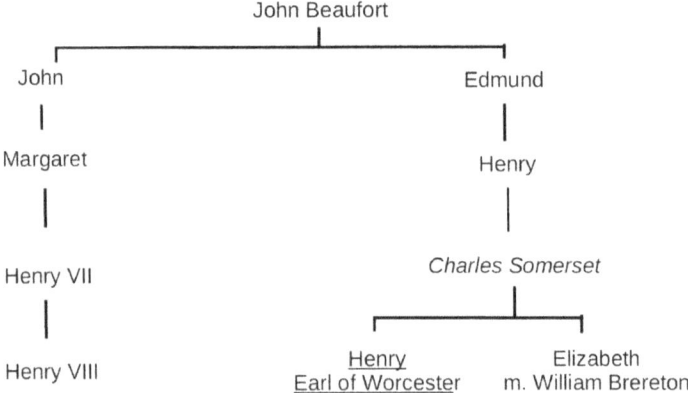

KEY RELATIONSHIPS

Brandon - Wingfields

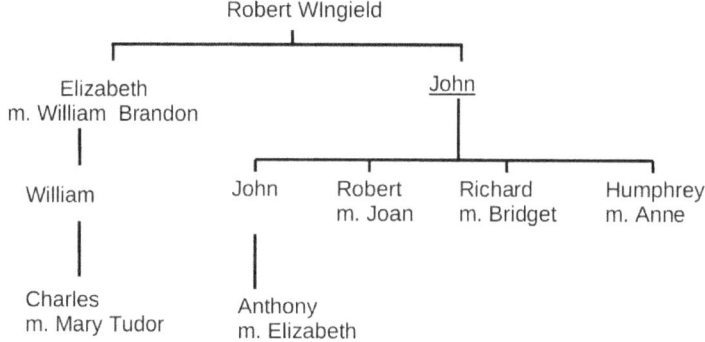

Carew - Norris

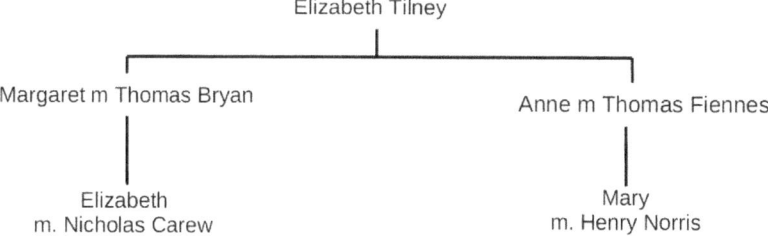

Cobham - Wyatt

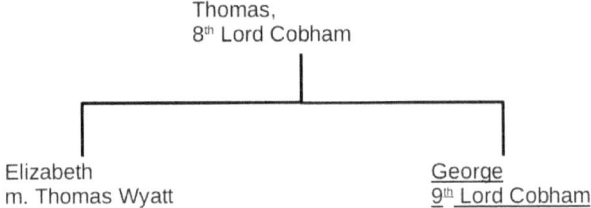

Fiennes – Clinton

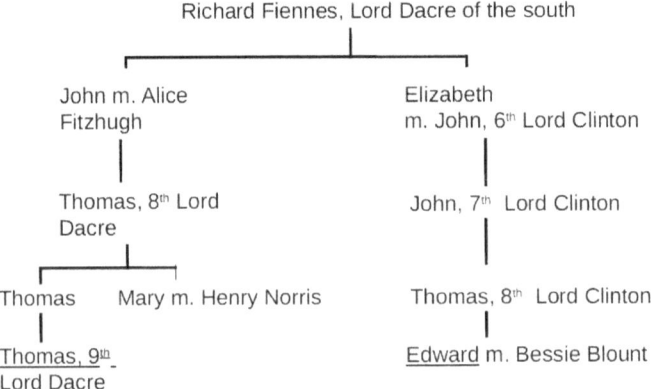

KEY RELATIONSHIPS

Norfolk - Oxford

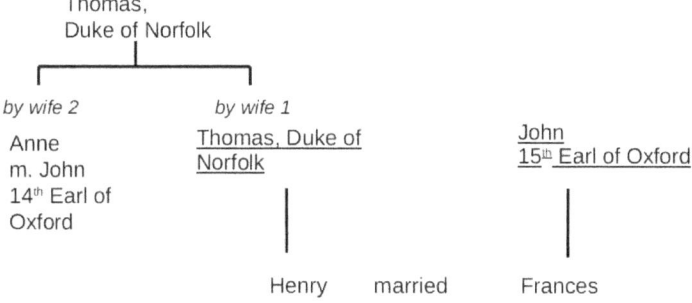

Emperor - Katherine

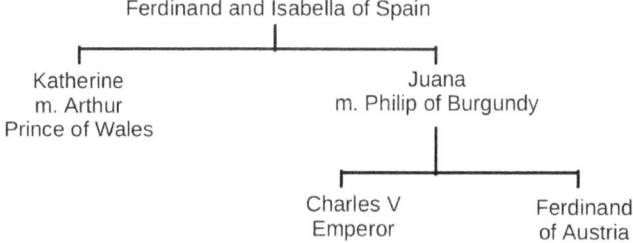

Emperor – Margaret - Francis

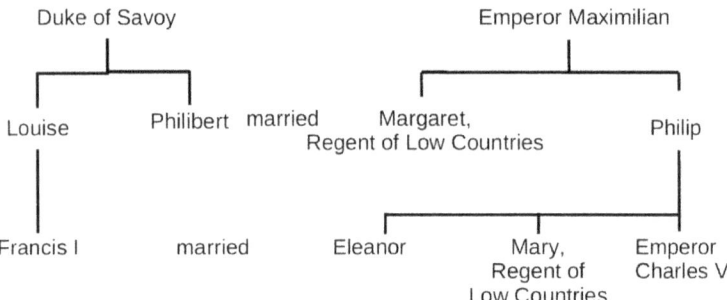

Medici

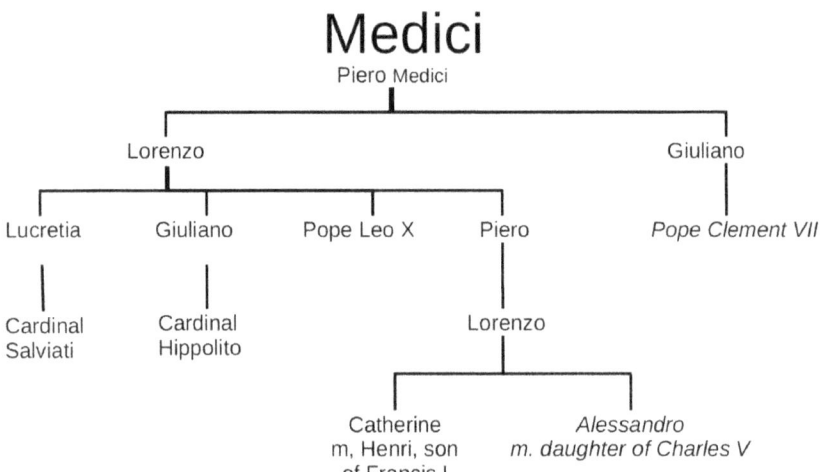

Appendix 7   Anne's Judges

As members of the nobility, Anne Boleyn and her brother were entitled to be judged by a jury comprised of their peers. Twenty-five men served on the jury reporting to the Duke of Norfolk. The details show the names of the jurors, their relationship if any with Henry or the Boleyns or the other accused, their age where known, and any other relevant information. For ease of reference, peers have been listed alphabetically rather than in order of seniority.

Name	Brandon, Charles	*Age*	52
Title	Duke of Suffolk	*Rank*	2
Relationship	Until 1533, brother-in-law of Henry VIII having married his sister, Mary, Dowager Queen of France. Cousin of the deceased Lady Wingfield.		

Name	Brook, George	*Age*	39
Title	Lord Cobham	*Rank*	18
Relationship	Brother-in-law of Thomas Wyatt. Second cousin of Anne and George Boleyn.		
Other	His kinswoman gave evidence against Anne. He had attended Mary Tudor in France in 1514 along with Anne and her sister.		

Name	Burgh, Thomas	*Age*	48
Title	Lord Burgh	*Rank*	25
Relationship	-		
Other	Lord Chamberlain of Anne's household. His son married Katherine Parr.		

Name	Courtenay, Henry	*Age*	37
Title	Marquess of Exeter	*Rank*	3
Relationship	First cousin of Henry VIII.		
Other	He and his wife were regular informers of Chapuys and strong supporters of Katherine and Mary.		

Name	Fiennes, Edward	*Age*	24
Title	Lord Clinton	*Rank*	21
Relationship	Following the death of his father, his mother had married Robert Wingfield who was first cousin of Charles Brandon. She thereby became sister-in-law of Anne's friend, Bridget. His father's second cousin had been the wife of Henry Norris.		
Other	Married to Bessie Blount, mother of Henry VIII's son, Richmond.		

Name	Fiennes, Thomas	*Age*	21
Title	Lord Dacre (of the south)	*Rank*	17
Relationship	His aunt had been the wife of Henry Norris.		

Name	Fitzalan, William	*Age*	60
Title	Earl of Arundel	*Rank*	5
Relationship	First cousin of Henry VIII's mother. Great uncle of Henry Percy by marriage.		
Other	Carried one of the sceptres at Anne's coronation.		

Name	Grey, Edward	*Age*	33
Title	Lord Powys	*Rank*	19
Relationship	Married to Brandon's daughter.		

Name	Hastings, George	*Age*	49
Title	Earl of Huntingdon	*Rank*	12
Relationship	Married to Henry VIII's second cousin.		

Name	Howard, Thomas	*Age*	63
Title	Duke of Norfolk	*Rank*	1
Relationship	Uncle to Anne and George Boleyn being their mother's brother. His daughter was married to Henry's illegitimate son, the Duke of Richmond. His first wife had been Henry's aunt being sister to Elizabeth of York.		

Name	Manners, Thomas	*Age*	40
Title	Earl of Rutland	*Rank*	10
Relationship	Second cousin of Henry VIII.		

Name	Mordaunt, John	*Age*	53
Title	Lord Mordaunt	*Rank*	26
Relationship	-		

Name	Nevill, Ralph	*Age*	38
Title	Earl of Westmorland	*Rank*	7
Relationship	Married to Henry VIII's second cousin.		

Name	Parker, Henry	*Age*	60
Title	Lord Morley	*Rank*	16
Relationship	Second cousin of Henry VIII. George Boleyn's father in law.		
Other	His daughter Jane was one of Anne's principal ladies.		

ANNE'S JUDGES

Name	Percy, Henry	*Age*	34
Title	Earl of Northumberland	*Rank*	4
Relationship	Third cousin of Henry VIII.		
Other	Had a romance with Anne before she became involved with the King.		

Name	Pole, Henry	*Age*	44
Title	Lord Montagu	*Rank*	15
Relationship	Second cousin of Henry VIII.		
Other	Brother of Reginald, friend of Chapuys.		

Name	Radcliffe, Robert	*Age*	53
Title	Earl of Sussex	*Rank*	11
Relationship	First cousin of Henry VIII's mother.		

Name	Sandys, William	*Age*	66
Title	Lord Sandys	*Rank*	22
Relationship	-		
Other	Actively sought an Imperial invasion to restore Katherine and Mary. Either the uncle or great-uncle of Francis Weston.[1]		

Name	Somerset, Henry	*Age*	40
Title	Earl of Worcester	*Rank*	9
Relationship	Third cousin of Henry VIII. His sister was the wife of William Brereton.		
Other	His wife served Anne Boleyn and was said to have been the first source of allegations about her impropriety. She was also cousin of Fitzwilliam.		

Name	Stanley, Edward	*Age*	27
Title	Earl of Derby	*Rank*	8
Relationship	Had married Anne and George's first cousin then their step-aunt		
Other	Cup bearer at Anne's coronation. He later urged Chapuys to encourage the Emperor to invade and depose her (LP 7.1206).		

Name	Stanley, Thomas	*Age*	29
Title	Lord Mounteagle	*Rank*	20
Relationship	Married to Brandon's daughter.		

---

1 Sources disagree on whether Francis' mother, Anne Sandys was the daughter of Oliver and niece of William or his sister.

Name	Tuchet, John	*Age*	53
Title	Lord Audley	*Rank*	13
Relationship	Third cousin once removed of Henry VIII.[2]		

Name	Vere, John de	*Age*	54
Title	Earl of Oxford	*Rank*	6
Relationship	His daughter was married to Norfolk's son.		
Other	Carried the crown at Anne's coronation.		

Name	West, Thomas	*Age*	64
Title	Lord de la Warre	*Rank*	14
Relationship	-		

Name	Windsor, Andrew	*Age*	69
Title	Lord Windsor	*Rank*	23
Relationship	-		

Name	Wentworth, Thomas	*Age*	35
Title	Lord Wentworth	*Rank*	24
Relationship	-		
Other	Cousin of Jane Seymour		

---

[2] Not to be confused with the Lord Chancellor.

Appendix 8   The Cardinals Involved

English, French and Imperial sources all made lists of which cardinals they believed to be loyal to their cause, particularly in 1530 when they thought Clement VII was about to die.[1] Their thoughts are the basis for the affiliation references below though in some cases, the individual's loyalty changed due to political developments.

Accolti (Ancona)
Dates   1455-1532   *Elected*   1511
Nationality Florentine   *Affiliation*   Neutral
Speciality   Law   *Age in 1530*   75
Notes   Papal secretary 1503-11. Wrote 1520 bull condemning Luther. Advised the pope on annulment but also expressed support for Henry.

Accolti (Ravenna)
Dates   1497-1549   *Elected*   1527
Nationality Florentine   *Affiliation*   Neutral
Speciality   Law   *Age in 1530*   33
Notes   Cardinal Protector of Scotland. Friend of Cardinal Mantua. Prosecuted for corruption in 1535. Took money from both sides during the annulment.

Bellay (Bayonne)
Dates   1492-1560   *Elected*   1535
Nationality French   *Affiliation*   Anglo-French
Speciality   Law   *Age in 1530*   38
Notes   French ambassador to England. Friend of Wolsey, Henry and Anne. Experienced diplomat and member of Francis I's privy council from 1530. Bishop of Bayonne 1524-1532, then Bishop of Paris. Present when Henry and Anne visited France. Opposed at Rome the verdict given against Henry in 1534. His brother, William de Langais, was also active in Henry's cause.

---

[1] CSPS 3.2.657; LP 4.5270; Joachim Le Grand, *Histoire du Divorce*, vol. 3 (Paris, 1688) pp.299-302; Nicholas Pocock, *Records of the Reformation*, vol 2 (1870) pp.605-6

Brandenburg

Dates	1490-1545	*Elected*	1518
Nationality	German	*Affiliation*	Imperial
Speciality		*Age in 1530*	40
Notes	Employed Tetzel whose preaching that as soon as the coin hit the tin, the soul was released from purgatory, prompted Luther to reform. Absentee from Rome.		

Campeggio

Dates	1474-1539	*Elected*	1517
Nationality	Milanese	*Affiliation*	Imperial
Speciality	Law	*Age in 1530*	56
Notes	Cardinal Protector of England from 1524 to 1531. Sat in legatine court with Wolsey. Professor of law at Padua where married and had five children before taking holy orders. Auditor of the Rota 1511. Served as papal nuncio to Emperor Charles V and his grandfather Emperor Maximilian. Spent considerable time in Germany and Austria with Charles and Ferdinand. Visited England 1518-19 to raise funds for crusade against the Turk and met Henry, Katherine and Wolsey. A teenage Gregory Casale was part of his retinue. Campeggio was Bishop of Salisbury 1524 to 1534. In January 1534, Imperial sources praised him for his loyalty to Katherine.		

Carafa

Dates	1477-1541	*Elected*	1527
Nationality	Neapolitan	*Affiliation*	Imperial
Speciality		*Age in 1530*	53
Notes	Bought his hat for 20,000 ducats.		

Cardona

Dates	1485-1530	*Elected*	1527
Nationality	Spanish	*Affiliation*	Imperial
Speciality		*Age in 1530*	45

Castelnau

Dates	1480-1541	*Elected*	1503
Nationality	French	*Affiliation*	Anglo-French
Speciality		*Age in 1530*	50
Notes	Absentee from Rome.		

Cesarini

Dates	1480-1542	*Elected*	1517
Nationality	Roman	*Affiliation*	Imperial
Speciality		*Age in 1530*	50

Notes Held hostage in 1527 by Imperialists. Believed to be a "sincere friend" of Henry in July 1532 but also known to be close to the Medici family.

Cesi

Dates	1481-1537	*Elected*	1517
Nationality	Roman	*Affiliation*	Anglo-French
Speciality	Law	*Age in 1530*	49

Notes Papal secretary 1502. One of the hostages given to Colonna at the end of December 1527. Following death of Ancona, appointed to work with Monte and Campeggio advising the pope on the annulment. Opposed to passing of a verdict in Katherine's favour in March 1534.

Chambre

Dates	c1490-1550	*Elected*	1533
Nationality	French	*Affiliation*	Anglo-French
Speciality		*Age in 1530*	40

Notes His mother was the widow of the Duke of Albany. Absentee from Rome.

Cibo

Dates	1491-1550	*Elected*	1513
Nationality	Genoese	*Affiliation*	Anglo-French
Speciality		*Age in 1530*	39

Notes Nephew of Pope Leo X and cousin of Pope Clement VII

Cles

Dates	1485-1539	*Elected*	1530
Nationality	Austrian	*Affiliation*	Imperial
Speciality	Law	*Age in 1530*	45

Notes Part of the regency council set up when Emperor Charles V was a minor. Suppressed the German Peasants Revolt, 1525.

Coligny

Dates	1517-1571	*Elected*	1533
Nationality	French	*Affiliation*	Anglo-French
Speciality		*Age in 1530*	13
Notes	Elected a cardinal when just sixteen and prior to ordination. Became a Calvinist in 1561. Absentee from Rome.		

Colonna

Dates	1479-1532	*Elected*	1517
Nationality	Roman	*Affiliation*	Imperial
Speciality		*Age in 1530*	51
Notes	Deprived following involvement in the attack on the Vatican in 1526. Became Regent of Naples for the Emperor in 1530.		

Contarini

Dates	1483-1542	*Elected*	1535
Nationality	Venetian	*Affiliation*	
Speciality	Theology	*Age in 1530*	47
Notes	Venetian ambassador to the Emperor. Much involved in the League of Cognac and the refusal of Venice to restore Ravenna and Cervia. Helped negotiate the pope's release in 1527.		

Cornaro

Dates	1478-1543	*Elected*	1527
Nationality	Venetian	*Affiliation*	Anglo-French
Speciality		*Age in 1530*	52
Notes	Soldier. Visited the Holy Land. Became Imperialist.		

De Cupis (Trani)

Dates	1493-1553	*Elected*	1517
Nationality	Roman	*Affiliation*	
Speciality	Law	*Age in 1530*	37
Notes	Recognised as the cardinal who took his faith most seriously and as a holy man. Advised pope to rule in Henry's favour, February 1531. Believed to be a "sincere friend" of Henry in July 1532 and opposed the passing of a verdict in Katherine's favour in March 1534.		

Doria

Dates	1495-1558	*Elected*	1529
Nationality	Genoese	*Affiliation*	Imperial
Speciality		*Age in 1530*	35

Du Prat

Dates	1463-1535	*Elected*	1527
Nationality	French	*Affiliation*	Anglo-French
Speciality		*Age in 1530*	67

Notes Tutor to Francis I, he later became Chancellor of France. Presided over peace talks at Cambrai with Louise of Savoy and Margaret of the Low Countries. Wrote an open letter of support for Henry in 1532. Present when Henry and Anne visited France. Argued Henry's case with Clement VII in France. Absentee from Rome.

Eberhard

Dates	1472-1538	*Elected*	1518
Nationality	Low Countries	*Affiliation*	Imperial
Speciality	Law	*Age in 1530*	58

Notes Supported Charles' election as Holy Roman Emperor in 1519 and appointed to his council. Absentee from Rome.

Egidio

Dates	1472-1532	*Elected*	1517
Nationality	Roman	*Affiliation*	Imperial
Speciality	Theology	*Age in 1530*	58

Notes Knew Greek and Hebrew and wrote extensively about Judaism. Worked with Ghinucci in 1531 to protect Jews from the Inquisition. His library was destroyed in the Sack of Rome. Served as papal legate in Germany and Spain to Emperor Maximilian and his grandson Charles V. Threatened experts writing in favour of Henry with death in 1530.

Enckenvoirt (Tortosa)

Dates	1464-1534	*Elected*	1518
Nationality	Low Countries	*Affiliation*	Imperial
Speciality	Law	*Age in 1530*	66

Farnese (Pope Paul III)
Dates 1468-1549 *Elected* 1493
Nationality Roman *Affiliation* Anglo-French
Speciality *Age in 1530* 62
Notes Papal secretary from 1491. Fathered four bastards before his conversion in 1513. Supported a General Council in 1530. Appointed a papal advisor in September 1533. In January and April 1534, Imperial sources praised him for his loyalty to Katherine. Elected pope 1534. Henry had supported his candidature to be pope but found him unfriendly toward him after election due to him having joined the Imperialists.

Farnese
Dates 1520-1589 *Elected* 1534
Nationality Roman *Affiliation*
Speciality *Age in 1530* 10
Notes Created a cardinal aged 14 by his grandfather Paul III.

Ferrero
Dates 1476-1543 *Elected* 1517
Nationality Savoyard *Affiliation* Anglo-French
Speciality *Age in 1530*

Gaddi
Dates 1499-1552 *Elected* 1527
Nationality Florentine *Affiliation* Anglo-French
Speciality *Age in 1530* 31
Notes Held hostage by Imperial troops at Naples for eighteen months 1527-28.

Gambara (Tortona)
Dates 1489-1549 *Elected* 1539
Nationality Venetian *Affiliation*
Speciality *Age in 1530* 41
Notes Nuncio to England in 1527 so knew Henry and Katherine and possibly met Anne Boleyn. Early supporter of Henry's case but changed side after war ended. Governor of Bologna 1528 to 1533 where he tried to prevent the English obtaining opinions.

Gattinara

Dates	1465-1530	*Elected*	1529
Nationality	Savoyard	*Affiliation*	Imperial
Speciality	Law	*Age in 1530*	65
Notes	Grand chancellor of Spain from 1518 to 1530. Councillor to the Emperor and his parents. A layman. Absentee from Rome.		

Ghinucci

Dates	1480-1541	*Elected*	1535
Nationality	Siennese	*Affiliation*	Anglo-French
Speciality	Law	*Age in 1530*	59
Notes	Secretary to Julius II. Sent by Leo X as papal nuncio to England and so impressed Henry that he appointed him Bishop of Worcester in 1522. English ambassador in Spain from 1526 to 1529. Auditor of the Apostolic Camera or Treasurer. Very active in obtaining opinions for Henry, Wrote the report on the "Spanish brief."		

GiacoBazzi

Dates	1444-1528	*Elected*	1517
Nationality	Roman	*Affiliation*	
Speciality	Law	*Age in 1530*	

Gonzaga (Ercole)

Dates	1505-1563	*Elected*	1527
Nationality	Mantuan	*Affiliation*	Neutral
Speciality		*Age in 1530*	25
Notes	Friend of the Casale family. Brother of the Marquis, later Duke, of Mantua. Mother bought him his cardinal's hat for 25,000 ducats when he was a layman. Became Cardinal Protector of Spain. Jesuit supporter.		

Gonzaga (Pirro)

Dates	1505-1529	*Elected*	1527
Nationality	Mantuan	*Affiliation*	Imperial
Speciality		*Age in 1530*	
Notes	Cousin of Ercole Gonzaga.		

Gorvod

Dates	1473-1535	*Elected*	1530
Nationality	Savoyard	*Affiliation*	
Speciality		*Age in 1530*	57

Gramont (Tarbes)

Dates	1486-1534	*Elected*	1530
Nationality	French	*Affiliation*	Anglo-French
Speciality		*Age in 1530*	44

Notes Bishop of Tarbes from 1524 until death. Experienced diplomat and keen supporter of annulment in England, France and at Rome. Some accused him of proposing the idea to Henry. Negotiated marriage of the Duke of Orleans to Princess Mary of England and then to Catherine de Medici. Present when Henry and Anne visited France. His second cousin, Antoine de Castelnau, was the French ambassador at Henry's court when Anne fell.[2]

Grimaldi

Dates	c1490-1543	*Elected*	1527
Nationality	Genoese	*Affiliation*	Imperial
Speciality		*Age in 1530*	40

Notes In January 1534, praised for his loyalty to Katherine.

Grimani

Dates	1489-1546	*Elected*	1527
Nationality	Venetian	*Affiliation*	Anglo-French
Speciality		*Age in 1530*	41

Notes Believed to be a "sincere friend" of Henry in July 1532.

Loaysa (Osma)

Dates	1478-1546	*Elected*	1530
Nationality	Spanish	*Affiliation*	Imperial
Speciality	Theology	*Age in 1530*	52

Notes Dominican and Inquisitor General of Spain. Confessor to the Emperor and after 1533 a member of his council. Active at Rome in support of Katherine.

Longwy

Dates	1481-1561	*Elected*	1533
Nationality	French	*Affiliation*	
Speciality	Law	*Age in 1530*	49

Notes Absentee from Rome.

---

2 Some books incorrectly list Gramont as Castelnau's uncle. Antoine was the son of Suzanne Gramont, wife of Louis de Castelnau, herself the daughter of Francois Gramont. Francois' sister Isabeau was the maternal grandmother of Gabriel Gramont, Bishop of Tarbes.

Lorraine

Dates	1498-1550	*Elected*	1518
Nationality	French	*Affiliation*	Anglo-French
Speciality		*Age in 1530*	32

Notes Present when Henry and Anne visited France. Absentee from Rome.

Medici (Pope Clement VII)

Dates	1478-1534	*Elected*	1513
Nationality	Florentine	*Affiliation*	
Speciality	Law	*Age in 1530*	52

Notes Studied canon law at Pisa. Prisoner of Emperor Charles V's grandfather in 1499 and of Charles V in 1527. Governed Florence with the advice of Machiavelli after the death of his uncle Lorenzo the Magnificent. Cardinal Protector of England 1513 to his election as pope in 1523. Considered at the outset of his papacy to be a friend of Wolsey and Henry.

Medici (Hippolito)

Dates	1511-1535	*Elected*	1529
Nationality	Florentine	*Affiliation*	Imperial
Speciality		*Age in 1530*	19

Notes Cousin of Clement VII. In January 1534, Imperial sources praised him for his loyalty to Katherine.

Mendoza

Dates	1489-1535	*Elected*	1530
Nationality	Spanish	*Affiliation*	Imperial
Speciality	Theology	*Age in 1530*	41

Notes Imperial Ambassador to England 1526 to 1529. Advised Katherine prior to the legatine court and gave her the "Spanish brief."

Merino (Jaen)

Dates	1472-1535	*Elected*	1533
Nationality	Spanish	*Affiliation*	Imperial
Speciality		*Age in 1530*	58

Notes Active supporter of Katherine at Rome from 1533 when he replaced Loaysa who had returned to Spain. He had been present on behalf of Cardinal Sforza at the conclave which elected Julius II

Monte
Dates	1462-1533	*Elected*	1511	
Nationality	Florentine	*Affiliation*	Anglo-French	
Speciality	Law	*Age in 1530*	68	
Notes	Auditor of the Rota 1493 and Apostolic Chamber 1504. Handled the investigations into the plot by certain cardinals to murder Leo X. Supported General Council. Very active for Henry at Rome. Appointed to deputise for the pope at Rome when Clement went to France in 1533, he died while he was away. His nephew was elected pope in 1550.			

Numai
Dates	1460-1528	*Elected*	1517	
Nationality	Roman	*Affiliation*	Anglo-French	
Speciality	Theology	*Age in 1530*		
Notes	Confessor to Francis I's mother. Mistreated by Imperial troops during Sack of Rome and died not long afterwards hence played no role in Henry's annulment.			

Orleans
Dates	1484-1533	*Elected*	1533	
Nationality	French	*Affiliation*		
Speciality		*Age in 1530*	46	
Notes	Died six months after election.			

Orsini
Dates	1473-1534	*Elected*	1517	
Nationality	Roman	*Affiliation*	Anglo-French	
Speciality		*Age in 1530*	57	
Notes	Nephew of Leo X and cousin of Clement VII			

Palmieri
Dates	1493-1527	*Elected*	1527	
Nationality	Neapolitan	*Affiliation*	Impetial	
Speciality		*Age in 1530*		
Notes	Bought his hat for 20,000 ducats.			

Pappacoda
Dates	1456-1536	*Elected*	1527	
Nationality	Neapolitan	*Affiliation*		
Speciality	Law	*Age in 1530*	74	
Notes	Confusion remains if he accepted the hat or not. Certainly he played no active role in the annulment debate at Rome.			

Passerini
Dates	1469-1529	*Elected*	1517
Nationality	Florentine	*Affiliation*	
Speciality		*Age in 1530*	

Piccolomini
Dates	1475-1537	*Elected*	1517
Nationality	Siennese	*Affiliation*	Imperial
Speciality		*Age in 1530*	55

Notes   Tried to prevent Decio writing in Henry's favour in 1530.

Pisani
Dates	1494-1570	*Elected*	1517
Nationality	Venetian	*Affiliation*	Anglo-French
Speciality		*Age in 1530*	36

Notes   Bought his hat for 20,000 ducats in 1517. Held hostage at Naples by the Imperialists for eighteen months 1527-28.

Portugal
Dates	1509-1540	*Elected*	1517
Nationality	Portuguese	*Affiliation*	
Speciality		*Age in 1530*	21

Notes   His father sought the hat for him when he was three years' old but was told to wait. Absentee from Rome.

Pucci (San Quatuor)
Dates	1458-1531	*Elected*	1513
Nationality	Florentine	*Affiliation*	Anglo-French
Speciality	Law	*Age in 1530*	72

Notes   Accused of misappropriating funds through the sale of indulgences and of making creative interpretations of canon law. Disciplined by Pope Adrian but restored by Clement VII. Involved in discussions about decretal commission. Patron of Michelangelo.

Pucci (Pistoia)
Dates	1484-1544	*Elected*	1531
Nationality	Florentine	*Affiliation*	
Speciality	Theology	*Age in 1530*	46

Notes   Sentenced to death by Imperial troops in 1527 but escaped. Papal nuncio to Spain and France.

Quinones (San Croce)

Dates	1475-1540	*Elected*	1527
Nationality	Spanish	*Affiliation*	Imperial
Speciality		*Age in 1530*	55
Notes	Relative, councillor and confessor of Emperor Charles V. Helped negotiate the pope's release in 1527. In January 1534, Imperial sources praised him for his loyalty to Katherine. Appointed one of her two legal advisors at Rome in 1529.		

Ridolfi

Dates	1501-1550	*Elected*	1517
Nationality	Florentine	*Affiliation*	Anglo-French
Speciality		*Age in 1530*	29
Notes	Held hostage after sack of Rome.		

Salviati

Dates	1490-1553	*Elected*	1517
Nationality	Florentine	*Affiliation*	Anglo-French
Speciality		*Age in 1530*	40
Notes	Nephew of Leo X and cousin of Clement VII. Papal legate to France in 1526 and involved in establishing League of Cognac.		

San Severino

Dates	1477-1543	*Elected*	1527
Nationality	Neapolitan	*Affiliation*	Imperial
Speciality		*Age in 1530*	53
Notes	A layman. Believed to be a "sincere friend" of Henry in July 1532.		

Schonberg (Capua)

Dates	1472-1537	*Elected*	1535
Nationality	German	*Affiliation*	Imperial
Speciality	Theology	*Age in 1530*	58
Notes	Cardinal Protector for Germany. In late 1520s travelled to Hungary, Poland, England, France and Spain so knew most of the rulers in Europe. Urged the election of John Fisher as a cardinal and excommunication of Henry.		

Sforza

Dates	1518-1564	*Elected*	1534
Nationality	Roman	*Affiliation*	
Speciality		*Age in 1530*	12
Notes	Became a cardinal at sixteen. Grandson of pope Paul III		

Simonetta

Dates	1475-1539	*Elected*	1535
Nationality	Milanese	*Affiliation*	Imperial
Speciality	Law	*Age in 1530*	55
Notes	Dean of the Rota 1525 to 1528. Appointed as advisor on the annulment by the Emperor. Accompanied pope to France in 1533.		

Solis (Seville)

Dates	1473-1538	*Elected*	1531
Nationality	Spanish	*Affiliation*	Imperial
Speciality		*Age in 1530*	57
Notes	Greek scholar. Opposed Ferdinand of Aragon but became councillor of Charles V. Succeeded Loaysa as Inquisitor General of Spain.		

Spinola (Perugia)

Dates	1482-1537	*Elected*	1527
Nationality	Genoese	*Affiliation*	Imperial
Speciality		*Age in 1530*	48

Tavera (Compostella)

Dates	1472-1545	*Elected*	1531
Nationality	Spanish	*Affiliation*	Imperial
Speciality	Law	*Age in 1530*	58
Notes	Negotiated the Emperor's marriage to Isabella of Portugal. President of the Royal Council from 1524 to 1539		

Tournon

Dates	1489-1562	*Elected*	1530
Nationality	French	*Affiliation*	Anglo-French
Speciality		*Age in 1530*	41
Notes	Councillor to Francis I. One of the negotiators of the Treaty of Madrid. Went to Spain to escort the French princes and Queen Eleanor home. Active in seeking to prevent break with Rome. Present when Henry and Anne visited France. Absentee from Rome.		

Trivulzio
Dates	1485-1548	*Elected*	1517
Nationality	Milanese	*Affiliation*	Anglo-French
Speciality	Law	*Age in 1530*	45
Notes	Cardinal Protector of France. Auditor of the Rota. Held hostage by Imperial troops for eighteen months at Naples 1527-8.		

Valle
Dates	1463-1534	*Elected*	1517
Nationality	Roman	*Affiliation*	Imperial
Speciality		*Age in 1530*	67
Notes	Governed Rome while pope at Bologna in 1529. In January 1534, Imperial sources praised him for his loyalty to Katherine.		

Vendome (Bourbon)
Dates	1493-1557	*Elected*	1517
Nationality	French	*Affiliation*	Anglo-French
Speciality		*Age in 1530*	37
Notes	Crowned Francis I's second queen. Absentee from Rome.		

Veneur
Dates	1470-1543	*Elected*	1533
Nationality	French	*Affiliation*	Anglo-French
Speciality		*Age in 1530*	60
Notes	Almoner to Francis I. Absentee from Rome.		

Vio (Cajetan[3])
Dates	1469-1534	*Elected*	1517
Nationality	Neapolitan	*Affiliation*	Imperial
Speciality	Theology	*Age in 1530*	61
Notes	Dominican. Wrote commentary on Thomas of Aquinas' *Summa*. Opposed Luther at Augsburg. In January 1534, Imperial sources praised him for his loyalty to Katherine. One of nineteen cardinals to condemn Henry in 1534 although he had been listed as one of his supporters in 1530.		

Wellenberg
Dates	1468-1540	*Elected*	1511
Nationality	German	*Affiliation*	Imperial
Speciality	Law	*Age in 1530*	62
Notes	Ambassador to Emperor Maximilian, the grandfather of Charles V. Opponent of Luther.		

---

3 Often spelt Gaietana in records of the period.

Wolsey

Dates	1473-1530	*Elected*	1515
Nationality	English	*Affiliation*	Anglo-French
Speciality		*Age in 1530*	57

Notes   Absentee from Rome. Henry's chief minister and leading European diplomat. Given responsibility for obtaining Henry's annulment from Katherine. Chaired the legatine court at Blackfriars with Campeggio.

INDEX

Abell, Thomas arguments against Henry's case: 96, 98, 104-106, 108-110, 112, 113, 121, 122, 126-129, 131, 132; dismissed from court: 340; Invicta Veritas: 385; released from Tower: 460; sent to Tower: 440

Agostini, Dr 350, 353, 357, 360, 379, 381, 434, 457

Ales, Alexander on Anne's fall: 563

Alphonso IX 461, 463, 488

Ancona, Cardinal advice to Henry: 342, 434; advice to pope: 298; blamed by pope: 477; career: 663; death: 457; greed: 414; promised reward by Henry: 405, 448; respect for: 457; rewarded by Emperor: 430; selected as papal advisor: 430; support for Henry: 293, 417, 434; support sought by Henry: 233, 235; upholds pre-eminence of canon law: 510; urges delay: 334, 404

Arthur, Prince death: 6; marriage to Katherine: 5

Basil of Caesarea 316

Baynton, Edward 475

Beaufort, Margaret opposition to Henry's marriage to Katherine: 8

Barlow, John and Bessie Blount: 71, 140, 176, 431, 432; consulted on annulment: 142; granted Sundridge: 255; role in annulment: 258

Bilney, Thomas 388

Blount, Bessie relationship with Henry: 138

Boleyn, Anne acknowledged to be virgin by Rome: 356; admits ill at ease: 528; alleged pre-contract with Percy: 436, 439; alleged threat from mob: 392-394; alleged to say too many priests in England: 433, 437; arrest: 574; as employer: 535; as stepmother: 532-534; asks Matthew Parker to care for daughter: 569; association with France: 219; attitude to dissolution: 529; attitude to prophecy: 337; becomes Lady Anne Rochford: 316; birth of daughter: 518; charges against: 594-597; charitable giving: 526, 527; childhood marriage: 58, 180; compared to Bessie Blount: 431, 432; complains her youth is being wasted: 314; coronation: 484, 529, 630-636; created Marquess of Pembroke: 443, 445; dances with Henry: 199; descriptions of: 70, 162, 234; entertains ambassadors: 318; exchange with Norris: 572; execution: 587; Field of the Cloth of Gold.: 152; gifts from Henry: 211, 215, 219, 222, 227, 230, 232, 234, 238, 332, 352, 358, 368, 376, 411, 430, 458, 473; gifts to Henry: 317, 320, 411, 571; gives Henry a copy of Tyndale's Obedience.: 279; grants: 476; hires Bridget Harvey: 335; household appointed: 472, 474, 524-526; in Low Countries: 57, 58; influence of: 307, 311; involvement in Wilton Abbey suit: 250; joins English court: 161; jointure: 473; letter from Tower: 584; letter to Lady Wingfield: 579; link to Henry Norris' family: 158; listens in on audience with Chapuys: 352; love song for Henry: 358, 361; marries Henry: 452; Maundy money: 69, 527; motto: 358, 361; moves into own apartment: 244; obtains wardship of Henry Carey: 272; planned visit to Dover: 570; portraits and images: 70; praised for obedience to Henry: 434; pregnancies: 473, 530-532, 558-559; proposed marriage to Butler: 152; publicly recognised as Queen: 477;

reaches out to Mary when Katherine dies: 559; receives ring from Henry: 211; relationship with Henry Percy: 69, 156; relationship with Wolsey: 248, 252, 254, 255, 315, 322; row with Guildford: 380, 382; seeks books about papal power: 454; sent to Hever: 260; shared interests with Henry: 152; skeleton: 72, 165; Suits handled: 388, 536; suits not handled: 160, 204, 415; support for education: 537; support for Thomas Cheyney: 236, 274, 275; taken ill with sweating sickness: 249; time spent with Queen Claude: 64; twenty-first birthday: 241; upset over Henry's shirts: 334; visits France with Henry: 448-450; weddings to Henry: 518-521, 622-629; whereabouts early 1520s: 158;

Boleyn, George account of Henry and Anne's wedding: 516; age: 67; announces marriage of Anne and Henry: 471; arrest: 574; becomes Viscount Rochford: 316; charges against: 594; confusion over annulment status: 321; execution: 586; Garter elections: 562; grants: 259, 267, 299, 385; position at court: 161; receives annuity from Wolsey: 314; sent to France: 313, 357, 417, 450; service to Henry: 583

Boleyn, Mary age: 68; in 1522 court masque: 154; marriage to William Carey: 140; need for support when widowed: 250; relationship with Henry VIII: 140

Boleyn, Thomas becomes Lord Privy Seal: 319; becomes Viscount Rochford: 149; brings portrait of French princess home: 202; calls Chapuys two-faced: 483; career: 161; created Earl of Wiltshire: 313; Durham Place: 393; fulminates against pope: 347; grants: 302, 304, 317, 368, 385, 395; income: 57, 193, 222, 223; involvement in Anglo-French treaty: 197, 348, 476; involvement in fall of Wolsey: 313; involvement in French marriage proposals, 1527: 193; keeps Anne's childhood letter: 62; marriage to Elizabeth Howard: 54; meets Charles V: 323; meets pope: 323; misses 1532 visit to France: 449; promises to Duke of Milan: 343, 351; promises to Duke of Savoy: 388; relationship with daughter, Mary: 250; report from Rome: 326; settles Ormond dispute: 227; sponsors anti-Wolsey farce: 363, 367

Bourges, Pragmatic Sanction of 212, 419

Brandon, Charles income: 194; legatine court: 298, 300; marital history: 246, 487; relationship with Anne: 331, 385, 387; sends daughter to Malines: 58; wardship of Henry Grey: 472, 474

Brereton, William arrest: 576; carries petition of nobles: 334; charges against: 594; conviction: 585; debt to Henry: 358, 443; execution: 586; grants: 197, 200, 222, 302, 340; inspects property for Henry: 456; marriage: 295; service to Henry: 583

Bribery and rewards philosophy 407, 452

Browne, Anthony 589

Buckingham, Duke of 146

Cajetan, Cardinal arguments against Henry's case: 104, 105, 108, 109, 112, 119, 125, 128; career: 676

Camden, William Anne Boleyn's birth date: 65

Campeggio, Cardinal anger at Katherine: 262, 301; bags searched: 308; Cardinal Protector of England: 379, 492; career: 664; departure for

England delayed: 247; first visit to England: 138; loyalty to Charles V: 203, 293; on Katherine's virginity: 301; ordered to delay annulment: 259, 290; prorogues legatine court: 298; reaches London: 261; receives bishopric from Emperor: 457; recognises Henry as expert theologian: 262; role in obtaining verdict against Henry: 508; supports Cranmer becoming Archbishop: 464; tries to persuade Katherine to become a nun: 262; upholds papal authority: 388

Capisucio, Paolo accepts money from Emperor: 385; lies to obtain verdict against Henry: 506

Carew, Nicholas elected to Garter: 562; encouragement of Jane Seymour: 561; message to Mary: 568

Carey, William appointments: 161; death: 248; grants: 197; income: 193; marriage to Mary Boleyn: 140; Wilton Abbey suit: 250

Carne, Edward 363, 367, 394, 397, 417, 421, 425, 435

Casale, Gregory appointed to handle annulment: 224; background: 194, 269; diplomatic efforts: 203; grants: 414; involvement in obtaining decretal commission: 251; meeting with Henry: 442, 448; meets Wolsey in France: 207; negotiations with pope: 237, 241, 406; Obtains proof of Julius II accepting bribe: 12; receives cramp ring from Anne Boleyn: 283; seeks advice: 457; sends Henry papal promise: 291; supported by colleagues: 470; view of Clement VII: 192, 226, 277, 295, 497; warnings to Henry: 277, 284, 294, 356, 378, 435

Casale, John Henry's efforts to get him elected cardinal: 315, 357; recommended by pope as cardinal: 351; sent to Ferrara: 192; stopped in Mantua: 364

Casale, Paul murder: 405

Catherine de Medici marriage proposals: 190, 331, 342, 375, 379, 380, 384, 398; marriage to Francis' son: 506; relationship to pope: 191; taken captive, 1527: 201

Cavendish, George on Henry Percy: 156; reliability as a source: 17, 67

Cervia 208, 314

Chapuys, Eustace accounts of Henry's wedding to Anne: 466, 477, 514; admits exaggerating the truth: 436; admits lacks credible information: 395, 410, 444, 459; admits weakness of Katherine's virginity argument: 368, 384; advocates bribery to find perjurers to support Katherine: 381; and astrology: 589; antisemitism: 101, 363, 372, 373; Calls Anne a Lutheran: 372, 416; claims Henry said Katherine was a virgin: 308; complains of inability to bribe Henry's councillors: 312, 395; confirms Anne a virgin: 384; credit for rumours: 409; decides to punish Henry by loss of his company: 357; defends coin clipping priest: 433; delusions: 444, 484; doubt of Anne's guilt: 602; fall of Wolsey: 350; false reports: 318, 321, 410, 433, 438, 462, 465, 470, 477, 479, 562, 571; hopes for Anne's execution: 315; income: 352, 478; jealousy of French: 347; obsession with Anne as a poisoner: 574, 575; papal letter to Henry: 427; reaction to Anne's arrest: 574; recognises Anne as Queen: 561; reliability as source: 44; rows with Henry: 477; seeks interdict: 358, 465; seeks to prevent debate at Rome: 314; suggested as ambassador to England: 228; summoned before Privy Council: 483; view of Anne: 322, 342, 350, 352, 369, 375, 384, 397, 425, 438, 444, 451, 559; view of Cromwell: 588; view of Practice of Prelates: 358; war mongering: 470, 477

Charles V advised to curb Chapuys: 478; arrests pope's nephew: 446; attacks on Rome: 189; attitude to mother Juana: 145; attitude to Sack of Rome: 200, 203, 205, 206, 210, 221, 223, 231; becomes Holy Roman Emperor: 147; blames Wolsey for annulment plan: 232; breaks betrothal to Mary: 149; challenges Francis to a duel: 240; character: 494; considers war on England: 234; debts to Henry: 189; excommunicated by pope: 389, 390, 496; fear of Henry and Francis: 357; given brief: 232; initial reaction to annulment plan: 206, 208; legitimises bastard daughter: 298; marries Isabella of Portugal: 149; meets with pope: 311; offers to pope: 265; orders new armour: 249; orders pope not to issue annulment: 225; praises Cranmer: 454; reaction to Katherine's death: 495, 559; refuses to pay debts to Henry: 231, 253; rejects legality of appeals to pope from his dominions: 222, 223; rejects Wolsey's peace plan: 242; response to declaration of war: 231; seeks General Council: 352; sends Katherine legal bill: 302; situation at start of 1527: 184; threatens cardinals: 470; treatment of French princes: 276; Treaty of Barcelona: 297; tries to sabotage legatine court: 264, 295, 297; use of financial rewards: 187, 213, 215, 226, 253, 298, 312, 340, 346, 385, 392; view of annulment: 277, 386; vows to call General Council: 196, 288; warned likely to lose war: 210, 214, 219, 226; willingness to accept Anne: 557, 561

Cheyney, Thomas grants: 262; relationship with Wolsey: 274; visited by Henry and Anne: 447; wardship dispute: 252, 259, 275

Cifuentes, Count of 465, 478

Clement VII admiration for Wolsey: 491; admits lack of cause for Julius' dispensation: 314, 344, 458, 466; admits to not being learned: 241; advises Henry to marry Anne: 231, 323, 379; advocation of Henry's case: 298; and Florence: 191, 260, 284, 286; and Machiavelli: 438; attitude to General Council: 352, 392; attitude to Henry VIII: 190; Cardinal Protector of England: 491; character: 496-499; cites Latvian case: 307, 309; desecration of tomb: 499; desire for Katherine to become a nun: 262, 284; determination to obtain Ravenna and Cervia: 215, 232, 234, 238, 244, 247, 252, 261, 265, 272, 290; duplicitous behaviour: 228, 231, 233, 238, 240, 325, 379, 412, 466, 469; forbids Henry to marry Anne: 356, 362; forms anti-Imperial league: 150; friendship for Ghinucci: 492; grants commission to Wolsey to hear annulment: 226; ill health: 274, 276; issues decretal commission: 237, 247, 251; issues dispensation for Henry to marry Anne: 226, 242; issues gagging order: 331, 332, 342; issues pollicitation: 252, 254; learns Henry has married Anne: 478; leaves captivity: 226; letters to Henry: 303, 343, 362, 410, 412, 453; meets with Charles V: 311; mistrust of: 256, 259, 277, 279, 284, 288, 290, 317, 383, 446, 464, 496; offers Henry a new dispensation: 262, 508; offers to permit communion in both kinds: 385; on decisions of predecessors: 217; orders Campeggio to delay annulment: 259; permits nuncio to avoid face to face meetings with Henry: 356; promises not to grant annulment: 285; promises not to issue verdict against Henry: 384; recalls letter to Henry: 477; receipt of financial rewards: 404; recommends Henry have two wives: 342; refuses to allow Cranmer to hear annulment case: 464; rejoins the League: 197; relationship with Charles V: 226, 321, 323, 349; sale of seats in college of cardinals: 226; simoniac: 101; situation after Sack of Rome: 203; situation at start of 1527: 184; suggests Henry's two children marry one another: 272; support for Emperor: 348, 411, 430; supports Henry's case: 279, 493; surrenders to Emperor: 222, 295; threatened by Imperialists: 279; threatens Henry with excommunication: 324; threatens to excommunicate Henry's supporters: 340; upsets the League: 192; validity of election: 329; wishes Katherine dead: 288

Clifford, Henry reliability as a source: 20

Commissions, general and decretal 230

Cranmer, Thomas annuls Henry's "marriage" to Katherine: 482; annuls Henry's marriage to Anne: 587, 604, 608; begins study of annulment: 304; chosen as Archbishop of Canterbury: 462; confirms Henry's marriage to Anne: 483; consecrated Archbishop: 472; joins royal service: 303; response to Anne's arrest: 576; testimony regarding Henry's wedding to Anne: 518

Cromwell, Thomas and destruction of Anne: 588; bribes and threats to Anne's accusers: 601; character: 433, 438; talks with Richard Sampson: 569

De Carles, Lancelot reliability as source: 22

Du Bellay, Jean becomes Bishop of Paris: 442; belief Wolsey wanted Renée as queen: 172, 257; blamed by Cavendish for annulment: 169; career: 663; concern for Wolsey: 289, 295, 305; gives verdict on annulment: 268; impressed by Henry's information network: 241; on start of annulment: 169; relationship with Henry: 172, 317; reports to Francis: 256; view of Paris verdict: 340; visits Henry and Anne: 395

Elizabeth, Princess marriage plans: 558

Ferdinand of Aragon agreement with Henry VII: 9; attitude to daughter Juana: 145; desire for dispensation: 7; letter to Rome: 10, 375; reassurance to Henry that union with Katherine legal: 15

Ferdinand of Austria elected King of the Romans: 357

Ferrara, Duke of 190-192, 194, 210, 219, 222, 232, 242, 260, 378, 392, 393, 418

Fish, Simon Supplication of the Beggars: 282, 437

Fisher, Bishop John alleged warned not to attend Parliament: 395, 396; arguments against Henry's case: 78, 103-106, 108, 109, 112, 115, 116, 118-120, 122-124, 127-129, 133; arrested: 476; attempted poisoning: 369; legatine court: 295; meets with Wolsey: 205, 206; response to annulment: 202; support for

Katherine: 322; votes against Henry: 479

Fitzroy, Henry attendance at court: 326; becomes Duke of Richmond: 148; birth: 141; joins French court: 453; marriage proposals: 190, 197, 210, 289, 314; suggested as heir to the throne: 228; trip to France: 431, 432

Forrest, William reliability as source: 23

Foxe, Edward becomes royal almoner: 393; returns from Rome: 245; sent to Rome: 233; university opinions published: 398

Foxe, John on Anne's fall: 563; reliability as source: 24; sources: 564

Foxe, Bishop Richard 197, 198, 261, 301

Francis advice to Henry: 471, 474; anger at pope: 431; asked about Wolsey and Campeggio: 293; brokers peace in Switzerland: 406; capture at Pavia: 147; challenges Charles V to a duel: 236; coronation gift to Anne: 484; dances with Anne Boleyn: 448; death of mother: 391; Imperial concerns about legality of marriage: 324; imprisons Imperial ambassador: 233; marriage to Eleanor: 195; offers armed support to Henry: 333, 430; on arrest of Wolsey: 350, 353; opposes citation of Henry: 391, 410, 451; proposal to marry Henry's daughter: 187, 190, 193; refusal to break with Rome: 558; rejects Wolsey's peace plan: 242; release of sons: 336; released from captivity: 150; situation at start of 1527: 184; support for annulment: 151, 234, 247, 289, 290, 293, 364, 372, 499, 558; treaty with England: 197; view of Anne: 564, 565

Frith, John 370, 449, 452, 476, 479, 502, 504

Gambara, Cardinal arrests Dr Pallavicini: 342; career: 668; integrity: 345; recommends bribes: 274; supports annulment: 226, 237

Garay, Dr 263, 327, 328, 336, 346, 348, 349

Gardiner, Stephen appointed bishop of Winchester: 391; negotiations with pope: 241; receives letter from Anne Boleyn: 283; sent to France: 412; sent to Rome: 233; summoned back from Rome: 286

Georgius, Francisco 321, 323, 331, 335

Ghinucci, Bishop Giralomo assists annulment: 213; background: 191; career: 669; diplomatic service: 187, 230, 253, 285, 307; discussions with cardinals: 334; Henry's efforts to get him elected cardinal: 190, 315, 324, 357, 426, 453, 470; placed under house arrest by Emperor: 232; prevented from testifying at legatine court: 295; recommended by pope as cardinal: 351, 392; report on Spanish brief: 286; researches in Italy: 317, 343; support for Gregory Casale: 473; view of Charles V: 197; view of pope: 497

Glass of Truth 356, 382, 444

Gruffydd, Rhys ap 404, 408, 409

Hall, Edward account of Henry and Anne's wedding: 514; reliability as source: 25

Hall, Richard reliability as source: 27

Harpsfield, Nicholas account of Henry and Anne's wedding: 515; arguments against Henry's case: 77, 104-108, 115, 116, 119, 126, 131, 132; reliability as source: 28

Harvey, Bridget birth of child: 417; marital history: 578

Henry VIII accepts submission of the clergy: 426; admits only fathered one bastard: 140; advised to bribe cardinals: 274; advised to financially punish pope: 414; advised to marry Anne by pope: 231; and Luther: 176; anger at clergy oath of loyalty to pope: 422; anger at daughter's rejection: 149; anger at pope: 245, 395, 443; appeals to General Council: 485; appoints legal counsel for Katherine: 268; argues with Anne: 572; arrest of Wolsey: 350, 353, 354; attitude to excommunication: 372, 375, 411; attitude to sister Margaret: 196; becomes Prince of Wales: 7; belief in Anne's guilt: 582, 583, 588, 591; betrothed to Katherine: 10; birth of Henry Fitzroy: 141; building works: 378, 385, 444, 445; children by Katherine: 137; claim to France: 149; comments on loss of his sons: 274; condemns Katherine's disobedience: 465; considers seeking Chapuys' removal: 326; contributes to godson's ransom: 318, 319; creates petition to the pope: 272; dances with Anne: 199; "Declare, I dare not": 159; demands fines from convocation: 368; denounces the pope as simoniacal: 327, 329; description of: 167, 398, 399; desire to reform church: 213, 347; dispensation to marry Katherine: 8; dispensations to marry Anne: 178, 180, 215-217, 229, 243; displays Anglo-Imperial treaties: 461, 466; doubts about union with Katherine: 142; encourages Francis to wage war: 557; English Bible: 330; expresses concern about legality of dispensation on accession: 15, 177; faith in Campeggio: 283; fall at joust: 559; final separation from Katherine: 384; first hearing of annulment: 201; gives Anne a ring: 211; happiness with Anne: 558; hires swordsman to execute Anne: 585; income: 399; letters to pope: 341, 356; line of succession: 146; loans Cranmer money: 460; love letters to Anne: 249, 258, 617-621; makes peace with France: 150; marries Anne Boleyn: 452, 455, 460, 513-521, 622-629; meeting with Katherine's physician: 575; mistakes made: 501; offered a new dispensation for Katherine: 262; on Katherine's virginity: 383; opposition to papal authority: 345, 372; orders investigation into Spanish brief: 266; petition of nobles and clergy to pope: 336, 338; planned visit to Dover: 570, 573; possible spiritual kinship with Anne: 179; praises Wolsey: 348; proposes seeking German support: 385, 412; protest at Julius' dispensation: 13; reaction to papal letters: 426; reaction to son's death: 559; receives Spanish brief: 279; refers to pope as Bishop of Rome: 349; refuses citation: 415; regrets marriage to Jane: 591; rejection of Imperial proposals: 561; rejects opportunity to marry Bessie Blount: 328; relationship with Bessie Blount: 138; relationship with Jane Seymour: 561; relationship with Jean du Bellay: 317; relationship with Mary Boleyn: 140, 315, 468; relationship with Mary Stafford: 139; relationship with Wolsey: 174, 315; religious beliefs: 76, 416; request to Castelnau: 566; rows with Chapuys: 326; rumours in 1514 of divorcing Katherine: 63; seeks Charles V's excommunication:

234; seeks decretal commission: 290, 383, 386; seeks for daughter Mary to remain legitimate: 225, 227; seeks new treaty with France: 412; seeks portrait of Francis and his sons: 415; seeks to save Norris' life: 573; sends Anglo-Imperial treaties to Rome: 461; sends excusator to Rome: 363; sends Richard Croke to Italy: 311; separates from Katherine's bed: 142; shared interests with Anne: 152; situation at start of 1527; 185; supreme head of church in England: 368, 371; tells Katherine has married Anne: 476; tells Katherine of separation: 204; threatens Emperor: 197; treaty with France: 197, 443; trust of pope: 233; understanding of nature of the Church: 428; use of financial rewards: 327, 346; use of Hebrew scholarship: 102; visit to France with Anne: 447-449; vows to annul own "marriage": 280; warned against Campeggio: 290; wedding to Katherine of Aragon: 15; weddings to Anne: 513-521, 622-629

Howard, Kathryn conviction: 597

Howard, Mary visit to France with Anne: 450

Howard, Thomas admits does not understand Henry's case: 461; arrest of Wolsey: 353; blames Henry's loss of sons on God: 348; Irish lands: 154; marriage to Henry VIII's aunt: 161; suggests Satan as instigator of annulment: 378

Hunne, Richard 319

Joachim, Jean 324, 326, 330, 350, 353, 354, 357, 364, 368, 385, 398, 499

John, King of England marital history: 490; surrenders England to papacy: 371, 470, 475

Julius II bribed to issue dispensation: 12, 263; grants dispensation: 11, 96; Julius Exclusus: 431; simoniac: 101

Katherine of Aragon admits many favour annulment: 291; appoints proctors at Rome: 291; arguments against Henry's case: 124, 129; blames annulment on malice: 305; children by Henry: 137; criticised by Chapuys: 314; death: 559; denied legal counsel by Charles V: 294; denies marriage to Arthur consummated: 262, 266, 291, 312, 380; desire for peace: 478; desire to be a nun: 13; dishonesty: 266, 270, 275, 308, 391, 397, 400, 500; disloyalty: 469; disobedience to Henry: 425; exaggerations: 388, 395, 396, 398, 401; faith in pope's integrity: 395; gives Spanish brief to Henry: 279; gives Campeggio the Spanish brief: 266; granted new household: 326; green sickness: 365, 366; income: 483; insists case heard at Rome: 380, 465; legatine court: 294, 297; letters to pope: 357; lies told by her lawyers: 394, 396; marriage to Arthur: 5; mistrust of: 261; objects to legatine court: 252; obtains legal advisers from Flanders: 271, 289; official appeal to pope: 284; orders new liveries: 485; reaction to separation news: 204; refuses to consider biblical case: 308; refuses to give jewels to Anne: 445; rejects legal advice: 210; rejects pope's letter to Henry: 421, 423; resides at The More: 389, 392; resumes title of Princess Dowager: 476; seeks Anne's removal from court: 334; seeks to limit parliamentary freedom: 268; seeks to prevent Cranmer becoming Archbishop: 464; seeks witnesses to non-consummation: 351; sees brief in 1504; 11; sends message to Charles V: 206, 454; threatens war: 260; upset by Henry's marriage plans: 266; upset by pope: 443; urged to become nun: 262; wedding to Henry VIII: 15

Latymer, William reliability as source: 30

Loaysa, Cardinal 187, 238, 324, 373, 417, 418, 432, 443, 446, 452, 457, 459, 470, 496, 670

Luther, Martin arguments against Henry's case: 101, 117, 118; view of Leviticus: 176

Mai, Miguel admits Anne is a virgin: 356; admits Imperial bias in papal court: 391; admits strength of Henry's case: 337, 363; advises out of court settlement: 363; appointed Katherine's legal representative: 291; arrives in Rome: 278; belief Henry will face revolt: 455; changes evidence: 372; describes cardinals as devils: 404; devises questions to be asked in Spain: 364; dissatisfaction with Spanish witness statements: 397; invents rumour of Katherine's life being endangered: 285; levirate marriage: 347, 348; on Katherine's virginity: 342, 374; replaced by Cifuentes: 465; supports revising 1504 dispensation: 298, 299; threatens pope: 279; upset Henry consulting Jews: 311; use of financial rewards: 334; view of pope: 288, 294, 392, 427

Mantua, Marquis of family: 468; marital history: 253, 327, 343, 346, 372, 375, 376, 489; seeks to frustrate Henry's case: 356, 364

Margaret Tudor, sister to Henry VIII annulment of marriage: 196, 236, 238, 239, 486; place in succession to English throne: 146

Mary Tudor, daughter of Henry VIII clothes: 391; marriage proposals: 186-188, 193, 195, 397; reaction to Anne's death: 589

Mary Tudor, sister of Henry VIII alleged dislike of Anne: 422, 424; betrothed to future emperor: 14; death: 485; in 1522 court masque: 155; letter to Henry: 242; marries Louis XII of France: 64; obtains bull regarding own marriage: 244, 303; place in succession to English throne: 146; selects staff for France: 63

Marguerite, sister of Francis I expresses love for Henry and Anne: 484; marriage to Henri of Navarre: 171, 186, 190; support for Henry and Anne: 485

Mendoza, Inigo de advises Katherine not to accept revised dispensation: 210; angers Henry: 282; arrival in England: 187; concern about Imperial debt: 193; created bishop: 238; created cardinal: 324; denies Sack of Rome: 203; mistrust of Campeggio: 277; opinion of Anne: 219; ordered to prevent legatine court opening: 262; placed under house arrest: 233; recommends Wolsey for pope: 207; reports investigation into royal marriage: 200; suggests Henry want to marry Anne: 209; warns Katherine against virginity defence: 262

Milan history 184

Modena 210, 232, 248, 378

Monte, Cardinal 225, 229, 233, 237, 363, 364, 410, 417, 430, 434, 454, 672

More, Thomas attitude to heretics: 472; justifies use of perjurers as witnesses: 601; resignation as Lord Chancellor: 426; response to

Submission of the Clergy: 428; says too many priests in England: 437
Naples history 184
Norfolk, Duke of:
see Howard, Thomas :
Norris, Henry arrest: 573; attendance at Henry and Anne's wedding: 515; charges against: 594; conviction: 585; education of son: 447; exchange with Anne: 572; execution: 586; friendship with Anne: 158; grants: 222, 267, 277, 280, 290, 295, 312, 322, 324, 381, 388, 395, 426; offered life by Henry: 573; receives annuity from Wolsey: 317; service to Henry: 583
Ortiz, Dr admits Katherine's alleged virginity irrelevant: 394; anticipates Henry's destruction: 427; anticipates Katherine being canonised: 456; arrival in Rome: 367; belief Katherine in poverty: 395; claims Anne is the conduit of Satan: 430; denies Leviticus divine law: 374; disagreements with pope: 411, 435, 440, 442; discovers Henry once slept with Mary Boleyn: 464; lies to pope: 405; opposes advocation in own case: 385, 386; rows with Mai: 380, 453; view of Katherine: 384
Oyer and terminer commissions 566-568
Page, Richard arrest: 576; grants: 295, 312, 336, 358
Parker, Matthew 390
Parliament Act in Restraint of Appeals: 481, 482; Act of Annates: 417; debate banning appeals to Rome: 472; grievances against clergy: 317, 319; hear university opinions: 372; opening of Reformation Parliament: 311; rebuked by Henry: 425; recalled regarding Anne's fall: 570; study clergy oaths: 422; supplication against clergy: 426
Paul III career: 668
Peace of Cambrai 305
Percy, Henry and Anne Boleyn: 69, 156; appointed Sheriff of Northumberland: 425; debts: 211, 391; denies pre-contract with Anne: 436, 573; elected to Garter: 375; grants: 227; relationship with Wolsey: 284; sent to arrest Wolsey: 350; separation from wife: 305
Peto, Friar William 140, 422, 423, 444, 468
Pole, Reginald arguments against Henry's case: 114, 115; on Mary Boleyn: 140; on start of annulment: 175; reliability as source: 31; suggestion be made Archbishop of York: 357; supports annulment: 323, 336
Praemunire 309, 334
Privy Chamber shift system: 420, 424, 577
Raphael, Marc 317, 337, 351, 363, 389, 411, 448
Ravenna 207, 208, 314
Ravenna, Cardinal career: 663; machinations: 457, 459, 466, 471; offered money by Emperor: 464
Renée, Princess of France marriage proposals: 172, 192; marries Ercole of Ferrara: 242; memories of Anne Boleyn: 65; plot to assassinate husband: 392; reported to be sterile: 207
Richmond, Duke of:
see Fitzroy, Henry:
Rochford, Jane 575, 600
Rome, sack of 199-201, 203
Salviati, Cardinal 330, 674
San Croce, Cardinal 291, 302, 674

San Quatuor, Cardinal 231, 233, 237, 239, 245, 247, 279, 296, 392, 673
Sander, Nicolas reliability as source: 33
Seymour, Edward grants: 280, 343, 434
Seymour, Jane gold coins charade: 561; granted annuity: 567; receives gifts from Henry: 560; removal to Beddington: 576; role in Anne's fall: 590; warned against political involvement: 589, 590
Simonetta, Giacomo 231, 237, 241, 279, 385, 507
Smeaton, Mark arrested: 573; conviction: 585; exchange with Anne: 571; execution: 587; service to Henry: 583
Spanish brief 232, 233, 260, 261, 266, 267, 274, 279, 283, 286, 290, 292, 293, 393, 459, 493
Spanish Chronicle reliability as source: 35
Staffileo, Joannes 213, 215, 225, 229, 232, 241, 245
Sweating sickness 246, 248
Tarbes, Bishop of and Anglo-French marriage: 196; career: 670; created cardinal: 333; death: 474; diplomatic work: 206; meetings with pope: 384; opposes citation of Henry: 410; reads declaration of war: 231; role in starting annulment: 168-170; sent to Rome: 293, 453; supports Henry at Rome: 346, 378, 392; taken ill: 472; witnesses papal coronation: 321
Throckmorton, George ignorance of Mary Boleyn as mistress: 140, 468; grants: 385; land dispute with Henry: 464; seeks position in Mary's household: 241; told by Peto of Henry's relationship with Mary Boleyn: 468

Tracy, William 369, 370, 373, 461, 462
Trani, Cardinal career: 666; seeks to become Cardinal Protector for England: 417; support for Henry: 368, 371
Treason Acts 592, 593
Treaty of Barcelona 297
Treaty of Madrid 150, 185, 192, 195, 206, 231, 260, 266, 305, 503
Tyndale, William Answer to More: 374, 377; arguments against Henry's case: 91, 92, 100, 103, 105, 109, 122, 131, 132; invited to England: 363; Obedience of a Christian Man: 279-281, 330, 504; Practice of Prelates: 358-360
Venice ambassador's report on England: 398-400, 402, 403; seeks to remain impartial on annulment: 330
Wakefield, Robert 206, 208
Warham, William death: 440; legatine court: 300; opposition to Henry's marriage to Katherine: 8; protests about anti papal measures: 414
Weston, Francis arrest: 576; charges against: 594; conviction: 585; execution: 586; knighted: 484; marriage: 332; receives wife's inheritance: 434; service to Henry: 583
Wingfield, Anne 159
Wingfield, Bridget 158
Wingfield, Humphrey appointed Speaker: 467
Wingfield, Lady identity: 577-579
Wolsey, Cardinal accused of breaching Praemunire: 310; admiration for pope: 491; arrest and death: 350; blamed for annulment plan: 232, 242; career: 677; commission to hear annulment: 226;

enthusiasm for annulment: 205, 245; final meeting with Henry: 306; first annulment hearing: 200; granted an official pardon: 321; ill health: 315; influence over Henry VIII: 174; learns of Spanish brief: 256, 258; legatine court: 291, 294, 298; loses power: 307; meets with Knight in France: 215; on indissolubility of marriage: 78; peace efforts: 187, 190, 191, 210, 238, 271; plans for church during pope's captivity: 206, 214; prorogation of legatine court: 301; receives ring from Henry: 307; role in annulment: 170; seeks advice on public honesty: 245; seeks decretal commission: 233, 244, 285; takes up work as Archbishop of York: 334; warned of Campeggio's real purpose: 259; warns Henry about impact of Sack: 206

Worcester, Countess of birth of child: 322; evidence against Anne: 599; role in Anne's fall: 565

Wyatt, George reliability as source: 38

Wyatt, Thomas: arrest: 576, 581; capture in Italy: 196, 198; on impact of imprisonment: 572; relationship with Anne: 332; sent to Calais: 334

Final Word

Many people will have picked up this book because they admired Anne Boleyn or they were fascinated by her. She is often seen as a tragic heroine but this is not how Anne wished to go down in history. She told those about her that "she prayed they would remember her words but not her fragility."[1] Her chaplain wrote that people should rejoice "that before she stepped from us, she did leave such mirrors behind, thereby our lives to frame."[2] It is said that imitation is the sincerest form of flattery. It may be supposed that Anne's greatest desire would be for those who consider themselves her fans to adopt the same charitable impulses and interest in the Gospel. Many people today may not share her religious faith but the desire to do good to others should not be controversial. It is hoped that this volume will encourage not just an appreciation for Anne but a practical application of that for the benefit of those alive today.

---

1   Lancelot de Carles, *Trial and Death of Queen Anne Boleyn* (1545) f43 lines 1191-92
2   Maria Dowling (ed.), *William Latymer's Cronickille of Anne Bulleyne* (Camden, 1990) p.65

www.ingramcontent.com/pod-product-compliance
Lightning Source LLC
Chambersburg PA
CBHW071849290426
44110CB00013B/1077